T0350655

Understanding Long-Run
Economic Growth

A National Bureau
of Economic Research
Conference Report

Understanding Long-Run Economic Growth
Geography, Institutions, and the Knowledge Economy

Edited by **Dora L. Costa and Naomi R. Lamoreaux**

The University of Chicago Press

Chicago and London

DORA L. COSTA is professor of economics at the University of California, Los Angeles; associate director of the California Population Research Center; and a research associate and director of the Cohort Studies Working Group at the NBER. NAOMI R. LAMOREAUX is professor of economics and history at Yale University, a fellow of the American Academy of Arts and Sciences, and a research associate of the NBER.

The University of Chicago Press, Chicago 60637
The University of Chicago Press, Ltd., London
© 2011 by the National Bureau of Economic Research
All rights reserved. Published 2011.
Printed in the United States of America
20 19 18 17 16 15 14 13 12 11   1 2 3 4 5
ISBN-13: 978-0-226-11634-1   (cloth)
ISBN-10: 0-226-11634-4   (cloth)

Library of Congress Cataloging-in-Publication Data

Understanding long-run economic growth : geography, institutions,
    and the knowledge economy / edited by Dora L. Costa and
    Naomi R. Lamoreaux.
        p. cm. — (National Bureau of Economic Research conference
    report)
    Includes bibliographical references and index.
    ISBN-13: 978-0-226-11634-1 (cloth : alk. paper)
    ISBN-10: 0-226-11634-4 (cloth : alk. paper) 1. Economic
development. 2. Economic history. 3. Sokoloff, Kenneth Lee.
I. Costa, Dora L. II. Lamoreaux, Naomi R. III. Series: National
Bureau of Economic Research conference report.
    HD78.U544 2011
    339.9′009—dc22
                                                          2010051605

Relation of the Directors to the
Work and Publications of the
National Bureau of Economic Research

1. The object of the NBER is to ascertain and present to the economics profession, and to the public more generally, important economic facts and their interpretation in a scientific manner without policy recommendations. The Board of Directors is charged with the responsibility of ensuring that the work of the NBER is carried on in strict conformity with this object.

2. The President shall establish an internal review process to ensure that book manuscripts proposed for publication DO NOT contain policy recommendations. This shall apply both to the proceedings of conferences and to manuscripts by a single author or by one or more co-authors but shall not apply to authors of comments at NBER conferences who are not NBER affiliates.

3. No book manuscript reporting research shall be published by the NBER until the President has sent to each member of the Board a notice that a manuscript is recommended for publication and that in the President's opinion it is suitable for publication in accordance with the above principles of the NBER. Such notification will include a table of contents and an abstract or summary of the manuscript's content, a list of contributors if applicable, and a response form for use by Directors who desire a copy of the manuscript for review. Each manuscript shall contain a summary drawing attention to the nature and treatment of the problem studied and the main conclusions reached.

4. No volume shall be published until forty-five days have elapsed from the above notification of intention to publish it. During this period a copy shall be sent to any Director requesting it, and if any Director objects to publication on the grounds that the manuscript contains policy recommendations, the objection will be presented to the author(s) or editor(s). In case of dispute, all members of the Board shall be notified, and the President shall appoint an ad hoc committee of the Board to decide the matter; thirty days additional shall be granted for this purpose.

5. The President shall present annually to the Board a report describing the internal manuscript review process, any objections made by Directors before publication or by anyone after publication, any disputes about such matters, and how they were handled.

6. Publications of the NBER issued for informational purposes concerning the work of the Bureau, or issued to inform the public of the activities at the Bureau, including but not limited to the NBER Digest and Reporter, shall be consistent with the object stated in paragraph 1. They shall contain a specific disclaimer noting that they have not passed through the review procedures required in this resolution. The Executive Committee of the Board is charged with the review of all such publications from time to time.

7. NBER working papers and manuscripts distributed on the Bureau's web site are not deemed to be publications for the purpose of this resolution, but they shall be consistent with the object stated in paragraph 1. Working papers shall contain a specific disclaimer noting that they have not passed through the review procedures required in this resolution. The NBER's web site shall contain a similar disclaimer. The President shall establish an internal review process to ensure that the working papers and the web site do not contain policy recommendations, and shall report annually to the Board on this process and any concerns raised in connection with it.

8. Unless otherwise determined by the Board or exempted by the terms of paragraphs 6 and 7, a copy of this resolution shall be printed in each NBER publication as described in paragraph 2 above.

Contents

Acknowledgments ix

Introduction 1
Dora L. Costa and Naomi R. Lamoreaux

1. **Once Upon a Time in the Americas: Land and
Immigration Policies in the New World** 13
Stanley L. Engerman and Kenneth L. Sokoloff

2. **The Myth of the Frontier** 49
Camilo García-Jimeno and James A. Robinson

3. **Differential Paths of Financial Development:
Evidence from New World Economies** 89
Stephen Haber

4. **Political Centralization and Urban Primacy:
Evidence from National and Provincial Capitals
in the Americas** 121
Sebastian Galiani and Sukkoo Kim

5. **History, Geography, and the Markets for Mortgage
Loans in Nineteenth-Century France** 155
Philip T. Hoffman, Gilles Postel-Vinay, and Jean-
Laurent Rosenthal

6. **Two Roads to the Transportation Revolution:
Early Corporations in the United Kingdom
and the United States** 177
Dan Bogart and John Majewski

7.   Premium Inventions: Patents and Prizes
            as Incentive Mechanisms in Britain and
            the United States, 1750–1930   205
            B. Zorina Khan

8.   The Reorganization of Inventive Activity in the United
            States during the Early Twentieth Century   235
            Naomi R. Lamoreaux, Kenneth L. Sokoloff,
            and Dhanoos Sutthiphisal

9.   Mass Secondary Schooling and the State:
            The Role of State Compulsion in the High
            School Movement   275
            Claudia Goldin and Lawrence F. Katz

10.   The Impact of the Asian Miracle on the Theory
            of Economic Growth   311
            Robert W. Fogel

11.   Ken Sokoloff and the Economic History
            of Technology: An Appreciation   355
            Joel Mokyr

12.   Kenneth Sokoloff on Inequality in the Americas   363
            Peter H. Lindert

13.   Remembering Ken, Our Beloved Friend   373
            Manuel Trajtenberg

            Contributors   375
            Author Index   377
            Subject Index   385

Acknowledgments

The editors of this volume owe a large debt of gratitude to the National Bureau of Economic Research, the Social Sciences Division and the Economics Department at the University of California, Los Angeles, and the All-UC Group in Economic History, joint sponsors of the conference at which these papers were originally presented. We particularly thank Martin Feldstein, James Poterba, Scott Waugh, Reynaldo Macias, Gary Hansen, and Alan Olmstead for their support. The papers benefited from the comments of the formal discussants: David Card, Jeffrey Frieden, Edward Leamer, Peter Lindert, Joel Mokyr, Ariel Pakes, Ronald Rogowski, Manuel Trajtenberg, Daniel Treisman, and John Wallis. They also benefited from the suggestions of anonymous referees and from the many ideas offered by conference participants. Finally, we would like to thank David Pervin of the University of Chicago Press and Helena Fitz-Patrick of the NBER for their advice and work on this volume.

Introduction

Dora L. Costa and Naomi R. Lamoreaux

This volume honors the memory of Kenneth L. Sokoloff with essays by colleagues, coauthors, students, teachers, mentors, and friends on themes associated with his work. The aim is to showcase Sokoloff's influence on the field of economic history and beyond and to carry forward the intellectual endeavors for which he was most renowned.

Sokoloff devoted his career to understanding the sources of long-run growth, particularly the role played by factor endowments and institutions in creating the conditions for sustained economic development. One of his most important contributions was his work with Stanley Engerman on the effect that initial factor endowments in different parts of the Americas had in shaping the subsequent development paths of the countries carved out of these regions (see Engerman and Sokoloff 2002). We open the volume with a new article from this project and then continue with two chapters that explore the argument and push it in new directions. The rest of the chapters in the volume range further afield, but all engage the central idea that underpinned Engerman and Sokoloff's work: that geography shapes patterns of institutional development and that one can use the resulting differences in growth trajectories to understand how institutions, as well as geography, matter for economic development.

There has been much scholarly debate in recent years about whether institutions are determined exogenously or whether they develop endogenously as

Dora L. Costa is professor of economics at the University of California, Los Angeles; associate director of the California Population Research Center; and a research associate and director of the Cohort Studies Working Group at the NBER. Naomi R. Lamoreaux is professor of economics and history at Yale University, a fellow of the American Academy of Arts and Sciences, and a research associate of the NBER.

We are grateful to Stanley Engerman and Claudia Goldin for their helpful comments.

1

part of the growth process. Sokoloff recognized that the answer could never be exclusively one or the other. Rather, he was primarily concerned with advancing the knowledge needed to further economic development by tracing out the implications for growth of particular sets of factor endowments and particular institutional choices. His usual modus operandi was to exploit aptly chosen comparisons, over time and across regions and countries, to make inferences about the direction of causation. The chapters in the volume pursue this basic method, using comparisons of different countries and also different parts of the same county to explore a number of topics that figure prominently in Sokoloff's work: how markets expand along both their extensive and intensive margins, the mechanisms that facilitate technological discovery, and the factors that encourage investment in human capital. As Sokoloff emphasized throughout his career, these topics are all interconnected. Ongoing technological change is the key to long-run economic growth, but it does not just happen. Inventors devote resources to technological discovery when expanding markets create new opportunities for profit and when there are institutions, like the patent system, that provide security for their intellectual property. They also need access to new sources of knowledge and incentives to make costly investments in human capital. Successful economies are those whose governments provide an infrastructure that facilitates the growth of markets, the security of property rights, and the development of human capital without encouraging rent seeking. How human societies create such successful economies is the larger question that structured Sokoloff's scholarly career. It is also the question that structures this volume in his honor.

At the time of his death, Engerman and Sokoloff had nearly completed their project on differential paths of economic growth in the Americas.[1] Their starting point was the observation that the societies with the best growth records in the nineteenth and twentieth centuries were generally those that had not been particularly well off during the colonial era, and they hypothesized that the pattern was not accidental. The richest, most prized colonies were those whose factor endowments were conducive to the production of high value crops using slave labor or the exploitation of large native populations in mining or other extractive activities. These colonies were characterized from the beginning by highly unequal distributions of wealth, and the elites at the top of the resulting social hierarchies put in place institutions that ensured their continued dominance. By contrast, in colonies where factor endowments were not so favorable to these high-value activities, wealth was more evenly distributed among the settler populations, and the institutions that developed were, for the time, more democratically structured. Engerman and Sokoloff argued that these early institutional differences were the key to the differential growth experi-

---

1. The book is forthcoming from Cambridge University Press under the title, *Economic Development in the Americas since 1500: Endowments and Institutions.*

ences of these economies after independence, and they developed this idea in a series of papers that looked at the implications of these differences for the subsequent evolution of suffrage rules and for the provision of public goods such as schooling (see Engerman and Sokoloff 2002, 2005; Engerman, Mariscal, and Sokoloff 2009).

The first chapter in this volume, "Once Upon a Time in the Americas," continues this work by exploring the connection between factor endowments and the policies colonial governments adopted toward immigration and the distribution of land. The basic argument is that elites allowed broad access to land only when it was necessary to attract labor. In the main Spanish colonies, where dense populations of Native Americans meant there was little need for additional European labor, the government actually imposed restrictions on immigration. Where land was suitable for the production of sugar and other similarly valued crops—in Brazil, for example, and the Caribbean islands—the forced migration of Africans solved the labor problem. Only in British North America, where labor had to be induced to come voluntarily, did governments pursue policies to make migration affordable (by regulating contracts for indentured servitude) and attractive (by making land available to migrants who completed their terms of servitude).

Engerman and Sokoloff argue that these different experiences mattered after independence because elites had much more power in societies where there had been no need to attract migrants during the colonial era. In Mexico and other places with large numbers of Native Americans, those in control ensured that their preferred access to labor would continue by grabbing the natives' land. In colonies that had depended on slave labor, they blocked policies that would distribute frontier lands to those further down on the social ladder, even as they subsidized immigrants to come work on their plantations. Elites in the former British North American colonies also tried to restrict access to land, but they did not prevail, and land distribution policies in the United States and Canada became more generous over time. Although factor endowments continued to play a role in shaping land policy in the nineteenth century, the institutional heritage of the colonial period was a more dominant factor. The United States and Argentina both had large frontiers, but their distribution policies were radically different. By the end of the century 75 percent of adult males residing in rural areas of the United States owned land. In Argentina the figure was only about a third as much.

The second chapter in the volume, "The Myth of the Frontier" by Camilo García-Jimeno and James A. Robinson, develops similar themes. Robinson and his coauthors, Daron Acemoglu and Simon Johnson, have been engaged in research closely related to that of Engerman and Sokoloff, and the two teams continually exchanged ideas and information. In this chapter with García-Jimeno, Robinson employs a cross-country regression framework to study the relationship between factor endowments (in this case the existence of a frontier) and institutions. Over a century ago, Frederick Jackson Turner delivered his famous paper connecting the emergence of democratic institutions in the United States to the availability of free land in the West (see Turner 1894). García-Jimeno and Robinson note that many countries in the Americas had large frontiers but did not develop similar democratic political systems, and they set out to try to understand whether Turner was wrong or if there was a more complex relationship between factor endowments and institutions. Their findings reinforce those of Engerman and Sokoloff in "Once Upon a Time in the Americas." What mattered was not simply whether there was a physical frontier, but how governments allocated frontier lands in the nineteenth century, and that in turn depended on the institutions the countries had inherited from the colonial period. According to García-Jimeno and Robinson's "conditional frontier thesis," frontiers are conducive to democracy only where existing institutions facilitate a wide distribution of land. Where existing institutions allow elites to engross the land themselves, frontiers can actually make outcomes worse by helping to entrench wealthy groups in power.

The degree to which elites were able to dominate the various American governments in the nineteenth century mattered for relative economic performance as well as for political structure. As Stephen Haber shows in "Differential Paths of Financial Development: Evidence from New World Economies," control by elites of the banking system was an important cause of financial underdevelopment. Haber worked with Sokoloff as a graduate student at UCLA and later collaborated with Engerman and Sokoloff on their comparative study of the Americas (see Engerman, Haber, and Sokoloff 2000). In this chapter, he uses case studies of three countries (Mexico, Brazil, and the United States) to explore the relationship between the institutional heritage of the colonial era and the structure of the financial system. In both Mexico and Brazil, he shows, nineteenth-century governmental leaders granted powerful members of the elite monopoly power over banks in exchange for the financial and political support they needed to stay in power. Although the banks financed industrial enterprises, access to capital was largely restricted to enterprises associated with the ruling coalition. In the United States, by contrast, similar efforts by elite groups to limit entry into banking did not succeed. The widespread franchise led instead to free entry into banking and a financial system composed literally of tens of thousands of small unit banks. Although such a system had its own problems, it effectively channeled savings into economic development.

Governments ruled by entrenched elites tend to be highly centralized, and Sebastian Galiani and Sukkoo Kim, who received his PhD under Sokoloff's direction at UCLA, explore the implications of this tendency for the structure of cities in "Political Centralization and Urban Primacy: Evidence from National and Provincial Capitals in the Americas." Inspired by Mark Jefferson's influential observation that in most countries the largest, most important city is also the political capital (Jefferson 1939), Galiani and Kim investigate the relationship between a city's political status (whether it was a national or provincial/state capital) and its relative size, controlling for other economic and geographic variables. Using data for the twentieth century, they find that the effect of a city's political status on the size of its metropolitan area was much stronger for most Latin American countries than for the United States. Following Engerman and Sokoloff, they attribute this difference to the kinds of institutions each region inherited from the colonial era. In Latin America political power was more concentrated in the hands of elites, both national and provincial, who were also more likely to reside in capital cities. One consequence was that government spending on public goods was much more concentrated in capital cities in Latin America than in the United States.

Urban structures matter because the concentration of population in cities can have agglomeration effects that foster economic growth. Adam Smith famously postulated that the expansion of markets made possible a more productive division of labor. Sokoloff took the idea further in his own work and, inspired by Jacob Schmooker (1966), used patenting data to show that the growth of markets encouraged inventive activity. He showed, for example, that patenting rates per capita were higher in cities than in other areas and that they soared wherever transportation improvements provided broader access to markets (Sokoloff 1988).

Similar agglomeration effects play an important role in the contribution to this volume by Jean-Laurent Rosenthal, Sokoloff's longtime colleague, and two other friends, Philip T. Hoffman and Gilles Postel-Vinay. The three coauthors have written extensively on the role notaries played in intermediating credit transactions in Paris before the twentieth century (see Hoffman, Postel-Vinay, and Rosenthal 2000). In "History, Geography, and the Markets for Mortgage Loans in Nineteenth-Century France," they examine the relationship between access to markets and the provision of medium- and long-term loans in mid-nineteenth century France, based on data they collected from notarial records for a large sample of villages and cities across the country. They find that the volume of lending was greatest in towns located near other towns. Geographic proximity mattered because it facilitated the development of networks among notaries that integrated the credit markets of neighboring localities. These networks alleviated problems of asymmetric information between borrowers and lenders and also reduced search costs. The result was significantly higher levels of lending per capita compared to towns of comparable sizes that were more geographically isolated.

In his work with Engerman, Sokoloff aimed to answer a question posed some years ago by Richard Easterlin, another of his longtime friends: "Why isn't the whole world developed?" (Easterlin 1981). Sokoloff was also interested, however, in comparing countries within the set that had successful records of economic growth. By studying the different development paths that rich economies had taken, he believed, one could gain an understanding of the alternative ways in which countries could make the transition to sustained economic growth. Sokoloff was particularly interested in understanding how the United States experience diverged from that of its former colonizer, Great Britain, given that the two countries had so much in common, culturally and institutionally. For example, he and his coauthor, David Dollar, sought to understand why early manufacturing growth primarily took the form of cottage industry in England, whereas small factories were much more important in the United States. They found that the difference owed to the greater seasonality of agriculture in England. British manufacturers could not afford to hire labor during peak periods of agricultural demand. Rather than invest their capital in plant and equipment that would lay idle part of the year, they focused instead on bringing manufacturing tasks to the farm (Sokoloff and Dollar 1997).

Dan Bogart and John Majewski explore another difference between the United States and the United Kingdom in their contribution to this volume. Bogart and Majewski both got their PhDs from UCLA and benefited greatly from Sokoloff's guidance as they worked on their dissertations. In "Two Roads to the Transportation Revolution: Early Corporations in the United Kingdom and the United States," they try to understand why state legislatures in the United States chartered many more transportation corporations in the late eighteenth and early nineteenth centuries than the British Parliament, and why charters in the United States were so much less costly to obtain than in Britain. Like Sokoloff and Dollar, they find much of the explanation in geography. The United States had a large, dispersed rural population. It badly needed a transportation system to bring agricultural goods from the interior to coastal markets, but its low population density meant that only a few of these projects were likely to be profitable to investors. If charters had been costly to get in the United States, no one would have sought them. By contrast, Britain's much higher population density made transportation projects profitable and provided a surplus that Parliament could extract. Institutions were also an important part of the story, according to Bogart and Majewski. Although the United States had inherited many institutions from Britain, its political structure differed from that of the parent country in two key respects: Its franchise was more democratic, and its decentralized federal system meant that power over matters like corporations resided largely with the states. The former difference forced state legislatures to be more responsive to popular demands for low-cost transportation; the latter put them in competition with each other to build transportation projects that would channel agricultural products from the interior to their own Atlantic ports.

Although much of Sokoloff's work emphasized the importance of factor endowments and other geographic factors for the course of economic development, he recognized that the choice of institutions could also play an important role. For example, he and B. Zorina Khan compared the features of the U.S. patent system with those of Britain and other European countries (Khan and Sokoloff 1998, 2004) and showed that the U.S. patent system provided better security for property rights in invention at lower cost than its counterparts elsewhere in the nineteenth century. The result was not just higher rates of patenting per capita, but greater involvement by nonelites—mechanics, artisans, and farmers—in the process of technological improvement. Khan and Sokoloff attributed the United States' more open system to a rejection of the European view that only a small part of the citizenry had the education and resources to generate valuable inventions. In Britain, for example, efforts to lower the cost of obtaining a patent ran up against the objection that lower fees would only encourage the common people to seek protection for trivial improvements. Khan explores the implications of this elitism further in "Premium Inventions: Patents and Prizes as Incentive Mechanisms in Britain and the United States, 1750–1930." Using data on great inventors in the United States and Britain that she and Sokoloff collected from biographical dictionaries and other sources, she compares systematically the attributes of those who won prizes for technological discovery with those who did not. British great inventors were far more likely than their American counterparts to come from elite backgrounds. But even given this difference, prizes were much more likely to be awarded to members of the elite in Britain than they were in the United States. In recent years, critics of the patent system have embraced prizes as a superior way of encouraging technological discovery, but Khan's findings suggest that prize committees can be "captured" by elite groups who bestow the awards on their own members to an extent disproportionate to merit.

The secure property rights that the American patent system conferred on inventors made possible the growth of a market for patented technology, which in turn facilitated a division of labor that allowed inventors to specialize in the generation of new technological ideas and sell or license those ideas to others better positioned to exploit them commercially. Sokoloff and Naomi R. Lamoreaux have documented the rise of this market (see Lamoreaux and Sokoloff 2003). They have also studied the factors that led to its decline in the early twentieth century. In their view, the new technologies of the second Industrial Revolution increased the amount of capital (both human and physical) required for effective invention, making it more difficult for technologically creative people to embark on careers as independent inventors. One consequence of the higher barriers to entry was the rise of in-house research laboratories in large firms, a familiar story in the literature. Another—less well known—was the emergence in the Midwest of a Silicon Valley-like economy where overlapping networks of venture capitalists, entrepreneurs, and inventors founded large numbers of high-technology startups (Lamoreaux and Sokoloff 2009; Lamoreaux, Levenstein, and Sokoloff 2007). In "The Reorganization of Inventive Activity in the United States During the Early Twentieth Century," Lamoreaux and Dhanoos Sutthiphisal, whose dissertation Sokoloff supervised at UCLA, continue this line of inquiry. The authors challenge the conventional scholarly wisdom that large firms' research and development (R&D) labs came to dominate inventive activity because they were a superior way of organizing technological discovery. Using a new sample of patent data from the late 1920s, they show that innovative regions in the Midwest held their own as sites of technological creativity until the 1930s. The ascendancy of large-firm R&D in the post–World War II period was a result more than anything else of the Great Depression, which disrupted the networks of venture capitalists that had fueled the small-firm economy of the Midwest. Large firms by contrast had more abundant internal resources. Not only did they survive the economic turmoil in greater proportions but during the Depression greatly expanded their investments in R&D, stockpiling technologies that would enable them to grow rapidly with the return of prosperity.

The continuous stream of new technological ideas spewed forth by American inventors, whether they operated independently or worked for large or small firms, would never have been possible without widespread schooling. The U.S. educational system enabled ordinary people to obtain the knowledge needed for effective invention, particularly in the science-based technologies of the second Industrial Revolution. Sokoloff had always been interested in understanding why countries differ so much in their willingness to invest in the human capital of their populations. In another paper on the Americas with Engerman and Elisa Mariscal (2009), he traced the relationship between initial factor endowments and colonial institutions, on the one hand, and literacy rates and the availability of schooling in the nineteenth and twentieth centuries on the other. In this comparison, the United States stands out for its high rates of literacy early on and for the extent of its public school system.

No one has done more to illuminate the United States' unique educational history than Claudia Goldin, Sokoloff's erstwhile coauthor and his teacher in graduate U.S. economic history, and Lawrence F. Katz (see Goldin and Katz 2008). In their chapter for this volume, Goldin and Katz study the provision of mass secondary schooling in the twentieth century. They are particularly interested in understanding the extent to which compulsory schooling and child labor laws were responsible for the high levels of secondary education attained by the U.S. population, as some had asserted. They find that although some aspects of the laws had a positive effect on enrollment, the effect was small relative to the enormous expansion in high school attendance during the period. Part of the reason for the small effect was that the laws' primary aim was not so much to encourage children to stay in school, but rather to ensure that they were either in school or in the workforce and not idle. The main explanation, however, was that school attendance was endogenous to economic opportunity. Most parents wanted their children to stay in school and reap the substantial pecuniary returns to additional education. Moreover, economic growth led to increases in family wealth that made it easier for parents to provide their children with this opportunity.

In much of his work, especially his project with Engerman, Sokoloff was concerned with understanding why some economies failed to make the transition to sustained economic growth. But he was also interested in the experience of countries that recently had negotiated the transition success-fully, particularly the so-called Asian Tigers. Sokoloff wrote several papers critiquing the notion that governmental industrial policy was behind these achievements (see, for example, Dollar and Sokoloff 1992), and he partici-pated in the design and execution of an industrial census, conducted by the World Bank in a number of Asian countries, to provide the raw data for further exploration of the issue.

Sokoloff's thesis advisor and mentor, the Nobel Prize–winning econo-mist Robert W. Fogel, takes up the topic of the Asian growth record in his contribution to this volume. "The Impact of the Asian Miracle on the Theory of Economic Growth" reviews the origins and evolution of growth theory, showing how theory has responded to, and often been surprised by, global events, and how the writings of economic historians have often antici-pated theoretical advances. Fogel begins with the seminal work of Robert Solow, which shifted the attention of economists from labor productivity to total factor productivity as the principal measure of changes in economic efficiency or technological change (Solow 1957). Moses Abramovitz, writ-ing prior to the publication of Solow's work, had discovered that increases in labor, capital, and land could account for only 14 percent of the increase in U.S. output over the 75 years between 1869 to 1878 and 1944 to 1953. The remaining 86 percent was due to an unexplained increase in productiv-ity, variously described as either the measure of our own ignorance or as technological change (Abramovitz 1956). Solow's model and other formal growth models of the 1950s and 1960s treated this technological change as exogenous, but again economic historians and other "verbal theorists" were out in front, writing about technological change as endogenous well before theorists began to write down formal models of endogenous technological change. Simon Kuznets, for example, pointed out that economic growth both required and produced major changes in the structure of the economy (Kuznets 1966). Increases in agricultural productivity were necessary for the growth of manufacturing and manufacturing in turn stimulated changes in agricultural technology.

Growth theory has not yet caught up with the Asian miracle and Fogel argues that growth theory needs to be informed by historical perspective. Growth theory in the 1980s was mainly responding to the post–World War II developments in Europe and the United States, and the debates were about convergence between Europe and the United States. In the first half of the

1990s attention shifted to Korea, Hong Kong, Singapore, and Taiwan, countries whose rapid growth rates in the preceding decades earned them the nickname of "Four Asian Tigers." Prior to the early 1990s, there was the widespread belief that these high growth rates were a fluke and could not last. China and India did not even enter the debate until the second half of the 1990s, but Fogel predicts that by 2040 China may be richer in terms of gross domestic product (GDP) per person than the current fifteen European Union nations and will have 40 percent of the world's GDP compared to 14 percent for the United States. Fogel emphasizes that much of the success of the developing countries was due to changes in labor productivity. Because most of China's labor force is still in agriculture, there is a substantial potential for growth through a shift to industry and services as China continues to catch up to the economic frontier. Agreeing with Dwight Perkins (2006), he argues that the main future challenge for China is to maintain a stable environment for economic growth while the Chinese political system evolves to one more suitable for an educated, high income country. Fogel points out that the United States is currently at the economic frontier, and its continued growth depends on the rate at which it can develop new technologies. Much therefore will depend on the willingness of the United States to invest heavily in scientific research and development and increase the share of the population educated in the sciences.

The volume concludes with three shorter chapters that convey the influential character of Sokoloff's scholarship and the critical role he played in the profession. Joel Mokyr surveys Sokoloff's contributions to the economic history of technology, Peter Lindert to the comparative history of inequality. Finally, Manuel Trajtenberg captures in a few broad brushstrokes the remarkable man who had such a deep impact on us all. As these memorials make clear, with Sokoloff's death, the profession lost not only an intellectual giant, but an important source of its vitality. By the sheer force of his personality, Sokoloff helped channel potentially divisive scholarly debates in productive directions that pushed out the frontiers of knowledge. We hope his memory will inspire others to do the same.

References

Abramovitz, Moses. 1956. "Resource and Output Trends in the United States Since 1870." *American Economic Review* 46:5–23.
Dollar, David, and Kenneth L. Sokoloff. 1992. "Labor Productivity Growth in Follower Countries: The Case of South Korea." In *Studies in Labor Markets and Institutions,* edited by Kenneth L. Sokoloff, 97–125. Los Angeles: Institute of Industrial Relations, University of California, Los Angeles.
Easterlin, Richard A. 1981. "Why Isn't the Whole World Developed?" *Journal of Economic History* 41:1–19.

Engerman, Stanley L., Stephen Haber, and Kenneth L. Sokoloff. 2000. "Inequality, Institutions, and Economic Growth: A Comparative Study of New World Economies Since the Sixteenth Century." In *Institutions, Contracts, and Organizations: Perspectives from New Institutional Economics,* edited by Claude Menard, 108–36. Cheltenham, UK: Edward Elgar.

Engerman, Stanley L., Elisa V. Mariscal, and Kenneth L. Sokoloff. 2009. "The Evolution of Schooling Institutions in the Americas, 1800–1925." In *Human Capital and Institutions: A Long Run View,* edited by David Eltis, Frank Lewis, and Kenneth L. Sokoloff, 93–142. New York: Cambridge University Press.

Engerman, Stanley L., and Kenneth L. Sokoloff. 2002. "Factor Endowments, Inequality, and Paths of Development among New World Economies." *Economia* 3:41–109.

———. 2005. "The Evolution of Suffrage Institutions in the New World." *Journal of Economic History* 65:891–921.

Goldin, Claudia, and Lawrence F. Katz. 2008. *The Race between Education and Technology.* Cambridge: Harvard University Press.

Hoffman, Philip T., Gilles Postel-Vinay, and Jean-Laurent Rosenthal. 2000. *Priceless Markets: The Political Economy of Credit in Paris, 1660–1870.* Chicago: University of Chicago Press.

Jefferson, Mark. 1939. "The Law of the Primate City." *Geographical Review* 29: 226–32.

Khan, B. Zorina, and Kenneth L. Sokoloff. 1998. "Two Paths to Industrial Development and Technological Change." In *Technological Revolutions in Europe, 1760–1860,* edited by Maxine Berg and Kristine Bruland, 292–313. Cheltenham, UK: Edward Elgar.

———. 2004. "Institutions and Democratic Invention in 19th-Century America: Evidence from 'Great Inventors,' 1790–1930." *American Economic Review* 94: 395–401.

Kuznets, Simon. 1966. *Modern Economic Growth: Rate, Structure, and Spread.* New Haven: Yale University Press.

Lamoreaux, Naomi R., Margaret Levenstein, and Kenneth L. Sokoloff. 2007. "Financing Invention during the Second Industrial Revolution: Cleveland, Ohio, 1870–1920." In *Financing Innovation in the United States, 1870 to the Present,* edited by Naomi R. Lamoreaux and Kenneth L. Sokoloff, 39–84. Cambridge: MIT Press.

Lamoreaux, Naomi R., and Kenneth L. Sokoloff. 2003. "Intermediaries in the U.S. Market for Technology, 1870–1920." In *Finance, Intermediaries, and Economic Development,* edited by Stanley L. Engerman, Philip T. Hoffman, Jean-Laurent Rosenthal, and Kenneth L. Sokoloff, 209–46. New York: Cambridge University Press.

———. 2009. "The Rise and Decline of the Independent Inventor: A Schumpeterian Story?" In *The Challenge of Remaining Innovative: Lessons from Twentieth Century American Business,* edited by Sally H. Clarke, Naomi R. Lamoreaux, and Steven Usselman, 43–78. Stanford: Stanford University Press.

Perkins, Dwight. 2006. "Stagnation and Growth in China over the Millennium: A Comment on Angus Maddison's 'China in the World Economy, 1300–2030.'" *International Journal of Business* 11:255–64.

Schmooker, Jacob. 1966. *Invention and Economic Growth.* Cambridge: Harvard University Press.

Sokoloff, Kenneth L. 1988. "Inventive Activity in Early Industrial America: Evidence from Patent Records, 1790–1846." *Journal of Economic History* 48: 813–50.

Sokoloff, Kenneth L., and David Dollar. 1997. "Agricultural Seasonality and the Organization of Manufacturing in Early Industrial Economies: The Contrast Between England and the United States." *Journal of Economic History* 57: 288–321.

Solow, Robert M. 1957. "Technical Change and the Aggregate Production Function." *Review of Economics and Statistics* 39:312–20.

Turner, Frederick Jackson. 1894. "The Significance of the Frontier in American History." In *Annual Report of the American Historical Association for the Year 1893,* 197–227. Washington, DC: Government Printing Office.

1

Once Upon a Time in the Americas
Land and Immigration Policies in the New World

Stanley L. Engerman and Kenneth L. Sokoloff

1.1 European Migrations

Once upon a time, more than five hundred years ago, Europeans began a grand, long-term campaign to extract material and other advantages from underpopulated or underdefended territories by establishing permanent settlements around the world.[1] There had been extensive migration within Europe, both eastward and westward, including settlements of areas within Europe conquered by both Europeans and non-Europeans.[2] In the eighteenth and nineteenth centuries there was also a large movement of contracted labor from east and central Europe to Russia, and to Siberia.[3] The radically novel and diverse environments they encountered offered great economic opportunities, but also posed formidable problems of organization. Such circumstances made adaptation and innovation essential, and enormous variety in the economic structures and institutions that evolved over time is evident across colonies, even among those of the same Euro-

Stanley L. Engerman is the John H. Munro Professor of Economics and professor of history at the University of Rochester, and research associate of the National Bureau of Economic Research. Kenneth L. Sokoloff (1952–2007) was professor of economics at the University of California, Los Angeles, and a research associate of the National Bureau of Economic Research.

1. See Engerman and Sokoloff (forthcoming, [2011]). For a recent description of the world economy since year 1000, see Findlay and O'Rourke (2007).

2. See the studies in Moch (1992), Emmer and Mörner (1992), Canny (1994) (particularly the essays by Phillips and Sánchez-Albornoz), and Altman and Horn (1991). There had earlier been movements into Europe by the Mongols and the Ottomans, among others.

3. For the earlier period, see Bartlett (1993), and for the later years see Bartlett (1979). Peter Lindert (2011) notes that the eastward movement of peasants in Russia led to a tying down of workers, not an enticement by the availability of small farms.

pean nation.[4] Inspired by the goal of improving understanding of the role of institutions in the processes of economic growth and development, many scholars have recently come to appreciate how the history of European colonization provides a rich supply of quasi-natural experimental evidence that can be analyzed to determine whether there were systematic patterns in how institutions or economies evolved with respect to initial conditions, and what causal mechanisms may be involved.[5] Our chapter is very much in this spirit.

The European movements into Africa and Asia, beginning at about the same time as did the colonization of the Americas, were to areas of high population density that provided more than ample native labor forces and left little need for extensive inflows of settlers or migrants from elsewhere. Few Europeans were to make the trek to these colonies, and their numbers, relative to the aboriginal populations, accordingly remained quite small (see table 1.1 for the population composition of colonies late in the nineteenth century). There were also extensive movements by the British after 1788 to Australia and then to New Zealand, both of which had population and settlement patterns somewhat similar to the Americas and, at the end of the nineteenth century, by Britain and other European nations to Africa and to Oceania.

In the Americas, however, the Europeans confronted very different sorts of environments than in Asia and Africa. Although conditions varied across space, overall low population density (labor scarcity) was the rule, and thus the economic problems of the colonizers (or authorities) centered on how to exploit the abundant land and other natural resources without initially having much labor on hand to do the actual productive work. Two fundamental and closely related issues were central to this challenge. First, how would ownership or use rights in land be allocated among the interested parties, such as the state or the corporate entity behind any particular colony, individual settlers, Native Americans, and the church? Land disposal policy not only affected the rate at which this critical resource was opened to investment and the generation of output, but also influenced the supply and location of labor, by measures such as making it easier for individuals to realize the returns to the land they worked (and might invest in) and subsidies via land granted to potential migrants (international as well as intranational). In some cases, land policies involved making unoccupied or unemployed land available; but not infrequently, ownership or use rights were transferred or seized from previous users—such as Natives or squatters—to other parties.

---

4. For discussion of institutional changes and their effects see Engerman and Sokoloff (1997, 2002). There had been nine European nations involved in the settlement of the Americas, some of whom were also involved with settlements in Asia and Africa.

5. See, for example, Acemoglu, Johnson, and Robinson (2001), Nugent and Robinson (2010), and Engerman and Sokoloff (2005a, 2006).

Table 1.1   **The composition of populations in European colonial domains**

		Non-whites	Whites	Ratio of whites to others
BRITAIN	1850			
Europe		15	347,691	23,179.400
Asia		97,356,000	62,162	0.001
Australasia		155,000	131,800	0.850
Africa		242,800	67,868	0.280
North America		120,000	1,410,400	11.753
South America		99,571	3,958	0.040
West Indies		639,708	71,350	0.112
TOTAL		98,613,094	2,095,229	0.021
FRANCE	1926			
Africa (all)		32,883,000	1,331,400	0.040
Americas (all)		492,500	48,500	0.098
Asia		20,415,000	23,500	0.001
Oceania		71,600	16,400	0.229
TOTAL		53,862,100	1,419,800	0.026
GERMANY	1913			
Africa		12,084,436	22,405	0.002
Pacific/Oceania		961,000	6,454	0.007
ITALY	1931			
Africa		2,380,560	69,441	0.029
BELGIUM	1900			
Africa		30,000,000	1,958	0.00007
NETHERLANDS	1900			
East Indies		36,000,000	75,927	0.002
West Indies		85,571	6,310	0.074
PORTUGAL	1935			
Africa		7,619,258	85,024	0.011

Sources: For Britain, Martin (1967); for France, Southworth (1931, 26); for Germany, Townsend (1930, 265–66); for Italy, Clark (1936, 35); for Portugal, Kuczynski (1936, 95); for Netherlands West Indies, Kuczynski (1936, 103); for Netherlands East Indies, *Statesman's Yearbook* (1909, 881–934); and for Belgium, *Statesman's Yearbook* (1901, 505). For a lower Belgian Congo estimate, see Hochschild (1998, 232–33).

Note: Given the periodic demographic and political changes, the racial compositions of the Spanish colonies, mainly in the Americas and the Philippines as well as in Africa, varied considerably over time. For estimates for 1570 and 1650, see table 1.4. In 1890, prior to the losses in the Spanish–American War, the colonies of Cuba, Puerto Rico, and the Philippines were 85 percent nonwhite.

Land policy had a major impact on the pace of regional development, but it was influenced by the degree of centralization of authority: whether the national government would have exclusive jurisdiction over land policy, or whether states, provinces, or other subnational districts permitted separate land policies.

Another critical issue that faced the colonial authorities was how to secure or attract enough labor to realize the potential fruits of the abundant land and natural resources. The colonies in the Americas were hardly unique in their attention to the adequacy of labor supply.[6] Indeed, population had been a longstanding concern of many elites and statesmen, especially those of a mercantilist bent, in many societies around the globe.[7] Some were concerned with underpopulation and introduced restrictions on emigration, although some national policymakers, as in England, believed that there was overpopulation and Malthusian difficulties within parts of Europe and encouraged outmigration.[8] The situation in the New World was quite different, however, because of the extreme scarcity of labor that the European colonizers found in the New World, either on contact, or soon afterward as the diseases they brought with them wrought depopulation of the Native Americans, estimated by some to be a decline of more than 80 percent of the population.[9] Prior to the great decline after 1492, it was possible that the population of the Americas exceeded the total of the twelve major Western European nations.[10] The recognition that labor was essential to extract income from colonies was one major reason (the wealth of the areas settled was another) why the Spanish, the first Europeans to organize colonies in the Americas, chose to focus their efforts on the more densely populated and richer areas we know as Mexico and Peru. There, the Spanish adapted some of the hierarchical institutions utilized by the Aztecs and Incas, and introduced their own systems (such as *encomienda*) involving grants to Spanish settlers of claims to labor or tribute from Native Americans, to obtain much of the desired labor supplies.

Colonies established later, after a period of about one century, whether British, French, Portuguese, Dutch, Swedish, or Danish, had to manage without much in the way of a native labor force, and therefore had to tap outside sources. Unconstrained by law or morality (no colony or country in the New World, for example, maintained more than a temporary prohibition on slavery or on the slave trade before 1777), those with climates and soils well suited for crops such as sugar or cacao obtained the dominant share of their labor forces from the African market in slaves.[11] Although

6. For discussions of settlement issues in British North America see Galenson (1996), Smith (1947), and Baseler (1998). For a description of the related problem in the Spanish colonies, see Elliot (2006). The French situation is described in Boucher (2008) and Prichard (2004).

7. See Heckscher (1935).

8. For England the major problem was seen to be overpopulation, leading to an encouragement of emigration. Elsewhere, as seen in the attempts to restrict outmigration, the problem was quite the opposite. For an examination of emigration restrictions, see Engerman (2002). For a general discussion of European population at this time, see De Vries (1976).

9. See the summary essay by Ubelaker in Denevan (1976). See also Livi-Bacci (2008).

10. For European population c. 1500, see Maddison (2003). The population of these twelve Western European countries is estimated at forty-eight million. For a survey of estimates made of the native populations of the Americas prior to European arrival see Sánchez-Albornoz (1974), with no firm conclusion presented within a range of 13.3 million to 112 million.

11. In 1777 the state of Vermont became the first locale to end slavery, but this did require a period of apprenticeships and freed, at most, nineteen slaves. Most slave emancipations did not lead to an immediate freeing, but did require a period of apprenticeship of some fifteen to thirty years for those considered to be born free.

their heavy reliance on slaves may have been encouraged somewhat by proximity to Africa, by far the factor most responsible seems to have been the development of the gang and other systems of organizing slave labor that gave large slave plantations a substantial efficiency advantage in producing those highly profitable commodities.[12] Colonies with the appropriate natural endowments soon came to specialize in these crops, and their demand for labor kept slave prices above what employers in areas more fit for grain or mixed agriculture could afford.[13] The result was that the relatively few colonies in the Americas that lacked either a large native population or the conditions conducive to growing sugar and other slave-intensive staples had to exert themselves to mobilize labor forces drawn from Europe and of European descent.

The British colonies on the North American mainland (above the Rio Grande) exemplify this pattern. Having been established in locales with only sparse numbers of Native Americans, especially after the Indians suffered from the introduction of diseases from Europe, and receiving only modest inflows of slaves until well into the eighteenth century (especially the states north of the Mason-Dixon Line), the thirteen colonies (or their ruling authorities) realized that they would have to increase their populations if they were to be successful. They quickly set about devising institutions and policies that would attract migrants from Europe. The basic foundation of their campaign was the institution of indentured servitude, which meant an exchange of the cost of transport for several years of labor, permitting those with inadequate funds to migrate. After a protracted process of passing and implementing laws aimed at improving the enforcement of both sides of the indenture contract (and improving terms to secure an edge over competitors), this was enormously effective and it accounted for more than 75 percent of arrivals from Europe to the thirteen colonies.[14] Other inducements, which were offered in some form for extended periods by all of these colonies, included easy and very low-cost access to owning land, and some forms of tax exemption.

The active pursuit of European migrants by the British colonies on the mainland contrasts sharply with the policies of Spanish America.[15] Although the first waves of settlers in Spain's colonies, particularly those from the mili-

---

12. Slavery was not an institutional innovation of the American settlers, since slavery had long existed in many places. Nor was the plantation production of sugar by slave labor new, since this had been important in the Mediterranean after the Crusades. See Galloway (1989) and Engerman (2007).

13. The development of slavery and sugar production in the British and French West Indies did take some twenty-five to fifty years, the initial period being based primarily on free white or indentured labor producing tobacco. For the French case see Boucher (2008) and for the British Appleby (1996).

14. See, among others, Smith (1947), and Grubb (1985). For a discussion of French indentured labor, see Boucher (2008).

15. See Elliot (2006), Haring (1947), and Altman and Horn (1991).

tary or from elite backgrounds, were rewarded with grants of land, claims on Native Americans, relief from taxes, and other incentives, the Crown began early in the sixteenth century to regulate and restrict the flow of European migrants to its colonies in the Americas.[16] The stringency of the limits did vary somewhat over time, due to the population changes and movements, such as the migration of expelled Moriscos in the early seventeenth century. There were occasionally interventions designed to effect specific movements of population from Europe as well as of slaves to specific colonies including Mexico and Peru, judged especially worthy or needy of support, but overall there is no doubt that Spanish policies limited, rather than encouraged, the migration of Europeans to the New World.[17] A salient illustration is the conspicuous failure of the Spanish Crown to approve proposals for indentured labor trading free transportation in return for future labor services. The starkly divergent approaches of the Spanish and British mainland colonies toward migration may appear puzzling, especially as their agricultural sectors were similar in consisting largely of grain and animal products, but we argue that the fundamental explanation for this difference is that the most important Spanish colonies (i.e., Mexico, Peru, and Colombia) were relatively abundant in labor as compared to their British mainland counterparts; the population density in 1700 in the three leading Spanish colonies was several times greater than for the British mainland colonies.[18] Their relatively substantial Native American populations kept returns to unskilled labor low, reducing the incentives for Spaniards who might have contemplated migration to the New World, and also meant that the elites in the colonies did not need to lobby the Crown to change its policies. The other important factor behind the maintenance of the strict limitations on immigration, in our view, was the greater centralization or concentration of political authority. Not only did the imposed controls apply to immigration to all of the Spanish colonies in the Americas, but centering the government structures for Spanish America in Mexico City and Lima meant that outlying areas with different conditions and demands for labor (such as Argentina) were largely deprived of autonomy or even influence in policy.

These contrasts in land and labor policies that had emerged early in the colonial period essentially endured into the nineteenth century, by which time most of the societies in the Americas were independent nations and nominal democracies, and at times, had moved beyond this politically.[19] Despite periodic spells of political tension (if not conflict) about immigration, generally coinciding with macroeconomic contractions (or focused on specific ethnic groups), the United States (and Canada) continued to pursue

16. Elliot (2006).
17. Moses ([1898] 1965) and Sánchez-Albornoz (1974). In the seventeenth century Spain also suffered from a population decline. See Parry (1966).
18. See estimates in McEvedy and Jones (1978), Maddison (2003), and Carter et al. (2006).
19. See Rout (1976) for the dates of Latin American independence.

policies that were generally extremely favorable to immigration. Although state (provincial) and local governments on or inside the western frontier of the time may have been the most aggressive in courting migrants, the importance of the consistently liberal stances of the U.S. and Canadian governments in making public land available in small plots at low cost to all who sought to settle should not be underestimated. The usefulness of offering easy access to land in attracting migrants was universally understood, and indeed helps to explain that in an era of labor scarcity, cities and long-settled areas in the East concerned about their labor supplies accounted for the major opposition to the federal government disposing of land out West on generous terms.

Despite most societies having achieved independence, and other radical changes in their political environment, there was much continuity in Latin America. Most notably perhaps, the region remained largely dependent on the population born there—whether of European or Native American descent. Immigration from abroad was not much more than a trickle, except for the experiences of Argentina, Uruguay, Brazil, Chile, and several of the smaller nations beginning late in the nineteenth century.[20] Responsibility for this failure to attract immigrants cannot be laid solely on the policies of the nations of Latin America. With the improving levels of material welfare and economic opportunity that the United States could offer as it industrialized, it was now an increasingly tough competitor for immigrants from Europe, and the United States was the major recipient of migrants from Europe.[21] That being said, however, it is striking that although there were many appeals for programs to entice more immigrants, inspired in part by the evident success of the United States, most of the programs purporting to achieve that goal were either framed very narrowly or flawed in design. Even when public lands were to be made available for purchase, the terms or other details of the laws tended to keep prices high or greatly advantage the wealthy and privileged in access. This evident lack of concern by the authorities with offering incentives to migrants was likely not unrelated to the generally poor record throughout Latin America (though better in Argentina, Uruguay, and Chile, which were relatively labor scarce for the region) in providing for public schooling, as well as to the policies that a number of countries, such as Mexico and Colombia, implemented late in the nineteenth century (when land values had risen) that transferred to large landowners the rights to land traditionally held and worked by Native Americans as community property.

20. See Willcox (1929), and Davie (1936).
21. See Maddison (2003) on the greatly widening gap between the per capita income of the United States and of Latin America during the nineteenth century. The increasing relative backwardness in Latin America seemingly occurs after independence from Spain, and amidst a series of civil and international wars. The changing political structure (or lack of same) requires more attention.

In this chapter, we lay out the basis for our view that the record of the evolution of land and immigration institutions in the Americas, since colonization, provides broad support to the idea that the initial factor endowments are of fundamental importance. We highlight, in particular, the significance of labor scarcity or abundance rather than placing exclusive weight on political factors, as in Lindert (2011). Where labor was scarce, even political and economic elites who may have had disproportionate power in shaping institutions were willing to extend privileges, including low-cost access to land, to ordinary people as a means of attracting or mobilizing them. Not only was the influence of labor scarcity direct and immediate, but it may also have had long-lasting effects in fostering greater economic and political equality and the different outcomes that might flow from such conditions. Where labor was relatively abundant, however, elites had less reason to share privileges as a means of attracting more labor, and likely were less constrained in their ability to shape institutions to advantage them. In section 1.2, we develop our argument with a brief sketch of the history of land and immigration institutions during the colonial period. In section 1.3, we discuss how these institutions evolved during the nineteenth century and devote some attention to detailing how variation across countries within Latin America and across the states of the United States is generally consistent with our hypothesis. Section 1.4 deals with several other British colonies, and section 1.5 concludes.

1.2   Migrations to the Americas

A central issue, for all of the colonies, was labor supply. This had obvious and substantial implications for the ability to take advantage of the abundant land and other natural resources. The seriousness of this constraint was a major reason why the Spanish, the first Europeans to arrive, chose to focus their efforts on the areas in the Americas with the largest and richest concentrations of native populations (see table 1.2). Another indication of the relative labor scarcity prevailing in the New World is the extensive and unprecedented flow of migrants from Europe and Africa (see table 1.3) that traversed the Atlantic despite high costs of transportation.[22] That about 70 percent of migrants between 1500 and 1760, increasing from roughly 25 percent prior to 1580 and rising to over 75 percent between 1700 and 1760, were Africans brought over involuntarily as slaves is a testament to the high productivity of labor (due to labor scarcity) in the Americas. With their prices set in competitive international markets, slaves ultimately flowed to those locations where their productivity was greatest—and their pro-

---

22. Table 1.3 is based upon the estimates of David Eltis (1999, 2002). For estimates through 1830, see Eltis (1983). Perhaps the most striking of Eltis's findings concerning settlement patterns is that down to 1830 about three times as many enslaved Africans as free Europeans arrived in the New World.

Table 1.2   The estimated distribution of the aboriginal American population, c. 1492

North America (the United States, Canada, Alaska, and Greenland)	4,400,000
Mexico	21,400,000
Central America	5,650,000
Caribbean	5,850,000
Central Andes	11,500,000
Lowland South America	8,500,000

Source: William N. Denevan (1976, 291).

ductivity tended to be greatest in areas with climates and soils well suited for the cultivation of sugar and a few other staple crops. There were no serious national or cultural barriers to owning or using them in any colony, since slavery was legal in all colonies, and welcome in the colonies of all the major European powers. The Spanish and British settlements each received between one-half and two-thirds of their pre-1760 immigrants from Africa. In contrast, the colonies of other nations were more dependent on slave labor, over 80 percent of all immigrants to the French and Dutch colonies were slaves, and the figure was about 70 percent for the Portuguese.

The areas in the Caribbean, the northern coast of South America, and Brazil had a comparative advantage in sugar, cacao, and a few other crops, and they relatively soon specialized in producing these commodities on large plantations, obtaining the majority of their labor force from the slave trade. These colonies had relatively little need for large numbers of European immigrants. For different reasons, the same was true for Spanish America. European immigrants (and *creoles*) were initially required to defeat the Native Americans, establish control over and then defend territory, and provide the basic political and economic structures, but the majority of the overall labor force was provided by the Native Americans.

With Spain the pioneer in establishing substantial settlements, over 70 percent of the migrants to the Americas between 1500 and 1580 landed in Spanish colonies. That share plunged over time, to almost 14 percent between 1700 and 1760. Part of this precipitous fall was due to the rise of the colonies of other European nations, but a more important factor was Spain's severe tightening of the restrictions on who was allowed to migrate to its colonies.[23] Unlike the other major European colonizers, Spain, with the support, if not instigation, of the *pensulares* and *creoles* already there, progressively raised more formidable obstacles to those who might have otherwise ventured to the New World to seek their fortunes. The authorities in Spain seem to have been motivated both by a desire to keep costs down by limiting the numbers of population centers to defend, as well as, politically, by the desires of those who had arrived early or descended from those who

23. Spain's relative decline, however, was at a time during which there remained absolute increases in the number of migrants.

Table 1.3   **European directed transatlantic migration, by European nation and continent of origin, 1500–1760**

	Africans leaving Africa on ships of each nation (net)	Europeans leaving each nation for Americas	Africans arriving in American regions claimed by each nation
Before 1580			
Spain	10	139	45
Portugal	56	58	13
Britain	2	0	0
Total	68	197	58
1580 to 1640			
Spain	0	188	289
Portugal	594	110	181
France	0	4	2
Netherlands	10	2	8
Britain	3	87	4
Total	607	391	484
1640 to 1700			
Spain	0	158	141
Portugal	259	50	225
France	40	23	75
Netherlands	151	13	49
Britain	379	285	277
Total	829	529	767
1700 to 1760			
Spain	1	193	271
Portugal	958	300	768
France	458	27	414
Netherlands	223	5	123
Britain	1,206	222	1,013
Total	2,846	747	2,589

Source: David Eltis (1999, 2002).

did, to maintain their privileged positions.[24] Early in the sixteenth century, they began to impose strict controls as reflected in requirement for licenses over who could settle in the Americas, with preference shown for relatives of those already there, and permission denied to citizens of European countries other than Spain as well as to non-Catholics. Licenses to emigrate were

24. Large blocks of land and claims on Native American labor were often granted as incentives or rewards to the early waves of settlers, especially military men, missionaries, and others of some prominence. Although smaller holdings could be obtained through sales, generally the more important were governmental land grants, the larger tended to be the holdings, and the more unequal the distributions of wealth and political power would become. The initial land grants were often nontradable by the recipients, but transferable by the Spanish Crown. Hence, later migrants to colonies might indeed have eroded the value of property rights held by earlier cohorts. It is not difficult to comprehend why the already established population of European descent was less than enthusiastic about a liberal immigration policy during the colonial era. On Spanish settlement of the Americas, see Elliott (2006) and Gibson (1966).

initially restricted to single men, but were ultimately extended to married men accompanied by their families; single white women were never allowed, influenced in part on the availability of Native American women.[25] It seems highly unlikely that such a restrictive stance toward immigration would have been retained if there had not already been a substantial supply of Indians to work the land and otherwise produce with the assets owned by the elites and the Spanish Crown. In this sense, at least, the preferred policy must have been ultimately due to the factor endowments.[26] Another mechanism through which the relatively ample local supply of labor provided by the Native Americans could have reduced immigration was through keeping the returns to unskilled labor low, and in so doing reducing the desire of Spanish unskilled labor to migrate.

What stands out from the estimates presented in table 1.4 is how small the percentages of populations composed of those of European descent were in Spanish America and in the economies focused on sugar until well into the nineteenth century. The populations of those colonies suitable for cultivating sugar, such as Barbados, Jamaica, and Brazil, came to be dominated by those of African descent imported to work on the large slave plantations.[27] The populations of the Spanish colonies were composed predominantly of Indians and *mestizos*. This was largely because these colonies had been established and built up in places where there had been substantial populations of Native Americans beforehand, and because flows of Europeans were constrained by the restrictive immigration policies of Spain. If not for these policies, it is probable that the societies in the southern cone of South America, such as Argentina and Chile, might well have attracted many more immigrants from Europe during the colonial period. As a result, less than 20 percent of the population in Spanish America was composed of whites as late as the beginning of the nineteenth century.[28]

25. See Moses ([1898] 1965), Elliott (2006), and Parry (1966).

26. At first it seems somewhat puzzling, or contradictory to the idea that the factor endowment was the crucial determinant of policy, that Spanish authorities did not actively encourage immigration to colonies without a substantial supply of readily available Indian labor, like Argentina. On reflection, however, it seems likely that Spanish policy toward immigration to places like Argentina was simply incidental, with the overall policy as regards immigration to the New World based on the factor endowments and politics in all of Spanish America together. Hence, Spanish policy was probably driven by conditions in Mexico and Peru—the most populous and valued colonies. Since these centers of Spanish America had an abundance of Indian labor, the local elites and the authorities in Spain were able to maintain restrictive policies.

27. See, in particular, Dunn (1972) on the English colonies and Schwartz (1985) on Brazil. In the early period of settlement in Brazil, slaves were also used in mining.

28. See the notes to table 1.4 for estimates of the shares of Indians and *mestizos* in the Spanish American populations. The immigration policies were especially restrictive toward single European women, and this too likely contributed over the long run to the small proportion of the population that was white. The Spanish Antilles did have a relatively large white population, reflecting the limited number of Indians after depopulation, and the long lag between the beginnings of the settlement and the sugar boom that developed there only after the start of the nineteenth century. On the Caribbean in general, and for a discussion of the patterns of Cuban settlement, see Knight (1990). For an ethnic breakdown of Caribbean populations in 1750, 1830, and 1880, see Engerman and Higman (1997).

Table 1.4   The distribution and composition of population in New World economies

Area	Year	White (%)	Black (%)	Indian (%)	Share in New World population
		A.			
Spanish America	1570	1.3	2.5	96.3	83.5
	1650	6.3	9.3	84.4	84.3
	1825	18.0	22.5	59.5	55.2
	1935	35.5	13.3	50.4	30.3
Brazil	1570	2.4	3.5	94.1	7.6
	1650	7.4	13.7	78.9	7.7
	1825	23.4	55.6	21.0	11.6
	1935	41.0	35.5	23.0	17.2
U.S. and Canada	1570	0.2	0.2	99.6	8.9
	1650	12.0	2.2	85.8	8.1
	1825	79.6	16.7	3.7	33.2
	1935	89.4	8.9	1.4	52.6
		B.			
Barbados	1801	19.3	80.7		
Mexico	1793	18.0	10.0	72.0	
Peru	1795	12.6	7.3	80.1	
Venezuela	1800–09	25.0	62.0	13.0	
Cuba	1792	49.0	51.0		
Brazil	1798	31.1	61.2	7.8	
Chile	1790	8.3	6.7	85.0	

Sources: A. The data for 1570, 1650, and 1825 are from Rosenblat (1954, 88 [1570], 58 [1650], and 35–6 [1825]); the data for 1935 are from Kuczynski (1936, 109–10). The Antilles have been included within Spanish America in all years. B. Line 1: Watts (1987, 311). Lines 2–5: Lockhart and Schwartz (1983, 342). Line 6: Merrick and Graham (1979, 29). Line 7: Mamalakis (1980, 7–9).

Notes: In 1825, the category "castas," which included "mestizajes, mulattos, etc.," and represented 18.17 percent of the total population in Spanish America, was divided two-thirds Indian, one-third black, except for the Antilles where all were considered to be blacks. In 1935, there were a number counted as "others" (generally Asian), so the distributions may not total to 100 percent.

It was the northern part of North America, the temperate-zone colonies that became the United States and Canada, that was distinctive in its reliance on attracting immigrants from Europe, a reliance forced to some extent later on the southern temperate-zone colonies of Argentina, Chile, and Uruguay. The northern temperate areas had only very small numbers of Native Americans on the eastern rim of the continent, where the most substantial European settlements were located, and thus the composition of their populations soon came to be essentially determined by the groups who immigrated and their respective rates of natural increase. This was of particular significance in New England, where net migration was negative over the colonial period, but the rate of natural increase very high. Although significant numbers of slaves were employed in the southern colonies, on the whole the factor endowments in the thirteen colonies and Canada were far more hospitable to the cultivation of grains, tobacco, and animal products than sugar (or other crops that were grown on large slave plantations during this era). The colonies in this area accordingly absorbed far more Europeans than they did African slaves, and they stood out in the hemisphere with whites accounting for roughly 85 percent of the population and labor force.

Perhaps because it was the one region in the New World that was dependent on attracting large numbers of voluntary migrants from Europe during the colonial period that the colonies in the northern part of North America distinguished themselves soon after their establishment for institutions supportive of immigration and attractive to immigrants. The willingness of the thirteen colonies to accept convict labor is an aspect of their history that Americans prefer to deemphasize, but a better known and important example of this pattern is indentured servitude, a contractual means of extending credit (primarily the cost of transportation across the Atlantic) whereby the servant promised to work for the recruitment agent (or the agent to which he assigned or sold the contract) in a specified colony and for a specified period of time. This system was first introduced by the Virginia Company, designed explicitly to attract potential migrants from Britain, but the innovation, which was related in legal basis to contracts as servants of husbandry (if not apprentices as well), soon spread to carry migrants from a variety of countries in Europe to British colonies.[29] Over the entire colonial period, upward of 75 percent of European migrants to British America came as indentured servants. Although some may regard the extensive use of indentured servitude in the British colonies as due primarily to a distinctive British heritage, this characterization seems unwarranted. Contractual forms similar to apprenticeships and servants of husbandry and migration of convicts existed in a number of European countries, including Spain, Portugal, France, and earlier in Northern Italy and Sicily. In Spain, however, the Crown chose not to implement a proposal to provide transport to its colonies in return for obligated labor services on arrival.[30] The evidence appears consistent with the view that the urgency of the demand for workers from Europe contributed to the institutional innovation and its diffusion among Europeans.

Another way in which the colonies in the northern part of North America strove to attract immigrants was through making ownership of plots of land rather accessible. Of course, with the enormous abundance of land relative to labor, land was relatively cheap, especially compared to the wage,

29. On convict labor in America see Ekirch (1987). See also Galenson (1981), Smith (1947), and Perry (1990).
30. See, for example, Reynolds (1957), Coates (2001), Boucher (2008), and Altman and Horn (1991).

and easy to obtain (by European standards) through the market. But the experience in the colonies on the North American mainland sometimes went well beyond that, with provincial authorities making obvious use of land grants to attract migrants. In the British colonies, the distribution of land was left to the individual colonies, once the land was transferred from the Crown to proprietors or the government of the crown colonies. Over time, some quite different, but persistent, regional patterns emerged. The New England colonies made grants, generally of small plots, to individuals, but land grants were not directly used to attract indentured servants (as they were elsewhere)—perhaps because of the relatively small number of immigrants who came or were needed to come to the region.[31]

It was in the Southern colonies (states), where staple crops such as tobacco and rice were grown and the demand for European field labor may have been especially high, that land grants were most targeted as attracting indentured servants and other migrants. During the seventeenth century, Virginia introduced the headright system (grants of land to settlers, or to those who enticed others to settle) to stimulate in-migration, with the only requirement a three-year period of settlement. Indentured servant laborers who came to Virginia were generally to be granted fifty acres when their term had expired. Variants of the headright system were adopted in Maryland and the Carolinas. The Middle Atlantic colonies of New Jersey and Pennsylvania also employed variants of the headright system, but, in both, the grants of land were subsidized, rather than free. Late in the eighteenth century, after independence, a number of what were now state governments extended their liberal land policies to include preemption for squatters.[32]

It is perhaps worth highlighting how different the attention to, and prevalence of, land ownership was in the northern part of North America as compared to Europe. Tenancy and farm labor were clearly much more common in Britain and France than in their American colonies on the mainland, with these European arrangements and other means of allocating land achieved over a very long history and in environments with rather different land-labor ratios.[33] The attempts to bring variants of the British manorial system to, for example, Maryland and Pennsylvania, and the French seigneurial system (in Canada), were, however, not successful given the land availability, crops to be grown, and their optimal scale of production. Thus, in the French and British mainland colonies, there was adaptation in land policy to allow for smaller units worked by owner-occupiers and for more flexibility in pro-

---

31. Bidwell and Falconer (1925), Harris (1953), and, on the Dutch case, Rife (1931).
32. Gray (1933), Gates (1968), and Ford (1910).
33. On England see Allen (1992), and for an examination of France contrasted with England see Heywood (1981). See also Nettels (1963), Barnes (1931), Craven (1970), Ackerman (1977), and Bond (1919).

duction.[34] These adaptations meant that the distribution and allocation of land were more similar across these colonies than they were with those in the metropolis in Europe. Because of the long tradition of property requirements for voting, the wider distribution of land was significant not just for economic purposes, but it also meant a broader base for voting.[35] Thus, not only could voting influence land policy, land policy could also influence voting.

There was, of course, no such liberality regarding land policy in Spanish America. Without any significant interest in attracting more immigration to its colonies, but with concern for maintaining control and a stream of revenue from the labor of the Native American labor force, the initial policy in nearly all of the colonies with substantial populations was the *encomienda* system, which consisted of Crown-awarded claims to tribute (in goods, service, time, and cash) from a specified body of natives working on the land where they had previously resided. Relatively small numbers, never many more than 500 in the first half of the sixteenth century, of these often enormous grants were awarded in any single colony. Cortes was assigned 115,000 natives in Mexico, and Pizarro 20,000 in Peru. In Peru, for example, only 5 percent of the Spanish population in the mid-sixteenth century held *encomiendas*.[36] These *encomanderos* and their families became, in effect, the aristocracy of Spanish America. When pressure from depopulation and movement toward a cash economy, as well as Church concern about treatment of Native Americans, began to alter the *encomienda* system, they were well positioned to assemble large private holdings of much of the best located and most fertile land. The high concentration of land holding that developed over time in Spanish America paralleled the extreme inequality that prevailed in wealth, human capital, political influence, and other dimensions.

1.3   Land and Immigration Policy in the Americas

As the United States became a sovereign nation and most of Spanish America gained independence from Spain over the late eighteenth and early nineteenth centuries, there were many important changes across the Americas in institutions and in the economic environment of great relevance to immigration and land policy. First, if not foremost, the structures of government institutions were radically altered. Although Canada remained a colony with limited autonomy until the 1860s, and Brazil was, after 1822, an

---

34. On the seigneurial system in French Canada, see Trudel (1967) and the literature cited there.

35. See Keyssar (2000) and Rusk (2001). See also Engerman and Sokoloff (2005b).

36. Burkholder and Johnson (2001). For discussions of the *economienda,* see, among other sources, Simpson (1982) and Himmerich y Valencia (1991), and on the *mita* system see Cole (1985).

independent monarchy, most of the major societies were both independent and at least nominally democratic and, if not free of slavery, with severe restrictions on slave imports.[37] The new national governments, and their ability to design policies targeted to the interests (as felt and expressed by various domestic groups) of their own individual countries and to implement them, were crucial and novel elements. Among those interests, of course, was the means of settling unoccupied territories within the national boundaries, if not expanding those boundaries, which led to costly wars in the nineteenth century.[38] This interest in new settlements gave impetus to both liberal immigration (and also intracountry migration as well) and land policies, particularly in countries where labor was especially scarce.

Also of great consequence for the formulation of immigration and land policy was the onset of industrialization in the United States and Western Europe and the acceleration of technological change. Economic growth and the decrease in the cost of transoceanic transportation increased the propensity of Europeans to migrate to the New World (without having to indenture themselves), but also increased the relative desirability of the United States as their destination as compared to other countries in the hemisphere.[39] These advances also spurred the growth of international trade, and increased the returns to the exploitation of the abundant land and natural resources in the New World. In so doing, they contributed to an increase in the value of land, a development that not only likely influenced the behavior of immigrants in countries where land was accessible, but also that of elites in countries where they exercised disproportionate political power.

Although there were frequent changes in the precise details, overall there was remarkable continuity in the basic orientation of U.S. policies in favor of immigration and relatively easy access to land in small plots. At the national level, there were periodic calls for restrictions, but except for ending the international slave trade in 1808, those measures imposed in the name of public health, and those (after 1880) on Japanese and Chinese immigration, serious obstacles were not introduced until the 1920s.[40] State policies differed substantially, however. Over the nineteenth century, those states new to the Union often sent abroad delegations or placed advertisements to attract immigrants to their environs, and highlighted liberal qualifications for residence and participation in local elections and commitments to public schools and other infrastructure of particular interest to poten-

37. On Latin American slavery see Rout (1976) and Klein (1986), and on the independence movement see Lynch (1986).
38. Gates (1968). On Latin American wars in the nineteenth century and data on wars with Indians in the United States, see Clodfelter (2008). For a survey of Indian-White relations in the United States and their impact on land changes see Washburn (1975).
39. See the data in Willcox (1929) and Davie (1936).
40. See Hutchinson (1981), Risch (1937), and Farnam (1938). See also Engerman (2002).

tial migrants.[41] Later in the nineteenth century, however, concentrations of immigrants in industrial cities led some states (mostly in the Northeast) to raise difficulties by introducing literacy tests for voting. Again, there seems a relation between labor scarcity and public policies toward immigrants.[42]

With the establishment of the United States, many of the original states gave up their claims to land in the West, and ceded principal authority in public land policy to the federal government. This may well have proved fortuitous for the maintenance of liberal land policies—which generally evolved over time through new legislations (see table 1.5) to make the terms for individuals seeking to acquire and settle on land progressively easier.[43] These changes were the basis of debate among the representatives of the different regions in Congress and elsewhere, often intertwined with other aspects of political disagreement. This reflected the broad range of issues that the controversies over land dealt with. For example, because of the government's budget constraint, there was a tradeoff between revenues from land sales and revenues from the protective tariffs favored by Northeastern manufacturers. Given that land policy could influence the distribution of population across regions (and thus wage rates), commodity prices, land value, and the location and structure of output, political disagreement should not have been surprising. What is most striking, perhaps, is that despite such political disagreements, a commitment to broad and easy access to those seeking to settle on public lands was generally sustained and deepened.[44]

What may have begun as an intended set policy, however, shifted numerous times over the antebellum period, and later, generally in more liberal directions.[45] From 1796 to 1820 the government provided credit to purchasers; this ended following the panic of 1819 and numerous defaults, but the growth of the banking system did minimize its impact. Other dimensions, however, went into a liberalized direction. The pace at which land was surveyed and made available increased. The Preemption Act of 1841, following a decade of more individualized legislation in which title was not specified beforehand, permitted settlers (squatters) to purchase settled lands before they would be auctioned, allowing them to keep the value of improvements made before title was legalized. The minimum size of purchases fell from 640 acres in 1796 to 40 acres as of 1832, before postbellum adjustments were made due to requirements for larger holdings for desert lands, timber culture, and related matters. With the minimum price per acre cut from $2 in 1796 to $1.25 after 1820, the minimum purchase price for a plot fell from

---

41. See discussions in, among other sources, Hibbard (1924), Robbins (1942), and Stephenson (1917).
42. See sources cited in footnote 35.
43. See Atack, Bateman, and Parker (2000) and Gates (1968).
44. See, among other sources, Wellington (1914) and Feller (1984).
45. Gates (1968).

Table 1.5   Significant public land laws, United States, 1785–1916

Year	Law	Min price/acre ($)	Minimum acreage	Maximum acreage	Conditions and terms
1785	Land Ordinance of 1785	1	640	none	Cash
1787	Northwest Ordinance of 1787	1	640	none	1/2 cash, balance in 3 months
1796	Land Act of 1796	2	640	none	1/2 in 30 days, balance in 1 yr
1800	Harrison Land Act	2	320	none	1/4 in 30 days, balance in 3 yrs at 6%
1804	Land Act of 1804	2	160	none	$1.64/acre for cash; credit terms as per Land Act of 1800
1812	General Land Office established				
1820	Land Act of 1820	1.25	80	none	Cash only
1830	Preemption Act of 1830	1.25		160	Permits squatters to purchase
1832	Land Act of 1832	1.25	40	none	Cash
1841	General Preemption Act of 1841	1.25	40	160	Pre-emption only. Cash.
1854	Graduation Act	0.125	40	none	Price progressively reduced on unsold lands to 12.5 cents/acre after 30 yrs
1862	Homestead Act	free	40	160	$10 registration fee. 5 yrs continuous residence on land for full title
1873	Timber Culture Act	free	160	160	Cultivation of trees on 1/4 of lot for title. Amended in 1878 to 1/16th of lot.
1877	Desert Land Act	1.25		640	Irrigation within 3 yrs; $0.25 per acre on entry, balance due upon compliance
1878	Timber and Stone Act	2.50	40	160	Stipulation that timber and stone for personal use only and not for speculation or other parties.
1909	Enlarged Homestead Act	Free		320	Five years residence with continuous cultivation
1912	Three-Year Homestead Act	Free		160	Seven months residence a yr for 3 yrs
1916	Stock Raising Homestead Act	Free		640	On land only suitable for grazing

Source: Atack, Bateman, and Parker (2000).

$1,280 in 1796 to $50 in 1832. Other policies that made land more available followed. The Graduation Act of 1854 established that land not yet sold could be sold at a price below $1.25, with the price prorated based on the length of time before sale (12.5 cents per acre after thirty years). And, in 1862, the Homestead Act (which was extended or liberalized several times more before 1920) provided 160 acres for each family head who either resided on land for five years or who paid $1.25 per acre after six months' residence. That the westward movement accelerated over the nineteenth century, and that more individuals from lower income groups were able to acquire land, was to no small degree attributable to the liberal land policies.

The government's choice between a high price and a low price land policy had a number of implications. Low prices or free land would make it easy for more people to acquire land, attracting more people to the West, either initially as landowners, or else as tenants with the hopes of becoming landowners in the future. Low prices would mean, in general, low revenues, leading to more reliance on alternative sources of income such as tariffs, which the Northeast would like. The encouragement to westward movement of workers would reduce the available labor supply and raise wage rates in the areas of outflow (which manufacturing interest in the Northeast would not like). The maintenance of liberal land policies was certainly not predestined in a complex political environment, but ultimately the highly democratic political institutions and the well-founded belief that such policies would enhance returns to labor generally and the gains from free immigration may have together been decisive.

That not everyone accepted the case for a liberal land policy, and that even in a country with labor scarcity it might not be advocated or adopted, is illustrated by the arguments for a high land price and/or slow settlement policy offered by two renowned economists: the American Henry Charles Carey and the Englishman Edward Gibbon Wakefield.[46]

Carey argued for high land prices to slow the pace of settlement and to benefit from the positive externalities he attributed to higher population density in urban and previously settled areas. A more influential set of policies, both in theory and in its effect upon policymakers, came from Wakefield. Wakefield was interested in British settlement of Australia and New Zealand, and thought that their growth and development would be aided by ensuring a labor force in older areas, while slowing down the pace of settlement by owners of land in the newer areas. This policy entailed a high price ("sufficient price") to limit the movement of labor from the older areas,

---

46. See Carey (1837–1840), and the discussion in Dorfman (1947, included in the five volume set, years 1946 to 1959). For Wakefield's arguments see his works in 1829 and 1849. Carey was familiar with Wakefield's writings. Wakefield had argued that the Spanish had failed in the Americas because of the absence of sufficient concentration of land. See Burroughs (1965). While Carey apparently had little direct impact on land policy, Wakefield's ideas were implemented in several cases, although of limited success.

with the use of funds collected tied to the payment to help subsidize new immigrants. Thus, Wakefield's proposals would have served to attract immigrants and yet create concentrations of labor with geographically limited settlement. Such a policy was in fact introduced in parts of both Australia and New Zealand, but, given the adaptability of institutions in response to the desires of smallholders, the land size requirements were reduced, and Wakefield's policies did not become a permanent fixture in either place.[47]

Another, and more long-lived, example of where Wakefield's ideas were embraced was in Brazil. In that country, after the grants policy (which also had provision for purchase of land at relatively low prices) of the colonial government had been abolished at independence in 1822, squatting became the dominant means by which individuals of all classes carved land to cultivate or settle in virgin territory. These arrangements were generally not recognized under the law, and came to be viewed as a significant obstacle to the growth of coffee production and development in general. Coffee plantations needed well-defined and secure rights to their land, but also required labor. The land law of 1850, the original draft of which was proposed in 1842, dealt with these issues in the ways prescribed by Wakefield.[48] Public lands were to be offered at high prices, with requirements that all plots purchased be surveyed at the expense of the purchaser. Although early drafts of the law provided for a land tax, which together with revenue from land sales and fees for surveying was intended to pay for the subsidies to immigrants from abroad, the tax was dropped in the final legislation. The impact of the law was to seriously limit access to public lands for ordinary people, including immigrants, and aided elites due to their differential capability of obtaining land and by lowering labor costs. Whether or not the land law of 1850 was a more effective stimulus to immigration than a policy of easy access to land would have been is unclear, but its particulars suggest that its passage and maintenance over time may have been at least partially due to the extreme political and economic inequality that prevailed in Brazil. Here, as in many other countries in Latin America, elites were more capable of shaping policies and institutions to serve their interests than in societies with more democracy and greater equality. The role of political power differences is crucial to understanding decisions made, but, it is argued, the nature of political power is itself influenced by the basic resource endowments.

As we have stressed, virtually all the economies in the Americas had ample supplies of public lands during the nineteenth century, especially when one acknowledges that land traditionally occupied and worked by Native Americans as community property was often viewed as public land—and as such completely unencumbered when depopulation or migration shifted

47. On Australia see Roberts (1968), Macintyre (1999), Wadham, Wilson, and Wood (1964), and Powell and Williams (1975), and for New Zealand see Jourdain (1925), Smith (2005), and McDonald (1952).
48. See Viotti da Costa (1985).

long-time occupants away. Since the respective governments of each colony, province, or nation were regarded as the owners of this resource, they were able to influence the distribution of wealth, as well as the pace of settlement for effective production, by implementing policies to control the availability of land, set land prices, establish minimum or maximum acreages, provide credit for such purposes, and design tax systems on land. Because agriculture was the dominant sector throughout the Americas during the nineteenth century, questions of how best to employ this public resource for the national interest, and how to make the land available for private use, were widely recognized as highly important and often became the subject of protracted political debates and struggles. Land policy was also used as a policy instrument to influence the size of the labor force, either by encouraging immigration through making land readily available or by influencing the regional distribution of labor (or supply of wage labor) through limiting access and raising land prices.

The United States never experienced major obstacles in this regard, and, as noted, the terms of land acquisition became easier over the course of the nineteenth century.[49] The Homestead Act of 1862, which essentially made land free in plots suitable for family farms to all those who settled and worked the land for a specified period, was perhaps the culmination of this policy of promoting broad access to land. Canada pursued similar policies: the Dominion Lands Act of 1872 closely resembled the Homestead Act in both spirit and substance.[50] Argentina and Brazil (as discussed), and also Chile, instituted similar changes as a means to encourage immigration but these efforts were much less directed, and while there were benefits, they were less successful at getting land to smallholders than the programs in the United States and Canada.[51] Thus in Argentina, where a comprehensive land law was passed in 1876 and followed by an extremely restrictive— applying only to Patagonia—Homestead Act in 1884, a number of factors seem to explain the contrast in outcomes. First, the elites of Buenos Aires (the city and province accounted for 40 percent of Argentina's population at the end of the nineteenth century), whose interests favored keeping scarce labor in the province, if not the capital city, were, because of the larger share of the urban population, much more effective at weakening or blocking programs than were their urban counterparts in North America. Second, even those policies nominally intended to broaden access tended to involve large grants to land developers, with the logic that allocative efficiency could best

49. See Gates (1968) for a comprehensive overview of United States land policy. See also Atack, Bateman, and Parker (2000).

50. Discussions of Canadian land policy include Martin (1938), Solberg (1987), Adelman (1994), and Pomfret (1981).

51. On Argentina see Adelman (1994), Amaral (1998), Castro (1991), and Solberg (1987), and on Chile see Solberg (1969) and Collier and Sater (1996). In addition to Viotti da Costa (1985), on Brazilian land policy see also Dean (1971), the excellent discussion in Adelman (1994), as well as Barickman (1998), Schwartz (1985), Summerhill (2003), and Alston, Libecap, and Mueller (1999).

be achieved through exchanges between private agents or transfers to occupants who were already using the land, including those who were grazing livestock. Although the debates over the land laws made frequent reference to the examples provided by the country's North American neighbors, the Argentine laws generally conveyed public lands to private owners in much larger and concentrated holdings than did the policies in the United States and Canada. Third, the processes by which large landholdings might have broken up in the absence of scale economies may have operated very slowly in Argentina: once the land was in private hands, the potential value of land in raising or harvesting livestock may have set too high a floor on land prices for immigrants and other ordinary would-be farmers to manage. Such constraints were exacerbated by the underdevelopment of mortgage and financial institutions more generally.[52] Since these nations maintained policies similar to those by the Spanish regarding education and other matters, they did not greatly benefit from growth after independence.

Indeed, as the growing volume and diversity of international trade during the mid- and late nineteenth century increased the value of land, there seems to have been a wave of policy changes throughout Latin America that not only eschewed the evidently successful U.S. example of liberal land policies, but instead worked to increase the concentration of ownership. At the end of the nineteenth century in Brazil, the abolition of slavery brought about an increased demand for European labor from Spain, Portugal, and Italy to produce coffee for export, now on smaller units than the plantations.[53] This demand for labor led to the provision of subsidies of transportation, cash, or land to attract migrants from southern Europe. Another pattern, but with limited subsidized labor from Spain and Italy developed in Argentina and in Chile, where slavery had ended much earlier and plantation crops had not developed to the extent that they did in Brazil.

Argentina, Canada, and the United States each had an extraordinary abundance of virtually uninhabited public lands to transfer to private hands in the interest of bringing this public resource into production and serving other general interests. In societies such as Mexico, however, the issues at stake in land policy were very different. Good land was relatively scarce, and labor was relatively abundant. Here the lands in question had long been controlled by Native Americans, but without individual private property

---

52. It is generally though, that the introduction of livestock to Argentina, when the Spanish first arrived in the sixteenth century, was the basis for widespread herds of feral cattle that were present during the nineteenth century and would eventually be harvested. Such production of animal products (hides and beef) was associated with scale economies and did not require much in the way of labor. These conditions may have increased the economic viability of large estates where labor was scarce and land abundant. In contrast, because the major crops produced in the expansion of the northern United States and Canada were grains, whose production was relatively labor intensive and characterized by quite limited scale economies, the policy of encouraging smallholding was effective. See Adelman (1994) and Engerman and Sokoloff (2002), for more discussion.

53. On the post-slave adjustment in Brazil, see Eisenberg (1974).

rights. Mexico was not unique in pursuing policies, especially near the end of the nineteenth and the first decade of the twentieth centuries, that had the effect of conferring ownership of much of this land to large non-Native American landholders.[54] Under the regime of Porfirio Díaz, between 1878 and 1908, Mexico effected a massive transfer of such lands (over 10.7 percent of the national territory) to large holders such as survey and land development companies, either in the form of outright grants for services rendered by the companies or for prices set by decree.

In table 1.6 we present estimates for four countries of the fractions of household heads (or of a near equivalent measure) that owned land in agricultural areas in the late nineteenth and early twentieth centuries. The figures indicate enormous differences across the countries in the prevalence of land ownership among the adult male population in rural areas. On the eve of the Mexican Revolution, the figures from the 1910 census suggest that only 2.4 percent of household heads in rural Mexico owned land. The number is quite low. The dramatic land policy measures in Mexico at the end of the nineteenth century may have succeeded in privatizing most of the public lands, but they left the vast majority of the rural population without any land ownership at all. The evidence obviously conforms well with the idea that in societies that began with extreme inequality, such as Mexico, institutions evolved so as to greatly advantage the elite in access to economic opportunities, and they thus contributed to the persistence of that extreme inequality.

In contrast, the proportion of adult males owning land in rural areas was quite high in the United States, at just below 75 percent in 1900. The prevalence of land ownership was markedly lower in the South, where blacks were disproportionately concentrated, with the share for whites being high. The overall picture for the United States is one of a series of liberal land policies, leading up to the Homestead Act of 1862, providing broad access to this fundamental type of economic opportunity. Canada had an even better record, with nearly 90 percent of household heads owning the agricultural lands they occupied in 1901. The estimates of landholding in these two countries support the notion that land policies made a difference, especially when compared to Argentina. The rural regions of Argentina constitute a set of frontier provinces, where one would expect higher rates of ownership than in Buenos Aires. The numbers, however, suggest a much lower prevalence of land ownership than in the two northernmost North American economies.[55] Nevertheless, all of these countries were far more effective than

54. For discussion of Mexican land policy, see McBride (1923), Tannenbaum (1929), and Holden (1994).

55. Our work with the data from the 1914 Argentina census yields the same qualitative results. It is worth noting that the proportions of families that owned land are exaggerated by the 1895 census figures. A close examination of the manuscripts indicates that double counting, in which both the husband and wife were listed as landowners, was prevalent in many parts of Argentina.

Table 1.6	Landholding in rural regions of Mexico, the United States, Canada, and Argentina in the early 1900s

Country, year, and selected regions	Proportion of household heads who own land[a]
Mexico, 1910	
North	3.4
Central	2.0
Gulf	2.1
South Pacific	1.5
Total rural Mexico	2.4
United States, 1900	
North Atlantic	79.2
South Atlantic	55.8
North Central	72.1
South Central	51.4
Western	83.4
Total United States	74.5
Canada, 1901	
Alberta	95.8
Saskatchewan	96.2
Manitoba	88.9
Ontario	80.2
Quebec	90.1
Total Canada	87.1
Argentina, 1895	
Chaco	27.8
Formosa	18.5
Missiones	26.7
La Pampa	9.7
Neuquén	12.3
Rio Negro	15.4
Chubut	35.2
Santa Cruz	20.2
Total for areas covered, Argentina	18.8

Sources: For Mexico: computed by the authors from the 1910 census figures reported in McBride (1923, 154); for the United States: U.S. Census Office (1902, part I, lxvi–xxxv); for Canada: Canada Bureau of Statistics (1914, vol. 4, xii, table 6); for Argentina: computed by the authors from 1895 census figures reported in Cárcano (1925) and Comisión Directiva del Censo de la República Argentina (1898, clvii, table IVd).

[a]Landownership is defined as follows: in Mexico, household heads who own land; in the United States, farms that are owner operated; in Canada, total occupiers of farmlands who are owners; and in Argentina, the ratio of landowners to the number of males between the ages of 18 and 50.

Mexico in making land ownership available to the general population. The contrast between the United States and Canada, with their practices of offering easy access to small units of land, and the rest of the Americas, as seen in the contrast with Argentina and Mexico, is consistent with the hypothesis that the initial extent of inequality influenced the way in which institutions evolved and in so doing helped foster persistence in the degree of inequality over time.[56]

1.4   Institutions and Policies

Economic historians and other social scientists have recently returned to the study of the role of institutions in the processes of economic growth and development. Much attention has been focused on where institutions come from, and why some societies seem to have institutions that are conducive to progress, while others seem plagued for extended periods with those that are less supportive, if not destructive. Some scholars argue that institutions are generally exogenous, arising from idiosyncratic events that led to distinctive institutional heritages that were remarkably durable, such as those from metropolitan areas or from major convulsions such as the French Revolution, which are difficult to predict and often have unexpected or unintended consequences. Others, however, suggest that there are powerful systematic patterns in the ways institutions evolve, shaped by how societies try to deal with the challenges and opportunities framed by the specific environment, state of technology, factor endowment, and other circumstances they face. Improving our knowledge of whether institutions are exogenous or endogenous, and of how flexible they are in adapting to changes in conditions, is crucial to gaining a good understanding of their role in economic development.[57]

Australia apparently had a relatively large population of aborigines when British settlement began in 1788, a number not achieved by Europeans until the 1850s, and after the decline with the English arrival, the aboriginal population has not yet reached the earlier total.[58] As in the Americas, the arrival

---

56. We have omitted here discussion of other Latin American countries for which we have some information on land policy and its changes. See, for example, on Colombia (Bergquist [1998], Bushnell [1993], McGreevey [1971], and Palacios [1980]), Peru (Davies [1984], Ford [1955], and Jacobson [1993]), Costa Rica (Gudmundson [1986]), Bolivia (Klein [1993]), El Salvador (Lindo-Fuentes [1990]), Guatemala (McCreery [1994]), Dominican Republic (Moya Pons [1995]), Central America (Pérez Brignoli [1989] and Roseberry, Gudmundson, and Samper Kutschbach [1995]), Ecuador (Pineo [1996]), and Venezuela (Yarrington [1997]). There is more generally useful material in volumes covering all of Latin America. See the various volumes edited by Bethell, *The Cambridge History of Latin America,* (particularly Bethell 1985 and 1986); Bulmer-Thomas (1994); Bulmer-Thomas, Coatsworth, and Cortés Conde (2006a, 2006b); Glade (1969); and Lockhart and Schwartz, (1983).

57. Engerman and Sokoloff (2008).

58. Vamplew (1987). For a considerably higher estimate of the aboriginal population at the time of contact, see Butlin (1983).

of European diseases led to a dramatic decline in the native population. The British settlement initially began with large numbers of convicts, and while there were attempts to negotiate land purchases with the aborigines, they did not work out and were soon followed by military actions to enable Europeans to acquire land. Each Australian state initially had its own land policies, but these tended to become more similar over time. While Wakefield had proposed his land policy be applied to all Australia, it was only in South Australia and Western Australia that Wakefield's policy was introduced early in settlement, and in both states it ended within several decades.[59] Initially, New South Wales, the most populous of the states, provided large grants to individuals or companies, but over time squatters, whose holdings tended to be small, were able to get permanent title to their land. Later it was policy to permit individuals to select between 40 and 320 acres by paying one quarter of the purchase price, the balance to be paid in three years, usually at a minimal price per acre.[60] There are several ways in which Australia resembled the United States, with a high ratio of land to population leading to the increased ease with which whites acquired land ownership over time. There was also a high percentage of ownership of relatively small farms, although the greater importance of sheep farming in Australia created a demand for larger units to permit pastoral agriculture. And, as in the United States, the original natives were pushed from the path of settlement and often relocated on reserves. Yet another similarity was the development of a sugar industry in the more tropical areas of both countries. This was based at first on some form of coerced labor, slaves in Louisiana before 1860 and indentured Pacific Islanders in Queensland, by the 1870s.[61] As elsewhere, these sugar-producing plantations in both nations were considerably larger that was the typical grain farm.

New Zealand, settled from Australia in the 1840s, also had a native population—the Maoris—although they did not suffer as severe a demographic decline after the Europeans arrived as did the natives in Australia (and the Americas).[62] Nevertheless, with the large immigration of whites, the Maoris represented less than 10 percent of the New Zealand population within several decades of white settlement. The Maoris reached better accommodation with the British, including selling land to whites, than did the Australian aborigines, but New Zealand remained a nation with a high ratio of land to population.

Land distribution in New Zealand was determined at the state level until 1876, and land was often used as a subsidy to immigrants. Homestead provi-

59. In addition to the sources cited in footnote 47, see also Powell (1970), Shaw (1966), Sinclair (1976), and Coghlan (1969).
60. See Powell (1970).
61. On the United States see Gray (1933) and Sitterson (1953). For Australia see Fitzgerald (1982), Shlomowitz (1996), and Graves (1993).
62. McLauchlan (1984).

sions required a set time of residence to acquire title to land and the governments provided credit arrangements, facilitating sales of land. After several decades it was a general policy to aim at establishing smaller units of up to 320 acres. The earlier settlement pattern was influenced by the policies proposed by Wakefield, including use of land revenues to subsidize immigration and the selling of large units at high prices, but, as elsewhere, this policy was modified over time to permit sales of cheap land to immigrants.[63] Thus in New Zealand, as in Australia, the general pattern over time was a liberalization of Wakefield's land policy to make land more easily accessible to smaller landholders.

Another interesting example of British colonialism, this time of adjacent areas of East Africa, demonstrates the variation in British colonial policy. The settlements of Kenya and Uganda at the end of the nineteenth century generated important differences in local institutions.[64] Both areas were populated almost entirely by black Africans. In Kenya, land was made available to white settlers in units from 160 to 640 acres, with five acres allotted to Africans and Asians for one year, with no ownership rights. By 1840 Europeans were about 1 percent of the population, and owned 18 percent of the land, that being regarded as the best land. Uganda, larger in area but with a similar African and European population mix, developed a rather different set of institutions for land distribution. There were few European settlers and landholders since, at the time of establishing the Protectorate in 1894, much of the land was given to local chiefs to be held under freehold. Unlike Kenya, with European-owned production of plantation crops such as coffee for export using African labor, Uganda produced mainly cotton on small-scale peasant farms. In part, these differences between Kenya and Uganda have been attributed to differences in climate and soil type, leading to the quite distinct set of institutions and political controls.

An earlier British African settlement with large amounts of land available, South Africa, finally seized from the Dutch in 1814, had a somewhat different pattern.[65] Slave labor was imported from elsewhere, mainly the Indian Ocean region, but important controls were imposed on the local natives, coerced into labor for whites by a combination of dispossession and limits on land purchases. Slavery ended in 1834, by the British Emancipation Act. Whites represented a higher percentage of the population than in East Africa, about 33 percent in the Cape Colony in 1836 and lower for the overall colony, but as in Kenya, whites took measures to own the land to pro-

63. In addition to the sources cited in footnote 47, see Condliffe (1930), Hawke (1985), and Sinclair (1959).
64. This paragraph draws upon the following books: Harlow, Chiver, and Smith (1965), van Zwanenberg and King (1975), Wa-Githumo (1981), and Ochieng' (1985). We have greatly benefited from the research of Tricia Redeker Hepner on these African colonies.
65. See Feinstein (2005), Elphick and Giliomee (1989), Wilson and Thompson (1969), Duly (1968), Ross (1993), and Hellman (1949).

duce for export.[66] By 1780, landholding was generally regarded as reserved for whites, with coerced labor left for slaves and "free" resident Africans. Later, by 1913, legislation placed the native population on reserves, which accounted for 7 percent of the land, where they remained laborers for white planters and miners.[67]

1.5   Institutions and Colonization

This chapter examines the colonization of the Americas as a quasi-natural experiment that can be exploited to learn more about where institutions come from. Its focus has been on the long-term evolution of immigration and land and labor policies or institutions, commonly recognized as important for paths of economic development. Much work remains to be done, but our results seem to accord with the notion that the colonies were powerfully influenced by their factor endowments in how they chose to formulate their policies regarding immigration and land. During the colonial period, Spanish America benefited from being centered on regions with rather large populations of Native Americans, and was accordingly much less dependent on immigration, both voluntary and involuntary, than other areas. Indeed, Spain maintained very severe restrictions on who and how many could come. Brazil and the islands in the Caribbean, specializing in sugar and a few other tropical crops well suited for production on large slave plantations, relied heavily on importing slaves to deal with their labor scarcity problem. It was only the northern part of North America that had to obtain the bulk of its labor force through voluntary migration from Europe. Rather than coincidental, or due exclusively to their British national heritage, the uses of the institution of indentured servitude and the liberal offering of land grants to migrants seems to have been policy instruments designed to solve the problem of labor scarcity and allow the colonies to take better advantage of their abundance of land and other resources.

After the independence movements swept across the Americas, there was a mixture of both continuity and change in the strategic land and immigration institutions. The United States, followed by Canada, continued to actively pursue immigrants from abroad. There was no longer a need or ability to acquire indentured servants, but both countries employed very liberal land policies to attract migrants. Again, it is striking that the regions most supportive of liberal land policies, and other policies that migrants were sensitive to, were the areas in the west of the United States and Canada that were most labor scarce. Of course, these boundaries evolved over time with settlement. The evidence for the endogeneity of these policies appears

---

66. Martin (1967). Feinstein (2005) provides an estimate of about 10 percent European in all of South Africa c. 1850. The first census, 1904, gave a figure of 21.6 percent white.
67. Feinstein (2005).

formidable. In contrast, the new nations of Spanish heritage (or Portuguese, in the case of Brazil), who were now free to formulate policies to suit their own interests, began to actively seek immigrants. Like their neighbors to the north (the United States and Canada), countries such as Brazil and Argentina were seemingly labor scarce and abundant in land available for agricultural and other purposes from early in settlement.

It is curious, however, that the programs they adopted were far less generous in offering land to immigrants or local residents than was the United States. This parsimony may be related to the general increase throughout Latin America in the value of land suitable for the production of agricultural exports, as was the movement in many other nations with large Native American populations regarding policies that in effect shifted control of land from Indians to elites. It may also be related to the extreme political and economic inequality that prevailed throughout Latin America, and that we have elsewhere attributed in large part to factor endowments broadly conceived.

References

Acemoglu, Daron, Simon Johnson, and James A. Robinson. 2001. "The Colonial Origins of Comparative Development: An Empirical Investigation." *American Economic Review* 91:1369–1401.

Ackerman, Robert K. 1977. *South Carolina Colonial Land Policies.* Columbia: University of South Carolina Press.

Adelman, Jeremy. 1994. *Frontier Development: Land, Labor, and Capital on Wheatlands of Argentina and Canada, 1890–1914.* New York: Oxford University Press.

Allen, Robert C. 1992. *Enclosure and the Yeoman.* Oxford: Clarendon Press.

Alston, Lee J., Gary D. Libecap, and Bernardo Mueller. 1999. *Titles, Conflict, and Land Use: The Development of Property Rights as Land Reform on the Brazilian Amazon Frontier.* Ann Arbor: University of Michigan Press.

Altman, Ida, and James Horn, eds. 1991. *"To Make America": European Emigration in the Early Modern Period.* Berkeley: University of California Press.

Amaral, Samuel. 1998. *The Rise of Capitalism on the Pampas: The Estancias of Buenos Aires, 1785–1870.* Cambridge: Cambridge University Press.

Appleby, John C. 1996. "English Settlement in the Lesser Antilles during War and Peace, 1603–1660." In *The Lesser Antilles in the Age of European Expansion,* edited by Robert L. Paquette and Stanley L. Engerman, 86–104. Gainesville: University Press of Florida.

Atack, Jeremy, Fred Bateman, and William N. Parker. 2000. "Northern Agriculture and the Westward Movement." In *Cambridge Economic History of the United States, Volume 2: The Long Nineteenth Century,* edited by Stanley L. Engerman and Robert E. Gallman, 285–328. Cambridge: Cambridge University Press.

Barickman, B. J. 1998. *A Bahian Counterpoint: Sugar, Tobacco, Casava, and Slavery in the Reconcava 1780–1860.* Stanford: Stanford University Press.

Barnes, Viola Florence. 1931. "Land Tenure in English Colonial Charters of the Seventeenth Century." In *Essays in Colonial History presented to Charles McLean Andrews by his students,* 4–40. New Haven: Yale University Press.

Bartlett, Robert. 1993. *The Making of Europe: Conquest, Colonization, and Cultural Change, 950–1350.* Princeton, NJ: Princeton University Press.

Bartlett, Roger P. 1979. *Human Capital: The Settlement of Foreigners in Russia, 1762–1804.* Cambridge: Cambridge University Press.

Baseler, Marilyn C. 1998. *"Asylum for Mankind": America 1607–1800.* Ithaca, NY: Cornell University Press.

Bergquist, Charles W. 1998. *Coffee and Conflict in Colombia, 1886–1910.* Durham, NC: Duke University Press.

Bethell, Leslie, ed. 1985. *The Cambridge History of Latin America, Volume 3: From Independence to c. 1870.* Cambridge: Cambridge University Press.

———. 1986. *The Cambridge History of Latin America, Volume 4: c. 1870 to 1930.* Cambridge: Cambridge University Press.

Bidwell, Percy Wells, and John I. Falconer. 1925. *History of Agriculture in the Northern United States, 1620–1860.* Washington: Carnegie Institution.

Bond, Beverley W., Jr. 1919. *The Quit-Rent System in the American Colonies.* New Haven: Yale University Press.

Boucher, Philip P. 2008. *France and the American Tropics to 1700.* Baltimore: Johns Hopkins University Press.

Bulmer-Thomas, Victor. 1994. *The Economic History of Latin America Since Independence.* Cambridge: Cambridge University Press.

Bulmer-Thomas, Victor, John H. Coatsworth, and Roberto Cortés Conde, eds. 2006a. *The Cambridge Economic History of Latin America, Volume 1: The Colonial Era and the Short Nineteenth Century.* Cambridge: Cambridge University Press.

———. 2006b. *The Cambridge Economic History of Latin America, Volume 2: The Long Twentieth Century.* Cambridge: Cambridge University Press.

Burkholder, Mark A., and Lyman L. Johnson. 2001. *Colonial Latin America.* 4th ed. New York: Oxford University Press.

Burroughs, Peter. 1965. "Wakefield and the Ripon Land Regulations of 1831." *Historical Studies* 11:452–66.

Bushnell, David. 1993. *The Making of Modern Colombia: A Nation in Spite of Itself.* Berkeley: University of California Press.

Butlin, Noel. 1983. *Our Original Aggression: Aboriginal Populations of Southeastern Australia, 1788–1850.* Sydney: G. Allen and Unwin.

Canny, Nicholas, ed. 1994. *Europeans on the Move: Studies in European Migration, 1500–1800.* Oxford: Clarendon Press.

Cárcano, Miguel Angel. 1925. *Evolución historica del régimen de la tierra pública, 1810–1916.* 2nd ed. Buenos Aires: Library "The Faculty," J. Roldán y c.a.

Carey, Henry Charles. 1837–1840. *Principles of Political Economy.* Philadelphia: Carey, Lea, and Blanchard.

Carter, Susan B., Scott Sigmund Gartner, Michael R. Haines, Alan L. Olmstead, Richard Sutch, and Gavin Wright, eds. 2006. *Historical Statistics of the United States: Earliest Times to the Present,* Millennial ed. Cambridge: Cambridge University Press.

Castro, Donald Steven. 1991. *The Development and Politics of Argentine Immigration Policy, 1852–1914: To Govern is to Populate.* San Francisco: Mellen Research University Press.

Clark, Grover. 1936. *The Balance Sheet of Imperialism: Facts and Figures on Colonies.* New York: Columbia University Press.

Clodfelter, Michael. 2008. *Warfare and Armed Conflicts: A Statistical Encyclopedia of Casualty and Other Figures, 1494–2007,* 2nd ed. Jefferson, NC: McFarland.

Coates, Timothy J. 2001. *Convicts and Orphans: Forced and State-Sponsored Colonizers in the Portuguese Empire, 1550–1755.* Stanford: Stanford University Press.

Coghlan, T. A. (1918) 1969. *Labour and Industry in Australia.* Melbourne: Macmillan.

Cole, Jeffrey A. 1985. *The Potosi Mita, 1573–1700: Compulsory Indian Labor in the Andes.* Stanford: Stanford University Press.

Collier, Simon, and William F. Sater. 1996. *A History of Chile, 1808–1894.* Cambridge: Cambridge University Press.

Condliffe, J. B. 1930. *New Zealand in the Making: A Survey of Economic and Social Development.* Chicago: University of Chicago Press.

Craven, Wesley Frank. 1970. *The Southern Colonies in the Seventeenth Century, 1607 1689.* Baton Rouge: Louisiana State University Press.

Davie, Maurice R. 1936. *World Immigration: With Special Reference to the United States.* New York: Macmillan.

Davies, Keith A. 1984. *Landowners in Colonial Peru.* Austin: University of Texas Press.

Dean, Warren. 1971. "Latifundia and Land Policy in Nineteenth-Century Brazil." *Hispanic American Historical Review* 57:606–25.

Denevan, William N., ed. 1976. *Native Populations of the Americas in 1492.* Madison: University of Wisconsin Press.

De Vries, Jan. 1976. *Economy of Europe in an Age of Crisis, 1600–1750.* Cambridge: Cambridge University Press.

Dorfman, Joseph. 1946–1959. *The Economic Mind in American Civilization* (5 Vols). New York: Viking Press.

Duly, Leslie Clement. 1968. *British Land Policy at the Cape: A Study of Administrative Policies in the Empire.* Durham, NC: Duke University Press.

Dunn, Richard S. 1972. *Sugar and Slaves: The Rise of the Planter Class in the English West Indies, 1624–1713.* Chapel Hill: University of North Carolina Press.

Eisenberg, Peter L. 1974. *The Sugar Industry in Pernambuco: Modernization without Change, 1840–1910.* Berkeley: University of California Press.

Ekirch, A. Roger. 1987. *Bound for America: The Transportation of British Convicts to the Colonies, 1718–1775.* New York: Oxford University Press.

Elliott, J. H. 2006. *Empires of the Atlantic World: Britain and Spain in America, 1492–1830.* New Haven: Yale University Press.

Elphick, Richard, and Hermann Giliomee, eds. 1989. *The Shaping of South African Society, 1652–1840,* 2nd ed. Middletown, CT: Wesleyan University Press.

Eltis, David. 1983. "Free and Coerced Transatlantic Migrations: Some Comparisons." *American Historical Review* 88:251–80.

———. 1999. "Slavery and Freedom in the Early Modern World." In *Terms of Labor: Slavery, Serfdom, and Free Labor,* edited by Stanley L. Engerman, 25–49. Stanford: Stanford University Press.

———. 2002. "Free and Coerced Migrations from the Old World to the New." In *Coerced and Free Migration: Global Perspectives,* edited by David Eltis, 33–74. Stanford: Stanford University Press.

Emmer, P. C., and M. Mörner. 1992. *European Expansion and Migration: Essays on the Intercontinental Migration from Africa, Asia, and Europe.* New York: Berg.

Engerman, Stanley L. 2002. "Changing Laws and Regulations and their Impact on Migration." In *Coerced and Free Migration: Global Perspectives,* edited by David Eltis, 75–93. Stanford: Stanford University Press.

———. 2007. *Slavery, Emancipation, and Freedom: Comparative Perspectives.* Baton Rouge: Louisiana State University Press.

Engerman, Stanley L., and Barry Higman. 1997. "The Demographic Structure of the Caribbean Slave Societies in the Eighteenth and Nineteenth Centuries." In *General History of the Caribbean,* vol. 3, edited by Franklin W. Knight, 45–104. London: UNESCO.

Engerman, Stanley L., and Kenneth L. Sokoloff. 1997. "Factor Endowments, Institutions, and Differential Paths of Growth Among New World Economies: A View from Economic Historians of the United States." In *How Latin America Fell Behind,* edited by Stephen Haber, 260–304. Stanford: Stanford University Press.

———. 2002. "Factor Endowments, Inequality, and Paths of Development among New World Economies." *Economia* 3:41–109.

———. 2005a. "Institutional and Non-Institutional Explanations of Economic Differences." In *Handbook of New Institutional Economics,* edited by Claude Ménard and Mary M. Shirley, 638–65. Dordrecht, Netherlands: Springer.

———. 2005b. "The Evolution of Suffrage Institutions in the Americas." *Journal of Economic History* 65:891–921.

———. 2006. "Colonialism, Inequality, and Long-Run Paths of Development." In *Understanding Poverty,* edited by Abhijit Vinayak Banerjee, Roland Benabou, and Dilip Mookherjee, 37–61. Oxford: Oxford University Press.

———. 2008. "Debating the Role of Institutions in Political and Economic Development: Theory, History, and Findings." *Annual Review of Political Science* 11: 119–35.

———. Forthcoming, 2011. "Five Hundred Years of European Colonization: Inequality and Paths of Development." In *Settler Economies in World History,* edited by Christopher Lloyd, Jacob Metzer, and Richard Sutch. Leiden, Netherlands: Brill Publishers.

Farnam, Henry W. 1938. *Chapters in the History of Social Legislation in the United States to 1860.* Washington, DC: Carnegie Institution.

Feinstein, Charles H. 2005. *An Economic History of South Africa: Conquest, Discrimination, and Development.* Cambridge: Cambridge University Press.

Feller, Daniel. 1984. *The Public Lands in Jacksonian Politics.* Madison: University of Wisconsin Press.

Findlay, Ronald, and Kevin H. O'Rourke. 2007. *Power and Plenty: Trade, War, and the World Economy in the Second Millennium.* Princeton, NJ: Princeton University Press.

Fitzgerald, Ross. 1982. *A History of Queensland from the Dreaming to 1915.* St. Lucia: University of Queensland Press.

Ford, Amelia Clewley. 1910. *Colonial Precedents of Our National Land System as it Existed in 1800.* Madison: University of Wisconsin Press.

Ford, T. R. 1955. *Man and Land in Peru.* Gainesville: University of Florida Press.

Galenson, David W. 1981. *White Servitude in Colonial American: An Economic History.* Cambridge: Cambridge University Press.

———. 1996. "The Settlement and Growth of the Colonies: Population, Labor, and Economic Development." In *The Cambridge Economic History of the United States, Volume 1: The Colonial Era,* edited by Stanley L. Engerman and Robert E. Gallman, 135–207. Cambridge: Cambridge University Press.

Galloway, J. H. 1989. *The Sugar Cane Industry: An Historical Geography from its Origins to 1914.* Cambridge: Cambridge University Press.

Gates, Paul W. 1968. *History of Public Land Law Development.* Washington, DC: Government Printing Office.

Gibson, Charles. 1966. *Spain in America.* New York: Harper and Row.

Glade, William P. 1969. *The Latin American Economies: A Study of Their Institutional Evolution.* New York: American Book.

Graves, Adrian. 1993. *Cane and Labour: The Political Economy of the Queensland Sugar Industry, 1862–1906.* Edinburgh: Edinburgh University Press.

Gray, Lewis Cecil. 1933. *History of Agriculture in the Southern United States to 1860.* 2 vols. Washington, DC: Carnegie Institution.

Grubb, Farley. 1985. "The Incidence of Servitude in Trans-Atlantic Migration, 1771–1804." *Explorations in Economic History* 22:316–39.

Gudmundson, Lowell. 1986. *Costa Rica Before Coffee: Society and Economy on the Eve of the Export Boom.* Baton Rouge: Louisiana State University Press.

Haring, C. H. 1947. *The Spanish Empire in America.* New York: Oxford University Press.

Harlow, Vincent, E. M. Chiver, and Alison Smith, eds. 1965. *History of East Africa, Volume 2.* Oxford: Clarendon Press.

Harris, Marshall. 1953. *Origin of the Land Tenure System in the United States.* Ames, IA: Iowa State College Press.

Hawke, G. R. 1985. *The Making of New Zealand: An Economic History.* Cambridge: Cambridge University Press.

Heckscher, Eli F. 1935. *Mercantilism* 2 vols. London: G. Allen and Unwin.

Hellmann, Ellen, ed. 1949. *Handbook on Race Relations in South Africa.* Cape Town: Oxford University Press.

Heywood, Colin. 1981. "The Role of the Peasantry in French Industrialization, 1815–1880." *Economic History Review* 34:359–76.

Hibbard, Benjamin Horace. 1924. *A History of the Public Land Policies.* New York: Macmillan.

Himmerich y Valencia, Robert. 1991. *The Encomenderos of New Spain, 1521–1555.* Austin: University of Texas Press.

Hochschild, Adam. 1998. *King Leopold's Ghost: A Story of Greed, Terror, and Heroism in Colonial Africa.* Boston: Houghton Mifflin.

Holden, Robert. 1994. *Mexico and the Survey of Modern Lands: The Management of Modernization, 1876–1911.* Dekalb, IL: Northern Illinois University Press.

Hutchinson, Edward P. 1981. *Legislative History of American Immigration Policy, 1789–1965.* Philadelphia: University of Pennsylvania Press.

Jacobson, Nils. 1993. *Mirages of Transition: The Peruvian Altiplano, 1780–1930.* Berkeley: University of California Press.

Jourdain, W. R. 1925. *History of Land Legislation in New Zealand.* Wellington: Government Printer.

Keyssar, Alexander. 2000. *The Right to Vote: The Contested History of Democracy in the United States.* New York: Basic Books.

Klein, Herbert S. 1986. *African Slavery in Latin America and the Caribbean.* New York: Oxford University Press.

———. 1993. *Haciendas and Ayllus: Rural Society in the Bolivian Andes in the Eighteenth and Nineteenth Centuries.* Stanford: Stanford University Press.

Knight, Franklin W. 1990. *The Caribbean: The Genesis of a Fragmented Nationalism,* 2nd ed. New York: Oxford University Press.

Kuczynski, Robert R. 1936. *Population Movements.* Oxford: Clarendon Press.

Lindert, Peter H. 2011 "Kenneth Sokoloff on Inequality in the Americas." *Understanding Long-Run Economic Growth: Geography, Institutions, and the Knowledge Economy.* Chicago: University of Chicago Press.

Lindo-Fuentes, Hector. 1990. *Weak Foundations: The Economy of El Salvador in the Nineteenth Century.* Berkeley: University of California Press.

Livi-Bacci, Massimo. 2008. *Conquest: The Destruction of the American Indios.* Cambridge: Polity.

Lockhart, James, and Stuart B. Schwartz. 1983. *Early Latin America: A History of Colonial Spanish America and Brazil.* Cambridge: Cambridge University Press.

Lynch, John. 1986. *The Spanish-American Revolutions, 1808–1826,* 2nd ed. New York: Norton.

Macintyre, Stuart. 1999. *A Concise History of Australia.* Cambridge: Cambridge University Press.

Maddison, Angus. 2003. *The World Economy: Historical Statistics.* Paris: Organization for Economic Cooperation and Development (OECD).

Mamalakis, Markos J. *Historical Statistics of Chile: Demography and Labor Force, vol. 2.* Westport, CT: Greenwood Press.

Martin, Chester. 1938. *"Dominions Lands" Policy.* Toronto: Macmillan Company of Toronto.

Martin, Robert Montgomery. (1834) 1967. *History of the Colonies of the British Empire.* London: Dawsons.

McBride, George McCutchen. 1923. *The Land Systems of Mexico.* New York: America Geographic Society.

McCreery, David. 1994. *Rural Guatemala, 1760–1940.* Stanford: Stanford University Press.

McDonald, J. D. N. 1952. "New Zealand Land Legislation." *Historical Studies* 5:195–209.

Merrick, Thomas W., and Douglas H. Graham. 1979. *Population and Economic Development in Brazil: 1800 to the Present.* Baltimore: Johns Hopkins University Press.

McEvedy, Colin, and Richard Jones. 1978. *Atlas of World Population History.* Harmondsworth, UK: Penguin Books.

McGreevey, William Paul. 1971. *An Economic History of Colombia, 1845–1930.* New York: Cambridge University Press.

McLauchlan, Gordon, ed. 1984. *Bateman New Zealand Encyclopedia.* Auckland, New Zealand: David Bateman.

Moch, Leslie Page. 1992. *Moving Europeans: Migration in Western Europe since 1650.* Bloomington: Indiana University Press.

Moses, Bernard. (1898) 1965. *The Establishment of Spanish Rule in America.* New York: Cooper Square Publishers.

Moya Pons, Frank. 1995. *The Dominican Republic: A National History.* New Rochelle, NY: Hispaniola Books.

Nettels, Curtis P. 1963. *The Roots of American Civilization: A History of American Colonial Life,* 2nd ed. New York: Appleton-Century-Crofts.

Nugent, Jeffrey B., and James A. Robinson. 2010. "Are Factor Endowments Fate?" *Journal of Iberian and Latin American Economic History* 28:45–82.

Ochieng', William R. 1985. *A History of Kenya.* London: Macmillan.

Palacios, Mario. 1980. *Coffee in Colombia, 1850–1970: An Economic, Social, and Political History.* Cambridge: Cambridge University Press.

Parry, J. H. 1966. *The Spanish Seaborne Empire.* New York: Knopf.

Pérez Brignoli, Héctor. 1989. *A Brief History of Central America.* Berkeley: University of California Press.

Perry, James R. 1990. *The Formation of a Society on Virginia's Eastern Shore, 1615–1655.* Chapel Hill: University of North Carolina Press.

Pineo, Ronn F. 1996. *Social and Economic Reform in Ecuador: Life and Work in Guayaquol.* Gainesville: University Press of Florida.

Pomfret, Richard. 1981. *The Economic Development of Canada.* Toronto: Methuen.

Powell, J. M. 1970. *The Public Lands of Australia Felix: Settlement and Land Appraisal in Victoria 1834–91 with Special Reference to the Western Plains.* Melbourne: Oxford University Press.

Powell, J. M., and M. Williams, eds. 1975. *Australian Space, Australian Time: Geographic Perspectives.* Melbourne: Oxford University Press.

Prichard, James. 2004. *In Search of Empire: The French in the Americas, 1670–1730.* Cambridge: Cambridge University Press.

Reynolds, Robert L. 1957. "The Mediterranean Frontier, 1000–1400." In *The Frontier in Perspective,* edited by Walker D. Wyman and Clifton B. Kroeber, 21–34. Madison: University of Wisconsin Press.

Rife, Clarence White. 1931. "Land Tenure in New Netherlands." In *Essays in Colonial History presented to Charles McLean Andrews by his students,* 41–73. New Haven: Yale University Press.

Risch, Erna. 1937. "Encouragement of Immigration as Revealed in Colonial Legislation." *Virginia Magazine of History and Biography* 45:1–10.

Robbins, Roy M. 1942. *Our Landed Heritage: The Public Domain, 1776–1936.* Princeton: Princeton University Press.

Roberts, Stephen H. (1924) 1968. *History of Australian Land Settlement 1788–1820.* New York: Johnson Reprint Corporation.

Roseberry, William, Lowell Gudmundson, and Mario Samper Kutschbach, eds. 1995. *Coffee, Society, and Power in Latin America.* Baltimore: Johns Hopkins University Press.

Rosenblat, Angel. 1954. *La Población Indígena v El Mestizaje en America, volume 1: La Población Indígena, 1492–1950.* Buenos Aires: Editorial Nova.

Ross, Robert. 1993. *Beyond the Pale: Essays on the History of Colonial South Africa.* Hanover, NH: Wesleyan University Press.

Rout, Leslie B. 1976. *African Experience in Spanish America: 1502 to the Present Day.* Cambridge: Cambridge University Press.

Rusk, Jerrold G. 2001. *A Statistical History of the American Electorate.* Washington, DC: CQ Press.

Sánchez-Albornoz, Nicolás. 1974. *The Population of Latin America: A History.* Berkeley: University of California Press.

Schwartz, Stuart B. 1985. *Sugar Plantations and the Formation of Brazilian Society: Bahia 1550–1835.* Cambridge: Cambridge University Press.

Shaw, A. G. L. 1966. *Convicts and the Colonies: A Study of Penal Transportation from Great Britain and Ireland to Australia and Other Parts of the British Empire.* London: Faber and Faber.

Shlomowitz, Ralph. 1996. *Mortality and Migration in the Modern World.* Aldershot, UK: Ashgate Variorum.

Simpson, Lesley Byrd. (1950) 1982. *The Encomienda in New Spain: The Beginning of Spanish Mexico.* Berkeley: University of California Press.

Sinclair, Keith. 1959. *A History of New Zealand.* Harmondsworth, UK: Penguin Books.

Sinclair, W. A. 1976. *The Process of Economic Development in Australia.* Melbourne: Longman Cheshire.

Sitterson, J. Carlyle. 1953. *Sugar Country: The Cane Sugar Industry in the South, 1753–1950.* Lexington: University of Kentucky Press.

Smith, Abbot Emerson. 1947. *Colonists in Bondage: White Servitude and Convict Labor in America, 1607–1776.* Chapel Hill: University of North Carolina Press.

Smith, Philippa Mein. 2005. *A Concise History of New Zealand.* Cambridge: Cambridge University Press.

Solberg, Carl E. 1969. "A Discriminatory Frontier Land Policy: Chile, 1870–1914." *The Americas* 26:115–33.

———. 1987. *The Prairies and the Pampas: Agrarian Policy in Canada and Argentina, 1880–1913.* Stanford: Stanford University Press.

Southworth, Constant. 1931. *The French Colonial Venture.* London: P. S. King and Son.

Stephenson, George M. 1917. *The Political History of the Public Lands from 1840 to 1862: From Pre-emption to Homestead.* Boston: Richard G. Badge.

Summerhill, William R. 2003. *Order Against Progress: Government, Foreign Investment, and Railroads in Brazil, 1854–1913.* Stanford: Stanford University Press.

Tannenbaum, Frank. 1929. *The Mexican Agrarian Revolution.* New York: Macmillan.

Townsend, Mary Evelyn. 1930. *The Rise and Fall of Germany's Colonial Empire, 1884–1918.* New York: Macmillan.

Trudel, Marcel. 1967. *The Seigneurial Regime.* Ottawa: Canadian Historical Association.

Vamplew, Wray, ed. 1987. *Australians, Historical Statistics.* Sydney: Fairfax, Syme and Weldon.

van Zwanenberg, R. M. A., and A. King. 1975. *An Economic History of Kenya and Uganda, 1800–1970.* London: Macmillan.

Viotti da Costa, Emilia. 1985. *The Brazilian Empire: Myths and Histories.* Chicago: University of Chicago Press.

Wadham, Samuel, R. Kent Wilson, and Joyce Wood. 1964. *Land Utilization in Australia,* 4th ed. London: Melbourne University Press.

Wa-Githumo, Mwangi. 1981. *Land and Nationalism: The Impact of Land Expropriation and Land Grievances upon the Rise and Development of Nationalist Movements in Kenya, 1885–1939.* Washington, DC: University Press of America.

Wakefield, Edward Gibbon. 1829. *Letter from Sydney: The Principal Town of Australia, Together with the Outline of a System of Colonization.* London: J. Cross.

———. 1849. *View of the Art of Colonization with Present Reference to the British Empire: In Letters Between a Statesman and a Colonist.* London: J. W. Parker.

Washburn, Wilcomb E. 1975. *The Indian in America.* New York: Harper and Row.

Watts, David. 1987. *The West Indies: Patterns of Development, Culture, and Environmental Change Since 1492.* Cambridge: Cambridge University Press.

Wellington, Raynor G. 1914. *The Political and Sectional Influence of the Public Lands, 1828–1842.* Cambridge, MA: Riverside Press.

Willcox, Walter with Imre Frencz. 1929. *International Migrations.* New York: National Bureau of Economic Research.

Wilson, Monica, and Leonard Thompson, eds. 1969. *The Oxford History of South Africa.* New York: Oxford University Press.

Yarrington, Doug. 1997. *A Coffee Frontier: Land, Society, and Politics in Duaca, Venezuela, 1830–1936.* Pittsburgh: University of Pittsburgh Press.

The Myth of the Frontier

Camilo García-Jimeno and James A. Robinson

2.1 Introduction

One of the great economic puzzles of the modern world is why, among a group of colonies founded at more or less the same time in the early modern period by more or less rapacious Europeans with more or less the same intentions, North America became such an economic and democratic success while Latin America did not. There is no shortage of candidates, of course, but one of the most prominent is the notion of the "frontier."[1] Many scholars have claimed that a crucial aspect of the uniqueness of the United States was the vastness of the open spaces (at least after the indigenous peoples had died (Mann [2005])), that heavily influenced the way society, economy, and polity evolved.

The most famous exposition of this view, first developed in 1893, was attributed to Frederick Jackson Turner. Turner, postulating what has become known as the "frontier (or Turner) thesis," argued that the availability of the frontier had attracted a particular type of person and had crucially determined the path of U.S. society.

Camilo García-Jimeno is a graduate student in the Economics Department at the Massachusetts Institute of Technology. James A. Robinson is the David Florence Professor of Government at Harvard University, a faculty associate at the Weatherhead Center for International Affairs, and a research associate of the National Bureau of Economic Research.

This chapter was written for the conference "Understanding Long-Run Economic Growth: A Conference Honoring the Contributions of Kenneth Sokoloff." Our biggest debt is to Ken for all his encouragement, friendship, and inspiration over the years. We miss him. We thank Ron Rogowski and Naomi Lamoreaux for their comments and suggestions. We also thank Giovanni Zambotti at the Center for Geographic Analysis at Harvard for his enormous help with the maps. We thank the Canadian Institute for Advanced Research for financial support.

1. For other ideas on this topic of the exceptionalism of the United States see Hartz (1955, 1964), Lipset (1996), and Engerman and Sokoloff (1997).

The existence of an area of free land, its continuous recession, and the advance of American settlement westward, explain American Development. Behind institutions, behind constitutional forms and modifications, lie the vital forces that call these organs into life and shape them to meet changing conditions. Turner (1920, 1–2)

Turner emphasized that the frontier created strong individualism and social mobility, and his most forthright claim is that it was critical to the development of democracy. He noted

the most important effect of the frontier has been to promote democracy. Turner (1920, 30)

and

These free lands promoted individualism, economic equality, freedom to rise, democracy . . . American democracy is fundamentally the outcome of the experiences of the American people in dealing with the West. Turner (1920, pp. 259, 266)

Moreover, the things that went along with democracy and helped to promote it, such as social mobility, most likely also stimulated economic performance.

Since Turner wrote it, the frontier thesis has become part of the conventional wisdom among historians and scholars of the United States.[2] Though the specific mechanisms that Turner favored, such as individualism, have become less prominent, arguments about the frontier have appeared in many places, particularly the literature on the democratization of the United States (Keyssar 2000; Engerman and Sokoloff 2005). Keyssar (2000, xxi) argues,

The expansion of suffrage in the United States was generated by a number of key forces and factors. . . . These include the dynamics of frontier settlement (as Frederick Jackson Turner pointed out a century ago).

Those who have contested this view (see Walsh [2005] for an excellent discussion) have tended to focus on the extent to which the frontier did or did not have the postulated effects within the United States.

At some level the acceptance of the frontier thesis and the nature of the debate is quite surprising. This is because the existence of a frontier clearly *did not* distinguish the United States from the other colonies of the Americas or, indeed, other societies such as Russia, South Africa, or Australia in the nineteenth century. Every independent South American and Caribbean country, with the exception of Haiti, had a frontier in the nineteenth century. These frontiers were usually inhabited by indigenous peoples and they went through the same pattern of expansion into this zone that, as in the United States, coincided with the expropriation and oftentimes annihilation

---

2. For some of the debate about the applicability of this thesis to the United States see Taylor (1956), Billington (1962, 1966, 2001), Hofstadter and Lipset (1968), and Walsh (2005).

of indigenous communities. In these cases, however, there seems to be much less reason to associate frontier expansion with democracy or economic development. Indeed, one could conjecture that if the frontier thesis had been developed by Latin American academics in the late nineteenth century it would have been formulated with a minus sign in front![3]

A small literature has examined the frontier hypothesis in comparative perspective, but it has come to inconclusive results. Turner did engage in some comparative observations but refers only to Europe, noting,

> The American frontier is sharply distinguished from the European frontier—a fortified boundary line running through dense populations. (Turner 1920, 3)

Hennessy (1978) specifically addresses the applicability of the frontier thesis to Latin America (see also the papers in Weber and Rausch [1994]).[4] Noting the absence of a literature on the frontier thesis in Latin America, Hennessy (1978, p 13) reasons,

> If the importance of the Turner thesis lies in its . . . ability to provide a legitimating and fructifying nationalist ideology, then the absence of a Latin American frontier myth is easy to explain. Without democracy, there was no compulsion to elaborate a supportive ideology based on frontier experiences.

Hennessy's general conclusion is that the thesis is irrelevant because

> Latin American frontiers have not provided fertile ground for democracy. The concentration of wealth and the absence of capital and of highly motivated pioneers effectively blocked the growth of independent small-holders and a rural middle class. (Hennessy 1978, 129)

The correlation between good outcomes and the frontier in the United States and Canada but the lack of such a correlation in Latin America raises the question of whether or not, in general, there is any connection between the frontier and economic and political development. Maybe the frontier was irrelevant? A myth?

We believe the answer to this is no. Some of the mechanisms described in the case of the United States certainly seem plausible, it is just that they do not seem to have operated in Latin America. The key to understanding why comes from examining how frontier land was allocated.[5] In the United

---

3. Though the issue of the role of the frontier has been considered in Latin American studies (see Hennessy [1978] and Weber and Rausch [1994]), it appears that nobody has made these comparative observations before.

4. Other work that looks, usually critically, at the frontier thesis as a comparative perspective include Winks (1971), Miller (1977), and Powell (1981). For more general discussions of frontier expansions in the modern world not focused on the Turner thesis see Richards (2003) and Belich (2010).

5. Differences in labor institutions developed in frontier areas may also have played an important role, and were no doubt related to how land was allocated.

States it was the 1862 Homestead Act, building on earlier legislation such as the Land Ordinance of 1785, which played a major role in governing who and on what terms had access to the frontier. In Latin America, on the other hand, only Costa Rica and Colombia passed and enforced legislation that resembled measures such as these. In a few other countries where some legislation was passed, it seems to have never been put into practice. Jefferson (1926, 167), for example, points out the difference between the "elevated aims and philanthropic language" of the Argentine legislation regarding landowning in frontier areas and "the actuality of events." More generally, frontier land was allocated in a relatively inegalitarian pattern by existing elites, and property rights over frontier lands of settlers were in many cases weak for nonelites. Though Turner continually talks about the frontier and "free land" as if they were the same thing, as Adelman (1994, 101) points out,

> Turner . . . overlooked two hard facts: land was not free, and workers had to be brought in from outside the region.

Outside of Costa Rica and Colombia, frontier land was not free in Latin America and, indeed, was allocated oligarchically by those with political power.[6] Hennessy (1978, 19) observed,

> Another contrast lies in the availability of "free land." Whereas free land was the magnet attracting pioneers into the North American wilderness, in Latin America most available land had been preempted by landowning patterns set in the sixteenth century.

The historical experience of Argentina is again revealing. Jefferson (1926, 175–8) describes several episodes in the Paraná basin, the Nequén region to the South, or even in La Pampa, where settlers found difficulties in maintaining their property rights over the lands they opened, both because state officials reneged on past promises or because of abuses from local elites. Interestingly, when Turner does discuss the issue of land laws with respect to the frontier, he seems to see these as an endogenous response to the existence of the frontier, for example, arguing that

> The disposition of the public lands was a third important subject of national legislation influenced by the frontier. Turner (1920, 25)

and

> It is safe to say that the legislation with regard to land . . . was conditioned on frontier ideas and needs. Turner (1920, 27)

---

6. There is a large historical literature on the oligarchic allocation of frontier lands in nineteenth century Latin America. For overviews of the Central American experience see Williams (1994), Gudmundson (1997), and Mahoney (2001); McCreery (1976, 1994) for the important Guatemalan experience; Parsons (1949) is the classic work on frontier expansion in Colombia, see also Christie (1978) and LeGrand (1986); Dean (1971) and Butland (1966) analyze the

The Latin American experience suggests to us not that the frontier is irrelevant, but rather that a more nuanced version of the frontier thesis is required. We refer to this as the "conditional frontier thesis." This takes into account the fact that the consequences of the frontier are conditional on the initial political equilibrium when frontier expansion occurred. Although the opening up of a frontier might bring new opportunities for the establishment of equitable societies in ways that could promote democracy and economic growth, as Turner suggested, in relatively oligarchic countries the existence of an open frontier gave the ruling elite a new valuable instrument that they could manipulate to remain in power. They did this through the structure of land and laws, policies toward immigrants and clientelistic access to frontier lands. When initial political institutions were different, as they were in the United States, Canada, Costa Rica, and Colombia, elites were less able to manipulate this resource and a more open society evolved. As Turner argued, it is quite likely in these circumstances that the existence of a frontier helped to induce further improvements in political institutions. In countries like Argentina or Mexico, it is possible that an oligarchically allocated frontier was worse than having no frontier at all.

In this chapter we propose what we believe is the first empirical test of the frontier thesis, and also our extended conditional frontier thesis. To do this we construct an estimate of the proportion of land that was frontier in each independent country in the Americas in 1850. We combine this with data on current income per capita, democracy, and inequality. Our first main finding is that our estimates of the relative size of the frontier are positively correlated with long-run economic growth and the extent to which countries were democratic over the twentieth century. The relative size of the frontier is also negatively correlated with income inequality. These initial results are quite consistent with the simple frontier thesis.

Nevertheless, we then test the conditional frontier thesis by interacting the proportion of frontier land in 1850 with measures of initial institutions, specifically constraints on the executive from the Polity data set that is available for every independent country in the Americas in 1850.[7] When the gross domestic product (GDP) per capita in 2007 is the dependent variable, we find that neither frontier land in 1850 nor constraints on the executive are themselves statistically significant, but their interaction is. Indeed, the results imply that for countries with the lowest level of constraints on the executive (which is almost half our sample in 1850), long-run economic growth is *lower* the larger the frontier. For higher levels of constraints, however, long-run growth is higher. These simple regressions are very consistent with the conditional frontier thesis. With respect to democracy, when we look at the

---

Brazilian case; Solberg (1969) presents the evidence for Chile; Coatsworth (1974, 1981) for Mexico. Solberg (1987) and Adelman (1994) discuss Argentina, and both books make interesting comparisons to the differential evolution of Canada.

7. Except for Canada, for which data is available starting in 1867.

average Polity Score from 1900 to 2007, we again find that once we add the interaction term neither frontier nor constraints themselves are significant. In this case we do not find that the frontier is ever bad for democracy, but rather its impact on democracy is greater the greater are constraints on the executive in 1850. These results suggest, again consistent with the conditional Frontier thesis, that the frontier on its own had no impact on democracy. When we turn to the democracy score averaged over the post–World War II period (1950 to 2007) we find different results. Here frontier on its own tends to be positively correlated with democracy while the interaction term is not statistically significant. Finally, when we examine contemporary inequality as the dependent variable we do not find robust results. Though frontier and constraints on the executive in 1850 are both negatively correlated with inequality, when we add the interaction term none of the variables is statistically significant.

Taken seriously, our results provide quite strong support to the conditional frontier thesis and suggest that the reason that Turner himself and so many subsequent scholars based in the United States may have accepted the simple frontier thesis is that they were living in a country that had relatively good institutions. Nevertheless, the size of our sample is small and we are limited to using cross-national variation, so our findings ought to be regarded as tentative.

Our argument about the conditional effect of the frontier is related to several important historical debates. For example, one interpretation of the arguments of Brenner (1976) is that large shocks in the Middle Ages, such as trade expansion or the Black Death, had conditional effects that depended on initial institutions. In Britain, where the serfs were relatively organized and where lords did not have large estates, the Black Death empowered the lower orders and led to the collapse of feudal institutions. In Eastern Europe, however, where the initial conditions were different, the Black Death ultimately led to the second serfdom. A related argument is presented in Acemoglu, Johnson, and Robinson (2005) who argue that the impact on Western Europe of trade and colonial expansion after 1492 depended on initial political institutions. In places where there were relatively strong political institutions, such as Britain and the Netherlands, trade expansion led to improvements of institutions and stimulated economic growth and further political change. In places that were more absolutist, such as Spain and France, trade expansion had opposite effects.[8]

The chapter proceeds as follows. In the next section we discuss how we measure the extent of the frontier and present some basic data about its extent and nature. In section 2.3 we examine the correlation between the frontier and long run economic and political outcomes. Section 2.4 investi-

---

8. This type of interaction also comes up in the literature of the impact of the resource curse; see Moene, Mehlum, and Torvik (2006).

gates whether or not there is a conditional effect of the frontier and section 2.5 concludes.

2.2   Measuring the Frontier

The literature on the frontier has been quite vague on how exactly to determine what was or what was not frontier. Turner himself noted (1920, 3),

> In the census reports it is treated as the margin of that settlement which has a density of two or more to the square mile. The term is an elastic one, and for our purposes does not need a sharp definition. We shall consider the whole frontier belt, including the Indian country and the other outer margin of the "settled area" of the census reports.

It was the definition of the frontier as areas with a population density of less than two people per square mile that led the Census Bureau to declare in 1890 that the U.S. frontier had closed.

Any attempt to measure the extent of the frontier across the Americas must confront several methodological issues. In the first place, frontiers in each country, and even within countries, looked very different around the mid-nineteenth century. Coming up with a measure of the frontier for each country therefore requires a compromise to select some basic simplifying but consistent criteria that will necessarily overlook many possibly important dimensions. Following the historical literature, the natural candidates for such a classification are the presence or absence of Native American communities not subject to state control and authority, overall population density (including any non-Native American settlers), and the presence or absence of state institutions. All of these conditions were important determinants of the potential availability of free land and of the possibilities for successful settlement. Obviously problematic is that we would like to think of the frontier as a dichotomous condition, whereas its defining variables are in most cases inherently continuous, and its boundaries usually not clear-cut.

When dealing with the frontier experience of South America another issue arises—settlement of frontier lands was not an absorbing state in some regions. Several areas in Paraguay, for example, were significantly settled and run by Jesuit missionaries during the colonial period. After the expulsion of Jesuits from the Spanish Empire in 1767, the Crown reassigned the control of these regions to other religious communities who failed to maintain the economic viability of the missions and the political control of the indigenous communities inhabiting the areas. As a result, in a matter of decades the missionary regions degenerated to a virtual absence of state control and became frontiers once again. They remained as such until late in the nineteenth century (Eidt 1971; Bandeira 2006). The case of Brazilian *bandeirantes* in the seventeenth and eighteenth centuries is similar. Brazil expanded its boundaries as these settlers moved west into the Amazon and its southwestern basin. Nonetheless, many of these areas were subsequently unsettled and remained like that until late in the republican period. As a result, Brazilian historiography refers to them as "hollow" frontiers (Katzman 1977). For our purposes we tried to include in our measure these regions, which around 1850 were in fact not controlled by republican states even if they had been so earlier in colonial times.

Once such decisions have been made, the second issue is related to the availability of information about location of frontier and nonfrontier lands. Not only is detailed information scarce by the very nature of the subject, but the comparability of the data across countries might also be problematic. We collected three types of information, based on which we constructed three alternative measures of the frontier; (a) historical cartographic data depicting directly information on frontier territories or on population density for several of the countries in our sample of independent republics, at different dates starting in the mid-nineteenth century; (b) geographic (and georeferenced) information on current-day administrative divisions (provinces, departments, or states); and (c) direct country or regional historical accounts on the settlement of frontier areas during the nineteenth century. The appendix contains a detailed description of the sources used for each country. The reason that making use of current administrative divisions is helpful is that, in fact, the formation of administrative units in many regions across the Americas was precisely driven by significant settlement and state presence. The best examples of this might be the straight lines marking the boundaries of the western states of the United States, put in place as a first effort to regulate and control the newly occupied territories as the westward expansion moved on, or the Amazon rainforest frontier provinces of countries like Colombia, Brazil, or Peru, which were designed precisely to delimit such frontier areas.

2.2.1   The Frontier in the United States and Canada

For these two countries we were able to find detailed cartographic information that allowed us to calculate the share of unsettled and settled land in 1850. More specifically, for the United States, the United States Census Office (1898) and Gerlach (1970) contain detailed maps of population density. Both sources use the nineteenth century United States Census data, and following the Census Bureau, classify as frontier land the territory with less than two people per square mile (0.7725 people per square kilometer). For Canada, the Dominion Bureau of Statistics (n.d.) contains maps for several years in the second half of the nineteenth century, depicting population density by points on the map. We directly georeferenced these maps using geographic information system (GIS) software, and computed the share of total land area of each country with population density below 0.7725 people per square kilometer, in 1850 for the United States and in 1851 for

Canada. Since these maps were based on detailed census data, we believe these frontier measures have the smallest possible measurement error, and are the only ones we consider for these two countries.

For the rest of countries in the Americas the information is not as detailed and is more scattered throughout different sources. As a result, we decided to create a set of alternative measures of the frontier, taking into account the differences we found when comparing the available information.

2.2.2   The Frontier in Central America

To measure the frontier in Central America we relied heavily on Hall and Pérez Brignoli (2003), which contains rich historical maps for Guatemala, El Salvador, Honduras, Nicaragua, Costa Rica, and Panama, of settlement during the nineteenth century, and also has a thorough historical discussion of the frontier expansion throughout the region. We merged the information of these maps, which depict the frontier regions in each country, with a georeferenced subnational level map of Central America, and coded each province/department/state as frontier or nonfrontier depending on whether or not it fell into the regions considered as unsettled in the Hall and Pérez Brignoli (2003) maps. Of course, with this procedure a considerable number of subnational units appeared as partially frontier areas. We thus created two different measures of the frontier, which we call narrow and wide. The narrow measure classifies as nonfrontier the subnational units for which an ambiguous coverage of the Hall and Pérez Brignoli (2003) maps had been obtained, while the wide measure classifies them a frontier. We further refined the classification of provinces using United States Bureau of the Census (1956a), which contains very detailed population density maps for all the Central American republics in 1950 at the province/department level. The comparison with these maps allowed us to reclassify provinces that might have been ambiguous, but which by 1950 clearly had a population density below 0.7725 people per square kilometer, and necessarily must have been frontier areas 100 years before. The appendix presents the coding of each subnational unit in its narrow and wide versions.

For the Mexican frontier we relied on the Bureau of Business Research (1975) population density map for 1900, a state-level map based on the 1900 Censo General de Población, together with Bernstein (1964) and Hennessy (1978). Since population density in 1900 was considerably higher than in 1850 everywhere in Mexico, we coded as frontier states not only those with less than 0.7725 people per square kilometer in 1900, but also any state with at most a population density of five people per square kilometer in 1900, which were at the same time mentioned in the complementary references as frontier areas. This resulted in a relatively straightforward classification except for the state of Chiapas, which we coded as nonfrontier in the narrow measure and as frontier in the wide measure.

2.2.3   The Frontier in the Caribbean Republics

Only Haiti and the Dominican Republic were independent by 1850, and as such are the only two Caribbean countries in our sample. Coding the frontier for them was a pretty straightforward job based on Anglade (1982) and Lora (2002). Anglade presents population density maps for the late eighteenth century and mid-nineteenth century, where it is clear that since the colonial period Haiti had population densities well above 0.7725 people per square kilometer, and almost everywhere significantly higher. Haiti, therefore, did not have a frontier. For the Dominican Republic the picture is very similar, except possibly for the provinces of Barahona and Pedernales in the southwestern tip of the country. The United States Bureau of the Census (1956b) also contains detailed province-level maps of these two countries in 1950, which show a low population density in the southwest of the Dominican Republic. As a result, the narrow measure considers Barahona and Pedernales as nonfrontier, while the wide measure codes them as frontier. All the rest of the country is coded as nonfrontier.

2.2.4   The Frontier in South America

To measure the frontier in the South American countries we followed a procedure very similar to the one we used for the Central American republics, merging the information in usually country-specific historical maps and accounts with current-day, subnational units. The appendix contains the historical references used for each country. When a subnational unit was partially covered by settlement, we again made the distinction by coding it as nonfrontier in the narrow measure and as frontier in the wide version. This is the case, for example, of the northeastern Brazilian province of Piaui or the Pacific coast province of Esmeraldas in Ecuador.

For South America we found an alternative source for the frontier. Butland (1966), which discusses in detail the frontier expansion in southern Brazil, presents a South American map depicting the frontier areas in the mid-nineteenth century. Unfortunately, he does not explain how this map was drawn, but it actually coincides to a quite large extent with our own province-level codings. We used GIS software to georeference the frontier map in Butland (1966) and directly computed the share of each country that was frontier in the mid-nineteenth century. As a result, we have three different frontier measures for South America: narrow, wide, and Butland.

Table 2.1 sums up the data from these calculations. For the United States and Canada we only have one number each, with 72.5 percent of the territory of the United States being frontier in 1850, while the corresponding number for Canada is 85.3 percent. Figure 2.1 shows exactly where the frontier and nonfrontier areas were. This is a pretty familiar picture with, for example, the United States being settled on the Eastern Seaboard and all the way west to the western boundaries of Arkansas and Missouri. Far

Table 2.1　　The frontier in the Americas

Country	Total number of subnational units	Total land area (square kms.)	Number of narrow frontier subnational units	Total narrow frontier land area (square kms.)	Narrow frontier share (%)	Number of wide frontier subnational units	Total wide frontier land area (square kms.)	Wide frontier share (%)	Total frontier from Butland (1966) and historical cartography	Frontier share from Butland (1966) and historical cartography (%)
Argentina	24	2,780,403	11	1,370,454	49.3	15	2,063,942	74.2	1,922,371	69.1
Bolivia	9	1,098,581	4	685,635	62.4	4	803,853	73.2	861,507	78.4
Brazil	27	8,498,331	15	6,354,737	74.8	17	7,192,601	84.6	7,606,006	89.5
Chile	13	756,095	5	398,745	52.7	5	398,745	52.7	562,762	74.4
Colombia	33	1,141,748	15	718,130	62.9	15	718,130	62.9	663,584	58.1
Costa Rica	7	51,102	4	32,870	64.3	5	43,011	84.2	32,870	64.3
Dominican Republic	32	46,891	0	—	0.0	2	3,665	7.8		
Ecuador	23	256,370	7	116,519	45.4	9	151,309	59.0	120,827	47.1
El Salvador	14	21,040	0	—	0.0	0	—	0.0		
Guatemala	22	108,889	2	44,892	41.2	7	69,692	64.0		
Honduras	18	112,492	3	45,262	40.2	6	64,904	57.7		
Haiti	9	27,700	0	—	0.0	0	—	0.0		
Mexico	32	1,970,774	11	1,131,990	57.4	12	1,207,619	61.3		
Nicaragua	17	120,339	4	77,129	64.1	7	91,601	76.1		
Panama	12	75,071	6	35,102	46.8	7	46,773	62.3		
Peru	25	1,285,199	4	595,813	46.4	7	709,235	55.2	786,028	61.2
Paraguay	18	406,752	3	246,925	60.7	13	378,370	93.0	365,955	90.0
Uruguay	19	175,016	19	175,016	100.0	19	175,016	100.0	175,016	100.0
Venezuela	25	916,445	6	598,945	65.4	8	707,231	77.2	655,533	71.5
United States	51	9,372,587							6,792,227	72.5
Canada	13	9,017,699							7,819,625	85.3

Source: www.geohive.com for land areas of subnational administrative units, Butland (1966), Dominion Bureau of Statistics (n.d.), Gerlach (1970), and Bureau of Business Research (1975). Frontier coding calculated by the authors.

Note: Dashed cells indicate that no information is available.

Settled Areas   Frontier Areas

Fig. 2.1   The frontier in North America circa 1850 (current administrative boundaries)

to the west, parts of coastal California and the central valley north of San Francisco were also settled. For the countries in South America we have three different estimates of the extent of the frontier. For example, table 2.1 shows that for Colombia the narrow definition of the frontier suggests that 62.9 percent of the territory was frontier in 1850 and this exactly coincides with the wide definition. Butland's map gives a fairly similar estimate of 58.1 percent. For other countries, however, the differences between these estimates are much larger. For example, for Argentina the narrow definition is 49.3 percent while the wide one is 74.2 percent. The reason for this large difference is easy to see from figure 2.2. Here the settled areas intersect with many departments. For instance, the narrow definition treats the depart-

▓ Settled Areas   ☐ Frontier Areas

Fig. 2.2   The frontier in South America circa 1850 (current administrative bound-aries)

ments of San Luis, Córdoba, Neuquén, Santiago del Estero, and Salta as settled, while the wide definition treats them as frontier. For Argentina, Butland's estimate is close to our wide definition. Finally, figure 2.3 looks at Central America and the Caribbean.

These calculations clearly illustrate our conjecture from the introduction,

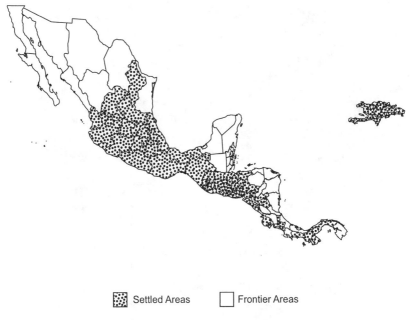

Settled Areas   Frontier Areas

Fig. 2.3   The frontier in Central America circa 1850 (current administrative boundaries)

which is that simply in terms of the size of the frontier, the United States is not distinct. Uruguay had a frontier that was quite a bit larger relative to the size of the country, and Brazil's frontier was also larger. Other countries such as Costa Rica, Nicaragua, or Venezuela had frontiers that were only about 15 percent or so less.

2.3   Other Data

Apart from the data we constructed on the extent of the frontier in 1850, we use some other readily obtainable data. For our measure of historical political institutions we use constraints on the executive in 1850 from the Polity IV Project.[9] This variable is defined as the extent of institutional restrictions on decision-making powers of the chief executive, whether individual or collective. In a democracy constraints would come from the legislative or judicial branches of government. In a dictatorship constraints may come from the ruling party in a one-party system, a council of nobles or powerful advisors in monarchies, or maybe the military in polities that are subject to the threat of military coups. The extent of constraints on the executive are coded as being between one, meaning "unlimited executive authority" and

9. http://www.systemicpeace.org/polity/polity4.htm.

Fig. 2.4   Constraints on the executive in 1850

seven, implying "executive parity or subordination." A country would be in the first category if "constitutional restrictions on executive action are ignored" or "there is no legislative assembly or there is one but it is called or dismissed at the executive's pleasure." A country would be in the latter category if "a legislature, ruling party or council of nobles initiates much or most important legislation" or "the executive is chosen by the accountability group and is dependent on its continued support to remain in office."

Figure 2.4 shows the distribution of constraints on the executive in 1850 for the twenty-one countries in our data set. One can see that nine countries are assigned the minimum score of one, while the United States and Canada have the maximum score of seven.[10] Interestingly for our hypothesis, Costa Rica and Colombia both have scores of three in 1850. The country with constraints of five in 1850 is Honduras.

We also use the Polity IV Project's measure of how democratic a country is, which they refer to as the Polity IV score, which is the difference between the Polity's democracy and autocracy indices.[11] The democracy index ranges from zero to ten and is derived from coding the competitiveness of political participation, the openness and competitiveness of executive recruitment, and constraints on the chief executive. The Polity autocracy index also ranges from zero to ten and is constructed in a similar way to the democracy score based on scoring countries according to competitiveness of political

10. As previously noted, Polity data for Canada only starts in 1867, at which point it has a 7, which we used as its 1850 number.
11. This measure is a very standard one in empirical work on democracy, and other definitions typically give very similar results (see Acemoglu, Johnson, Robinson, and Yared [2008]).

participation, the regulation of participation, the openness and competitiveness of executive recruitment, and constraints on the chief executive. This implies that the Polity IV score ranges from −10 to 10.

The other data we use is GDP per capita in 2007 purchasing power parity (PPP) adjusted from the World Bank's World Development Indicators CD Rom, and from the same source we also take information of the Gini coefficient for income distribution that we average over the period 1996 to 2005.

Table 2.2 shows some basic descriptive statistics of the data. The rows correspond to our different dependent and key explanatory variables and we divide the sample according to the median extent of frontier land in 1850 according to our narrow definition. The first set of columns show the average data for countries with greater than median frontier land, while the last set of columns in the table show the data for less than median frontier land. The median country here is Mexico, 57 percent of whose land was frontier in 1850 according to our narrow definition. Note that for countries below the median the average amount of land that was frontier was 32 percent (with a standard deviation of 0.22), while for countries above the median the average proportion of frontier land was 70 percent (with standard deviation of 0.12).

The comparison of low and high frontier countries is quite revealing. For instance, looking at the third row of table 2.2 we see that GDP per capita in 2007 on average was $11,466 for above median frontier societies, while it was only $3,744 for below median. The data shows that those countries that had a relatively large frontier in 1850 now have substantially higher income per capita. In row four we show the average Polity IV score over the period 1900 to 2007. This is 2.43 for above median countries and −0.35 for below median. In the next row we instead look at the average Polity IV score for the period 1950 to 2007. Though there is a clear upward trend in the extent of democracy, the comparison looks quite similar with above median frontier countries that have an average polity score of 3.96 while below median countries have a score of 1.05. As with income per capita, there seems to be a clear pattern with countries that had relatively large frontiers in 1850 being today more democratic than those that had relatively small frontiers in 1850.

Finally, the last row examines average inequality over the period 1996 to 2005. The average Gini coefficient for high frontier countries is 49.1 while for low frontier countries it is 53.4. Just as countries with relatively large frontiers are more prosperous and democratic, they also appear to be more equal.

These raw numbers are quite consistent with the basic frontier thesis. It is interesting to examine them in figures. Figure 2.5 plots the share of frontier (narrow definition) against GDP per capita in 2007. There is a pronounced positively sloped relationship that remains even if the United States and Canada are dropped. Figure 2.6 examines the raw relationship between the

Table 2.2   Descriptive statistics

Variable	Countries with frontier share $\geq$ sample median frontier share					Countries with frontier share $<$ sample median frontier share				
	Obs	Mean	Std. dev.	Min	Max	Obs	Mean	Std. dev.	Min	Max
Share of frontier land circa 1850	11	0.700	0.127	0.574	1	10	0.322	0.225	0	0.527
Constraints on the executive 1850	11	2.636	2.335	1	7	10	2.600	1.265	1	5
Per capita income 2007	11	11,466.36	15,725.61	980	46,040	10	3,744	2,296.15	560	8,350
Polity score average 1900 to 2007	11	2.427	5.325	-3.537	10	10	-0.350	1.935	-3.107	2.333
Polity score average 1950 to 2007	11	3.964	5.008	-3.293	10	10	1.052	2.482	-5.339	3.828
Income Gini average 1996 to 2005	11	49.113	8.389	32.560	58.770	10	53.435	2.614	50.630	59.2

Note: The sample median country for frontier share is Mexico, with a frontier share of 0.574 (based on our preferred measure of frontier). For the years in which the Polity score records a political transition we assign the average score of the years before and after the transition, and years in which the Polity score assigns interruption or interregnum periods are excluded from the averages.

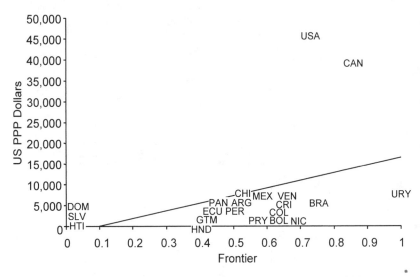

Fig. 2.5   Share of frontier land circa 1850 versus GDP per capita in 2007

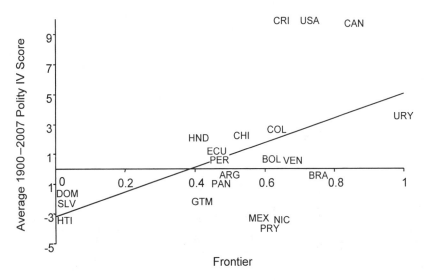

Fig. 2.6   Share of frontier land circa 1850 versus Polity IV score (average 1900 to 2007)

share of frontier land against the Polity score over the period 1900 to 2007. The picture is rather similar with a distinct positive correlation and with North America and Costa Rica far off the regression line. Figure 2.7 shows the same picture, but now with the Polity IV score averaged over the post–World War II period, 1950 to 2007. This is very similar to figure 2.7. Finally, figure 2.8 examines inequality and the extent of the frontier. This figure sug-

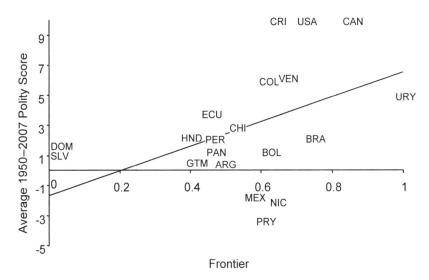

Fig. 2.7   Share of frontier land circa 1850 versus Polity IV score (average 1950 to 2007)

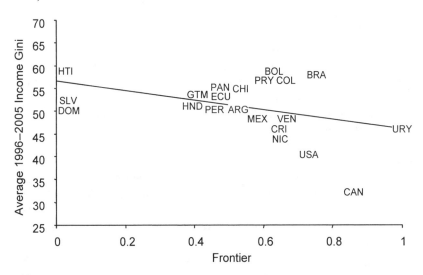

Fig. 2.8   Share of frontier land circa 1850 versus income Gini (average 1996 to 2005)

gests that there is a negative correlation between the extent of the frontier and contemporary inequality.

All of the previously mentioned figures give support to the Turner thesis. We now turn to regression analysis to investigate how robust they are and whether these numbers may also be consistent with our conditional frontier thesis. As we shall see, the image that emerges from the descriptive statistics and simple scatterplots is not general.

2.4   Empirical Results

We now examine some simple regression models to examine the long-run consequences for economic and political development of having a frontier. In all cases we estimate Ordinary Least Squares (OLS) regressions of the form

$$(1) \qquad y_i = \alpha + \beta F_{i,1850} + \gamma C_{i,1850} + \delta(F_{i,1850} \times C_{i,1850}) + \varepsilon_i,$$

where y_i is the dependent variable of interest for country i. This is respectively GDP per capita in 2007, the democracy score of Polity averaged over different periods, or the Gini coefficient of inequality averaged over some period. Variable $F_{i,1850}$ is the proportion of the country that was frontier land around 1850, $C_{i,1850}$ is constraints on the executive from Polity in 1850, and ε_i is a disturbance term that we assume to have the usual properties. Here, following the discussion earlier, we also allow for the interaction between constraints on the executive and frontier land in 1850.

2.4.1   Income Per Capita

We first look at regressions where y_i is GDP per capita for country i in 2007. These are recorded in table 2.3. The table is split into three sets of columns where each set uses a different definition of the frontier. The first three columns use our narrow definition of the frontier, the second three our wide definition, and the final three columns use the Butland definition.[12]

The first column shows the most parsimonious OLS regression of GDP per capita on the proportion of land that was frontier in 1850. The coefficient $\beta = 18324.1$ (with a standard error of 9953.3) is statistically significant. To see what this coefficient implies, consider Mexico, which is the median frontier country, with 57 percent of its territory comprised of frontier. This coefficient implies a GDP per capita for Mexico of $-1738 + 18324 \times 0.57 = \$8706$, which is pretty close to the actual value for Mexico, which is $8340. The coefficient on the frontier share implies that if one changed the frontier from the median level to the level of the United States, which is 0.72, GDP per capita would increase by $(0.72-0.57) \times 18324 = \$2748$, which is a 31 percent ($= 2748/8706$) increase of the predicted income for the median country. Alternatively, if Mexico's frontier increased by 10 percent, from 57 percent to 62.7 percent, income would increase by $(0.627-0.57) \times 18324 = \$1,044.5$.

It is important to note, however, that one should be very cautious about proposing any type of causal interpretation of the data. For example, we

12. Since the Butland data are only available for the South American countries, the Butland frontier definition uses the narrow frontier measure for the rest of the sample.

Table 2.3   Per capita income regression results

	Narrow frontier			Wide frontier			Butland frontier		
	Dependent variable: Per capita GDP 2007 (PPP adjusted)								
Frontier share	18324.10	15777.35	−13849.29	10535.48	10397.26	−12590.71	12611.73	14272.81	−10397.47
	(9953.30)	(4900.72)	(7835.69)	(6043.12)	(3884.45)	(8253.17)	(6934.05)	(4840.60)	(6118.02)
Constraints on the executive 1850		4405.86	−3657.29		4579.16	−3029.61		4708.54	−2663.75
		(1346.50)	(2228.71)		(1526.40)	(3360.24)		(1371.11)	(2332.80)
Constraints 1850 × Frontier Share			11843.70			10391.53			10341.30
			(3015.50)			(3765.30)			(2880.38)
R-squared	0.162	0.631	0.773	0.061	0.571	0.655	0.094	0.632	0.738
No. observations	21	21	21	21	21	21	21	21	21

Note: Robust standard errors in parentheses. All regressions include a constant (omitted).

have treated the extent of the frontier in 1850 as econometrically exogenous, while in fact it may be the endogenous outcome of other factors that influence economic or political development. Perhaps countries that had good fundamentals had expanded more, for instance, by attracting greater numbers of migrants and thus tended to have relatively small frontiers in 1850. Of course, if this form of omitted variable bias were important, it actually suggests that we might be underestimating the effect of the frontier because it suggests that relatively small frontiers ought to be associated with factors that also lead to good long-run development. We are also treating constraints on the executive as exogenous, which is again unlikely to be the case.

In column (2) we add constraints on the executive in 1850. This greatly increases the extent of variation explained by the model and both constraints and frontier are significant, though the estimated coefficient on frontier falls. The coefficient on constraints, $\gamma = 4405.86$ (s.e. $= 1346.5$) is statistically significant.

Column (3) then adds the interaction term. This term is highly significant; $\delta = 11843.7$ (s.e. $= 3015.5$) and the estimated coefficient on frontier now changes sign so that $\beta = -13489.29$ (s.e. $= 7835.69$). One can see here that when constraints on the executive are equal to 1 (which is the case in 9 out of our 21 countries in 1850) the total effect of frontier is $\beta + \delta \times 1 = -13489.29 + 11843.7 = -1,645.59 < 0$. In other words, for countries with the lowest value of constraints on the executive, representing "unlimited executive authority," the greater is the relative size of the frontier in 1850, the poorer is the country today. However, as long as constraints are two or above, frontier land is positively correlated with long-run growth.

It is also interesting to examine the quantitative impact of these results. For example, if we held the extent of frontier fixed and increased the level of constraints on the executive in a country from one to seven then this would imply a change in income of

$$(-13849 \times F_{1850}) + (11843 \times F_{1850} \times 6) - (3657 \times 6)$$
$$= (-13849 \times F_{1850}) + (71058 \times F_{1850}) - 21942$$
$$= (57209 \times F_{1850}) - 21942.$$

Hence, a country with median frontier would increase its current income by $0.57 \times 57209 - 21942 = \$10667$, which would eliminate about one third of the income gap between Mexico and the United States.

Columns (4) to (6) then reestimate the same three models using our wide definition of the frontier. The results are very similar to those in the first three columns with the narrow definition except that now neither frontier nor constraints on the executive are significant when they are entered with the interaction. The final three columns use the Butland definition of the frontier with similar results.

In all specifications, when we enter the interaction term, it is robustly estimated and very significant and in all cases suggests that when constraints are at their minimum the presence of the frontier was bad for economic development, while at higher levels of constraints the frontier was good for long-run economic growth. The results in this section are not consistent with the frontier thesis but they are consistent with the conditional frontier thesis.

2.4.2   Democracy

We now turn to regressions where y_i is the Polity score for country i averaged over different periods. We look at two such periods, one is 1900 to 2007 and the other is 1950 to 2007. These regressions are in tables 2.4 and 2.5 respectively. As with table 2.3, each table is split into three sets of columns where each set uses a different definition of the frontier.

Table 2.4 column (1) shows the simplest regression of the Polity score 1900 to 2007 on frontier in 1850. There is a significant positive correlation with $\beta = 8.189$ (s.e. $= 2.458$). The second column adds constraints on the executive in 1850. Constraints are also significantly positively correlated with democracy in the twentieth century with an estimated coefficient of 1.474 (s.e. $= 0.195$).

The third column then adds our interaction term. The interaction term is marginally significant with a t-statistic of 1.78 and has a positive coefficient of $\delta = 1.263$. However, unlike in the regressions where income per capita was the dependent variable, the frontier share on its own remains positive and significant, even if the magnitude of the coefficient falls by 50 percent.

The rest of table 2.4 shows that these results are not completely robust. The interaction terms remain positive and basically significant, but when we use the wide definition of the frontier, frontier entered on its own is not statistically significant in column (6), or using the Butland definition in column (9). Nevertheless, there is no evidence here of any negative effect of the frontier, unlike in the income regressions. The results in table 2.4 suggest that even for the lowest level of constraints on the executive, the greater was the frontier in 1850, the more democratic the country was in the twentieth century. Nevertheless, the greater are constraints in 1850, the larger the quantitative effect.

In table 2.5 we reestimate the same models as in table 2.4 except that now we average the dependent variable only over the post–World War II period. As is quickly seen, this gives some quite different results. When we just control for frontier and constraints on the executive, the results in terms of the size and significance of the coefficients are very similar to those in table 2.4. However, once we control for the interaction we find that the interaction term is never close to significant, while the estimated coefficient on frontier on its own remains more or less the same quantitatively and mostly significant (only marginally so in column [6]). This table shows that the conditional effect on democracy is actually a phenomenon of the first half of the twentieth century. In the second half, the simpler version of the frontier thesis captures the patterns in the data quite nicely.

Table 2.4   Polity score 1900–2007 regression results

	Narrow frontier			Wide frontier			Butland frontier		
				Dependent variable: Polity IV score, average 1900 to 2007					
Frontier share	8.189	7.337	4.178	5.886	5.839	0.281	5.608	6.176	3.159
	(2.458)	(1.297)	(2.243)	(2.317)	(1.789)	(2.975)	(2.180)	(1.424)	(2.454)
Constraints on the executive 1850		1.474	0.615		1.554	−0.285		1.611	0.710
		(0.195)	(0.552)		(0.240)	(0.798)		(0.192)	(0.487)
Constraints 1850 × frontier share			1.263			2.512			1.265
			(0.708)			(1.074)			(0.706)
R-squared	0.256	0.672	0.685	0.151	0.617	0.655	0.147	0.646	0.659
No. observations	21	21	21	21	21	21	21	21	21

Note: Robust standard errors in parentheses. All regressions include a constant (omitted). The Polity score for Panama is average over the 1903 to 2007 period.

Table 2.5   Polity score 1950–2007 regression results

	Narrow frontier			Wide frontier			Butland frontier		
	Dependent variable: Polity IV score, average 1950 to 2007								
Frontier share	8.213	7.455	9.809	5.822	5.780	6.474	5.304	5.815	7.597
	(2.960)	(1.851)	(2.676)	(3.119)	(2.151)	(4.388)	(2.873)	(1.865)	(3.866)
Constraints on the executive 1850		1.313	1.954		1.394	1.624		1.448	1.980
		(0.254)	(0.959)		(0.282)	(1.197)		(0.252)	(1.080)
Constraints 1850 × frontier share			−0.941			−0.314			−0.747
			(1.120)			(1.514)			(1.354)
R-squared	0.262	0.599	0.606	0.150	0.533	0.533	0.134	0.545	0.550
No. observations	21	21	21	21	21	21	21	21	21

Note: Robust standard errors in parentheses. All regressions include a constant (omitted).

2.4.3   Inequality

Finally, we let y_i in equation (1) be the average Gini coefficient for country i over the period 1990 to 2007. The results of estimating this model are reported in table 2.6. A quite robust pattern emerges in all three sets of columns, irrespective of how we measure the extent of the frontier. When entered on its own, frontier is negatively and significantly correlated with contemporary income inequality, as are constraints on the executive. These results suggest that either having a bigger frontier in 1850 or better political institutions is associated with lower inequality today. However, as columns (3), (6), and (9) indicate, once the interaction term is included none of the coefficients are statistically significant.

2.5   Conclusion

In this chapter we have developed what to our knowledge is the first test of the frontier (or Turner) thesis. Turner argued that it was the existence of the frontier that generated the particular path of development that the United States followed in the nineteenth century. Though his work on the United States has been criticized, it still appears to heavily influence the ways scholars think about these issues. The starting point of our assessment of this thesis is the observation that every country in the Americas, with the possible exception of El Salvador and Haiti, had a frontier in the nineteenth century. The United States was certainly not exceptional in either this or the relative extent of the frontier. In consequence, seen in comparative context, the existence of a frontier does not seem to be obviously correlated with long-run economic and political development.

We hypothesized, however, that there may be a conditional relationship between the extent of the frontier and political institutions at the time of the allocation of frontier land. Historical evidence suggests that even if most countries in the Americas had an open frontier, how that frontier land was allocated differed a lot. For example, while the United States, Costa Rica, and Colombia passed Homestead Acts or something approximating them, in places like Argentina, Chile, or Guatemala, political elites allocated frontier lands to themselves or associates in a very oligarchic manner. This indicates that the impact of the frontier might be conditional on the existing political institutions that influenced how the land was allocated—a notion we dubbed the conditional frontier thesis. Our hypothesis suggests that if political institutions were bad at the time of frontier settlement, the existence of such frontier land might actually lead to worse development outcomes, probably because it provides a resource that nondemocratic political elites can use to cement themselves in power.

To investigate more systematically the relationship between the frontier and long-run development, we constructed measures of the extent of fron-

Table 2.6 Inequality regression results

	Narrow frontier			Wide frontier			Butland frontier		
			Dependent variable: Income Gini, average 1996 to 2005						
Frontier share	−10.585	−9.579	−2.755	−7.086	−7.030	−1.901	−5.923	−6.596	1.723
	(5.632)	(4.126)	(7.922)	(4.628)	(3.520)	(8.094)	(4.897)	(3.707)	(9.226)
Constraints on the executive 1850		−1.740	0.117		−1.845	−0.147		−1.906	0.580
		(0.676)	(1.745)		(0.767)	(2.347)		(0.745)	(2.220)
Constraints 1850 × frontier share			−2.728			−2.319			−3.487
			(2.727)			(3.523)			(3.207)
R-squared	0.177	0.417	0.442	0.091	0.362	0.376	0.068	0.358	0.397
No. observations	21	21	21	21	21	21	21	21	21

Note: Robust standard errors in parentheses. All regressions include a constant (omitted).

tier land for twenty-one independent countries in the Americas in 1850. Using some simple regressions we showed that the data does indeed support our conditional hypothesis. With respect to both income per capita today and democracy over the twentieth century, it is the interaction between the extent of the frontier in 1850 and constraints on the executive in 1850 that plays the primary explanatory role. For example, for a country with the lowest level of constraints on the executive, the larger is the relative size of the frontier, the lower is GDP per capita today. For countries with higher constraints, however, a larger frontier is positively correlated with current GDP per capita. With respect to democracy, we found that for a given level of constraints in 1850, greater size of the frontier is correlated with greater democracy in the twentieth century, though this effect comes primarily from the first half of the century.

There are many caveats with these findings. For example, we did not control for variation in the quality of the frontier. For instance, there may be a big difference between Oklahoma in the United States and the Atacama Desert in northern Chile, both of which were frontiers in 1850. Still, the United States also had large areas of the Rocky Mountains that were not high quality lands. Trying to control or adjust for this explicitly is an important area for future research. Moreover, while 1850 seemed to us to be an interesting year to focus on because it marked the beginning of the period of the rapid expansion of world trade that created such huge frontier movements in the Americas, one could argue it is too late. An important area for future research is a more intensive sensitivity analysis than is presented here.

Nevertheless, results suggest that the role of the frontier is much more complex than the original Turner thesis suggests. The consequences of the existence of a frontier for different countries in the Americas depended a lot on the nature of political institutions that formed in the early independence period. If these institutions featured few constraints on the executive, having a frontier was actually bad for economic development. If El Salvador and Haiti had had frontiers in the nineteenth century, this would have made them poorer today, not richer. Though we found no such negative effect for democracy, we did find that the impact of the frontier on the democratization of a society was conditional on initial political institutions. If Turner thought that the United States frontier had a strong democratizing effect, this was only because it was in a country that already had good political institutions. This effect was severely muted in Latin America.

Though our results are not consistent with a large part of the Turner thesis, they are consistent with the research of Brenner (1976) and Acemoglu, Johnson, and Robinson (2005), which emphasized that the implications of large shocks or new economic opportunities depends on the initial institutional equilibrium. More specifically in the Americas, they are also consistent with the work of Engerman and Sokoloff (1997) and Acemoglu,

Johnson, and Robinson (2001, 2002) who emphasized the critical importance of the creation of institutions in the colonial period and their path-dependent consequences. In a sense, our results on income per capita show how different paths were reinforced by the availability of frontier lands in the nineteenth century.

Appendix

Table 2A.1   Sources for frontier

Country	Cartographic Source	Historical references
Argentina	Butland (1966)	Eidt (1971), Bandeira, (2006), Jefferson, (1926), Moniz (2006)
Bolivia	Butland (1966)	Gill (1987), Fifer (1982)
Brazil	Butland (1966)	Bandeira (2006), Katzman (1977), Katzman (1975), James (1941)
Canada	Dominion Bureau of Statistics (n.d.)	Silver (1969), Landon (1967)
Chile	Butland (1966)	James (1941), Villalobos (1992)
Colombia	Butland (1966)	James (1941), LeGrand (1986), Rausch (1993)
Costa Rica	Hall and Pérez Brignoli (2003), United States Bureau of the Census (1956a)	Hall and Pérez Brignoli (2003), James (1941)
Dominican Rep.	United States Bureau of the Census (1956b)	Lora (2002)
Ecuador	Butland (1966)	Dueñas (1986), Sampedro (1990)
El Salvador	Hall and Pérez Brignoli (2003), United States Bureau of the Census (1956a)	Hall and Pérez Brignoli (2003)
Guatemala	Hall and Pérez Brignoli (2003), United States Bureau of the Census (1956a)	Hall and Pérez Brignoli (2003), McCreery (1976)
Haiti	United States Bureau of the Census (1956b)	Anglade (1982)
Honduras	Hall and Pérez Brignoli (2003), United States Bureau of the Census (1956a)	Hall and Pérez Brignoli (2003), Davidson (2006)
Mexico	Bureau of Business Research (1975)	Bernstein (1964)
Nicaragua	Hall and Pérez Brignoli (2003), United States Bureau of the Census (1956a)	Hall and Pérez Brignoli (2003), Aguirre (2002)
Panama	Hall and Pérez Brignoli (2003), United States Bureau of the Census (1956a)	Hall and Pérez Brignoli (2003)
Paraguay	Butland (1966)	Moniz (2006)
Peru	Butland (1966)	Milla (1995)
United States	United States Census Office (1898), Gerlach (1970)	Billington (2001), Billington (1962), Wyman and Kroeber (1965)
Uruguay	Butland (1966)	Moniz (2006), Bollo (1896)
Venezuela	Butland (1966)	

Table 2A.2   Frontier classification by subnational administrative units

Country	Province/state/department	Land area (square kms.)	Narrow frontier	Wide frontier
Argentina	Buenos Aires	307,571	0	1
	Catamarca	102,602	0	0
	Chaco	99,633	1	1
	Chubut	224,686	1	1
	Ciudad De Buenos Aires	203	0	0
	Córdoba	165,321	1	1
	Corrientes	88,199	1	1
	Entre ríos	78,781	1	1
	Formosa	72,066	1	1
	Jujuy	53,219	0	0
	La Pampa	143,440	1	1
	La Rioja	89,680	0	0
	Mendoza	148,827	0	0
	Misiones	29,801	1	1
	Neuquén	94,078	0	1
	Río Negro	203,013	1	1
	Salta	155,488	0	1
	San Juan	89,651	0	0
	San Luis	76,748	0	0
	Santa Cruz	243,943	1	1
	Santa Fe	133,007	0	0
	Santiago Del Estero	136,351	0	1
	Tierra Del Fuego	21,571	1	1
	Tucumán	22,524	0	0
Bolivia	Beni	213,564	1	1
	Chuquisaca	51,524	0	0
	Cochabamba	55,631	0	0
	La Paz	133,985	0	0
	Oruro	53,588	0	0
	Pando	63,827	1	1
	Potosí	118,218	0	1
	Santa Cruz	370,621	1	1
	Tarija	37,623	1	1
Brazil	Acre	152,522	1	1
	Alagoas	27,819	0	0
	Amapá	142,816	1	1
	Amazonas	1,570,947	1	1
	Bahia	564,272	0	0
	Ceará	145,712	0	0
	Distrito Federal	5,802	1	1
	Espírito Santo	46,047	0	0
	Goiás	340,119	1	1
	Maranhão	331,919	1	1
	Mato Grosso	903,385	1	1
	Mato Grosso Do Sul	357,140	1	1
	Minas Gerais	586,553	0	1
	Pará	1,247,703	1	1
	Paraíba	56,341	0	0
	Paraná	199,282	1	1

Table 2A.2   (continued)

Country	Province/state/department	Land area (square kms.)	Narrow frontier	Wide frontier
	Pernambuco	98,526	0	0
	Piauí	251,311	0	1
	Rio De Janeiro	43,797	0	0
	Rio Grande Do Norte	53,077	0	0
	Rio Grande Do Sul	268,836	1	1
	Rondónia	237,565	1	1
	Roraima	224,118	1	1
	Santa Catarina	95,286	1	1
	São Paulo	248,177	0	0
	Sergipe	21,962	0	0
	Tocantins	277,297	1	1
Chile	Antofagasta (II)	126,049	0	0
	Atacama (III)	75,176	0	0
	Aysén (XI)	108,494	1	1
	Bío-Bío (VIII)	37,063	0	0
	Coquimbo (IV)	40,580	0	0
	La Araucanía (IX)	31,842	1	1
	Los Lagos (X)	67,013	1	1
	Magallanes y Antártica Chilena (XII)	132,297	1	1
	Maule (VII)	30,296	0	0
	O'higgins (VI)	16,387	0	0
	Santiago	15,403	0	0
	Tarapacá (I)	59,099	1	1
	Valparaíso (V)	16,396	0	0
Colombia	Amazonas	109,665	1	1
	Antioquia	63,612	0	0
	Arauca	23,818	1	1
	Atlantico	3,388	0	0
	Bogota	1,587	0	0
	Bolivar	25,978	0	0
	Boyaca	23,189	0	0
	Caldas	7,888	1	1
	Caqueta	88,965	1	1
	Casanare	44,640	1	1
	Cauca	29,308	0	0
	Cesar	22,905	0	0
	Choco	46,530	1	1
	Cordoba	25,020	0	0
	Cundinamarca	22,623	0	0
	Guainia	72,238	1	1
	Guajira	20,848	0	0
	Guaviare	42,327	1	1
	Huila	19,890	0	0
	Magdalena	23,188	0	0
	Meta	85,635	1	1
	Nariño	33,268	0	0
	Norte De Santander	21,658	0	0

(continued)

Table 2A.2   (continued)

Country	Province/state/department	Land area (square kms.)	Narrow frontier	Wide frontier
	Putumayo	24,885	1	1
	Quindio	1,845	1	1
	Risaralda	4,140	1	1
	San Andres	44	1	1
	Santander	30,537	0	0
	Sucre	10,917	0	0
	Tolima	23,562	0	0
	Valle Del Cauca	22,140	0	0
	Vaupes	65,268	1	1
	Vichada	100,242	1	1
Costa Rica	Alajuela	9,758	1	1
	Cartago	3,125	0	0
	Guanacaste	10,141	0	1
	Heredia	2,657	1	1
	Limón	9,189	1	1
	Puntarenas	11,266	1	1
	San José	4,966	0	0
Dominican Republic	Azua	2,688	0	0
	Bahoruco	1,244	0	0
	Barahona	1,647	0	1
	Dajabón	1,004	0	0
	Distrito Nacional	91	0	0
	Duarte	1,640	0	0
	El Seibo	1,775	0	0
	Elias Piña	1,397	0	0
	Espaillat	825	0	0
	Hato Mayor	1,324	0	0
	Independencia	1,754	0	0
	La Altagracia	3,001	0	0
	La Romana	656	0	0
	La Vega	2,274	0	0
	María Trinidad Sánchez	1,212	0	0
	Monseñor Nouel	992	0	0
	Monte Cristi	1,886	0	0
	Monte Plata	2,613	0	0
	Pedernales	2,018	0	1
	Peravia	785	0	0
	Puerto Plata	819	0	0
	Salcedo	430	0	0
	Samaná	845	0	0
	San Cristóbal	1,240	0	0
	San Jose De Ocoa	853	0	0
	San Juan	3,360	0	0
	San Pedro De Macorís	1,255	0	0
	Sánchez Ramírez	1,191	0	0
	Santiago	2,809	0	0
	Santiago Rodriguez	1,152	0	0
	Santo Domingo	1,302	0	0
	Valverde	809	0	0

Table 2A.2   (continued)

Country	Province/state/department	Land area (square kms.)	Narrow frontier	Wide frontier
Ecuador	Azuay	7,995	0	0
	Bolívar	3,926	0	0
	Cañar	3,142	0	0
	Carchi	3,750	0	0
	Chimborazo	6,470	0	0
	Cotopaxi	5,985	0	0
	El Oro	5,817	0	0
	Esmeraldas	15,896	0	1
	Galápagos	8,010	0	0
	Guayas	20,566	0	0
	Imbabura	4,615	0	0
	Loja	10,995	0	0
	Los Ríos	7,151	0	0
	Manabí	18,894	0	1
	Morona Santiago	23,797	1	1
	Napo	12,483	1	1
	Orellana	21,675	1	1
	Pastaza	29,325	1	1
	Pichincha	13,270	0	0
	Región Zonas No Delimitadas	775	1	1
	Sucumbíos	18,008	1	1
	Tungurahua	3,369	0	0
	Zamora Chinchipe	10,456	1	1
El Salvador	Ahuachapán	1,240	0	0
	Cabañas	1,104	0	0
	Chalatenango	2,017	0	0
	Cuscatlán	756	0	0
	La Libertad	1,653	0	0
	La Paz	1,224	0	0
	La Unión	2,074	0	0
	Morazán	1,447	0	0
	San Miguel	2,077	0	0
	San Salvador	886	0	0
	San Vicente	1,184	0	0
	Santa Ana	2,023	0	0
	Sonsonate	1,225	0	0
	Usulután	2,130	0	0
Guatemala	Alta Verapaz	8,686	0	1
	Baja Verapaz	3,124	0	1
	Chimaltenango	1,979	0	0
	Chiquimula	2,376	0	0
	El Petén	35,854	1	1
	El Progreso	1,922	0	1
	El Quiché	8,378	0	1
	Escuintla	4,384	0	0
	Guatemala	2,126	0	0
	Huehuetenango	7,400	0	0

(continued)

Table 2A.2   (continued)

Country	Province/state/department	Land area (square kms.)	Narrow frontier	Wide frontier
	Izabal	9,038	1	1
	Jalapa	2,063	0	0
	Jutiapa	3,219	0	0
	Quetzaltenango	1,951	0	0
	Retalhuleu	1,856	0	0
	Sacatepéquez	465	0	0
	San Marcos	3,791	0	0
	Santa Rosa	2,955	0	0
	Sololá	1,061	0	0
	Suchitepéquez	2,510	0	0
	Totonicapán	1,061	0	0
	Zacapa	2,690	0	1
Honduras	Atlántida	4,372	0	1
	Choluteca	3,923	0	0
	Colón	4,360	1	1
	Comayagua	8,249	0	0
	Copán	5,124	0	0
	Cortés	3,242	0	0
	El Paraíso	7,489	0	1
	Francisco Morazán	8,619	0	0
	Gracias a Dios	16,997	1	1
	Intibucá	3,123	0	0
	Islas De La Bahía	236	0	0
	La Paz	2,525	0	0
	Lempira	4,228	0	0
	Ocotepeque	1,630	0	0
	Olancho	23,905	1	1
	Santa Bárbara	5,024	0	0
	Valle	1,665	0	0
	Yoro	7,781	0	1
Haiti	Artibonite	4,984	0	0
	Centre	3,675	0	0
	Grand' Anse	3,310	0	0
	Nord	2,106	0	0
	Nord-Est	1,805	0	0
	Nord-Ouest	2,176	0	0
	Ouest	4,827	0	0
	Sud	2,794	0	0
	Sud-Est	2,023	0	0
Mexico	Aguascalientes	5,569	0	0
	Baja California Norte	70,113	1	1
	Baja California Sur	73,677	1	1
	Campeche	56,859	1	1
	Chiapas	75,629	0	1
	Chihuahua	247,087	1	1
	Coahuila De Zaragoza	151,571	1	1
	Colima	5,455	0	0
	Distrito Federal	1,499	0	0
	Durango	119,648	1	1

Table 2A.2   (continued)

Country	Province/state/department	Land area (square kms.)	Narrow frontier	Wide frontier
	Guanajuato	30,350	0	0
	Guerrero	63,749	0	0
	Hidalgo	20,987	0	0
	Jalisco	80,137	0	0
	México, Estado De	21,461	0	0
	Michoacán De Ocampo	59,864	0	0
	Morelos	4,941	0	0
	Nayarit	27,336	0	0
	Nuevo Léon	64,555	0	0
	Oaxaca	94,964	0	0
	Puebla	33,919	0	0
	Querétaro De Arteaga	11,769	0	0
	Quintana Roo	50,843	1	1
	San Luis Potosí	60,547	0	0
	Sinaloa	58,092	1	1
	Sonora	184,934	1	1
	Tabasco	24,661	0	0
	Tamaulipas	79,829	1	1
	Tlaxcala	4,061	0	0
	Veracruz-Llave	72,815	0	0
	Yucatán	39,337	1	1
	Zacatecas	74,516	0	0
Nicaragua	Boaco	4,177	0	1
	Carazo	1,081	0	0
	Chinandega	4,822	0	0
	Chontales	6,481	0	0
	Estelí	2,230	0	0
	Granada	1,040	0	0
	Jinotega	9,222	1	1
	León	5,138	0	0
	Madriz	1,708	0	0
	Managua	3,465	0	0
	Masaya	611	0	0
	Matagalpa	6,804	0	1
	Nueva Segovia	3,491	0	1
	Region Autónoma Atlántico Norte	33,106	1	1
	Region Autónoma Atlántico Sur	27,260	1	1
	Río San Juan	7,541	1	1
	Rivas	2,162	0	0
Panama	Bocas Del Toro	4,644	1	1
	Chiriquí	6,548	0	0
	Coclé	4,927	0	0
	Colón	4,868	1	1
	Comarca Emberá	4,384	1	1
	Comarca Kuna Yala	2,341	1	1
	Comarca Ngöbe Buglé	6,968	1	1

(*continued*)

Table 2A.2 (continued)

Country	Province/state/department	Land area (square kms.)	Narrow frontier	Wide frontier
	Darién	11,897	1	1
	Herrera	2,341	0	0
	Los Santos	3,805	0	0
	Panamá	11,671	0	1
	Veraguas	10,677	0	0
Peru	Amazonas	39,249	1	1
	Ancash	35,915	0	0
	Arequipa	63,345	0	0
	Ayacucho	43,815	0	0
	Cajamarca	33,318	0	0
	Cusco	71,987	0	0
	Departamento Apurímac	20,896	0	0
	El Callao	147	0	0
	Huancavelica	22,131	0	0
	Huánuco	36,849	0	1
	Ica	21,328	0	0
	Junín	44,197	0	0
	La Libertad	25,500	0	0
	Lambayeque	14,213	0	0
	Lima	34,802	0	0
	Loreto	368,852	1	1
	Madre De Dios	85,301	1	1
	Moquegua	15,734	0	0
	Pasco	25,320	0	1
	Piura	35,892	0	0
	Puno	71,999	0	0
	San Martín	51,253	0	1
	Tacna	16,076	0	0
	Tumbes	4,669	0	0
	Ucayali	102,411	1	1
Paraguay	Alto Paraguay	82,349	1	1
	Alto Paraná	14,895	0	1
	Amambay	12,933	0	1
	Asunción	117	0	0
	Boquerón	91,669	1	1
	Caaguazú	11,474	0	1
	Caazapá	9,496	0	1
	Canindeyú	14,667	0	1
	Central	2,465	0	0
	Concepción	18,051	0	1
	Cordillera	4,948	0	0
	Guairá	3,846	0	1
	Itapúa	16,525	0	1
	Misiones	9,556	0	1
	Ñeembucú	12,147	0	0
	Paraguarí	8,705	0	0
	Presidente Hayes	72,907	1	1
	San Pedro	20,002	0	1

Table 2A.2   (continued)

Country	Province/state/department	Land area (square kms.)	Narrow frontier	Wide frontier
Uruguay	Artigas	11,928	1	1
	Canelones	4,536	1	1
	Cerro Largo	13,648	1	1
	Colonia	6,106	1	1
	Durazno	11,643	1	1
	Flores	5,144	1	1
	Florida	10,417	1	1
	Lavalleja	10,016	1	1
	Maldonado	4,793	1	1
	Montevideo	530	1	1
	Paysandú	13,922	1	1
	Río Negro	9,282	1	1
	Rivera	9,370	1	1
	Rocha	10,551	1	1
	Salto	14,163	1	1
	San José	4,992	1	1
	Soriano	9,008	1	1
	Tacuarembó	15,438	1	1
	Treinta y Tres	9,529	1	1
Venezuela	Amazonas	180,145	1	1
	Anzoátegui	43,300	0	1
	Apure	76,500	1	1
	Aragua	7,014	0	0
	Barinas	35,200	1	1
	Bolívar	238,000	1	1
	Carabobo	4,650	0	0
	Cojedes	14,800	0	0
	Delta Amacuro	40,200	1	1
	Dependencias Federales (DF)	120	0	0
	Distrito Federal	433	0	0
	Falcón	24,800	0	0
	Guárico	64,986	0	1
	Lara	19,800	0	0
	Mérida	11,300	0	0
	Miranda	7,950	0	0
	Monagas	28,900	1	1
	Nueva Esparta	1,150	0	0
	Portuguesa	15,200	0	0
	Sucre	11,800	0	0
	Táchira	11,100	0	0
	Trujillo	7,400	0	0
	Vargas	1,497	0	0
	Yaracuy	7,100	0	0
	Zulia	63,100	0	0

References

Acemoglu, Daron, Simon Johnson, and James A. Robinson. 2001. "The Colonial Origins of Comparative Development: An Empirical Investigation." *American Economic Review* 91:1369–1401.

———. 2002. "Reversal of Fortune: Geography and Institutions in the Making of the Modern World Income Distribution." *Quarterly Journal of Economics* 118:1231–94.

———. 2005. "The Rise of Europe: Atlantic Trade, Institutional Change and Growth." *American Economic Review* 95:546–79.

Acemoglu, Daron, Simon Johnson, James A. Robinson, and Pierre Yared. 2008. "Income and Democracy." *American Economic Review* 98:808–42.

Adelman, Jeremy. 1994. *Frontier Development: Land, Labour, and Capital on the Wheatlands of Argentina and Canada, 1890–1914.* Oxford: Clarendon Press.

Aguirre, Francisco Xavier. 2002. *Un Atlas Histórico de Nicaragua.* Managua, Nicaragua: Fundación Vida.

Anglade, Georges. 1982. *Atlas critique d'Haiti.* Montréal: Université du Québec à Montréal.

Bandeira, Moniz. 2006. *La Formación de los Estados en la Cuenca del Plata: Argentina, Brasil, Uruguay, Paraguay.* Buenos Aires: Grupo Editorial Norma.

Belich, James. 2010. "Exploding Wests: Boom and Bust in Nineteenth-Century Settler Societies." In *Natural Experiments of History,* edited by Jared Diamond and James A. Robinson, 53–87. Cambridge: Harvard University Press.

Bernstein, Marvin D. 1964. *The Mexican Mining Industry, 1890–1950.* Albany: State University of New York Press.

Billington, Ray Allen. 1962. *The Far Western Frontier, 1830–1860.* New York: Harper and Row.

———. 1966. *The Frontier Thesis: Valid Interpretation of American History?* New York: Holt, Rinehart and Winston.

———. 2001. *Westward Expansion: A History of the American Frontier.* Albuquerque: University of New Mexico Press.

Bollo, Luis Cincinato. 1896. *Atlas Geográfico y Descripción Geográfica y Estadística de la República Oriental del Uruguay.* Montevideo, Uruguay: A Barreiro y Ramos.

Brenner, Robert. 1976. "Agrarian Class Structure and Economic Development in Preindustrial Europe." *Past and Present* 70:30–75.

Bureau of Business Research. 1975. *Atlas of Mexico.* Austin: University of Texas Press. Available at: http://www.lib.utexas.edu/maps/atlas_mexico/index.html.

Butland, G. J. 1966. "Frontiers of Settlement in South America." *Revista Geografica* 65:93–108.

Christie, Keith H. 1978. "Antioqueño Colonization in Western Colombia: A Reappraisal." *Hispanic American Historical Review* 58:260–83.

Coatsworth, John H. 1974. "Railroads, Landholding, and Agrarian Protest in the Early Porfiriato." *Hispanic American Historical Review* 54:48–71.

———. 1981. *Growth Against Development: The Economic Impact of Railroads in Porfirian Mexico.* DeKalb: Northern Illinois University Press.

Davidson, William. 2006. *Atlas de Mapas Históricos de Honduras.* Managua, Nicaragua: Fundación Uno.

Dean, Warren. 1971. "Latifundia and Land Policy in Nineteenth Century Brazil." *Hispanic American Historical Review* 51:606–25.

Dominion Bureau of Statistics. n.d. *Distribution of Population, 1851–1941.* Available at: http://atlas.nrcan.gc.ca/site/english/maps/archives/3rdedition/peopleandsoci ety/population/046.

Dueñas, Carmen. 1986. *Historia Económica y Social del Norte de Manabí.* Quito, Ecuador: Abya Yala.

Eidt, Robert C. 1971. *Pioneer Settlement in Northeast Argentina.* Madison: University of Wisconsin Press.

Engerman, Stanley L., and Kenneth L. Sokoloff. 1997. "Factor Endowments, Institutions, and Differential Growth Paths among New World Economies." In *How Latin America Fell Behind,* edited by Stephen H. Haber, 260–306. Stanford: Stanford University Press.

———. 2005. "The Evolution of Suffrage Institutions in the New World." *Journal of Economic History* 65:891–921.

Fifer, J. Valerie. 1982. "The Search for a Series of Small Successes: Frontier Settlement in Eastern Bolivia." *Journal of Latin American Studies* 14:407–32.

Gerlach, Arch C. 1970. *The National Atlas of the United States of America.* Washington, DC: U.S. Department of the Interior.

Gill, Lesley. 1987. "Frontier Expansion and Settlement in Lowland Bolivia." *Journal of Peasant Studies* 14:380–98.

Gudmundson, Lowell. 1997. "Lord and Peasant in the Making of Modern Central America." In *Agrarian Structures and Political Power in Latin America,* edited by A. Evelyn Huber and Frank Safford, 151–176. Pittsburgh: University of Pittsburgh Press.

Hall, Caroline, and Héctor Pérez Brignoli. 2003. *Historical Atlas of Central America.* Norman: University of Oklahoma Press.

Hartz, Louis. 1955. *The Liberal Tradition in America: An Interpretation of American Political Thought since the Revolution.* New York: Harcourt Brace and Company.

———. 1964. *The Founding of New Societies: Studies in the History of the United States, Latin America, South Africa, Canada, and Australia.* New York: Harcourt, Brace and World.

Hennessy, C. Alistair M. 1978. *The Frontier in Latin American History.* London: Edward Arnold.

Hofstadter, Richard, and Seymour Martin Lipset, eds. 1968. *Turner and the Sociology of the Frontier.* New York: Basic Books.

James, Preston E. 1941. "Expanding Frontiers of Settlement in Latin America." *Hispanic American Historical Review* 21:183–95.

Jefferson, Mark. 1926. *Peopling the Argentine Pampa.* New York: American Geographical Society.

Katzman, Martin. 1975. *The Brazilian Frontier in Comparative Perspective.* New York: Cambridge University Press.

———. 1977. *Cities and Frontiers in Brazil: Regional Dimensions of Economic Development.* Cambridge: Harvard University Press.

Keyssar, Alexander. 2000. *The Right to Vote: The Contested History of Democracy in the United States.* New York: Basic Books.

Landon, Fred. 1967. *Western Ontario and the American Frontier.* Toronto: McClelland.

LeGrand, Catherine. 1986. *Frontier Expansion and Peasant Protest in Colombia, 1850–1936.* Albuquerque: University of New Mexico Press.

Lipset, Seymour Martin. 1996. *American Exceptionalism: A Double-edged Sword.* New York: W. W. Norton.

Lora, Quisqueya. 2002. *Atlas Histórico de la República Dominicana.* Santo Domingo, Dominican Republic: Editorial Santillana.

Mann, Charles C. 2005. *1491: New Revelations of the Americas before Columbus.* New York: Knopf.

Mahoney, James L. 2001. *The Legacies of Liberalism: Path Dependence and Political Regimes in Central America.* Baltimore: The Johns Hopkins University Press.

McCreery, David J. 1976. "Coffee and Class: The Structure of Development in Liberal Guatemala." *Hispanic American Historical Review* 56:438–60.

———. 1994. *Rural Guatemala, 1760–1940.* Stanford: Stanford University Press.

Milla, Carlos. 1995. *Atlas Histórico y Geográfico del Peru.* Lima: Editorial Milla Batres.

Miller, David H., ed. 1977. *The Frontier: Comparative Studies.* Norman: University of Oklahoma Press.

Moene, Karl Ove, Halvor Mehlum, and Ragnar Torvik. 2006. "Institutions and the Resource Curse." *The Economic Journal* 116:1–20.

Moniz, Luis Alberto. 2006. *La Formación de los Estados en la Cuenca del Plata.* Buenos Aires: Norma.

Parsons, James J. 1949. *Antioqueño Colonization in Western Colombia.* Berkeley: University of California Press.

Powell, Philip W. 1981. *Essays on Frontiers in World History.* Austin: University of Texas Press.

Richards, John F. 2003. *The Unending Frontier.* Berkeley: University of California Press.

Sampedro, Francisco. 1990. *Atlas Histórico-geográfico del Ecuador.* Quito, Ecuador: P Bustos.

Silver, A. I. 1969. "French Canada and the Prairies Frontier, 1870–1890." *Canadian Historical Review* 50:11–36.

Solberg, Carl E. 1969. "A Discriminatory Frontier Land Policy, Chile 1870–1914." *The Americas* 26:115–33.

———. 1987. *The Prairies and the Pampas: Agrarian Policy in Canada and Argentina, 1880–1930.* Stanford: Stanford University Press.

Taylor, George R. 1956. *The Turner Thesis Concerning the Role of the Frontier in American History,* rev. ed. Boston: Heath.

Turner, Frederick Jackson. 1920. *The Frontier in American History.* New York: H. Holt and Co.

United States Bureau of the Census. 1956a. *Census Atlas Maps of Latin America.* Washington, DC: U.S. Department of Commerce.

———. 1956b. Census Maps of Latin America, Part II, Greater Antilles. Washington, DC: U.S. Department of Commerce.

United States Census Office. 1898. *Statistical Atlas of the United States: Based Upon the Results of the Eleventh Census.* Washington, DC: GPO.

Villalobos, Sergio. 1992. *La Vida Fronteriza en Chile.* Madrid: Mapfre.

Walsh, Margaret. 2005. *The American West: Visions and Revisions.* New York: Cambridge University Press.

Weber, David J., and Jane M. Rausch, eds. 1994. *Where Cultures Meet: Frontiers in Latin American History.* Wilmington, NC: SR Books.

Williams, Robert G. 1994. *States and Social Evolution: Coffee and the Rise of National Governments in Central America.* Chapel Hill: University of North Carolina Press.

Winks, Robin W. 1971. *The Myth of the American Frontier: Its Relevance to America, Canada, and Australia.* The Sir George Watson lecture. Leicester, UK: Leicester University Press.

Wyman, W. D., and C. B. Kroeber, eds. 1965. *The Frontier in Perspective.* Madison: The University of Wisconsin Press.

3

Differential Paths of Financial Development
Evidence from New World Economies

Stephen Haber

One of the central questions of economic history is the impact of inequality on long-run paths of economic development. Ideas about the impact of inequality on growth have a long pedigree, but one of its most powerful recent articulations can be found in the work of Stanley Engerman and Kenneth Sokoloff, most particularly their 1997 paper "Factor Endowments, Institutions, and Differential Paths of Growth Among New World Economies." Engerman and Sokoloff hypothesize that natural environments that gave rise to social structures of evenly matched citizens produced, over the long run, institutions conducive to sustained economic growth, while natural environments that gave rise to social structures characterized by small elites dominating economically and politically disenfranchised masses produced institutions that benefited incumbent elites, at the expense of long-run growth.

This chapter builds upon the theme of inequality and long-run paths of growth by focusing on how differences in initial levels of inequality in human capital and political power affected the development of financial systems—the network of banks and markets that mobilize capital for both private investment and government spending—across three New World economies, Mexico, Brazil, and the United States. While one can point to mechanisms by which inequality affects financial development via the demand for credit, the emphasis of this chapter is the supply side: when human capital and political power is unequally distributed, elites can lobby on entry in order

Stephen Haber is the A. A. and Jeanne Welch Milligan Professor in the School of Humanities and Sciences and director of the Social Science History Program at Stanford University. He is also the Peter and Helen Bing Senior Fellow at the Hoover Institution, senior fellow of the Stanford Institute for Economic Policy Research, senior fellow of the Center for International Development, and research economist at the National Bureau of Economic Research.

to control the flow of capital and its terms. The barriers to entry they erect not only generate rents in the financial sector itself, but also preserve rents earned by elites in any area of the economy in which access to finance is crucial.

The institutions that govern entry in the financial sector are inherently complex, but their basic shape is dictated by the degree to which the consumers of credit—farmers, artisans and manufacturers, merchants, and households—are able to project sufficient power to force political elites into coalitions that broaden access to capital. The task facing the consumers of credit is difficult. Financial incumbents and political elites are natural allies: Financial incumbents want to earn rents, and they therefore need the government to create and enforce regulatory barriers to entry; political elites need to finance the state or risk losing power, and their control of the government means that they regulate banks and securities markets. What is to stop political elites from imposing controls on the licensing of banks and the formation of publicly traded limited liability companies in order to preserve the rents of financial incumbents, in exchange for which the incumbent financial elite make loans to the government at attractive terms? Indeed, what is to prevent the financial incumbents from aligning the incentives of political elites by sharing some of the their rents directly with political elites through bribes, corporate board seats, or business partnerships?

There is, as yet, no real science of this, but a partial answer is that the consumers of credit have to be able to structure the incentives of political elites, which means that they have to be able to credibly threaten elites with removal from power. This implies, in turn, that the consumers of credit have to be informed enough to understand the game that is being played and powerful enough to create the political institutions necessary to sanction political elites who act against their interests. Foremost among these institutions are universal suffrage, free and fair elections, and freedom of association, which eases the creation of political parties.

The implication, I hope, is clear: the study of finance cannot be separated from the study of political power without serious analytical loss. Just as one can define finance as a set of contracts that are inextricably linked to the legal system, the entire financial, contractual, and legal apparatus is embedded in a political system. That political system is, in turn, shaped by the distribution of power among members of society—and that distribution of power is in no small part an outcome of the distribution of human capital.

Tracing the complex ways in which inequality in human capital and power becomes embedded in institutions, how those institutions then affect the coalitions that can be formed by financial incumbents and political elites, and how those coalitions then result in institutions that regulate entry and structure the flow of capital is a task better suited to historical narrative than it is to econometric hypothesis testing. Thus, the bulk of this chapter focuses on the process by which coalitions between political elites and financial incumbents were formed in three New World economies—Mexico, Brazil, and the United States—during the period from independence to roughly 1914. We will, at the end of the chapter, explore whether the patterns revealed by the case studies are supported by the large-N literature.

We focus on Mexico, Brazil, and the United States for three reasons. First, they allow us to observe variation across countries in terms of the distribution of human capital. Second, they allow us to observe variation over time in their political institutions, including the breadth of the suffrage. Third, they allow us to observe variation both across cases and over time within cases in terms of the specific features of financial regulation, as well as the size and structure of their resulting financial systems.

3.1   Mexico

Mexico is one of the cases that looms large in Ken's papers on inequality, institutions, and long-run growth. And for good reason: Colonial Mexico was extremely wealthy, but that wealth was distributed unequally between a small elite of Spanish descent and a large mass of illiterate and politically disenfranchised Indians and Mestizos. The weakness of the latter group is underlined by the process of Mexican independence. An independence movement that championed their rights, and that directly threatened the Spanish elite—the Hidalgo Rebellion of 1810—was soundly defeated by the elites, who quickly made common cause with the Spanish Viceroy and his army. When Mexico achieved independence eleven years later, it was as a reaction to a successful liberal revolution in Spain that threatened the colonial status quo. As a result, Mexico's independence did not produce a republic, but a constitutional monarch, who quickly proclaimed himself emperor and closed Congress.

Emperor Iturbide lasted only eight months in power, but even after he was removed political power remained concentrated among a narrow elite. One subgroup of this elite, the conservatives, sought to maintain all of the political and economic institutions of the colony, including the centralization of political power and exemptions from trial in civil courts for the army and clergy. A second subgroup, the liberals, wanted a federal republic in which states would be granted considerable autonomy and in which the political economy of the country would be guided by laissez faire principles. Both sides agreed on one issue: suffrage would be restricted and European-ized elites should run the country (Costeloe 2002). Not surprisingly, the right to vote in nineteenth century Mexico was constrained by both literacy and wealth requirements (Engerman and Sokoloff 2001). These were binding constraints, because there were no public schools and most of the population eked out a living as subsistence farmers and day laborers.

While the conservatives and liberals agreed on the disenfranchisement of the mass of the population, they could not agree on much else. They therefore engaged in a series of coups, countercoups, and civil wars from independence to 1876. In the fifty-five years after independence Mexico had seventy-five presidents. For every constitutional president there were four interim, provisional, or irregular presidents. One military figure, Antonio López de Santa Ana, occupied the presidential chair on eleven different occasions. All sides in these conflicts preyed on the property rights of their opponents. Every government that came to power also inherited a depleted treasury and no ready source of income. To meet their need for large infusions of cash, Mexico's nineteenth century governments borrowed from the country's wealthy merchant-financiers. When governments changed, or when governments faced sufficient threat, they reneged on these debts (Tenenbaum 1986; Walker 1987).

Given this environment, the country's financial incumbents—the wealthy merchant-financiers—had very weak incentives to obtain bank charters: deploying their capital in a visible manner would only create a target for expropriation via forced loans. The severity of this problem is made evident by one of the Mexican government's most desperate moves. Precisely because there was so little bank credit, in 1830 the country's manufacturers pressured the government into founding a government-owned industrial development bank—the Banco de Avío. In 1842, desperate for cash, the government ransacked its vaults, which is to say that it expropriated its own bank (Potash 1983). Not surprisingly, Mexico had no private, chartered banks at all until 1863. To the degree that there was any financial intermediation, it was via notaries—who, as Levy (2003) shows, linked mortgagees with mortgagors, much in the way that Hoffman, Postel-Vinay, and Rosenthal (2001) document for eighteenth century France. In addition, credit was available for short-term commercial transactions via the private banking houses of the country's merchant-financiers. Neither of these forms of intermediation possessed the advantages of a chartered bank: the ability to mobilize capital by selling equity to outside investors who would be protected by limited liability, primacy as a creditor in the event of borrower bankruptcy, and the ability to issue banknotes that had the status of legal tender. These notarial and private banking operations were thus necessarily limited in scale. When Mexico did finally charter its first bank in 1863 it was to a foreign entity (the British Bank of London, Mexico, and South America) and the charter was granted by the puppet government of a foreign power (the Emperor Maximilian, who had been installed by the French).

In the last decades of the nineteenth century, a political-military leader, Porfirio Díaz, finally brought political stability to Mexico—but he did so by creating a dictatorship that endured from 1877 to 1911. The Díaz dictatorship was characterized by three phenomena: the centralization of political power, heightened inequality, and rapid economic growth centered in large-scale enterprises owned by politically connected elites. Mexico nominally remained a federal republic, but Díaz quickly undermined whatever bite the institutions of federalism and suffrage had. He gradually appointed men loyal to him as governors—typically choosing individuals who were from outside the state and had few local ties, and thus owed their political survival to Díaz (Haber, Razo, and Maurer 2003, chap. 3). He then had the governors and other local officials he had appointed rig the elections for the federal Congress and Senate, even sending them a list of the desired outcomes before the election took place. As Razo (2008) has shown, by 1888 the federal Congress and Senate were little more than rubber stamps for Díaz's decrees.

Centralized political power then became a vehicle to transfer wealth upward in order to create incentives for investment in an economy that had been moribund since independence. One area where this phenomena has been intensively studied is agriculture, where a host of studies all point in the same direction: state governors and other members of the local political elite allied with a subset of the large landowners in the state to dispossess small farmers and Indian villages. In some cases—Chihuahua being the most notorious—governors ran their states as family business enterprises, using their power to expropriate everything worth owning. Though the data on land tenure for this period are rough, the evidence indicates that by 1910 95 percent of rural heads of families had no land of their own. Attempts by small farmers to resist the onslaught of the planters were dealt with by state-administered brutality (Womack 1969; Wasserman 1984; Markiewicz 1993; Holden 1994; Katz 1998).

Even with the growth created by the special deals between political and economic elites, Díaz still confronted the same problem as every government before him: he lacked sufficient tax revenues to finance a government capable of unifying the country and putting an end to internecine warfare. Borrowing his way out of this situation was difficult, because Mexico had a long history of defaulting on its debts to its international and domestic creditors. In fact, Díaz himself had reneged on debts to some of the banks that had been founded in Mexico City during the early years of his rule (Marichal 2002; Maurer and Gomberg 2004).

The solution that Díaz and Mexico's financiers hit upon was one that had been used by European governments since the late seventeenth century: create a semiofficial super bank whose investors would be compensated for the risk of expropriation by extremely high rates of return. They did this by engineering the merger of the two largest banks in Mexico City in order to establish the Banco Nacional de México (Banamex). The deal was simple: Banamex got a charter from the government that gave it a set of extremely lucrative privileges and, in return, Banamex extended a credit line to the government. These privileges included the right to issue banknotes up to three times the amount of its reserves, to act as the treasury's fiscal agent, to tax farm customs receipts, and to run the mint. In addition, the government established a 5 percent tax on all banknotes, and then exempted Banamex notes from the tax. Díaz simultaneously got congress to pass a commercial code that removed the authority of state governments to issue bank charters. Any bank that wanted to compete with Banamex had to obtain a charter from Díaz's Secretary of the Treasury (Maurer 2002; Haber, Razo, and Maurer 2003, chap. 4; Maurer and Gomberg 2004).

Mexico's already extant banks, some of which were owned by powerful provincial politicians, realized that the commercial code and Banamex's special privileges put them at a serious disadvantage. They therefore obtained an injunction against the 1884 Commercial Code, citing the 1857 Constitution's antimonopoly clause. The ensuing legal and political battle ground on for thirteen years, until Secretary of Finance José Yves Limantour finally hammered out a compromise in 1897. Under this agreement, Banamex shared many (although not all) of its special privileges with the Banco de Londres y México, state governors chose which business group in the state would receive a bank charter from the federal government, and that state bank would effectively be granted a local monopoly. Legal barriers to entry into banking could not be eroded by competition between states, or between states and the federal government, because states did not have the right to charter banks (Maurer 2002, chap. 5).

Mexico's 1897 banking law was deliberately crafted to limit the number of banks that could compete in any market. First, the law specified that bank charters (and additions to capital) had to be approved by the secretary of the treasury *and* the federal Congress, which was a rubber stamp for the dictator. Second, the law created high minimum capital requirements—more than twice the amount for a national bank in the United States (Haber 1991). Third, the law established a 2 percent annual tax on paid-in capital. The first bank granted a charter in each state, however, was granted an exemption from the tax. Fourth, banks with territorial charters were not allowed to branch outside of their concession territories, preventing banks chartered in one state from challenging the monopoly of a bank in an adjoining state. In short, the only threat to the monopoly of a state bank could come from a branch of Banamex or the Banco de Londres y México (Maurer 2002).

These segmented monopolies were made incentive compatible with the interests of Mexico's political elite, who received seats on the boards of the major banks (and thus were entitled to director's fees and stock distributions). The board of directors of Banamex, for example, was populated by members of Díaz's coterie, including the president of Congress, the undersecretary of the treasury, the senator for the federal district, the president's chief of staff, and the brother of the secretary of the treasury. Banks with limited territorial concessions were similarly populated with powerful politicians, the only difference being that state governors, rather than cabinet ministers, sat on their boards (Haber, Razo, and Maurer 2003, chap. 4; Razo 2008).

The resulting banking system had one major advantage, and one major

Table 3.1   The Mexican banking industry, 1897–1913

Year	Number of banks[a]	Total assets (millions of nominal pesos)	Assets as percent GDP	Average equity ratio[b] (%)	Deposits as % of assets[c]	Bank of issue assets as % of total assets
1897	10	147	12	32	2	93
1898	16	175	15	32	3	94
1899	18	211	18	31	2	90
1900	20	259	20	31	5	90
1901	24	264	15	35	4	87
1902	25	317	19	31	5	88
1903	31	380	20	31	4	86
1904	32	435	24	30	3	88
1905	32	535	24	28	6	87
1906	32	629	28	32	9	88
1907	34	724	31	30	9	83
1908	34	757	31	31	9	81
1909	32	917	35	26	16	80
1910	32	1,005	32	24	16	80
1911	33	1,119		22	13	81
1912	34	1,086		23	15	78
1913	28	1,105		21	15	77

Source: Calculated from Secretaria del Estado y del Depacho de Hacienda, y Credito Publico y Comercio, *Anuario de Estadistica Fiscal, 1912–1913.*
[a]Includes banks of issue, mortgage banks, and investment banks (bancos refaccionarios). The 1913 figure does not include six banks that did not report because of the revolution.
[b]Weighted by assets.
[c]Weighted by market capitalization.

disadvantage. The advantage was that the construction of Banamex created, for the first time in Mexican history, a stable banking system. As table 3.1 shows, this banking system was, by the standards of typical less developed countries (LDC) banking systems today, quite sizable: in 1910, bank assets were 32 percent of gross domestic product (GDP)—about the same ratio as in 2006. Moreover, this banking system provided the government with a stable source of public finance, which allowed Díaz the financial breathing room he needed to slowly redraft tax codes and increase tax revenues to the point that he ran balanced budgets. It also allowed Díaz, with the help of Banamex's directors, to renegotiate Mexico's foreign debt—which had been in default for several decades. State governors obtained a similar advantage: the banks within their borders were a steady source of loans to the state government (Marichal 2002; Maurer 2002; Aguilar 2003; Cerutti 2003; Gamboa Ojeda 2003; Ludlow 2003; Oveda 2003; Rodríguez López 1995, 2003; Romero Ibarra 2003).

The disadvantage was that Mexico had a concentrated banking system. In 1911, there were only thirty-four incorporated banks in the entire coun-

Table 3.2   Industrial concentration in cotton textiles—Mexico, Brazil, India, and the United States

| | Four firm ratio | | | | | Herfindahl index | | |
| | Mexico (%) | Mexico Expected (%) | Brazil (%) | India (%) | U.S.A. (%) | Mexico | Brazil | Indi\|
Circa								
1888	18	19	37		8	0.022	0.058	
1893	29	15				0.038		
1895	33	17	35			0.042	0.059	
1896	30	16				0.041		
1900	30	14		19	7	0.038	0.028	0.01
1904	33	15	21			0.042		
1909	38	15				0.045		
1912	30	14		19	8	0.039		0.01
1913	31	14	14			0.041	0.014	

Source: Maurer and Haber (2007).

try. Half of all assets were held in just two banks: Banamex and Banco de Londres y México (Mexico, Secretaria de Hacienda 1912, 236, 255). The vast majority of markets had, at most, three banks: a branch of Banamex, a branch of the Banco de Londres y México, and a branch of the bank that held that state's territorial concession. The high level of concentration of the banking system had a variety of negative effects on the rest of the economy. As Maurer (2002) has shown, Banamex and the Banco de Londres y México acted like inefficient monopolists, driving up their rates of return by holding excess liquidity. As Haber (1991, 1997) and Maurer and Haber (2007) have shown, the concentrated nature of the banking industry gave rise to concentration in the rest of the economy. Mexico's banks tended only to allocate credit to firms owned by their own board members. The logical implication of a small number of banks and insider lending was that there was a reduced number of firms in finance-dependent, downstream industries. The phenomenon is shown in the structure of Mexico's cotton textile industry as compared to the cotton textile industries of the United States, Brazil, and India (see table 3.2). Not only did Mexico have higher concentration indices than Brazil, India, and the United States, but concentration actually increased as the industry grew in size. This is not the result that one would anticipate from an industry characterized by constant returns to scale technology—but it is what one would expect when the largest firms in the industry shared directors with the largest banks in the country.

Financial markets did not serve as a substitute for the banking system. The reason was that it was very difficult for outside investors to monitor the activities of firm directors and managers because financial reporting requirements were not enforced. As a result, individuals tended to invest only in publicly traded firms if those enterprises were founded and controlled by important financial capitalists with proven track records. As a practical matter, this meant that they only bought stock in firms that were already tied to a bank, which is to say that there were very few publicly traded companies. Cotton textile manufacturing provides a relevant case in point. Of the 100 firms operating in the industry in 1910, only five were publicly traded companies, and all of these were tied to a bank.

The coalition that supported the Díaz dictatorship fell apart after three decades. The same set of institutions that underpinned growth in banking—an alliance between economic and political elites that came at the expense of everyone else—also existed in other sectors of the economy. Indeed, restrictions on bank charters were a fundamental weapon in the arsenal of tactics employed by the country's largest industrialists to constrain competition in manufacturing (Haber, Razo, and Maurer 2003, chap. 5). As was the case in banking, the resulting growth in those sectors tended to heighten inequality, and produced, in time, organized resistance to the dictatorship. That resistance took up armed force in 1910, removing Díaz from power in 1911, and opening up a decade-long period of coups, rebellions, and civil wars.

Every side in the Mexican Revolution preyed upon the banking system. The lack of political stability meant, once again, that it was not possible for Mexico's bankers to forge durable coalitions with the country's political elites. By 1916 the financial system had become a shell, stripped of its liquid assets (Maurer 2002; Haber, Razo, and Maurer 2003, chap. 4). The outcome can be seen clearly in table 3.3: circa 1921 the total assets of Mexico's banks were only 5 percent of the GDP, as compared to 32 percent in 1910.

Space constraints prevent us from exploring in detail how Mexico's revolution did little to broaden the distribution of wealth, increase investment in human capital, or decrease the degree to which political power was centralized. Suffice to say, however, that Díaz was replaced by a party-based dictatorship—the Partido Revolucionario Institucional (PRI), which ruled until 2000. While the PRI was rhetorically redistributionist, as a practical matter its major accomplishments were to centralize power even more effectively than Díaz and to provide very little in the way of public education or other public goods. It also managed to create an alliance of convenience with Mexico's financial incumbents (Haber, Klein, Maurer, and Middlebrook 2008, chap. 2). One basic element of that coalition was the creation of a banking system that was remarkably similar to the one that had existed under Díaz: the number of banks was limited, bankers tended to make loans to enterprises that they controlled, and everyone else was starved for credit (Del Ángel-Mobarak 2005). These features of the Mexican banking system have been loosened only in recent years, as a result of the country's transition to democracy (Haber 2009).

Table 3.3   The Mexican banking industry, 1897–1929

Year	Assets as Percent GDP
1897	12
1898	15
1899	18
1900	20
1901	15
1902	19
1903	20
1904	24
1905	24
1906	28
1907	31
1908	31
1909	35
1910	32
1921	5
1922	3
1923	3
1924	4
1925	4
1926	8
1927	10
1928	10
1929	12

Source: Haber, Razo, and Maurer (2003, chap. 4); Maurer and Haber (2007).

3.2   Brazil

Brazil is a prime example of a country in which political elites and financial incumbents forged a durable coalition to limit competition and constrain access to capital. One key to the durability of this coalition was binding constraints on suffrage. These arrangements came under threat only once, when the monarchy was overthrown in 1889 and the new government allowed virtually unlimited access to bank charters. Nevertheless, within a few years of the creation of the republic, the old set of arrangements was re-created and Brazil went back to a system in which the government limited the number of banks, and, in exchange, the banks extended credit to the government. Indeed, Brazil ultimately created a banking system that was dominated by a single bank of issue that was the country's largest commercial bank and the government's fiscal agent.

Banking in colonial Brazil was handled by the private banking houses of the merchant-financiers who dominated the import-export trade. This pattern was broken in 1808, when King Dom João VI was transported to Brazil by the British Navy following the invasion of Portugal by Napoleon. Dom João faced a difficult problem: he needed a source of revenues to run his court and administer his empire, but Brazil lacked an administrative structure to collect sufficient taxes. He therefore adopted a solution that European monarchs had long used when expenses outran their ability to tax: charter a bank whose purpose was to finance the government. This created an obvious commitment problem from the point of view of the investors in the Banco do Brasil, because Dom João could repudiate the bank's loans with impunity. He therefore had to coax Brazil's financial incumbents into deploying their capital by granting the bank lucrative privileges. These included a monopoly on the issuance of paper money, a monopoly on the export of luxury goods, a monopoly on the handling of government financial operations, the right to have debts to the bank treated as having the same legal standing as debts owed to the royal treasury, and the right to collect new taxes imposed by the king—and to then hold those taxes as interest free deposits for a period of ten years (Peláez 1975, 460–61).

The problem was that there was nothing to stop the king from reneging on these privileges. The merchants and landowners who the government needed to buy the bank's shares remained so wary that the Banco do Brasil was unable to achieve its original capitalization goals until 1817, eleven years after it was founded. Their wariness was well founded: most of the bank's business consisted of printing banknotes that were then used to buy bonds issued by the imperial government. As the amount of banknotes increased, so too did inflation. In effect, the bank was the government's agent in creating an inflation tax, and that inflation tax hit everybody, including the bank's shareholders, who likely did not receive an inflation-adjusted rate of return adequate to compensate them for the opportunity cost of their capital. As table 3.4 shows, the nominal rate of return on owner's equity in the Banco do Brasil from 1810 to 1820 averaged 10 percent per year, which, as near as it can be known, probably did not exceed the rate of inflation by a wide margin. Not surprisingly, as table 3.4 shows, the shareholders of the bank paid out virtually all of the available returns to themselves as dividends. Worse, in 1820, Dom João reneged on the arrangement by which the bank could hold the proceeds from the new taxes that he had created. The following year he returned to Portugal and took with him all of the metals that he and his court had deposited in the bank, exchanging them for whatever banknotes they had in their possession. The Banco do Brasil then continued to function through the rest of the 1820s and was used by Dom João's son, the Emperor Dom Pedro I, much in the same way as it had been used previously—to finance government budget deficits through note issues (Peláez 1975).

In 1822 Dom Pedro, at the urging of local elites and with the consent of his father, declared Brazil independent. Independence did not do much to change the status quo ante for the great mass of slaves, free blacks, and native-born Brazilians of humble social origin. It did, however, allow the incumbent financial elites to constrain the emperor, forcing him into a

Table 3.4   Accounts of the First Banco do Brasil, all units in thousands of contos de reis

	Subscribed capital	Reserve fund	Annual taxes transferred to bank as deposits	Owner's equity[a]	Estimated earnings[b]	Return on equity (%)	Dividends as % earnings
1809	116	0	0	116	0	0	
1810	120	0.3	0	120	1.3	1	77
1811	122	1	0	123	4.7	4	85
1812	172	2	0	174	6	3	83
1813	397	5.6	63	403	21.6	5	83
1814	502	14	58	516	51.4	10	84
1815	581	29	62	610	89	15	83
1816	690	53	88	743	144	19	83
1817	1,189	83	65	1,272	183	14	84
1818	1,719	122	75	1,841	241	13	84
1819	2,037	163	73	2,200	249	11	84
1820	2,215	207	16	2,422	271	11	84
1821	2,235	275	0	2,510	421	17	84
1822	2,248	329	0	2,577	336	13	84
1823	2,357	404	0	2,761	467	17	84
1824	2,662	482	0	3,144	502	16	84
1825	3,600	570	0	4,170	539	13	84
1826	2,600	692	0	3,292	762	23	84
1827	3,600	819	0	4,419	796	18	84
1828	3,600	954	0	4,554	851	19	84
1829	3,600	1083	0	4,683	815	17	84

Source: Calculated from data in Peláez (1975, tables 3 and 4).
[a]Capital plus reserve fund.
[b]Dividends plus change in reserves from previous year.

coalition. The elites who drafted the Constitution of 1824 gave parliament, and not the emperor, the ultimate responsibility to tax, spend, and borrow. They also specified an elected lower house of parliament, and restricted the vote on the basis of wealth so that the lower house represented their interests. As Summerhill (forthcoming) has pointed out, this had two consequences: the emperor could not default on loans that he had contracted from the incumbent financial elites, and the financial elite could use its influence in parliament to make sure that competing economic groups could not obtain bank charters. In point of fact, from the closing of the Banco do Brasil by parliament in 1829 to the mid-1850s, parliament permitted only seven new banks to be formed—all of which had limited provincial charters that created local banking monopolies.

This set of arrangements worked well for the incumbent bankers, but it came at a cost to the emperor: after 1829 the imperial government did not have a bank that it could use to finance budget deficits. Finding a solution was difficult because creating a national bank large enough to finance the government required aligning the incentives of all the incumbent bankers— some of whom were able to use their influence in parliament to undo whatever deals the emperor struck. Thus, parliament authorized a second Banco do Brasil in 1853, but then removed its right to issue banknotes just four years later (Peláez and Suzigan 1976, 82–87).

A compromise was only reached in the 1860s when a coalition was formed between the bankers and the imperial government. An 1860 law specified that corporate charters, including those for banks, not only needed the approval of parliament and the emperor's cabinet, they also required approval from the emperor's council of state, whose members enjoyed life tenure. In 1863, the Second Banco do Brasil merged with two other Rio de Janeiro banks, the Banco Comercial e Agrícola and the Banco Rural e Hipotecario, which transferred to the Banco do Brasil their rights of note issue, thereby creating something that the emperor had been seeking for a decade: a note-issuing bank that acted as the government's fiscal agent (Peláez and Suzigan 1976, 103). The government got its bank, and the economic elite got their banks, but no one else could get a bank charter—and no one from outside the small group of "barons" who sat on a bank board was eligible for a loan (Hanley 2005; Summerhill, forthcoming).

Some sense of how restricted the banking industry in Brazil was can be gleaned from table 3.5, which contains estimates of the size of the Brazlian banking system based on information retrieved from the Rio de Janeiro stock exchange. In 1875 there were only twelve banks in the entire country. The number of banks then increased at a snail's pace throughout the rest of the imperial period: at the end of the first semester of 1888 there were only twenty-seven. Moreover, their combined capitalization had only increased by 53 percent over the thirteen-year period since 1875. Twenty-two percent of this capital was concentrated in one bank, the third Banco do Brasil. Let

Table 3.5   Size estimates of the Brazilian banking system, 1875–1935

Year	Operating banks	Estimated total paid-in capital (millions 1900 milreis)
1875	12	234
1880	12	197
1882	22	296
1888	27	358
1889	81	1,447
1890	112	2,048
1891	133	1,413
1892	127	922
1893	116	576
1894	110	486
1895	106	537
1896	0	487
1897	104	455
1898	102	384
1899	96	400
1900	86	311
1901	84	385
1902	81	445
1903	70	422
1904	67	380
1905	63	413
1906	62	356
1907	62	363
1908	55	326
1909	50	336
1910	51	341
1911	45	327
1912	46	393
1913	48	438
1914	48	563
1925	49	346
1926	50	323
1927	47	382
1929	47	369
1930	46	406
1931	45	486
1934	45	397
1935	36	237

Source: Berg and Haber (2009).

us put this into comparative perspective. In 1888, bank assets per capita in Brazil totaled $2.40 U.S. In Mexico in 1897, they were nearly three times this level, at $6.74. In the United States, in 1890, they were $85.

The coalition between the political elites who ran the government and the incumbent financial elite came under threat when the monarchy was overthrown and a federal republic was created in 1889. Space constraints prevent us from exploring how and why the coalition that had supported the emperor fell apart, but one crucial piece of the story was the abolition of slavery in 1888. Abolition drove a wedge between Brazil's planter class and the imperial government. In an effort to placate the planters by making credit more easily available, the imperial government awarded concessions to twelve banks of issue and provided seventeen banks with interest-free loans. The easy credit policies of 1888 were not enough, however, to stem the tide of Brazil's Repúblican movement. In November of 1889, Dom Pedro II was overthrown in a military coup and a federal republic was created.

The creation of a federal republic undermined for a time the arrangements that had supported a small and concentrated banking industry. The 1891 Constitution gave each of Brazil's twenty states considerable sovereignty, ending the central government's monopoly on the chartering of banks. This put the federal republic's first finance minister, Rui Barbosa, under considerable pressure: if he did not grant additional charters to new banks in order to satisfy the demand for credit from Brazil's growing regional economic elites—most particularly planters and manufacturers—those elites would get their own state governments to do so. As a result, Rui Barbosa quickly pushed through a series of financial reforms, one of whose features was that the federal government allocated bank charters to virtually all comers through a general incorporation law, and another of whose features was that banks could engage in whatever kind of financial transactions they wished. The results of these reforms were dramatic. Recall that in 1888 there were only twenty-seven banks in the entire country. In 1891, as table 3.5 indicates, there were 133. Moreover, their total real capitalization (in 1900 milreis) was four times that of the 1888 banks.

Brazil's central government soon found itself in a difficult position. The 1891 Constitution denied it access to a crucial source of tax income, revenues from export taxes, which were now collected directly by states. The government therefore contracted gold-denominated foreign loans to make up for the budget shortfall. The government also allocated the right to issue banknotes to a number of banks, each of which aggressively printed and lent currency. Their note issues, in addition to driving a speculative boom in the stock market, also drove up inflation (Hanley 2005). The result was a currency mismatch: a hard-currency denominated debt, a domestic-currency denominated source of income (taxes paid in Brazilian milreis), and an inflation that drove down the international value of the domestic currency. The central government had three options: spend less, raise taxes, or curtail the growth of the money supply. It chose options two and three. In 1896 the government decided once again to restrict the right to issue currency to a single bank—the Banco da República, which was a private commercial bank that had a special charter that made it the agent of the treasury. Two years later, the government increased taxes and restructured its foreign debt.

These moves, coupled with the already shaky financial situation of many of the banks, produced a massive contraction of the banking sector. In 1891, as table 3.5 shows, there were 133 banks operating in Brazil. Ten years later there were eighty-four, and their combined capital was only one quarter that of the 1891 banks. The numbers kept falling, so that by the end of 1905 there were only sixty-three banks in operation with a total capital still only one quarter that of 1891. Moreover, one-third of this capital was concentrated in the single bank that served as the government's financial agent, the Banco da República.

The contraction of the banking sector brought about yet another round of reform—one that recreated the coalition between financial incumbents and political elites. End users of credit lost out in this reform, and they did so because they had weak levers with which to structure the incentives of political elites. In the first place, less than 5 percent of the population had the right to vote. In the second place, power was concentrated in a strong presidency: Congress was more a consultative forum than a legislative body (Triner 2000, 18). In the third place, Congress selected the president, which allowed the political elites of the two largest states, Minas Gerais and Sao Paulo, to form a coalition and trade the presidency between them.

Essentially, the government nationalized the insolvent Banco da República, converting debts owed by the bank to the treasury into equity and created a new bank, the Fourth Banco do Brasil. Like the Banco da República, the fourth Banco do Brasil was a commercial bank fully capable of taking deposits and making private loans. It differed from the Banco da República, however, in that the central government was a major stockholder, owning almost one-third of its shares, and the president of the republic had the right to name the president of the bank, along with one of its four directors (Topik 1980). In addition, the Fourth Banco do Brasil was not permitted to make loans with terms greater than six months and was not allowed to purchase stock in other companies. These restrictions were designed to guarantee that the bank would retain high levels of liquidity so that it could purchase treasury notes and bills, as well as to act as a lender of last resort in times of economic crisis (Topik 1987, 39).

For the better part of the next six decades, the Brazilian banking system was dominated by the Fourth Banco do Brasil, which acted both as a commercial bank and as the treasury's financial agent. The charter that created the bank included a number of lucrative privileges, including the right to hold federal balances, issue banknotes, and have a monopoly on interstate branching. These privileges appear to have constituted a barrier to entry: the Banco do Brasil earned a rate of return on equity more than twice that of its competitors (Berg and Haber 2009). As a result, to the degree that there were competing banks in Brazil they were few in number. As table 3.5 shows, as late as 1930, when the First Republic was overthrown in a coup, Brazil had fewer banks than it had in 1899.

In short, the political economy of Brazilian banking was not dramatically different from that of Mexico: regardless of which particular political elite was in power, that elite forged a coalition with incumbent financiers, and the arrangements they created provided bankers with oligopoly rents and the central government with a bank to fund its budget deficits. In the years following World War I, state governments began to copy the model of the Banco do Brasil, establishing joint state-private banks whose purpose was to finance their budget deficits. That is, the banks took deposits from private individuals, and then invested the proceeds in the bonds of state governments. The disadvantage of this system was that it allocated credit very narrowly: to state governments, the federal government, and large business enterprises whose owners were tied to the banks (Bornstein 1954, 312–13).

Brazil did, however, depart from the experience of Mexico in terms of the degree to which securities markets served as substitutes for banks. Rui Barbosa's general incorporation law gave rise to the widespread sale of equity and bonded debt to the investing public in order to mobilize long-term capital. Thus, Brazil had, by 1913, a well-developed stock and bond market. This market was used to make public offerings for a wide variety of enterprises including large-scale manufacturing, railroads, shipping, and land colonization companies. This market, however, began to go into decline in the 1910s as the government's strategy of inflationary finance made it increasingly difficult for investors to value their assets. By the late 1920s the markets were no longer important sources of new capital (Haber 1998; Musacchio, 2009).

3.3   The United States

One of the central themes of Ken and Stan's work on differential paths of growth was the impact of a society of highly literate and evenly matched citizens in New England and the Middle Atlantic States on the course of American economic development. The United States may have had a plantation economy in the South, but even the U.S. South never became as reliant on slave labor as Brazil—nor did colonial Brazil have the equivalent of a Massachusetts or New York to balance the regions dominated by slavery, as the United States did. The upshot was that at independence the United States already had a much more democratic political economy than either Brazil or Mexico. Indeed, the percentage of adult white males voting in America's first elections was extraordinarily high—more than 80 percent in some states (Engerman and Sokoloff 2001). American states restricted the suffrage to property owners, but at least until the country began to fill up with immigrants in the 1810s and 1820s that was not a binding constraint in a frontier society where a large percentage of the population were property owners.

This is not to suggest that America's elites did not try to blunt the political power of ordinary citizens. That was the whole point of creating a bicameral legislature and selecting the upper house by indirect election. It was also the motivation behind the creation of the institution of the presidency—an indirectly elected, temporary monarch who could veto any populist legislation that got past the indirectly elected Senate. The president and the Senate then appointed the Supreme Court, crucially without any input from the directly elected lower house of Congress. Institutions at the state level had a similar antipopulist design, but added another twist: states decided the laws regarding the suffrage, and all of them initially imposed restrictions based on wealth or social standing.

This is also not to suggest that America's elites did not use their political power in order to generate rents for themselves by constraining access to finance. As we shall discuss in detail, the initial organization of U.S. banking was predicated on explicit deals between bankers and politicians, both at the state and national level, to create and share rents.

It is to suggest, however, that the underlying distribution of human capital in the United States was inconsistent with an elite-dominated political economy. Elites in the United States were forced to bargain with citizens. One reflection of this was the political annihilation of the Federalist Party. A second reflection was the ascendance of the Jacksonians, America's first genuinely populist political movement. A third reflection was that the laws that blocked access to finance by limiting the number of banks began to be undermined as early as the 1810s. America's bankers did not, of course, passively accept the idea that they should allow all of their rents to be dissipated by competition. They found ways to join coalitions—ironically, with antibank populists—that afforded them local monopolies and quasi-monopolies. The history of U.S. banking is, in fact, the story of how these monopolies were progressively made smaller and their rents disspated—until they were finally undermined entirely in the 1990s.

Governments need banks in order to finance their survival, and banks need governments to grant them the privileges that make them attractive investments. America's first chartered bank, the Bank of North America (BNA), was not an exception to this general pattern. In order to finance the war for independence, in 1781 the Congress of the Confederation granted a charter to a group of shareholders to create a commercial bank that would also serve as the government's fiscal agent, the BNA. Right from the beginning, however, the idea of a privately owned national bank that had a special relationship with the central government ran into trouble. The fundamental problem was that the BNA competed with local banks that operated without charter (meaning that their shareholders had unlimited liability). The wedge that local banks were able to drive between the BNA and its charter was that the Articles of Confederation were ambiguous as to whether the central government actually had the authority to charter a bank. The BNA, therefore, had to be rechartered by the state of Pennsylvania. No sooner was this charter granted, however, that, at the behest of local unchartered banks, the BNA came under attack in the Pennsylvania State Legislature, which revoked the bank's charter in 1785. The legislature restored the charter two years later, following an agreement by the BNA to accept a series of restrictions on its activities that effectively meant that it could not serve as the banker to the central government (Bodenhorn 2003, 128).

The Articles of Confederation were soon replaced by the Constitution of 1789, but the basic problem of state finance remained. The new central government lost little time in chartering a bank to replace the BNA—the Bank of the United States (BUS), founded in 1791. The BUS was a commercial bank that took deposits and made loans to private parties. The federal government subscribed 20 percent of the BUS's capital without paying for those shares; instead, it received a loan from the bank and then repaid the loan out of the stream of dividends it received as a shareholder in the bank. In exchange, the BUS received a set of valuable privileges that were afforded no other bank: the right to limited liability for its shareholders, the right to hold federal government specie balances, the right to charge the federal government interest on loans from the bank (notes issued by the bank to cover federal expenses), and the right to open branches throughout the country. In short, the BUS was the product of a deal: the bankers financed the state, and the state gave the bankers a set of lucrative privileges.

Had America's political institutions granted the federal government the sole right to charter banks, the BUS might have completely dominated the financial system. The federal organization of the U.S. government prevented that from happening, however. The Constitution provided that any power not explicitly delegated to the federal government could be exercised by the states. Under the Constitution, the states lost both the right to tax imports and exports and the right to coin money—both of these powers were vested with the federal government, in exchange for which the federal government assumed the considerable debts that the states had amassed under the Articles of Confederation. Having been denied their traditional sources of finance, the states began to search for alternative sources of revenue. The Constitution said nothing about the state's right to charter banks of issue, whose banknotes would circulate as currency.

States, therefore, had strong fiscal incentives to sell bank charters—and strong incentives to do whatever was necessary to maximize the value of those charters. States obviously received no charter fees from banks incorporated in other states; therefore, they prohibited interstate branching (Kroszner and Strahan 1999). States could earn income by selling the charter and by owning stock in the bank; therefore, they were almost universally major owners of bank shares, and they typically paid for those shares with a loan from the bank, which they then repaid out of the dividend stream. States received a larger stream of dividends when the banks earned monopoly rents; so, they constrained the number of banks within their own borders.

Table 3.6   State-chartered banks in the United States, 1790–1835

	New England		South		U.S. total	
Year	Number of banks	Authorized capital (millions)	Number of banks	Authorized capital (millions)	Number of banks	Authorized capital (millions)
1790	1	0.8			3	3.1
1795	11	4.1			20	13.5
1800	17	5.5			28	17.4
1805	45	13.2	6	3.5	71	38.9
1810	52	15.5	13	9.1	102	56.2
1815	71	24.5	22	17.2	212	115.2
1820	97	28.3	25	28.6	327	159.7
1825	159	42.2	32	33.3	330	156.1
1830	186	48.8	35	37.3	381	170.4
1835	285	71.5	63	111.6	584	308.3

Source: Sylla (2007).

States might extract additional income from banks by threatening them with new entrants to the banking market; in that event, they accepted "bonuses" from incumbent banks to deny the charter applications of potential competitors (Bodenhorn 2003, 17, 244). While there was a high degree of variance across states circa 1810 to 1830, bank dividends and bank taxes often accounted for one-third of total state revenues (Sylla, Legler, and Wallis 1987; Wallis, Sylla, and Legler 1994).

Banking in the early republican United States was therefore characterized by segmented monopolies. The four largest cities in the United States in 1800—Boston, Philadelphia, New York, and Baltimore—had only two banks apiece. Smaller markets typically had only one bank, if they had a bank at all. As table 3.6 shows, in 1800 there were only 28 banks (with a total capital of only $17.4 million) in the entire country (Wallis, Sylla, and Legler 1994, 135–9; Bodenhorn 2003, 142; Majewski 2004).

The system of a single national bank and segmented state monopolies was not stable given American political institutions. One crucial source of friction was the different incentives that faced the states and the central government. Bankers with state charters, and hence state legislatures, had opposed the BUS from the time of its initial chartering in 1791. The reason for their opposition was straightforward: branches of the BUS undermined local banking monopolies. State bankers, therefore, had incentives to form a coalition with the Jeffersonians, who were ideologically opposed to chartered corporations and "aristocratic" bankers, to oppose the BUS. They initially tried to tax the banknotes of the BUS in order to constrain it from competing against their own state-chartered banks. When that failed, they successfully lobbied state representatives to not renew its charter, which expired in 1811 (Lane 1997, 601–12; Wettereau 1942; Sylla 2000; Rockoff 2000). The War of 1812 demonstrated, however, the importance of a bank that could serve as the financial agent of the federal government, and thus a new charter (for a Second Bank of the United States) was granted in 1816. The Second Bank of the United States was founded on the same principles as the first bank, and it met the same fate when Andrew Jackson successfully vetoed the renewal of the bank's charter, forcing it to close in 1836 (Hammond 1947; Temin 1968; Engerman 1970; Rockoff 2000).

A second source of friction was the interaction of federalism, an expanding frontier, and a broad suffrage. States had incentives to compete against one another for business enterprises and population—and this pushed their legislatures to undertake steps that ultimately undermined the monopoly banks they had earlier erected. First, state legislatures sought to construct canals that would funnel commerce from the expanding interior of the country through their states. They tended not, however, to have sufficient tax revenues to fund those public works projects. One response by states was to issue bonds, but another response was to charge a "charter bonus" on new bank charters. Such charter bonuses created, of course, an incentive for state legislatures to renege on the monopoly deals that they had already made with the incumbent banks (Grinath, Wallis, and Sylla 1997; Sylla 2000; Bodenhorn 2003, 86, 148, 152, 228–34). Second, state legislatures had an incentive to ratchet downward restrictions on the right to vote. New states, eager to attract population, eliminated or reduced voting restrictions, forcing the original thirteen states to match their more permissive voting laws, or risk losing population. By the mid-1820s, property qualifications had been dropped or dramatically reduced in virtually all of the original states (Engerman and Sokoloff 2001; Keyssar 2000). The extension of the suffrage, in turn, allowed citizens to bring pressure to bear on legislatures, voting in legislators who were willing to remove constraints on the chartering of banks.

Political competition within and among states undermined the incentives of state legislatures to constrain the numbers of charters they granted. Massachusetts began to increase the number of charters it granted as early as 1812, abandoning its strategy of holding bank stock as a source of state finance and instead levying taxes on bank capital. Pennsylvania followed Massachusetts's lead with the Omnibus Banking Act of 1814. The act, passed over the objections of the state's governor, ended the cozy Philadelphia-based oligopoly that, until then, had dominated the state's banking industry. Rhode Island also followed Massachusetts's lead. In 1826 it sold its bank shares, increased the numbers of charters it granted, and began to tax bank capital as a replacement for the income it had earned from dividends. It soon became, on a per capita basis, America's most heavily banked state.

These reforms did not allow all comers to charter banks or permit banks to open branches at will. Pennsylvania's Omnibus Banking Act of 1814, for example, divided the state into twenty-seven banking districts and then allocated charters to forty-one banks, with each district receiving at least one bank charter. A crucial aspect of the law was that banks were constrained from lending more than 20 percent of their capital to borrowers outside their districts, thereby limiting the amount of competition within any particular banking district. Additional restrictions placed on the banks favored local economic incumbents: 20 percent of banks' capital had to be lent to farmers, mechanics, and manufacturers; interest rates were capped by statute; bank indebtedness was capped by statute; and no more than 20 percent of capital could be invested in corporate or government securities. The rents earned by these local banking monopolies were then shared with the state government. Banks had to pay a 6 percent tax on dividends, and banks were required by law to pay dividends or risk the revocation of their charter. In addition, the banks had to make loans to the state government, at the government's discretion, at an interest rate that could not exceed 5 percent (Bodenhorn 2003, 142–3). In short, Pennsylvania's Omnibus Banking Act was a compromise between potential debtors who sought increased access to credit; incumbent bankers who sought rents by limiting competition; and the state government, which needed a source of income and a mechanism to fund a public debt. The core feature of the deal was that banking monopolies would be allowed to persist: they would just be made smaller.

While the rate at which states reformed varied—with Southern states lagging the Northeast by a wide margin—the U.S. banking system grew remarkably quickly. As table 3.6 shows, in 1820 there were 327 banks in operation with $160 million in capital—roughly three times as many banks and four times as much bank capital as in 1810. By 1835, there were 584 banks with $308 million in capital—a nearly two-fold increase in just 15 years. At this point, larger cities often had a dozen or more banks, while small towns had as many as two or three (Bodenhorn 2003). As the density of banks increased, competition among them increased as well, so much so that they began to extend credit to an increasingly broad class of borrowers. Banks, particularly in the Mid-Atlantic States, lent funds to a wide variety of merchants, artisans, and farmers (Wang 2006). Even in New England, where insider lending dominated, the shear number of banks and ease of new bank formation removed access to credit as a barrier to entry in the real economy (Lamoreaux 1994).

The result, as Rousseau and Sylla (2005) have made clear, is that the United States banking system outgrew that of England and Wales—which is usually though of as the world's nineteenth century financial center. In 1825, the United States had a slightly smaller population than England and Wales (11.1 versus 12.9 million), but it had roughly 2.4 times England and Wales' banking capital (Rousseau and Sylla 2005). Indeed, Rousseau and Sylla suggest that the early nineteenth century United States was a successful example of "finance led growth."

By the late 1830s the de facto policies of Northeast states to grant virtu-ally all requests for bank charters became institutionalized in a series of laws known as free banking. Under free banking, bank charters no longer had to be approved by state legislatures. Rather, individuals could open banks provided that they registered with the state comptroller and deposited state or federal bonds with the comptroller as a guarantee of their note issues. Readers may wonder how such a system of free entry could have been com-patible with the fiscal needs of state governments. The answer lies in the fact that under free banking all banknotes had to be 100 percent backed by high-grade securities that were deposited with the state comptroller of the currency. Free banks were forced, in essence, to grant a loan to the state government in exchange for the right to operate.

The first state to make the switch to de jure free banking was New York, in 1838. From the 1810s to the late 1830s, bank chartering in New York was controlled by the Albany Regency—a political machine run by Martin Van Buren. Bank charters were only granted to friends of the Regency, in exchange for which the legislators received various bribes, such as the abil-ity to subscribe to initial public offerings of bank stock at par, even though the stock traded for a substantial premium (Bodenhorn 2003, 134, 186–8; Bodenhorn 2006; Gatell 1966, 26; Moss and Brennan 2004). The Regency's hold on bank chartering came to an end when the state's voting laws were amended in 1826, allowing universal manhood suffrage. Within a decade the Regency lost its control of the state legislature, and in 1837 the now domi-nant Whig Party enacted America's first free banking law. By 1841, New Yorkers had established 43 free banks, with a total capital of $10.7 million. By 1849, the number of free banks mushroomed to 111 (with $16.8 million in paid capital). By 1859 there were 274 free banks with paid in capital of $100.6 million (Bodenhorn 2003, 186–92; Wallis, Sylla, and Legler 1994; Moss and Brennan 2004). Other states soon followed New York's lead—with the liberalization of banking laws correlating with the liberalization of suffrage laws (Benmelech and Moskowitz 2005). By the early 1860s, twenty-one states adopted some variant of the New York law, and as they did so, they encouraged bank entry and increased competition (Bodenhorn 1990, 682–6; Bodenhorn 1993, 531–5; Economopoulos and O'Neill 1995; Ng 1988; Rockoff 1974; Rockoff 1985).

Free banking did not mean that the supply constraints on the credit mar-ket were completely eliminated. The free banking laws of most states pre-cluded the chartering of branch banks. Thus, with the exception of Southern states, where free banking did not catch on, the banking systems of virtually all states were composed of unit (single branch) banks. This unusual orga-nization of the banking system was the outcome of an unlikely political coalition: populists opposed to aristocratic bankers allied with bankers who wanted to create local monopolies. In short, free banking was not a com-plete rethinking of the earlier system of segmented monopolies. It simply expanded the number, and reduced the size, of those monopolies. The results were twofold: some of the rents that had been earned by bankers were dissipated, and borrowers who had earlier been closed out of credit markets now had access to finance, though it came from a bank that had a great deal of local market power.

Readers may wonder why, if banks could not open branches in underserved markets, farmers, merchants, and manufacturers in those markets did not simply obtain credit from banks in larger towns? The answer is that, until the computer revolution, obtaining information about the quality of potential borrowers was very costly. Bankers assessed the creditworthiness of borrowers on the basis of personal relationships: sets of repeated interactions that allowed the banker to assess what was going on inside an informationally opaque enterprise or household. As a result, until the 1990s most small business loans were made by banks that were less than fifty-one miles away (Petersen and Rajan 2002).

Readers may also wonder why the South lagged the North when it came to the passage of free banking laws. Recent work by Rajan and Ramcharan (forthcoming) provides the answer. The U.S. South was characterized by concentrated landholding and large landowners opposed legislation designed to facilitate bank entry because, in the absence of banks, they were the only source of credit and could therefore extract rents from small, tenant farmers.

From the point of view of the federal government, allowing the states to charter banks had a major drawback: it did not provide the federal government with a source of finance. This problem came to the fore during the Civil War, when the financial needs of the federal government skyrocketed. The federal government therefore passed laws in 1863, 1864, and 1865 that were designed to eliminate the state-chartered banks and replace them with a system of national banks that would finance the government's war effort. Federally chartered banks had to invest one-third of their capital in federal government bonds, which were then held as reserves by the comptroller of the currency against note issues. That is, banks had to make a loan to the federal government in exchange for the right to issue notes. Consistent with the goal of maximizing credit to the federal government, the National Banking Act made the granting of a charter an administrative procedure. As long as minimum capital and reserve requirements were met, the charter was granted. It was free banking on a national scale (Sylla 1975).

The federal government could neither abrogate the right of states to charter banks, nor could it prevent state-chartered banks from issuing banknotes. It could, however, impose a 10 percent tax on banknotes, and then exempt federally chartered banks from the tax, thereby giving state banks strong incentives to obtain new, federal charters. In the short run, the response of private banks was as the federal government expected. As table 3.7 shows, the number of state-chartered banks declined from 1,579 in 1860 to 349 by

Table 3.7   Number of U.S. commercial banks, 1860–1934

Year	State-chartered banks		National banks		Total banks		National banks as % of total	
	Number	Assets (millions $)	Number	Assets (millions $)	Number	Assets (millions $)	Number	Assets (millions $)
1860	1,579	423			1,579	423		
1865	349	231	1,294	1,127	1,643	1,358	79	83
1870	325	215	1,612	1,566	1,937	1,781	83	88
1875	1,260	1,291	2,076	1,913	3,336	3,204	62	60
1880	1,279	1,364	2,076	2,036	3,355	3,400	62	60
1885	1,661	2,005	2,689	2,422	4,350	4,427	62	55
1890	4,717	3,296	3,484	3,062	8,201	6,358	42	48
1895	6,103	4,139	3,715	3,471	9,818	7,610	38	46
1900	9,322	6,444	3,731	4,944	13,053	11,388	29	43
1905	13,103	10,186	5,664	7,325	18,767	17,511	30	42
1910	18,013	13,030	7,138	9,892	25,151	22,922	28	43
1914	20,346	15,872	7,518	11,477	27,864	27,349	27	42

Sources: Lamoreaux (1994, 540); Davis and Gallman (2001, 268); Calomiris and White (1994, 151). U.S. Federal Reserve (1943, 24).

1865. Federal banks grew dramatically from zero in 1860 to 1,294 in 1865. They then continued growing, reaching 7,518 by 1914, controlling $11.5 billion in assets in that year.

In the long run, however, the political institutions of the United States frustrated the federal government's goal of a single, federally chartered banking system. They also undermined the barriers to entry in banking that had been created by the National Banking System. The federal government had effectively nationalized the right to issue banknotes by creating a 10 percent tax on the notes of state-chartered banks in 1865. The law did not, however, say anything about checks drawn on accounts in state-chartered banks. State banks, therefore, aggressively pursued deposit banking and checks drawn on those accounts became an increasingly common means of exchange in business transactions (Moss and Brennan 2004; Sylla 1975, 62–73; Davis and Gallman 2001, 272). The result was that state-chartered banks actually outgrew federally chartered banks during the period 1865 to 1914. As table 3.7 shows, in 1865 state banks accounted for only 21 percent of all banks and 13 percent of total bank assets. By 1890 there were more state banks than national banks, and state banks controlled the majority of assets. Circa 1914, 73 percent of all banks were state banks, and state banks controlled 58 percent of assets.

The result was a banking system with a most peculiar competitive structure. In 1914 there were 27,349 banks in the United States, 95 percent of which had no branches! The banks that did have branches tended to be small; the average number of branches operated by these banks was less than five (Calomiris and White 1994, 145–88; Davis and Gallman 2001, 272). The reason for the preponderance of "unit banks" was that most states had laws that prevented branch banking, even by nationally chartered banks. Those states that did not explicitly forbid branch banking had no provision in their laws for branches. In fact, unit bankers formed numerous local and state organizations to lobby against the relaxation of branch banking restrictions. Restrictions on branching likely had little effect on urban consumers of credit because there were usually multiple unit banks operating in any mid-sized city. But, these restrictions had real bite in rural markets where consumers faced a local monopolist.

Why did rural consumers go along with this arrangement? Why didn't they form a coalition with urban bankers who wanted to open branches in their underserved markets? Calomiris (2010) summarizes a long line of research on this question. One reason is that unit bankers formed a coalition with agrarian populists, who viewed big city business enterprises—as well as their plutocrat owners—as a threat to their way of life. One reflection of this coalition was the fact that William Jennings Bryan, the presidential candidate for both the Populist and Democratic Parties in 1896, was a strong antibranch banking advocate. A second reason is that one particular subgroup of farmers—those in prosperous farming districts, who used unit banks to fund their operations and acquisitions—calculated that they had something to gain from unit banking. A local banker who was not part of a branch network had to lend to them, or lend to no one. From their point of view, unit banking provided loan insurance. The higher interest rate they paid the unit banker for the loan was simply the premium for the insurance policy.

In sum, the outcome in the United States was dramatically different from that in Mexico and Brazil. This was not because there were not attempts by bankers to constrain supply. Rather, it was because attempts by bankers to form coalitions with political elites to constrain supply were undermined by countercoalitions, composed of the consumers of credit and political elites with populist orientations. America's bankers responded in the only way possible: they joined the coalition, at times making common cause with populists who were opposed to banks of any kind, and in so doing were able to preserve monopolies at the local level.

3.4   Conclusions and Implications

This chapter has looked at the political and economic histories of three New World economies in order to assess how the distribution of power across society shaped the institutions that governed entry into banking. The results are broadly consistent with the view that the distribution of human capital and the ability to project power exert an effect on an economy's economic institutions. One clear pattern that emerges from these case studies is that representative institutions alone—such as Brazil's parliament in the nineteenth century—are necessary but not sufficient conditions to generate economic institutions that give rise to broadly based financial development. Financial incumbents can either capture the representative institutions or form coalitions with their members; effective suffrage is necessary in order to align the incentives of political elites with the end users of credit.

Are these results generalizable? Obviously, more detailed case studies beyond the three studied here are necessary before any firm conclusions should be drawn, but the available evidence from large-N studies is broadly consistent with the patterns we find in Mexico, Brazil, and the United States. Barth, Caprio, and Levine (2006) analyze a cross section of sixty-five countries in 2003 and find that democratic political institutions are associated with greater ease in obtaining a bank charter and fewer restrictions on the operation of banks. They also find that the tight regulatory restrictions on banks created by autocratic political institutions are associated with lower credit market development and less bank stability, as well as with more corruption in lending. Bordo and Rousseau (2006) analyze a panel of seventeen countries over the period 1880 to 1997, and produce similar results: there is a strong, independent effect of proportional representation, frequent elections, female suffrage, and political stability on the size of the financial sector. The result, while qualified because of the small cross-country sample, is impressive as it is robust to controlling for initial per capita income. Quintyn and Verdier (2010) analyze more than 200 episodes of "financial acceleration" around the world since 1960, and find that the likelihood of an acceleration leading to sustained financial development increases when the underlying political system is democratic. Taken together, the case studies offered here, and the available statistical studies point in the same direction, and provide, we hope, a guide for further research.

References

Aguilar, Gustavo. 2003. "El sistema bancario en Sinaloa (1889–1926): Su influencia en el crecimiento economico." In *La banca regional en Mexico, 1879–1930,* edited by Mario Cerutti and Carlos Marichal, 47–100. Mexico: Fondo de Cultura Económica.

Barth, James R., Gerard Caprio Jr., and Ross Levine. 2006. *Rethinking Bank Regulation: Till Angels Govern.* Cambridge: Cambridge University Press.

Benmelech, Efrain, and Tobias J. Moskowitz. 2005. "The Political Economy of Financial Regulation: Evidence from U.S. State Usury Laws in the 18th and 19th Century." Harvard University. Working Paper.

Berg, Aaron, and Stephen Haber. 2009. "Always Turkeys: Brazil's State-Owned Banks in Historical Perspective." Stanford University. Unpublished Manuscript.

Bodenhorn, Howard. 1990. "Entry, Rivalry, and Free Banking in Antebellum America." *Review of Economics and Statistics* 72:682–6.

———. 1993. "The Business Cycle and Entry into Early American Banking." *Review of Economics and Statistics* 75:531–5.

———. 2003. *State Banking in Early America: A New Economic History.* New York: Oxford University Press.

———. 2006. "Bank Chartering and Political Corruption in Antebellum New York: Free Banking as Reform." In *Corruption and Reform: Lessons from America's Economic History,* edited by Edward Glaeser and Claudia Goldin, 231–57. Chicago: University of Chicago Press.

Bordo, Michael D., and Peter Rousseau. 2006. "Legal-Political Factors and the Historical Evolution of the Finance-Growth Link." NBER Working Paper no. 12035. Cambridge, MA: National Bureau of Economic Research, February.

Bornstein, Morris. 1954. "Banking Policy and Economic Development: A Brazilian Case Study." *The Journal of Finance* 9:312–3.

Calomiris, Charles W. 2010. "The Political Lessons of Depression-Era Banking Reform." *Oxford Review of Economic Policy* 26 (3): 540–60.

Calomiris, Charles W. and Eugene N. White. 1994. "The Origins of Federal Deposit Insurance." In *The Regulated Economy: A Historical Approach to Political Economy,* edited by Claudia Goldin and Gary D. Libecap, 145–88. Chicago: University of Chicago Press.

Cerutti, Mario. 2003. "Empresarido y banca en el norte de Mexico, 1879–1910: La fundacion del Banco Refaccionario de la Laguna." In *La banca regional en Mexico, 1870–1930,* edited by Mario Cerutti and Carlos Marichal, 168–215. Mexico: Fondo de Cultura Económica.

Costeloe, Michael. 2002. *The Central Republic in Mexico, 1835–1846: Hombres de Bien in the Age of Santa Anna.* Cambridge: Cambridge University Press.

Davis, Lance E., and Robert E. Gallman. 2001. *Evolving Financial Markets and International Capital Flows: Britain, the Americas, and Australia, 1865–1914.* Cambridge: Cambridge University Press.

Del Ángel-Mobarak, Gustavo. 2005. "La banca mexicana antes de 1982." In *Cuando el estado se hizo banquero: Consecuencias de la nacionalización bancaria en México,* edited by Gustavo del Ángel-Mobarak, Carlos Bazdresch Parada, and Francisco Suárez Dávila. Mexico City: Fondo de Cultura Económica.

Economopoulos, Andrew, and Heather O'Neill. 1995. "Bank Entry during the Antebellum Period." *Journal of Money, Credit, and Banking* 27:1071–85.

Engerman, Stanley L. 1970. "A Note on the Economic Consequences of the Second Bank of the United States." *The Journal of Political Economy* 78:725–8.

Engerman, Stanley L., and Kenneth L. Sokoloff. 1997. "Factor Endowments, Institutions, and Differential Paths of Growth among New World Economies: A View from Economic Historians of the United States." In *How Latin America Fell Behind: Essays on the Economic Histories of Brazil and Mexico, 1800–1914,* edited by Stephen Haber, 260–304. Stanford: Stanford University Press.

———. 2001. "The Evolution of Suffrage Institutions in the New World." NBER Working Paper no. 8512. Cambridge, MA: National Bureau of Economic Research, October.

Gamboa Ojeda, Leticia. 2003. "El Banco Oriental de Mexico y la formacion de un sistema de banca, 1900–1911." In *La banca regional en Mexico, 1870–1930,* edited by Mario Cerutti and Carlos Marichal, 101–33. Mexico: Fondo de Cultura Económica.

Gatell, Frank Otto. 1966. "Sober Second Thoughts on Van Buren, the Albany Regency, and the Wall Street Conspiracy." *The Journal of American History* 53: 19–40.

Grinath, Arthur, John Joseph Wallis, and Richard E. Sylla. 1997. "Debt, Default, and Revenue Structure: The American State Debt Crisis in the Early 1840s." NBER Historical Working Paper no. 97. Cambridge, MA: National Bureau of Economic Research, March.

Haber, Stephen. 1991. "Industrial Concentration and the Capital Markets: A Comparative Study of Brazil, Mexico, and the United States, 1830–1930." *The Journal of Economic History* 51:559–80.

———. 1997. "Financial Markets and Industrial Development: A Comparative Study of Governmental Regulation, Financial Innovation, and Industrial Structure in Brazil and Mexico, 1840–1930." In *How Latin America Fell Behind: Essays on the Economic Histories of Brazil and Mexico, 1800–1930,* edited by Stephen Haber, 146–78. Stanford: Stanford University Press.

———. 1998. "The Efficiency Consequences of Institutional Change: Financial Market Regulation and Industrial Productivity Growth in Brazil, 1866–1934." In *Latin America and the World Economy Since 1800,* edited by John H. Coatsworth and Alan M. Taylor, 275–322. Cambridge: Harvard University David Rockefeller Center for Latin American Studies. Harvard University Press.

———. 2009. "Why Banks Don't Lend: The Mexican Financial System." In *No Growth without Equity? Inequality, Interests, and Competition in Mexico,* edited by Santiago Levy and Michael Walton, 283–320. Washington, DC: The World Bank and Palgrave Macmillan.

Haber, Stephen, Herbert S. Klein, Noel Maurer, and Kevin Middlebrook. 2008. *Mexico Since 1980.* Cambridge: Cambridge University Press.

Haber, Stephen, Armando Razo, and Noel Maurer. 2003. *The Politics of Property*

Rights: Political Instability, Credible Commitments, and Economic Growth in Mexico, 1876–1929. Cambridge: Cambridge University Press.

Hammond, Bray. 1947. "Jackson, Biddle, and the Bank of the United States." *The Journal of Economic History* 7:1–23.

Hanley, Anne G. 2005. *Native Capital: Financial Institutions and Economic Development in Sao Paulo, Brazil, 1850–1905.* Stanford: Stanford University Press.

Hoffman, Philip T., Gilles Postel-Vinay, and Jean-Laurent Rosenthal. 2001. *Priceless Markets: The Political Economy of Credit in Paris, 1660–1870.* Chicago: University of Chicago Press.

Holden, Robert H. 1994. *Mexico and the Survey of Public Lands: The Management of Modernization, 1876–1911.* Dekalb: Northern Illinois University Press.

Katz, Friedrich. 1998. *The Life and Times of Pancho Villa.* Stanford: Stanford University Press.

Keyssar, Alexander. 2000. *The Right to Vote: The Contested History of Democracy in the United States.* New York: Basic Books.

Kroszner, Randall S. and Philip E. Strahan. 1999. "What Drives Deregulation? Economics and Politics of the Relaxation of Bank Branching Restrictions." *Quarterly Journal of Economics* 114:1437–67.

Lamoreaux, Naomi. 1994. *Insider Lending: Banks, Personal Connections, and Economic Development in Industrial New England.* Cambridge: Cambridge University Press.

Lane, Carl. 1997. "For a 'Positive Profit': The Federal Investment in the First Bank of the United States, 1792–1802." *William and Mary Quarterly* 54:601–12.

Levy, Juliette. 2003. "Yucatan's Arrested Development: Social Networks and Credit Markets in Merida, 1850–1899." PhD diss., University of California, Los Angeles.

Ludlow, Leonor. 2003. "El Banco Mercantil de Veracruz, 1898–1906." In *La banca regional en Mexico, 1870–1930,* edited by Mario Cerutti and Carlos Marichal, 134–67. Mexico: Fondo de Cultura Económica.

Majewski, John. 2004. "Jeffersonian Political Economy and Pennsylvania's Financial Revolution from Below, 1800–1820." University of California, Santa Barbara. Unpublished Manuscript.

Marichal, Carlos. 2002. "The Construction of Credibility: Financial Market Reform and the Renegotiation of Mexico's External Debt in the 1880's." In *The Mexican Economy, 1870–1930: Essays on the Economic History of Institutions, Revolution, and Growth,* edited by Jeffrey L. Bortz and Stephen H. Haber, 93–119. Stanford: Stanford University Press.

Markiewicz, Dana. 1993. *The Mexican Revolution and the Limits of Agrarian Reform, 1915–1946.* Boulder, CO: Lynne Rienner Publishers.

Maurer, Noel. 2002. *The Power and the Money: The Mexican Financial System, 1876–1932.* Stanford: Stanford University Press.

Maurer, Noel, and Andrei Gomberg. 2004. "When the State is Untrustworthy: Public Finance and Private Banking in Porfirian Mexico." *Journal of Economic History* 64:1087–107.

Maurer, Noel, and Stephen Haber. 2007. "Related Lending and Economic Performance: Evidence from Mexico." *The Journal of Economic History* 67:551–81.

Mexico, Secretaria de Hacienda. 1912. *Anuario de Estadistica Fiscal, 1911–12.* Mexico City: Imprenta del Gobierno.

Moss, David, and Sarah Brennan. 2004. "Regulation and Reaction: The Other Side of Free Banking in Antebellum New York." Harvard University, Harvard Business School. Working Paper 04-038.

Musacchio, Aldo. 2009. *Experiments in Financial Democracy: Corporate Governance and Financial Development in Brazil, 1882–1950.* Cambridge: Cambridge University Press.

Ng, Kenneth. 1988. "Free Banking Laws and Barriers to Entry in Banking, 1838–1860." *The Journal of Economic History* 48:877–89.

Oveda, Jaime. 2003. "Bancos y banqueros en Guadalajara." In *La banca regional en Mexico, 1870–1930,* edited by Mario Cerutti and Carlos Marichal. Mexico: Fondo de Cultura Económica.

Peláez, Carlos Manuel. 1975. "The Establishment of Banking Institutions in a Backward Economy: Brazil, 1800–1851." *The Business History Review* 49:446–72.

Peláez, Carlos Manuel, and Wilson Suzigan. 1976. *Historia Monetária do Brasil: Análise da Política, Comportamento e Instituições Monetárias.* Brazil: Editora Universidade de Brasília.

Petersen, Mitchell A., and Raghuram G. Rajan. 2002. "Does Distance Still Matter? The Information Revolution In Small Business Lending." *Journal of Finance* 57:2533–70.

Potash, Robert. 1983. *The Mexican Government and Industrial Development in the Early Republic: The Banco de Avío.* Amherst: University of Massachusetts Press.

Quintyn, Marc, and Geneviève Verdier. 2010. "Mother Can I Trust the Government? Sustained Financial Deepening—A Political Institutions View." IMF Working Paper no. WP/10/210. Washington, DC: International Monetary Fund, September.

Rajan, Raghuram, and Rodney Ramcharan. Forthcoming. "Land and Credit: A Study of the Political Economy of Banking in the United States in the Early 20th Century." *Journal of Finance.*

Razo, Armando. 2008. *Social Foundations of Limited Dictatorship: Networks and Private Protection During Mexico's Early Industrialization.* Stanford: Stanford University Press.

Rockoff, Hugh. 1974. "The Free Banking Era: A Reexamination." *Journal of Money, Credit, and Banking* 6:141–67.

———. 1985. "New Evidence on Free Banking in the United States." *The American Economic Review* 75:886–9.

———. 2000. "Banking and Finance, 1789–1914." In *The Cambridge Economic History of the United States Volume II,* edited by Stanley Engerman and Robert Gallman, 643–84. Cambridge: Cambridge University Press.

Rodríguez López, María Guadalupe. 1995. "La banca porfiriana en Durango." In *Durango (1840–1915): Banca, transportes, tierra e industria,* edited by Mario Cerruti, 7–34. Monterrey, Nuevo León, Mexico: Impresora Monterrey.

———. 2003. "Paz y bancos en Durango durante el Porfiriato." In *La banca regional en Mexico, 1870–1930,* edited by Mario Cerutti and Carlos Marichal, 254–90. Mexico: Fondo de Cultura Económica.

Romero Ibarra, Maria Eugenia. 2003. "El Banco del Estado de Mexico 1897–1914." In *La banca regional en Mexico, 1870–1930,* edited by Mario Cerutti and Carlos Marichal, 216–51. Mexico: Fondo de Cultura Económica.

Rousseau, Peter L., and Richard Sylla. 2005. "Emerging Financial Markets and Early U.S. Growth." *Explorations in Economic History* 42:1–26.

Summerhill, William. Forthcoming. *Inglorious Revolution: Political Institutions, Sovereign Debt, and Financial Underdevelopment in Imperial Brazil.* New Haven: Yale University Press.

Sylla, Richard. 1975. *The American Capital Market, 1846–1914: A Study of the Effects of Public Policy on Economic Development.* New York: Arno Press.

———. 2000. "Experimental Federalism: The Economics of American Government, 1789–1914." In *The Cambridge Economic History of the United States Vol-*

ume II, edited by Stanley Engerman and Robert Gallman, 483–542. Cambridge: Cambridge University Press.

———. 2007. "The Political Economy of Early U.S. Financial Development." In *Political Institutions and Financial Development,* edited by Stephen Haber, Douglass C. North, and Barry R. Weingast, 60–91. Palo Alto: Stanford University Press.

Sylla, Richard, John B. Legler, and John Wallis. 1987. "Banks and State Public Finance in the New Republic: The United States, 1790–1860." *The Journal of Economic History* 47:391–403.

Temin, Peter. 1968. "The Economic Consequences of the Bank War." *The Journal of Political Economy* 76:257–74.

Tenenbaum, Barbara. 1986. *The Politics of Penury: Debt and Taxes in Mexico, 1821–1856.* Albuquerque: University of New Mexico Press.

Topik, Steven. 1980. "State Enterprise in a Liberal Regime: The Banco do Brasil, 1905–1930." *Journal of Interamerican Studies and World Affairs* 22:401–22.

———. 1987. *The Political Economy of the Brazilian State, 1889–1930.* Austin: University of Texas Press.

Triner, Gail D. 2000. *Banking and Economic Development: Brazil, 1889–1930.* New York: Palgrave.

United States Board of Governors of the Federal Reserve System. 1943. *Banking and Monetary Statistics.* Washington, DC: Federal Reserve.

Walker, David W. 1987. *Business, Kinship, and Politics: The Martinez del Rio Family in Mexico, 1824–1867.* Austin: University of Texas Press.

Wallis, John, Richard Sylla, and John B. Legler. 1994. "The Interaction of Taxation and Regulation in Nineteenth Century U.S. Banking." In *The Regulated Economy: A Historical Approach to Political Economy,* edited by Claudia Goldin and Gary D. Libecap, 122–44. Chicago: The University of Chicago Press.

Wang, Ta-Chen. 2006. "Courts, Banks, and Credit Market in Early American Development." PhD diss., Stanford University.

Wasserman, Mark. 1984. *Capitalists, Caciques, and Revolution: Elite and Foreign Enterprise in Chihuahua, Mexico, 1854–1911.* Chapel Hill: University of North Carolina Press.

Wettereau, James. 1942. "The Branches of the First Bank of the United States." *Journal of Economic History* 2:66–100.

Womack, John. 1969. *Zapata and the Mexican Revolution.* New York: Alfred A. Knopf.

4

Political Centralization and Urban Primacy
Evidence from National and Provincial Capitals in the Americas

Sebastian Galiani and Sukkoo Kim

> "All over the world it is the Law of the Capitals that the largest city shall be super-eminent, and not merely in size, but in national influence."
> —Jefferson (1939) "The Law of the Primate City"

4.1 Introduction

In his pioneering article, Jefferson (1939) extolled the virtues of the largest or the primate city of each nation. For Jefferson, in almost every country, the primate city, usually a capital city, housed the finest wares, the rarest articles, the greatest talents and skilled workers and, more importantly, was the center of its national culture, pride, and influence. According to Jefferson's calculations, the national capitals of many Latin American nations such as Mexico, Peru, Argentina, Cuba, Bolivia, and Chile followed this pattern as did those of many European nations. Jefferson was also aware that America was a major exception to this rule. While "capital" was synonymous with "primate city" almost everywhere else, it was not so in America. In America, the word capital was limited to political capitals, often very unimportant towns. But at the same time that America distinguished itself from the rest of the countries—or, at least those of its same hemisphere—because of the unimportant cities where political authorities had their seat, it also enjoyed a highly superior level of welfare. Could these two facts be related?

In this chapter we intend to present an answer to that question by exploring the causes of urban primacy in the Americas and linking them to the long-run determinants of growth. To study these issues we use Jefferson's

Sebastian Galiani is professor of economics at Washington University in St. Louis. Sukkoo Kim is associate professor of economics at Washington University in St. Louis, and a research associate of the National Bureau of Economic Research.

We are grateful to Ed Leamer, Naomi Lamoreaux, two anonymous referees, and participants of the conference honoring the contributions of Kenneth Sokoloff at UCLA for their comments. Maximiliano Appendino, Andres Drenik, Fernando Yu, and Ivan Torre provided excellent research assistance. We thank the Weidenbaum Center at Washington University in St. Louis and the Bradley Foundation for invaluable research support.

general insight that urban primacy is often characterized by a disproportionate concentration of population in capital cities.[1] However, unlike Jefferson's
and most other studies that focus on the impact of national capitals, we also
investigate the role of provincial or state capitals in Latin America and the
United States. In Latin America, not only is the national capital often the
largest city in the nation, its provincial capitals are also often the largest
cities in its provinces. By contrast, in the United States, where urban primacy
is not a major feature of its urban development, its national capital is not
the largest city in the nation and the majority of its state capitals are often
quite small.

We suggest that these differing patterns of capital city development in the
Americas is most likely caused by differing levels of political centralization
that can be traced back to colonial times. When political power is centralized
in the executive branches of the federal and provincial governments, as is the
case in much of Latin America, government resources and regulations are
most likely to benefit the capital cities at the expense of noncapital cities and
rural areas. On the contrary, when political power is decentralized in state
and local governments, as is the case in the United States, the distribution of
government resources will often depend on the competitive ability of local
and state governments to raise revenues from their economic bases. In the
United States, the devolution of political power has also tended to redistribute incomes from the wealthy to poor areas. To the point that urban primacy
boosted by centralized regimes may entail productivity losses—namely, by
misallocating resources—it is clear that certain institutional arrangements
may be less conducive to growth in the long-term. In fact, urban primacy
may be one of the factors that account for the persistence of institutions
across time. Acemoglu, Johnson, and Robinson (2001) have shown that the
present institutional structure in most developing countries mirrors the one
set up by European colonial empires between the sixteenth and the eighteenth centuries and is responsible for present differences in income between
countries. In terms of our analysis, it could be said that centralized colonial
regimes resulted in unbalanced and inefficient distributions of population
that, at the same time, hindered growth, and conditioned and limited further
institutional change.

We motivate our empirical study by considering some theoretical argu-

---

1. In Latin America, Morse (1971), using the share of the population of the largest city as
a measure of primacy, finds that urban primacy arose in Argentina and Cuba around 1800, in
Colombia, Mexico, and Peru in 1850, and in Brazil and Venezuela by 1900. In all of these cases,
the primate city was also the national capital. McGreevey (1971), using a measure based on the
Pareto distribution of city sizes, dates the rise of urban primacy in Mexico to as early as 1750,
Cuba to 1825, Chile to 1830, Argentina to 1850, Brazil to 1880, Peru to 1925, and Venezuela and
Colombia to 1950. By 1970, Portes (1976) argues, most Latin American countries, except per-
haps Brazil and Colombia, exhibited significant urban primacy characteristics. In the United
States, by contrast, urban primacy is rarely seen as a key feature of its urban development; the
distribution of city sizes have favored the medium- to small-size cities over time (Kim 2000).

ments that suggest that urban primacy depends on productivity and political centralization. On the one hand, in assuming a politically decentralized region where the mainland and the hinterland independently choose their level of taxes and of public goods investment, primacy only arises if the mainland is more productive than the hinterland. On the other hand, in a nation/region said to be politically centralized—where the mainland government has the power to set taxes and levels of expenditures on the public goods of both mainland and hinterland economies—primacy depends on productivity and on the relative importance the government gives to the welfare of each location's residents. If mainland citizens are considered more important than hinterland citizens, then urban primacy will arise; however, if the government is more balanced in its valuation of the different citizens' welfare, then urban primacy is lower than in the decentralized scenario. Thus, we suggest that the relationship between political centralization and urban primacy depends critically on the relative weight given to the mainland relative to the hinterland economy in a central government's welfare function. We also sketch some arguments that explain why urban primacy may be associated to resource misallocation and, in the long run, productivity losses. This is particularly important since it may partly explain differences in long-term growth performance between British North America and Latin America after both regions gained independence from their metropolis.

In order to estimate the impact of capital cities on urban primacy in the Americas, we construct extensive data on all cities greater than 2,500 and 25,000 for seven Latin American countries in 1900 and for eighteen Latin American countries and the United States in 1990. It is important to note that our data set differs significantly from those of earlier studies such as Ades and Glaeser (1995) and Henderson (2002) whose samples consist only of the largest national capital and noncapital cities around the world. Unlike these studies, we are able to estimate the impact of national and provincial capital city status on population in comparison to the full sample of noncapital cities within each country controlling for other factors that might cause population concentration.[2] As controls, we include geographic variables such as land area, longitude, latitude, coastal perimeter, and nearness to port or navigable river, climate variables such as temperature, rainfall, and sunshine and, in the case of the United States, some economic variables as well.

Our estimates indicate that the impact of national capital status on population concentration in Latin America was already quite significant by the beginning of the twentieth century and only grew in importance over time. Using only land area as the control variable to maintain consistency across

2. For example, in Ades and Glaeser's (1995) sample, seventy-seven out of eighty-five cities are national capitals; thus, when they drop noncapital cities from their analysis, their results are unchanged.

countries, we find that in 1900 the national capital status increased population by 523 percent, but by 1990 the figure rose to 677 percent for the same sample (919 percent for the full sample).[3] On the other hand, the impact of provincial capital status in Latin America was quite modest in 1900 as it increased population by 70 percent; however, its impact rose to 353 percent by 1990 (232 percent for the full sample).

The relative importance of national and provincial capital statuses on population concentration also varied by countries in Latin America. In 1900, the national capital city status increased population concentrations by extraordinary amounts for Argentina and Brazil but slightly less so for Cuba, Chile, and Uruguay. However, for provincial capitals, the impact was only significant for Brazil. In 1990, for which we have data for a larger sample, the national capital city effect was most significant for Mexico followed by Argentina, Paraguay, Colombia, and Peru. The provincial capital city effect generally increased for most countries over time, but it was much more significant for Brazil, Colombia, and Mexico than countries like Nicaragua, Guatemala, El Salvador, Paraguay, Honduras, and Panama.

For the United States, by contrast, the impact of national and state capital statuses on population concentration was quite modest in 1900 as they increased population by 70 percent and 15–29 percent, respectively. However, by 1990, the impact of the national capital status on population grew sharply to 475 percent whereas the figure remained relatively modest for state capital status at only 38 percent. Thus, according to our estimates, the main difference between the United States and Latin America by the end of the twentieth century was in the differing importance of provincial or state capital status on population concentration.

The fact that differences in the degrees of urban primacy between the United States and Latin America grew over time is particularly interesting since it is correlated with the growing income gap between the same regions during the same period. In fact, while in 1900 the United States income per capita was about 3.67 times the Latin American one, in 1990 it was 4.57 times (data from Maddison 2003).

While the lack of generally accepted measures of political centralization makes it extremely challenging to link this factor to our empirical evidence on national and state capital statuses, we believe that there is a variety of evidence that can be used to support our hypothesis that urban primacy is caused by political centralization. With some important variations, whether

3. In general, the estimated coefficients on capital city dummy variable is relatively robust to the inclusion of other control variables. While the use of land area as a control variable might be seen as problematic as land area is partly endogenous, our results are even sharper if land area is excluded. In addition, most other studies such as Ades and Glaeser (1995) and Henderson (2002) also include land area as one of the independent variables. More recently, Campante and Do (2009) propose a new method for studying the impact of spatial concentration around a center or capital point. For important earlier cross-country studies on urban primacy, see Rosen and Resnick (1980) and Wheaton and Shishido (1981).

unitary or federal, most scholars believe that political power is highly centralized in the executive branches of federal and provincial governments in Latin America (Nickson 1995). First, most of the powerful political and economic elites, including large landowners, live, work and socialize in capital cities. Second, the power to generate tax revenue is highly centralized in the federal government and the provincial and local governments rely on national transfers that are determined politically rather than economically (Sokoloff and Zolt 2006). Third, until recent times, the political and policing powers of the national capital city was under the control of the president and the federal government in many countries (Meyers and Dietz 2002).

Moreover, as we suggest in our theoretical section, there is considerable evidence that political centralization in the national and provincial capitals led to a significant bias in the distribution of government resources to the capital cities in Latin America (Myers 2002). Most scholars consider Mexico to be one of the most politically centralized in Latin America as the federal government collects more than 90 percent of government revenues. Most of the revenues were likely to be funneled to capital cities and the remaining local governments received only 4 percent of those revenues in 1990 (Nickson 1995; Diaz-Cayeros 2006). In the earlier period under Porfirio Díaz, the era between 1876 to 1911, it is estimated that Mexico City received more than 80 percent of all government investments in infrastructure (Kandell 1988). While Argentina is seen to be less centralized than Mexico (Diaz-Cayeros 2006), economic development was also severely biased in favor of capital cities due to centralized government decisions.

In the United States, by contrast, political power was highly decentralized toward states and localities until the second half of the twentieth century when the federal government became more centralized (Skowronek 1982). However, U.S. state governments, unlike Latin American provincial governments, remain relatively decentralized as state legislatures continue to be strongly influenced by state-wide constituents. Political decentralization, as predicted by our model, also led to the competitive distribution of public goods across localities. Thus, between 1840 and 1990, local government expenditures represented the highest shares of government expenditures in the United States (Wallis 2000). In the second half of the twentieth century, federal taxes and expenditures rose significantly, suggesting the growing centralization of power in the federal government. However, due to checks and balances on executive power stemming from local congressional representation, the relative weight given to states and localities is likely to be much more balanced in the United States than in most of Latin America.

Finally, a last concern for our chapter is the fact that the capital city effect we capture in our regression may be, nevertheless, subject to endogeneity issues. To deal with them we show evidence that, unlike Europe and elsewhere, where endogeneity of the location of capital cities may be a major problem (Ades and Glaeser 1995), the forces that led to the location of political capitals in the Americas were largely exogenous from an economic point of view. In Latin America, national and provincial capitals were almost always important political capitals of the Spanish and Portuguese empires, most of which were initially chosen for military reasons (Portes 1976; Cortés Conde 2008). In the United States, by contrast, the majority of capitals were founded or relocated in geographically central but undeveloped areas for political reasons. To illustrate our case, we trace the political factors that led to the founding of the locations of political capitals in Argentina and the United States.

This chapter is organized as follows. In section 4.2, we present our theoretical arguments about political centralization and population distribution. In section 4.3, we estimate the impact of national and state/provincial capital statuses on population concentration for Latin America and the United States between 1900 and 1990. In section 4.4, we explore the historical link between political centralization, capital city concentration, and urban primacy. In section 4.5, we examine in some detail the forces that led to the founding of capital cities in the United States and Argentina. In section 4.6, we conclude our chapter with a summary.

4.2   Centralization and Urban Primacy—an Analytical Framework

In this section we will discuss theoretical considerations based on a model of political centralization and population distribution that is presented in the appendix of this chapter.

First of all, suppose a political region divided into two locations—the main city and the hinterland, in which a central government doesn't exist—an arrangement akin to a loose confederation that is fully economically integrated and where migration between locations is costless. What should be the pattern of distribution of the population? As there is complete labor mobility, wages are expected to be the same across the region—to achieve that, initial differentials in productivity should be compensated by population movements. Therefore, intrinsically more productive locations—because of geographical reasons, for instance—are expected to be relatively more populated than less productive locations. This result also holds if we include in our analysis local governments that tax and provide public goods. As long as they perform those activities within their location—that is, the hinterland or the mainland governments only tax their respective inhabitants and provide public goods only to them—the population will distribute according to differences in productivity; the level of public goods provision in the more productive region is expected to be higher as the level of taxes that can be withstood is higher. Initial productivity differentials may remain unaltered or be magnified—but never reversed.

The situation is different when local governments are replaced by a unique central government that taxes economic activity across the region and decides the distribution of public goods across locations. This last issue is crucial to our analysis: as long as public goods have a positive effect on productivity, some particular patterns of allocation in their provision may reverse geographically driven differences in productivity, thus having consequences on the distribution of population. This brings us to a fundamental question: what are the determinants of public goods allocation across a political region? A simple political economy assumption would be to consider a central government with a welfare function that includes both the welfare of hinterland and mainland citizens. The importance the central government gives to each one will necessarily impact on the allocation of public goods: if the welfare of mainland citizens is considered to be more important to the central government than that of hinterland citizens, the practical consequence would be that mainland inhabitants will be provided with a relatively higher level of public goods than residents of the hinterland. If the mainland is initially more productive than the hinterland, then the productivity gap between them would be exacerbated and, consequently, the population will move accordingly. If, in a similar initial context, the central government is more worried about the hinterland residents' welfare, then the situation would be opposite: public goods provision would be greater in the hinterland, something that would contribute to a reversal in the productivity differentials and, therefore, a distribution of population biased toward the hinterland. Within the framework we have just sketched, then, urban primacy may arise from a centralized government that caters mainland citizens in a disproportionate way, exacerbating or even reversing productivity differentials in favour of capital cities and thus triggering incentives for the population to establish themselves physically close to political authorities.

Central governments that care about the mainland more than the hinterland not only cause urban primacy but also have economic consequences in the long run. In fact, they may entail an inefficient distribution of population. Suppose a case where the hinterland is vastly more productive than the mainland. In a decentralized regime, the former would be expected to be more populated than the latter. If, then, a centralized government emerges and taxes equally all the country but concentrates its investment in the mainland, what happens is practically a transfer of resources from the more productive region to the less productive one. The capital city becomes crowded with migrants coming from the hinterland, who leave their original site in order to have a better access to public goods. But if the productivity-enhancing effect of public goods is assumed to be variable—for instance, high productivity locations may benefit more from an additional unit of public good than low productivity locations—then there may be an efficiency loss in reducing the provision of public goods in the hinterland and raising it in the mainland; the transfer implies a misallocation of resources. In particular, suppose the productivity-enhancing effect of public goods has the shape of an inverted U—very low and very high productivity locations enjoy a small effect, while middle productivity locations benefit the most from public goods provision. In this sense, reallocating public goods provision away from the hinterland can entail efficiency costs both in situations where the mainland is compara-tively more productive or less productive. As long as these efficiency costs persist in time, the urban primacy that emerges from a centralized regime may be partly responsible for long-term differences in productivity across countries with different political regimes. The case of British North America and Latin America, as we present in section 4.4, is particularly relevant in that respect.

4.3   Capital Cities and Urban Primacy

The analytical framework sketched in the previous section suggests that urban primacy is due to two important factors: economic factors that affect productivity and political factors that affect the geographic distribution of public goods. In this section, we attempt to identify the impact of political factors by estimating the influence of capital city status, both national and state/provincial, on population concentration after controlling for other factors that might affect productivity. In nations with centralized political power, the political and economic elites often reside in political capitals and have the means and the incentives to place a higher weight, γ, which increases urban primacy. Thus, capital city status is likely to capture the influence of political centralization on population.

The literature on urban primacy also provides a variety of reasons for why capital cities contribute to primacy. Capital cities may become signifi-cantly larger due to their advantage as the centers of governments.[4] First, government agencies and workers are concentrated in capital cities. Second, since governments make laws and redistribute income, capital cities may attract significant lobbying activity. To the extent that political corruption or rent-seeking behavior contributes to primacy, their impact is likely to be manifested in the growth of capital cities.[5] Finally, capital cities may attract a disproportionate share of government resources for local infrastructure and amenities. In many Latin American countries, the political and economic elites who disproportionately reside in capital cities may have little political incentives to distribute resources to smaller cities.[6]

---

4. Ades and Glaeser (1995) argue that the political power of the capital city is greater when governments are weak and respond to local pressure, have large rents to dispense, and do not respect the political rights of the hinterland. They also argue that the benefits of proximity to political actors are likely to increase when influence comes from the threat of violence, distance makes illegal action more difficult to conceal, and distance lowers access to information and communication between political agents and government.

5. The primacy of Seoul, Korea, has been associated with the need to locate in the capital city to lobby and obtain export and import licenses and loans from the Korean government bureaucracy (Henderson 2002).

6. In Argentina, for example, Walter (1993) writes that economic and political elites, includ-ing the agricultural landowners of the Pampas, live in their capital city of Buenos Aires. A similar story unfolds in Chile where the landed and capitalist elites intermarried and formed tight political bonds in their capital city of Santiago (Zeitlin and Ratcliff 1988; Walter 2005).

We estimate the following equation:

(5) $\ln(\text{pop})_i = \alpha_1 + \beta_1 N\text{capital}_i + \beta_2 P\text{capital}_i + \beta_3 Ex\text{capital}_i$
$+ \beta_3 \ln(\text{landarea}_i) + \beta_4 X_i + \varepsilon_i,$

where the Ncapital and Pcapital are dummy variables for whether a city is a national or provincial/state capital, Excapital for whether a city was a ex-national capital, landarea is the area of the city in km^2, and X_i are exogenous controls. For Latin America, the X_i control variables consist of the positional variables, latitude, longitude, altitude; the geographic variables, coastline and river dummies; and the climate variables, January, July, annual average temperatures and annual average precipitation. For the United States, our control variables differ somewhat due to data availability.

The data consist of all cities with populations greater than 25,000 for seven Latin American countries and the United States circa 1900, and for eighteen Latin American countries and the United States in 1990. For Latin American countries, we also have data for cities with populations greater than 2,500. Cities in general are defined as municipalities rather than as urban or metropolitan areas. In Latin America, we use the second administrative division; in the United States, we use the municipality. We provide detailed information on definitions and sources of our data in the appendix.

Table 4.1 presents the basic descriptive information on the provinces and states of the countries in the Americas. There were considerable variations in

Table 4.1	Descriptive statistics of the provinces/states in the Americas	
	Number	Population (1,000) average (sd)
Argentina	24	1,510.8 (2,757.6)
Bolivia	9	919.4 (820.0)
Brazil	27	6,809.7 (8,184.0)
Chile	53	285.2 (647.1)
Colombia	32	1,295.9 (1,831.2)
Costa Rica	7	544.3 (382.0)
Cuba	15	749.3 (467.0)
Ecuador	24	503.5 (704.7)
El Salvador	14	410.3 (365.1)
Guatemala	22	510.0 (497.4)
Honduras	18	337.6 (298.4)
Mexico	32	3,228.6 (2,793.7)
Nicaragua	17	300.7 (268.6)
Panama	12	236.6 (376.4)
Paraguay	18	286.8 (315.5)
Peru	26	1,003.8 (1289.1)
Uruguay	—	—
Venezuela	24	960.5 (756.9)
United States	49	5,042.0 (5,486.6)

Note: Dashed cells indicate no entry.

the number, average population, and land area of provinces/states across the countries. In general, the larger countries such as the United States, Brazil, and Mexico generally had a greater number of provinces/states as well as higher average population per province/state.

Table 4.2 reports descriptive statistics of the cities in our regression data sample. As expected, the data suggest an increase in the urban concentration of population in the largest cities in Latin America as compared to those in the United States over time. In 1900, for cities with populations greater than 25,000, the average size of cities in Latin America was less than half of those in the United States; however, by 1990, it was larger than those of the United States. In addition, whereas the number of cities in this size category rose over ninefold for the United States during this period, the increase in the number of cities in Latin America was much more modest.

In table 4.3, we report the regression estimates for the pooled sample of Latin American countries for the period around 1900 and 1990. In tables 4.4 and 4.5, we present similar regressions for the United States and the individual countries in Latin America, respectively.

The national and provincial capital statuses increased population in all countries but did so to a much greater extent in Latin America than in the United States. Based on the seven subset of Latin American countries in 1900, the data show that the importance of national capital status on population was already very high in 1900 and remained so through 1990; however, the relative importance of provincial capital status rose significantly over this period. By contrast for the United States, the importance of national capital status rose over time but that of state capital status remained relatively unimportant over time.

The absolute values of the capital city coefficients were sensitive to the choice of sample size (population greater than 2,500 or 25,000). When cities are defined as having a population greater than 2,500, the national capital and provincial capital coefficients were much larger, especially for the latter.

The national capital status increased population by 523 percent for the seven Latin American countries in 1900; in 1990, for the same sample of countries as in 1900, the figure rose slightly to 677 percent, whereas for the full sample of the eighteen Latin American countries, the national capital status increased population by 918 percent. By contrast, in the United States, national capital status increased population by only 70 percent in 1900, but by 493 percent (216 percent for 1900 sample) in 1990.

Provincial capital status increased population by 70 to 127 percent for the seven Latin American countries in 1900, but the figure rose markedly to 353 percent in 1990 for the same sample of cities. For the full sample of eighteen countries in 1990, the impact was slightly smaller at 232 percent. For the United States, state capitals remained a much less influential magnet for population as their impact rose from 15 percent to 42 percent between 1900

Table 4.2 Descriptive statistics: Cities in the Americas

	1910* urbanization	2000	c1900 number	(2,500+) average (sd)	c1900 number	(25,000+) average (sd)	c1990 number	(2,500+) average (sd)	c1990 number	(25,000+) average (sd)
Argentina	31.2%	89.4%	365	21,257 (84,654)	73	67,779 (182,644)	489	74,074 (180,553)	245	136,022 (239,671)
Bolivia	4.3	64.8	—	—	—	—	109	75,865 (190,537)	68	113,769 (233,706)
Brazil	10.7	81.3	1,469	28,764 (60,656)	566	51,163 (93,238)	5,270	34,777 (203,018)	1,222	116,848 (411,056)
Chile	14.5	84.6	79	41,016 (48,918)	50	54,250 (57,539)	52	290,655 (652,191)	44	341,547 (698,033)
Colombia	7.1	74.9	—	—	—	—	1,054	39,256 (237,976)	251	130,904 (476,827)
Costa Rica	9.0	51.9	29	8,261 (7,887)	2	32,505 (9,344)	81	47,039 (49,751)	49	67,783 (54,715)
Cuba	15.1	75.3	124	17,418 (29,380)	17	60,058 (64,878)	155	72,510 (180,618)	134	80,959 (192,978)
Ecuador	9.1	62.4	—	—	—	—	214	56,454 (191,369)	97	110,426 (275,365)
El Salvador	6.3	46.6	159	7,986 (10,577)	5	53,572 (30,379)	244	23,425 (38,601)	54	71,327 (60,901)
Guatemala	5.1	40.4	—	—	—	—	327	34,294 (62,755)	141	61,554 (88,378)
Honduras	3.9	46.9	—	—	—	—	285	21,235 (61,564)	46	82,289 (138,620)
Mexico	7.6	74.4	—	—	—	—	2,049	50,174 (228,685)	689	128,414 (382,572)
Nicaragua	7.0	64.7	—	—	—	—	151	33,847 (79,242)	61	65,866 (117,904)
Panama	11.1	57.7	—	—	—	—	72	39,354 (92,250)	20	111,664 (155,245)
Paraguay	14.1	56.0	—	—	—	—	217	23,740 (45,541)	47	72,851 (80,402)
Peru	5.0	72.8	—	—	—	—	195	133,843 (508,984)	162	158,037 (555,587)
Uruguay	28.7	91.3	19	54,878 (63,493)	17	59,216 (65,916)	19	170,579 (295,890)	19	170,579 (295,890)
Venezuela	3.6	87.4	—	—	—	—	322	71,549 (188,929)	179	116,782 (244,356)
Latin America	45.6		2,244	25,831 (61,622)	730	53,396 (102,350)	11,305	44,463 (213,113)	3,528	119,283 (370,595)
United States		79.2	—	—	160	123,243 (322,758)	—		1,066	97,697 (289,637)

Sources: Urbanization for circa *1910–1914 is defined as proportion of population living in major cities; in 2000, as proportion living in urban areas by various national definitions. See Bulmer-Thomas (2003, 7, 85).

Note: Dashed cells indicate no entry.

Table 4.3   Log of population on capital city status for pooled Latin America: 1900 and 1990

	1900				1990 (1900 sample)				1990			
	2,500+		25,000+		2,500+		25,000+		2,500+		25,000+	
National capital	2.69*** (0.60)	2.81*** (0.50)	1.83*** (0.56)	2.05*** (0.43)	2.67*** (0.64)	2.71*** (0.48)	2.05*** (0.52)	2.06*** (0.42)	2.78*** (0.34)	2.74*** (0.32)	2.32*** (0.29)	2.29*** (0.27)
Provincial capital	0.82*** (0.13)	1.14*** (0.11)	0.53*** (0.11)	0.75*** (0.12)	2.72*** (0.12)	2.32*** (0.13)	1.51*** (0.12)	1.48*** (0.11)	2.14*** (0.07)	1.93*** (0.07)	1.20*** (0.07)	1.22*** (0.07)
Ex. national capital	—	—	—	—	—	3.03*** (0.20)	—	3.16*** (0.20)	—	3.58*** (0.13)	—	3.32*** (0.13)
ln(landarea)	0.14*** (0.01)	0.11*** (0.01)	0.01 (0.01)	0.05*** (0.02)	0.18*** (0.01)	0.13*** (0.01)	-0.04*** (0.01)	-0.06*** (0.01)	0.19*** (0.01)	0.18*** (0.01)	-0.006 (0.009)	-0.03*** (0.01)
Latitude	—	0.02*** (0.00)	—	0.02*** (0.01)	—	0.02*** (0.003)	—	0.02*** (0.004)	—	-0.005** (0.002)	—	0.010*** (0.002)
Longitude	—	-0.02*** (0.00)	—	-0.02*** (0.00)	—	-0.001 (0.001)	—	-0.012*** (0.001)	—	0.003*** (0.001)	—	-0.004*** (0.001)
Altitude	—	-0.00*** (0.00)	—	-0.00 (0.00)	—	-0.00*** (0.00)	—	-0.00 (0.00)	—	-0.00* (0.00)	—	-0.00 (0.00)
Coastline dummy	—	0.16** (0.07)	—	0.11 (0.11)	—	0.72*** (0.09)	—	0.19** (0.09)	—	0.77*** (0.07)	—	0.21*** (0.07)
Coast line perimeter (0-1)	—	-0.49** (0.21)	—	0.06 (0.37)	—	-0.24 (0.27)	—	-0.42 (0.28)	—	-0.43** (0.21)	—	-0.25 (0.21)
River dummy	—	0.05 (0.04)	—	0.01 (0.04)	—	0.31*** (0.04)	—	0.17*** (0.04)	—	0.07*** (0.02)	—	-0.01 (0.03)

Summer avg. temperature	—	-0.04*** (0.01)	—	0.01 (0.01)	—	0.03*** (0.01)	—	-0.02 (0.01)	—	-0.007 (0.006)	—	0.008 (0.007)
Winter avg. temperature	—	0.04*** (0.01)	—	0.01 (0.01)	—	-0.02*** (0.006)	—	0.00 (0.00)	—	-0.011** (0.004)	—	-0.02*** (0.005)
Average annual temperature	—	-0.04*** (0.01)	—	-0.00 (0.01)	—	0.04*** (0.008)	—	0.01 (0.01)	—	0.002 (0.005)	—	0.007 (0.007)
Average annual precipitation	—	0.00*** (0.00)	—	0.00 (0.00)	—	0.00 (0.00)	—	-0.00*** (0.00)	—	-0.000*** (0.000)	—	-0.000*** (0.000)
R^2	0.15	0.42	0.24	0.31	0.16	0.22	0.21	0.29	0.20	0.24	0.22	0.27
Number of observations	2,232	2,222	728	726	6,309	6,307	1,767	1,767	11,300	11,286	3,528	3,525
F-test	—	117.90	—	3.67	—	44.23	—	16.59	—	68.25	—	20.15

Notes: Robust standard errors are shown in parentheses. The F-test tests the joint significance of the controls included in the regression. Dashed cells indicate no entry.

***Significant at the 1 percent level.

**Significant at the 5 percent level.

*Significant at the 10 percent level.

Table 4.4   Log of population on capital city status for United States: 1900 and 1990

	1900		1990 (1900 sample)		1990	
	25,000+		25,000+		25,000+	
National capital	0.53***	0.52**	1.15***	0.80***	1.78***	1.82***
	(0.18)	(0.26)	(0.10)	(0.23)	(0.05)	(0.05)
State capital	0.14	0.26**	0.10	0.20*	0.35***	0.37***
	(0.13)	(0.11)	(0.14)	(0.11)	(0.11)	(0.11)
ln(landarea)	0.58***	0.58***	0.66***	0.72***	0.52***	0.48***
	(0.08)	(0.08)	(0.07)	(0.09)	(0.03)	(0.03)
Latitude	—	0.02	—	0.11*	—	0.02***
		(0.04)		(0.06)		(0.01)
Longitude	—	–0.02***	—	–0.03***	—	–0.01***
		(0.01)		(0.01)		(0.00)
Port dummy	—	0.50***	—	0.44***	—	0.71***
		(0.14)		(0.15)		(0.09)
River dummy	—	0.21**	—	–0.03	—	0.22***
		(0.10)		(0.10)		(0.06)
Precipitation	—	–0.00	—	–0.00***	—	–0.00***
(annual avg)		(0.00)		(0.00)		(0.00)
Temperature	—	0.06	—	0.16**	—	0.03***
(annual avg)		(0.05)		(0.08)		(0.01)
R^2	0.44	0.54	0.59	0.69	0.46	0.54
Number of Observations	160	160	157	157	1,066	1,066
F-test	557	217	531	284	8,875	3,632

Notes: Robust standard errors are shown in parentheses. The F-test tests the joint significance of th controls included in the regression. Dashed cells indicate no entry.
***Significant at the 1 percent level.
**Significant at the 5 percent level.
*Significant at the 10 percent level.

and 1990. However, for the sample of 1900 cities, the impact of state capitals on population continued to remain tiny at 11 percent, even in 1990.

As shown in table 4.6, there were significant variations with the Latin American countries. For the smaller sample of countries in 1900, national capital city effect was already quite significant for Argentina and Brazil and, to a lesser extent for Cuba, Chile, and Uruguay. On the other hand, provincial capital effect was only sizeable for Brazil. By 1990, the data indicate that the national and provincial capital city effects for a great majority of Latin American countries were greater than those for the United States. In some countries like Mexico, Colombia, and Peru, both national and provincial capitals played important roles; in Argentina and Chile, national capitals were more important than provincial capitals; and in Bolivia and Brazil, provincial capitals were more important than national capitals. However, Brazil's case is rather unusual since its national capital was changed from

Log of population on capital city status by country in Latin America, 1900 and 1990

		1900				1990			
		2,500+		25,000+		2,500+		25,000+	
		(1)	(2)	(1)	(2)	(1)	(2)	(1)	(2)
Argentina	National capital	4.95***	4.52***	3.54***	3.42***	3.93***	3.82***	3.17***	3.56***
	Provincial capital	0.59**	0.69***	0.49**	0.65***	2.02***	2.05***	1.10***	1.17***
	R^2	0.11	0.32	0.56	0.66	0.25	0.35	0.35	0.41
	Number of observations	365	365	73	73	489	489	245	245
	F-test	—							
Bolivia	National capital					1.11	0.58	1.12	1.14
	Provincial capital					1.97***	2.20***	1.35***	1.43***
	R^2					0.31	0.51	0.45	0.51
	Number of observations					109	106	68	67
	F-test								
Brazil	National capital	4.48***	4.85***	3.81***	3.94***	0.89***	1.87***	1.39***	1.30***
	Provincial capital	1.72***	1.89***	1.14***	1.30***	3.89***	3.46***	2.54***	2.46***
	R^2	0.13	0.30	0.30	0.36	0.13	0.23	0.23	0.28
	Number of observations	1469	1459	566	564	5269	5267	1222	1222
	F-test	—							
Chile	National capital	2.20***	2.00***	2.05***	1.97***	2.35***	2.12***	2.33***	2.00***
	Provincial capital	0.62***	0.60***	0.38***	0.41***	1.51***	1.44***	0.95***	1.13***
	R^2	0.39	0.52	0.45	0.55	0.33	0.75	0.46	0.70
	Number of observations	79	79	50	50	52	52	44	44
	F-test	—							
Colombia	National capital					3.50***	3.34***	3.31***	3.03***
	Provincial capital					2.49***	2.64***	1.73***	1.87***
	R^2					0.26	0.42	0.46	0.50
	Number of observations					1052	1051	251	251
	F-test								
Costa Rica	National capital	1.10***	1.08***			1.07***	1.19***	1.01***	0.95***
	Provincial capital	0.94**	0.96***			1.31***	1.11***	0.80***	0.77***
	R^2	0.66	0.80			0.25	0.41	0.37	0.61
	Number of observations	29	29			81	81	49	49
	F-test	—							

(continued)

Table 4.5 (continued)

		1900				1990			
		2,500+		25,000+		2,500+		25,000+	
		(1)	(2)	(1)	(2)	(1)	(2)	(1)	(2)
Cuba	National capital	2.23***	2.11***	1.96***	1.45	2.28***	2.33***	2.28***	2.36***
	Provincial capital	1.42***	1.49***	0.40***	0.77	1.70***	1.71***	1.56***	1.55***
	R^2	0.42	0.47	0.63	0.96	0.60	0.62	0.71	0.73
	Number of observations	120	120	16	16	155	155	134	134
	F-test								
Ecuador	National capital					2.78***	3.19***	2.66***	2.73***
	Provincial capital					1.54***	1.47***	1.04***	1.15***
	R^2					0.29	0.50	0.42	0.53
	Number of observations					214	212	97	96
	F-test								
El Salvador	National capital	1.84***	1.67***			1.90***	1.45***	1.45***	1.20***
	Provincial capital	1.11***	1.02***			1.31***	1.11***	0.40*	0.42**
	R^2	0.52	0.67			0.31	0.54	0.21	0.44
	Number of observations	151	151			244	244	54	54
	F-test	—				—			
Guatemala	National capital					2.79***	2.53***	2.63***	2.34***
	Provincial capital					0.89***	0.84***	0.45***	0.46***
	R^2					0.41	0.50	0.30	0.43
	Number of observations					327	327	141	141
	F-test								
Honduras	National capital					2.49***	2.48***	2.30***	2.19***
	Provincial capital					0.87***	0.70***	0.31	0.36
	R^2					0.53	0.73	0.47	0.65
	Number of observations					284	284	46	46
	F-test								
Mexico	National capital					5.86***	5.52***	4.95***	5.09***
	Provincial capital					2.94***	2.88***	1.97***	1.94***
	R^2					0.22	0.32	0.25	0.31
	Number of observations					2049	2049	689	689
	F-test					—			

Nicaragua	National capital			2.87***	2.01***	2.69***	2.06***
	Provincial capital			1.21***	1.13***	0.57***	0.60***
	R^2			0.51	0.64	0.59	0.70
	Number of observations			151	151	61	61
	F-test			—			
Panama	National capital			2.80***	2.34***	2.46***	1.88***
	Provincial capital			0.89***	0.81*	0.25	0.80**
	R^2			0.28	0.49	0.52	0.90
	Number of observations			72	72	20	20
	F-test			—			
Paraguay	National capital			3.76***	3.93***	2.25***	2.30***
	Provincial capital			1.25***	1.30***	0.34	0.57***
	R^2			0.17	0.34	0.34	0.52
	Number of observations			217	214	47	47
	F-test			—			
Peru	National capital			3.44***	2.97***	3.40***	3.03***
	Provincial capital			1.58***	1.52***	1.30***	1.28***
	R^2			0.39	0.55	0.48	0.57
	Number of observations			195	193	162	161
	F-test			—			
Uruguay	National capital	2.12**	3.44**	1.71	3.61*	1.71	3.61*
	Provincial capital	—	—	—	—	—	—
	R^2	0.62	0.87	0.57	0.85	0.57	0.85
	Number of observations	19	19	19	19	19	19
	F-test	—	—				
Venezuela	National capital			2.66***	2.49***	2.54***	2.38***
	Provincial capital			1.89***	1.90***	1.34***	1.41***
	R^2			0.27	0.35	0.38	0.45
	Number of observations			321	320	179	179
	F-test			—			

Note: The F-test tests the joint significance of the controls included in the regression. Dashed cells indicate no entry.

***Significant at the 1 percent level.

**Significant at the 5 percent level.

*Significant at the 10 percent level.

Table 4.6 Rank order of national and provincial/state capital coefficients, 1900 and 1990

N. capital (≥2,500)		P. capital (≥2,500)		N. capital (≥25,000)		P. capital (≥25,000)	
				1900			
Argentina	4.95	Brazil	1.72	Brazil	3.81	Brazil	1.14
Brazil	4.48	Cuba	1.42	Argentina	3.54	Argentina	0.49
Cuba	2.23	El Salvador	1.11	Chile	2.05	Cuba	0.40
Chile	2.20	Costa Rica	0.94	Cuba	1.96	Chile	0.38
Uruguay	2.12	Chile	0.62	U.S.	0.53	U.S.	0.14
El Salvador	1.84	Argentina	0.59				
Costa Rica	1.09						
				1990			
Mexico	5.86	Brazil	3.89	Mexico	4.95	Brazil	2.54
Argentina	3.93	Mexico	2.94	Peru	3.40	Mexico	1.97
Paraguay	3.76	Colombia	2.49	Colombia	3.31	Colombia	1.73
Colombia	3.50	Argentina	2.02	Argentina	3.17	Cuba	1.56
Peru	3.44	Bolivia	1.97	Nicaragua	2.69	Bolivia	1.35
Nicaragua	2.87	Venezuela	1.89	Ecuador	2.66	Venezuela	1.34
Panama	2.80	Cuba	1.70	Guatemala	2.63	Peru	1.30
Guatemala	2.79	Peru	1.58	Venezuela	2.54	Argentina	1.10
Ecuador	2.78	Ecuador	1.54	Panama	2.46	Ecuador	1.04
Venezuela	2.66	Chile	1.51	Chile	2.33	Chile	0.95
Honduras	2.49	El Salvador	1.31	Honduras	2.30	Costa Rica	0.80
Chile	2.35	Costa Rica	1.31	Cuba	2.28	Nicaragua	0.57
Cuba	2.28	Paraguay	1.25	Paraguay	2.25	Guatemala	0.45
Brazil[a]	2.19	Nicaragua	1.21	Brazil[a]	2.24	El Salvador	0.40
El Salvador	1.90	Panama	0.89	U.S.	1.78	U.S.	0.35
Bolivia	1.11	Guatemala	0.89	El Salvador	1.45	Paraguay	0.34
Costa Rica	1.07	Honduras	0.87	Brazil	1.39	Honduras	0.31
Brazil	0.89			Bolivia	1.12	Panama	0.25
				Costa Rica	1.01		

Notes: Regression coefficient of the log of population on capital dummies with land area control

Salvador to Rio de Janeiro and then to Brasilia. In general, the importance of provincial capitals in Latin America seems have grown over time. This result is particularly important since it can be considered a proof of the historical persistence of urban primacy. As long as the determinants of population distribution haven't changed during the twentieth century, the empirical evidence can also be the reflection of a set of institutional incentives that has remained unchanged—something in line with the arguments of Acemoglu, Johnson, and Robinson (2001) about the colonial origins of present differences in income.

In 1990, the impact of national capital status on population was the highest for Mexico (Mexico City) at 14,017 percent and then for Peru (Lima), Colombia (Bogota), and Argentina (Buenos Aires) at over 2,281 percent. By contrast, capitals in El Salvador (San Salvador), Brazil (Brasilia), Bolivia (Santa Cruz), and Costa Rica (San Jose) had lower impact than those of the United States (Washington, DC) and Canada (Ottawa). Interestingly, Brazil's previous capital, Rio de Janeiro, enjoyed greater ex-capital status benefits than its current capital. For the same year, provincial capital status increased population by 1,167 percent in Brazil, 617 percent in Mexico, 464 percent in Colombia, and 376 percent in Cuba. In Bolivia, Venezuela, and Peru, the figure was around 282 percent; Argentina, Ecuador, and Chile was around 200 percent; only Honduras and Panama's provincial capitals had smaller impacts than the United States' state capitals.

4.4   The Historical Roots of Urban Primacy in the Americas

Having presented the empirical results of our study, it is useful now to explore the historical process that is behind the present outcome. To do so, in this section we compare and contrast the forces that led to differences in political centralization in the Americas and, ultimately, to divergent patterns in urbanization. Central and South America had historically more centralized regimes than North America, which is deeply decentralized—even at municipal levels. As we will see, these differences may have emerged from different patterns of colonial administration, which at the same time have also been determined by factor endowments as Engerman and Sokoloff (1997) suggest.

The modern United States was, in the sixteenth century, a vast and scarcely populated territory deprived of mineral resources considered valuable in the European continent in those times; the soil quality and climate made the region apt only for grain cultivation and livestock raising. Given the set of relative prices existent in that period—with precious metals and tropical products being highly valuated—those activities were not particularly profitable and, therefore, the flow of resources toward British North America was significantly lower than the one directed to the silver-mining regions of Mexico and Bolivia or to the coffee plantations in Brazil. In fact, the first settlers of North America were not economic migrants but, rather, political migrants, while the millions of Africans brought to Central and South America were used as slaves in mines and plantations. In this context, British North America saw the emergence of a *market-preserving federalism,* as explained in North, Summerhill, and Weingast (2000). Northern American colonies faced strong competition between one another for scarce capital and labor and any colony that failed to promote and protect markets simply failed to grow and was ultimately lead to disappear; as North, Summerhill, and Weingast indicate, successful colonies adapted local institutions to suit local needs. Colonial assemblies—where settlers were represented—were central in the administration system, which was funded with local taxes and provided for economic and religious freedom to the inhabitants. When independence was achieved in the late eighteenth century, the newly founded United States was organized as prescripted by market-preserving federalism. The national government's powers were limited to truly national public goods such as national security and market integration; decisions influencing everyday economic and social issues were reserved to the states, whose different preferences could allow them to enact different laws. In terms of the theoretical arguments mentioned in previous sections, then, the value given to the mainland's welfare by the federal authorities was quite low; the hinterland's welfare was key for the political stability of the country, given the great deal of autonomy the states enjoyed under the British Empire and expected to preserve after independence. In fact, as North, Summerhill, and Weingast point out, the revolutionary wars were triggered by the sudden eagerness for funding by the Crown after the Seven Years War—something seen by Americans as a challenge to their financial autonomy. If such a pattern was to be reproduced at the federal level—a central government eager for taxes collected from the states—then the stability of the union itself could be threatened. Urban primacy in the United States was limited not only by the relatively balanced interest of the authorities on the welfare of its citizens, but also by the rather uniform productivities across the original thirteen colonies. In fact, *market-preserving federalism* resulted in the failure of unproductive colonies and, ultimately, in the survival of the most productive ones—whose productivity should have been similar in a competitive common market.

The pattern for Spanish America was radically different. As indicated by Cortés Conde (2008), the Spanish colonial administration was completely centered on the exploitation of silver mines in New Spain (modern Mexico) and the Upper Perú (Bolivia). As the mines were located far from coasts and navigable rivers, the Spanish were forced to establish a transport network formed by several cities that served as waypoints on the long journeys and provided the mining areas with basic supplies. The centrality of silver mining owed not only to the high intrinsic value of its produce, but also to the short-term horizon of the Spanish Crown, which was not interested in the long-term economic development of its colonies. All these geographical and political considerations resulted in a large and heavily centralized administration. In order to ensure the flow of bullion to Spain, the Crown concentrated trade only in four ports across two continents (one in Spain and three in the Americas) and restricted intercolonial trade. As Cortés Conde points out, the local representative of the King, the Viceroy, did not share his power with local assemblies, which lacked any autonomy. Taxes were decided by officials appointed in Spain and its revenues were sent to the Crown after deducting the expenses of local administration. When the Spanish American colonies became independent in the early nineteenth century, the institutional organization they inherited was, thus, heavily centralized. As the colonial political system was based on the exchange of economic and political rights by support and loyalty to the Crown (North, Summerhill, and Weingast 2000), rent-seeking lobbyists were expected to locate themselves close to the Viceroy's seat. The cities that were the seat of Viceroys and General Captains during the Spanish domination became the capitals of the new countries, whose organization intended to reproduce at local scale the old colonial system. In this sense, the welfare of the mainland—as opposed to the hinterland—was of special importance for the new independent authorities, since the most important corporations and lobbyists that the previous regime had catered for with privileges in exchange for loyalty were located in the national capitals. The organization of Latin American states was nevertheless not a rapid process; in spite of the centralizing forces of the new institutional regime, the disappearance of the Spanish colonial authority led many subnational entities to revolt and claim their autonomy—only after several years of internal fighting did the new nations find a stable political equilibrium which, in almost all of the cases, mirrored the colonial organization. Except for Mexico, Argentina, and Venezuela, the rest of the Spanish Latin American countries organized themselves in a unitary system. And even in the federal countries, the capital cities were among the winner parties of the civil wars.

After the dust had settled, the historical comparison of the economic development of the United States and Latin America showed a strikingly growing gap between them: in 1700, the per capita income of both regions was the same; in 1820 the U.S. average was 1.81 times the Latin American average, in 1870 it was 3.61 times, in 1900 3.67 times, and in 1990 4.57 times (data from Maddison 2003). If the different institutional arrangements of both regions may explain this growing income gap over time, then the politically driven patterns of population distribution can account for a share of that difference. As we have described in the previous paragraphs, the institutional settings of British North America and Latin America were radically different and, while the former favored a more balanced distribution of population, the other one laid incentives toward concentration around the capital city.

4.5 Case Studies: United States and Argentina

One last point of concern to our analysis is the fact that political capitals may have been chosen because of particular economic characteristics that we did not take into account in our empirical analysis carried out in section 4.3. In order to rest assured that it was not the case, in this section we describe the historical process by which two different countries in the region, the United States and Argentina, determined both their national and provincial capitals, showing that mainly political factors—and not economical ones—were behind those decisions. The events surrounding the establishment of the national capitals of the United States and Argentina are a clear depiction of their different political and economic settings. In the first case, market-preserving federalism had created a series of productive and autonomous colonies, whereas in the second case the old viceroyal seat, Buenos Aires, was the center of all the economic and political activity of the country, with the rest of the urban agglomerations being almost deprived of resources.

In the United States, the representatives of the newly formed thirteen states debated repeatedly and contentiously over the location of the nation's capital between 1774 and 1790. The debate pitted the northern federalists who desired a strong federal government against southern antifederalists who favored a loose federation of decentralized state governments. Several factors militated against locating the capital in a major commercial center. Because of a famous incident in Philadelphia, the Congress unanimously agreed that the federal government rather than the state in which it is located would have complete jurisdiction of the federal city.[7] Given the lack of representation of the citizens of the federal district, many antifederalists feared the corrupting influences of locating the capital in a major commercial center.[8] Moreover, locating a federal district in a major commercial center created greater conflicts with the state in which it is located. Indeed, Philadelphia was removed as a candidate because Pennsylvania refused to yield its jurisdiction over its major port city. In the end, in 1790 James Madison, in a political bargain with Alexander Hamilton, secured the national capital in the South.

The Compromise of 1790, which established the location of the U.S. capital, is well-known. Hamilton, desiring a strong central government, desperately wanted the new national government to assume the state debts incurred during the Revolutionary War. The assumption of state debts,

7. In 1774, when the Continental army soldiers with arms demanded their pay and surrounded the Philadelphia State House where the Congress met, the congressmen requested the Philadelphia Council to disband the soldiers using their state militia. However, the Council refused and the Congress adjourned to Princeton, New Jersey. This famous incident caused Congress to seek exclusive jurisdiction over the federal district.

8. When Congress voted in 1783 to create a federal district with exclusive jurisdiction over no more than thirty-six square miles, antifederalists feared that the nation's capital would be larger and potentially more corrupt than Philadelphia or even London (see Bowling 1988).

Hamilton believed, would align the incentives of the creditors with a strong federal government. However, Madison and other southerners viewed assumption as usurpation of state authority by the federal government and blocked it accordingly. In a well-known dinner mediated by Thomas Jefferson, Madison and Hamilton reached a compromise. If Hamilton could deliver the location of the nation's capital in the South along the Potomac, Madison would allow the assumption bill to go through the House.

In Argentina, the fight over the location of the national capital was less about where to locate it than who would rule it, as few places could compete against Buenos Aires. From its early beginnings, Buenos Aires was a commercial and administrative center for Spain. In 1618, it became the seat of a governorship over a vast territory; in 1776, it became a viceroyal capital that controlled the present-day areas of Argentina, Bolivia, Paraguay, Uruguay, and northern parts of Chile. The primacy of Buenos Aires was based on the control of the Potosi silver trade through its port which was, nevertheless, not the best one in the Rio de la Plata Basin due to its extremely shallow draft. With the concentration of lawyers, bureaucrats, priests, military officers, artisans, soldiers, laborers, and slaves, Buenos Aires possessed 40,000 inhabitants by the end of the eighteenth century. Thus, when Argentina became independent in the early nineteenth century, Buenos Aires had been the dominant political capital of the region for almost 200 years.

With independence from Spain in 1810, the federalists of the hinterland provinces and the centralists of the Buenos Aires province fought repeatedly for the control of the city of Buenos Aires. Yet, no matter who won, the city of Buenos Aires remained the de facto capital. The collapse of the central government in 1820 led to more than thirty years of a virtual acephalic government, in which the powerful governor of Buenos Aires, Juan Manuel de Rosas, exercised most of the ordinary powers attributed to national authorities. When Argentineans established a constitutional government with strong centralized powers in the office of the presidency in 1853, presidents consistently vetoed attempts to locate the capital in Córdoba or Rosario—a port city with even better conditions for the docking of ships than Buenos Aires—and chose Buenos Aires as the capital city (Rock 1987). Since the only substantial and reliable government revenue came from duties and tariffs collected at the port in Buenos Aires, Scobie (1974, 105) writes that the "control of the city became virtually synonymous with control of the nation, and any truly national authority took the city as its seat."[9] Initially, the constitution also designated the city of Buenos Aires

9. In 1790, New York City, like Buenos Aires in 1880, was a major commercial port city with a rich agricultural hinterland. It also possessed a sizeable potential government income from taxes on foreign trade. Why did New York City not evolve into a major political capital city like Buenos Aires? First, unlike Buenos Aires, a city that wielded significant influence over its province, New York City was a creature of the New York state. In the colonial period, the actions of the city council needed the approval of the governor (Burrows and Wallace

as the federal capital to be independent of the province of Buenos Aires. But when Buenos Aires province refused to cede the control of its port city, the two governments shared the capital. When the dual use of the capital city proved unsatisfactory, the issue was finally resolved militarily as the federal forces claimed the city of Buenos Aires and detached it from the province of Buenos Aires in 1880.

In the United States, political decentralization was a major force at both the national and at the state level in the choice of capital city locations. In the national sphere, states' rights decentralized power to the states, and in the state arena, power was further decentralized to small towns and rural areas as state legislatures limited the powers of the executive branch by locating capitals away from population centers and by implementing apportionment schemes favoring small localities. In the American colonies prior to independence, legislatures often met in major coastal cities such as Boston, New York, and Philadelphia. With independence, however, the antifederalist state legislatures fought successfully to move state capitals to central locations that were largely rural.[10] Thus, except for Massachusetts and Maryland, the other eleven former colonies moved their state capitals from the eastern coast to a geographically more central location.

In Argentina, many of the cities that became provincial capitals after independence, like Buenos Aires, were initially located by the Spanish Crown to serve as administrative and military centers. Because the Potosi silver mines in Upper Peru were in a remote location, this network of cities located in intervals of 150 miles started with fewer than 100 settlers each (Cortés Conde 2008; Scobie 1988). However, with the growth of the silver trade, these Spanish cities grew in administrative and commercial importance. At the time of independence from Spain, because of their size and political influence, these cities acquired territorial hegemony over their provincial areas and essentially became de facto provincial capitals. As in Buenos Aires, the provincial landowners and elites resided in the capital and used their power to concentrate provincial resources in their city. But, unlike Buenos Aires, these provincial capitals often lacked sufficient fiscal resources and relied on provincial and national governments for expenditures of local public goods (Scobie 1988). In most provinces, except for their capital, there were no other competing secondary cities.

In the United States, cities were creatures of states, and state governments

---

1999). Second, the state's tax policies were dominated by small towns and farms who controlled the state assembly (Brown 1993). Import taxes acted as a subsidy to the hinterland in terms of lower property taxes. Indeed, New York City could not even maintain its standing as its own state capital. Third, New York City, unlike Buenos Aires, could not create an artificial monopoly because it could not hinder trade to other port cities.

10. James Madison in 1790: "In every instance where the seat of Government has been placed in an uncentral position, we have seen people struggling to place it where *it ought to be*." Because travel in the eighteenth century was difficult and time consuming, equal rights of inhabitants required the government to be as central as possible. See Zagarri (1987).

possessed authority over cities and other local governments. In Argentina, as elsewhere in Latin America, cities began as military outposts designed to control the indigenous population in the countryside. Thus, the jurisdiction of the city was not restricted to a specific area and often extended to the rural countryside (Portes 1976). In Argentina, the capital cities controlled the hinterlands; in the United States, hinterlands often controlled the capital cities. In both cases, nevertheless, capital cities were chosen not because of economic considerations but, rather, by political considerations. This allows us safely to conclude that, for the cases of the United States and Argentina, the long-run economic consequences of having a determined political regime—decentralized in one case, centralized in the other—are independent of the particular cities that were to become their national and provincial capitals.

4.6   Conclusion

This chapter examines the causes of urban primacy in the Americas using the insight that the law of primacy is highly correlated with the "Law of Capitals." Using extensive data on cities in Latin America and North America, we estimate the impact of national and provincial capital city dummies on population controlling for a variety of factors that might contribute to urban productivity. We find that national and provincial capital city statuses played a much greater role in causing population concentration in Latin America than in North America. However, there were important variations across the countries within Latin America. The "Law of Capitals" seems to have held to a much greater extent in countries like Mexico, Argentina, and Brazil but to a lesser extent in countries like Paraguay and El Salvador.

Our findings suggest that urban primacy in major Latin American countries such as Mexico, Argentina, Chile, and others were caused by political centralization that placed greater weight on the welfare of capital city residents. In many Latin American countries, especially in those whose land-ownership was concentrated, major landowners often resided permanently in the national and provincial capitals. In these places, the political and economic interests of landowners and capitalists were intimately intertwined by marriage and many sought to control national and provincial affairs from their capital cities (Zeitlin and Ratcliff 1988). For example, in Argentina, the powers of the federal government were centralized in Buenos Aires, and as the capital city had substantial representation in national politics as it elected 20 percent of the congressional deputies and two of thirty senators. The president was the "immediate and local head of the Capital of the Nation" and appointed the municipal executive or the intendente (Walter 1993).

In the United States, by contrast, political and economic elites rarely resided in capital cities. Washington, DC remained dismally backward and small well into the nineteenth century and has only recently become a major center of political lobbyists (Green 1962). In most states, capitals were intentionally located in the small towns and rural areas in geographically central locations. Because rural and small town interests were often overrepresented in state legislatures, the large urban centers, unlike their counterparts in Latin America, did not possess disproportionate political advantages. Consequently, national and state expenditures on infrastructures such as roads and highways and education were often biased toward rural areas and small towns and fostered the growth of smaller municipalities.

The variations in political centralization in the Americas is likely to have deep colonial roots (North 1991; Engerman and Sokoloff 1997, 2002; Acemoglu, Johnson, and Robinson 2001). In colonial Iberian Latin America, in contrast to colonial British North America, many contend that the Spanish and, to a lesser extent, the Portuguese, left a deep imprint of strong central governments and weak local governments (Portes 1976; Nickson 1995). Whereas the cities and towns in the British American colonies, especially in the North, possessed considerable political autonomy in the election of city leaders, those in Latin America were often appointed or auctioned. Sokoloff and Zolt (2006) argue that the differences in early colonial inequality influenced the sources of revenues and expenditures for federal, state, and local governments in the Americas. In the United States, localities were allowed to choose instruments of taxation such as property tax (Becker 1980) whereas those in Latin America possessed a weak capacity to raise revenues as direct taxes on property were not allowed (Nickson 1995).

Data Appendix
Definitions and Sources

Latin America

Population is the total for second administrative division (municipality in general).

Sources for 1900: Argentina: National Census (1914); Brasil: National Census (1937); Chile: National Census (1907); Costa Rica: National Census (1892); Cuba: National Census (1097); El Salvador: National Census (1930); Uruguay: National Census (1908).

Sources for 1990: Argentina: INDEC, Censo Nacional de Población, Hogares y Viviendas (2001); Bolivia: INE, Censo Nacional de Población y Vivienda (2001); Brazil: IBGE, Contagem da População (2007) y Estimativas da População (2007); Chile: INE, XVII Censo Nacional de Población y VI de Vivienda (2002); Colombia: DANE, Censo General (2005); Costa Rica: INEC, IX Censo Nacional de Población y V de Vivienda (2000); Cuba: ONE, Anuario Estadístico Cuba (2006); Ecuador: INEC, VI Censo de Población y V de Vivienda (2001); El Salvador: DIGESTYC, VI Censo Nacional de Población y V de Vivienda (2007); Guatemala: INE, XI Censo Nacional de Población y VI de Habitación (2002); Honduras: INE, Censo de Población y Vivienda (2001); Mexico: INEGI, II Conteo de Población y Vivienda (2005); Nicaragua: INEC, VIII Censo Nacional de Población y IV de Vivienda (2005); Panama: DEC, X Censo de Población y VI de Vivienda (2000); Paraguay: DGEEC, Censo Nacional de Población y Viviendas (2002); Peru: INEI, X Censo de Población y V de Vivienda (2005); Uruguay: VIII Censo General de Población, IV de Hogares y VI de Viviendas—Fase I (2004); Venezuela: INE, XIII Censo General de Población y Vivienda (2001).

Land area is squared kilometers for second administrative division.

Sources for 1900: Except for the case of Brazil, where the data were available, the land area of other countries was estimated using that of the contemporary second administrative division.

Sources for 1990: Argentina: INDEC, Censo Nacional de Población, Hogares y Viviendas (2001); Bolivia: INE, Estadísticas Departamentales (2005); Brazil: IBGE; Chile: INE, División Político-Administrativa y Censal (2001); Colombia: DANE, Costa Rica: Nonofficial website (www. sitiosdecostarica.com); Cuba: ONE, Anuario Estadístico (2007); Ecuador: INEC; El Salvador: DIGESTYC; Guatemala: INE; Honduras: Asociación de Municipios de Honduras; Mexico: INEGI; Nicaragua: Instituto Nicaragüense de Estudios Territoriales; Panama: DEC; Paraguay: DGEEC; Peru: INEI; Venezuela: INE.

Latitude, Longitude, Altitude.

Sources: Google Earth: Release 4.3. Sea dummy, coastal perimeter (coast perimeter divided by total perimeter), river dummy were defined using country maps.

Average summer temperature (January), average winter temperature (July), average annual temperature, precipitation (mm).

Sources: World Meteorological Organization and National Statistical Institutes.

United States

1900: U.S. Census Bureau, Abstract of the 12th Census 1900. The river and port variables constructed using Google. map. Longitude, latitude from various websites.

1950: U.S. Census Bureau, Statistical Abstract of the U.S., 1955.

1990: U.S. Department of Commerce, City and County Data Book, 1994.

Appendix

A Simple Model of Political Centralization and Urban Primacy

In this section we propose a simple model of political centralization and population distribution. As in Ades and Glaeser (1995), we will divide each political region into two locations, the main city and the hinterland, and model the behavior of the local governments. However, and in line with our empirical strategy, a political region may not necessarily mean a country, but can also imply a province and its municipalities. Following Ennis, Pinto, and Porto (2006), each agent has an endowment of one unit of labor that they supply inelastically, and derives utility from its net income (wage minus taxes). Each of the two locations produces the same homogeneous good with a Cobb-Douglas production function:

$$q_i = A_i L_i^\alpha G_i^{1-\alpha} \qquad \alpha \in (0,1) i = M, H,$$

where M implies mainland, H means hinterland, A_i is the productivity of each location, L_i is the population, and G_i is the level of a public good that contributes to the production of the homogeneous good. Normalizing the output price, the profit maximizing condition determines the real wage level:

$$w_i = \alpha A_i \left(\frac{G_i}{L_i} \right)^{1-\alpha}.$$

Note that the wage level is decreasing in population, reflecting the decreasing marginal returns of labor. This result can also encompass the congestion effect in Ades and Glaeser (1995). However, wages will be higher the more productive a region is and the more it invests in the public good.

Decentralization

In a decentralized scenario, the government in each location chooses the level of public good G_i and taxes the population with a uniform lump sum tax τ_i to finance this investment. The objective of the government is to maximize the net income $w_i - \tau_i$ and the budget constraint is given by $G_i = \tau_i L_i^\beta$, where parameter $\beta \in (0,1)$ reflects scale inefficiencies in revenue raising by the local powers. Given this, the local government problem can be stated as

$$\max_{\tau_i} \alpha A_i \left(\frac{G_i}{L_i} \right)^{1-\alpha} - \tau_i$$

$$\text{s.t. } G_i = \tau_i L_i^\beta,$$

which gives a maximized objective function for the two locations:

$$w_i^*(A_i, L_i) = [\alpha^{1+\alpha}(1 - \alpha)^{1-\alpha} A_i L_i^{(\beta-1)(1-\alpha)}]^{1/a}$$

We will assume costless migration between locations, which implies that in equilibrium net income in both locations will be equalized:

$$w_M^*(A_M, L_M) = w_H^*(A_H, L_H)$$

This gives a relation between L_M and L_H:

(1)
$$\frac{L_M}{L_H} = \left(\frac{A_M}{A_H}\right)^{1/[(1-\alpha)(1-\beta)]}$$

and the condition $L_M + L_H = L$ closes the model.

As a secondary result, we get that the tax level in both locations will be the same:

$$\tau_i^* = \left\{\alpha(1-\alpha)\left[\frac{A_M^{1/[(1-\alpha)(1-\beta)]} + A_H^{1/[(1-\alpha)(1-\beta)]}}{L}\right]^{(1-\alpha)(1-\beta)}\right\}^{1/\alpha}.$$

This means that the level of public goods in the more populated location will be higher and that wage levels will be equalized in both locations. Thus, the distribution of population will serve to compensate productivity differences between areas. As we can see in equation (1), the population distribution will be given by the relative productivity differences between both locations. In a decentralized scenario, the mainland will be more populated only if it is more productive than the hinterland.

Centralization

In the centralized case, there is one central government that rules on both locations and has the power to excise taxes and decide on the level of expenditure on public goods. We will simplify this twofold decision of tax and expenditure level on both locations by assuming that the central government chooses the same tax level in both locations but can provide different quantities of the public good. Thus, total revenue will be given by $G_M + G_H = \tau L^\beta$ and we will define $\theta = G_M/(G_M + G_H)$ as the share of expenditure of the public good in the mainland. The central government problem will be:

$$\max_{\theta, t} \gamma\left[aA_M\left(\frac{G_M}{L_M}\right)^{1-\alpha} - \tau\right] + (1-\gamma)\left[\alpha A_H\left(\frac{G_H}{L_H}\right)^{1-\alpha} - \tau\right]$$

$$\text{s.t. } G_M = \theta\tau L^\beta, G_H = (1-\theta)\tau L^\beta,$$

where parameter $\gamma \in (0,1)$ represents the level of political centralization in the region. A larger γ will imply that the mainland has more political power and is therefore more relevant in the political considerations of the central government.

The maximizing condition for θ is independent of the tax level:

$$(2) \qquad \frac{\theta^*}{1-\theta^*} = \left[\frac{A_M}{A_H} \frac{\gamma}{1-\gamma} \left(\frac{L_H}{L_M} \right)^{1-\alpha} \right]^{1/\alpha}.$$

The costless migration assumption implies in this case that:

$$\alpha A_M \left(\frac{G_M}{L_M} \right)^{1-\alpha} - \tau = \alpha A_H \left(\frac{G_H}{L_H} \right)^{1-\alpha} - t$$

and using $G_M = \theta \tau L^\beta$, $G_H = (1-\theta)\tau L^\beta$ gives

$$(3) \qquad \frac{L_M}{L_H} = \left(\frac{A_M}{A_H} \right)^{1/(1-\alpha)} \frac{\theta}{1-\theta}.$$

Using equations (2) and (3) we arrive at $\theta^* = \gamma$ and

$$(4) \qquad \frac{L_M}{L_H} = \left(\frac{A_M}{A_H} \right)^{1/(1-\alpha)} \frac{\gamma}{1-\gamma}.$$

The model is closed with the condition $L_M + L_H = L$.

The tax rate is given by

$$\tau^* = \left\{ \frac{\alpha(1-\alpha)}{L^{(1-\alpha)(1-\beta)}} [\gamma A_M^{1/(1-\alpha)} + (1-\gamma) A_H^{1/(1-\alpha)}]^{(1-\alpha)} \right\}^{1/\alpha}$$

which can easily be shown to be smaller than τ_i^*, the tax rate in the decentralized case. With a central government, there is no competition among political authorities between localities and as a result there is a lower provision of public goods: $\tau^* L^\beta < \tau_M^* L_M^\beta + \tau_H^* L_H^\beta$.

The main result is equation (4), which shows that the population distribution in the centralized case is given by productivity differences and also by the level of political centralization. Urban concentration will be higher the larger is γ. However, the model does not predict that a centralized structure will always imply a larger degree of urban concentration. If the central authority assigns a sufficiently balanced weight to the welfare of both localities, urban primacy will be lower in the centralized scenario.[11] Comparing equation (4) with equation (1), we show that urban concentration will be higher if and only if γ exceeds a certain threshold:

$$\gamma > \frac{A_M^{\beta/[(1-\beta)(1-\alpha)]}}{A_M^{\beta/[(1-\beta)(1-\alpha)]} + A_H^{\beta/[(1-\beta)(1-\alpha)]}}.$$

The results of the model are illustrated in figure 4A.1.

11. As an example, take $\gamma = 1/2$.

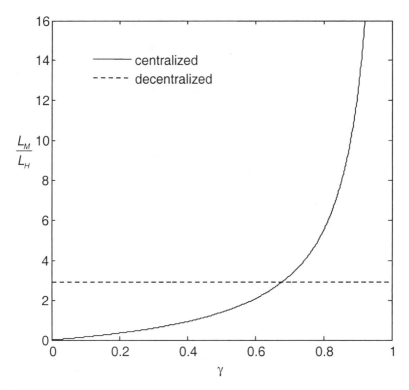

Fig. 4A.1   Population ratios
Notes: α = 0.3, β = 0.7, A_M = 5, A_H = 4, L = 100

References

Acemoglu, Daron, Simon Johnson, and James A. Robinson. 2001. "The Colonial Origins of Comparative Development: An Empirical Investigation." *American Economic Review* 91:1369–1401.

Ades, A. F., and E. L. Glaeser. 1995. "Trade and Circuses: Explaining Urban Giants." *Quarterly Journal of Economics* 110:195–227.

Becker, Robert A. 1980. *Revolution, Reform, and the Politics of American Taxation, 1763–1783.* Baton Rouge: Louisiana State University Press.

Bowling, Kenneth R. 1988. *Creating the Federal City, 1774–1800: Potomac Fever.* Washington, DC: American Institute of Architects Press.

Brown, Roger H. 1993. Redeeming the Republic: Federalists, Taxation, and the Origins of the Constitution. Baltimore: Johns Hopkins University Press.

Bulmer-Thomas, Victor. 2003. *The Economic History of Latin America Since Independence.* 2nd ed. New York: Cambridge University Press.

Burrows, Edwin G. and Mike Wallace. 1999. Gotham: A History of New York City to 1898. New York: Oxford University Press.

Campante, Filipe R., and Quoc-Anh Do. 2009. "A Centered Index of Spatial Concentration: Expected Influence Approach and Application to Population and Capital Cities." Harvard University. Working Paper.

Cortés Conde, Roberto. 2008. "Spanish America Colonial Patterns: The Rio de la Plata." Universidad de San Andrés, Department de Economia. Working Paper.

Diaz-Cayeros, Alberto. 2006. *Federalism, Fiscal Authority, and Centralization in Latin America.* Cambridge: Cambridge University Press.

Engerman, Stanley L., and Kenneth L. Sokoloff. 1997. "Factor Endowments, Institutions, and Differential Paths of Growth Among New World Economies: A View From Economic Historians of the United States." In *How Latin America Fell Behind: Essays on the Economic Histories of Brazil and Mexico 1800–1914,* edited by Stephen Haber, 260–306. Stanford: Stanford University Press.

———. 2002. "Factor Endowments, Inequality, and Paths of Development Among New World Economies." *Economia* 3:41–102.

Ennis, Huberto M., Santiago M. Pinto, and Alberto Porto. 2006. "Choosing a Place to Live and a Workplace." *Económica* 52:15–50.

Green, Constance M. 1962. *Washington: Village and Capital, 1800–1878.* Princeton, NJ: Princeton University Press.

Henderson, J. Vernon. 2002. "Urbanization in Developing Countries." *World Bank Research Observer* 17:89–112.

Jefferson, Mark. 1939. "The Law of the Primate City." *Geographical Review* 29: 226–32.

Kandell, Jonathan. 1988. *La Capital: The Biography of Mexico City.* New York: Random House.

Kim, Sukkoo. 2000. "Urban Development in the United States, 1690–1990." *Southern Economic Journal* 66:855–80.

Maddison, Angus. 2003. *The World Economy: Historical Statistics.* Paris: OECD.

McGreevey, William P. 1971. "A Statistical Analysis of Primacy and Lognormality in the Size Distribution of Latin American Cities, 1750–1960." In *The Urban Development of Latin America 1750–1920,* edited by Richard Morse. Stanford: Stanford University Press.

Morse, Richard M. 1971. "Latin American Cities in the 19th Century: Approaches and Tentative Generalizations." In *The Urban Development of Latin America 1750–1920,* edited by Richard Morse. Stanford: Stanford University Press.

Myers, David J. 2002. "The Dynamics of Local Empowerment: An Overview." In *Capital City Politics in Latin America: Democratization and Empowerment,* edited by D. Myers and H. Dietz. Boulder, CO: Lynne Rienner Publishers.

Myers, David J. and Henry A. Dietz, eds. 2002. *Capital City Politics in Latin America: Democratization and Empowerment.* Boulder, CO: Lynne Rienner Publishers.

Nickson, R. Andrew. 1995. *Local Government in Latin America.* Boulder, CO: Lynne Rienner Publishers.

North, Douglass C. 1991. *Institutions, Institutional Change and Economic Performance.* Cambridge: Cambridge University Press.

North, Douglass C., William Summerhill, and Barry R. Weingast. 2000. "Order, Disorder, and Economic Change: Latin America versus North America." In *Governing for Prosperity,* edited by Bruce Bueno de Mesquita and Hilton L. Root, 17–58. New Haven: Yale University Press.

Portes, Alejandro. 1976. "The Economy and Ecology of Urban Poverty." In *Urban Latin America,* edited by A. Portes and J. Walton. Austin: University of Texas Press.

Rock, David. 1987. *Argentina 1516–1987: From Spanish Colonization to Alfonsin.* Berkeley: University of California Press.

Rosen, Kenneth T., and Mitchel Resnick. 1980. "The Size Distribution of Cities: An

Examination of the Pareto Law and Primacy." *Journal of Urban Economics* 8: 165–86.

Scobie, James R. 1974. *Buenos Aires: Plaza to Suburb, 1870–1910.* New York: Oxford University Press.

———. 1988. *Secondary Cities of Argentina: The Social History of Corrientes, Salta, and Mendoza, 1850–1910.* Stanford: Stanford University Press.

Skowronek, Stephen. 1982. *Building a New American State: The Expansion of National Administrative Capacities 1877–1920.* Cambridge: Cambridge University Press.

Sokoloff, Kenneth L., and Eric M. Zolt. 2007. "Inequality and the Evolution of Institutions of Taxation: Evidence from the Economic History of the Americas." In The Decline of Latin American Economies: Growth, Institutions, and Crises, edited by S. Edwards, G. Esquivel, and G. Márquez, 83–138. Cambridge, MA: National Bureau of Economic Research.

Wallis, John J. 2000. "American Government Finance in the Long Run: 1790 to 1990." *Journal of Economic Perspectives* 14:61–82.

Walter, Richard J. 1993. *Politics and Urban Growth in Buenos Aires: 1910–1942.* Cambridge: Cambridge University Press.

———. 2005. *Politics and Urban Growth in Santiago, Chile 1891–1941.* Stanford: Stanford University Press.

Wheaton, W., and H. Shishido. 1981. "Urban Concentration, Agglomeration Economies and the Level of Economic Development." *Economic Development and Cultural Change* 30:17–30.

Zagarri, Rosemarie. 1987. *The Politics of Size: Representation in the United States, 1776–1850.* Ithaca, NY: Cornell University Press.

Zeitlin, Maurice, and Richard E. Ratcliff. 1988. *Landlords and Capitalists: The Dominant Class of Chile.* Princeton, NJ: Princeton University Press.

5

History, Geography, and the Markets for Mortgage Loans in Nineteenth-Century France

Philip T. Hoffman, Gilles Postel-Vinay, and Jean-Laurent Rosenthal

5.1 Introduction: Inequality, Endowments, and Market Institutions

From his early articles on Early American manufacturing onward, much of Kenneth Sokoloff's research focused on how access and distance to markets changed individual behavior and in turn influenced subsequent market development. In particular, he emphasized the positive effects of large, competitive markets (1984, 1988). We take up this theme in a different context—mid-nineteenth-century French mortgage markets. Credit markets are often thought to benefit from larger scale, most simply because borrowers and lenders will benefit from having access to more potential counterparties. Such a larger population of potential partners in transactions might arise in a large city or if the countryside is dense with small market towns. It would also arise if individuals were willing to travel some distance to secure investment opportunities or capital.

In the case of credit, however, the large competitive markets do carry a danger: as markets get bigger, asymmetric information becomes an increasingly serious problem. In particular, a lender rarely knows whether borrow-

Philip T. Hoffman is the Rea A. and Lela G. Axline Professor of Business Economics and professor of history at the California Institute of Technology. Gilles Postel-Vinay is director of research at the National Institute for Agricultural Research (INRA) and director of studies at the School for Advanced Studies in Social Sciences (EHESS). Jean-Laurent Rosenthal is the Rea A. and Lela G. Axline Professor of Business Economics and executive officer for the Social Sciences at the California Institute of Technology, and a research economist at the National Bureau of Economic Research.

The authors would like to thank Macha Chichtchenkova, Alena Lapatiovna, and Asli Sumer for many a trip to local archives and for assistance in coding the data. The authors are grateful for the support of the National Science Foundation, the Russell Sage Foundation, the Dean of Social Sciences and the Department of Economics at UCLA, the Division of Humanities and Social Sciences at Caltech, and INRA.

ers will repay or whether forfeited collateral will compensate for default. As a result, an individual may prefer to participate in a small market where information is good than in a large one where it is poor.

One solution is to have the lender investigate borrowers, but if the borrowers are not nearby, the lender will likely rely on agents to carry out the investigation. If so, then the lender will be vulnerable to the agents' misbehavior. Such moral hazard is not just a recent creation of venal mortgage originators eager to sign virtually anyone up for subprime loans. It is in fact an old problem, as shown by the history of the east coast mortgage companies who hired agents to originate loans in the Great Plains in the late nineteenth century. A land boom and competition from new mortgage companies led the agents to relax their lending standards, which provoked huge losses after a drought struck the Plains (Snowden 1995).

Instead of having a lender or his agents investigate borrowers, the borrowers can conceivably seek out lenders and convince them of their creditworthiness. If the borrowers do not employ agents in their search, they will avoid the sort of moral hazard problems afflicting lenders. But if (as is likely) they operate on a smaller scale than lenders, then the costs of searching may make it relatively expensive for them to look far from home. If so, they will borrow nearby, and the lenders will risk having too many local loans in their portfolios, which will leave them vulnerable to local economic shocks. Only large scale loans will offer an escape from this dilemma and at the same time help integrate the credit market across space.

Both alternatives then have advantages and disadvantages. Having lenders hire agents to probe borrowers runs the risk of moral hazard; having borrowers seek out lenders penalizes small loans and puts lenders at risk from local shocks. Which of the two alternatives prevails will depend upon history, institutional details, and the extent and location of local credit markets. With mortgages on the Great Plains, the first alternative prevailed, with lenders hiring agents. In France, by contrast, borrowers, as we shall see, sought out lenders, although there was some searching going on by lenders, too. But the French borrowers (and lenders) did not look on their own. They benefited from a network of intermediaries who helped borrowers find and convince lenders of their creditworthiness. The intermediaries were notaries—semi-public, semi-private officials who drew up loan contracts and other legal and financial documents and kept official copies for court proceedings. They created a positive externality in lending so that borrowers who were close to multiple credit markets could take out more loans, and lenders could make more investments than would otherwise have been possible. The externality resembles that found by Sokoloff for inventors who lived close to product markets, who ended up filing more patents. In France, the externality made possible a thriving mortgage market.

We proceed in three steps. We begin by summarizing the sources of our data and our aggregate findings of our research on French credit markets.

We next move to an analysis of local credit markets and then search for the positive externality by examining loans between inhabitants of different cities and towns. We show that there was indeed a positive network externality in credit markets, and we demonstrate that it is consistent with a queuing model. Our data suggests that competition and market integration were supported by two different sets of institutions. Individuals who engaged in small scale transactions relied on the dense network of notaries who referred business to one another and were all within an afternoon's walk. Individuals who wanted to participate in larger deals tended to meet in larger cities and rely on formal lien registries. While the local networks were dense enough to obviate the idiosyncrasies of local demand, market integration depended upon the capacity of larger transactions to move capital from one region to another. The reason for this complex pattern of behavior, we argue, were the costs borrowers and lenders faced. There were fixed costs involved in arranging loans, which made it advantageous for a borrower to avoid dividing up his loan among several lenders. The cost of waiting for an appropriate lender to appear would be high for unusually small or large loans. Borrowers wanting small or large loans would therefore have an incentive to seek lenders elsewhere (and particularly in large cities), but travel costs could rule out such a search for small scale borrowers.

5.2 Mortgage Markets and Notarial Credit in France as a Whole

As we have explained in a book on Paris and in articles on rural lending, mortgages were a fundamental component of the European financial system from the Middle Ages to the first World War; so were other sorts of medium- and long-term loans secured by other forms of collateral. Most of this lending involved loans arranged by notaries, who provided legal advice and served as financial intermediaries. Unlike the stock market or the banking system, the study of this financial system has most often been left to historians who have examined the evolution of credit in one market, region, or for a particular social group. While time and again these scholars have emphasized the local importance of credit, little has been done to assess its overall importance or draw out conclusions about the aggregate sums involved, which, as we will see, were enormous.

Notaries were private individuals who after some training purchased the right to draft and authenticate private contracts in a given location. Other elements of their activity vary from country to country in continental Europe, and in France, before the French Revolution, from region to region. By the mid-nineteenth century, their number in France had stabilized at two to five per rural canton, with a larger number in cities as a function of the urban population. (Here the canton is the second smallest of the administrative subdivisions of France, one just above that of the municipality. The country as a whole was divided into approximately one hundred roughly equal-sized divisions called departments, each of which contained several smaller subdivisions called arrondissements. The arrondissements, which took roughly a day of travel to cross on foot, were in turn divided up into several cantons, which typically contained a town and several villages.)

In contrast to other parts of the world, the French government encouraged competition by ensuring that notaries were not local monopolists and by allowing individuals to draw up contracts in front of whatever notary they wanted. Parties to all sorts of contracts—not just loans—had a strong incentive to consult a notary, for in civil litigation the burden of proof weighted heavily against anyone wanting to overturn a notarized contract. Even mortgages between family members or friends were often notarized, for otherwise the lenders would have had difficulty getting control of collateral or pursuing a defaulting debtor in court. Lending that did not involve notaries certainly did exist, but it was likely minimal, although the exact amount at stake cannot be measured precisely.[1]

Notaries also had the advantage that their records gave them unparalleled information about individuals' asset position, which revealed who was a good credit risk and who had money to lend. The records included all previous contracts they and their predecessors had drawn up, from loans and land sales to wills, estate settlements, and prenuptial agreements. Unlike banks, they could not take a position in the contracts they drafted, and so they served not as bankers, but as brokers of information. Yet, as we have shown for Paris, that role was extensive.

To study the notarial market, we selected a stratified set of 103 cantons and collected data on all the new loans recorded in these cantons in 1840 and 1865. The data come from the registers of the *Enregistrement* tax (Actes Civils Publics). This tax was collected on all notarial contracts at Bureaux de l'Enregistrement, which were dispersed throughout France. The registers maintained by officers of the *Enregistrement* contain a great deal of detail about the financial terms of notarial contracts; for credit, they reveal social characteristics of borrowers and lenders and tell which notary drew up the loan.

The cantons include very large cities (e.g., Paris, Lyon, and Rouen), towns (e.g., Montpellier, Evreux, Vannes), and villages (e.g., Baud, Estissac) and are drawn from eleven departments (the Aube, Eure, Gard, Haute Garonne, Herault, Morbihan, Rhone, Sarthe, Seine, Seine Maritime, and Vaucluse) split evenly between northern and southern France. We focus on data from

1. For notarial lending between family members and friends, see Hoffman, Postel-Vinay, and Rosenthal (2000). Debt that did not involve notaries included informal consumption loans and certain forms of merchant credit that were not subject to the registration requirements. For an individual merchant, the mercantile credit could be important, but because only a small number of people took out such loans, they would count for very little in the per capita calculations below. They would count for even less if we weight loans by duration and consider debt stock, for the mercantile debt was short term (typically ninety days or less), while the mortgages had durations of several years (table 5.1).

these 103 cantons to avoid a problem in the literature, which often assumes that local credit markets can be treated as isolates. We, however, have learned that the local credit markets were interconnected. We thus needed to include regions where we had a large number of contiguous cantons so that we could observe individuals lending or borrowing both 'at home' and 'away.' A dense sample is particularly important if borrowers' and lenders' behaviour is affected by search costs, which would encourage them (and financial intermediaries such as notaries) to find potential lending partners in nearby communities. If borrowers, for instance, were seeking out lenders, then we would overlook what the borrowers were doing if they found matches in a medium-sized city that happened to be adjacent to one of our cantons but not in the data set.

The data set we constructed to avoid such problems includes some 55,000 loans that give addresses (or more precisely, the municipality of residence, which might be a village, a town, or a city) for borrowers, lenders, and notaries. These addresses have, to the extent possible, the geographical information system (GIS) codes showing precise location, which is useful for studying spatial transaction costs. The location of all 103 cantons in our panel are displayed in figure 5.1.

To gauge the importance of notarial credit, we turned to another, larger sample of notarial loans to estimate total notarial credit for France as a whole (Hoffman, Postel-Vinay, and Rosenthal 2008).[2] Ours come extremely close the government's estimates.[3] We then employ the reported duration of the loan contracts and evidence about contract renewals to estimate the stock of loans. If we compare these numbers to the gross domestic product (GDP), the stock of notarial loans outstanding amounted to 27 percent of the GDP in 1840 and 20 percent in 1865 (table 5.1). There is thus no doubt notarial credit was large. Indeed, given the huge number of notarial loans that were made, we estimate that about one quarter of French households were involved in this market either as lenders or more likely as borrowers.

This rosy picture of a broad credit market was clouded by one darker trend, for by our estimates the number of new loans fell between 1840 and 1865. If there was a loan outstanding for every fourteen persons or so in 1840, that number had fallen to one in twenty by 1865. While it is conceivable that the maturing banking industry was siphoning away some business from notaries, such a turn of events is unlikely, for even the first banks to offer mortgages worked hand in hand with notaries. Indeed, as the history of the first such major mortgage bank (the Crédit Foncier) shows, the new intermediaries were dependent upon the system for registering liens, which

---

2. For our estimate, we divided the data from the lending offices in our larger sample into four categories based on population (Paris, large cities, cities, and rural markets). We then computed per capita levels of lending for each category and then used French population data to estimate total lending for France as a whole.

3. See Martin du Nord (1844) and Allinne (1978).

■ Paris (debt stock 450 million Francs)
◇ Markets with debt stock>10million francs
○ Markets with debt stock>1million francs
• Markets with debt stock<1million francs
——North South Boundary

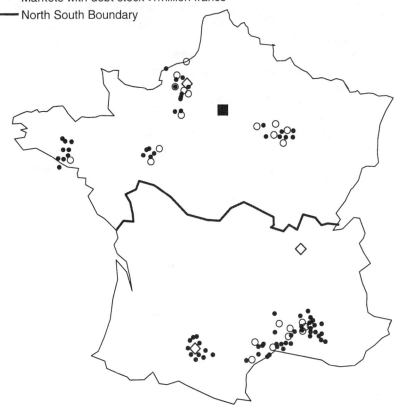

Fig. 5.1   Cantons in our sample

the notaries controlled, and in any case, the figure here for the number of loans in 1865 excludes those made by the Crédit Foncier (henceforth CFF).[4] A more likely explanation was a rise in wealth inequality (Piketty, Postel-Vinay, and Rosenthal 2006). That process, which has been documented with data from wealth at death, included both a jump in the value of large estates and an increase in the fraction of the population dying without any wealth. If the distribution of wealth among the living was not appreciably different, then a declining fraction of the population had assets, which were a pre-

4. Adding the CFF would not change the number of loans per capita appreciably, but it would increase their size and duration (table 5.1).

Table 5.1   **Estimates of mortgage lending in France, 1840–1865**

	1840 total	1865 notaries	1865 CFF	1865 total
Number of loans (000)	653	452	1	454
Amount lent (million francs)	817	919	53	972
Number of outstanding loans (000)	2,314	1,958	40	1,997
Number of outstanding loans per capita	0.07	0.05	0.00	0.05
Total stock of loans (millions of francs)	3,675	4,097	581	4,678
Stock of loans/GDP	0.27	0.19	0.03	0.23
Average duration (years)	4	4	31	6
Average loan size (francs)	1,251	2,031	45,926	2,143
Average loan size/GDP per capita	2.7	3.5	83.6	3.9

Source: Hoffman, Postel-Vinay, and Rosenthal 2008.

Note: The CFF (Crédit Foncier de France), which was founded in 1852, was essentially the only bank that made mortgage loans in 1865. For details, see the text and Hoffman, Postel-Vinay, and Rosenthal 2000.

requisite for accessing notarial credit. The lack of collateral plus growth in average wealth for those who did have some assets might well have led to fewer notarial debt contracts in total and a larger average loan size for the smaller number of notarial credit contracts that were being drafted. That is precisely what we observe.

The size of the debt stock implies that notarial credit was extremely important to the French economy. Some loans were, of course, small—the 100 francs that the vintner François Meunier and his wife borrowed in 1840 from their neighbor, the laborer François Gressin, or 160 francs that the laborer Etienne Desgens owed the landowner François Poubeau in the same year.[5] But even the 100 francs represented 50 days of work for an unskilled day laborer, and overall notarial lending, we know, was sizeable and mattered to a significant number of French families. Our laconic records rarely mention what the loans were used for, but the occupations of borrowers and lenders suggest that notarial credit was important to local industry, such as textiles in Lyon. And occasional indications in the records of the tax offices reveal that notarial credit could be used for the newest investments, such as installing gas lights in the city of Dijon.[6] How, then, were all these loans arranged? How did borrowers and lenders manage to overcome the problems of asymmetric information and move such large sums of money? The rest of this chapter attempts to answer these two questions.

5. The examples here come from the records for the office of Dun-sur-Auron at the Archives départementales du Cher, 1 Q 4025 (6 January 1840).
6. Records of the office of Lyon, 2e arrondissement, at the Archives départementales du Rhône, 3Q18 9 (11 June 1840).

5.3   The Externality in Credit Markets

It is easy to understand why access to large credit markets might generate a positive externality. With a large market nearby, both borrowers and lenders would have more financial transactions to choose from and hence more that would be appealing. Their search costs would be lower, too. Lenders might be able to do without agents—and the attendant moral hazard problems—and if borrowers sought out lenders, they might have an easier time convincing them of the value of their collateral, provided the lenders were locals who were familiar with the local property market. In either case, we would then see more lending (other things being equal) when large credit markets were close by.

We wanted to see if such a positive externality appeared in our data. To do so, we created three measures of access for each of the municipalities in our sample and then regressed the per capita stock of lending in the municipality on the access measures. If there is a positive externality, the regressions should yield large and significant positive coefficients for at least one of the three measures.

The first access measure is simply an index that gauges whether a given municipality has large cantons (over 20,000 inhabitants) nearby. The other two measures are indexes for having medium-sized cantons (10,000 to 20,000 inhabitants) or small-sized cantons (under 10,000 inhabitants) nearby. The regressions (which we do not report here) also include fixed effects to control for local economic conditions, and they were run separately for groups of municipalities with different population levels.[7]

The regressions do point toward a strong positive network externality, but only one that benefited small- or medium-sized municipalities when they were surrounded by small- and medium-sized cantons. Only then was per capita stock of loans boosted by a statistically significant and economically sizeable amount.[8] One might worry that we were simply picking up

7. The first index simply takes the population of each canton in our sample with over 20,000 inhabitants and divides it by the distance to a given municipality. This index will therefore be large if the municipality has large cantons (over 20,000 inhabitants) nearby. The other two indexes are calculated in a similar fashion using medium-sized and small cantons. To avoid problems of endogeneity, the calculations used 1806 populations, and to dampen noise from annual shocks to local markets, the dependent variable was the sum of the per capita stock of loans in 1840 and 1865. Alternative measures for the stock of loans were calculated using figures for local borrowing and local lending, and the regressions were run for each measure. The regressions were also run separately for the following groups of municipalities: those with over 5,000 inhabitants, those with populations between 2,000 and 5,000, those between 2,000 and 1,000, those between 500 and 1,000, and finally those under 500. The full regression results and further information about the variables are available from the authors.

8. For example, a one standard deviation increase in our second index (which measured having medium-sized cantons nearby) boosted per capita borrowing by 158 percent in municipalities with populations between 2,000 and 5,000, and by 468 percent in the smallest muncipalities. The externality affected both per capita lending and per capita borrowing, but it disappeared when the regressions were run for municipalities with over 5,000 inhabitants.

the effect of trade between a municipality and the population in nearby cantons, which might raise incomes and therefore generate more lending, but if that were the case, then we would also expect more lending when large cantons were nearby. But having large cantons close by did not boost lending significantly. Furthermore, the pattern of lending was not consistent with a gravity model of trade, as one would expect if positive externality simply reflected trade effects.[9]

If we accept this evidence, where do the externalities come from? One possibility is that the externality is generated from the greater number of opportunities that appear when a small- or medium-sized municipality is surrounded by a dense network of small or medium cantons. The cantons give the residents of the municipality access to potential financial transactions that they could find in their municipality, and the cantons do so at relatively low cost since they are not far away. The effect then disappears in larger municipalities, where the population is large enough to furnish appealing financial partners without leaving the community, and the resulting pattern of transactions would not necessarily fit a gravity model. But how then do borrowers and lenders seek out the matches, whether at home or in neighboring cantons? Do the borrowers search, or the lenders? And do they seek the assistance of intermediaries?

5.3.1   Individual Loans

To see how borrowers and lenders might find matches and how the externality in credit markets might arise, let us consider what happened in the market for mortgage loans. First, most mortgage loans paid interest at close to 5 percent, since collateral requirements served to equalize the risk profile of borrowers (Hoffman, Postel-Vinay, and Rosenthal, forthcoming). The dimensions of a loan that mattered more were its duration, its size (someone who wanted to borrow a significant sum could do so in one or several loans, but transaction costs would be lower for a single loan), the amount of time that it would take to complete the transaction, and the distance between the borrower and the lender (while the two need not have met, they still had to sign documents in presence of the notary).

Distance between borrower and lender was more important that one might think, because the modern solution to the problem of matching borrowers and lenders—going to a bank that would raise capital from investors and then use the pooled money to fund mortgages—was a rarity, both in France and in other parts of Europe, until at least the 1850s. As we have previously shown, there were banks in many cities in France, and although the number of banks in a city was positively correlated with the volume of local mortgage lending, the banks were making short-term loans, not writing mortgages (Hoffman, Postel-Vinay, and Rosenthal 2008). The reason

---

9. Evidence from a gravity model regression is available from the authors.

was simple, as the recent mortgage meltdown in the United States shows: it was risky to fund medium- and long-term loans with the sort of demand deposits that banks relied on.

Visiting a bank was thus not an option for most borrowers. That was true even in 1865, when the major mortgage bank in France (the CFF) might have originated what we estimate to be some 12 percent of the stock of loans (table 5.1). Most of these CFF mortgages were large loans for Parisian or other urban borrowers; outside such large cities, the CFF was responsible for only 3 percent of the stock. At the time, there were really no other significant mortgage banks (Hoffman, Postel-Vinay, and Rosenthal 2000, 2008).

If the vast majority of borrowers and lenders were not matched up by a bank that conveniently pooled the lenders' deposits, they faced a queuing problem. Somehow, a borrower had to find a saver who happened to be interested in making a loan of the right size, right duration, and right interest rate. A lender faced the same problem, and it would be costly for the two to find one another if they lived apart. The problem would be particularly severe in smaller markets, because the arrival rate of demands for new loans would be slow, and the same would hold for offers to supply new loans. In larger markets the interval of time between new loan demands or between offers to supply new loans would be less.

Now consider a lender who lives in a settlement of a given size. In equilibrium, she faces transaction costs incurred in determining the characteristics of a potential partner and a given wait time for completing a desired transaction in her home market. If that wait time is long enough, she may want to see if there is another market nearby where she can arrange the transaction quickly. However, doing so raises three costs. First, since there are many alternative markets, she needs to find out where there are borrowers who are likely to suit her needs. She also faces the travel costs needed to complete the deal, both when trying to find a suitable borrower and when concluding the transaction. Finally, she must worry about the possibility of adverse selection and moral hazard. A borrower would face similar problems, and in particular would have to overcome adverse selection and moral hazard problems in convincing lenders that he was a good credit risk.

In the absence of intermediaries, the first and third problem are likely to prevent nearly anyone from arbitraging the wait times, for no one knows where to go, and people will worry about facing a lemons problem in the foreign market. The evidence from our credit markets suggests as much. It was rare to see loans between borrowers and lenders who had the sort of personal ties (belonging to the same family or profession, living in the same village or city neighborhood) that we would expect if they were arranging loans on their own without the help of intermediaries. In a big city like Paris, where the first and second sorts of costs would be irrelevant, borrowers and lenders had ceased relying on such personal ties back in the early eighteenth century (Hoffman, Postel-Vinay, and Rosenthal 2000). Evidence from Lyon suggests much the same. There a sample of loans suggests that only 14 percent of lenders had obvious personal ties in 1840.[10]

Borrowers and lenders could therefore try to overcome their queuing problem, but they would then face even more serious trouble with asymmetric information. Demand would therefore rise for intermediaries who could furnish the desired information. We cannot demonstrate that notaries always stepped in to fill the necessary role, but we can show that markets were too big to allow every participant to maintain accurate knowledge of what others were doing. Most French people interacted in mortgage markets that spanned 10,000 people or more. In Paris, Lyon, and Toulouse, most loans involved borrowers and lenders who lived in the same city, but these metropolises were too big for borrowers and lenders to know one another, and in particular for lenders to be able to keep track of what borrowers were doing. In smaller communities, a lender's capacity to keep tabs on everyone rose, but the fraction of loans made with individuals who lived elsewhere increased. In fact, in our sample only 17 percent of borrowers in municipalities under 2,000 people ended up taking out a loan from a lender in the same community even though it was such communities that we would expect personal ties to be strongest.

Some 83 percent of the loans involved individuals who contracted with someone not from their own village, and for them, the median distance between borrower and lender was nine kilometers. Borrowers thus had access to a wide variety of potential lenders, but that in turn would have posed a serious problem for any lender who was considering making a loan. With so many other potential lenders around, how could a lender know what other loans a borrower had taken out? How could he assure himself that collateral was not overmortgaged or that earlier loans were not going to leave him a junior creditor? In all likelihood, he would have to turn to some sort of intermediary who knew the local mortgage market.

Evidence from the department of the Vaucluse in southeastern France suggests that it is what lenders were doing, and borrowers, too. If we use network software to plot the municipalities that were linked by mortgages between a borrower in one community and a lender in the other (figure 5.2), we see that the ties do not bind the small municipalities to the department's cities (Avignon, Apt, Carpentras, Orange). That is what we might expect if borrowers or lenders were employing personal ties to arrange loans, for the personal ties would presumably follow either migration, which typically

10. The calculation comes from the enregistrement records of 842 loans with complete information about borrowers' and lenders' professions and residences. The borrowers and lenders were considered to have personal ties if they were related, had the same profession (except when they were both in the broad categories of propriétaire and rentier), or lived in the same municipality (except in cases where they both lived in the large city of Lyon). There may, of course, have been instances in which borrowers and lenders lived in the same Lyon neighborhood or worked in related professions (such as wine merchants and café owners). Similarly, there may have been some family ties that were not evident in our sources, but such cases were likely rare.

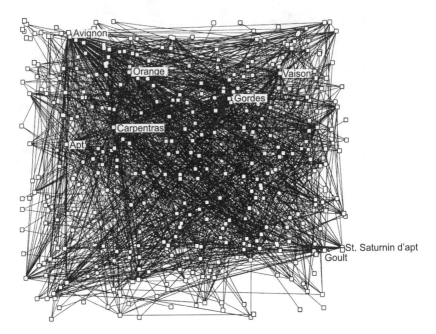

Fig. 5.2   Municipalities in the Vaucluse that were linked by mortgage loans

Notes: The figure, which is plotted using network software (Borgatti, Everett, and Freeman 2002), displays the municipalities in the French department of the Vaucluse without regard for their actual geographic location. There is a line between two municipalities if a borrower resides in one of the municipalities and a lender in another. Loans between residents of the same community are also shown. The lines do not take into account the number or size of loans, or the direction in which funds flowed. The largest cities in the department (Avignon, Apt, Carpentras, and Orange) are labeled, along with several other sizeable towns.

ran from smaller municipalities to cities, or lines of business, which also connected cities and the countryside. Instead, the small municipalities are all bound to one another, as well as to the cities. That pattern would not be what one would expect if borrowers and lenders were unaided by intermediaries.

If borrowers and lenders did in fact rely on local and distant intermediaries who cooperated in the regional redistribution of credit, then the situation would be very different. Our lender, for example, would know which nearby town would offer her opportunities for investing her funds, she could be assured that her concerns about adverse selection were moot, and the intermediary could monitor the borrower and remit his payments of interest and principal. In this case, beyond paying the intermediary for his services, our lender would only bear the cost of travel to the distant market and would in return face a much shorter wait time. Borrowers would enjoy similar benefits.

Who then could act as an intermediary? Notaries are the obvious candidates, for they knew who had money to lend and who was a creditworthy borrower, with little debt and excellent collateral. The notaries acquired this information in the course of their business. They drew up loan contracts and investigated property titles and existing mortgages on collateral, so they knew who might be overburdened with debt. They also handled land sales and inheritances, which revealed who had savings to invest. Having amassed this information in the course of business, they could use it to match borrowers and lenders and do so at low marginal cost, and they could share information with one another by referring clients and opportunities. We know they played such a role in Paris, and the evidence (as we shall see) is consistent with their doing the same elsewhere in France. Elsewhere, other intermediaries had a similar informational advantage—attorneys in England, for example, who dominated the early mortgage market across the English Channel, or town registrars, who recorded mortgages in much of northern Europe.[11] But in France, it was notaries. Potentially, they could play a similar role in other countries influenced by Roman Law or the French legal tradition. But they would only be able to do so when other intermediaries (such as town registrars) had no informational advantage and only when inequality did not restrict lending. Inequality could have that effect because few borrowers had collateral, or because political leaders had an incentive to limit the supply of loans, as Steven Haber shows elsewhere in this volume.

To return then to the problems facing our borrowers and lenders, it is worth noticing that most of the costs involved in interregional intermediation are fixed. As a result, if the notary acted as an intermediary and shared information with a fellow notary about his net demands for credit transactions, then the costs involved would not depend on the size of the loans. Neither would the travel costs that he or the borrowers and lenders would face. Although the cost of investigating collateral would increase with loan size, it would be the same in the home market and in a distant one. Thus, if notaries were organized in a network in which information was traded, lenders would face a fixed transaction cost for distant deals, as would borrowers.

Now let us consider the lender's wait time, which depends on the population of her municipality and the distribution of wealth. (The problem of the borrower's wait time will lead to similar conclusions.) Suppose the municipality is small and wealth very evenly distributed. Wait times are then going to be higher for smaller and larger loans than for "middling" ones. Clearly, a lender who wants to invest a large sum will likely want to see what deals are available in nearby towns, provided the local wait times at home are long enough. Since small loans are rare, so will a lender who wants to lend out a small sum, but for her the interregional fixed costs of intermediation loom comparatively large, making her much less mobile. If travel costs are

---

11. For notaries in Paris and attorneys in England, see Hoffman, Postel-Vinay, and Rosenthal (2000, 287).

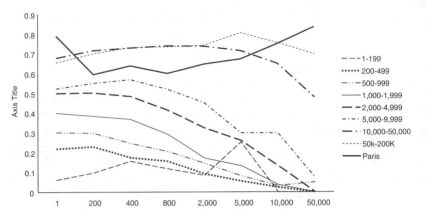

Fig. 5.3   Fraction of loans where borrowers and lenders co-reside

small, middling lenders are therefore the most likely to do their business at home, while small and large lenders will make loans to borrowers in other towns. The same will hold for borrowers. If, however, travel costs are large, then only individuals who seek larger transactions will do business with counterparties outside the home market. The integration of markets should thus vary systematically with loan size and municipal population. All other things being equal, individuals living in large municipalities should engage in credit transactions in their home community (because they have more potential partners), while individuals with less representative loan demands should be less loyal to their own municipality, provided their transactions are not too small.[12]

To explore the effects of these costs and wait times, we computed the fraction of loans in which the lender, the borrower, and the notary resided in the same municipality. We added the notaries since they were the most likely intermediaries. We performed the calculation for various-sized loans and municipalities (figures 5.3 and 5.4). Figure 5.4 reports the fraction of loans in which the borrower, the lender, and the notary all reside in the same municipality. Figure 5.3 modifies the calculation by including cases in which the borrower and lender resided in the same municipality but ended up traveling to a notary in another community. The cases added would include loans in which the borrower and lender lived in a small village with no notary, for they always had to go elsewhere to see a notary, even if they arranged a loan among themselves. Figure 5.3 would also include instances in which a borrower and lender from a municipality with a notary decided to do their business before a notary elsewhere.

12. Municipalities with railroads would have lower transport costs in 1865. We are currently gathering the data to test that hypothesis rather than just relying on physical distance.

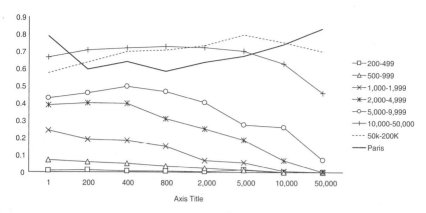

Fig. 5.4 **Fraction of loans where borrower, notary, and lender co-reside**

We expect both fractions to rise with the size of the municipality and to decrease with loan size. The data for the calculations come from 52,000 transactions in our sample for which residences could be recovered. The municipal populations are those of the community where the borrower resided; computations using the lender's residence lead to a similar conclusion, with the caveat that lenders are more urban and thus more likely to live in the same settlement as their notary.

The data confirm that individuals who live in large municipalities do more business at home, and that the fraction of loans arranged within a municipality diminishes for large loans (figures 5.3 and 5.4). In the very largest municipalities the share of the population that coreside with their notary and partners approaches 80 percent and is not sensitive to loan size except for the largest loans. Nevertheless, even for the largest municipalities in our sample some 20 percent of loans had either a borrower or lender who did not reside in the same municipality as the notary. If we consider borrowers who lived in municipalities with between 1000 and 2000 inhabitants, the fraction of loans arranged with a lender and notary in the same community falls from 40 percent to nearly nothing as loan size passes from 100 to 50000 francs (figure 5.4). Clearly, transaction costs seem to matter according to what types of loans involve distant partners.

The other dimension of the spatial distribution of loans involves distance. Figure 5.5 traces the average distance between borrower and lender (for those loans where it is positive) given loan and city size. Here the reverse pattern holds. In small and medium municipalities where people travel often, they do not go very far: usually less than fifty kilometers. How far one travels, however, increases with city size, so that individuals from smaller municipalities rarely go beyond thirty kilometers whatever the loan size, while in larger cities people may travel 100 kilometers or more (well over a day's travel before the advent of railroads). Such lengthy voyages are more

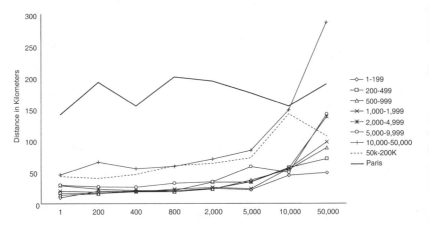

Fig. 5.5   Average distance borrower-lender for loans where distance > 0 by borrower residence and loans size categories

common with larger loans, for the distance traveled also rises steadily with loan size. That relationship between distance and loan size is precisely what one would expect if travel and search costs are largely fixed. The fixed costs will add less to the relative cost of large loans, and that in turn will make individuals seeking larger loans or investments more willing to bear the costs of a search in return for shorter queuing times.

Averages can be misleading, in particular for small municipalities. One can have an inordinate number of loans made to local borrowers by men in the military, who happen to be posted in distant garrisons. Or one can run into an unusual number of migrants who return home to invest. To filter out unusual cases of this sort, we examine the seventy-fifth percentile of the distribution of the distance borrowers and lenders travelled, conditional on their voyaging at all. We interpret this value as the outer range of how far people are willing to go to join a short queue for a match in the credit market. The results are displayed in figure 5.6. Once again, distance is increasing in loan size and municipal population, so long as the city is not too large. The striking finding, however, is that for all loans under 2000 francs (a category that account for 85 percent of all transactions) and for all municipalities with less than 5,000 inhabitants, this seventy-fifth percentile is 17.6 kilometers. The explanation for this upper bound on how far most people would travel is simple: it is the outer limit of a long day's round trip on foot. Only for the largest loans and the largest municipalities do individuals want to travel further. That large loans involved more distant travel is easy to understand, because a large loan dilutes the fixed cost of travel. That individuals in large cities are willing to voyage longer distances (for a given loan size) may reflect improved transportation between larger cities, as they connected to the national transport grid. In other words, the pattern of market integration

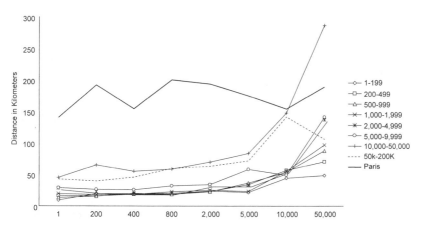

Fig. 5.6 **Seventy-five percentile value of distance between borrower and lendeer conditional on distance > 0 by city and loan size**

seems to reflect the fixed costs of travel, which weigh more heavily on small loans than larger ones.

That the same outer limits to travel applied to most loans and all but the largest municipalities is consistent with our belief that the notaries formed a network in which a notary whose shingle hung in a village of 1000 people had more or less the same information as a colleague in a town of 3000. Notaries knew not only what deals were available in their own municipality or canton but in nearby cantons as well. In larger municipalities more deals could be completed with coresidents, but when that failed, lenders and borrowers faced the same conditions as their rural brethren. Travel costs, however, made it undesirable to go far beyond a location that could be reached in a day, because they would then rise sharply.

One can surely imagine that individuals would sometimes have secured the information themselves without the help of notaries, but in that case it would be hard to understand why borrowers were less likely than lenders to live in the same municipality as the notary who drew up the loan contract. Lenders and notaries resided in the same municipality in 59 percent of the loans, yet borrowers and notaries did so only 44 percent of the time. If borrowers and lenders were seeking one another out with no help from intermediaries, we might expect no such difference in coresidence. After all, it would presumably be just as easy for a borrower to seek out a distant lender, persuade him that he was creditworthy, and then draw up a loan before the lender's notary as it would for a lender to go through a similar process of investigating the borrower's collateral and then signing the loan documents before the borrower's notary. But with a network of notaries, borrowers might more often than not be given an introduction from their notary and all the requisite paperwork and then be sent off to meet their lenders. The borrowers would then be the ones to travel. That appears to be what was happening in France.

Thus, even for small loans, notaries worked to match lenders and borrowers in a series of overlapping markets that covered all of France. Market integration resulted from how ready borrowers and lenders in large loans were to travel. They could rarely arrange loans with someone in their hometown, and the large loan sizes made it economical for them to travel long distances in search of a suitable partner. Because the sums were big, the capital flows between regions (or actually between urban regional centers) were huge. Excluding Paris, but including Lyon and Rouen, some 53 percent of all loans greater than 5,000 francs (about seven times per capita income) involved borrowers and lenders who did not live in the same municipality. The average distance between a borrower and lender in a loan over 5,000 francs was thirty-six kilometers, and if we calculate that distance when parties did not live in the same place it was seventy-two kilometers.

These loans over 5000 francs amounted to only 7 percent of the loans in the sample, but they constituted 57 percent of the value of loans, and almost two-thirds of the stock. (The calculations here omit Paris because loans there were so large; if we include Paris, loans over 5000 francs amount to 73 percent of the value of the loans in the sample and 89 percent of the stock). When new opportunities arose, a large scale borrower could rely on the notarial system to raise capital from distant investors via mortgages backed by his real assets.

5.3.2   Change and Structure

The preceding sections have taken the data set as if it were a single cross section and then used it to shed light on the spatial structure of notarial lending. The evidence that individuals could, and frequently did, travel to meet partners in loans has important implications for research on the growth of mortgage markets. To begin with, most of the research implicitly studies these markets as island economies where changes in fundamental variables like wealth or economic structure interact with scale of the local market. The earlier evidence suggests that we must reconsider these implicit assumptions not just for the American Midwest or Latin America but also for the long-settled economies of continental Europe.

To see why, consider for a moment an economy where lending increases with wealth. Such a relationship could arise for a variety of reasons: land rents might be rising, individuals might be buying more valuable housing, more people might be taking out mortgages to purchase or build housing, or entrepreneurs might be turning to long-term markets to build manufactures. In a closed economy, such an increase in the demand for financial intermediation must be met locally and thus we expect the local credit market to grow. To some extent this is the story revealed by the astounding developments in the canton of Montcenis. One of France's largest iron and steel firms, Schneider, had its main plant in Le Creusot, a town that soon became the largest of the canton. Between 1840 and 1865, as the works grew into the largest firm in France, the population doubled in the canton, and the credit market pretty much matched this growth, since the stock of loans per capita remained constant. Yet local credit did not finance the growth of Schneider, for the local supply of funds was simply too small. Instead, the Schneider family and their firm financed themselves in Paris and through retained earnings. Other inhabitants of Montcenis who wanted to borrow could turn to the nearby towns of Macon or Chalon-sur-Saone. Thus, the resources available for borrowing and lending in Le Creusot or in the canton of Montcenis are only a limited part of the story of financial change there. Instead, what mattered most was the interactions of Le Creusot with other areas of France, and in particular Paris, three hundred and fifty kilometers away.

The tale of Le Creusot is not as extreme as it might seem: the twenty-fold growth in the value of loans in the municipality of Aigues Mortes is solely due to a loan taken out by a corporation that intended to turn nearby marshes into vineyards and salt flats. The collapse of lending in the famous wine-producing town of Nuits Saint Georges (lending there collapsed by 91 percent) was not due to a sudden decline in demand for high quality Burgundy wines, but to an exceptionally large loan taken by a Dijon banking family in 1840 for more than a million francs. Such a huge loan was unheard of outside of Paris, and there was, of course, never anything like it again in Nuits.

The seemingly random walk of the development of our credit markets is not due to the chance arrival of large loans alone. If that were so, then larger markets would be more predictable than small ones, which is not the case. Rather, it is a direct consequence of the intense spatial integration of what are commonly taken to be closed and traditional markets. While a very large fraction of all loans matched local borrowers and lenders, even small loans could be transacted at some distance. Thus, when lending boomed in Mauguio (another canton with endowments favorable to salt marshes and wine) between 1840 and 1865, the inhabitants of the canton also appear in the two nearby markets of Montpelier and Lunel, where they took out twenty-five loans worth 40,000 francs. Beyond the smaller markets, if we take into account the growth of inequality between 1807 and 1899 and the redistribution of population from villages to cities, it is likely that this spatial integration was growing. As wealth inequality increased, the number of loans outstanding per capita fell while their size and duration increased. Longer and bigger loans made borrowers and lenders more willing to travel in order to find suitable counterparties. But the loans where partners met after some travel most likely depended both on notaries' information and on the formal registration of liens, which could be exploited by a new mortgage bank founded in the 1850s, the Crédit Foncier. In large settlements, many notaries may well have decided to drop arranging smaller loans because there was more money to be made in dealing with rich clients, a move that would have increased inequality over time.

Evaluating the welfare consequences of the spatial scale of credit markets is thus complex. On the one hand, the progressive disappearance of smaller, shorter term loans was costly, in particular in areas where alternative institutions (savings banks, pawnshops) were scarce. On the other, the larger loans served to integrate the economy and to redistribute capital across different rural areas and toward the more rapidly growing urban centers. In the countryside, participation in local mortgage markets remained widespread through the 1860s, in part because demand was too small for alternative intermediaries to enter, and in part because the scale of farms and firms guaranteed that a very large number of entrepreneurs needed access to long term credit. In cities a completely different economy emerged, one where most of the population rented their lodgings and worked for large firms where the entrepreneur provided the capital. That was true even in Paris where much of manufacturing occurred on a contract basis, with workers toiling away in very small shops and owning their own tools. Most often it was the wholesale merchant (fabricant) who organized production and provided the working capital. Hence, cities could grow and grow quickly without credit markets serving small scale lenders.

The structure that our spatial analysis revealed suggests a final element to the process of change: competition. Although a notary might seem to control the local market, the increasing capacity of borrowers and lenders to direct their business to notaries in other municipalities gave him an incentive to exchange information in order to better serve his clients. The resulting competition was enhanced by the growing size of loans in the nineteenth century, since clients involved in big loans were more willing to travel in search of a better deal. The same clients were also more likely to have the loans inscribed on lien registries, which provided an alternative to using a notary to resolve problems of asymmetric information. The common thread here is that all these local markets were deeply interconnected.

5.4   Conclusion

The study of financial markets, in general, and of credit markets in particular, often focuses either on countries or on localities. Here we have broken with both traditions, for we wanted to study mortgage markets in France as a whole, even though we knew that mortgage markets rely on information that is inherently local. Inspired by Sokoloff's work on the importance of access to markets, we chose to assemble groups of markets that were geographically close together. This chapter shows that except for the very largest localities, nineteenth century mortgage markets cannot be understood in isolation; to a very large extent their capacity to serve borrowers and lenders came from their interconnection.

Although by American standards capital did not move any great distance, our study documents two kinds of integration. The first involved tens of thousands of small loans and took place within areas some twenty kilometers across. This local process helped obviate the noncoincidence of demand and supply in small localities where the market was thin. The second kind of integration, by contrast, involved large loans. They were rarer but they spanned much longer distances. Because the sums involved were large, it is likely that it is the second process that integrated different regions. All these important elements to the mortgage market would have been missed if one had focused only on familiar forms of intermediation such as banks, or on computing an aggregate value of credit transacted.

Because the frequency of interaction decreased with distance, regions that were dense (either in local markets or in medium-sized cities) did see more lending than others. We can therefore confirm Sokoloff's arguments about the beneficial aspects of access to markets. The French credit markets were highly competitive. While the state limited entry into particular forms of financial intermediation (most famously corporate banks and the stock exchange), it did not cartelize the whole of the system. In fact, entry into private banking was always free, and beyond the banks, more than 10,000 notaries competed for the business of intermediating private mortgages and markets for assets such as the real estate market.

Although the notaries were seemingly "traditional" intermediaries, they had the information that could make mortgage markets run smoothly. They were, in a sense, like a beneficial endowment—in their case, an endowment of information—which helped them raise enormous amounts of capital and integrate a national credit market. How this happened was a complicated process, but by the mid-nineteenth century, the notaries were helping to integrate French credit markets. In future work we hope to show that this was also the case before the French Revolution.

References

Allinne, Jean-Pierre. 1978. "Le Crédit Foncier de France 1852–1920." Doctoral thesis. University of Paris II Law Faculty.

Borgatti, Stephen P., Martin G. Everett, and Linton C. Freeman. 2002. *UCINET for Windows: Software for Social Network Analysis.* Lexington, KY: Analytic Technologies.

Hoffman, Philip T., Gilles Postel-Vinay, and Jean-Laurent Rosenthal. 2000. *Priceless Markets: The Political Economy of Credit in Paris, 1662–1869.* Chicago: University of Chicago Press.

———. 2008. "The Old Economics of Information and the Remarkable Persistence of Traditional Credit Markets in France 1740–1899." California Institute of Technology, Division of Humanities and Social Sciences. Working paper.

————. forthcoming. "Is Trust an Ultimate Cause? Its Role in the Long Run Development of Financial Markets in France." In *Trust,* edited by Karen S. Cook, Russell Hardin, and Margaret Levi. New York: Sage Foundation.

Martin du Nord, Nicolas M. F. L. J., ed. 1844. *Documents relatifs au régime hypothécaire et aux réformes qui ont été proposées.* 3 vols. Paris: Imprimerie Royale.

Piketty, Thomas, Gilles Postel-Vinay, and Jean-Laurent Rosenthal. 2006. "Wealth Concentration in a Developing Economy: Paris and France, 1807–1994." *American Economic Review* 96:236–56.

Snowden, Kenneth A. 1995. "The Evolution of Interregional Mortgage Lending Channels, 1870–1940: The Life Insurance-Mortgage Company Connection." In *Coordination and Information: Historical Perspectives on the Organization of Enterprise,* edited by Naomi R. Lamoreaux and Daniel M. G. Raff, 209–47. Chicago: University of Chicago Press.

Sokoloff, Kenneth L. 1984. "Was the Transition from the Artisanal Shop to the Non-Mechanized Factory Associated with Gains in Efficiency? Evidence from the U.S. Manufacturing Censuses of 1820 and 1850." *Explorations in Economic History* 21:351–82.

————. 1988. "Inventive Activity in Early Industrial America: Evidence From Patent Records, 1790–1846." *The Journal of Economic History* 48:813–50.

Two Roads to the Transportation Revolution
Early Corporations in the United Kingdom and the United States

Dan Bogart and John Majewski

6.1 Introduction

The complex relationship between geography and institutions was a key theme of Ken Sokloff's work. In analyzing the development of the Americas, Sokoloff and Engerman famously argued that factor endowments like geography and population density profoundly influenced the evolution of important economic institutions. The cultivation of highly profitable staple crops—and a readily available pool of exploitable labor—created high levels of inequality in Latin America and the Caribbean. Powerful groups of influential insiders had little to gain (and often much to lose) from open incorporation, public schooling, expanded suffrage, and other institutions associated with long-term development. In North America (especially in the U.S. North and Canada), environmental conditions prevented the cultivation of staple crops, which encouraged entrepreneurs to focus on raising long-term land values via settlement. Landowners created relatively open political institutions, which led to the development of open, competitive economies with higher levels of public goods.[1] While Sokloff saw an intimate connection between geography and institutions, he also realized that institutions (once created) could have their own independent impact. Sokoloff and Khan, for example, argued that the British government established a complex patenting system with high fees that essentially limited patenting to those with access to capital and specialized information regarding patenting procedures.[2] Inventors in the United States paid far less in patenting fees and could rely upon

Dan Bogart is associate professor of economics at the University of California, Irvine. John Majewski is chair and professor of history at the University of California, Santa Barbara.

1. Engerman and Sokoloff (1997).
2. Khan and Sokoloff (1998, 298).

far more efficient judicial protection of their claims. Patenting rates in the United States, not surprisingly, were far higher than in Britain.

Following Sokoloff's example, we explore the interaction of factor endowments and institutions through a comparison of the transportation revolution in the United Kingdom and the United States. A long and vibrant literature has recognized that the transportation revolution—the emergence of turnpikes, improved bridges, canals, and railroads in the eighteenth and nineteenth centuries—helped generate economic growth.[3] Improvements in transportation expanded markets, thus setting the stage for productivity advances in both agriculture and manufacturing. Although new technologies, like steam locomotives, played an important role in the transportation revolution, many of the key breakthroughs involved institutional and organizational changes. Common law, which insisted that landowners near roads and rivers should pay for their maintenance, restricted collective efforts to improve transport. To overcome the limitations of common law, legislative bodies in Britain and the United States chartered trusts, joint-stock companies, and corporations to build and oversee transportation improvements. Individual promoters collected tolls and user fees, which in turn allowed capital to be raised from a wider variety of sources. Flexible and adaptable to a wide range of improvements, these organizations provided incentives for private individuals to invest in projects with high rates of social return. Institutions, in essence, created the framework in which new transportation technologies could be developed and implemented.

Our comparison of transportation organizations in the United Kingdom and the United States seeks to shed light on the critical question of how the United States managed to overtake the United Kingdom as a global economic leader. Both nations are rightly considered "success stories," but by the late nineteenth century the United States had shed its status as a settler economy to become one of the world's preeminent economies. A leading question is whether the United States overtook the United Kingdom as the global economic leader because of its political institutions or differences in factor endowments. Analyzing the evolution of transportation improvements offers a unique lens because they were closely linked with population densities and natural resources and had "natural monopoly" characteristics that often led to government regulation.

Our comparison begins in the early nineteenth century long after Britain's Parliament wrestled the authority to grant charters away from the Crown. Parliament jealously guarded its right to grant charters and was the sole authority for obtaining rights-of-way and the authority to collect tolls. Parliament was quite open to passing bills creating transportation organizations, but promoters paid handsomely for their rights through fees to clerks and solicitors.

---

3. Freeman (1983, 1–30).

The United States adapted (with considerable revision) Britain's basic institutions for improving transport. Following the American Revolution state governments from Massachusetts to South Carolina viewed it as their right to issue charters. Unlike Parliament, U.S. states extracted little in the way of rents—fees, bribes, or other charges were marginal. With corporate charters cheap and relatively easy to obtain, incorporations in the United States proceeded as a series of dramatic booms. In the first part of this chaper, we show that U.S. state governments incorporated far more transport companies per person with far lower fees than did the U.K. Parliament.

The second part of the chapter focuses on why it was relatively more expensive to get a transport charter from Parliament and why more charters were issued per person in the United States. We view these outcomes as a political economy equilibrium, in which there was different demand for charters in each country and different political institutions governing supply. We argue that differences in urbanization and urban structure were key factors in determining the profitability of transport investments and the transaction costs associated with authorizing transport investments. The United States had a largely rural population dispersed over a large area. Most transportation projects paid little in the way of direct returns. Investors, almost all of whom lived close to the improvement in question, instead hoped for "indirect" returns captured through higher land values. While it might have been possible for legislatures to force organizers to pay a portion of their expected higher land values in the way of fees and bribes, in reality the speculative nature of U.S. transportation improvements made the extraction of rents far less likely. The dearth of direct profits for U.S. transportation companies, in other words, created a highly elastic demand in which charging for charters would dramatically lower the number of organized companies. The United States also lacked a central city that could act as a natural anchor for a transportation network. Cities competed to develop their transport links to the West. The emerging urban network fostered boosterism and the developmental impetus behind early U.S. transport development.

The United Kingdom, on the other hand, was a far more developed and densely populated country. It also had a wealthy central city—London—which dominated the structuring of the network and yielded more certain revenue streams. Most U.K. transportation projects paid investors some direct return in the form of interest on bonds or dividends on equity and because they expected some direct return, organizers could more readily pay the fees that Parliament demanded. The urban environment in the United Kingdom created more opportunities for rent extraction. Operating in a more developed and thickly settled country also meant that transportation projects in Britain confronted more vested interests, whether property owners who feared eminent domain damages or merchants and artisans who feared new projects would endanger their livelihood. Parliament's desire to sort out of these conflicts—which might be thought of as political transactions costs—helped give long-term credibility to Britain's transportation revolution, but they also added to the cost of getting charters.

Differences in political institutions were another key factor. The United States had an active democratic political system where a large percentage of white males could vote. Disgruntled constituents denied a corporate charter could vent their frustrations at the next election. Indeed, they often voiced their opposition to corporations that they perceived as "monopolists" or as "privileged." Approval of turnpikes, toll bridges, and other transportation corporations soon became routine legislative business. Larger corporations such as railroads generated more substantial controversy, but the democratic political culture in the United States allowed different groups and localities to successfully pursue charters for "their" railroads.

British politics were far less democratic. Voting was restricted to a smaller percentage of males and seats in the House of Commons were often uncontested. Moreover, elections were rarely swayed by populist rhetoric that corporations represented monopoly and privilege. Popular uprisings against transport authorities did occur, but they were exceptional compared to the United States.

Political decentralization was also relevant to chartering regimes in the United States and United Kingdom. The British Parliament issued all charters in England, Wales, and Scotland. Facing no domestic political competition, it could charge promoters dearly for its blessing without fearing a substantial loss of economic activity to neighboring jurisdictions. U.S. state governments, on the other hand, faced a competitive environment that worked to dissipate rents. Failure to improve transportation might result in the loss of commerce and population to other states, thus encouraging state legislators to facilitate local projects. In support of this view, we show that the British and Irish Parliament facilitated the passage of acts in their competing counties relatively more before 1801, when the Irish Parliament lost its independent authority to issue charters. Qualitative evidence also indicates that greater decentralization in the United States facilitated transport acts in areas where economic competition was greatest.

An important general point of our story was the ultimate success of both the United States and Britain. Each nation had enough flexibility to tailor corporate institutions to fit their differing economies. The more open chartering environment in the United States helped a relatively sparsely populated country rapidly develop, leading to what one scholar has described as a remarkable "release of energy." It is not clear, however, that the same permissive system would have worked equally well in the United Kingdom. We conclude with a brief assessment of the costs and benefits of decentralized, open chartering in the United States with the greater centralization and somewhat less open system in Britain.

6.2 Background

In both the United Kingdom and the United States, improving transportation involved creating organizations that relied heavily on private capital. Local governments in each nation possessed neither the revenue streams nor the administrative ability to improve long-distance transportation routes. A locality that wanted to improve a road or a river in its jurisdiction faced a pronounced coordination problem—if adjoining towns failed to keep up the road or river, the effort of any single town or parish would largely be wasted. There was strikingly little enthusiasm in either Britain or the United States for creating centralized government bureaucracies powerful enough to improve roads, clear rivers, or construct canals.[4] Instead, both nations established private and quasi-private organizations to build projects such as turnpike roads, toll bridges, and river improvements. The U.K. Parliament authorized trusts, which had the power to issue bonds and collect tolls, to oversee turnpike construction and operation. Other British transportation improvements, such as canals and railways, organized themselves as joint-stock companies or corporations that could issue equity or debt. The corporate form was especially popular in the United States, where state legislatures chartered most turnpikes, toll bridges, and river improvements as corporations. States sometimes chartered U.S. canals as corporations as well, but the governments of New York, Pennsylvania, Ohio, and several other states owned and operated large-scale canal systems.[5] The profusion of different organizational types—private corporations, mixed enterprises, and outright state ownership—reflects the degree to which decentralization allowed states to experiment with different organizational forms.

Even when organized as private corporations, most of the transportation organizations involved a complex mix of private initiative and public authority that often defied our modern dichotomy of private and public. While the trusts and corporations allowed groups of private individuals to raise capital, governments in Britain and the United States made clear that such organizations depended upon government authority for their existence. Theoretically, transportation organizations acted as agents of the state, which gave Parliament and U.S. state governments authority to heavily regulate these organizations. As befitting the public nature of transportation trusts and corporations, British and U.S. state governments approved specific routes, detailed procedures for resolving eminent domain disputes, and instituted complex regulations governing tolls and fees. Political and judicial authorities in both Britain and the United States saw transportation

4. The U.S. national government financed the National Road and scattered funding for other projects, but such spending was only 10 percent of state investment in internal improvements and banks. Wallis (1999, 283).

5. Goodrich (1960, 270–71).

improvements, even when improved via private capital, as a public affair that demanded regulatory oversight.

6.3   The Low Price of Transport Charters in the United States

In the United States, it was surprisingly easy to secure legislative permission for a transportation project. We focus on Middle Atlantic states (New York, New Jersey, Maryland, and Pennsylvania) plus the relatively new state of Ohio. The economies of these states—containing a mix of farming, manufacturing, and commerce—resembled the United Kingdom far more than the slave states or newly settled states in the West. Readily available data for these states shows that the number of charters for turnpikes, toll bridges, canals, and railroads is astounding (see table 6.1). These five states chartered more than a total of 1,800 companies between 1800 and 1840. The 1810s and the 1830s stand out as particularly significant; these two decades saw rapid growth that eventually ended in financial panic and recession. New York led in the absolute number of charters, and was well ahead in per capita terms until the number of corporate charters had trouble keeping pace with the state's tremendous population growth. Ohio, settled by Americans for less than a generation, was the per capita leader in the 1830s. Charters for U.S. transportation companies seemed cheap and easy to secure.

The corporate charters themselves bear out this point. States rarely (if ever) charged companies for the privilege of incorporation. The secondary literature on turnpikes and toll bridges—as well as a review of a sample of charters—reveals that legislatures did not even bother to assess modest administrative fees for transportation charters. The absence of such fees is striking. In Pennsylvania, for example, the state legislature required a corporation to sell a certain percentage of its stock before it could begin operations. To insure these requirements were met, the incorporators often had to send the governor a list of initial share subscribers. Such a process afforded the state government a perfect opportunity to collect fees in addition to the names of initial stockholders, but the legislature failed to do so.

Perhaps it is possible that individual members of the legislature—as opposed to the legislature as an institution—collected fees via bribes. The secondary literature does not associate charters for early transportation with widespread legislative corruption, but then again neither incorporators nor the legislators had any incentive to leave behind a readily visible paper trail.[6] One important fact, however, militates against the story of widespread (but hidden) bribery: most of the transportation corporations chartered in the United States did not become operating concerns. In New York, for ex-

---

6. Individual companies might have had corruption among corporate officers—say a treasurer or president using company funds for their own personal use—but that is far different than legislators taking bribes for charters.

Table 6.1   Corporate charters for U.S. transport companies in selected states, 1800–1839

	1800–09	1810–19	1820–29	1830–39
A. Number of charters				
Ohio	2	18	28	241
New Jersey	29	29	13	49
Maryland	10	46	31	32
New York	145	185	143	240
Pennsylvania	45	153	101	284
TOTAL	231	431	316	846
B. Number of charters per 10,000 residents				
Ohio	0.146	0.443	0.368	1.961
New Jersey	1.338	1.149	0.441	1.416
Maryland	0.396	1.616	0.962	0.883
New York	1.921	1.603	0.871	1.104
Pennsylvania	0.638	1.646	0.842	1.848
TOTAL	1.117	1.423	0.749	1.497

Sources: Evans (1948).

ample, only about one-third of chartered turnpikes actually built enough roadway to justify a toll gate.[7] Many projects, moreover, received multiple charters. When a company failed to sell a certain percentage of its stock before beginning operations, they sometimes went back to the legislature and asked for a new charter, perhaps with modifications to the route that might help attract new investors.[8] Such behavior suggests that corporate charters were sufficiently inexpensive that organizers secured their charter first and worried about viability later.

To say that corporate charters were inexpensive is not to say that they were free. Lobbying the legislature for a corporate charter took time and effort. Typically, organizers of a given project initiated a series of organizational meetings—usually advertised in local newspapers—and collected signatures for petitions. Organizers then incorporated these petitions to the state legislature, setting into motion the incorporation process. As the articles of incorporation made their way from committee to a general legislative vote, substantial political opposition might arise. A rival locality could oppose the bill, as might some local residents who resented paying tolls for a local road, bridge, or river improvement. Such opposition was particularly significant in the 1790s when the corporate form was relatively new and untested, but it tended to dissipate after 1800. Local travelers won significant toll exemp-

7. Klein and Majewski (1992, 482).
8. To cite but one example: The Rivanna Navigation Company, a rather small company located in central Virginia, had its charter changed numerous times. See Majewski (2000, 88–97).

tions that muted opposition, and state legislatures often adopted logrolling schemes that made it difficult for one locality to block the improvements of another.

6.4   The British Parliament: Charging for Corporations

How did the chartering regime differ in the United Kingdom? Data on the clerical summaries of all acts affecting local roads, bridges, canals, and railways can illuminate the patterns.[9] The clerical summaries identify acts creating authorities to improve transport and acts authorizing an existing trust or joint-stock company to undertake new projects or improvements. For the purposes of comparison we counted original acts creating new transport authorities along with acts that authorized more projects for an existing transport organization because U.S. charters contained similar information.[10]

Table 6.2 shows the number of turnpike, bridge, canal, and railway improvement acts in absolute and per capita terms for various subperiods from 1800 to 1839. The data cover the regions of England, Wales, Scotland, and Ireland with a combined land area of 121,124 square miles. For comparison, table 6.3 shows the number of turnpike, bridge, canal, and railroad charters in Ohio, New Jersey, Maryland, New York, and Pennsylvania for all years between 1800 and 1839. The combined land area of these five states is 150,167 square miles. During the nineteenth century there were far fewer acts per capita in the United Kingdom than charters per capita in the U.S. states we examine. Even if all the transport improvement acts in the eighteenth century were added to the U.K. total, it would still come to around 40 percent fewer transport improvement acts per 10,000 residents than the U.S. states analyzed above.

Comparing railroad charters is particularly illuminating because this technology evolved in both countries at roughly the same time. Ohio, New Jersey, Maryland, New York, and Pennsylvania together had far more railroad charters per capita than the United Kingdom by 1840—in fact, nearly ten times as many. The higher number of acts translated into a higher number of railroad miles per capita. By 1840 the United States had 1.65 railroad miles per 10,000 residents. The United Kingdom had 0.69 railroad miles per 10,000 residents.[11]

Unlike U.S. corporations, U.K. projects paid significant costs to secure permission to operate. Promoters often hired solicitors or agents who paid

9. See Bogart and Richardson (2006).
10. Some acts in the second category simply extended the term of a transport authority. For example, a turnpike trust often obtained a renewal act after their original authority expired in twenty-one years.
11. The data on railroad miles in Britain and the United States comes from Mitchell (1988).

Table 6.2   Acts for U.K. transportation authorities, 1800–1839

	1800–09	1810–19	1820–29	1830–39	1800–39
	A. Number of acts for new transport improvements				
Turnpike	185	199	363	207	954
Bridges	18	21	38	37	114
Canals	47	36	28	33	144
Railways	10	11	42	94	157
TOTAL	260	267	471	371	1369
	B. Number of acts per 10,000 residents				
Turnpike	0.11	0.102	0.161	0.084	0.388
Bridges	0.01	0.01	0.016	0.015	0.046
Canals	0.027	0.018	0.012	0.013	0.058
Railways	0.005	0.005	0.018	0.038	0.063
TOTAL	0.154	0.137	0.209	0.151	0.557

Sources: Bogart and Richardson (2006).

Table 6.3   U.S. transport charters by mode, 1800–1839

A. Number of transport charters	
Turnpike	997
Bridges	361
Canals	153
Railways	364
Total	1875
B. Number of charters per 10,000 residents	
Turnpike	1.764
Bridges	0.638
Canals	0.270
Railways	0.644
Total	3.317

Sources: See tables 6.1 and 6.2.

all the fees and guided their bill through Parliament. The fees include payments to officers in the Commons and Lords as well as other expenses. Table 6.4 reports the bills paid to solicitors and agents for a sample of transport acts from 1825 to 1833. The average solicitors' or agents' bill was £505 or $2,405. For comparison, annual incomes for white-collar workers in Britain were between £175 and £500 in the 1820s. Manufacturing workers earned between £60 and £80 per year in the same period.[12] Thus, the fees for charters were well beyond the means of most individuals.

The evidence suggests that the high price of acts in Britain encouraged promoters to select projects that were more likely to be completed. Table

12. For annual earnings see Lindert and Williamson (1983, 4).

Table 6.4   Solicitor and agents bills for the passage of transport improvement acts

Act	Year	Bill in (in £)
Birmingham Roads	1825	740
Limerick Railway	1828	723
Shipley Roads	1828	325
Hammersmith Bridge	1829	363
Finchley Roads	1829	416
Highham Bridge	1830	359
Rickmansworth Roads	1830	74
Festiniog Railway	1832	667
Bradford and Leeds Railway	1832	903
Hull and Hedon Roads	1832	495
East London and London Railway	1828	458
East London and London Railway	1829	535
Average solicitors' and agents' bills		505

Source: Great Britain, House of Commons (1833, 424–29).

6.5 shows the completion history for a sample of canal projects identified from a 10 percent random sample of canal acts.[13] The vast majority of canal projects authorized by acts were implemented within five years. Only two (or 10 percent) were never completed. The percentage of turnpike acts that were implemented can be estimated by the number of trusts that obtained renewal acts after twenty-one years. Since renewal acts were expensive, they would only be sought if the trust was still in operation. Table 6.6 shows that among all trusts created before 1729, only 7 percent failed to obtain a renewal act before their term expired. Unlike the U.S. states, the vast majority of projects that Parliament authorized were actually completed.

6.5   The Role of Urbanization

Urbanization contributed to the differences in chartering regimes by affecting the profitability of transport projects and the transaction costs of implementing projects. We begin by analyzing the link between urbanization, profitability, and the willingness to pay for charters.

Although formally organized as for-profit corporations, most U.S. companies paid little in the way of direct profits (dividends and stock appreciation). This was especially true of turnpikes, which typically generated just enough revenue to pay for operating expenses. In 1825, the Pennsylvania state government (which invested heavily in transportation companies) held just over $1.8 million in turnpike stock, yet received only $540 in dividend

13. The percentage of canal acts that were implemented can be estimated using the detailed histories put together by Jim Shead (2008) and Joseph Priestley (1831).

Table 6.5   The completion rate for U.K. canal projects authorized by acts

Projects identified in 10% random sample of canal acts	Year original act	Year when completed
Cromford	1789	1794
Kennet and Avon	1796	1810
Birmingham to Bilstone to Autherley	1768	before 1784
Neath canal	1791	1795
Trent and Mersey Canal, tunnel Harecastle Hill	1823	c1825
Birmingham and Liverpool Junction Canal	1826	1835
Birmingham and Liverpool Junction Canal, Newport Branch	1827	1835
Lough Corrib to Galway Bay canal	1830	c1835
Sankey Bridges to Widnes branch canal	1830	1833
Chard Canal	1834	1842
Canal from Forth and Clyde to Campsie in Stirling	1837	never built
Montgomershire canal, Newton Branch	1815	1819
Edinburgh to Falkirk	1821	c1825
Bradford canal	1771	1774
Wyrley and Essington Canal	1792	1797
Rochdale canal	1794	1804
Bath to Bristol	1811	never built
Between Birmingham and Worcester and Birmingham Canals	1815	c1820
Calder and Hebble, Halifax branch	1825	1828
Forth and Cart Canal	1836	1840
Stourbridge Extension Canal	1837	1840
Number of canal projects		21
% that were not started or completed		10%

Sources: Priestly (1831); Shead (2008).
Notes: Canal projects were identified through a 10% random sample of acts.

payments—a rate of return of far less than 1 percent. Not surprisingly, there was little in the way of a secondary market for these unprofitable stocks. In 1817, Biddle and Company of Philadelphia, one of the nation's biggest securities brokers, traded a grand total of 118 shares in transportation companies, a tiny fraction of the 71,369 total shares that the company handled.[14] In Virginia, an 1847 government report declared that stock of the state's turnpike and navigation companies "had no public value." No systematic data exists for other states, but observers frequently noted that turnpike stock was unprofitable. Speaking of New York's turnpikes, DeWitt Bloodgood noted in 1838 that, "Generally they have never remunerated their proprietors, nor paid much more than the expense of their actual repairs."[15] Even in New England, where high population densities resulted in more

14. Calculated from Wright (2002, 155).
15. Klein and Majewski (1992, 499).

Table 6.6   English turnpike trusts before 1730 that did not obtain a renewal act
before their term expired

Turnpike road	Year created	Term expired	Year authority was resumed
Great North Road in Hert., Cam. and Hunt.	1663	1672	1693
Ryegate and Crawley in Surrey	1697	1712	1755
Barnhill and Hutton Heath in Cheshire	1706	1727	?
London Norwich road, St. Stephen to Norfolk	1726	1747	1767
Roads into Tewkesbury in Gloucester	1726	1747	1756
Roads into Bridgewater in Somerset	1730	1751	1758
Number of trusts created between 1663 and 1730			87
% that did not renew their authority			7%

Sources: The data for Turnpike acts come from 1663 and 1750 in *Statutes of the Realm.* (Great Britain, various years).

traffic and more revenue, turnpikes made little money. According to one historian, "it is doubtful whether more than five or six [New England's turnpikes] paid their proprietors even reasonably well."[16]

Other types of early U.S. corporations generated more direct profits, but not much more. Table 6.7 summarizes the share prices in Pennsylvania, when the state government tried to auction off its stock in various improvements in 1842. Turnpike stock sold for an average of $3.35 per share, well below the initial par value (what investors initially paid for each share) of $50 to $100. What's more, the state found it impossible to auction off thousands of other turnpike shares—no buyers could be found at any price. The profitability of toll bridges was better, as they sometimes held quasi-monopoly status in large urban areas divided by rivers.[17] The state auctioned its toll bridge stock for $9.66 per share, which still represented a steep loss for shares that it initially paid $25 to $100 apiece. The same pattern held true of navigation and canal companies—the state managed to unload most of its shares, but at a substantial loss.

It is more difficult to find comprehensive data on the profitability of early U.S. railroads. Railroads would eventually pay far higher dividends than other improvements, but it took several years for them to generate revenues and profits. Most of the railroads chartered in the 1830s were hit particularly hard by the Panic of 1837, which depressed revenues and profitability. The shares of three companies sold by the state of Pennsylvania—which fetched the rock-bottom price of $2.37 per share—reflected the rather dire short-term outlook for railroad stocks.

16. Taylor (1934, 266).
17. It was also far easier for bridges to collect tolls. Unlike turnpikes, toll bridges did not have to worry about informal "shunpikes" skirting around toll gates.

Table 6.7   Stock prices for Pennsylvania corporations at 1842 state auctions

Corporation type	Number of companies	Number of shares sold	Average price of shares	Par value of shares ($)
Turnpikes	40	16,069	$3.35	50–$100
Toll bridges	21	17,046	$9.66	25–$100
Canals and navigation companies	6	7,350	$12.35	50–$100
Railroads	3	710	$2.37	50

Source: Hartz (1948).

The poor profitability of early U.S. transportation companies (at least from the standpoint of direct returns) stands in sharp contrast to their British counterparts. The dividends paid by joint-stock canal companies have been extensively studied in the literature. Duckham summarizes the results of an 1825 report by the *Quarterly Review* on the dividends of eighty canal companies.[18] The average divided equaled 5.7 percent of total capital. Studying the average is somewhat misleading because some canal companies paid very large dividends and most others paid less than 4 percent. Nevertheless, the fact that U.K. canal companies paid some dividends stands in stark contrast to the U.S. case. U.K. turnpike authorities did not issue shares, but they issued bonds secured on the income of the tolls. How well did these bonds pay? Albert has argued that a large percentage of trusts in 1821 and 1837 were in adverse financial condition.[19] Many trusts (more than half), nevertheless, regularly paid interest on their bonds. Charity Commission records also suggest that turnpike bonds were not being traded at a heavy discount like U.S. turnpike shares.[20]

Underlying population densities are surely one reason why British transportation organizations generated direct returns for investors while U.S. companies did not. Figure 6.1 compares British population densities with those of the Middle Atlantic states and Ohio. The differences were striking. British population densities in 1800 were some five to fifteen times higher than the various U.S. states; by 1840, British population density was still five times greater than that of the United States. The differences in population density resulted in a far larger urban population. In 1801, the proportion of British residents living in cities of at least 5,000 was 25 percent. More people lived in London (900,000) than all U.S. residents in census-defined

18. Duckham (1983, 123) and Ward (1974).
19. Albert (1972).
20. Charity commission records report the prices paid for assets by charities in England from the 1500s to the early 1900s. The prices of turnpike bonds were often purchased or sold at prices around £25 or £50, which was their usual denomination. See Clark (1998) for more details on the source.

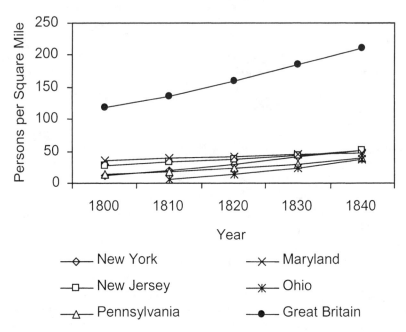

Fig. 6.1   Population per square mile, 1800–1840 Great Britain vs. selected U.S. States
Sources: Mitchell (1988, 1998).

urban areas (322,371).[21] America's urban population and manufacturing output would expand dramatically over the next three decades, but even in 1830 London's 1.9 million residents surpassed the 1.3 million persons living in all U.S. cities.[22] British transportation improvements could rely on more people—and hence great economic activity—to generate more revenue for each mile of turnpike, canal, or railroad. No wonder that few U.S. companies could hope for even minimal direct profits, while British companies typically rewarded investors well.

The financial difficulties of U.S. transport authorities lessened the incentives for U.S. legislatures to extract fees for their charters. The demand for charters in the rural United States was effectively elastic. Higher fees would have resulted in far fewer charters. Even in the case of railroads, where construction costs were far higher, greater fees could discourage marginal projects. In urban Britain, Parliament could charge higher fees for acts. Demand was less elastic because the financial prospects were far brighter.

Differences in demand elasticity suggest one straightforward explanation for the differences in chartering between the United States and Britain.

21. U.S. Bureau of the Census (1998a,14).
22. B. R. Mitchell (1988, 25), (1998, 14). U.S. Bureau of the Census (1998b).

Assuming that Parliament acted as a monopolist, it would set the fees at the point where the marginal revenue from acts equaled the marginal cost. At this fee level, some promoters would not petition for acts because they had a low willingness to pay. Parliament did not mind the loss in revenues from the marginal project because it was more than compensated by the higher fees charged to other petitioners willing to pay for the act. In the United States, monopolistic state legislatures had greater difficulty extracting rents because more promoters would have exited the market if fees were raised to the British level. By undermining profits, low population density reduced the profit-maximizing fee in the United States.

The pure rent-extraction hypothesis has some qualitative support in the data. For example, promoters often complained about the fees charged by Parliament and the resulting erosion of their profits.[23] However, simply having the ability to charge higher fees does not necessarily account for why Parliament charged so much more for transportation charters. The higher fees in the United Kingdom also reflected the expenses incurred in convincing members of Parliament (henceforth MPs) of a project's merits and in negotiating with opposition groups. This view is suggested by the relatively small proportion of total costs directly charged by Parliament. Promoters were required to pay fees to clerks in the Commons and Lords, who drafted the legal documents and ensured that MPs received copies of the bills. The fees paid to clerks were generally smaller than the fees paid to solicitors and parliamentary agents who were not employed by Parliament.[24]

Solicitors and agents handled a variety of tasks for promoters and were especially important when bills were opposed. In such cases, committee proceedings in Parliament resembled a courtroom. Expert witnesses were selected by each side and were examined and cross-examined by MPs. The Birmingham to Worcester canal bill in 1791 provides an illustrative example. It was opposed by a rival canal company, by mill owners and landowners along the route, merchants in neighboring cities who feared trade diversion, and a segment of the manufacturing community in Birmingham who feared higher prices for coal once it was exported.[25] Seventeen witnesses were examined resulting in a lengthy proceeding. Solicitors of agents helped to organize the witnesses who were favorable to the project. Behind the scenes the solicitors were also involved in negotiation with opposition groups. The act for the Birmingham and Worcester canal, for example, contained a clause prohibiting the company from building close to its rival

23. Clifford (1968, 734).

24. Turnpike acts between £50 and £100 went to fees for House of Commons officers. Bridge acts between £95 and £180 went to fees for House of Commons officers. For railway and canal acts, officer fees were between £60 and £330. See table 6.4 for data sources.

25. Counterpetitions and the details of the proceedings for this bill in the House of Lords are available at the Parliamentary Archives in the House of Lords, Main Papers, 30/3/04, May 1791.

canal and even required they provide compensation in the event their rival's profits fell.[26]

The time and resources required to argue against opponents' claims were "political transaction" costs. Transaction costs were higher in Britain than the United States because of its greater urbanization. Land is more valuable in urbanized societies, making rights-of-way problems more difficult. Opposition is also greater because more is invested in mills, coal mines, neighboring cities, and rival transport operators. U.K. transport charters were more expensive, in part, because it is costly to reorganize property rights in a highly urbanized society.

6.6 Developmental Aims and Inter-City Competition

The different chartering regime in the United States was driven by additional factors that were related to its frontier context and emerging urban structure. U.S. improvements promised substantial indirect benefits from higher property values. Many contemporary observers noted a strong relationship between transportation improvements and higher land values. Pennsylvania gazetteer Thomas F. Gordon reported in 1832 that, "None [of the turnpikes] have yielded profitable returns to the stockholders, but everyone feels that he has been repaid for his expenditures in the improved value lands, and the economy of business."[27] An article in the *Poughkeepsie Journal* urged residents to invest in the New Paltz Turnpike not because of dividend payments, "but from an expectation that the investment would be returned with treble interest, in the addition which would be made to business and the value of property." A number of scholarly studies confirm such assessments; they have found that transportation improvements such as navigation companies and early railroads raised land values anywhere from 4 to 10 percent. Property owners living closest to the lines of improvement typically benefited the most.[28]

The combination of poor direct profits and high indirect returns made early U.S. transportation companies, to some degree, public goods. If many local landowners benefited from the improvements, then why buy unprofitable stock? Why not let neighbors buy shares that would quickly depreciate in value? Historians have documented how a vigorous spirit of civic boosterism—including rousing speeches, well-attended public meetings, and widespread publicity in local newspapers—helped to motivate local investment.[29] Analysis of shareholder lists bolsters that interpretation. Investors tended to live near the improvement in question, which makes sense given that those

26. Priestly (1831, 1691).
27. Gordon (1832, 35).
28. Coffman and Gregson (1998, 191–204); Craig, Palmquist, and Weiss (1998, 173–189); Majewski (2000, 28–32); Wallis (2003, 238–244).
29. Klein (1990); Majewski (1996).

owning property closest to the project stood to gain the most. The distribution of shares tended to reflect the distribution of property. The top 10 percent of investors (typically large local landowners and prominent merchants) owned around 40 percent of a given company's shares, while a large number of more modest investors purchased the rest.[30] In Pennsylvania, for example, the average holding of turnpike investors was around $200, while the median holding was $100. The large number of modest investors seemed to be spreading the pain of low-direct returns as widely as possible, while still contributing to a project that promised to deliver substantial indirect benefits.[31]

The strong developmental impetus of early U.S. corporations helps account for why state legislatures never attached fees for charters. U.S. transportation companies could ill afford additional costs, especially up-front costs that would have forced many local organizers to raise a substantial sum of capital even before formally organizing their company. Obtaining a corporate charter cheaply and easily allowed local organizers to gauge the depth of community sentiment and their ability to attract investment into what were essential nonprofit enterprises that still promised significant economic benefits to the community at large. That so many companies obtained charters, yet never built the actual project, suggests the underlying fragility of these enterprises. State governments had no incentive to see more fail, in part because individual legislators—who owned land in the localities they represented—had considerable incentive to speedily approve transportation corporations.

The more "open" urban hierarchy in the United States added to the boisterous booster spirit that animated early transportation companies. Commercial and urban growth, of course, would fuel capital gains resulting in urban real estate speculation. On the flip side, cities that failed to keep pace might suffer absolute declines in trade and population. Urban boosters exaggerated such fears, but an overwhelming amount of qualitative evidence indicates that civic leaders saw the race for commerce as a zero-sum game in which some cities would win while others would lose. On the national level, New York, Philadelphia, Boston, and Baltimore battled for commercial supremacy, while scores of small towns and cities sought to become preeminent within their own region or county. Civic leaders who feared losing population, wealth, and prestige to rival cities could hardly tolerate restrictive and expensive corporate-chartering policies. Urban rivalries, in fact, may have led to too much investment in transportation. The great success of New York's Erie Canal led Philadelphia, Baltimore, and Richmond to try to emulate the Empire State's great success. The resulting state-financed canals ultimately failed in their quest to redirect trade and saddled Pennsylvania, Maryland, and Virginia with significant debt.

30. Hilt (2008, 664).
31. Majewski (2006, 309).

The developmental impetus was also present in the United Kingdom, but it appears to have been weaker. The absence of strong boosterism suggests that transport improvements were viewed as complements to property values and urban status rather than a fundamental determinant of wealth and comparative advantage. The dominance of London in the British urban hierarchy is perhaps one reason. No British city envisioned that it would overtake the metropolis in terms of its economic and political functions. Philadelphia, Boston, and Richmond all had such ambitions vis-à-vis New York. Down the urban ladder there was more competition in the United Kingdom, like that between Bristol and Liverpool who both vied for leadership in the Atlantic trade, but there was no equivalent to the race to link the Eastern Seaboard with western areas in the United States.

6.7   The Role of Democracy

Thus far we have focused on economic differences. There were also, of course, significant political differences, with the United States being more democratic than the United Kingdom. Although the various colonies had significant restrictions on white male suffrage, states slowly began to relax these restrictions once the United States had won its independence. Tax-based qualifications, which were significantly easier to meet, replaced property qualifications in many of the original states. New western states, eager to attract new migrants, generally adapted universal white manhood suffrage. Older states followed their lead. In 1840, 78 percent of all adult white males voted in the presidential election.[32] In Britain, the franchise was far more restricted. In 1774, the estimates are that 13.9 percent of adult males in England and Wales voted and in 1831 only 12.2 percent of adult males voted.[33] Even that number does not fully capture the relative lack of democracy in Britain, as many parliamentary seats were simply given to members of prominent families or their political allies. In 1774, 18 percent of seats in the Commons were contested (i.e., more than two candidates ran for a two seat constituency); in 1818 the figure was the same.[34]

Not only was the United States more democratic, but its wealth was also distributed more equally than Britain's more hierarchal and aristocratic society. In 1810, the top 1 percent of British households owned almost 55 percent of marketable net worth, a figure that rose to 61 percent by 1875. For the United States, the top 1 percent in 1860 owned 29 percent of all assets.[35] State and local studies are consistent with the aggregate U.S. figures. Steckel and Moehling, for example, have recently calculated that the total taxable

32. Engerman and Sokoloff (2005, 906).
33. Jupp (2006, 236).
34. Jupp (2006, 236).
35. Lindert (2000, 181, 188).

wealth owned by the top 1 percent of households in Massachusetts fluctuated between the range of 20 to 33 percent between 1820 and 1860.[36]

The greater degree of democracy and economic equality in the United States made it more difficult to limit the availability of corporate charters. Aggrieved citizens denied corporate charters could use their power at the ballot box to make their voices heard. Those seeking corporate charters used a republican rhetoric suspicious of "privilege," "corruption," and "monopolists" to paint political opponents as "aristocrats" who used political power for individual gain. Such rhetoric was most indentified with Jeffersonian Republicans and Jacksonian Democrats, but it could be used by any group who believed that they had been unfairly denied access to corporate charters.[37] Rather than risk the mobilization of potential political opponents, legislators found it expedient to issue new charters. Restricting access to charters became politically difficult. Local communities flooded the legislature with requests for charters and approval for turnpikes, toll bridges, and other local improvements became routine.

There is some quantitative evidence within the United States that greater democracy contributed to higher numbers of charters for transport improvement. Table 6.8 shows the number of transport charters per capita in the 1820s and 1830s for five U.S. states as well as the average percentage of males who voted in the presidential elections in the same decades. If greater democracy contributed to lower fees for acts or greater effort by politicians, then there should have been a higher increase in acts per capita from the 1820s to the 1830s in states where there was a greater increase in the percentage of males who voted. The bottom panel of table 6.8 shows that this was indeed the case. Ohio had the greatest increase in acts per capita and the greatest increase in the percentage of males who voted. Maryland had the lowest increase in acts per capita and it had the lowest increase in the percentage of males who voted. It is difficult to draw strong conclusions from this analysis because of the myriad of factors influencing relative chartering rates across U.S. states, but it is notable that the correlation between the change in transport charters per capita and the change in the percent voting was 0.78.

Conditions were quite different in Britain where democracy was more muted. The small proportion of males who voted has already been noted. Consistent with this fact, the general view among historians is that elections had little influence on economic policies in the early nineteenth century.[38] This conclusion seems to apply to charters as well. In Britain the number of contested seats provides a local measure of democracy, as data on the number of males who voted in each county is lacking. If elections mattered

36. Steckel and Moehling (2001, 167).
37. Wallis (1999, 294–99); Wood (1992, 305–25); Majewski (2000, 85–110).
38. Jupp (2006, 245).

Table 6.8   Democracy and transport acts across five U.S. states

A. Voting rates and acts per capita

State	Period	Acts per capita	Voting rate
Ohio	1820s	0.368	55.3
New Jersey	1820s	0.441	51
Maryland	1820s	0.962	64.95
New York	1820s	0.871	50.75
Pennsylvania	1820s	0.842	38.1
Ohio	1830s	1.961	74.65
New Jersey	1830s	1.416	65.1
Maryland	1830s	0.883	61.55
New York	1830s	1.104	66.15
Pennsylvania	1830s	1.848	52.9

B. Changes from 1820s to 1830s

State	(1) Change in transport acts per capita	(2) Change in vote rate
Ohio	1.593	19.35
New Jersey	0.975	14.1
Maryland	−0.079	−3.4
New York	0.233	15.4
Pennsylvania	1.006	14.8
Correlation between (1) and (2)		0.776

Sources: For voting rates see Engerman and Sokoloff (2005, 906).

in Britain, then one would expect a positive relationship between the number of transport charters and the number of contested seats in a county. This relationship can be tested using Thorne's data on contested elections in each county around 1800.[39] A simple regression analysis was performed using the number of road acts and the number of contested elections for all constituencies in each English county in two separate periods, 1790 to 1806 and 1807 to 1818. The results show that the change in the number of road acts between the 1790 to 1806 and 1807 to 1817 periods is insignificantly related to the change in contested elections over the same period after controlling for the change in population growth for the county from 1791 to 1801 and 1811 to 1821 (see table 6.9). The same result holds for canal acts over the same two periods. Thus a preliminary analysis of the data suggests little evidence linking electoral competition and transport acts in Britain. The difference with the United States is not surprising. In early nineteenth century Britain,

39. Thorne (1986, 358–67).

Table 6.9   **The effect of contested elections on transport acts across English counties c. 1800**

Variable	Road acts coeff (*t*-stat)	Canal acts coeff (*t*-stat)
Dependent variable: Change in number of transport acts between 1790 to 1806 and 1807 to 1821		
Change in contested elections between 1790–1806 and 1807–1821	0.633 (1.33)	–0.25 (–1.39)
Change in population growth between 1791–1801 and 1801–1811	245 (1.82)	9.22 (0.09)
constant	–1.3 (–2.01)	–2.33 (–4.25)
N	39	39
R-Square	0.13	0.05

Notes: For data on acts see the text. For data on contested elections see Thorne (1986). For data on county level population growth, see Wrigley (2007).

there was a striking absence of the republican rhetoric focusing on privilege, corruption, and monopoly.

A greater degree of democracy in the United States, it should be stressed, did not always lead to more open economic institutions. Some states restricted charters as part of a fiscal strategy of asset finance. Instead of levying taxes, state governments sometimes borrowed money to invest in enterprises that could generate large and steady rates of return. Investment in banks, which frequently generated healthy profits, was the most common strategy. States such as Pennsylvania essentially granted a few favored banks quasi-monopoly status in return for generous bonuses and grants of bank stock. Such practices smacked of giving privileges to favored insiders, but politicians aggressively defended such practices as a means of eliminating taxation. In Pennsylvania, the state derived 23 percent of its revenue from bank investments, which essentially allowed the state to forgo a property tax.[40] Such arrangements broke down in the late 1830s, when bank panics, falling land values, and declining economic activity put many asset finance states near the edge of bankruptcy.

Could transportation enterprises fulfill the same function as banks? New York's famously successful Erie Canal supplied most of the state's revenue for many years, and legislators were therefore leery of chartering railroads that might cut into its operating profits. New Jersey's Camden and Amboy Railroad and Delaware and Raritan Canal were even better examples. In 1830, the New Jersey legislature granted the two corporations (which became known as the Joint Companies) a monopoly on the immensely profitable traffic between New York City and Philadelphia. In return, the state received preferred shares and levied transit duties on goods and passengers. The

40. Wallis (2003b, 239–40); Wallis (1999, 291–94); Wallis (2000, 40–1).

resulting revenue allowed the state to abolish the property tax and expand state support for public education.[41]

New Jersey's unusual arrangement with the Joint Companies was clearly exceptional. The Joint Companies obviously benefited from New Jersey's peculiar geography. Lying between New York and Philadelphia, the Joint Companies monopolized a lucrative route to produce profits that most other transportation companies could not generate. Shippers and passengers residing in New York and Philadelphia—and not residents of New Jersey—suffered the most from the monopoly. In many ways, the monopoly was a crafty means of levying a tax on interstate commerce. Rival entrepreneurs, hoping to charter competing railroad companies, resented the Joint Companies' monopoly status, yet their pleas fell on deaf ears. The stockholders of the Joint Companies managed to align their own interests with the interests of the state's taxpayers and politicians. The state legislature, in fact, explicitly adopted the policy of "the principle of protection as means of revenue" in defending the monopoly.[42] New Jersey's Jacksonian Democrats, usually hostile to privilege, readily supported the state's arrangement as an antitax measure. Despite campaigns to end the monopoly, it persisted until 1870. The political insiders who controlled the Joint Companies certainly benefited from their legal monopoly, but with the public support.

6.8   The Role of Political Decentralization and Centralization

One reason why few states emulated New Jersey was the fear that people and commerce might relocate to another state. Pennsylvania, for example, viewed New York and Maryland as rivals in the race to attract trade from the newly settled West. Granting a legislative monopoly to a company or even restricting access to charters might ultimately result in the loss of new trade opportunities, stoking fears of economic and political decline relative to other states. In the United Kingdom regions also competed with one another, but there was a potentially important difference in how competition was mediated through the political system of each country. In the United States, state legislatures had the authority to issue charters for transport improvement in their state only. They could neither authorize nor prevent the authorization of projects in nearby states. By contrast, United Kingdom regions like England, Wales, and Scotland did not have the direct authority to pass transport acts. This right belonged to the British Parliament as a whole before 1801 and the U.K. Parliament after 1801 when Ireland was incorporated. Thus, in the United States several legislatures possessed monopolies on charters in their own territory, while in the United Kingdom only a single legislature held such power.

41. Cadman (1949, 50–61).
42. Quoted in Cadman (1949, 58).

How did these differences in political structure influence transport acts or charters? One hypothesis is that U.S. state legislators did not charge higher fees because it would lead to a diversion of economic activity to other U.S. states, which would affect legislators' incomes adversely in the long run. In the United Kingdom, Parliament did not face the same cost because trade would be diverted to other areas in the United Kingdom that remained under its control. Parliament could therefore keep the fees high.

The effects of political structure are not easy to test. Ideally, one would like to observe the United States with one legislature or the United Kingdom with many regional parliaments. Irish unification offers one such test case. Ireland had its own parliament before 1801, when it was unified with Great Britain. The Irish Parliament was abolished and all acts relating to transport were passed in London through the U.K. Parliament. Prior to unification, the Irish Parliament might have kept fees low to prevent trade from being diverted to competing areas like the northwestern coast of Wales and England and the southwestern coast of Scotland. The British Parliament would have been sensitive to similar considerations in these same counties that competed with those in Ireland. However, after unification, the U.K. Parliament might have treated the competing regions the same as others because economic activity remained within the United Kingdom.

The preceding argument suggests that if the centralization of the U.K. Parliament mattered, then counties in Ireland, the northwestern coast of Wales and England, and the southwestern coast of Scotland should have had relatively fewer transport acts after unification in 1801 than before when compared to all other counties in Britain. Table 6.10 shows the number of road, canal, and harbor acts for each of the affected regions ten years before and after unification in 1801. The same comparison is made twenty years before and after unification to allow for a delayed response due to the Napoleonic Wars. The key comparison is between the treated counties (i.e., Ireland, the Welsh border, the Scottish border, and the English border) and the control counties (i.e., all other counties in Britain). There was a 57.3 percent drop in road acts in the treated counties between the 1790s and the 1800s, but in the control counties there was a 12.4 percent increase. The difference-in-difference in the percentage change was minus 69.7 percent. A similar set of results holds for canal acts that decreased in Ireland and the English border counties ten years after unification. In the control group canal acts decreased as well, but the difference-in-difference shows that canal acts declined more in the treatment group of counties in Ireland, the Welsh border, the Scottish border, and the English border. For harbor acts the results are mixed. In the ten-year period before and after unification harbor acts decreased more in the treatment counties, but in the twenty-year period before and after unification harbor acts increased more in the treatment counties.

Overall, the calculations provide suggestive evidence that British and Irish

Table 6.10   Changes in transport acts before and after unification of the Irish and British Parliaments in 1801

Act type	Ireland	Welsh border	Scottish border	English border	Total treatment	Treatment % diff	Control % diff	Diff-n-diff
Road acts								
1791 to 1800	33	6	12	24	75	−57.3	12.4	−69.7
1801 to 1810	5	4	3	20	32			
1781 to 1800	41	7	15	32	95	−37.9	35.9	−73.8
1801 to 1820	8	7	8	36	59			
Canal acts								
1791 to 1800	5	0	1	17	23	−69.6	−48.6	−21
1801 to 1810	0	1	3	3	7			
1781 to 1800	8	1	1	18	28	−64.3	−23	−41.3
1801 to 1820	1	1	3	5	10			
Harbor acts								
1791 to 1800	1	3	1	2	7	28.6	57.1	−28.5
1801 to 1810	2	4	3	0	9			
1781 to 1800	1	4	1	3	9	155.6	135.3	20.3
1801 to 1820	8	4	8	3	23			

Sources: Bogart and Richardson (2006).

Notes: Welsh border counties include Flint, Denbigh, Anglesey, Carnarvon, Merioneth, Cardigan, and Pembroke. English border counties include Cheshire, Lancashire, and Cumberland. Scottish border counties include Dumfireshire, Kirkcudbrightshire, Wigtownshire, Ayrshire, Renfrewshire, Dumbartonshire, Argyll, Bute, and Iverness-shire. The control group includes all British counties except Cheshire, Lancashire, and Cumberland.

MPs kept fees relatively low to facilitate transport acts in their respective counties that competed with one another before unification in 1801. More broadly, the results suggest that the high degree of political centralization in the United Kingdom tended to impede transport charters. In terms of the United States, the analysis is generally consistent with the view that political decentralization contributed to the higher number of transport charters. The potent combination of competitive urban rivalries and political decentralization reinforced one another and contributed to liberal chartering policies.

6.9   Concluding Thoughts

The nineteenth century United States had a similar institutional framework as the United Kingdom because of its colonial heritage. In the arena of transport policy the United States followed the British model in issuing charters to private organizations for specific projects. The United Kingdom and the United States differ considerably, however, in how they implemented their chartering regimes. The United States adopted a lower cost and more open charter policy than the United Kingdom.

We suggest that a number of different factors led to this outcome. Differences in urbanization and urban structure were primary factors. In the United States, state legislatures could not charge high fees because the low level of urbanization reduced the profitability of transport projects. The more open urban hierarchy and a highly competitive booster mentality also fueled the desire for cheap and readily available transportation charters. British companies, operating in a wealthier, more densely populated country, generated higher direct profits. British companies could more readily pay fees for charters. These fees might well have reflected the high costs of achieving political consensus in a more densely populated countryside with a greater variety of conflicting interests. In a more negative light, the fees may also have represented a way for Parliament to enrich itself and its members. Differences in political institutions were also contributing factors. The more democratic and decentralized political system in the United States readily responded (with some notable exceptions related to asset financing) to the demand for more charters. The more aristocratic and centralized political structure of Britain, on the other hand, created a more conservative chartering, which helped justify parliamentary fees.

In the end, what is the ultimate importance of understanding the two paths to the transportation revolution? On one level, our comparison comports with James W. Hurst's famous arguments that legal and political institutions led to a "release of energy" that transformed the U.S. economy.[43] The story, though, is more complex than celebrating the democratic and entrepreneur-

---

43. Hurst (1964, 3–32).

ial ethos of the United States while denigrating conservative and aristocratic Great Britain. British chartering policies undoubtedly slowed the pace of the transportation revolution, as the high costs of charters meant that more marginal projects were built slowly and sometimes not at all. While the British economy would have probably benefited from a more open chartering policy, Parliament still allowed considerable institutional innovation to take place. The U.S. system's emphasis on decentralization, moreover, produced its own set of problems. States sometimes prevented out-of-state rivals from obtaining charters, thus restraining competition. State competition sometimes encouraged desperate investment in transportation projects—such as the Pennsylvania Mainline Canal—that had little chance for success. The "release of energy" from open chartering policies certainly contributed to the rapid development of the U.S. economy, but the United States still had to grapple with its own institutional shortcomings.

In the United Kingdom the chartering regime had a number of shortcomings, but it was arguably more open than many of the chartering regimes in continental Europe in the early nineteenth century. It was difficult in most societies to form a corporation or organization without close ties to the monarchy. British transport policy had also progressed greatly from the seventeenth century when conflicts between the Crown and Parliament made it difficult to obtain acts and uncertainty in enforcement was substantial.[44] The two paths of the transportation revolution had their own potential pitfalls, but nevertheless allowed each nation to harness a complex mixture of political authority and private capital to jump-start economic development.

References

Albert, William. 1972. *The Turnpike Road System in England 1663–1840.* Cambridge: Cambridge University Press.

Bogart, Dan. 2010. "Did the Glorious Revolution Contribute to the Transport Revolution? Evidence from Investment in Roads and Rivers, 1600–1750." University of California, Irvine. Working Paper.

Bogart, Dan, and Gary Richardson. 2006. "Parliament and Property Rights: A Database." University of California, Irvine, Department of Economics. Unpublished Manuscript.

Cadman, John W. 1949. *The Corporation in New Jersey: Business and Politics, 1791–1875.* Cambridge: Harvard University Press.

Clark, Gregory. 1998. "The Charity Commission as a Source in English Economic History." *Research in Economic History* 18:1–52.

Clifford, Frederick. 1968. *A History of Private Bill Legislation.* London: Routledge.

44. Bogart (2010).

Coffman, Chad, and Mary Eschelbach Gregson. 1998. "Railroad Development and Land Value." *Journal of Real Estate Finance and Economics* 16:191–204.

Craig, Lee A., Raymond B. Palmquist, and Thomas Weiss. 1998. "Transportation Improvements and Land Values in the Antebellum United States: A Hedonic Approach." *Journal of Real Estate Finance and Economics* 16:173–89.

Duckham, Baron F. 1983. "Canals and River Navigations." In *Transport in the Industrial Revolution,* edited by D. H. Aldcroft and M. J. Freeman, 100–141. Manchester: Manchester University Press.

Engerman, Stanley L., and Kenneth L. Sokoloff. 1997. "Factor Endowments, Institutions, and Differential Paths of Growth Among New World Economies: A View from Economic Historians of the United States." In *How Latin America Fell Behind: Essays on the Economic Histories of Brazil and Mexico, 1800–1914,* edited by Stephen Haber, 260–304. Stanford: Stanford University Press.

———. 2005. "The Evolution of Suffrage Institutions in the New World." *Journal of Economic History* 65:891–921.

Evans, George Heberton, Jr. 1948. *Business Incorporations in the United States, 1800–1943.* New York: National Bureau of Economic Research.

Freeman, Michael J. 1983. "Introduction." In *Transport in the Industrial Revolution,* edited by Derek Aldcroft and Michael Freeman, 1–30. Manchester: Manchester University Press.

Goodrich, Carter. 1960. *Government Promotion of American Canals and Railroads, 1800–1900.* New York: Columbia University Press.

Gordon, Thomas F. 1832. *A Gazetteer of the State of Pennsylvania.* Philadelphia: T. Belknap Press.

Great Britain, House of Commons. 1833. "Report from the Select Committee on House of Commons Officers and Fees." British Parliamentary Papers 12:424–9.

Hartz, Louis. 1948. *Economic Policy and Democratic Thought: Pennsylvania 1776–1860.* Cambridge, MA: Harvard University Press.

Hilt, Eric. 2008. "When did Ownership Separate from Control? Corporate Governance in the Early Nineteenth Century." *Journal of Economic History* 68:645–85.

Hurst, James Willard. 1964. *Law and the Conditions of Freedom in the Nineteenth-Century United States.* Madison: University of Wisconsin Press.

Jupp, Peter. 2006. *The Governing of Britain 1688–1848.* London: Routledge.

Kahn, B. Zorina, and Kenneth L. Sokoloff. 1998. "Patent Institutions, Industrial Organization, and Early Technological Change: Britain and the United States, 1790–1850." In *Technological Revolutions in Europe,* edited by Maxine Berg and Kristine Bruland, 292–314. Northampton, MA: Edward Elgar.

Klein, Daniel B. 1990. "The Voluntary Provision of Public Goods? The Turnpike Companies of Early America." *Economic Inquiry* 28:788–812.

Klein, Daniel B., and John Majewski. 1992. "Economy, Community, and Law: The Turnpike Movement in New York, 1797–1845." *Law & Society Review* 26:469–512.

Lindert, P. H. 2000. "Three Centuries of Inequality in Britain and America." In *Handbook of Income Distribution,* vol. 1, edited by Anthony B. Atkinson and Francois Bourguignon, 167–216. New York: Elsevier.

Lindert, P. H., and J. G. Williamson. 1983. "English Workers' Living Standards during the Industrial Revolution: A New Look." *Economic History Review* 36:1–25.

Majewski, John. 1996. "Who Financed the Transportation Revolution? Regional Divergence and Internal Improvements in Antebellum Pennsylvania and Virginia." *Journal of Economic History* 56:763–88.

———. 2000. *A House Dividing: Economic Development in Pennsylvania and Virginia before the Civil War.* New York: Cambridge University Press.

———. 2006. "Toward a Social History of the Corporation: Shareholding in Pennsylvania, 1800–1840." In *The Economy of Early America: Historical Perspectives and New Directions,* edited by Cathy Matson, 294–316. University Park, PA: Pennsylvania State University Press.

Mitchell, B. R. 1988. *British Historical Statistics.* Cambridge: Cambridge University Press.

———. 1998. *International Historical Statistics: The Americas,* 4th ed. New York: Stockton Press.

Priestly, Joseph. 1831. *Historical Account of the Navigable Rivers, Canals, and Railways, Throughout Great Britain.* London: Longman, Rees, Orme, Brown and Green.

Shead, Jim. 2008. "Jim Shead's Waterways Information." Available at: http://www.jim-shead.com/waterways/index.php.

Steckel, Richard H., and Carolyn M. Moehling. 2001. "Rising Inequality: Trends in the Distribution of Wealth in Industrializing New England." *Journal of Economic History* 61:160–83.

Taylor, Philip E. 1934. "The Turnpike Era in New England." PhD diss. Yale University.

Thorne, R. G. 1986. *The House of Commons 1790–1820.* London: History of Parliament Trust.

U.S. Bureau of the Census. 1998a. "Population of the 33 Urban Places: 1800." Released June 15. http://www.census.gov/population/www/documentation/twps0027/tab03.txt.

———. 1998b. "Population of the 90 Urban Places: 1830." Released June 15. http://www.census.gov/population/www/documentation/twps0027/tab06.txt.

Wallis, John Joseph. 1999. "Early American Federalism and Economic Development, 1790–1840." In *Environmental and Public Economics: Essays in Honor of Wallace E. Oates,* edited by Arvind Panagariya, Paul R. Portney, and Robert M. Schwab, 283–309. Northampton, MA: Edward Elgar.

———. 2000. "State Constitutional Reform and the Structure of Government Finance in the Nineteenth Century." In *Public Choice Interpretations of American Economic History,* edited by Jac. C. Heckelman, John C. Moorhouse, and Robert M. Whaples, 33–52. Boston: Kluwer Academic Publishers.

———. 2003a. "The Property Tax as a Coordinating Device: Financing Indiana's Mammoth Internal Improvement System, 1835–1842." *Explorations in Economic History* 40:223–5.

———. 2003b. "The Promotion of Private Interest (Groups)." In *Collective Choice: Essays in Honor of Mancur Olson,* edited by Jac. C. Heckelman and Dennis Coates, 219–46. New York: Springer.

Ward, J. R. 1974. *The Finance of Canal Building in Eighteenth Century England.* Oxford: Oxford University Press.

Wood, Gordon. 1992. *The Radicalism of the American Revolution.* New York: Knopf.

Wright, Robert E. 2002. *The Wealth of Nations Rediscovered: Integration and Expansion in American Financial Markets, 1780–1850.* Cambridge: Cambridge University Press.

Wrigley, E. A. 2007. "English County Populations in the Later Eighteenth Century." *Economic History Review* 60:35–69.

Premium Inventions
Patents and Prizes as Incentive Mechanisms in Britain and the United States, 1750–1930

B. Zorina Khan

7.1 Introduction

Technological advances make a critical contribution to the wealth and well-being of nations, so it is not surprising that its analysis and study has long attracted the notice of scholars and policymakers. Kenneth Sokoloff's research portfolio includes a number of significant papers demonstrating that the rate and direction of inventive activity and innovation were endogenous. In particular, both important and incremental inventions responded to incentives, and this was especially true of patent policies that promoted a decentralized market-orientation and offered opportunities for a broad spectrum of the population to benefit from their technological creativity. Sokoloff's pioneering 1988 paper showed that improvements in market access led to a greater proportionate response among rural residents who were new to invention. Further evidence on the identities of nineteenth-century patentees suggested that the specific design of the patent system played a substantial role in inducing relatively ordinary individuals to reorient their efforts toward exploiting market opportunities (Sokoloff and Khan 1990; Khan and Sokoloff 1998). Studies of the great inventors (Khan and Sokoloff 1993; Khan 2005) revealed that technologically and economically

B. Zorina Khan is professor of economics at Bowdoin College, and a research associate of the National Bureau of Economic Research.

The great inventors project was initially coauthored with Kenneth L. Sokoloff and funded by a grant from the National Science Foundation. I am grateful for comments from Greg Clark, Stanley Engerman, Naomi Lamoreaux, Peter Lindert, Joel Mokyr, Manuel Tratjenberg, and participants at the UCLA/NBER conference to honor Kenneth Sokoloff. Thanks for excellent research assistance are due to Brian Amagai, Nathaniel Herz, Brittney Langevin, Storey Morrison, Birgitta Polson, Sherry Richardson, Christine Rutan, Peter Smith, and Anne Tolsma. Liability for errors is limited to the author.

important contributions exhibited similar patterns to those of less eminent inventors. Moreover, extensive markets in invention facilitated the appropriation of benefits, especially for inventors who were not well-endowed in terms of formal schooling and financial capital (Lamoreaux and Sokoloff 1996; Khan and Sokoloff 2004). This was not to say that the U.S. patent system and the related legal and market institutions were in any way optimal, but rather that they were appropriate for the circumstances of a newly-developing society and sufficiently flexible to respond to the evolution of economic and social needs.

A number of economists would agree with the view that strong protection of intellectual property rights induced rapid rates of technological and cultural progress during the early industrial period. Indeed, North and Thomas (1976) went as far as suggesting that the patent system was a crucial reason why Britain was the first country in the world to industrialize. A recent paper (Acemoglu, Bimpikis, and Ozdaglar 2008) proposes that patents may facilitate experimentation and diffusion to a greater extent than such alternatives as subsidies. Nevertheless, the historical record is still contested, and debates continue today regarding the design of appropriate mechanisms to encourage potential inventors, innovators, and investors to contribute to expansions in technological knowledge and economic development. Skepticism has increased of late about the efficacy of state grants of property rights in patents and in copyright protection as incentives for increasing creativity and invention. In a reprise of the nineteenth century, extremists today refer to patent systems as "an unnecessary evil," creating "costly and dangerous" intellectual monopolies that should be eliminated (Boldrin and Levine 2008). Among users of intellectual products the open-source movement advocates free access and the elimination of state-mandated rights of exclusion. At the same time, a growing roster of theorists who have been persuaded by models of prizes and subsidies have begun to lobby for these nonmarket-oriented policies as complements or superior alternatives to intellectual property rights. Economic historians who reach similar conclusions tend to extrapolate from the European experience with technological institutions (Clark 2003; Mokyr 1991). As such, it seems timely and relevant to engage in a more systematic comparison of the record of patents and prizes as incentive mechanisms for generating important technological innovation in Europe and America.

This chapter therefore explores the performance of alternative social schemes for promoting inventive activity in Britain and the United States. The evidence suggests that the efficacy of any set of rules and standards will depend on the specific nature of their implementation and on the metasocial context. The early American patent system provided an impressive route to rapid technological progress and economic development, in part because of the supportive network of effective legal, educational, and commercial institutions. In direct contrast, European intellectual property systems imposed constraints and rules that resulted in patterns that ultimately reflected the oligarchic nature of their social and political institutions. These variations in outcome indicate that policies cannot be selected based entirely on abstract conceptualization from models that are not calibrated to determine their sensitivity to institutional design. In particular, mathematical models fail to incorporate one of the most significant differences between patent systems and prizes: their relationship to, and implications for, participation in markets in inventions.

History provides a natural experiment for studying the evolution and effects of patent institutions and prizes. The prevailing view of the leading countries in Europe maintained that only a very narrow group of the population was capable of truly important contributions to technological knowledge. The British patent system was representative in favoring high transactions and monetary costs in order to confine access to a select few. Advocates well understood that patent systems with these sorts of restrictive features would mean that only a limited selection of inventions and inventors would receive patent protection, but the objectives and their outcomes were routinely defended. Moreover, in such countries as England and France prizes were frequently offered as inducements and as rewards for socially-valued contributions. For, the argument went, members of the special class of geniuses would respond more to honors and prizes rather than to mere material incentives, or else they would find it easy to raise the large amounts of funding needed for investments in exclusive rights to inventions. The U.S. institutions, on the other hand, reflected the democratic orientation of the new Republic, in the belief that broad access to property rights and economic opportunities more generally, mediated through the market mechanism, would allow society to better realize its potential. Consequently, in the United States prizes were not as prevalent as in Europe and, indeed, the most prominent of these honorific awards were introduced in the United States at the instigation of foreigners.

This chapter compares the evidence from patent institutions and the bestowal of prizes and their implications for inventors and inventions at the forefront of technological discovery during the early industrial era. The analysis in this chapter draws on samples of so-called "great inventors" from Britain and the United States in the eighteenth and nineteenth centuries. I discuss the extent to which the differences in patent systems across countries were manifested in the award of prizes, and examine the factors that influenced the patterns of patenting and prizes. Given the prevailing orientation of its socioeconomic institutions, it is perhaps not unexpected that the results for England suggest that both patent grants and prizes were primarily associated with recipients from privileged backgrounds. By way of contrast, among the American great inventors, the grant of prizes seemed related more to the nature of the technology rather than the identity of their recipients. Nevertheless, in the United States as well the conferral of prizes was neither as systematic nor as market-oriented as the patterns associated with patents.

7.2   Patent Systems in the Early Industrializers

The grant of exclusive property rights vested in patents developed from medieval guild practices in Europe, and England and France were early leaders in the grant of royal privileges that led to monopolies. According to the 1624 Statute of Monopolies, British patents were granted "by grace of the Crown" and were subject to any restrictions that the government cared to impose.[1] Patents were granted for fourteen years to applicants, including the importers of inventions that had been created abroad, and employers who wished to claim property rights in their workers' inventions. The fees for a full-term patent covering England, Scotland, and Wales amounted to over ten times annual per capita income, until well into the nineteenth century.[2] To a large degree by design, features such as extremely high fees and a lack of examination of applications implied that British patent institutions offered rather limited incentives to inventors who did not already command substantial capital and to creators of incremental inventions. In general, the British approach to encouraging private agents to invest in discovering and developing new technologies reflected a view that significant (in the sense of technologically important, and not being easily discoverable by many people) advances in technical knowledge were unlikely to be created by individuals who did not already have access to the means to absorb the high cost of obtaining a patent or to exploit the invention directly through a commercial enterprise.

These constraints restricted the use of the patent system to inventions of high value, and favored the elite class of those with wealth, political connections, or exceptional technical and scientific qualifications, whereas they deliberately generated disincentives for inventors from humble backgrounds. Indeed, in the Parliamentary debates regarding the patent system, some

---

1. 21 Jac. I. C. 3, 1623, Sec. 6. For the history of the British patent system, see MacLeod (1988) and Dutton (1984).

2. Patent fees for England alone amounted to £100 to £120 ($585), or approximately four times per capita income in 1860. The fee for a patent that also covered Scotland and Ireland could cost as much as £350 pounds ($1,680). Adding a coinventor was likely to increase the costs by another £24. Patents could be extended only by a private Act of Parliament, which required political influence, and extensions could cost as much as £700. The complicated administrative procedures that inventors had to follow added further to the costs: patent applications for England alone had to pass through seven offices, from the home secretary to the lord chancellor, and twice required the signature of the sovereign. Coverage of Scotland and Ireland required that the applicant negotiate another five offices in each country. The cumbersome process of patent applications afforded ample material for satire, but obviously imposed severe constraints on the ordinary inventor who wished to obtain protection for his discovery. These features testify to the much higher monetary and transactions costs, in both absolute and relative terms, of obtaining property rights to inventions in England.

witnesses regarded this restrictiveness by class as one of the chief *merits* of higher fees, since they did not wish patent applications to be cluttered with trivial improvements by the "working class."[3] The Comptroller General of Patents even declared that most inventions induced by low fees were likely to be for "useless and speculative patents; in many instances taken merely for advertising purposes."[4] Patent fees provided an important source of revenues for the Crown and its employees, and created a class of administrators who had strong incentives to block proposed reforms.

Other obstacles in the market for inventions related to policies toward trade in intellectual property rights such as patent assignments. Ever vigilant to protect an unsuspecting public from fraudulent financial schemes on the scale of the South Sea Bubble, ownership of patent rights was limited to five investors (later extended to twelve). Nevertheless, the law did not offer any relief to the purchaser of an invalid or worthless patent, so potential purchasers were well advised to engage in extensive searches before entering into contracts. When coupled with the lack of assurance inherent in a registration system and the scarcity of relevant information, the purchase of a British patent right involved a substantive amount of risk and high transactions costs—all indicative of a speculative instrument. Moreover, the state could expropriate a patentee's invention without compensation or consent, although in some cases the patentee was paid a royalty. In 1816, Sir William Congreve was allowed to violate a legal injunction that prevented him from manufacturing gunpowder barrels without the permission of the patentee, on the grounds that the infringement was in the public service on behalf of the ordnance office of the British Government.[5] It is therefore not surprising that the market for assignments and licences seems to have been quite limited.

By the second half of the eighteenth century, nationwide lobbies of manufacturers and patentees were expressing dissatisfaction with the operation of the British patent system. However, it was not until the middle of the nineteenth century that their concerns and requests for reforms were formally addressed. The creativity and efficiency of the U.S. inventions on display at the Crystal Palace Exhibition of 1851 deeply impressed Europeans, and many observers credited this favorable achievement in part to the innovative American patent institution. As a direct result, in 1852 the British patent laws were revised in the first major adjustment of the system in two centuries. The patent application process was greatly simplified, and a renewal system was adopted, making it cheaper to initially obtain a patent. Before 1852

---

3. Thus, in the 1829 Report of the British Committee on the Patent System, one of the questions was, "Do not you think that if it became a habit among that class of people to secure patent rights for those small discoveries at low rates, it would be very inconvenient?" (The answer was in the affirmative.)

4. Great Britain Patent Office (1858), p. 5.

5. Walker v. Congreve, 1 Carp. Pat. Cas. 356.

patent specifications were open to public inspection only on payment of a fee per patent but afterwards, following the U.S. model, they were indexed and published.

Reforms were limited and hesitant, in part because of other institutional obstacles. The system remained one based on registration rather than examination through the end of the nineteenth century, and this absence of a centralized examination system likely had important consequences. Without examination, there was great uncertainty about what a patent was really worth, and this increased the transactions costs involved in either trading the rights to the underlying technology or in using the patent to mobilize capital financing. Moreover, a patent taken to full term remained just as expensive as before and it was not until the 1880s that the total cost was significantly lowered. Still, as figure 7.1 indicates, when Britain changed the features of its patent system in line with the U.S. rules, British patentees—ordinary and more eminent inventors alike—did respond by increasing their investments in patentable property. A striking feature of the second part of this figure is that the patterns for scientist-inventors, generally held to be motivated by nonmaterial factors, were also responsive to the incentives provided by the changes in institutional design.

Sir Henry Sumner Maine regarded it as self-evident that "if for four centuries there had been a very widely extended franchise and a very large electoral body in this country [Britain]. . . . The threshing machine, the power loom, the spinning jenny, and possibly the steam-engine, would have been prohibited," and "all that has made England famous, and all that has made England wealthy, has been the work of minorities, sometimes very small ones . . . the gradual establishment of the masses in power is of the blackest omen for all legislation founded on scientific opinion."[6] However, even as stringent a critic of democratic ideals as Maine conceded that the federal grant of patent rights was one of the "provisions of the Constitution of the United States which have most influenced the destinies of the American people," and was moreover responsible for the finding that the United States in 1885 was "the first in the world for the number and ingenuity of the inventors by which they have promoted the useful arts."[7]

The framers of the U.S. Constitution and statutes were certainly familiar with, and influenced by, the European experience with technological incentives (Khan 2009). It is telling that they made important departures in the ways in which property rights in technology were defined and awarded, and nearly all of their alterations can be viewed as strengthening and extending inducements and opportunities for inventive activity by classes of the population that would not have enjoyed them under traditional intellectual property institutions. From what record of their thinking survives, the framers were intent on crafting a new type of patent system that would promote

---

6. Sir Henry Sumner Maine (1976 reprint of 1885, 112).
7. Sir Henry Sumner Maine (1976 reprint of 1885, 241–42).

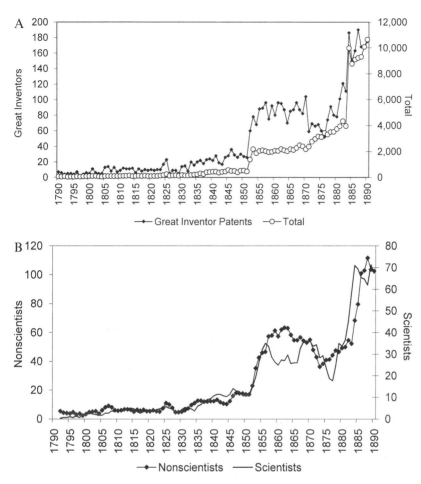

Fig. 7.1   Patenting in Britain, 1790–1890: *A*, **Patenting by British great inventors and all patentees, 1790–1890;** *B*, **Great inventor patents by scientific orientation (three-year moving average, 1790–1890)**

Notes: See text for sample of great inventors. Patent data before 1852 are from Bennett Woodcroft, Chronological Index; patents after 1851 are from the Annual Reports of the Commissioners of Patents. Total patents filed before 1852 comprise patent applications and patent grants after 1851. *Scientists* include great inventors who were listed in a dictionary of scientific biography, those who received college training in medicine, mathematics, or the natural sciences, and Fellows of the Royal Society.

learning, technological creativity, and commercial development, as well as create a repository of information on prior art. Their chosen approach to accomplishing these objectives was based on providing broad access to property rights in new technology, primarily through the medium of low fees and an application process that was impersonal and relied on routine administrative procedures. Incentives for generating new technological knowledge were also fine-tuned by requiring that the patentee be "the first and true inventor" anywhere in the world.[8] Moreover, a condition of the patent award was that the specifications of the invention be available to the public immediately on issuance of the patent. This latter condition not only enhanced the diffusion of technological knowledge, but also—when coupled with strict enforcement of patent rights—aided in the commercialization of the technology. That strict enforcement was indeed soon forthcoming, for within a few decades the federal judiciary evolved rules and procedures to enforce the rights of patentees and their assignees. The key players in the American legal system clearly considered the protection of the property right in new technological knowledge to be of vital importance for the promotion of progress in "the useful arts."

Another distinctive feature of the U.S. system of great significance was the requirement that all applications be subject to an examination for novelty. Each application was scrutinized by technically trained examiners to ensure that the invention conformed to the law and constituted an original advance in technology. Approval from technical experts reduced uncertainty about the validity of the patent, and meant that the inventor could more easily use the grant to either mobilize capital to commercially develop the patented technology, or to sell or license the rights to an individual or firm better positioned to directly exploit it. Private parties could always, as they did under the registration systems prevailing in Europe, expend the resources needed to make the same determination as the examiners; but there was a distributional impact, as well as scale economies and positive externalities, associated with the government's absorbing the cost of certifying a patent grant as legitimate and making the information public. One would, accordingly, expect technologically creative people without the capital to go into business and directly exploit the fruits of their ingenuity to be major beneficiaries under a patent examination system such as the one the U.S. pioneered.

One reason for believing that the design of the patent system (and other institutions relevant to the rewards individuals can realize from their contributions to technology), should matter for who generates new technological knowledge is the now substantial accumulation of evidence that inventive activity in nineteenth-century America was indeed responsive to the prospects for material returns. Working with a general sample of patent records and manufacturing firm data, Sokoloff (1992) argued that both the geographic and cyclical patterns of inventive activity in early industrial America were profoundly influenced by the extent of the market, and had measurable impacts on manufacturing productivity. Skeptics objected that

8. The law employed the language of the British statute in granting patents to "the first and true inventor," but unlike in Britain, the phrase was used literally, to grant patents for inventions that were original in the world, not simply within U.S. borders. This feature of the U.S. was another way in which the technologically creative without much wealth were offered more incentives than were their counterparts in Britain. In the latter country (effectively), and in most of the rest of the world, the first able to file and pay the fee had a right to the patent. This seems to have meant that employers could obtain patents on inventions their employees had actually invented.

analyses based on patent counts were flawed by the inability to distinguish between important and trivial inventions, but our study of the behavior of great inventors born before 1820 showed that these inventors were even more attuned to economic conditions than were ordinary inventors (Khan and Sokoloff 1993). Not only were these great inventors energetic in their use of the patent system to appropriate the returns to their efforts, but their entrepreneurial and inventive activity were also heavily concentrated in geographic areas with low-cost transportation access to markets.[9] If technologically creative individuals are indeed sensitive to the prospects for material returns, then one would expect that the existence and specific design of a patent system would provide incentives that influenced the rate and/or direction of inventive activity.

Another indication that the design of a patent system matters is apparent in the contrast between the United States and Britain in the volume of trade in patented technologies. It was not coincidental that the U.S. system was extraordinarily favorable to trade in patent rights. From the special provision made in the 1793 law for keeping a public registry of all assignments onward, it is clear that the framers of the system expected and desired an extensive market in patents to develop. It was well understood that the patent system enhanced potential private and social returns to invention all the more, by defining and extending broad access to tradable assets in technological knowledge to a wide spectrum of the population. A market-orientation enabled patentees to extract income (or raise capital) from their ideas by selling them to a party better positioned for commercial exploitation, and thereby encouraging a division of labor that helped creative individuals specialize in their comparative advantage. The U.S. system extended the protection of property rights to a much broader range of inventions than obtained in Britain or elsewhere in Europe (largely through the lower costs and diffusion of information) and, when coupled with effective enforcement of the rights of the "first and true inventor," this meant that inventors could advantageously reveal information about their ideas to prospective buyers even before they received a patent grant. As seen in figure 7.2, trade in patents was indeed much more extensive—even on a per patent basis—in the United States than in Britain. The markedly higher ratio of assignments to patents displayed for the United States is all the more striking, both because the British numbers are biased upward by the inclusion of licenses, and because the higher expense of obtaining a patent in Britain should, at least in principle, have led to patents of higher average quality. By the mid-1840s,

9. Such locations must have been particularly attractive to technologically-creative individuals seeking to extract the returns to their talents, and part of the high patenting by "great inventors" in these locations was due to in-migration. However, since the "great inventors" were disproportionately born in the same areas, the extent of markets does seem to have had real independent effects on the rates of inventive activity. Overall, the strong association of patenting with the market, in the case of both ordinary patentees and (even more) great inventors, supports the notion that expected returns played a major role in the processes generating inventions both big and small.

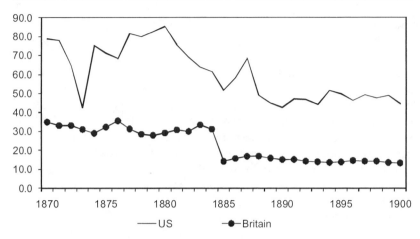

Fig. 7.2   The ratio of all assignments to patents in the United States as compared to the ratio of all assignments and licenses to patents in Britain, 1870 to 1900

Sources: U.S. Patent Office, Annual Report of the Commissioner of Patents. Washington, DC: GPO, various years; and Great Britain Patent Office. Annual report of the Commissioners of Patents (after 1883: Annual Report of the Comptroller-General of Patents, Designs and Trade Marks) London: HMSO., various years.

trade in U.S. patents (and patenting) was booming, and growing legions of patent agents or lawyers had materialized in major cities and other localities where rates of patenting were high. Although these agents focused initially on helping inventors obtain patents under the new system, it was not long before they assumed a major role in the marketing of inventions.[10] In short, the institutional design of the American system created incentives that were more conducive to the development of a market in technology than was the costly registration system in Britain, and this created incentives for specialization and commercialization that proved especially beneficial to inventors with more creativity than capital.

7.3   Great Inventors and Technological Innovation

Kenneth Sokoloff and I compared the patterns of inventive activity for ordinary patentees and for great inventors in the United States, and also investigated the impact of the structure of intellectual property institutions on their behavior and socioeconomic standing. The data set used in this chapter is more extensive than in our previous publications: it includes a

10. Patent agents and lawyers became increasingly specialized and were drawn into activities such as the provision of advice to inventors about the prospects for various lines of inventive activity, and the matching not only of buyers with sellers of patents but also of inventors with venture capital. As the extent of the market for technology expanded over the course of the nineteenth century, creative individuals with a comparative advantage in technology appear to have increasingly specialized in inventive activity. This tendency was likely reinforced by the increasing importance to inventors of specialized technical knowledge as technology became

sample of British great inventors who contributed to technological advances in the early industrial era, in addition to the important inventors who were active in the United States during the long nineteenth century. The U.S. sample consists primarily of all the individuals born before 1886 and listed in the *Dictionary of American Biography* (DAB) on the strengths of their careers as inventors.[11] For each of the U.S. inventors the sample comprises biographical information including places and dates of birth and death, family background such as father's occupation, level and course of formal schooling, a series of variables reflecting work experience and career length, and means (if any) of realizing a return on inventions, total numbers of patents ever received, and, for patentees, the years of first and last patent. Also collated were the individual records of a proportion of the patents (4,500 out of 16,900) they were awarded over their careers (approximately 97 percent received at least one). These individual patent records provide a description of the invention (classified by industry of final use), the residence of the inventor at the date of the patent award, as well as the identity and location of the individual or firm to which the inventor assigned (if he did) his rights at the date the patent was issued. In addition, the sample includes information on prizes that these inventors received.

The parallel sample of great inventors from Britain incorporates information on 435 inventors who were credited with at least one invention between 1790 and 1930. The British sample was compiled from a broader series of biographical dictionaries, including the *Oxford Dictionary of National Biography* (DNB) (Goldman 2005), and the *Biographical Dictionary of the History of Technology* (BD) (Day and McNeil 1996), among others. The objective was to assemble a sample of individuals who had made significant contributions to technological products and productivity. This accorded more with the intent of the BD, whose contributing authors were specialists in the particular technological field that they examined. The DNB's objective was somewhat different and more diffuse, and their selection criteria were less aligned with variables that might conduce to economic or technological significance (and also diverged from the classification of inventions in the DAB). Such inconsistent terminology in the description of occupations and basis for inclusion in the DNB biographies made it necessary to refer

---

more complex. For evidence and more discussion, see Lamoreaux and Sokoloff (1996) and Khan (2005).

11. A small number of inventors were added from other sources, such as dictionaries of engineers, and a few entries from the *Dictionary of American Biography* were dropped because closer examination implied that they had been listed for reasons other than the significance of their inventions. As a way of examining whether there might have been a bias resulting from the procedures the editors (at Columbia University) of the DAB followed in selecting which inventors to include (such as a lower threshold for the inclusion of inventors from New York, or from urban areas generally), I examined whether the number of modern patent citations to the great inventors varied with their characteristics (such as residence), and found that the only significant correlation was with the year of the invention (the later the year, the more likely it was to be cited). Also reassuring was that roughly 40 percent of the U.S. great inventors were cited at least once since the late 1970s.

to a larger number of other historical dictionaries, and also required more cross-checking to compile the sample of great inventors in Britain than for the U.S. counterpart.[12] The information from the DNB and BD volumes was supplemented with other biographical compilations, and numerous books that were based on the life of a specific inventor.[13] Although a few of the entries in any such sample would undoubtedly be debatable, this triangulation of sources minimizes the possibility of egregious error. In addition to the standard variables, it was also possible to collect general information on the prizes and other sorts of official recognition the British great inventors received, including membership in the Royal Society. In short, biographical coverage of the resulting records for the British great inventors is quite comparable to the United States sample.

Even a casual perusal of these data indicates significant contrasts in the characteristics of British and American great inventors, and in the nature of important technological contributions in the two countries. The American sample demonstrates a higher propensity to patent, and greater numbers of average patents per inventor. Top U.S. patentees include Thomas Edison (1,093 patents), Carleton Ellis (753 patents), Elihu Thomson (696), Henry A. Wood (440), Walter Turner (343), and George Westinghouse (306), with numerous other inventors who filed over 100 patents. Among the British inventors, although Sherard Cowper-Coles stands out with a portfolio of some 900 patents, and inventors such as Sir Henry Bessemer, Samuel Lister, and Robert Mushet were also prolific patentees, the ranks of the numbers of patents per person rapidly decline. George Stephenson, Henry Fourdrinier, and Henry Shrapnel each barely mustered a half-dozen patented inventions, and fully forty-seven of the British patentees failed to obtain patent protection for their discoveries (compared to thirteen of the American inventors). American great inventors contributed to technologies in a wide range of industries that included varying degrees of capital intensity, engaged in more experimentation, and were quick to switch to emerging and riskier fields of invention. British inventors, however, were heavily specialized in a narrow range of already leading capital-intensive industries such as textiles, heavy metals, engines, and machinery.

The comparison presented in table 7.1 suggests that throughout most of

12. For instance, the DNB listings included Walter Wingfield ("inventor of lawn tennis"); Rowland Emett (cartoonist and "inventor of whimsical creations"); as well as the inventors of Plasticine, Pimm's cocktail, self-rising flour, and Meccano play sets. At the same time, Henry Bessemer is described as a steel manufacturer, Henry Fourdrinier as a paper manufacturer, and Lord Kelvin as a mathematician and physicist. A large fraction of the technological inventors are featured in the DNB as engineers even though the majority had no formal training. Other inventors are variously described as pioneers, developers, promoters, or designers. Edward Sonsadt is omitted altogether, although elsewhere he is regarded as an "inventive genius." See McNeil (1990, 113).

13. Approximately 15 percent of the sample from these alternative sources was missing altogether from the DNB.

Table 7.1   **Social backgrounds of great inventors in Britain and the United States: By birth cohort, 1700 to 1910**

Birth Cohorts	Farmer or agri. row (%)	Professional or elite row (%)	Manufacturer or skilled worker row (%)	Other white collar row (%)	Unskilled worker or miscellaneous row (%)	n
		Britain, distribution of inventors				
1709–1780	10.0	45.7	21.4	10.0	12.9	70
1781–1820	7.8	37.9	38.8	11.2	4.3	116
1821–1845	8.6	42.9	35.7	4.3	8.6	70
1846–1870	7.3	45.5	21.8	18.2	7.3	55
1871–1910	5.0	57.5	12.5	7.5	17.5	40
		United States, distribution of inventors weighted by patents				
1739–1794	40.5	9.3	22.7	12.6	11.2	259
1795–1819	37.4	19.8	27.9	12.8	2.0	494
1820–1845	39.0	18.7	32.1	7.0	3.2	918
1846–1865	11.0	28.1	31.8	23.3	7.7	1,115
1866–1885	0.2	54.9	8.2	36.7	—	463

Notes: These estimates were computed for all of the great inventors included in the U.S. and British samples, where information about the father's occupation was available. See the text for more information about the samples. Because many of the British great inventors did not obtain patents, the distribution of great inventors for Britain is reported. However, the distribution of great inventors weighted by patents is provided for the United States, because only a small number (less than 5 percent) of the great inventors there did not obtain patents. For tables 7.1 through 7.4, a dashed cell implies there is no entry.

the nineteenth century the great inventors in the United States were drawn from a much broader spectrum of the population than were their British counterparts. For example, among the great inventors born between roughly 1820 and 1845, nearly 43 percent of those in Britain had fathers who were in elite or professional occupations, whereas less than 19 percent of those in the United States came from such privileged backgrounds. The substantial disparity in the social origins of those responsible for important inventions continued until the cohort born after 1865—a group that would have been most active at invention after the major reforms of the British patent system during the 1880s and 1890s. It must be noted, however, that much of this convergence does not seem to be attributable to a shift in the social origins of British great inventors, but rather to an increased proportion of their counterparts in the United States whose fathers were of elite, professional, or other white-collar occupations. This reflects in part the growing importance of a high level of formal schooling for becoming a productive inventor, and the pattern that children of such fathers were more likely to attend institutions of higher learning than children from different backgrounds.

Indeed, another way of gauging the socioeconomic class of the great inventors is to utilize the information on the formal schooling they received. For most of the eighteenth and nineteenth centuries, especially for Europe, whether (and how far) an individual advanced beyond primary schooling was highly correlated with the income and social class of his parents. Another reason for examining the formal schooling attained by the great inventors is that it bears directly on the notion underlying many of the European intellectual property institutions of the nineteenth century—so ably depicted by Dava Sobel in her book *Longitude*—that people from humble backgrounds without much in the way of formal schooling (or scientific knowledge) were generally not capable of making truly significant contributions to technological knowledge. Those adhering to such views, as well as those who believe that advances in science were the driving force behind the progress of early industrialization, might well be surprised by the distributions of the U.S. great inventor patents, arrayed by birth cohort and the amount and type of formal schooling they received. Table 7.2 reveals that, from the very earliest group (those born between 1739 and 1794) through the birth cohort of 1820 to 1845, roughly 75 to 80 percent of patents went to those with only primary or secondary schooling.[14] So modest were the educational backgrounds of these first generations of great U.S. inventors, that 70 percent of those born during 1739 to 1794 had at best a primary edu-

---

14. Primary education comprises those who spent no time in school to those who attended school until about age twelve. Secondary schooling indicates those who spent any years in an academy or who attended school after the age of twelve (but did not attend a college or seminary). Inventors who attended college were either counted in the college category, or—if they were academically trained in engineering, medicine, or a natural science—in the engineering/natural science group.

Table 7.2   **Distribution of U.S. great inventor patents by level of education and the major way in which the inventor extracted returns over their careers: By birth cohorts, 1739–1885**

Birth cohort	Level of education				
	Primary	Second	College	Eng/natsci.	Total
1739–1794 (row %)	69.5	6.8	12.5	11.3	400
Avg. career patents	5.6	3.8	6.5	5.2	75
Sell/license (col. %)	54.9	11.1	84.0	17.7	51.4%
Prop/direct (col. %)	36.5	74.1	2.0	44.7	35.6%
Employee (col. %)	6.2	7.4	—	—	4.8%
1795–1819 (row %)	59.1	19.3	5.4	16.2	709
Avg. career patents	20.0	14.4	17.3	12.1	80
Sell/license (col. %)	58.2	81.0	42.1	60.4	62.1%
Prop/direct (col. %)	33.2	10.2	47.4	24.3	28.1%
Employee (col. %)	8.4	8.8	—	13.5	8.8%
1820–1845 (row %)	39.2	34.7	16.3	9.7	1,221
Avg. career patents	41.8	44.0	29.4	23.7	145
Sell/license (col. %)	50.7	31.8	37.4	72.8	44.0%
Prop/direct (col. %)	42.3	55.2	47.7	19.3	45.5%
Employee (col. %)	7.7	13.0	14.9	7.0	10.2%
1846–1865 (row %)	22.2	24.5	20.9	32.4	1,438
Avg. career patents	158.3	73.6	78.6	55.3	80
Sell/license (col. %)	94.5	68.5	46.2	57.1	66.0%
Prop/direct (col. %)	5.5	18.6	52.8	16.9	22.6%
Employee (col. %)	—	12.9	—	23.6	10.4%
1866–1885 (row %)	0.2	17.9	21.4	60.5	574
Avg. career patents	—	144.5	53.6	155.7	26
Sell/license (col. %)	—	1.0	46.3	40.1	34.3%
Prop/direct (col. %)	100.0	98.1	49.6	18.7	39.7%
Employee (col. %)	—	1.0	4.1	41.2	26.0%

Notes: See the text.

cation, with the proportion dropping to only just above 59 percent among those who entered the world between 1795 and 1819. Given that these birth cohorts were active and, indeed, dominant until the very last decades of the nineteenth century, these numbers unambiguously indicate that people of rather humble backgrounds were capable of making important contributions to technological knowledge.

The evidence suggests that these features and the market-orientation of the U.S. patent system were highly beneficial to inventors, and especially to those whose wealth would not have allowed them to directly exploit their inventions through manufacturing or other business activity. As seen in table 7.2, a remarkably high proportion of the great inventors, generally near or above half, extracted much of the income from their inventions by selling or licensing the rights to their inventive property. Moreover, it was just those groups that one would expect to be most concerned to trade their intellectual property that

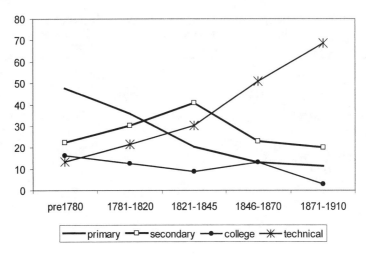

Fig. 7.3   Distribution of British great inventors, by level of education and birth cohort

Note: See text.

were indeed the most actively engaged in marketing their inventions. Specifically, the great inventors with only a primary school education were most likely to realize the income from their inventions through sale or licensing, whereas those with a college education in a nontechnical field were generally the least likely to follow that strategy. Overall, the reliance on sales and licensing was quite high among the first birth cohort (51.4 percent on average), and remained high (62.1, 44.0, and 66.0 percent in the next three cohorts), until a marked decline among the last birth cohort (those born between 1866 and 1885). The proportion of great inventors who relied extensively on sales or licensing of patented technologies then fell sharply, and there was a rise in the proportion that realized their returns through long-term associations (as either principals or employees) with a firm that directly exploited the technologies.

Consistent with what one would expect from the design of their patent system, British institutions do not appear to have been nearly as favorable to those who did not, or could not, attend universities. After the change in the laws toward the American model, an increasing proportion of these eminent British inventors went on to obtain at least one patent over their career. Britain lagged the United States considerably in literacy and other gauges of schooling amongst the general population (thus, biasing the results against the case being made here). Nevertheless, as figure 7.3 indicates, individuals with low levels of schooling were far less well represented among the British great inventors, and those with university degrees in technical fields such as engineering, natural sciences, or medicine were far more represented than they were in the U.S. sample. Primary school education accounted for roughly 40 percent of the patents that were granted to the U.S. cohort

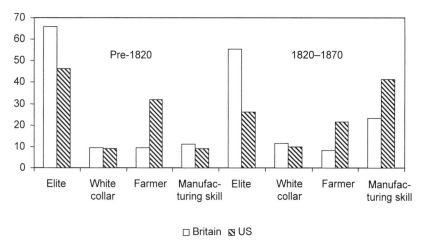

Fig. 7.4   British and U.S. great inventors who attended college, by occupational class of father and birth cohort
Note: See text.

born between 1820 and 1845, while those with university education in a technical field garnered only 10 percent. The analogous shares for the British great inventors (computed over inventors because many did not patent) were roughly 20 percent and over 30 percent, respectively. The evidence in figure 7.4 on the occupations of the fathers of the great inventors who attended university likewise signals that the British universities recruited their students from far more privileged backgrounds than institutions of higher education in the United States.

Circumstances changed over time with the evolution of technology. Knowledge of science clearly became increasingly important, particularly in the late nineteenth century with the beginning of the Second Industrial Revolution (Khan 2008). Although this development can be overemphasized, such systematic knowledge inputs made significant contributions at the technological frontier and perhaps occurred in the context of R&D programs. For instance, individuals with technical degrees rapidly began to dominate among the later birth cohorts of great inventors in both countries (figure 7.5). Although there is substantial convergence in the distributions of great inventors by formal schooling during this period, this may overstate the extent to which the social origins of the inventors likewise converged. As reported earlier, it seems the great inventors in Britain who received degrees at universities were continually drawn overwhelmingly from extremely privileged backgrounds.[15] The U.S. educational institutions may have evolved

15. See also Khan (2008): The British patent records are consistent with the notion that at least until 1870 a background in science did not add a great deal to inventive productivity of

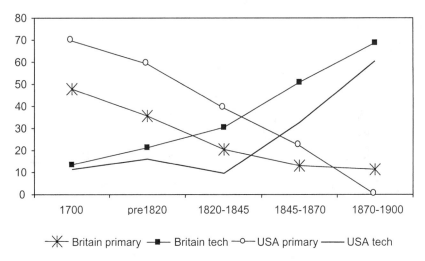

Fig. 7.5   Educational attainment of British and U.S. great inventors, by birth cohort
Note: See text.

more readily to support broader access to the increasingly valuable training in technical fields than did those in Britain. Land-grant state universities began expanding rapidly in the United States during the late-nineteenth century, and these institutions of higher learning are recognized both for offering open access as well as for having a disproportionate number of programs in the natural sciences and in engineering. Britain was much slower in extending entry to educational opportunities, as well as in establishing new universities, and the emphasis was decidedly on a more "classical" orientation. Thus, even after the patent systems in the United States and Britain became more similar, the contrasts in the social origins of those active at invention may have persisted because of other institutional differences.

7.4   Prizes in Britain and America

Observers commonly propose that scientists are primarily motivated by the recognition of their peers, and that solutions to previously intractable

British great inventors. If scientific knowledge gave inventors a marked advantage, it might be expected that they would demonstrate greater creativity at an earlier age than those without such human capital. Inventor scientists are marginally younger than nonscientists, but both classes of inventors were primarily close to middle age by the time they obtained their first invention (and note that this variable tracks inventions rather than patents). Productivity in terms of average patents filed and career length are also similar among all great inventors irrespective of their scientific orientation. Thus, the kind of knowledge and ideas that produced significant technological contributions during British industrialization seem to have been rather general and available to all creative individuals, regardless of their scientific training.

problems yield an innate satisfaction. The implication is that supply elasticities with respect to economic incentives are rather low and that honors might be more appropriate than material gains for eliciting or rewarding contributions at the frontiers of knowledge. In recent years, economists have paid increasing attention to prizes as alternatives to patents as a means of encouraging creativity and innovation without incurring the inefficiency of deadweight losses. In the absence of asymmetries in information regarding costs and benefits, theoretical models suggest that prizes, public funding, or payment on delivery might be preferable to the temporary monopoly associated with intellectual property rights (Maurer and Scotchmer 2004). Wright (1983) found that prizes are optimal if the success probability is moderately high, if the supply elasticity of inventions is low, and in circumstances where awards can be adjusted ex post. Shavell and van Ypersele (2001) argued that subsidies were likely the most effective means of calibrating rewards for innovations according to social value, whereas some versions of this subsidy mechanism center on discounting the price to consumers who value the patented product above its marginal cost. Kremer (1998) suggested an ingenious hybrid that transforms the patent into a prize that is auctioned to the highest bidder in a process that reveals the underlying value of the invention. The government could then engage in patent buyouts of high-valued discoveries and turn them over to the public domain. The theoretical and practical problems with prizes are well recognized, however, and they include challenges in assessing the value of the invention (such as those that arise from asymmetric information, delays in the determination of value, and the difficulty of aggregating benefits that might accrue from sequential innovations). Even if these issues were resolved, the credibility or efficiency of bureaucrats in holding to contracted promises might be questioned, leading to a diminution in the expected return from a prize.

Much of this work has relied on illustrative anecdotes based on isolated historical events. Proponents of patent buyouts, the hybrid patent-prize model, point to the example of the daguerrotype in France, where the state purchased the patent and made it available to the public. Other popular examples of prizes are drawn from the aviation industry in the early twentieth century, most notably the Orteig prize that Charles Lindbergh secured in 1927 for the first transatlantic flight. Ironically, the example that is most frequently cited in favor of prizes, the problem of determining longitude at sea, and the experience of the humble artisan John Harrison with the Board of Longitude, instead demonstrates the disadvantages of administered award systems.[16] More systematic studies of prizes include Petra Moser's (2005) work on the Great Exhibition of 1851, and Brunt, Lerner,

---

16. See Sobel (1995) for more details. The Longitude Act awarded as much as £20,000 for a "Practical and Useful" means of determining longitude at sea. Candidacy for the award was judged by a Board of Longitude, members of whom were drawn from the scientific, military, and public elite, some of whom were themselves competing for the prize. These individuals were

and Nicholas, (2008) who conclude that prizes offered by the Royal Agricultural Society of England comprised a "powerful mechanism" in inducing technological innovation. Nevertheless, closer inspection of the British and French historical records gives ample reason to question the efficacy of prizes during this period, especially in the case of inventors who were not politically astute or who were more likely to have been drawn from the "lower classes."[17]

In Europe, an extensive array of prizes were conferred on "deserving" inventors, such as the premium offered for margarine and food preservation, and the sums directed toward the process to make soda from sodium chloride.[18] European inventors or introducers of inventions could benefit from the award of pensions that sometimes extended to spouses and offspring, loans (some interest-free), lump-sum grants, bounties or subsidies for production, exemptions from taxes, cash, and more honorary items such as titles or medals. The biographies of the British great inventors include information about honors and awards they earned. Altogether, 171 of the inventors in the sample (close to 40 percent) received such recognition, ranging from the recipients of gifts of silver plate from the Crown to two winners of the Nobel Prize (Sir Edward Appleton and Guglielmo Marconi). Unlike patents, it is impossible to trace and compile comprehensive counts of prizes that inventors received over their careers, but the omissions seem to be random. Although they are not as detailed or complete as one would like, these data still allow us to obtain insights into the advantages and drawbacks of patents and alternative incentive/reward mechanisms in the case of technologically important discoveries.

As a number of scholars have reminded us, elites and talented innovators can engender social benefits and growth; however, rent-seekers in privileged positions might not only redistribute wealth but also have the potential to

---

scornful of Harrison as a common uneducated artisan, and hindered his attempts to collect the prize, which was never actually awarded. Instead, as Harrison was close to death, the King intervened and provided payment for achieving the task that had eluded the finest theoretical scientific minds up to that date.

17. In 1775 the French government and the Académie des Sciences offered a prize of 2,400 livres for a process of making artificial soda from sodium chloride. Numerous attempts were made to solve the problem until Nicholas Leblanc finally succeeded and obtained a patent for the discovery in 1791. However, he never obtained the prize from the Académie, his factory was seized, and he died as an impoverished suicide in 1806. The British government promised Lord George Murray £16,500 pounds for his telegraph but they only gave him £2,000 and he died in debt. As for the famed Henry Shrapnel, the DNB notes that "a narrow, bureaucratic interpretation of the terms of the award ensured that, in reality, he enjoyed scant financial gain."

18. Premiums from the state did not preclude inventors from also pursuing profits through other means, including patent protection. For instance, Napoleon III offered a prize for the invention of a cheap substitute for butter that allegedly induced Hippolyte Mège to make significant improvements in margarine production. In assessing the efficacy of this prize it should be noted that many inventors worldwide were already pursuing the idea of a cheap and longer-lasting substitute for butter. Mège not only won the prize but also obtained patent protection for fifteen years in France in 1869, and patented the original invention and several improvements in England, Austria, Bavaria, and the United States.

reduce growth (Murphy, Shleifer, and Vishny 1991). If potential inventors are aware that prize winners will be drawn from the more privileged classes, such awards are less likely to induce the more humble inventors to make contributions to new technologies. Table 7.3 presents ordinary least squares (OLS) regressions where the dependent variable is the likelihood that a British great inventor is the recipient of at least one prize (the analysis here does not distinguish between different types of awards).[19] The results highlight the potential inefficiencies of administered awards, which were highly susceptible to the possibility of bias, personal prejudices, or even corruption. The grants of prizes to British great inventors seem to have been primarily connected to elite status itself rather than to factors that might have enhanced productivity.[20] The most significant variable affecting the possession of a prize was an elite or Oxbridge education, which substantially increased the odds of getting an award, despite the traditional hostility of such institutions to pragmatic or scientific pursuits.[21] It is worth noting the contrast with specialized education in science and engineering, patentee status, and employment in science or technology, which had little or no impact on the probability of getting a prize. Instead, such accolades were more linked to residence close to the capital, or to publications in the annals of the "learned societies," which resembled gentlemen's social clubs where membership simply depended on connections and payment of substantial dues.

An interesting facet of the relationship between privilege, science, and technological achievement in Britain is reflected in the experience of the ninety great inventors who were also Fellows of the Royal Society.[22] The

19. Ideally, one would like to distinguish between different categories of awards, especially between those that were bestowed as an ex post reward for career achievements and those that were offered as ex ante inducements. One would also wish to allow for variation in their objectives, value, timing, and frequency. However, the biographical information is unfortunately not sufficiently detailed to allow such disaggregation.

20. Samuel Sidney (1861) thought that "the prize system has invariably broken down" (375), and "[t]he theory that prizes encourage humble merit is only a theory, for experience shows that in a series of yearly contests wealth wins, as it must be when hundreds of pounds must be expended to win ten" (376).

21. See Roy Macleod and Russell Moseley (1980). As late as 1880 only 4 percent of Cambridge undergraduates read for the NSTs (Natural Science Tripos) and most were destined for occupations such as the clergy and medicine. The method of teaching eschewed practical laboratory work, and there was a general disdain among the dons for the notion that science should be directed toward professional training; so it is not surprising that only 4 percent of the NST graduates entered industry. Students who did take the NSTs tended to perform poorly because of improper preparation and indifferent teaching, especially in colleges other than Trinity, Caius, and St. John's. Chairs in engineering were created in Cambridge in 1875 and in Oxford in 1907, whereas MIT alone had seven engineering professors in 1891.

22. The variable indicates whether the inventor was inducted into the Royal Society at any point in his lifetime. Although the society was associated with some of the foremost advances in science, many of the projects the Royal Society funded were absurd or impractical. James Bischoff (1842) notes that the Society distributed £544 12s in premiums "for improving several machines used in manufacturers, vis. The comb-pot, cards for wool and cotton, stocking frame, loom, machines for winding and doubling, and spinning wheels. None of these inventions of spinning machines, however, succeeded."

Table 7.3 Likelihood of British great inventor receiving prize (OLS linear probability), dependent variable: Probability of receiving prize

	(1)	(2)	(3)	(4)
Intercept	0.43	0.40	0.38	0.29
	(9.75)***	(6.23)***	(5.90)***	(1.83)
Time period				
Before 1800	−0.22	−0.22	−0.23	−0.17
	(2.88)***	(2.62)***	(2.77)***	(1.93)*
1800–1819	−0.12	−0.13	−0.13	−0.09
	(1.59)***	(1.51)	(1.54)	(1.07)
1820–1839	−0.18	−0.20	−0.23	−0.19
	(2.68)***	(2.63)***	(3.11)***	(2.58)***
1840–1849	−0.12	−0.08	−0.10	−0.06
	(1.31)	(0.84)	(1.03)	(0.60)
1850–1859	−0.11	−0.07	−0.10	−0.09
	(1.43)	(0.83)	(1.13)	(0.95)
1860–1869	0.02	−0.03	−0.01	−0.03
	(0.19)	(0.31)	(0.11)	(0.28)
Education				
Elite schooling	0.33	0.30	0.21	0.20
	(5.24)***	(4.06)***	(2.88)***	(2.63)***
Science degree	—	0.02	−0.04	−0.02
		(0.28)	(0.63)	(0.22)
Technical degree	—	0.03	0.00	0.01
		(0.33)	(0.00)	(0.08)
Residence				
London and home counties	—	0.16	0.12	0.13
		(3.27)***	(2.50)***	(2.64)***
Patentee	—	−0.04	−0.06	−0.11
		(0.64)	(0.97)	(1.81)
Fellow of Royal Society	—	—	0.15	0.15
			(2.43)***	(2.23)***
Publications	—	—	0.16	0.16
			(3.04)***	(3.02)***
Employment				
Scientific	—	—	—	0.06
				(0.37)
Professional	—	—	—	−0.01
				(0.05)
Engineering	—	—	—	−0.00
				(0.02)
Manufacturing	—	—	—	0.06
				(0.40)
Inventive Career	—	—	—	0.003
				(2.19)*
	$N = 435$	$N = 394$	$N = 390$	$N = 385$
	$R^2 = 0.09$	$R^2 = 0.11$	$R^2 = 0.15$	$R^2 = 0.16$

Notes: T-statistics are in parentheses. Prizes consist of all nonpatent awards including medals and ex-post or ex-ante cash grants. Patentee is a dummy variable that indicates whether the inventor had ever received a patent through 1890, and coinvention was counted as one patent. Publications comprise a count of articles in professional journals and nonfiction books. London and the Home Counties include Berkshire, Middlesex, Sussex, Essex, Kent, Oxford, Bedfordshire, and Hertfordshire. Elite education refers to education at Cambridge, Oxford, Durham, the Royal Colleges, or graduate education in Germany. Science education includes college training in mathematics, sciences, or medicine, whereas technical education comprises postsecondary education in engineering or metallurgy. Career length is measured as the period between the first and last invention plus one year.

***Significant at the 1 percent level.

**Significant at the 5 percent level.

*Significant at the 10 percent level

likelihood that an inventor had received prizes and medals was higher for scientific men who had gained recognition as famous scientists or Fellows of the Royal Society. The Royal Society itself was the target of persistent criticism throughout this period, including scathing assessments by its own members such as Sir William Grove and Charles Babbage. Many were disillusioned with these award systems, attributing outcomes to arbitrary factors such as personal influence, the persistence of one's recommenders, or the self-interest of the institution making the award. Grove, a great inventor and member of the Royal Society, was only one of the many contemporary observers who "lambasted both the Royal Society and the increasingly influential specialist scientific societies for their nepotism and corruption, calling for full-scale reform of England's scientific institutions."[23] The bias in the award of technological premiums was widespread and was not merely limited to privileges for members of the Royal Society. William Sturgeon, an electricity pioneer who was the son of a Lancashire shoemaker, was ignored by the scientific elites because of his social background. The uneducated George Stephenson resolved the problem of a safety lamp using practical methods, whereas Sir Humphry Davy applied scientific principles. According to the DNB, "in 1816 Davy received a public testimonial of £2,000 and Stephenson the relatively paltry sum of 100 guineas." The growing disillusionment in Europe with the prize system as an incentive mechanism for generating innovation—and its subsequent decline in the twentieth century—are consistent with the coefficients on the time trend over the course of the nineteenth century.

In the United States the statutes from the earliest years of the Republic ensured that the progress of science and useful arts was to be achieved through a complementary relationship between law and the market in the form of a patent system. Notable Americans such as Benjamin Franklin and Alexander Hamilton advocated the award of prizes and subsidies for invention and innovation but, despite their support, the premium system in the United States has always been sporadic and limited in scope. For instance, the New York Society for Promoting Arts, Agriculture, and Economy, founded in 1764, offered £600 in premiums for innovations in spinning flax, manufactures, and agricultural products, but was dissolved only a decade later. The state of New York provided premiums in 1808 for textile goods but similarly ceased after a few years, whereas the Pennsylvania Society for the Encouragement of Manufactures and the Useful Arts occasionally offered gold medals and cash disbursements. Little success met the proposals that were repeatedly submitted to Congress throughout the nineteenth century to replace the patent system with more centralized systems of national prizes, awards, or subsidies by the government. In general, the granting of premiums was far more prevalent in agriculture rather than

23. Gillespie (1980, vol. 5, 559).

in manufacturing, possibly because many agricultural innovations were not patentable.

Annual fairs for a variety of agricultural and mechanical exhibits were organized by the American Institute of New York (founded in 1828), and the Massachusetts Charitable Mechanic Association (founded in 1795 but with an inaugural exhibition in 1837), whereas numerous state fairs of varying scale sporadically raised funds to reward the best improvements in diverse categories among the exhibits.[24] The occasional exhibitions of the Franklin Institute, founded in 1824 to promote mechanics and manufactures, comprised the most significant of such prizes for technological innovations, but these had largely ceased by the middle of the nineteenth century. Prizes in the form of medals and diplomas were similarly featured at international and national exhibitions, notably the Crystal Palace Exhibition in London in 1851; the Paris expositions of 1855, 1867, and 1889; the Centennial Exhibition of 1876 in Philadelphia; and the World's Columbian Exposition of 1893 in Chicago.

Individual benefactors also offered prizes for advances in American technology. The most prominent awards included the medals funded by Elliott Cresson's 1848 endowment, the Longstreth Medal in 1890, and the John Scott Medal and premium. The latter was funded by a legacy from a London pharmacist, who bequeathed $4,000 in 1815 to the corporation (city) of Philadelphia for "premiums to ingenious men or women who make useful inventions." Noted recipients of the Scott Medal included George Westinghouse, Nikola Tesla, and Thomas Edison, but some contend the award was administered with "generally low standards and a certain narrowness" (Fox 1968, 416). Other prizes were designed to address specific problems, such as "Ray Premiums" offered by F. M. Ray for innovations "to improve the conveniences and safety of railroad travel." Nevertheless, more extensive proposals to enhance the premium system failed to persuade, because it was argued that the process of rapid technological change was most likely to be attained through decentralized decision making by inventors themselves, impersonal filtering of value by the market, and through legal enforcement by judges confronting individual conflicts on a case-by-case basis. The general conclusion is that Americans tended to be far more skeptical about premiums as incentives for invention than their European counterparts.[25]

24. In 1841 New York state authorized $8,000 annually to promote agriculture and domestic manufactures, allocated through individual counties. Other states followed the same model, including Ohio (1846), Michigan and New Hampshire (1849), Indiana and Wisconsin (1851), Massachusetts and Connecticut in 1852, Maine (1856), Iowa (1857).

25. For instance, Charles B. Lore of Delaware submitted H.R. 5,925 in 1886 to set up an alternative system of rewards for inventors, to be administered by an "Expert Committee." The editors of *Scientific American* were critical of the proposal and pointed out that "[t]he Expert Committee would have a very delicate duty to perform in fixing the cash valuations, and they would constantly be subjected to risks and probabilities of making egregious errors. For instance, if they were to allow $10,000 as the value of the patent for the thread placed in the crease of an envelope to facilitate opening the same, how much ought they to allow for the

Of the great inventors in the United States, 30 percent received prizes, mainly awards from the Franklin Institute, medals from exhibitions, and overseas honors. Amasa Marks and Thaddeus Fairbanks, assiduous exhibitors, won over thirty medals for prosthetics and improvements to scales, respectively. Contributors to electricity innovations such as Elihu Thomson, Thomas Edison, and George Westinghouse were overwhelmed with numerous medals, tributes, and titles. Edison was made a Chevalier of the French Legion of Honor, the Royal Society of Arts in London bestowed the Albert Medal for his career achievements, and Congress presented him with a gold medal in recognition of his "development and application of inventions that have revolutionized civilization in the last century." The inventors of military implements, in particular, were accorded favors both in the United States and throughout the rest of the world: Samuel Colt received a Telford Medal, Hiram Maxim was knighted in England, and by order of the King of Belgium John M. Browning was created a Chevalier de l'Ordre de Léopold for his improvements to armaments.

The first regression in table 7.4 shows the factors influencing the probability that an American great inventor would obtain a prize. It is striking that the regression has very little explanatory power, with an adjusted R-square of only 7 percent, suggesting that the conferral of prizes was largely unsystematic. Individual variables that one might expect would signal the potential for higher economic or technical productivity—schooling, science and technology training, industry—are not significantly different from zero. Location is not influential, neither is birth cohort or prolific patenting. However, in regressions of prizes that great inventors received at industrial exhibitions (not reported here), a higher likelihood of winning prizes tended to be associated with higher number of patents, perhaps because judges used patent records as a signal of greater merit or because multiple patentees who were adept at commercialization also sought to be eligible for prize contests at exhibitions to better market their discoveries. Finally, in all types of prizes, contemporary citations to the inventor's innovations increased the probability of receiving an award, indicating that prizes were in part given because judges were persuaded by the currency of "the next new thing."[26] As the coefficient on long-term citations shows, inventors who made contributions to more lasting technological innovations were not so distinguished.

---

second patent, that was granted for the little knot that was tied on the end of the thread, so that the finger nail could easily hold the thread? Then, again, how much ought the committee allow for a simple device like the patent umbrella thimble slide, a single bit of brass tubing that costs a cent and a quarter to make? Probably the committee would think that one thousand dollars would be a most generous allowance, while two hundred thousand dollars—the limit of the bill—would, of course, be regarded as a monstrous and dishonest valuation. But the real truth is, the patent for this device is actually worth nearer one million dollars than two hundred thousand" (*Scientific American* 54 [April, 1886]: 208).

26. Sidney Smith (1861–1862) referred to the "number of colourable alterations and improvements, devised to satisfy the passion for 'something new,' which is the peculiar failing of amateur judges" (376).

Table 7.4   **Determinants of prizes and career patents among U.S. great inventors**

Dependent variable	(1) Prob. of prize		(2) Log of total patents	
Intercept	0.142	(0.90)	1.516	(6.72)***
Birth Cohort				
1820s and 1830s	0.094	(0.91)	0.021	(0.13)
1840s	0.010	(0.08)	0.034	(0.19)
1850s	0.106	(0.98)	0.219	(1.29)
Region				
Northern New England	0.083	(0.77)	0.217	(1.27)
Southern New England	−0.152	(1.72)	0.111	(0.80)
Middle West	−0.049	(0.49)	0.035	(0.23)
West	−0.001	(0.00)	0.301	(0.56)
South	−0.093	(0.58)	−0.217	(0.87)
Education				
Secondary school	−0.022	(0.24)	0.189	(1.33)
College	−0.007	(0.09)	0.095	(0.77)
Science	0.002	(0.02)	−0.186	(1.03)
Engineering	−0.055	(0.48)	0.065	(0.36)
Citations (index of technical value)				
Contemporary citations	0.010	(2.69)***	0.020	(3.53)***
Long-term citations	0.006	(1.21)	0.038	(5.65)***
Industry				
Construction and engineering	0.054	(0.46)	−0.069	(0.37)
Electrical and communications	0.164	(1.39)	0.329	(1.77)
Heavy industry	0.041	(0.49)	0.227	(1.71)
Light manufacturing	0.126	(1.15)	0.073	(0.42)
Transportation	−0.028	(0.29)	0.061	(0.41)
Patenting				
Log (total patents)	−0.034	(0.77)	—	—
Patent litigation	−0.001	(0.16)	−0.008	(0.72)
Percent of patents sold	0.002	(1.51)	0.007	(4.70)***
Inventive career	0.003	(1.12)	0.036	(4.70)***
Prize dummy	—	—	−0.085	(0.77)
	$R^2 = 0.1605$		$R^2 = 0.67$	
	Adj $R^2 = 0.0677$		Adj $R^2 = 0.63$	
	$N = 231$		$N = 231$	

Notes: These OLS regressions are estimated over a sample of great inventors from the United States from the birth cohorts of the 1820s through 1885. T-statistics are in parentheses. See notes to other tables. Contemporary citations refer to patent citations by other inventors of the same period to the great inventor's work, whereas "long-term citations" refer to citations that were made to the great inventor's work by modern-day patentees (between 1975 and the present). Patent litigation indicates the total number of lawsuits in which the great inventor was involved either as a plaintiff or a defendant. Percent of patents sold (assigned) is an index of commercial success. Career length is measured as the period between the first and last invention plus one year.

***Significant at the 1 percent level.

**Significant at the 5 percent level.

*Significant at the 10 percent level.

By contrast, the second regression assesses the determinants of variation in the total number of patents that the great inventors received (only three in this sample were not patentees). Patent grants appear to have been more systematic, for two-thirds of their overall variation can be explained by the included variables. Patents were positively associated with higher numbers of both contemporary and long-term citations. Thus, a greater propensity to invest in patented inventions was indicative of contributions to technology that were not only important in their own time but also still matter to technical progress today.

7.5 Conclusion

Institutions such as property rights comprise rules and standards that create incentives and constraints that influence behavior. This chapter uses parallel data sets of great inventors from Britain and the United States to explore the nature and consequences of different institutions for generating technological progress. At least three results stand out. First, the inventors in the United States were drawn from a much broader spectrum of the population than were their counterparts in Britain, consistent with the view that the more restrictive provision of property rights in new technological knowledge under the British patent system did matter for who was involved in inventive activity. Although other differences in institutions and economy-wide circumstances undoubtedly contributed to this pattern, it is striking that so much of the important invention in the United States was carried out by individuals from humble backgrounds until very late in the nineteenth century. For these inventors, the patent system and the related market for property rights in invention were critical to their expected and actual ability to appropriate returns from their efforts.

Second, the analysis of the prizes that the great inventors were accorded for their discoveries highlights the potential for "capture" whereby select groups of prize givers bestow prizes on members from their own background, independently of merit. In Britain the most decisive determinants for whether the inventor received a prize were which particular university he had graduated from and membership in the Royal Society of Arts, characteristics that seem to have been somewhat uncorrelated with technological productivity. Thus, rather than being calibrated to the value of the inventor's contributions, prizes to British inventors appear to have been largely determined by noneconomic considerations. If petty politics and social connections were perceived to have played a major role in selecting recipients, this likely undermined the efficacy of such incentives in eliciting efforts by creative individuals without the requisite links or influence. And here it is worth repeating that inventors from undistinguished backgrounds were indeed capable of making discoveries at the frontiers of technology, as the record of the great inventors in the United States amply demonstrates.

Finally, apart from such factors, the determination of prizes seems to have been largely idiosyncratic and difficult to predict, both in Britain and in the United States. In the American case, the only systematic factor influencing their award was whether the innovator operated in the newest technology field, as opposed to discoveries that had lasting technical value. The contrast with patenting is quite marked, especially given that the grant of property rights in patented inventions was related more to the nature of the technology than to the personal characteristics of the inventors. If inventors respond to expected benefits, the implication is that prizes may have been less effective as inducements for investments in inventive activity than other alternative mechanisms. It is therefore not surprising that technological prizes declined in popularity over the course of the nineteenth century. The French Academy of Sciences ultimately switched from a system of prestigious prizes toward more dispersed funding of projects for younger researchers (Crosland and Galvez 1989). Similarly, by 1900 the Council of the Royal Society decided to change its emphasis from the allocation of medals to the financing of research.[27]

These results support the view of those economists who argue that institutions matter, but they also function within a political and economic context that can dramatically influence outcomes. In the context of institutional mechanisms to promote the progress of useful arts, society is likely to benefit most when rewards are tailored to objective technological contributions rather than to the identities of the inventors. Markets for patented inventions in the period of early industrialization in the United States were effective in mobilizing the efforts of creative men and women from all social classes and backgrounds. By contrast, British patent institutions were designed to elicit contributions from only a select class, thus providing fewer incentives for incremental inventions or for the efforts of more humble inventors. The experience of the great inventors in both Britain and America suggests that the institutional structure of prize systems should be calibrated to be more predictable and correlated with productivity, with specific measures to avoid the potential for capture and corruption to which their administration is susceptible. For, as Thomas Jefferson long ago pointed out, perhaps one of the most crucial elements of achieving growth is to ensure that institutions are sufficiently open and flexible to respond to the needs of the developing society.

---

27. The council stated that its experience in the award of medals had revealed that adding to the number of such awards would be "neither to the advantage of the Society nor in the interests of the advancement of Natural Knowledge." See MacLeod (1971, 105).

References

Acemoglu, Daron, Kostas Bimpikis, and Asuman Ozdaglar. 2008. "Experimentation, Patents, and Innovation." NBER Working Paper no. 14408. Cambridge, MA: National Bureau of Economic Research, October.

Bischoff, James. 1842. *A Comprehensive History of the Woollen and Worsted Manufactures.* London: Smith, Elder & Co.

Boldrin, Michele, and David K. Levine. 2008. *Against Intellectual Monopoly.* Cambridge and New York: Cambridge University Press.

Brunt, Liam, Josh Lerner, and Tom Nicholas. 2008. "Inducement Prizes and Innovation." CEPR Working Paper no. 6917. London: Centre for Economic Policy Research.

Clark, Gregory. 2003. "The Great Escape: The Industrial Revolution in Theory and in History." Unpublished Manuscript.

Crosland, Maurice, and Antonio Galvez. 1989. "The Emergence of Research Grants within the Prize System of the French Academy of Sciences. 1795–1914." *Social Studies of Science* 19:71–100.

Day, Lance, and Ian McNeil. 1996. *Biographical Dictionary of the History of Technology.* New York: Routledge.

Dictionary of American Biography. 1928–36. New York: Charles Scribner's Sons.

Dutton, Harold I. 1984. *The Patent System and Inventive Activity during the Industrial Revolution, 1750–1852.* Manchester: Manchester University Press.

Fox, Robert. 1968. "The John Scott Medal." *Proceedings of the American Philosophical Society* 112:416–30.

Gillispie, Charles D., ed. 1980. *Dictionary of Scientific Biography.* 16 volumes. New York: Scribner.

Goldman, Lawrence, ed. 2005. *Oxford Dictionary of National Biography,* online edition. London: Oxford University Press.

Great Britain Patent Office. Various years. *Annual Report of the Comptroller General of Patents.* London: HMSO.

Khan, B. Zorina. 2005. *The Democratization of Invention: Patents and Copyrights in American Economic Development, 1790–1920.* New York: Cambridge University Press and NBER.

———. 2008. "Science and Technology in the British Industrial Revolution: Evidence from Great Inventors, 1750–1930." Unpublished Paper.

———. 2009. "Founding Choices: The Sources of U.S. Policies toward Innovation and Intellectual Property Protection." Unpublished Paper.

Khan, B. Zorina, and Kenneth L. Sokoloff. 1993. "'Schemes of Practical Utility': Entrepreneurship and Innovation among 'Great Inventors' in the United States, 1790–1865." *Journal of Economic History* 53:289–307.

———. 1998. "Two Paths to Industrial Development and Technological Change." In *Technological Revolutions in Europe, 1760–1860,* edited by Maxine Berg and Kristine Bruland, 292–313. Cheltenham: Edward Elgar.

———. 2004. "Institutions and Democratic Invention in 19th Century America." *American Economic Review* 94:395–401.

Kremer, Michael. 1998. "Patent Buyouts: A Mechanism for Encouraging Innovation." *Quarterly Journal of Economics* 113:1137–67.

Lamoreaux, Naomi R., and Kenneth L. Sokoloff. 1996. "Long-Term Change in the Organization of Inventive Activity." *Proceedings of the National Academy of Sciences* 93:12686–92.

MacLeod, Christine. 1988. *Inventing the Industrial Revolution.* Cambridge: Cambridge University Press.

MacLeod, Roy M. 1971. "Of Medals and Men: A Reward System in Victorian Science, 1826–1914." *Notes and Records of the Royal Society of London* 26: 81–105.

MacLeod, Roy M., and Russell Moseley. 1980. "The 'Naturals' and Victorian Cambridge: Reflections on the Anatomy of an Elite, 1851–1914." *Oxford Review of Education* 6:177–95.

Maine, Sir Henry Sumner. 1976. *Popular Government.* Indianapolis: Liberty Classics.

Maurer, Stephen M., and Suzanne Scotchmer. 2004. "Procuring Knowledge." In *Intellectual Property and Entrepreneurship: Advances in the Study of Entrepreneurship, Innovation and Growth,* volume 15, edited by Gary Libecap, 1–31. Bingley: Emerald Group Publishing Limited.

McNeil, Ian, ed. 1990. *Encyclopaedia of the History of Technology.* London: Routledge.

Mokyr, Joel. 1991. *The Lever of Riches.* New York: Oxford University Press.

Moser, Petra. 2005. "How Do Patent Laws Influence Innovation? Evidence from Nineteenth-Century World's Fairs." *American Economic Review* 95:1214–36.

Murphy, Kevin M., Andrei Shleifer, and Robert W. Vishny. 1991. "The Allocation of Talent: Implications for Growth." *Quarterly Journal of Economics* 106: 503–30.

North, Douglass, and Robert Thomas. 1976. *The Rise of the Western World: A New Economic History.* New York: Cambridge University Press.

Shavell, Steven, and Tanguy van Ypersele. 2001. "Rewards versus Intellectual Property Rights." *Journal of Law and Economics* 44:525–47.

Sidney, Samuel. 1861–1862. "On the Effect of Prizes on Manufactures." *Journal of Society of Arts* 10:376–80.

Sobel, Dava. 1995. *Longitude: The True Story of a Lone Genius Who Solved the Greatest Scientific Problem of His Time.* New York: Penguin Books.

Sokoloff, Kenneth L. 1988. "Inventive Activity in Early Industrial America: Evidence from Patent Records. 1790–1846." *Journal of Economic History* 48: 813–50.

———. 1992. "Invention, Innovation, and Manufacturing Productivity Growth in the Antebellum Northeast." In *American Economic Growth and Standards of Living before the Civil War,* edited by Robert E. Gallman and John J. Wallis, 345–78. Chicago: University of Chicago Press.

Sokoloff, Kenneth L., and B. Zorina Khan. 1990. "The Democratization of Invention during Early Industrialization: Evidence from the United States." *Journal of Economic History* 50 (2): 363–78.

Wright, Brian D. 1983. "The Economics of Invention Incentives: Patents, Prizes, and Research Contracts." *American Economic Review* 73:691–707.

8

The Reorganization of Inventive Activity in the United States during the Early Twentieth Century

Naomi R. Lamoreaux, Kenneth L. Sokoloff, and Dhanoos Sutthiphisal

According to the standard view of U.S. technological history, large firms reorganized inventive activity during the early twentieth century. Previously, individuals had dominated the process of technological discovery, but as the economy shifted from the mechanical technologies of the first industrial revolution to the science-based technologies of the second, the capital requirements (both human and physical) for successful invention soared. Large firms were better able to muster the resources needed for successful invention. Moreover, their in-house research laboratories solved technological problems more efficiently. Although individual inventors never completely disappeared, they came to play a secondary role in technological

Naomi R. Lamoreaux is professor of economics and history at Yale University, a fellow of the American Academy of Arts and Sciences, and a research associate of the NBER. Kenneth Sokoloff (1952–2007) was professor of economics at the University of California, Los Angeles, and a research associate of the National Bureau of Economic Research. Dhanoos Sutthiphisal is assistant professor of economics at McGill University, and a faculty research fellow of the National Bureau of Economic Research

We would like to express our thanks to Oana Ciobanu, Shogo Hamasaki, Scott Kamino, and Ludmila Skulkina for their able research assistance, to Yun Xia for his help with programming, and above all to Shih-tse Lo for his suggestions and other assistance. We have also benefited from comments by Michael Darby, Rochelle Dreyfuss, Harry First, Louis Galambos, Timothy Guinnane, Paul Israel, Daniel Kevles, Zorina Khan, Margaret Levenstein, Tom Nicholas, Jean-Laurent Rosenthal, Mary O'Sullivan, Ariel Pakes, Ross Thomson, Eugene White, Lynn Zucker, members of the audience at the UCLA conference in honor of Kenneth Sokoloff in November 2008 and at the 2009 World Economic History Congress in Utrecht, and participants in seminars at the NYU Law School, UC Merced, and UCLA's Anderson School of Management. We also gratefully acknowledge the financial support provided by the Social Sciences and Humanities Research Council of Canada (SSHRC), Le Centre interuniversitaire de recherche en économie quantitative (CIREQ) in Montréal, the Harold and Pauline Price Center for Entrepreneurial Studies at the UCLA Anderson School of Management, and the UCLA Center for Economic History.

change, as did the small entrepreneurial ventures that had commercialized their ideas (see, for example, Schumpeter 1942 and Hughes 1989).

This standard view has come under criticism in recent years, and there are a growing number of studies questioning both the advantages of large firms' in-house research laboratories and whether the labs were ever really the dominant source of new technological discoveries (see, for example, Lamoreaux and Sokoloff 1999, 2007; Nicholas 2009, 2010; Hintz 2007). There is also another, largely unrelated literature on capital markets that has very different implications for our understanding of trends in the location of innovative activity. This literature portrays the early twentieth century as a period when more and more Americans were investing their savings in equities and, as a result, a broader range of companies could raise capital from the general public (see, for example, O'Sullivan 2007). One hypothesis that can be drawn from this scholarship is that improved access to finance made it possible for small- and medium-sized enterprises (SMEs) to continue to make important contributions to technological discovery, even as the capital requirements for effective invention rose.

The purpose of this chapter is to bring systematic evidence to bear on this hypothesis. Analyzing data on the assignment (that is, sale or transfer) of patents, we find that large firms with industrial research labs obtained a rising share of patents during the first third of the twentieth century, but that so did small entrepreneurial enterprises. Rather than the former surpassing the latter, these two alternative modes of organizing technological discovery seem to have developed in parallel in different regions of the country. Large firms accounted for the lion's share of the inventions in the Middle Atlantic. By contrast, in the East North Central region smaller entrepreneurial enterprises predominated.

Geography thus mattered for the organization of invention as it did for many of the other economic activities analyzed in this volume. Small entrepreneurial firms could not raise funds on the nation's main equity markets, but they benefited from the regional exchanges that emerged to compete for investment dollars with the New York Stock Exchange (NYSE). They benefited particularly from the networks of venture capitalists that sprung up around these exchanges to exploit the superior information they could collect about local enterprises. Geography mattered in another sense as well because the networks of financiers that supported small entrepreneurial start-ups in the East North Central were much more vulnerable to macroeconomic shocks than the large firms of the Middle Atlantic. Large firms would come to dominate technological discovery more completely over the middle third of the century, but contrary to the standard literature, the change was more a result of the differential effect of the Great Depression than of the inherent superiority of in-house R&D.

8.1   The Literature on Large Firms' Industrial Research Labs

Until the last decade or two, most economists and business historians would have agreed with Joseph Schumpeter (1942) that large firms had become the drivers of innovation in the U.S. economy.[1] The avidity with which big businesses built industrial research laboratories from the 1920s into the 1960s (see Mowery and Rosenberg 1989) indicates that their executives believed that in-house labs were a superior way of organizing technological discovery. Moreover, there seemed to be good theoretical reasons to think they were right. In the first place, the electro-chemical technologies of the second industrial revolution were much more complex than the mechanical technologies of the first. Successful invention now required much greater investments in both physical and human capital and also the kind of coordinated teamwork at which industrial research labs excelled. Second, as a general rule, inventors are better able to solve production problems or create desirable new products if they have access to knowledge gained in manufacturing and marketing. Because this kind of knowledge is largely firm-specific, it is not easily acquired by outsiders, but it can readily be transmitted to researchers in a firm's own R&D facilities. Third, moving R&D in-house can solve the information problems that make it difficult for independent inventors to sell their discoveries to firms that will commercialize them. Before buyers will invest in an invention, they need to be able to estimate its value—to assess, for example, the extent to which a new process will lower production costs, or whether a novel product is likely to appeal to consumers. But sellers of inventions have to worry that buyers will steal their ideas, so they may not be willing to reveal enough information about their discoveries to effectuate a sale. These problems can be avoided by moving the process of technological discovery in-house.[2]

Of course, there were always dissenters who argued that the value of in-house R&D for large firms was less a matter of efficiency than of market dominance through the control of important technologies (see, for example, Reich 1977, 1980, and 1985). Other scholars have also questioned the relationship between firm size and innovation and suggested that most big businesses were considerably larger than the threshold at which size conferred advantages (see, for example, Scherer 1965 and Cohen, Levin, and Mowery 1987). However, it was not until the 1990s, when large firms began to cut back their R&D expenditures and even shut down their labs, that scholars began seriously to question the idea that in-house R&D was a superior way of organizing technological discovery (Rosenbloom and Spen-

---

1. Examples from different parts of the literature include Jewkes, Sawers, and Stillerman (1958); Chandler (1977); Hughes (1989); Lazonick (1991); Teece (1993); Cohen and Klepper (1996).

2. For examples of scholars who have made these arguments, see Nelson (1959); Arrow (1962); Teece (1986, 1988); Mowery (1983, 1995); Hughes (1989); and Zeckhauser (1996).

cer 1996). As some then pointed out, there were important information and contracting problems associated with the movement of R&D in-house that were different from those that afflicted the market exchange of technological ideas but were potentially just as troublesome. In order to learn about and gain control of new technologies developed in their facilities, for example, firms had to invest in monitoring their employees' activities and to create incentives that aligned employees' interests with those of the firms. It was not easy, however, to design a reward structure that induced employees to work hard at generating new technological ideas without discouraging cooperation and the sharing of information within the firm (Lamoreaux and Sokoloff 1999). The problems of managing research employees were greatly magnified, moreover, when firms started hiring university trained scientists who wanted to raise their status in the academic community by publishing discoveries their employers would prefer to keep proprietary, and who were more interested in working on scientifically interesting problems than in improving their firm's profitability (Leslie 1980; Wise 1985; Smith and Hounshell 1985; Hounshell and Smith 1988). In addition, the informational advantages of locating R&D inside the firm turned out not to be as great as expected because research labs were often sited at a remove from the company's other facilities. It required considerable and continuous managerial effort to keep communication flowing across the different units of the firm (Hounshell and Smith 1988; Usselman 2007; Lipartito 2009).

At the same time as scholars were highlighting the problems faced by industrial research laboratories, they were also showing that the difficulties associated with transacting for technology in the marketplace were not as great as hitherto believed. Although patent rights are never perfectly enforced, they provide enough protection to enable inventors to engage in market exchange. Moreover, the information problems that afflict this kind of trade can be solved in a number of ways. Firms seeking to purchase outside technologies can invest in facilities for assessing them and can work to cultivate a reputation for safeguarding inventors' interests; intermediaries who possess the trust of parties on both sides of the market can take charge of facilitating exchange; and talented inventors can establish track records that give buyers confidence in the worth of their discoveries (Gans and Stern 2003; Lamoreaux and Sokoloff 1999 and 2007). Naomi Lamoreaux and Kenneth Sokoloff (1996, 2001, and 2003) demonstrated that a vibrant trade in patented inventions developed during the second half of the nineteenth century, intermediated by patent agents and lawyers, that enabled talented independent inventors to specialize in technological discovery. Steven Usselman (2002) and Stephen Adams and Orville Butler (1999) provided examples of firms that built reputations that encouraged inventors to bring them their ideas. Ashish Arora, Andrea Fosfuri, and Alfonso Gambardella (2001) documented the revival of trade in patented technology in high-tech industries in the late twentieth century. Moreover, scholars have uncovered considerable evidence that large firms continued to purchase inventions from outsiders even after they created industrial research laboratories. David Mowery (1995) has shown that the original function of most in-house R&D facilities was to keep abreast of (and vet for purchase) externally generated technology (see also Lamoreaux and Sokoloff 1999 and 2007). Tom Nicholas (2009) has used geo-coded data on the location of inventors and research labs to show that a significant fraction of the most valuable patents acquired by large firms during the 1920s were most likely *not* generated in the firms' research laboratories. Eric Hintz (2007) has provided case-study evidence showing that, even in the heyday of the industrial research lab in the 1950s, large firms transacted for important technologies with outside inventors who insisted on maintaining their independence.

8.2   The New History of Equity Markets

If the 1920s was the decade when large firms first began to build industrial research laboratories in significant numbers, it was also the decade when securities markets began to channel funds to firms on the technological cutting edge. To the extent that the recipients of these funds were the very same enterprises that were building in-house R&D facilities, the history of the growth of equity markets would simply reinforce the standard view that large firms were the main drivers of innovation in the twentieth century. But recent research has shown that small entrepreneurial enterprises also obtained access to equity markets during this period, a development that is not consistent with the dominant narrative of American technological history.

During the nineteenth century, trading on the markets was pretty much limited to the securities of banks, railroads (bonds, not equities), other transportation companies, and utilities (Navin and Sears 1955; Cull et al. 2006). The number of industrials whose securities were listed on the New York Stock Exchange could be counted on one's fingers, and the number whose unlisted securities traded in New York was also very low (Baskin and Miranti 1997). Industrials had a greater presence on regional exchanges such as Boston's, but even there their shares were traded only infrequently (Martin 1898). The general view among scholars is that problems of asymmetric information limited the public's appetite for equities. Markets were unregulated, firms reported little information about their affairs, and insiders manipulated both the flow of information and corporate decisions to their advantage (De Long 1991; Baskin and Miranti 1997; White 2003). Even the savvy could get taken, as Commodore Vanderbilt found when officers of the Erie Railroad responded to his attempt to buy control by cranking up the printing press and turning out more and more new shares of Erie stock (Adams 1869).

By the turn of the century, however, private parties with an interest in expanding the reach of the securities markets were taking steps to increase the confidence of investors. The New York Stock Exchange, for example, instituted a rule change in 1896 requiring firms listed on the exchange to publish audited balance sheets. A few firms had already begun to provide this kind of information on their own, but the new rule helped to make the exchange an imprimatur of quality, increasing trading, the value of listed shares, and not coincidentally, the price of a seat on the exchange (Neal and Davis 2007). At the same time, investment bankers such as J. P. Morgan exploited the reputations for probity they had built up over the years to expand the market for specific securities. Morgan had worked out a technique for building investors' confidence when he reorganized bankrupt railroads during the 1890s, putting his own people on the boards of directors to reassure stockholders that the business would be run in their interests (Carosso 1987). The railroads' return to profitability enhanced his reputation and the market for their securities, and Morgan used the same method to promote the securities of the giant consolidations he orchestrated at the turn of the century. Studies by J. Bradford De Long (1991) and Miguel Simon (1998) suggest that stockholders responded by flocking to buy the securities of "Morganized" firms and also profited handsomely from their purchases.[3]

This record of profitability whetted investors' appetites for securities, but it was not until the 1920s that the market really took off. Investment bankers had developed new techniques during World War I to sell Liberty Bonds. With the return of "normalcy" in the 1920s, they applied what they had learned to the sale of equities. Eager to enter this business, commercial banks circumvented laws that prevented them from dealing in stocks by setting up affiliates to sell securities to their customers. At the same time, enterprising financiers brought large numbers of small investors into the market for the first time by creating new investment vehicles that gave them access to diversified portfolios. The most important of these, the investment trust, served much the same purpose as mutual funds do today (Carosso 1970; White 1984, 1990; De Long 1991; O'Sullivan 2007). Sales were also fueled during this period by competition between the NYSE and the New York Curb Exchange (which, like the NASDAQ more recently, specialized in issues of newer firms in technologically dynamic industries), by the growth of regional exchanges such as Cleveland's (which promoted the securities of local enterprises), and by the development of a national network of dealers that sold securities "over the counter" (O'Sullivan 2007; Lamoreaux, Levenstein, and Sokoloff 2006, 2007; Federer 2008).

---

3. De Long's argument that Morgan added value to firms by monitoring management's activities has recently been challenged by Leslie Hannah (2007), who claimed that the added value came instead from market power and inside deals. For our purposes, all that is important is that shareholders' appetite for these securities increased.

As investors lapped up what the bankers initially had to offer, firms began to issue more and more new securities. Mary O'Sullivan (2007) has shown that the number and size of new corporate stock issues soared in the early twentieth century, reaching levels during the late 1920s that in real terms were not attained again until the 1980s. Even if one leaves out the bubble years of 1928 and 1929, issues were higher as a proportion of gross domestic product (GDP) during the 1910s and 1920s than in any other period of American history except the recent dot-com boom. By the late 1920s, moreover, the great bulk of the issues consisted of common stock, with investors seeking to profit as much or more from a run-up in share prices as from dividend payments.

It might be thought that the primary beneficiaries of this growth in the securities markets would be large, well-established firms for the simple reason that investors could readily gather information about them (Calomiris 1995). Certainly, as Tom Nicholas (2003, 2007, 2008) has shown, during the 1920s investors particularly favored the equities of large firms with R&D facilities and substantial portfolios of patents in cutting-edge technologies (see also White 1990). But this appetite for technology stocks seems to have spilled over to smaller firms as well. The most obvious evidence is the enormous expansion in the number of firms about which the financial press reported information. Whereas only a handful of industrials were even mentioned in the pages of the *Commercial and Financial Chronicle* in the 1890s, during the late 1920s *Moody's* devoted more than three thousand pages of its annual securities manual to financial information on individual industrial enterprises. O'Sullivan (2007) has shown that investors were particularly attracted to new firms in "high-tech" industries such as radios and aviation. The advent of commercial broadcasting stimulated a craze for radio stocks during the early 1920s that led to so many initial public offerings (IPOs) that wags estimated the number of new shares to be about equal to the number of radios sold. Similarly, after Charles Lindbergh's transatlantic flight captivated the public's imagination, soaring interest in aviation stocks elicited about 125 additional offerings of securities, many of them from new entrants to the industry. O'Sullivan has calculated that the medium age of the issuers was only 0.4 years! Most of the new securities promoted during the 1920s were not listed on the NYSE, but were instead traded on regional exchanges, on the curb market, over the counter, or through more informal channels.

It is important to recognize that offerings by new firms in high-tech industries constituted only a minority of new issues during the 1920s. Nonetheless, the growth of equity markets during this period may have increased the ability of SMEs on the technological cutting edge to finance their inventive activities—either directly by issuing equities or indirectly by attracting venture capital from investors who hoped to be able to make a public offering down the line. If so, this effect is difficult to square with the standard argument that industrial research laboratories had already begun to displace entrepreneurial enterprises as the locus of technological discovery. Our aim in the rest of the chapter is to bring systematic evidence to bear on this problem—to determine whether there was a reorganization of technological discovery during the early twentieth century in favor or large firms, or whether SMEs (and perhaps also independent inventors) continued to play an important role in the generation and exploitation of new technologies.

8.3   Data Sources

We approach this problem through the analysis of patent data.[4] The starting point for our analysis is four random cross-sectional samples of patents that we drew from the *Annual Reports of the Commissioner of Patents* for the years 1870 to 1871, 1890 to 1891, 1910 to 1911, and 1928 to 1929.[5] For each patent in the samples we recorded a brief description of the invention, the name and location of the patentee(s), and the names and locations of any assignees who obtained rights to the invention before the patent was actually issued. We then linked the patents to other information we collected on the assignees to whom the patentees transferred their patent rights. For example, we looked up each company that received a patent in the directories of industrial research laboratories compiled by the National Research Council (NRC). We also collected information about companies receiving patents from financial publications: the *Commercial and Financial Chronicle* for the 1870 to 1871 and 1890 to 1891 cross-sections; *Poor's Manual of Industrials* for 1910 to 1911; and *Moody's Manual of Investments* for 1928 to 1929. Finally, we looked up both individual and company assignees wherever possible in city directories.

The information we obtained from these financial publications and city directories enabled us to classify a large number of the companies who obtained patents by size, measured in terms of the firms' total assets (or in a few cases where that information was not available, total capitalization). We were also able to determine for a large number of firms whether the inventor

---

4. We recognize that some scholars would object that large firms often eschewed patenting in favor of secrecy, taking advantage of the new legal protections for trade secrets that emerged during the early twentieth century (Fisk 2001), but we see no reason to assume a priori that large firms were more likely to favor secrecy than small firms. Indeed, economists working on late twentieth-century data have sometimes found precisely the opposite. Using survey data, they have shown, for example, that small enterprises worry that they will be not be able to protect their intellectual property against infringement by large firms—that for all practical purposes they will be defenseless against giants with the resources to hire the best legal talent (Lerner 1995; Cohen, Nelson, and Walsh 2002; Arora, Ceccagnoli, and Cohen 2007). Some scholars might also object that large firms devoted a significant proportion of their R&D resources to systematizing and elaborating new technologies in ways that often were not patentable (see Usselman [2002] on the railroads, for example). That may well have been the case, but our primary aim in this chapter is to understand whether large firms with R&D facilities were the dominant source of new technologies discoveries by the late 1920s.

5. The 1870 to 1871 sample amounts to about 6 percent of total patents; the other samples about 4 percent.

was an officer, director, or proprietor of the company to which he (or in rare cases she) assigned the patent. Our basic strategy was to use this information to look for changes over time in the relationship between patentees and their assignees and in the types of companies obtaining assignments. Were inventors increasingly less likely over time to be principals in the firms obtaining their patents? Were they more likely to be employees? Was there a shift over time in the types of firms obtaining assignments toward very large firms or toward firms with in-house research laboratories?

8.4   The Organization of Inventive Activity before the Great Depression

If there was a reorganization of inventive activity during the early twentieth century in favor of large firms with their own R&D facilities, one would expect to find, first of all, that inventors were assigning an increasing proportion of their patents to companies by the time of issue (because employees typically had to transfer their patents automatically to their firms), and second, that large firms with research labs would account for a growing proportion of patent assignments.[6] Certainly, the evidence bears the first expectation out. As table 8.1 shows, the fraction of patents assigned at issue increased quite steeply over time, rising from 16.1 percent in the 1870 to 1871 cross section to 56.1 percent in 1928 to 1929, with 87.2 percent of assignments at issue in the latter sample going to companies. The proportion of patents that went to large companies also increased dramatically. For the 1928 to 1929 cross section, the proportion assigned to enterprises reported by *Moody's* as having assets of at least $10 million was 20.5 percent, and 16.1 percent went to companies in that category listed by the NRC as having industrial research laboratories.[7]

These last figures represented a significant increase over those for 1910 to 1911, when few large firms had labs and the proportion of patents that went to firms with more than $10 million in assets was only 3.4 percent. The question, however, is whether the 1928 to 1929 numbers are big enough to make the case that such enterprises were coming to dominate the process of technological discovery. Over the same period, the proportion of patents assigned to companies not covered by publications like *Moody's*

---

6. Contracts requiring employees to assign all patents to their employers became increasingly prevalent by the 1920s. See Fisk (1998) and Lamoreaux and Sokoloff (1999). In the remainder of the chapter we use the descriptor "large" to mean firms included in *Moody's* that had at least $10 million in assets.

7. It is important to bear in mind that assignments to companies can come from outside inventors as well as from employees, so our figures overestimate the proportion of patents generated by the firms concerned. Our analysis includes only utility patents granted to residents of the United States. Adding patents awarded to foreigners would not change the analysis because there were so few of them. Even in 1930 there were only about forty in the sample, and intriguingly, somewhat more of them were acquired by firms not reported in *Moody's* than by large firms. We also exclude from the analysis the small number of patents that were assigned to foreign companies and the small number of patents that were reissued.

Table 8.1   **Distribution of patents and assignments at issue by type of company**

				Distribution (row percentages)				
				Assigned to a company with a financial report				
				Assets ≥ $10 million		Assets < $10 million		
Sample year	Number of observations	% not assigned	% assigned to individual	% with R&D lab	% with no R&D lab	% with R&D lab	% with no R&D lab	% assigned to other company
A. Percent of patents								
1870–1871	1,425	83.9	13.4	0.0	0.1	0.0	0.0	2.6
1890–1891	2,022	70.8	15.7	0.0	0.4	0.0	0.0	13.0
1910–1911	2,498	69.2	11.0	1.2	2.2	0.2	2.6	13.5
1928–1929	2,297	43.9	7.2	16.1	4.4	2.0	4.4	22.1
B. Percent of patents assigned to companies								
1870–1871	38			0.0	2.6	0.0	0.0	97.4
1890–1891	273			0.4	2.9	0.0	0.4	96.3
1910–1911	494			6.3	11.3	0.8	13.2	68.4
1928–1929	1,124			32.8	8.9	4.1	9.1	45.1
C. Percent of companies that obtained assignments								
1870–1871	35			0.0	2.9	0.0	0.0	97.1
1890–1891	220			0.5	1.4	0.0	0.5	97.7
1910–1911	372			3.2	5.6	0.8	11.6	78.8
1928–1929	787			14.5	8.9	5.0	11.3	60.4

Notes: The observations in panels A and B are random samples of patents taken from the *Annual Reports of the Commissioner of Patents* for the years 1870–1871, 1890–1891, 1910–1911, and 1928–1929. We report only utility patents awarded to residents of the United States, excluding patents assigned to foreign companies and patents that were reissued. "Not assigned" means that the patent was not sold or otherwise transferred by the time it was issued. We break assignments at issue into categories according to the identity of the assignee: first, whether the assignee was an individual or a company; and second, if it was a company, whether it was the subject of a report in a financial publication (the *Commercial and Financial Chronicle* for the 1870–1871 and 1890–1891 cross sections; *Poor's Manual of Industrials* for 1910–1911; and *Moody's Manual* for 1928–1929). We divided companies for which financial reports existed into two classes according to the amount of assets on their balance sheets. If no information on assets was reported for a firm, we used its total capitalization instead. If the firm was a subsidiary of a larger company, wherever possible we used the data for the parent on the grounds that that information better reflected the financial resources available to the enterprise. Information on whether a company had a research lab came from the surveys published in the *Bulletin of the National Research Council* for 1921, 1927, and 1946. We considered the firm to have a research lab if it was listed as having one in a survey conducted before the year of the cross-section. A few firms in the category "other company" had industrial research labs, though to save space we do not provide the breakdown in this table. The observations in panel C are the companies to which the patents in the respective cross-sectional samples were assigned. In a few cases more than one of the assignee companies were subsidiaries of the same larger company.

also rose—from 13.5 to 22.1 percent. The latter number is slightly greater than the proportion of patents that went to large firms in the same year, so it would seem that these other firms were holding their own as generators of patentable technology.

There was also a dramatic increase between 1910 and 1911 and 1928 and 1929 (from 4 to 9 percent) in the share of patents acquired by firms where the patentee was an officer, director, or proprietor or that bore the patentee's surname (table 8.2, panel A).[8] We treat the existence of a patentee-principal as a sign of the entrepreneurial character of the company. Sometimes the patentee was clearly the moving force behind the enterprise and held a position (such as president or secretary/treasurer) that indicated his active involvement in running the business. Sometimes, however, another person played the role of entrepreneur, and the patentee received an ownership interest and a largely honorific title (such as vice president) in order to ensure his continuing participation in developing and improving the technology.[9]

As table 8.2 indicates, there was relatively little overlap between the firms we are defining as entrepreneurial and the large firms covered by *Moody's,* particularly those that NRC surveys indicated had industrial research labs. In 1928 to 1929 only 4 percent of the assignments to large firms with R&D labs involved patentee-principals, as opposed to 26 percent of the assignments to firms in the "other" category. Moreover, from table 8.3 we can see that fully 66.3 percent of the assignments by patentee-principals went to "other" companies and only 7.1 percent to large firms with R&D labs. The "other" category consists of firms for which we were not able to find reports in *Moody's.* Although *Moody's* included reports on many small firms, the journal's coverage of large firms was much more comprehensive. We assume, therefore, that firms in the "other" category were smaller on average than those for which there were published financial reports.

Yet another striking difference between the entrepreneurial firms and the large-scale enterprises found in *Moody's* is that they tended to be located in different parts of the country. Whereas large firms were disproportionately concentrated in the Middle Atlantic region, enterprises in which the patentee was a principal were more likely to be found in the East North Central

8. Information on directors' identities comes from city directories and from financial publications such as *Moody's.* Our figures understate the number of patents awarded to principals of firms because we are not able to identify the officers and directors of small companies located in areas without city directories. Our figures are also underestimates because we miss companies with inventor-principals in which the inventor did not happen to receive a patent in 1928 or 1929. Some of the increase we observe may simply be a result of the growth in the number of firms covered by national financial publications. It is doubtful, however, that this expansion in coverage explains a big part of the change because relatively few of the firms for which financial reports are available actually had patentee principals.

9. For examples, see Lamoreaux, Levenstein, and Sokoloff (2006). In the remainder of the chapter, we use the descriptor "entrepreneurial" to refer to firms with a patentee-principal. We do not mean by this terminology to imply that firms without patentee-principals (most large firms, for example) were not innovative.

Table 8.2   Characteristics of patents by type of assignee

| | | | | Assigned to company with a financial report | | | | |
| | | | | Assets ≥ $10 million | | Assets < $10 million | | |
Sample year	All patents	Not assigned	Assigned to individual	Had R&D Lab	No R&D lab	Had R&D lab	No R&D lab	Assigned to other company
				A. Proportion where the patentee was a principal of the company				
1910–1911	0.04	n.a.	n.a.	0.06	0.02	0.50	0.22	0.26
1928–1929	0.09	n.a.	n.a.	0.04	0.11	0.20	0.31	0.26
				B. Proportion cited by a patent obtained in 1975–2002				
1910–1911	0.23	0.25	0.18	0.03	0.18	0.25	0.11	0.18
1928–1929	0.33	0.36	0.35	0.25	0.31	0.30	0.30	0.32
				C. Proportion high-tech1				
1910–1911	0.32	0.29	0.36	0.39	0.77	0.25	0.38	0.34
1928–1929	0.50	0.37	0.58	0.78	0.53	0.57	0.55	0.52
				D. Proportion high-tech2				
1910–1911	0.15	0.13	0.17	0.19	0.52	0.00	0.14	0.19
1928–1929	0.24	0.18	0.24	0.46	0.15	0.37	0.20	0.21
				E. Proportion collaborative				
1910–1911	0.08	0.08	0.07	0.10	0.11	0.50	0.06	0.08
1928–1929	0.10	0.07	0.14	0.14	0.10	0.11	0.12	0.10

Notes: For a description of the cross-sectional samples of patents and the categories of assignees, see notes to table 8.1. We considered the patentee to be a principal if the company obtaining the assignment bore the surname of the inventor or if information in a financial publication or city directory revealed that the patentee was an officer, director, or proprietor of the company. Data on citations from 1975–2002 come from Hall (2006). See Hall, Jaffe, and Trajtenberg (2002) for further information. We classified patents in the 1910–1911 and 1928–1929 samples by technology in two different ways. For high-tech1, we categorized a patent as high tech if, based on our reading of the patent, it pertained to electrical machinery and products, chemicals, petroleum, plastics and rubber, automobiles, primary metals, mining machinery, and transportation equipment, as well as the machinery used in production in these industries. For high-tech2, we defined as high tech patents that were classified by Hall, Jaffe, and Trajtenberg (2002) as falling in technology subclasses 11–49 (based on the U.S. Patent and Trademark Office's classification scheme). These subclasses include patents in chemicals, computers and communication technology, drugs and medical devices, and electrical and electronics. We consider a patent to have been collaborative if the number of patentees on the grant was greater than one. n.a. = not applicable.

Table 8.3   Distribution of patents and patent claims by type of assignee (row percentages)

| | | | Assigned to company with a financial report | | | | |
| | | | Assets ≥ $10 million | | Assets < $10 million | | |
Sample year	Not assigned	Assigned to individual	Had R&D lab	No R&D lab	Had R&D lab	No R&D lab	Assigned to other company
A. Distribution of patents where the patentee was a principal of the company							
1910–1911	n.a.	n.a.	1.9	0.9	1.9	13.2	82.1
1928–1929	n.a.	n.a.	7.1	5.6	4.6	16.3	66.3
B. Distribution of patents cited by a patent obtained in 1975–2002							
1910–1911	76.9	8.9	0.2	1.8	0.2	1.2	10.8
1928–1929	48.3	7.7	12.2	4.1	1.9	4.0	21.8
C. Distribution of patents classified as high-tech1							
1910–1911	62.9	12.4	1.5	5.4	0.1	3.2	14.4
1928–1929	32.4	8.3	24.8	4.6	2.3	4.9	22.7
D. Distribution of patents classified as high-tech2							
1910–1911	60.2	11.9	1.6	7.5	0.0	2.3	16.5
1928–1929	33.5	7.1	30.7	2.7	3.1	3.6	19.3
E. Distribution of patent claims							
1910–1911	59.1	11.7	3.6	4.6	0.2	3.2	17.6
1928–1929	34.7	7.4	19.5	7.1	2.3	5.2	23.8

Notes: See notes to tables 8.1 and 8.2. We do not report the distribution for collaborative patents because the number of patents that named more than one inventor was so small. Patent claims are the number of individual claims for novel technological contributions that the Patent Office approved in the text of the patent. n.a. = not applicable.

states (tables 8.4 and 8.6). Hence in 1928 to 1929, 53.5 percent of the patents acquired by large firms went to assignees located in the Middle Atlantic and only 29.0 percent to those in the East North Central region. By contrast, 43.9 percent of the patents assigned by patentee-principals went to firms in the East North Central states and only 23.5 percent to those in the Middle Atlantic.[10]

The Middle Atlantic and the East North Central regions were the nation's two main technology centers by the late 1920s, each accounting for roughly one-third of total patents (table 8.4). The two regions had comparable rates of patenting per capita (figure 8.1) and similar overall rates of assignment (table 8.5). In both, moreover, large firms obtained a greater share of assignments in 1928 and 1929 than they had in 1910 and 1911. Nonetheless, to the extent that there was a reorganization of inventive activity in favor of large-firm R&D during this period, the change seems to have gone a lot further in the Middle Atlantic region than in the East North Central. In the Middle Atlantic 32.5 percent of all patents went to large firms and only 19.5 percent to "other" companies in 1928 and 1929; in the East North Central the proportions were reversed, with 19.7 going to large firms and 27.5 to "other" companies (table 8.5). Moreover, the proportion of assignments that went to entrepreneurial firms (that is, to firms where the patentee was a principal) was more than twice as high in the East North Central as in the Middle Atlantic (table 8.5). Rather than a complete reorganization of technological discovery, therefore, the data suggest that two alternative modes of organizing technological discovery coexisted during the early twentieth century. Large firms may have dominated the acquisition of patents in the Middle Atlantic, but entrepreneurial firms were more important in the East North Central.

8.5   Questions of Significance and Technological Sector

Before one can conclude definitively that two alternative modes of technological discovery coexisted during the early twentieth century, one must consider the possibility that the patents assigned to entrepreneurial firms were on the whole less significant than those acquired by large firms with R&D labs. After all, patent counts can be notoriously misleading because they weight inventions of varying importance equally. One must also consider the possibility that entrepreneurial firms operated in different technological sectors than large firms with R&D labs—that is, that the patents they acquired were less "high tech."

The question of importance is difficult to resolve for the early twentieth century because patents were not subject to renewal fees and it was not yet common practice for inventors to cite prior art in their applications.

10. On this point, see also Lamoreaux and Sokoloff (2009).

Table 8.4   Regional shares of patents by assignee type (column percentages)

Region	All patents	Not assigned	Assigned to individual	Assigned to company with financial report		Assigned to other company	Company assignment by principal	Company assignment with missing information on principal	Patent cited during 1975–2002	Patent is high-tech1	Patent is high-tech2	Total number of claims
				Assets ≥ $10 million	Assets < $10 million							
A. 1910–1911												
West	10.6	12.3	11.6	1.1	0.0	5.9	8.5	4.8	12.3	10.5	9.0	8.9
West North Central	11.2	13.6	8.7	4.6	5.8	4.1	5.7	4.8	9.4	11.0	8.3	9.1
East North Central	26.1	25.9	23.9	14.9	23.2	32.5	40.6	15.6	27.9	27.1	23.5	26.4
New England	9.7	7.6	11.2	2.3	33.3	16.3	19.8	19.9	9.1	8.0	11.9	11.1
Middle Atlantic	29.8	26.2	28.3	75.9	36.2	36.1	18.9	51.6	29.5	32.8	37.7	34.8
South Atlantic	2.1	2.0	4.0	1.1	0.0	2.1	0.9	2.2	2.1	2.5	1.8	2.1
Other South	10.4	12.4	12.3	0.0	1.4	3.0	5.7	1.1	9.8	8.1	7.8	7.7
B. 1928–1929												
West	10.4	16.4	15.8	1.7	2.7	6.9	5.1	8.2	11.6	7.5	10.0	8.1
West North Central	6.9	9.6	12.1	1.9	4.1	5.3	6.1	3.1	7.4	6.3	3.8	5.4
East North Central	30.1	26.4	20.0	29.0	44.6	37.5	43.9	32.8	29.3	32.0	27.3	30.5
New England	10.0	6.6	9.1	11.5	20.3	12.4	14.8	10.9	9.4	6.9	8.7	12.2
Middle Atlantic	33.7	28.6	27.3	53.5	25.7	29.8	23.5	35.5	33.3	38.0	42.0	37.2
South Atlantic	2.4	1.5	4.8	1.7	2.0	4.3	3.6	6.3	1.9	2.9	3.3	2.3
Other South	6.6	10.9	10.9	0.6	0.7	3.7	3.1	3.1	7.0	6.3	4.9	4.3

Notes: See notes to tables 8.1, 8.2, and 8.3. Regions are the locations of the assignees. The West includes Arizona, California, Colorado, Idaho, Montana, Nevada, New Mexico, Oregon, Utah, Washington, and Wyoming. The West North Central includes Iowa, Kansas, Minnesota, Missouri, Nebraska, North Dakota, and South Dakota. The East North Central includes Illinois, Indiana, Michigan, Ohio, and Wisconsin. New England is Connecticut, Maine, Massachusetts, New Hampshire, Rhode Island, and Vermont. The Middle Atlantic is New Jersey, New York, and Pennsylvania. The South Atlantic is Delaware, the District of Columbia, and Maryland. The Other South is Alabama, Arkansas, Florida, Georgia, Kentucky, Louisiana, Mississippi, North Carolina, Oklahoma, South Carolina, Tennessee, Texas, Virginia, and West Virginia.

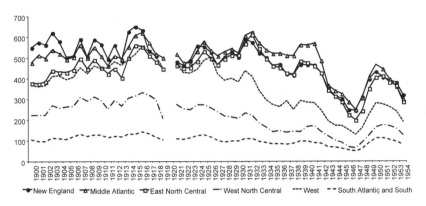

"•"New England   "△"Middle Atlantic   "□"East North Central   "—·West North Central   "···West   "‑‑South Atlantiç and South

Fig. 8.1   Patenting rates by region

Notes: Patent rates are number of patents per million residents of the region. Patent counts come from U.S. Commissioner of Patents, *Annual Reports,* 1900–1925, 1946, and 1955. Population figures are from U.S. Census Bureau (2002). We compiled the regional breakdowns by aggregating state-level patent counts. There are no state-level data for 1920. For definitions of the regions, see table 8.4.

We employ two alternative measures, both unfortunately highly imperfect, to assess whether the patents assigned to large firms were generally more significant than those assigned to their entrepreneurial counterparts. First, following Nicholas (2003), we use information on whether or not a patent in our sample was cited much later on (by a patent granted between 1975 and 2002). Second, we collect information on the number of claims allowed in the patent grant (Lerner 1994; Lanjouw and Schankerman 2004).

As table 8.2 (panel B) shows, the first measure does not favor large firms with industrial research laboratories. Only 25 percent of the patents assigned at issue in 1928 and 1929 to this type of firm were cited by a patent granted between 1975 and 2002, whereas the proportion for firms not included in *Moody's* was 32 percent.[11] This result, however, may not be all that surprising. We know that large firms like the American Telephone and Telegraph Company (AT&T) patented virtually all the inventions devised by their employees, whether important or not, for morale reasons and because even minor patents could be useful for blocking rivals' incursions in their markets (Lamoreaux and Sokoloff 1999; Reich 1977, 1980, 1985). Even in absolute terms, however, large companies with R&D laboratories accounted for a much smaller proportion of patents cited after 1975 than did firms in the "other" category: 12.2 versus 21.8 percent (see table 8.3, panel B). Intriguingly, patents that were not assigned at issue accounted for almost half (48.3) of those cited after 1975 (table 8.3) and had a higher probability of being

11. None of our results change when we use the number of later citations as a measure of importance rather than simply whether or not the patent was ever cited.

Table 8.5 Distribution of patents within regions by assignment categories and by patent characteristics

| | | | | Assigned to a company with a financial report | | | | | | | | | Row percent of company assignments | |
| | | | | Assets ≥ $10 million | | Assets < $10 million | | | | | | | | |
Region	No. of patents	Not assigned	Assigned to individual	Had R&D lab	No R&D lab	Had R&D lab	No R&D lab	Assigned to other company	Cited during 1975–2002	That are high-tech1	That are high-tech2	Made by principal	Missing information on principal
						A. 1910–1911							
West	266	80.1	12.0	0.0	0.4	0.0	0.0	7.5	25.9	31.2	13.2	42.9	42.9
West North Central	281	83.6	8.5	0.0	1.4	0.0	1.4	5.0	18.9	31.0	11.4	27.3	40.9
East North Central	652	68.6	10.1	0.8	1.2	0.0	2.5	16.9	24.1	32.8	14.0	30.9	20.9
New England	242	54.1	12.8	0.4	0.4	1.2	8.3	22.7	21.1	26.0	19.0	26.3	46.3
Middle Atlantic	744	60.9	10.5	3.2	5.6	0.1	3.2	16.4	22.3	34.8	19.6	9.4	45.1
South Atlantic	53	64.2	20.8	1.9	0.0	0.0	0.0	13.2	22.6	37.7	13.2	12.5	50.0
Other South	260	82.7	13.1	0.0	0.0	0.0	0.4	3.8	21.2	24.6	11.5	54.5	18.2
						B. 1928–1929							
West	238	69.3	10.9	1.7	1.7	0.4	1.3	14.7	36.6	36.6	23.1	21.3	44.7
West North Central	159	61.0	12.6	2.5	3.1	1.9	1.9	17.0	35.2	45.9	13.2	28.6	19.0
East North Central	691	38.5	4.8	14.9	4.8	2.5	7.1	27.5	32.0	53.4	21.7	21.9	21.4
New England	229	29.3	6.6	16.6	7.0	3.9	9.2	27.5	31.0	34.9	21.0	19.7	19.0
Middle Atlantic	773	37.3	5.8	27.2	5.3	1.8	3.1	19.5	32.5	56.7	29.9	10.5	20.7
South Atlantic	56	26.8	14.3	14.3	0.0	1.8	3.6	39.3	25.0	58.9	32.1	21.2	48.5
Other South	151	72.8	11.9	1.3	0.7	0.7	0.0	12.6	35.1	48.3	17.9	26.1	34.8

Notes: See notes to tables 8.1 through 8.4.

Table 8.6 Regional distribution of assignee companies by type

Region	No. of firms	Column percentages			Row percentages		
		Company had a financial report		Other company	Company had a financial report		Other company
		Assets ≥ $10 million	Assets < $10 million		Assets ≥ $10 million	Assets < $10 million	
A. 1910–1911							
West	20	3.1	0.0	6.5	5.0	0.0	95.0
West North Central	17	3.1	8.5	4.1	5.9	23.5	70.6
East North Central	116	18.8	29.8	32.8	5.2	12.1	82.8
New England	63	6.3	25.5	16.7	3.2	19.0	77.8
Middle Atlantic	138	65.6	34.0	34.5	15.2	11.6	73.2
South Atlantic	7	3.1	0.0	2.0	14.3	0.0	85.7
Other South	11	0.0	2.1	3.4	0.0	9.1	90.9
B. 1928–1929							
West	43	2.7	3.1	7.2	11.6	9.3	79.1
West North Central	38	3.8	4.7	5.3	18.4	15.8	65.8
East North Central	288	32.1	43.8	36.4	20.5	19.4	60.1
New England	107	12.5	18.8	12.6	21.5	22.4	56.1
Middle Atlantic	262	45.7	26.6	30.3	32.1	13.0	55.0
South Atlantic	26	1.6	2.3	4.2	11.5	11.5	76.9
Other South	23	1.6	0.8	4.0	13.0	4.3	82.6

Notes: See notes to tables 8.1, 8.2, and 8.4. We assigned companies that had facilities in different states to a region on the basis of the location recorded on the earliest patent they received in the sample years.

referenced by late-twentieth-century patents (36 percent) than those in any of the other assignment categories (table 8.2). The explanation may be that inventors sought to maintain control of their most valuable discoveries in order to profit more from exploiting them. This possibility fits with work by Lamoreaux, Levenstein, and Sokoloff (2006, 2007) showing that important inventors in the Cleveland region often had considerable bargaining power vis-à-vis their financial backers and that they exercised that power by licensing rather than assigning their patent rights to their companies.

Regression analysis of the 1928 to 1929 sample confirms the descriptive finding that the patents acquired by large firms with R&D labs were no more likely to be cited by late-twentieth-century patents than those acquired by "other" firms. To keep the focus on the different types of enterprises, we restrict our attention to patents assigned at issue to companies.[12] The dependent variable is a dummy that takes a value of one if the invention was cited by a patent awarded in 1975 to 2002. The independent variables include dummies for the size category of firms in terms of total assets (the omitted category is firms for which we have no financial information[13]), whether the NRC listed the firm as having an industrial research lab, whether the inventor was a principal of the firm, the region in which the assignee was located (the omitted category is the Middle Atlantic), and whether the patent was in a high-tech industry for the time.[14] The estimations are probits, and the reported figures are the marginal effects of changes in the independent variables.

As the first four columns in table 8.7 show, none of the coefficients is statistically significant.[15] Patents assigned to firms with more than $10 million in assets were no more likely to be cited at the end of the century than those that went to firms not included in *Moody's,* and firms with R&D labs were no more likely to acquire patents that would be cited later than those without. Indeed, the point estimates suggest that patents acquired by large firms with R&D labs were somewhat less likely to be cited. We obtained the same results when we included dummies for the individual technology subclasses (not shown). In other words, even within subclasses, the patents of large firms with R&D labs were no more likely to be cited later on than those of small firms.[16] Nor were there any significant regional differences in the frequency of citations. Patents assigned to firms in the Middle Atlantic were no more or less likely to be cited than those assigned to firms in the East North Central

12. The results in table 8.7 do not change when we run the estimations on all patents, except that the coefficients on the dummy for high tech in the first two estimations become consistently negative and weakly significant.

13. This category includes firms for which *Moody's* did not include information on assets or capital, as well as firms that *Moody's* did not cover.

14. See table 8.2 for an explanation of the two alternative definitions of high tech.

15. Including interactions between the R&D and size variables does not change the result. We do not report these estimations, however, because of serious problems of multicolinearity.

16. We do not report these results because of small cell sizes.

Table 8.7   Whose patents were important?

| | Patent was cited in 1975–2002 | | | | Number of claims | | | |
| | Using high-tech1 | | Using high-tech2 | | Using high-tech1 | | Using high-tech2 | |
	(1)	(2)	(3)	(4)	(5)	(6)	(7)	(8)
High-tech patent	-0.001	0.006	-0.036	-0.035	-0.059	-0.058	-0.093	-0.098
	(0.05)	(0.19)	(1.15)	(1.12)	(1.24)	(1.21)	(1.76)*	(1.85)*
Large national firm	-0.042	-0.040	-0.041	-0.038	0.277	0.239	0.272	0.235
	(1.08)	(1.00)	(1.06)	(0.97)	(4.32)***	(3.69)***	(4.27)***	(3.63)***
Small national firm	-0.020	-0.022	-0.020	-0.021	0.087	0.066	0.086	0.067
	(0.47)	(0.52)	(0.47)	(0.50)	(1.18)	(0.89)	(1.17)	(0.90)
Had R&D lab	-0.023	-0.020	-0.016	-0.012	-0.104	-0.101	-0.086	-0.082
	(0.63)	(0.54)	(0.42)	(0.32)	(1.72)*	(1.69)*	(1.41)	(1.35)
Patentee was principal	0.012	0.010	0.010	0.009	0.055	0.064	0.053	0.062
	(0.32)	(0.26)	(0.28)	(0.24)	(0.86)	(1.00)	(0.82)	(0.96)
West		0.072		0.074		-0.160		-0.126
		(0.99)		(1.03)		(1.31)		(1.04)
West North Central		-0.003		-0.009		-0.305		-0.317
		(0.04)		(0.12)		(2.35)**		(2.45)**
East North Central		0.028		0.024		-0.072		-0.075
		(0.85)		(0.73)		(1.31)		(1.36)
New England		0.044		0.038		0.050		0.053
		(0.96)		(0.84)		(0.67)		(0.72)
South Atlantic		0.019		0.017		-0.012		-0.012
		(0.23)		(0.21)		(0.08)		(0.08)
Other South		0.013		0.005		-0.457		-0.462
		(0.13)		(0.05)		(2.61)***		(2.64)***
Constant					2.051	2.108	2.037	2.095
					(43.66)***	(35.83)***	(50.26)***	(39.71)***
Observations	1,124	1,124	1,124	1,124	1,124	1,124	1,124	1,124

Notes: The absolute value of z-statistics are in parentheses. Columns (1) through (4) are probits, and the reported figures are the marginal effects. Columns (5) through (8) are negative binomial regressions. Observations are patents in the 1928–1929 cross section that were assigned to companies. The omitted categories are firms for which we have no financial information and the Middle Atlantic region. For definitions of the variables, see notes to tables 8.1 through 8.4.

***Significant at the 1 percent level.

**Significant at the 5 percent level.

region. Regardless of how we define high-tech, moreover, patents in the cutting-edge industries of the time were no more likely to be cited than other patents, and most of the point estimates have the wrong sign.

This last result in particular raises the question of whether citations from a much later period are a good measure of importance. It is at least possible that technology was changing more rapidly in high-tech industries than in low-tech ones, making inventions in the former obsolete more quickly and thus less likely to be relevant to patents granted in the late twentieth century. For example, Lee de Forest's patents for amplifiers were unquestionably important at the time, but because the devices used vacuum-tube technology they were not cited after 1974.[17] On the other hand, one could argue that patents in old industries circa 1930 were even more likely to be irrelevant by the late twentieth century and hence still less likely to be cited.

Because of our doubts about the validly of late-twentieth-century citations as an indication of a patent's importance, we collected data for an alternative measure that has been suggested in the literature—the number of claims allowed in each patent grant (Lerner 1994; Lanjouw and Schankerman 2004). The estimations (here negative binomial regressions) are reported in table 8.7, columns (5) through (8). Large firms had more claims per patent than those not covered in national financial publications, which by this measure would seem to indicate that large firms' patents were more important on average than those obtained by small firms. Another interpretation, however, is that large firms had superior access to legal expertise and thus were able to secure approval for more claims during the examination process.[18] Regardless, patents acquired by firms that had R&D labs were not more important by this measure than those acquired by firms that did not; the point estimates have the wrong sign and are weakly significant in the first two specifications. Moreover, the negative coefficients on the high-tech dummies (weakly significant for the second of our two classification schemes) raise doubts about the validity of the number of claims as a measure of importance, just as they did for late-twentieth-century citations.

As for the question of whether the patents acquired by large firms with industrial research laboratories were more likely to be in high-tech industries than those acquired by firms operating below the financial radar screen, the answer is yes. For the years 1928 and 1929, fully 78 percent of the patents acquired by the former were in high-tech industries according to our first definition and 46 percent according to our second (table 8.2, panels C and D). The figures for firms not found in *Moody's* were only 52 percent and 21 percent, respectively. As the probit regressions in table 8.8 show, by our

---

17. We searched in Google patents for de Forest's patents that included the word "vacuum." Unlike de Forest's other patents, none of these were cited in the late twentieth century.

18. When we presented this chapter at the NYU Law School, faculty and students in the audience were skeptical that the number of claims reflected anything other than the skill of the patent lawyer.

Table 8.8   Whose patents were high-tech? Collaborative?

	Patent was high-tech				Patent was collaborative			
	Using high-tech1		Using high-tech2		Using high-tech1		Using high-tech2	
	(1)	(2)	(3)	(4)	(5)	(6)	(7)	(8)
High-tech patent					-0.005	-0.007	-0.023	-0.026
					(0.22)	(0.35)	(1.09)	(1.19)
Large national firm	0.113	0.100	0.003	-0.008	0.020	0.021	0.021	0.021
	(2.72)***	(2.36)**	(0.09)	(0.21)	(0.73)	(0.74)	(0.75)	(0.74)
Small national firm	0.006	0.018	-0.012	0.002	0.009	0.014	0.009	0.014
	(0.13)	(0.38)	(0.26)	(0.05)	(0.28)	(0.44)	(0.28)	(0.46)
Had R&D lab	0.135	0.119	0.238	0.234	0.017	0.014	0.021	0.019
	(3.41)***	(2.98)***	(6.23)***	(6.06)***	(0.63)	(0.54)	(0.79)	(0.70)
Patentee was principal	-0.018	-0.012	-0.057	-0.045	0.028	0.029	0.027	0.028
	(0.45)	(0.29)	(1.49)	(1.14)	(1.04)	(1.06)	(1.00)	(1.04)
West		-0.278		0.104		-0.011		-0.007
		(3.54)***		(1.43)		(0.23)		(0.14)
West North Central		-0.054		-0.172		-0.028		-0.032
		(0.68)		(2.42)**		(0.55)		(0.64)
East North Central		-0.067		-0.095		-0.017		-0.019
		(1.87)*		(3.05)***		(0.76)		(0.86)
New England		-0.290		-0.113		-0.028		-0.029
		(5.97)***		(2.74)***		(0.95)		(1.01)
South Atlantic		-0.126		-0.035		-0.002		-0.001
		(1.38)		(0.43)		(0.03)		(0.01)
Other South		-0.165		-0.208		0.053		0.048
		(1.54)		(2.24)**		(0.75)		(0.68)
Observations	1,124	1,124	1,124	1,124	1,124	1,124	1,124	1,124

Notes: The absolute value of z-statistics are in parentheses. The estimates are probits, and the reported figures are marginal effects. Observations are patents in the 1928–1929 cross section that were assigned to companies. The omitted categories are firms for which we have no financial information and the Middle Atlantic region. For definitions of the variables, see notes to tables 8.1 through 8.4.

***Significant at the 1 percent level.
**Significant at the 5 percent level.
*Significant at the 10 percent level.

first definition both large firms and firms with R&D labs were significantly more likely to acquire high-tech patents than firms without financial reports in *Moody's*. By our second measure, however, only firms with R&D labs were significantly more specialized in cutting-edge technology. The point estimates for entrepreneurial firms were negative, though not significant, in all of the regressions. Finally, firms in the Middle Atlantic, where most of large enterprises with industrial research labs were located, were generally more likely to acquire high-tech patents than were firms in other regions, including the East North Central, and the differences were particularly apparent for our second measure.

Before one leaps to the conclusion that large firms with industrial research laboratories were dominating inventive activity in the high-tech sectors of the economy by the late 1920s, it is important to note that firms not included in *Moody's* still accounted for a substantial proportion of high-tech patents: 22.7 percent of the total for high-tech1 and 19.3 percent for high-tech2, compared respectively to 24.8 and 30.7 percent for large firms with R&D labs (table 8.3, panels C and D). So did firms in the East North Central: 32.0 percent for high-tech1 and 27.3 percent for high-tech2, compared respectively to 38.0 and 42.0 percent for the Middle Atlantic (table 8.4, panel B). Moreover, large firms were disproportionately high-tech as early as 1910 and 1911, when few of them had R&D labs. Indeed, in 1910 and 1911 large firms without R&D labs were much more likely to acquire high-tech patents than the firms that pioneered in establishing in-house research facilities (table 8.2, panels C and D). In addition, it is not at all clear how many of the patents acquired by large firms with R&D facilities actually originated in the companies' labs. For the 1928 and 1929 cross section, 36.9 percent of the patents assigned to large firms with research labs came from patentees who were located in a completely different state from any of their assignees' labs.[19] This result is consistent with, though somewhat larger, than that of Nicholas (2009), who found that a significant fraction of patents acquired by a sample of large firms came from inventors who resided beyond commuting distance from the firms' labs.[20] It is also consistent with the argument that one of the major reasons many firms established R&D labs in the first place

19. Adding a variable for whether the patentee resided in the same state as one of the company's labs does not change the estimations in tables 8.7 or 8.8. The variable was never significant, though intriguingly the point estimates suggest that patents by inventors located in the same state as a lab were less likely to be cited than those by inventors who resided in other states.

20. Nicholas found that a quarter of the inventions assigned during the 1920s to sixty-nine large firms operating ninety-four industrial research labs came from inventors who resided beyond commuting distance of the labs. Nicholas also found that the patents obtained from distant inventors were substantially more important on average (more likely to be cited by late twentieth-century patents) than those acquired from inventors who lived within commuting distance. In the case of the General Electric Company (GE), Nicholas was able to check his list of inventors against employment records and found that about a fifth of the patents GE acquired came from inventors who were not employees.

was to improve their ability to assess inventions offered for sale by outside inventors (Mowery 1995; Lamoreaux and Sokoloff 1999). To give one example, at the end of World War I Standard Oil of New Jersey founded its first research department on the principle that "new ideas and inventions . . . would arise in the main from external sources, and that [the department's] primary job . . . would be to uncover these ideas, test them out, and carry them forward to some practical end"—not, as has been generally assumed, to foster "primary research" (Gibb and Knowlton 1956).

Finally, our data enable us to test one of the arguments that scholars have offered for the superiority of research laboratories—that they facilitated the teamwork required for effective innovation in the complex, science-based technologies of the Second Industrial Revolution. If we take the presence of multiple inventors on a patent to be an indication that the patent was a team effort, we find that large firms, even those with industrial research laboratories, had only slightly more such inventions. Fourteen percent of the patents acquired by large firms with R&D facilities were granted to more than one inventor, as opposed to 10 percent of those acquired by firms not included in *Moody's* (table 8.2, panel E). The difference, moreover, is not statistically significant, as the regressions in the last four columns of table 8.8 show.[21]

To recap the results thus far, by the 1920s there seem to have been two main regions of inventive activity in the United States, each organized along different lines. In the Middle Atlantic, large firms with in-house R&D facilities predominated, whereas the East North Central was characterized by entrepreneurial start-ups. Assignments to large firms with R&D facilities accounted for an increased proportion of patents by the late 1920s, but assignments to firms without access to national capital markets represented a larger (and still growing) share of patents. Moreover, it is by no means clear that the patents acquired by large firms with research labs were more important than those acquired by firms in other categories. Large firms' patents were, if anything, less likely to be cited by late-twentieth-century patents than those of other firms, and though they included more claims on average, that was not the case for patents assigned to firms with R&D labs. Although large firms' patents (and those in the Middle Atlantic) were more likely to be in high-tech industries than those of small firms (and firms in the East North Central), the latter maintained a significant presence in these industries, especially according to our first, broader definition. Moreover, the direction of the relationship between large firms' investments in industrial research labs and the generation of high-tech inventions is by no

21. There may have been some bias against filing joint patents because they could pose special legal difficulties. For example, in cases where establishing priority was critical, the date of the invention could not precede the date when the inventors first started working together. Nonetheless, patents for inventions that were the joint product of more than one inventor were invalid unless all the inventors were named in the patent, and firms with R&D laboratories would have had to be very careful on this point. By the 1920s, moreover, the courts were no longer penalizing inventors who inadvertently, without fraudulent intent, mistakenly listed a joint inventor on a patent. See Robb (1922, 113–114); and Robinson (1890, I, 561–73).

means certain.[22] Large firms disproportionately acquired high-tech patents in 1910 and 1911, when only a few of them had research labs; many of the patents acquired by large firms with R&D labs came from inventors located in a different state from the companies' labs; and there was no significant association between large-firm R&D and collaborative invention. Rather than enabling large firms to dominate the process of technological discovery, it may simply be, as Mowery and others have argued, that in-house research labs helped them make better decisions about which of the complicated Second Industrial Revolution technologies being proffered on the market they should buy.

8.6   The Role of Equity Markets

For entrepreneurial firms to make important contributions to technological discovery, especially in the complex science-based technologies of the second industrial revolution, they needed to be able to raise capital. One clear advantage that large firms with R&D labs had over their entrepreneurial counterparts was ready access to the nation's main financial markets. As table 8.9, panel B shows, the vast majority of patents assigned to large firms (69.9 percent) and to firms with R&D labs (60.1 percent) went to enterprises whose shares were listed on the NYSE. By contrast, the proportion of patents acquired by entrepreneurial firms that were listed on the NYSE was comparatively miniscule (7.2 percent), and even if one adds to that firms whose equities traded on the secondary or regional exchanges, the total was still only 19.5 percent. Nonetheless, it is still possible that the growth of equity markets during the 1920s facilitated the formation of entrepreneurial start-ups. The promise of being able to go to the capital markets down the road may well have encouraged local financiers to invest in firms formed to exploit new technological discoveries.

If such a promise did help entrepreneurial start-ups obtain financing, the equity markets that mattered most would have been the regional exchanges and secondary New York markets like the Curb or the Produce Exchange—not the NYSE. Few entrepreneurial firms would have been able to jump directly to the Big Board because the requirements for listing were too stringent. Firms had to submit five years of financial statements as well as documents detailing their assets and liabilities, and relatively few passed the listing committee's muster. In 1927 the committee accepted 116 of 300 applications, in 1928 16 out of 571, and in 1929 80 out of 759 (White 2009). As a general rule, the only *new* firms that could meet the NYSE's standards were combinations formed by merger or firms with extensive financial backing that were born large in order to operate efficiently in industries characterized by economies

---

22. In other words, large firms may have dominated these industries for reasons that have nothing to do with the technological prowess of their labs. Their advantages may have resided elsewhere; for example, in production or marketing economies or a superior ability to negotiate favorable regulatory outcomes. See Chandler (1977) and Galambos with Sewell (1995).

Table 8.9   Distribution of patents by companies' access to equity markets in 1929

Exchanges where the firm's equities traded in 1929	No. of patents/share of patents	Patents assigned to firms with assets ≥ $10 million	Patents assigned to firms with assets < $10 million	Patents assigned to firms with R&D labs	Patents assigned to firms with inventor principals	Patents assigned to firms without inventor principals	Patents that were cited in 1995–2002	Patents that were high-tech1	Patents that were high-tech2
				A. Row percentages of patents					
NYSE and regional exchanges	201	98.5	1.0	92.5	3.5	96.5	22.4	89.1	60.7
NYSE only	137	94.9	5.1	65.7	5.1	94.9	31.4	69.3	24.1
Secondary NY and regional exchanges	63	79.4	20.6	63.5	11.1	88.9	15.9	52.4	17.5
Secondary NY exchanges only	58	60.3	39.7	55.2	12.1	87.9	37.9	56.9	34.5
Regional exchanges only	41	31.7	68.3	46.3	24.4	75.6	29.3	70.7	22.0
Unknown	121	35.5	62.0	40.5	23.1	76.9	31.4	45.5	22.3
All assignees found in Moody's	*621*	*75.5*	*23.8*	*67.0*	*10.6*	*89.4*	*27.4*	*68.3*	*35.7*
Assignees not found in Moody's	*503*	*n.a.*	*n.a.*	*8.5*	*25.8*	*74.2*	*32.0*	*51.5*	*20.9*
				B. Column percentages of patents					
NYSE and regional exchanges	17.9	42.2	1.4	40.5	3.6	20.9	13.6	26.2	37.3
NYSE only	12.2	27.7	4.7	19.6	3.6	14.0	13.0	13.9	10.1
Secondary NY and regional exchanges	5.6	10.7	8.8	8.7	3.6	6.0	3.0	4.8	3.4
Secondary NY exchanges only	5.2	7.5	15.5	7.0	3.6	5.5	6.6	4.8	6.1
Regional exchanges only	3.6	2.8	18.9	4.1	5.1	3.3	3.6	4.2	2.8
Unknown	10.8	9.2	50.7	10.7	14.3	10.0	11.5	8.1	8.3
All assignees found in Moody's	*55.2*	*100.0*	*100.0*	*90.6*	*33.7*	*59.8*	*51.4*	*62.1*	*67.9*
Assignees not found in Moody's	*44.8*	*0.0*	*0.0*	*9.4*	*66.3*	*40.2*	*48.6*	*37.9*	*32.1*

Notes: The table includes patents in the 1928–1929 cross section that were assigned to companies. Information on the markets where the assignee companies traded comes from *Moody's Manual of Investments* for 1929. The category "unknown" includes companies that were covered by *Moody's* but for which the report did not include information on where the equities traded. The stock of these companies was probably either closely held or traded privately. If the assignee was a subsidiary of a larger company, wherever possible we reported the information for the parent company. The variable "patents assigned to firms with inventor principals" includes firms that bore the patentees' surnames, as well as firms for which we know the patentee was an officer, director, or proprietor. All remaining firms are included in "patents assigned to firms without inventor principals." For definitions of the other variables, see notes to tables 8.1 and 8.2. n.a. = not applicable.

of scale. Entrepreneurial start-ups would have had a much easier time listing on a regional exchange or a secondary market in New York because these exchanges deliberately adopted laxer standards in order to attract this kind of business (White 2009; Ripley 1927). Moreover, unlike the NYSE, listing was not a requirement for trading on these other exchanges. Whether there was a market for a firm's securities depended less on such formalities than on whether investors had sufficient information to evaluate the enterprise's prospects. Reports in national financial publications like *Moody's* helped, but the kind of local knowledge that business people could accumulate about firms in their immediate vicinities probably mattered more.

It is difficult to get directly at the role that regional and secondary exchanges played in encouraging entrepreneurial enterprises because the equities of most such firms in our sample did not trade on any of the markets, at least not at the time we observe them (tables 8.9 and 8.10). Indeed, most were too small even to be noticed by a publication such as *Moody's*. We can, however, get a sense of the importance of the different exchanges by focusing our attention on the smaller firms for which we do have financial reports. In 1928 and 1929 enterprises with assets of less than $10 million look much more like companies not covered by *Moody's* than they do firms with more than $10 million in assets. Whereas most of the assignments to firms in the larger asset category went to enterprises with R&D labs, most of the assignments to these "small cap" firms went to companies that did not show up in the NRC lists as having industrial research facilities (table 8.1). The proportion of their patents classified as high tech was also more like that of companies in the "other" category than large cap firms: for high-tech1, 56 percent for small cap firms and 52 percent for other companies, compared to 74 percent for large-cap firms; and for high-tech2, 25 and 21, compared to 40 percent (table 8.2, panels C and D, and table 8.1).[23] The small cap firms also look very different from the larger firms in that a much greater share of the patents they acquired came from inventors who were principals in the enterprise. In 1928 and 1929 inventor principals generated 28 percent of the patents acquired by small cap firms, compared to 26 percent for other companies and only 6 percent for large cap firms (table 8.2, panel A, and table 8.1). Finally, small cap firms, like firms with inventor-principals more generally, were disproportionately located in the East North Central region of the country, whereas large firms were concentrated in the Middle Atlantic (table 8.4).

For each of the small cap and large cap firms covered by *Moody's*, we collected information on the markets where the firm's equities traded (table

23. The comparisons in this paragraph of all small cap and all large cap firms can be calculated using the counts in table 8.1 as weights to add up the subcategories in table 8.2. For the firms not included in *Moody's*, our figures on the proportion of inventors who were principals in the firms receiving their assignments are probably underestimates because we obtained this information by looking up the firms in city directories and thus were not able to check assignments to firms located in areas not covered by this source.

Table 8.10   Companies' access to equity markets in 1929

Exchanges where the firm's equities traded in 1929	Number of firms/Share of firms	Assignee firms with assets ≥ $10 million	Assignee firms with assets < $10 million	Assignee firms with R&D labs
A. Row percentages of firms				
NYSE and regional exchanges	45	93.3	4.4	73.3
NYSE only	75	93.3	6.7	49.3
Secondary NY and regional exchanges	29	65.5	34.5	58.6
Secondary NY exchanges only	42	54.8	45.2	59.5
Regional exchanges only	32	21.9	78.1	37.5
Unknown	93	24.7	72.0	32.3
All assignees found in Moody's	*316*	*58.2*	*40.5*	*48.7*
Assignees not found in Moody's	*471*	*n.a.*	*n.a.*	*7.4*
B. Column percentages of firms				
NYSE and regional exchanges	5.7	22.8	1.6	17.5
NYSE only	9.5	38.0	3.9	19.6
Secondary NY and regional exchanges	3.7	10.3	7.8	9.0
Secondary NY exchanges only	5.3	12.5	14.8	13.2
Regional exchanges only	4.1	3.8	19.5	6.3
Unknown	11.8	12.5	52.3	15.9
All assignees found in Moody's	*40.2*	*100.0*	*100.0*	*81.5*
Assignees not found in Moody's	*59.8*	*n.a.*	*n.a.*	*18.5*

Notes: See notes to tables 8.1, 8.2, and 8.9. n.a. = not applicable.

8.10). Not surprisingly, unlike the case for large cap firms, very few of the patents assigned to small cap firms (only 6.1 percent) went to companies listed on the Big Board (table 8.9, panel B). However, over half went to a firm whose equities traded on at least one other exchange: 18.9 percent to firms that traded on a regional exchange, 15.5 percent to firms that traded on a secondary New York market, and 8.8 percent to firms that traded on both a regional exchange and a secondary New York market. The rest went to firms for which Moody's did not provide listing information, and it is likely that the stock of these companies was closely held or that it traded only privately. If we go further and break the data down regionally, we see that the securities of small cap firms in the East North Central states were more likely to trade on regional equity markets, whereas those of small cap firms in New England and the Middle Atlantic were more likely to trade on a secondary New York market.[24]

When we trace the listing histories of the firms in our sample in earlier financial publications (table 8.11), we find that relatively few of them jumped from regional or secondary markets to the Big Board. The large cap firms whose equities traded on the NYSE in 1929 were not just small cap firms that grew big and shifted their listing. These firms for the most part were born large (often as a result of mergers), and their listing history seems to have begun on the NYSE. Similarly, most of the firms whose stock traded on regional exchanges in 1929 were first listed there, and the same was true for firms that traded on the secondary New York markets. The main exceptions were firms whose equities traded both on the secondary New York markets and on regional exchanges in 1929. A significant proportion of those firms started on a regional exchange and only later gained access to New York capital through a secondary market. Some firms, it seems, were able to market their equities on a local exchange and then, as investors accumulated more information about the firm's business, tap into broader markets in other regions. But most firms' access to capital markets remained local, with small firms in the East North Central turning primarily to exchanges in that region and those in the Middle Atlantic to secondary markets in New York.

Although the evidence is by no means conclusive, the information on listing locations is consistent with the idea that the growth of regional capital markets, especially in the East North Central states, encouraged investment in entrepreneurial start-ups. The most successful of these firms could anticipate being able to market their securities on exchanges in their home cities and perhaps move from there to one of the secondary markets in New York, and it may well be that this anticipation was enough to spur business people in such areas to risk some of their assets in new enterprises. Certainly, studies of Cleveland and Detroit by Lamoreaux, Levenstein, and Sokoloff

24. We do not show these further breakdowns to save space and because of small cell sizes.

Table 8.11   Earlier trading histories of assignee companies found in Moody's in 1929

	NYSE and regional exchanges		NYSE only		Secondary NY and regional exchanges		Second NY exchanges only		Regional exchanges only		Unknown		No financial report	
	1924	1912	1924	1912	1924	1912	1924	1912	1924	1912	1924	1912	1924	1912
A. Row percentages of firms														
NYSE and regional exchanges	**55.6**	**15.6**	2.2	2.2	6.7	0.0	0.0	0.0	6.7	15.6	6.7	17.8	22.2	48.9
NYSE only	4.0	4.0	**37.3**	**12.0**	0.0	0.0	6.7	4.0	2.7	2.7	20.0	21.3	29.3	56.0
Secondary NY and regional exchanges	6.9	0.0	0.0	0.0	**10.3**	**0.0**	6.9	0.0	31.0	17.2	27.6	37.9	17.2	44.8
Secondary NY exchanges only	4.8	0.0	0.0	0.0	2.4	0.0	**23.8**	**0.0**	0.0	2.4	42.9	38.1	26.2	57.1
Regional exchanges only	0.0	0.0	0.0	0.0	0.0	0.0	0.0	0.0	**31.3**	**9.4**	25.0	21.9	43.8	68.8
Unknown	0.0	0.0	0.0	0.0	0.0	0.0	0.0	0.0	2.2	3.2	**57.0**	**19.4**	40.9	77.4
All categories of equities	*10.1*	*3.2*	*9.2*	*3.5*	*2.2*	*0.0*	*5.4*	*0.9*	*8.2*	*6.6*	*33.2*	*24.1*	*31.6*	*61.7*
B. Column percentages of firms														
NYSE and regional exchanges	**78.1**	**70.0**	3.4	9.1	42.9	n.a.	0.0	0.0	11.5	33.3	2.9	10.5	10.0	11.3
NYSE only	9.4	30.0	**96.6**	**81.8**	0.0	n.a.	29.4	100.0	7.7	9.5	14.3	21.1	22.0	21.5
Secondary NY and regional exchanges	6.3	0.0	0.0	0.0	**42.9**	**n.a.**	11.8	0.0	34.6	23.8	7.6	14.5	5.0	6.7
Secondary NY exchanges only	6.3	0.0	0.0	9.1	14.3	n.a.	**58.8**	**0.0**	0.0	4.8	17.1	21.1	11.0	12.3
Regional exchanges only	0.0	0.0	0.0	0.0	0.0	n.a.	0.0	0.0	**38.5**	**14.3**	7.6	9.2	14.0	11.3
Unknown	0.0	0.0	0.0	0.0	0.0	n.a.	0.0	0.0	7.7	14.3	**50.5**	**23.7**	38.0	36.9
All categories of equities	*100.0*	*100.0*	*100.0*	*100.0*	*100.0*	*n.a.*	*100.0*	*100.0*	*100.0*	*100.0*	*100.0*	*100.0*	*100.0*	*100.0*

Notes: The table includes firms assigned patents in 1928–1929 for which there were reports in *Moody's* for 1929. Trading information comes from *Moody's Manual of Investments* for 1924 and 1929 and *Poor's Manual of Industrials* for 1912. The percentages of firms listed on the same categories of exchanges in 1912 and 1924 as in

(2006, 2007) and Steven Klepper (2007), respectively, point to the existence of local networks of notables eager to supply venture capital to innovative start-ups.

8.7   The Reorganization of Inventive Activity

We began this chapter by discussing two literatures that have very different implications for our understanding of how the process of technological discovery was reorganized in the United States in the early twentieth century. On the one hand, the literature on the rise of industrial research labs claims that invention was increasingly moving into large firms' R&D facilities. On the other, the literature on the growth of equity markets suggests that broadened access to funding may have enabled entrepreneurial firms to raise the capital they needed to play an ongoing role in technological discovery.

Our analysis of the patent data indicates that there is some truth to both of these perspectives. In the Middle Atlantic region of the country inventive activity was indeed moving into large firms' industrial research facilities. The East North Central, however, was home to a dynamic economy of entrepreneurial start-ups, supported (there is good reason to believe) by booming regional exchanges. Neither of these centers of inventive activity seems to have had a particular edge over the other during the 1920s, as the two regions accounted for roughly equivalent shares of total patents and had similar rates of patenting per capita. It is true that large firms in the Middle Atlantic were somewhat more specialized in the technologies associated with the second industrial revolution, but they had already developed this characteristic before they built most of their industrial research labs. Moreover, the inventions acquired by large firms with R&D facilities were no more likely than those of firms without labs to be the product of teamwork, as measured by the presence of more than one name on the patent, and large firms still acquired a significant proportion of their patents from inventors whose state of residence indicates that they were unlikely to be employees of their assignees' labs.

Why, then, has the literature on the history of technology focused on the large firms of the Middle Atlantic region and ignored the vibrant entrepreneurial economy further west? The answer, we think, lies in the events of the Great Depression, which hit small firms in the East North Central region much harder than large firms in the Middle Atlantic.[25] To measure the differential impact of the financial catastrophe on the two regions, we looked up the companies covered by *Moody's* in 1929 in the edition of the manual published in 1935. We then estimated the probability that firms that obtained patents in 1929 would suffer financial distress by 1935. In the first four columns of table 8.12, the dependent variable is a dummy that takes

---

25. On this point, see also Lamoreaux and Levenstein (2008).

Table 8.12   Effects of the Great Depression by type of firm and region

	Bankrupt, in reorganization, or dropped from *Moody's*				Bankrupt, in reorganization, dropped from *Moody's*, or access to financial markets deteriorated			
	Using high-tech1		Using high-tech2		Using high-tech1		Using high-tech2	
	(1)	(2)	(3)	(4)	(5)	(6)	(7)	(8)
High-tech patent	0.020	0.022	0.025	0.031	−0.103	−0.089	−0.029	−0.017
	(0.66)	(0.74)	(0.79)	(0.96)	(2.76)***	(2.37)**	(0.77)	(0.44)
Large firm	−0.185	−0.177	−0.184	−0.175	−0.220	−0.205	−0.228	−0.210
	(4.79)***	(4.63)***	(4.78)***	(4.61)***	(4.85)***	(4.53)***	(4.99)***	(4.60)***
Had R&D lab	−0.210	−0.200	−0.215	−0.205	−0.154	−0.142	−0.162	−0.150
	(5.88)***	(5.66)***	(5.85)***	(5.66)***	(3.81)***	(3.52)***	(3.91)***	(3.61)***
Patentee was principal	0.003	−0.005	0.003	−0.005	0.078	0.062	0.075	0.064
	(0.06)	(0.12)	(0.06)	(0.14)	(1.39)	(1.12)	(1.35)	(1.14)
West		0.233		0.221		0.192		0.205
		(1.97)**		(1.91)*		(1.45)		(1.51)
West North Central		0.366		0.365		0.431		0.454
		(3.07)***		(3.07)***		(3.25)***		(3.38)***
East North Central		0.065		0.067		0.085		0.083
		(1.90)*		(1.96)*		(2.04)**		(1.99)**
New England		−0.012		−0.014		0.081		0.105
		(0.28)		(0.34)		(1.45)		(1.87)*

South Atlantic	0.071		0.061		−0.013		−0.011	
	(0.58)		(0.50)		(0.09)		(0.07)	
Other South	0.464		0.463		0.362		0.381	
	(2.00)**		(2.01)**		(1.48)		(1.54)	
Observations	621	621	621	621	621			

Notes: The absolute value of z-statistics are in parentheses. The estimates are probits, and the reported figures are the marginal effects. The observations are patents in the 1928–1929 cross section that were assigned to companies for which there were reports in *Moody's* for 1929. Because our observations are patents, the estimations are effectively *weighted* by the number of patents each company was assigned. In the first four columns, the dependent variable is a dummy that takes a value of one if *Moody's* no longer published a report on the firm obtaining the patent or if the report indicated that the firm was in bankruptcy or being reorganized. Seventeen percent of patents were assigned to firms classified as distressed by this definition. In the last four columns, the dependent variable is a dummy that aims to capture deterioration in an assignee's access to financial markets using the following coding scheme: firms that were listed on the NYSE were coded 5; those listed on both a regional market and a secondary New York market, 4; those listed on either a regional market or a secondary New York market but not both, 3; those for which no listing information was given, 2; and those without any report in *Moody's*, 1. The dependent variable obtained a value of 1 if the firm obtaining the patent had a numerical code that was lower in 1935 than in 1929 or if the firm was in bankruptcy or reorganization, and a 0 in all other cases. Twenty-four percent of patents were assigned to firms classified as distressed by this second definition. The omitted category is the Middle Atlantic region. For definitions of the independent variables, see notes to tables 8.1, 8.2, and 8.4.

***Significant at the 1 percent level.

**Significant at the 5 percent level.

*Significant at the 10 percent level.

a value of one if the patent was assigned to a firm for which *Moody's* no longer published a report in 1935, or if the report indicated that the firm was in bankruptcy or being reorganized.[26] In the second four columns, the dependent variable also includes firms whose access to capital markets seems to have deteriorated over the period 1929 to 1935.[27] All of the estimates are probits, and the independent variables have the same definitions as in the previous tables.

The differential impact of the Depression is clear from the estimations. Although entrepreneurial firms do not seem to have been more negatively affected by the crisis than firms without patentee-principals, large firms were significantly less likely to suffer financial distress than small firms.[28] Moreover, firms with their own R&D facilities also came through the Depression comparatively well. As we have seen, both large firms and firms with R&D facilities were disproportionately located in the Middle Atlantic region. Yet even when we control for these characteristics, it is apparent that the Depression hit firms in that region less severely than it did other parts of the country. Of particular interest, of course, are the coefficients for the East North Central region. The point estimates are all suggestive of financial distress. They are significant at the 5 percent level in the second set of estimations and at the 10 percent level in the first.[29]

The effect of the Depression is also apparent in regional patenting rates (figure 8.1), which held up much better during the 1930s in the Middle Atlantic than in the East North Central region.[30] Given the low levels of demand during the Great Depression, large firms did not find building new productive capacity an attractive strategy. As Mowery and Nathan Rosenberg (1989) have shown, however, they greatly expanded their investments in R&D.[31] The number of new industrial research laboratories grew by 590 between 1929 and 1936, an increase that compares favorably with the 660 new labs founded between 1919 and 1928. Moreover, employment in industrial research labs shot up even more rapidly, multiplying nearly five times between 1927 and 1940 and raising the number of research employees per 1,000 wage earners in firms with R&D facilities from 0.83 to 3.67. As a result

26. Most of the firms for which there were no reports were listed explicitly as dropped. If small firms ran into financial trouble, *Moody's* was likely to stop publishing information about them, but the journal usually continued to cover large firms in the same condition because the prospects of these enterprises were of interest to significant numbers of readers.

27. For the precise definition of this variable, see the notes to table 8.12.

28. This result, of course, is not at all surprising. On large firms' high survival rates from the 1920s to the 1960s, see Edwards (1975). More generally, see also Averitt (1968).

29. We do not report estimations that control for technology subclasses because of small cell sizes, but the results are the same except that the coefficient on the East North Central dummy increases in significance.

30. Patenting rates in any given year reflect applications made several years before. Hence the rise in patenting rates in most regions during the early years of the Depression was a consequence of inventions generated mainly in the late 1920s.

31. On this point, see also Bernstein (1987).

of these investments, large firms in the Middle Atlantic emerged from the depression with a stockpile of new technologies that enhanced their competitive position, whereas the smaller firms that survived in the East North Central had not been able to maintain the same level of patenting activity.

Although the economy of the East North Central region prospered during World War II and its aftermath, it never regained its entrepreneurial character. The reason why must be a subject for future research. One possibility is that government procurement policy during the war favored large firms with industrial research labs, further encouraging the reorganization of inventive activity (Blum 1976; Vatter 1985; Mowery and Rosenberg 1989). Another is that the regulatory apparatus put in place as a result of the Great Depression killed the regional exchanges that had supported local venture capitalists (White 2009). Yet another is that the innovative economy of the 1920s depended on highly specific human capital that was destroyed during the 1930s along with the networks of inventors, entrepreneurs, and financiers in which it was embedded (Lamoreaux and Levenstein 2008).

Regardless, by the 1950s little remained of the alternative entrepreneurial economy that had flourished during the 1920s in the East North Central part of the country. Its contributions to technological discovery have been largely erased from our historical memory, and the scholarship of the late twentieth century has been written as if innovative regions like Silicon Valley were something entirely new. Now that financial crises are once again buffeting the economy, it is useful to revisit this forgotten history. The differential impact of the Great Depression on the large firm economy of the Middle Atlantic and the entrepreneurial economy of the East North Central is a stark reminder of the competitive advantages that large firms can reap under such circumstances as a consequence of their superior access to capital. It is also a useful warning about the dire consequences that macroeconomic shocks can have for innovative regions.

References

Adams, Charles F., Jr. 1869. "A Chapter of Erie." *North American Review* 109:30–106.
Adams, Stephen B., and Orville R. Butler. 1999. *Manufacturing the Future: A History of Western Electric.* New York: Cambridge University Press.
Arora, Ashish, Marco Ceccagnoli, and Wesley M. Cohen. 2007. "Trading Knowledge: An Exploration of Patent Protection and Other Determinants of Market Transactions in Technology and R&D." In *Financing Innovation in the United States, 1870 to the Present,* edited by Naomi R. Lamoreaux and Kenneth L. Sokoloff, 365–403. Cambridge, MA: MIT Press.
Arora, Ashish, Andrea Fosfuri, and Alfonso Gambardella. 2001. *Markets for Technology: The Economics of Innovation and Corporate Strategy.* Cambridge, MA: MIT Press.

Arrow, Kenneth J. 1962. "Economic Welfare and the Allocation of Resources for Invention." In *The Rate and Direction of Economic Activity: Economic and Social Factors,* Universities-National Bureau Committee for Economic Research, 609–26. Princeton, NJ: Princeton University Press.

Averitt, Robert T. 1968. *The Dual Economy: The Dynamics of American Industry Structure.* New York: W. W. Norton.

Baskin, Jonathan Barron, and Paul J. Miranti Jr. 1997. *A History of Corporate Finance.* New York: Cambridge University Press.

Bernstein, Michael A. 1987. *The Great Depression: Delayed Recovery and Economic Change in America, 1929–1939.* New York: Cambridge University Press.

Blum, John Morton. 1976. *V Was for Victory: Politics and Culture during World War II.* San Diego: Harcourt Brace Jovanovich.

Bulletin of the National Research Council. 1921. Pt. 1, No. 16 (December). Washington, DC: National Research Council.

———. 1927. No. 60 (July). Washington, DC: National Research Council.

———. 1946. No. 113 (July). Washington, DC: National Research Council.

Calomiris, Charles W. 1995. "The Costs of Rejecting University Banking: American Finance in the German Mirror, 1870–1914." In *Coordination and Information: Historical Perspectives on the Organization of Enterprise,* edited by Naomi R. Lamoreaux and Daniel M. G. Raff, 257–315. Chicago: University of Chicago Press.

Carosso, Vincent P. 1970. *Investment Banking in America: A History.* Cambridge, MA: Harvard University Press.

———. 1987. *The Morgans: Private International Bankers, 1854–1913.* Cambridge, MA: Harvard University Press.

Chandler, Alfred D., Jr. 1977. *The Visible Hand: The Managerial Revolution in American Business.* Cambridge, MA: Harvard University Press.

Cohen, Wesley M., and Steven Klepper. 1996. "A Reprise of Size and R&D." *Economic Journal* 106:925–51.

Cohen, Wesley M., Richard C. Levin, and David C. Mowery. 1987. "Firm Size and R&D Intensity: A Re-examination." *Journal of Industrial Economics* 35:543–65.

Cohen, Wesley M., Richard Nelson, and John P. Walsh. 2000. "Protecting their Intellectual Assets: Appropriability Conditions and Why U.S. Manufacturing Firms Patent (or Not)." NBER Working Paper no. 7552. Cambridge, MA: National Bureau of Economic Research, February.

Commercial and Financial Chronicle. 1870–72 and 1890–91. New York: William P. Dana and Co.

Cull, Robert, Lance E. Davis, Naomi R. Lamoreaux, and Jean-Laurent Rosenthal. 2006. "Historical Financing of Small- and Medium-Size Enterprises." *Journal of Banking and Finance* 30:3017–42.

De Long, J. Bradford. 1991. "Did J. P. Morgan's Men Add Value? An Economist's Perspective on Financial Capitalism." In *Inside the Business Enterprise: Historical Perspectives on the Use of Information,* edited by Peter Temin, 205–36. Chicago: University of Chicago Press.

Edwards, Richard C. 1975. "Stages in Corporate Stability and the Risks of Corporate Failure." *Journal of Economic History* 35:428–57.

Federer, J. Peter. 2008. "Advances in Communication Technology and Growth of the American Over-the-Counter Markets, 1876–1929." *Journal of Economic History* 68:501–34.

Fisk, Catherine L. 1998. "Removing the 'Fuel of Interest' from the 'Fire of Genius': Law and the Employee-Inventor, 1830–1930." *University of Chicago Law Review* 65:1127–98.

———. 2001. "Working Knowledge: Trade Secrets, Restrictive Covenants in

Employment, and the Rise of Corporate Intellectual Property, 1800–1920." *Hastings Law Journal* 52:441–535.

Galambos, Louis, with Jane Eliot Sewell. 1995. *Networks of Innovation: Vaccine Development at Merck, Sharp & Dohme, and Mulford, 1895–1995.* New York: Cambridge University Press.

Gans, Joshua, and Scott Stern. 2003. "The Product Market and the Market for 'Ideas': Commercialization Strategies for Technology Entrepreneurs." *Research Policy* 32:333–50.

Gibb, George Sweet, and Evelyn H. Knowlton. 1956. *History of Standard Oil Company (New Jersey), Volume 2, The Resurgent Years, 1911–1927.* New York: Harper and Brothers.

Hall, Bronwyn H. 2006. "2002 Updates to NBER Patent Data." Accessed October 2008. http://elsa.berkeley.edu/~bhhall/bhdata.html.

Hall, Bronwyn H., Adam B. Jaffe, and Manuel Trajtenberg. 2002. "The NBER Patent-Citation Data File: Lessons, Insights, and Methodological Tools." In *Patents, Citations, and Innovations: A Window on the Knowledge Economy,* edited by Adam B. Jaffe and Manuel Trajtenberg, 403–59. Cambridge, MA: MIT Press.

Hannah, Leslie. 2007. "What Did Morgan's Men Really Do?" CIRJE Discussion Paper F-465. Tokyo: Centre for International Research on the Japanese Economy, the University of Tokyo.

Hintz, Eric S. 2007. "Independent Researchers in an Era of Burgeoning Research & Development." *Business and Economic History On-Line* 5. http://www.h-net.org/~business/bhcweb/publications/BEHonline/2007/hintz.pdf.

Hounshell, David A., and John Kenley Smith Jr. 1988. *Science and Corporate Strategy: Du Pont R&D, 1902–1980.* New York: Cambridge University Press.

Hughes, Thomas Parke. 1989. *American Genesis: A Century of Invention and Technological Enthusiasm, 1870–1970.* New York: Viking.

Jewkes, John, David Sawers, and Richard Stillerman. 1958. *The Sources of Invention.* London: Macmillan.

Klepper, Steven. 2007. "The Organizing and Financing of Innovative Companies in the Evolution of the U.S. Automobile Industry." In *Financing Innovation in the United States, 1870 to Present,* edited by Naomi R. Lamoreaux and Kenneth L. Sokoloff, 85–128. Cambridge, MA: MIT Press.

Lamoreaux, Naomi R., and Margaret Levenstein. 2008. "The Decline of an Innovative Region: Cleveland, Ohio, in the Twentieth Century." Unpublished Manuscript.

Lamoreaux, Naomi R., Margaret Levenstein, and Kenneth L. Sokoloff. 2006. "Mobilizing Venture Capital During the Second Industrial Revolution: Cleveland, Ohio, 1870–1920." *Capitalism and Society* 1. http://www.bepress.com/cas/vol1/iss3/art5/.

———. 2007. "Financing Invention during the Second Industrial Revolution: Cleveland, Ohio, 1870–1920." In *Financing Innovation in the United States: 1870 to Present,* edited by Naomi R. Lamoreaux and Kenneth L. Sokoloff, 39–84. Cambridge, MA: MIT Press.

Lamoreaux, Naomi R., and Kenneth L. Sokoloff. 1996. "Long-Term Change in the Organization of Inventive Activity." *Proceedings of the National Academy of Sciences of the United States of America* 93:12686–92.

———. 1999. "Inventors, Firms, and the Market for Technology in the Late Nineteenth and Early Twentieth Centuries." In *Learning by Doing in Markets, Firms and Countries,* edited by Naomi R. Lamoreaux, Daniel M. G. Raff, and Peter Temin, 19–57. Chicago: University of Chicago Press.

———. 2001. "Market Trade in Patents and the Rise of a Class of Specialized Inventors in the Nineteenth-Century United States." *American Economic Review, Papers and Proceedings* 91:39–44.

———. 2003. "Intermediaries in the U.S. Market for Technology, 1870–1920." In *Finance, Intermediaries, and Economic Development,* edited by Stanley L. Engerman, Philip T. Hoffman, Jean-Laurent Rosenthal, and Kenneth L. Sokoloff, 209–46. New York: Cambridge University Press.

———. 2007. "The Market for Technology and the Organization of Invention in U.S. History." In *Entrepreneurship, Innovation, and the Growth Mechanism of the Free-Enterprise Economies,* edited by Eytan Sheshinski, Robert J. Strom, and William J. Baumol, 213–43. Princeton, NJ: Princeton University Press.

———. 2009. "The Rise and Decline of the Independent Inventor: A Schumpeterian Story?" In *The Challenge of Remaining Innovative: Insights from Twentieth Century American Business,* edited by Sally H. Clarke, Naomi R. Lamoreaux, and Steven W. Usselman, 43–78. Stanford: Stanford University Press.

Lanjouw, Jean O., and Mark Schankerman. 2004. "Patent Quality and Research Productivity: Measuring Innovation with Multiple Indicators." *Economic Journal* 114:441–65.

Lazonick, William. 1991. *Business Organization and the Myth of the Market Economy.* New York: Cambridge University Press.

Lerner, Josh. 1994. "The Importance of Patent Scope: An Empirical Analysis." *Rand Journal of Economics* 25:319–33.

———. 1995. "Patenting in the Shadow of Competitors." *Journal of Law and Economics* 38:463–95.

Leslie, Stuart W. 1980. "Thomas Midgley and the Politics of Industrial Research." *Business History Review* 54:480–503.

Lipartito, Kenneth. 2009. "Rethinking the Invention Factory: Bell Laboratories in Perspective." In *The Challenge of Remaining Innovative: Insights from Twentieth Century American Business,* edited by Sally H. Clarke, Naomi R. Lamoreaux, and Steven W. Usselman, 132–59. Stanford: Stanford University Press.

Martin, Joseph G. 1898. *A Century of Finance: Martin's History of the Boston Stock and Money Markets.* Boston: Privately printed.

Moody's Manual of Investments and Security Rating Service. 1924, 1929, and 1935. New York: Moody's Investors Service.

Mowery, David C. 1983. "The Relationship between Intrafirm and Contractual Forms of Industrial Research in American Manufacturing, 1900–1940." *Explorations in Economic History* 20:351–74.

———. 1995. "The Boundaries of the U.S. Firm in R&D." In *Coordination and Information: Historical Perspectives on the Organization of Enterprise,* edited by Naomi R. Lamoreaux and Daniel M. G. Raff, 147–76. Chicago: University of Chicago Press.

Mowery, David C., and Nathan Rosenberg. 1989. *Technology and the Pursuit of Economic Growth.* New York: Cambridge University Press.

Navin, Thomas R., and Marian V. Sears. 1955. "The Rise of a Market for Industrial Securities, 1887–1902." *Business History Review* 29:105–38.

Neal, Larry, and Lance E. Davis. 2007. "Why Did Finance Capitalism and the Second Industrial Revolution Arise in the 1890s?" In *Financing Innovation in the United States, 1870 to Present,* edited by Naomi R. Lamoreaux and Kenneth L. Sokoloff, 129–61. Cambridge, MA: MIT Press.

Nelson, Richard R. 1959. "The Simple Economics of Basic Scientific Research." *Journal of Political Economy* 67:297–306.

Nicholas, Tom. 2003. "Why Schumpeter Was Right: Innovation, Market Power, and Creative Destruction in 1920s America." *Journal of Economic History* 63:1023–58.

———. 2007. "Stock Market Swings and the Value of Innovation, 1908–1929." In *Financing Innovation in the United States, 1870 to Present,* edited by Naomi R. Lamoreaux and Kenneth L. Sokoloff, 217–45. Cambridge, MA: MIT Press.

———. 2008. "Does Innovation Cause Stock Market Runups? Evidence from the Great Crash." *American Economic Review* 98:1370–96.

———. 2009. "Spatial Diversity in Invention: Evidence from the Early R&D Labs." *Journal of Economic Geography* 9:1–31.

———. 2010. "The Role of Independent Invention in U.S. Technological Development, 1880–1930." *Journal of Economic History* 70:57–82.

O'Sullivan, Mary A. 2007. "Funding New Industries: A Historical Perspective on the Financing Role of the U.S. Stock Market in the Twentieth Century." In *Financing Innovation in the United States, 1870 to Present,* edited by Naomi R. Lamoreaux and Kenneth L. Sokoloff, 163–216. Cambridge, MA: MIT Press.

Poor's Manual of Industrials. 1910 and 1912. New York: Poor's Railroad Manual Co.

Reich, Leonard S. 1977. "Research, Patents, and the Struggle to Control Radio: A Study of Big Business and the Uses of Industrial Research." *Business History Review* 51:208–35.

———. 1980. "Industrial Research and the Pursuit of Corporate Security: The Early Years of Bell Labs." *Business History Review* 54:504–29.

———. 1985. *The Making of American Industrial Research: Science and Business at GE and Bell, 1876–1926.* New York: Cambridge University Press.

Ripley, William Z. 1927. *Main Street and Wall Street.* Boston: Little, Brown and Co.

Robb, John F. 1922. *Patent Essentials for the Executive, Engineer, Lawyer and Inventor.* New York: Funk and Wagnalls.

Robinson, William G. 1890. *The Law of Patents for Useful Inventions.* 3 volumes. Boston: Little, Brown and Company.

Rosenbloom, Richard S., and William J. Spencer. 1996. "Introduction: Technology's Vanishing Wellspring." In *Engines of Innovation: U.S. Industrial Research at the End of an Era,* edited by Richard S. Rosenbloom and William J. Spencer, 1–9. Boston: Harvard Business School Press.

Scherer, F. M. 1965. "Firm Size, Market Structure, Opportunity, and the Output of Patented Inventions." *American Economic Review* 55:1097–125.

Schumpeter, Joseph A. 1942. *Capitalism, Socialism, and Democracy.* New York: Harper.

Simon, Miguel Cantillo. 1998. "The Rise and Fall of Bank Control in the United States: 1890–1939." *American Economic Review* 88:1077–93.

Smith, John K., and David A. Hounshell. 1985. "Wallace H. Carothers and Fundamental Research at Du Pont." *Science* 229:436–42.

Teece, David J. 1986. "Profiting from Technological Innovation: Implications for Integration, Collaboration, Licensing, and Public Policy." *Research Policy* 15:285–305.

———. 1988. "Technological Change and the Nature of the Firm." In *Technical Change and Economic Theory,* edited by Giovanni Dosi, Christopher Freeman, Richard Nelson, Gerald Silverberg, and Luc Soete, 256–81. London: Pinter.

———. 1993. "The Dynamics of Industrial Capitalism: Perspectives on Alfred Chandler's Scale and Scope." *Journal of Economic Literature* 31:199–225.

U.S. Census Bureau. 2002. "Demographic Trends in the 20th Century." Census 2000 Special Reports, Series CENSR-4. Washington, DC: U.S. Government Printing Office. http://www.census.gov/prod/2002pubs/censr-4.pdf.

U.S. Commissioner of Patents. 1870–71, 1890–91, 1900–25, 1946, 1955. *Annual Report.* Washington, DC: U.S. Government Printing Office.

Usselman, Steven W. 2002. *Regulating Railroad Innovation: Business, Technology, and Politics in America, 1840–1920.* New York: Cambridge University Press.

———. 2007. "Learning the Hard Way: IBM and the Sources of Innovation in Early Computing." In *Financing Innovation in the United States, 1870 to Present,* edited by Naomi R. Lamoreaux and Kenneth L. Sokoloff, 317–63. Cambridge, MA: MIT Press.

Vatter, Harold G. 1985. *The U.S. Economy in World War II.* New York: Columbia University Press.

White, Eugene N. 1984. "Banking Innovation in the 1920s: The Growth of National Banks' Financial Services." *Business and Economic History,* Second Series 13: 92–104.

———. 1990. "The Stock Market Boom and Crash of 1929 Revisited." *Journal of Economic Perspectives* 4:67–83.

———. 2009. "Competition Among the Exchanges Before the SEC: Was the NYSE a Natural Hegemon?" Unpublished Manuscript.

White, Richard. 2003. "Information, Markets, and Corruption: Transcontinental Railroads in the Gilded Age." *Journal of American History* 90:19–43.

Wise, George. 1985. *Willis R. Whitney, General Electric, and the Origins of U.S. Industrial Research.* New York: Columbia University Press.

Zeckhauser, Richard. 1996. "The Challenge of Contracting for Technological Information." *Proceedings of the National Academy of Sciences of the United States of America* 93:12743–48.

9

Mass Secondary Schooling and the State
The Role of State Compulsion in the High School Movement

Claudia Goldin and Lawrence F. Katz

From 1910 to 1940, a period known in U.S. educational history as the high school movement, the fraction of youths enrolled in public and private U.S. secondary schools increased from 18 to 71 percent. The fraction graduating nationwide soared from 9 to 51 percent (see figure 9.1) and the increase was even greater in most northern and western states (see figure 9.2 for U.S. regional data). Such increases are as large as those achieved in the recent histories of nations undergoing the most rapid of transitions to mass secondary schooling. In South Korea, for example, the fraction graduating from upper secondary school increased from 25 percent to 88 percent in the three decades from 1954 to 1984.[1]

Claudia Goldin is the Henry Lee Professor of Economics at Harvard University and director of the Development of the American Economy program at the National Bureau of Economic Research. Lawrence F. Katz is the Elisabeth Allison Professor of Economics at Harvard University and a research associate of the National Bureau of Economic Research.

We gratefully acknowledge financial support from the Spencer Foundation (Major Grant no. 200200007) on parts of our book, *The Race between Education and Technology* (Harvard Press, 2008), which includes material on compulsory schooling in chapter 6. Adriana Lleras-Muney generously provided her data on compulsory schooling and child labor. Joshua Angrist and Daron Acemoglu kindly made available their coding of the laws, as did Stefanie Schmidt. We thank them all. We are grateful to Damon Clark, Edward Glaeser, Robert Willis, participants in the Harvard Labor Workshop, and especially our discussant, David Card, for helpful comments.

1. The increase for males was from 41 to 90 percent, but the increase for females was 10 to 86 percent. See the Organization for Economic Cooperation and Development (OECD 1998), tables A1-2a and A1-2b. The figures are for individuals in two age groups in 1996: fifty-five to sixty-four years old and twenty-five to thirty-four years old. If graduation occurred around eighteen years old, these data would approximately refer to the years from 1954 to 1984. A U.S.-style educational system was imposed in 1949 in Korea. Schooling was of the 6-3-3 variety, with six-year elementary schools, three-year middle schools, and three-year senior high schools. Compulsory education in Korea was six years until 1969, when it was expanded to nine years.

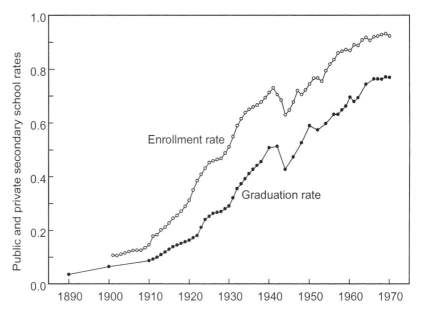

Fig. 9.1   Public and private secondary school enrollment and graduation rates, 1890 to 1970

Source: U.S. Department of Education (1993) and Goldin (1994, 1998) for graduation rates from 1910 to 1930.

Notes: Enrollment figures are divided by the number of fourteen- to seventeen-year-olds; graduation figures are divided by the number of seventeen-year-olds. Data include males and females in public and private schools (excluding preparatory departments of colleges and universities). Year given is end of school year.

An important difference between the experience of the United States in mass secondary schooling from 1910 to 1940 and that of other countries in the post–World War II era is the role played by government, especially the central government. In most nations the central or federal government largely coordinated the transformation. In the United States, it did not.

The U.S. educational bureaucracy was, and largely is, decentralized, diffuse, and diverse. The federal government is a relatively minor player in K–12 education, and within each of the states the various school districts have had considerable freedom regarding regulations, taxes, and expenditures.[2] School districts, moreover, are exceptionally numerous. Today there are about 15,000 school districts. But in 1932, when the federal government

2. The fraction of total public K–12 revenues accounted for by the federal government has never exceeded 10 percent in any year. In the 1920s less than 0.5 percent of total revenue came from the federal government. With the passage of the National Defense Education Act of 1964, the federal role increased from 4.4 in 1964 to 8.8 percent in 1968. The federal share of public K–12 revenues peaked at 9.8 percent in 1980, declined throughout the 1980s, and has risen since to 9.2 percent in 2005. See U.S. Department of Education (2008, table 162).

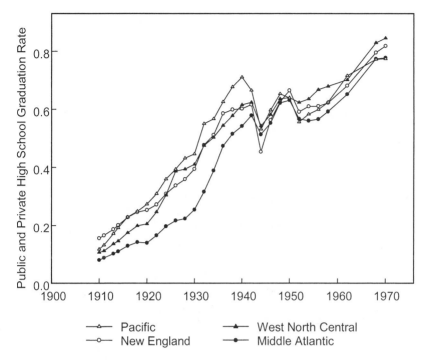

Fig. 9.2   Public and private high school graduation rates for four regions, 1910 to 1970

Sources: State-level high school graduation data set from various sources; see Goldin (1994, 1998).

Notes: Includes males and females in public and private schools (including preparatory departments of colleges and universities). The number of graduates is divided by the approximate number of seventeen-year-olds in the state. Constant growth rate interpolations of population data are made between decennial census years.

first made a count of the nation's school districts, they numbered almost 130,000. Although the great majority of them were tiny common school districts of the "open country," about 20 percent contained a high school.[3] Despite the large number of school districts in the United States and the absence of strong federal control, the "state" (and here we mean the various states) did mandate and coordinate various details concerning secondary school education.

Early in the period of the high school movement various states required that every district provide for the public high school education of its citizens (through the establishment of "free tuition" laws), just as states in the nine-

3. The Office of Education also reported in 1932 that there were 26,409 public secondary schools. At most, therefore, 21 percent of all school districts had a public secondary school, whereas the rest contained only elementary or common schools.

teenth century had required that all districts provide a common school education. States coordinated secondary education across the various districts by setting standards for what constituted a high school, which credentials were required of high school teachers, and what performance was demanded for grade advancement and high school graduation. Each of these laws and regulations compelled districts to take a particular action. Some states even passed legislation compelling the state university to accept the state's high school graduates without further preparation.

State governments were also involved in a host of ways that effectively decreased the supply price of secondary schooling to certain individuals and districts. Some states gave grants to poorer districts for teacher salaries, high school buildings, textbooks, and transportation. States often offered financial incentives for the consolidation of districts to increase the scale of secondary schools and for high school buildings. But of all the ways in which state legislation might have advanced secondary schooling, compulsory education and child labor laws have received the most attention.

Compulsory education and child labor laws were first passed in the United States in the mid-nineteenth century. Massachusetts, in 1852, was the earliest state to have a compulsory schooling law. By 1890 twenty-seven states (out of the forty-eight that would eventually exist by 1912) had already passed a compulsory schooling law and in 1918, with the passage of a law by Mississippi, all forty-eight states (plus the territories of Hawaii and Puerto Rico, and the District of Columbia) had a law.[4]

But it was not until the early twentieth century that compulsory education and child labor laws could have had a direct impact on secondary schooling. The ages that the laws were intended to constrain, the bureaucracy allotted to enforce them, and the coordination of the education and labor portions of the laws changed in the early twentieth century and gave the laws new bite to constrain the behavior of youth of secondary school age.

The federal government was removed from legislating against child labor until 1938. The U.S. Supreme Court ruled unfavorably on two federal child labor acts—the Keating-Owen Child Labor Bill of 1916, which it struck down in 1918, and the Child Labor Tax Law of 1918, which was to replace Keating-Owen but which was similarly overturned in 1922.[5] A child labor constitutional amendment failed to be ratified by the states in 1925. Not until the National Industrial Recovery Act (passed in 1933 but declared unconstitutional in 1935) and later the Fair Labor Standards Act (1938), upheld by the Supreme Court in 1941, did the federal government have a role in legislating against child labor. The states, in the meantime, were quite active.

What was the role of state compulsion in the expansion of secondary

4. For a timeline of compulsory education laws see, for example, Steinhilber and Sokolowsi (1966).

5. The ages covered by federal legislation before 1938 were those to fourteen years. The Keating-Owen Bill, for example, prohibited the interstate commerce of the products of children under fourteen years and those of older children in specific industries.

schooling from 1910 to 1940? It would appear from the timing of the laws and the high school movement that compulsion mattered a great deal. The laws became more effective and constrained youths in the secondary school ages just as youths were entering and graduating from high schools in considerably greater numbers. This coincidence has led many fine historians to accord compulsory schooling and child labor laws an enormous role in the large increase of school enrollment and attendance during the Progressive Era. For example, in his widely cited volume *The One Best System,* David Tyack states: "Attendance in high schools increased [from 1890 to 1918] . . . The curve of secondary school enrollment and graduation continued to soar: in 1920, 61.6 percent of those 14 to 17 were enrolled . . . in 1930, the [figure was] 73.1 percent . . . As these statistics suggest, during the first two decades of the twentieth century compulsory schooling laws were increasingly effective" (Tyack 1974, 183).[6]

In previous work we explored the reasons for the expansion of secondary school enrollment and graduation using a simple supply-demand framework for a quasi-public good.[7] We found, using repeated cross sections and panel data on states in reduced-form models, that high school graduation and enrollment rates increased with income and wealth per capita, decreased with greater youth employment opportunities, and increased with greater homogeneity of community. We had relied on the findings of several other researchers to support our sense that changes in compulsory schooling and child labor laws could account for only a small fraction of the increase in high school enrollments and graduation rates. The studies on which we depended (including Acemoglu and Angrist 2000; Lleras-Muney 2002; and Schmidt 1996) used microdata on educational attainment from the U.S. censuses to explore the impact of compulsory schooling and child labor laws that were in effect in the state of birth of native-born adults when they would have been constrained by the laws (at age fourteen).[8]

Our primary objective in this chapter is to uncover the effects of state compulsory schooling and child labor laws from 1910 to 1939 on secondary schooling rates. In contrast to prior work, we relate the laws to contempo-

6. Selwyn Troen, in his well-received history of the St. Louis public school system, gives the fraction of youths at various ages who attended school at some time during the census year. The fractions attending from seven to thirteen years old increased from 1880 to 1930 (although it is unlikely that all fractions were 97.7 percent in 1930, as Troen reports). Troen concludes, "the legislation was very effective. Due to vigorous enforcement, nearly all children were in school continuously from age six or seven until fourteen by the 1910s" (Troen 1975, 202, table 12). Because Troen uses decennial census data, his evidence does not necessarily indicate that children were at school "continuously" in the ages considered. More important is that there is no evidence that the laws caused enrollment to increase.

7. See, for example, Goldin and Katz (1999, 2009).

8. A large related literature uses U.S. state compulsory schooling and child labor laws as instruments for years of schooling in attempts to estimate the causal impacts of education on a wide range of outcomes. See Angrist and Krueger (1991) and Oreopoulos (2009) on earnings, Lleras-Muney (2005) on mortality, Lochner and Moretti (2004) on crime, and Moretti, Milligan, and Oreopoulos (2004) on citizenship.

raneous administrative data on secondary school enrollments, which we compiled for our work on the high school movement. In addition, and in a manner similar to others who have addressed these issues, we estimate the impact of the laws on the overall educational attainment of birth cohorts reaching high school age from around 1910 to 1939 (those born from 1896 to 1925), using microdata from the 1960 Census of Population. We have corrected the coding of the laws and use a somewhat different (and we believe more accurate) set of summary measures of the legal variables to highlight the aspects of the laws most likely to have constrained school attendance choices. Our estimation approach exploits cross-state differences in the timing of changes in state laws and controls for state fixed effects, birth cohort (or year) fixed effects, and other time-varying state level covariates.

We find that changes in state compulsory schooling and child labor laws from 1910 to 1939 had a positive impact on schooling but that the effect was modest, especially in comparison with the increase in high school enrollments and overall educational attainment. The potential endogeneity of law changes to other (unmeasured) determinants of increased schooling suggests our approach overestimates the "causal" impact of law changes. We also explore the role of enforcement. By 1928 all states had some form of state school census, but it is always possible that enforcement increased in ways that elude measurement.

The ideas in this contribution are closely connected to Kenneth Sokoloff and Stanley Engerman's work on economic growth and institutions.[9] A key mediating factor in the relationship between initial conditions and the path-dependency of economic growth is the type of educational institutions. If income is fairly evenly distributed and the franchise is relatively widespread, then publicly-provided and publicly-funded schools generally arise, as they did in much of North America since the colonial period. But if, as Engerman and Sokoloff point out, income is unequally distributed and the franchise is limited, publicly-provided and publicly-funded schools will be less apt to appear. Lower levels of education for the poorer members of society mean that class differences and income inequality will be reinforced. In addition, many of the nations that had early and relatively complete public education had decentralized control over schooling decisions whereas those that had limited public education had centralized control.

An interesting implication of the relationship between democratic and egalitarian institutions, on the one hand, and educational institutions, on the other, is that compulsory education laws should play a smaller role in established democracies with decentralized control than in expanding democracies with centralized control. And educational compulsion should be rarely found in autocratic regimes.

9. See Engerman and Sokoloff (forthcoming), in particular the chapter on education and schooling.

Individual parents, in established democracies with decentralized educational control, decide on the optimal levels of schooling and educational funding and they often sort into fairly homogeneous districts or neighborhoods. In an established democratic nation with decentralized educational institutions what role is there for educational compulsion? Why would any majority group vote to constrain itself? The majority might decide to constrain various minorities, but it would probably not constrain itself.

Our findings are fully consistent with the notion that established democracies with widespread franchise and decentralized control would not have compulsory education laws that constrain a large part of the population. On the other hand, members of democracies that suddenly expand the franchise (and where there is centralized educational control) might want compulsory legislation to compel the central government to provide school resources. We end with such an example—a comparison between the impacts of compulsory education in the United States and Great Britain.

9.1   Compulsory Schooling and Child Labor Laws

9.1.1   What Were the Laws?

The typical compulsory schooling law set down the ages during which youths had to be in school. That is, the typical law included a minimum age (the required school entry age) and a maximum age (the school leaving age). But the laws began to be more complicated in the early twentieth century when the maximum age of compulsory schooling (the earliest age for school leaving) increased in many states. The typical law was then altered to include a level of education that would exempt a youth from the maximum age of compulsory schooling. The grade needed for exemption, not the maximum age, became the binding constraint in many states. But that was not always the case, particularly for some foreign-born children who did not meet the grade standard before reaching the maximum age. Almost all laws also included exemptions for those with mental or physical impairments and some exempted youths with impoverished parents or who lived far from the closest school.

Child labor laws modified the compulsory schooling laws in various ways. They generally exempted older youths, who were constrained by the compulsory schooling law, so they could work. They set down the method by which youths could obtain a work permit and they often contained a minimum level of schooling required to do so. (The minimum amount of school required to leave school for work was almost always *lower* than the level of schooling that otherwise exempted a child from attending school.) Youths who worked at home and in agriculture were freed from many of the usual constraints concerning work permits.

When the two types of laws are viewed together, as they generally were by the authorities, the child labor laws are almost always the binding constraint, not the maximum age of compulsory schooling or the educational requirement for school exemption. Another important change in the early twentieth century was the better articulation of the two laws and of the inclusion of the child labor laws in the compulsory schooling legislation in some states.

Another important change during the Progressive Era was the addition of statutes mandating or enabling continuation (or part-time) schools. Continuation schools were established to educate the youth who had left school to work but who was still below the maximum age of compulsory schooling.[10] The legislation typically required that youths attend the continuation school from four to eight hours per week and that these hours occur during the usual workday, not at night or on Sundays. These schools were to be established in municipalities having a sufficient number of school-aged youths (often more than twenty) who had work permits. These laws increased the cost to employers of hiring such youths since they would have to be excused from work during part of an afternoon each week or up to an entire day each week.[11]

The child labor laws typically were more complex than the compulsory schooling laws. They often listed occupations from which youths were barred and the times of the day they could not be employed. Child labor laws often had complicated procedures to ensure compliance. For example, children who wanted to obtain a work permit had to find employment, have their prospective employer fill out a form, prove that they were above some required age, and be certified by a physician to be healthy. Their work permit remained with their employer, who was to surrender it when the youth left voluntarily or was fired.[12]

Some writers have interpreted the compulsory education and child labor laws as being inconsistent because the binding constraint was often the child labor law rather than the maximum age of compulsory education or the education required for exemption. But the laws were not in conflict. In fact, the laws were often sections of identical legislation.[13] The so-called inconsistencies were deliberate ways of compelling youths to be either at school or at work. Child labor and compulsory education laws were, in large measure, consistently written and were designed to ensure that youths were not idle.

Consider the modal state law in the 1920s. It had a minimum age of seven

---

10. Continuation schools often gave a combination of academic and vocational courses.

11. Emmons (1926, 134) contains a summary of the required attendance each week in continuation schools. Of the twenty-three states having a mandatory continuation school law in 1925, eight required up to eight hours per week, nine required four hours, and six were at the five or six hours level.

12. Bermejo (1923) has a step-by-step description of how youths could obtain employment status in states with effective child labor laws.

13. See, for example, Stambler (1968) and numerous contemporaneous studies, often by advocates, including Clapp and Strong (1928) on Massachusetts and Gibbons (1927) on Indiana. In California, for example, the 1931 general laws of the states included Act 7519 ("school code"), which contained separate articles on compulsory education and on work permits. Other states had separate laws passed by the legislature, often at separate times. One reason for the greater connection in some states is that the superintendent of schools was responsible for issuing work permits to certain minors.

years, a maximum age of sixteen years, an educational standard for exemption of eight years of school, and a work permit age of fourteen years, as long as the youth had completed six years of school. A youth could drop out of school at fourteen years old if he or she had finished six years of school and was legally employed. But an out-of-school fourteen-year-old would be deemed a truant unless he had a job (and a work permit). In order to avoid both school and work, a youth would have to complete eight years of school, making him fifteen years old at the time of school leaving (assuming that such a youth had advanced a grade during each year of school).

Compulsory schooling and child labor acts in most states were antitruancy and antivagrancy laws rather than strongly proactive education laws. The laws were, nevertheless, "pro-child" and made youth employment more costly through limitations on their hours, industries, and occupations. The political opposition to state compulsory schooling laws tended to emphasize that such laws interfered with the personal liberty and rights of parents, although some anticompulsion advocates argued that education was not valuable and was irrelevant to many youths (Deffenbaugh and Keesecker 1935; Reed 1927).

9.1.2   Specific Aspects of the Laws from 1910 to 1939

We have compiled information on seven aspects of these laws for all states for each year between 1910 and 1939 (see the data appendix) and have extended some variables back to 1900 to compute the analysis data. The variables are:

1. Minimum age of compulsory schooling, known as the school entrance age (also compiled for 1900 to 1909).
2. Maximum age of compulsory schooling, known as the school leaving age (also compiled for 1900 to 1909).
3. Education for exemption from maximum age rule.
4. Age at which youth can obtain a work permit (for work during normal school hours).
5. Education required to receive a work permit (for work during normal school hours).
6. Whether state has mandatory continuation schools.
7. Maximum age of continuation school attendance (and whether the state permitted municipalities to mandate continuation schools).

These details of the laws do not exhaust all possible variables pertaining to child labor and compulsory schooling laws. They are, however, the most important and are among those that can be obtained for most of the years under consideration.[14]

Figure 9.3 contains graphical depictions of the seven legal variables. The

---

14. Other variables of importance are: excluded occupations and industries, restrictions on hours of work for minors, exemptions for other factors and court interpretations of them, the state (or municipal) apparatus for enforcing the laws (e.g., number of attendance officers, quality of the school census).

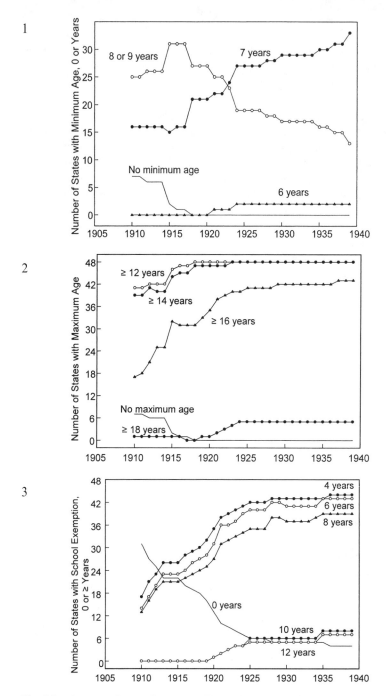

Fig. 9.3   Aspects of compulsory schooling and child labor laws (1910 to 1939): *1,* Minimum age of compulsory schooling (0 or number of years); *2,* Maximum age of compulsory schooling (0 or greater than or equal to given number of years); *3,* Education for exemption from maximum age rule (greater than or equal to given number

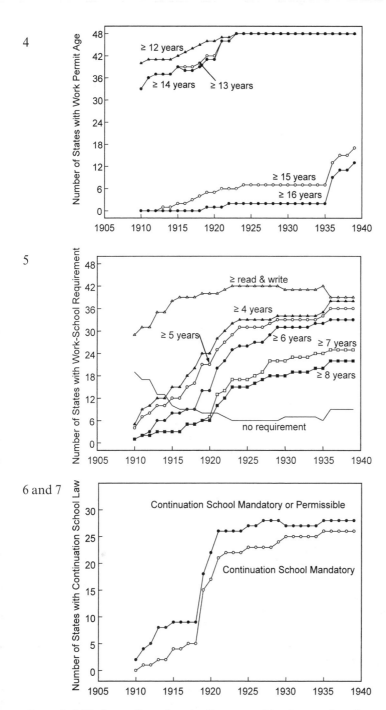

of years); *4*, Work permit age (greater than or equal to given number of years); *5*, Education required to obtain a work permit (none or greater than or equal to years given); *6 and 7*, Continuation School Mandatory or Permissible

Sources: See the data appendix.

maximum age (2) continued to increase to around 1930, when forty-two states set their maximum age at fourteen years or higher. The minimum age (1), on the other hand, decreased throughout the period.[15] At the start of the period shown, 60 percent of the states with compulsory schooling laws had a minimum age of entry set at eight or more years. At the end, however, almost 75 percent had a minimum age of seven or fewer years. The minimum age of entry served to constrain school districts to provide classrooms and teachers for youngsters and may have enabled teenagers to accumulate an additional year or two of schooling before they exited from the system, often around puberty.

The level of completed schooling required to be exempt from the maximum age of compulsory education (3) is somewhat complicated because it had to be consistent with the maximum age. At the start of the period, thirty-one (or almost two-thirds) of the states did not have such a provision in their laws and only thirteen states required eight years or more for the exemption. By 1925 only six states did not have such a provision and thirty-five states required eight years or more. As states increased the education required for exemption, they generally increased the school leaving age. Because the maximum age of compulsory education in most of the states with an eight-year exemption had increased to sixteen years, the requirement that youths remain in school for eight years meant that most would have been fifteen or sixteen years old at the time of school leaving anyhow.

The age at which youths could get a work permit (4) contains two periods of change: around World War I and after 1935. The eight states that did not have work permit regulations in 1910 adopted them from 1915 to the early 1920s, and by 1925 all states had at least a fourteen-year-old rule for work permits. The slow early movement to later ages for work permits rapidly changed around 1935, with eleven states increasing the age to at least sixteen years. Complementing the work permit age is the education required to obtain the permit (5). Sometimes expressed in years of schooling and other times as a grade, it increased primarily in the 1920s. By 1930 eighteen states had a requirement of eighth grade (or eight years of school) and thirty-one had at least a sixth grade (or a six year) requirement. But seven states still had no requirement in 1930 and seven others had only a basic literacy require-ment. In 1939 ten states still had no requirement or simple literacy.

The final two variables (6 and 7) depicted concern continuation or part-time school. Continuation schools—generally housed within the communi-ty's public high school—were intended to educate the youth who had exited the system to work before the maximum age of compulsory schooling, or in some cases, the legal age of majority. These schools were similar to other

15. In our estimation of the impact of the laws on school enrollment, graduation, and edu-cational attainment we use minimum ages to 1902 because a youth who was fourteen years old in 1914, for example, would have most likely entered school in 1908 if the minimum age of school entry were eight.

types of continuing education schools, such as night, adult, and vocational schools, but they differed in requiring the youth to attend school during the usual workday. In this respect, mandating attendance at these schools increased the cost to an employer of hiring a youth below the maximum age of compulsory schooling. Wisconsin, the home of the Progressive Party's Robert LaFollette, was the first state to approve mandatory continuation schools in 1911. As is obvious in figure 9.3 (6 and 7), the vast majority of states joined the continuation school bandwagon during or directly following World War I.[16] By 1921 twenty-one states had mandatory continuation school attendance and an additional four states allowed municipalities to establish compulsory attendance at continuation schools.

How could compulsory education and child labor laws have impacted secondary school enrollments? The most obvious way is by increasing the school leaving age to at least fifteen or requiring nine years of school. In 1920 thirty-one states had a school leaving age of sixteen, but only one paired that law with nine years of required school; all others were less. By 1925 six states had the nine year or more exemption and by 1935 eight did. Given the additional exemptions from the child labor law, only two states had legislation from 1925 to 1934 that would have compelled youths to attend a secondary school. But there are other ways that the legislation could have had an effect. We have already mentioned the potential effects of a mandatory continuation school law. In addition, junior high schools were established in most large cities by the 1920s and gave youths a compelling reason to remain in school until age fifteen to obtain a diploma. Laws that compelled youths to attend school to age fourteen, therefore, could have had further impacts to age fifteen for this reason and also because of indirect effects that showed youths the gains from further education.

9.2   Impact of Compulsory Schooling and Child Labor Laws on Schooling and Educational Attainment

9.2.1   Previous Findings and Empirical Strategies

Our work is most closely related to that of Lleras-Muney (2002) and Schmidt (1996), both of whom link the eventual schooling of individuals to the laws that existed in their state of birth when they were fourteen years old. Both authors exploit the complexity of the laws and focus on the 1915 to 1939 period.[17] Lleras-Muney uses the 1960 U.S. Census microdata

16. In Britain, which long had various types of continuation schools, the Education Act 1918 (known as the Fisher Act) and the Education Act 1921 mandated part-time attendance at continuation schools by those who left school between ages fourteen and eighteen (Ringer 1979).

17. Margo and Finegan's (1996) study of compulsory education laws using the 1900 census microdata files also uses the complexity of the laws to uncover why youths in certain states were more constrained by compulsory schooling laws. They find that the combination of child

files to estimate the impact of the laws on educational attainment, whereas Schmidt uses the 1940 Census. Acemoglu and Angrist (2000) also estimate the impact of the laws using fewer features of the laws, but expanding the time period to cover youth cohorts educated through the 1960s. These and other studies of compulsory schooling laws in the United States find impacts on educational attainment that are positive but modest at best and small in comparison with the enormous increases in educational attainment during the period studied.

All three studies, as well as ours, use an empirical strategy that includes state and cohort (year of birth) fixed effects, thereby taking out main levels and trends and thus identifying the effect of the laws off law changes within states.[18] The identification strategy has virtues, but it also has some drawbacks. The cohort effects, for example, will absorb factors that are common shocks to all states. For example, the reduction in the labor force in agriculture and domestic service and the decrease in industrial homework should have strengthened the impact of compulsory schooling laws by reducing employment in uncovered sectors and in workplaces that had costly surveillance. Furthermore, changes in enforcement, not changes in the laws, may have mattered, and we (as well as the others mentioned) have not yet secured a variable that captures enforcement expenditures and efforts for all states during the period of interest.[19] We have compiled some relevant information on enforcement that we report at the end of this chapter.

Although we have not yet circumvented the problems just mentioned, we can sidestep several others in the literature. In previous studies, the linkage of individuals to their state of birth probably caused attenuation bias because of geographic mobility. Similarly, linkage to state of birth has meant that the foreign born had to be excluded, although their children should not have been if they attended U.S. schools.

---

labor laws with compulsory education laws made the latter more effective. See also Eisenberg (1988) on the complexity of nineteenth-century compulsory schooling laws. Other previous studies on the effects of U.S. compulsory schooling laws on educational outcomes include Landes and Solmon (1972), who explore the impact of late nineteenth-century compulsory schooling laws using state cross-section differences and decadal changes for the 1870 to 1890 period; Edwards (1978), who examines the impact of compulsory schooling laws on enrollment from 1940 to 1960; Lang and Kropp (1986), who analyze compulsory schooling laws and the enrollment of sixteen- and seventeen-year-olds using population census data from 1910 to 1970 in an attempt to test signaling versus human capital models of educational investment; and Angrist and Krueger (1991, 1992), who exploit the differential effects of U.S. compulsory schooling laws by quarter of birth to estimate the impacts of age of school entry on completed schooling. Stigler (1950, appendix B) presents suggestive evidence that compulsory education laws did not causally affect schooling in 1940.

18. Oreopoulos (2003) uses a similar methodology in a parallel study of the impact on educational attainment in Canada of changes in provincial compulsory schooling laws. Oreopoulos finds a larger impact on years of schooling from changes in Canadian compulsory schooling laws than we, and others, do for the United States.

19. On the impact of enforcement resources on the effectiveness of compulsory schooling laws in New York State, see Schmidt (1996).

Our contribution to this literature is to analyze the effects of the state laws using contemporaneous data on secondary school enrollments that we have collected for our study of the high school movement.[20] By doing so, we do not have to restrict the analysis to the native born and we do not have to rely on matching individuals to their state of birth.[21] The contemporaneous data we use include enrollments in grades nine to twelve in both public and private schools, including the preparatory divisions of colleges and universities, and grade nine when a public junior high school was in existence.

Another contribution of ours concerns the coding of the laws. We have compared several independent compilations of the laws (including our own), reconciled differences among them, and corrected various coding errors.[22] We have, in addition, extended all aspects of the laws back to 1910 and the minimum age back to 1900. We did the latter to correct the definition of two key variables in most of the studies—the difference between the age at which a youth could obtain a work permit and the minimum age of compulsory school attendance and the analogous difference between the maximum and minimum ages of compulsory school attendance. The minimum age (that is, the relevant required school entry age) should reflect the laws in existence about eight years prior to when the youth could drop out of school to work, although previous studies mistakenly used the same year for both laws. Because of our changes to the laws and the definitions of some variables, we have also reestimated the effects of the laws on educational attainment using 1960 micro-level Census data.

9.2.2   Compliance and Constraints, 1910 and 1920

Before we examine the effects of compulsory schooling and child labor laws, it is useful to ask what fraction of youths would have been constrained by the laws and what fraction were in compliance with existing laws. We can address these questions for 1910 and 1920 using the micro-level data of the U.S. population censuses.

Both the 1910 and 1920 censuses requested information on the school attendance (for any length of time) of children and youths during the preceding academic year.[23] The included group could, in addition, have listed an occupation. We define "full-time" school attendance as attending school but

20. Goldin (1994, 1998) and Goldin and Katz (2008). The public school data are drawn from the annual reports from 1910 to 1918 and then from the biennial reports of the Office of Education, but the coverage in the early period is incomplete and the data set can best be described as being biennial.

21. See also Schmidt's (1996) work on New York State using administrative enrollment data.

22. See the data appendix.

23. Specifically, the schooling question in both the 1910 and 1920 censuses focused on persons five to twenty-one years of age and asked about any school attendance since the previous September 1. Census enumerators were instructed to write a "Yes" for anyone of any age attending school and a "No" only for those aged five to twenty-one years who had not attended school since the previous September 1.

not listing an occupation and "part-time" attendance as attending school and listing an occupation. The information in the Census does not reveal when the youth worked during the year. Therefore, it is impossible to determine whether the work was done in the summer, after school hours, or during vacation, all of which were legal work periods even within the constrained ages (often requiring a work permit, however). It is also impossible to know whether the youth attended school at the start of the school year and then dropped out to take a job. For youths older than ten years we give the results both for any school attendance and for full-time attendance.

Table 9.1 contains the fractions of youth attending school at various ages arrayed by the ages given by the laws existing in their current state of residence. We examine two laws: the minimum compulsory schooling age (panel A) and the age at which a youth could obtain a work permit (panel B). We also give the number of states in each category.

About 85 percent of children aged seven, in states having a minimum age of seven years, attended some school, and between 85 and 90 percent did at age eight, in states having a minimum age of eight. Although the fraction of children attending school in 1910 and 1920 by state was rarely above 95 percent, the shortfall was likely due to small rates of misreporting and exemptions for children due to distance to the closest school and disabilities. Compliance, by and large, appears to have been the norm. Moreover, the fraction who would have been constrained had the law been more stringent is relatively low for states with a minimum age of eight. In 1910 the fraction attending school at age seven in states with a minimum age of eight was just 9 percentage points lower than it was at age eight (0.775 vs. 0.865). In 1920 it was just 6 percentage points lower (0.847 vs. 0.904).

In both 1910 and 1920 the vast majority of states granted work permits to fourteen-year-olds. In both years the fraction of youth who attended school at all ("full-time" plus "part-time" attendance) was extremely high. Decreased attendance between ages thirteen and fourteen was about 7 percentage points. Put differently, only about 7 percent of all youths who attended school at age thirteen dropped out by age fourteen. The effect is somewhat greater using the "full-time" definition of school attendance, for which about 10 to 12 percent of thirteen-year-olds dropped out between ages thirteen and fourteen in states that granted work permits to fourteen-year-olds.

Although these data afford only a rough sense of compliance, they appear to indicate that the vast majority of youth were in compliance. Furthermore, a large fraction of youths in the unconstrained ages were already attending school. Changes in the laws could have made a difference, but the effects could not have been as large as they were in countries like Great Britain, where youths in the unconstrained ages were largely not attending school at all.[24]

24. See Oreopoulos (2006, 2007) on compulsory schooling law impacts in the Britain and Ireland.

Table 9.1 School attendance by age for white youths, by state compulsory schooling and child labor law ages: 1910 and 1920

A Minimum compulsory schooling age

Child's age	Minimum age, 1910				Minimum age, 1920		
	None	7	8	9	7	8	9
6	0.334	0.675	0.523	0.417	0.738	0.624	0.644
7	0.611	0.844	0.775	0.741	0.886	0.847	0.867
8	0.747	0.902	0.865	0.886	0.921	0.904	0.974
9	0.819	0.925	0.897	0.976	0.941	0.926	0.948
no. of states	7	16	24	1	21	26	1

B Work permit age

Youth's age	Work permit age, 1910			Work permit age, 1920					
	None	12	14	None	12	13	14	15	16
	Full-time or part-time school attendance								
11	0.894	0.925	0.958	0.932	0.904	0.986	0.965	0.976	0.915
12	0.847	0.901	0.943	0.929	0.902	0.964	0.961	0.973	0.893
13	0.854	0.893	0.934	0.946	0.877	0.925	0.953	0.972	0.912
14	0.803	0.828	0.868	0.846	0.843	0.820	0.883	0.938	0.882
15	0.723	0.704	0.721	0.793	0.736	0.611	0.739	0.806	0.778
16	0.617	0.568	0.517	0.586	0.588	0.329	0.506	0.526	0.646
17	0.454	0.384	0.354	0.476	0.441	0.263	0.345	0.358	0.445
	Full-time school attendance								
11	0.661	0.825	0.923	0.932	0.841	0.973	0.950	0.969	0.870
12	0.606	0.789	0.900	0.912	0.810	0.959	0.938	0.959	0.843
13	0.583	0.713	0.874	0.913	0.782	0.890	0.921	0.953	0.830
14	0.494	0.637	0.759	0.838	0.727	0.775	0.825	0.912	0.792
15	0.467	0.504	0.589	0.724	0.620	0.578	0.671	0.760	0.677
16	0.360	0.354	0.400	0.560	0.482	0.276	0.433	0.467	0.550
17	0.280	0.249	0.263	0.427	0.352	0.220	0.287	0.315	0.370
no. of states	8	7	33	2	4	1	36	4	1

Sources: See the data appendix for sources on compulsory schooling and child labor laws. School enrollment data are from the IPUMS of the U.S. federal population census for 1910 and 1920. See Ruggles et al. (2008).

Notes: "School attendance" in the U.S. censuses of 1910 and 1920 means that the youth had been in a school for at least one day during the previous year. Respondents could list an occupation in addition to school attendance. We define "full-time school attendance" as attendance but no occupation. "Full-time and part-time school attendance" means that the youth was listed as attending school but also could have an occupation. Youths who listed an occupation and stated that they had attended school during the year could have worked during the summer, school vacation, or after school hours. But they also could be youths who dropped out of school to work during the year or worked and attended school on a limited

9.2.3   Effects of Law Changes Using Contemporaneous Evidence on Enrollment

We examine the effects of state child labor and compulsory schooling laws on contemporaneous high school enrollment during the period of the high school movement using data on public and private enrollments in grades nine to twelve (divided by the number of fourteen- to seventeen-year-olds in the state) for even numbered years from 1910 to 1938.[25] A standard panel data model is estimated, including state and year fixed effects, state law variables, and other state time-varying economic and demographic control variables. The state fixed effects capture unmeasured time-invariant state characteristics that could have affected the adoption of schooling laws and enrollment rates. The year effects capture aggregate trends (and birth cohort effects) driving high school enrollment rates. Thus, our identification of the effects of state child labor and compulsory schooling laws is driven by differential law changes across states, conditional on a range of time varying state controls.

Our regression specifications are of the form

$$\text{ENR}_{st} = L_{st}\delta + Z_{st}\beta + \alpha_s + \gamma_t + \varepsilon_{st},$$

where ENR_{st} is the high school enrollment rate for state s in year t, L_{st} is a vector state child labor and compulsory schooling law variables, Z_{st} is a vector of state time-varying covariates, α_s are state fixed effects, and γ_t are year fixed effects. The state control variables include those found by Goldin and Katz (1999, 2009) to have substantial effects on high school enrollment and graduation rates during the time period considered here. We include basic demographic controls for age structure (fraction young, fraction old), nativity (fraction foreign born), and race (fraction black). We also include several time varying economic controls: automobile registrations per capita and manufacturing employment per capita. Automobile registrations per capita, in this early period in the history of the car, represent a crude proxy for state wealth (or income) and their distributions. The variable is a measure of the "middle class" share of the state population (the fraction able to afford a car) after conditioning on state demographics and urbanization. We include, as well, a full set of census division linear time trends in our basic specification, and we assess the sensitivity of our results to the inclusion of state-specific linear time trends. We report robust standard errors clustered by state to account for serial correlation in the residuals (as suggested by Bertrand, Duflo, and Mullainathan [2004], and Kézdi [2001]). All regres-

---

25. Goldin (1998) constructs state public and private secondary school enrollment rates for 1910, 1911, 1913, and even years from 1914 to 1950. We impute the 1912 rates using the average of 1911 and 1913.

sions are weighted by the contemporaneous number of fourteen-year-olds in the state.[26]

Regression estimates for different specifications of the state child labor and compulsory schooling law variables affecting high school age youth are presented in table 9.2. The national high school enrollment rate (for the forty-eight states in the sample) increased by more than 50 percentage points during the sample period, rising from 18.7 percent in 1910 to 69.1 percent in 1938. In all the specifications, we include a dummy variable for a "permissible" state continuation school law, meaning one that mandated municipalities establish continuation schools or permitted them to do so. Both types of continuation school laws set a maximum age below which working youths, who had not met the educational standard, could be required to attend. The number of states with "permissible" continuation school laws increased from two in 1910 to twenty-eight in 1938. The share of the high school age population covered by continuation school laws increased from 9 percent to 69 percent from 1910 to 1938.

The first column of table 9.2 follows Lleras-Muney (2002), who summarized the effects of the laws using a variable defined as the number of years a child would be compelled to attend school had he entered school at the compulsory entry age, given in year t, and had he left precisely when he could obtain a work permit, also given in year t. Since youths of secondary school age would have been affected by age of entry laws when they were about seven or eight years old, we construct our variable in a slightly different way. We use the difference in the work permit age at time t and the school entrance age prevailing in their state in year $t - 8$. The variable ranges from zero to ten years with a (population weighted) mean that increases from 4.0 years in 1910 to 7.5 years in 1938; the most stringent school attendance requirement in 1910 using this definition was seven years and by 1938 fourteen states required eight or more years.

The estimates in table 9.2, column (1) show noticeable and statistically significant positive effects of the continuation school law indicator. The adoption of a continuation school law is associated with a 2.4 percentage point increase in the high school enrollment rate. An increase of a year in our initial summary variable of child labor laws (i.e., work permit age – school entrance age) raises the high school enrollment rate by a modest (and not quite statistically significant) 0.3 percentage point.[27]

---

26. The regression results are not sensitive to weighting. In all cases, unweighted regressions yield estimates that are quite similar to the reported estimates. The results are also almost identical if, for each year, a state's share of all fourteen-year-olds in the United States is used as the weight.

27. We also find (consistent with Goldin and Katz 1999, 2009) a substantial and positive effect of auto registrations per capita and significant impacts of the state's age structure at the upper and lower ends.

Table 9.2   **Impact of state compulsory schooling and child labor laws on secondary school enrollment rates, 1910 to 1938 (biennially, 48 states)**

	(1)	(2)	(3)	(4)	(5)
Dependent variable: Fraction of state's 14- to 17-year-olds enrolled in public and private secondary schools (mean = 0.441)					
Continuation school law	0.0244	0.0271	0.0245	0.0271	0.0247
	(0.00899)	(0.00917)	(0.00846)	(0.00917)	(0.0110)
Child labor school years[a]		0.00522		0.00498	0.00422
		(0.00192)		(0.00231)	(0.00243)
Compulsory school years[b]				0.000324	−0.000890
				(0.00170)	(0.00171)
(Work permit age) − (school entrance age$_{t-8}$)	0.00297				
	(0.00223)				
Child labor school years = 8			0.00630		
			(0.0102)		
Child labor school years ≥ 9			0.0533		
			(0.0190)		
Compulsory school years = 8			−0.000112		
			(0.00759)		
Compulsory school years ≥ 9			0.00987		
			(0.0100)		
Autos per capita	0.987	0.979	0.856	0.978	1.011
	(0.208)	(0.204)	(0.184)	(0.201)	(0.268)
Manufacturing employment per capita	−0.0349	0.0123	0.0482	0.0224	−0.0355
	(0.412)	(0.409)	(0.398)	(0.412)	(0.465)
Fraction ≥ 65 years	2.44	2.67	2.69	2.69	3.58
	(1.55)	(1.54)	(1.35)	(1.54)	(2.72)
Fraction ≤ 14 years	−1.83	−1.74	−2.01	−1.75	−2.04
	(0.601)	(0.591)	(0.605)	(0.596)	(0.915)
Other state demographic controls[c]	Yes	Yes	Yes	Yes	Yes
State dummies	Yes	Yes	Yes	Yes	Yes
Year dummies	Yes	Yes	Yes	Yes	Yes
Census division trends	Yes	Yes	Yes	Yes	No
State trends	No	No	No	No	Yes
R^2	0.977	0.977	0.978	0.977	0.984
Standard error	0.0326	0.0325	0.0318	0.0325	0.0286
Number of observations	720	720	720	720	720

Sources: Secondary school enrollments, see Goldin (1994, 1998); compulsory school and child labor laws, see the data appendix. Data on percent black, percent foreign born, and percent urban were provided by Adriana Lleras-Muney, see http://www.econ.ucla.edu/alleras/papers.htm, and are from the 1910, 1920, 1930, and 1940 Censuses of Population (linearly imputed in intervening years). For other variables, see Goldin and Katz (2009).

Notes: All regressions have been weighted by the number of fourteen-year-olds in the state. The number in parentheses are robust standard errors clustered by state. The 1912 enrollment rate is the average of that in 1911 and 1913.

[a]Child labor school years$_t$ = *max* [(education required for work permit$_t$), (work permit age$_t$ − school entrance age$_{t-8}$)].

[b]Compulsory school years$_t$ = *min* [(education for exemption$_t$), (maximum age of compulsory schooling − entry age$_{t-8}$)].

[c]Includes fraction black, fraction foreign born, fraction urban.

The summary variable of the laws that we just defined (work permit age – school entrance age) does not account for other potentially important constraints that were part of the state child labor and compulsory school laws. Many state laws mandated a minimum amount of schooling, in addition to the age requirement, to receive a work permit. In some cases the mandated number of years was greater than the difference between the work permit age and the age of school entry. Thus, following Acemoglu and Angrist (2000), we define a more accurate measure of the mandated number of school years as follows:

Child Labor School Years$_{st}$ = max[(education required for work permit)$_{st}$, (work permit age$_{st}$ − school entrance age$_{s,t-8}$)].

A read and write requirement for a work permit is coded as the equivalent of requiring four years of completed schooling.[28] The (fourteen-year-old weighted) mean of child labor school years increased from 4.5 years in 1910 to 7.8 years in 1938. Only one state (Washington) required eight years of schooling for a work permit in 1910 and no state required more. By 1938, the majority of states required eight to ten years of schooling for a work permit.

The estimates in table 9.2, column (2) include this more accurate variable for measuring the constraints on schooling of child labor laws. The impact of our modified child labor law measure is both positive and statistically significant with each one-year increase in "child labor school years" associated with a 0.5 percentage point increase in the secondary school enrollment rate. The continuation law indicator remains significant and is associated with a 2.7 percentage point increase in the enrollment rate, similar to the column (1) estimate.

We next examine the impacts of state compulsory schooling laws as well as child labor laws. The specification in column (4) includes a summary measure of the minimum number of school years required by the state's compulsory schooling laws:

Compulsory School Years$_{st}$ = min[(education for exemption)$_{st}$, (maximum age of compulsory schooling$_{st}$ − school entrance age$_{s,t-8}$)].

In constructing this variable, we follow the procedure mentioned before and code an education exemption for "read and write" as four years of schooling. If state s at year t had no educational exemption, then Compulsory School Years$_{st}$ is given by (maximum age of compulsory schooling$_{st}$ − school

28. If there is no law regarding the school entrance age or the work permit age, then the "child labor school years" variable is set equal to zero or to the education required for a work permit, if such a requirement exists. The inclusion of a separate dummy variable for a read and write requirement yields a small and statistically insignificant coefficient and does not impact the other coefficients in any detectable manner.

entrance age$_{s,t-8}$).[29] The mean of "compulsory school years" is 6.9 over the sample and ranges from zero to twelve. The estimates in column (4) show a small and statistically insignificant effect of "compulsory school years" on high school enrollments with the same child labor and continuation school controls as in the core specification in column (2). A one-year increase in "compulsory school years" is associated with only a 0.03 percentage point rise in the high school enrollment rate as compared with a 0.50 percentage point rise from a one-year increase in "child labor school years."

The effects of "child labor school years" and continuation laws on secondary school enrollment rates are robust to controlling for state and census division (or region) trends and to a wide range of control variables. For example, in column (5), we replace the census division trends with a full set of state-specific linear time trends. The impacts of the "child labor school years" and continuation law variables are only slightly reduced in magnitude and the effect of "compulsory school years" remains insignificant.

We have also examined the discrete effects of child labor and compulsory schooling law requirements that were sufficiently stringent to directly impact high school enrollment decisions. We focus on state child labor laws requiring eight or more years of schooling to get a work permit and compulsory schooling law provisions requiring eight or more years to leave school. In column (3), we include dummy variables for eight years and nine or more years (fewer than eight years is the omitted category) for both "child labor school years" and "compulsory school years."

The estimates in column (3) reveal a substantial positive effect of child labor laws that mandated nine or more years of schooling. The high school enrollment rate increases by 5.3 percentage points when nine or ten years of school are required to leave school with a work permit. The coefficients on the "compulsory school years" indicators are small and insignificant.

In summary, changes in state child labor and compulsory schooling laws appear to have had some impact on high school enrollment rates from 1910 to 1938. But the impacts are modest relative to the rapid rise in secondary schooling rates during the era of the high school movement.[30] Continuation school laws, possibly because they imposed costs on the employers of high school-age youth, have the most consistently positive effects on enrollment rates. Other child labor law requirements had some impact, especially

29. If there is no law in place, setting a maximum age of compulsory schooling or a school entrance age, then the "compulsory school years" variable is set to zero. If there is no education for exemption statute, then the compulsory school variable is set equal to maximum age of compulsory schooling minus the school entrance age. Almost all states with no educational exemption in 1910 later added that clause to their compulsory education laws. Enforcement of the maximum age was probably lax in the absence of the exemption.

30. In our NBER working paper version (Goldin and Katz 2003) we allow for nonlinear effects of child labor and compulsory schooling laws by including dummy variables for no child labor law and no compulsory school law. The conclusions from that analysis are almost identical to those presented here.

those that required nine or more years of schooling for a work permit, since permit rules typically undermined compulsory schooling laws.

How large was the contribution of child labor and compulsory schooling laws to the 50.4 percentage point increase in the high school enrollment rate from 1910 to 1938? We take the coefficients from the specification in column (4) of table 9.2, which includes controls for continuation laws, child labor laws, and compulsory schooling laws, to predict the effects of the laws on high school enrollment rates using the change in the mean of the law variables from 1910 to 1938.

The share of youth in states with continuation school laws increased by 60 percentage points from 1910 to 1938, and that increase can explain a 1.6 percentage point increase in the high school enrollment rate. The combined effects of changes in child labor and compulsory schooling laws adds 1.8 percentage points driven almost entirely by the effects of the mean increase of 3.4 in "child labor school years." About 3.4 percentage points (or 6 to 7 percent) of the overall increase in the high school enrollment rate from 1910 to 1938 can therefore be accounted for by changes in child labor and compulsory schooling laws. In contrast, the estimates in column (4) imply that the crude proxy from improved economic status represented by the increase in automobiles per capita from under 0.01 in 1910 to 0.22 in 1938 can explain a 21 percentage point rise in the high school enrollment rate.

9.2.4 Effects of Law Changes Using Census Data on Educational Attainment

We next examine the effects of state compulsory schooling and child labor laws on the eventual educational attainment of the birth cohorts who were of high school age during the high school movement era. We focus on the 1896 to 1925 birth cohorts since they reached high school entry age between 1910 and 1939. Overall educational attainment increased rapidly for the cohorts affected by the high school movement in the first half of the twentieth century. Estimates from the 1960 federal population census for U.S.-born individuals indicate an increase of 2.45 in mean years of schooling, rising from 8.59 years for the birth cohort of 1896 to 11.04 years for the birth cohort of 1925. The increase in the high school grades (nine to twelve) accounts for the majority (1.42 years or 58 percent) of the rise in schooling over this time period.

Our empirical approach is to link our data on state laws and other state-level covariates to individual level data on educational attainment, state of birth, and individual demographics (race, sex, and parent's nativity) for the U.S.-born in the birth cohorts of 1896 to 1925 from the 1960 Census of Population IPUMS (Integrated Public Use Microdata Series). We match each individual to the state child labor and compulsory schooling requirement that prevailed in their state of birth at the relevant ages. Thus, we use the school entrance age law existing in their state of birth when they were seven years old and the other components of the laws prevailing when they were fourteen years old.

The Census microdata allow us to estimate the impact of the laws on the long-run educational attainment of the affected cohorts, although there are some disadvantages with this approach, as previously mentioned. For example, we have information on each individual's state of birth and not on their state of residence when they were of school age. Interstate migration (about 14 percent of fourteen-year-olds in 1920 were living in a state different from their state of birth) can lead to modest attenuation bias from standard measurement error, but it could also generate more subtle biases from non-random migration from states with different patterns of law changes. In addition, we cannot measure the effects of the laws on foreign-born children, who were about 5 percent of high school-age youth in 1920.[31] We focus our analysis on the 1960 Census because it contains large samples for all the relevant cohorts with a consistent measure of years of schooling.[32]

Our basic regression specification for analyzing the effects of state laws on years of schooling is:

$$E_{ics} = X_{ics}\beta + L_{cs}\delta + Z_{cs}\pi + \alpha_s + \gamma_c + \mu_{ics},$$

where E_{ics} is the years of completed schooling of individual i from birth cohort c and state-of-birth s, X_{ics} are individual-level demographic controls (race and sex dummies and an indicator variable for foreign-born parents), L_{cs} is the vector of state child labor and compulsory schooling law variables affecting those born in state s from cohort c, Z_{cs} are time-varying state covariates, α_s are state fixed effects, and γ_c are birth cohort fixed effects. We also include census division linear time trends.[33] The state law variables are the same as those from our core specification for high school enrollment rates from table 9.2, column (4). We report robust standard errors clustered by state of birth to account for any state-level serial correlation in the residuals.

The key results on educational attainment for the entire sample and for various subsamples (whites versus blacks, males versus females) are presented in table 9.3. The core specification for the full sample is shown in

31. Estimates of the interstate migration rates of families with youth and of the share foreign born of fourteen- to seventeen-year-olds in 1920 are from the 1920 Census of Population IPUMS.

32. We have also performed a similar analysis for the educational attainment of the same birth cohorts measured at similar ages (from forty to forty-nine years of age) using data from the 1940, 1950, 1960, and 1970 censuses. The results are similar but less precisely estimated than the estimates using the 1960 Census. The disadvantage of this approach is smaller sample sizes for the earlier cohorts since the 1940 Census only provides information on parents' nativity (a key control variable) for sample-line individuals and the 1950 Census only provides educational attainment information for sample-line individuals. There are also some differences in the measures of educational attainment available in the different census years. The educational variable in the 1940 Census does not distinguish whether the highest grade attended was actually completed, and the 1940 and 1950 Census educational attainment data are top coded at seventeen years as opposed to eighteen years in the 1960 Census.

33. Estimates are similar, but slightly attenuated, including a full set of census region-year fixed effects.

	All (1)	1901–1925 cohorts (2)	Whites (3)	Blacks (4)	Males (5)	Females (6)
	Dependent variable: Completed years of schooling (mean for all = 10.01)					
Continuation school law	0.147	0.140	0.134	0.220	0.162	0.131
	(0.0552)	(0.0524)	(0.0579)	(0.0977)	(0.0624)	(0.0549)
Child labor school years[a]	0.0148	0.0396	0.0162	-0.00549	0.00913	0.0219
	(0.0124)	(0.0130)	(0.0141)	(0.0145)	(0.0136)	(0.0144)
Compulsory school years[b]	0.00225	-0.0121	-0.00630	0.00670	-0.00654	0.00996
	(0.00757)	(0.00796)	(0.00763)	(0.00957)	(0.00860)	(0.0105)
Autos per capita	0.725	0.497	0.753	1.92	0.582	0.875
	(0.760)	(0.695)	(0.710)	(2.32)	(0.853)	(0.793)
Manufacturing employment per capita	-3.32	-4.26	-2.45	-6.42	-4.29	-1.12
	(1.63)	(1.72)	(1.56)	(2.63)	(1.86)	(1.71)
State demographic controls	Yes	Yes	Yes	Yes	Yes	Yes
Person demographic controls	Yes	Yes	Yes	Yes	Yes	Yes
State of birth dummies	Yes	Yes	Yes	Yes	Yes	Yes
Birth cohort dummies	Yes	Yes	Yes	Yes	Yes	Yes
Census division trends	Yes	Yes	Yes	Yes	Yes	Yes
R^2	0.160	0.150	0.099	0.160	0.172	0.151
Standard error	3.19	3.17	3.14	3.53	3.36	3.01
Number of observations	536,628	478,591	483,993	50,912	260,884	275,744

Sources: IPUMS of the 1960 federal population census (Ruggles et al. 2008). See the data appendix for state compulsory schooling and child labor laws. The sources of the other variables are given in the notes to table 9.2.

Notes: State demographic controls are fractions foreign born, black, urban, greater than sixty-four years old, and less than fifteen years old. Individual demographic controls include dummy variables for female, black, other race, and parents foreign-born. Robust standard errors are in parentheses clustered by state of birth. The school entrance law refers to that in existence in the individual's state of birth at age seven, whereas all other law variables are for age fourteen.

[a]Child labor school years$_t$ = *max* [(education required for work permit$_t$), (work permit age$_t$ − school entrance age$_{t-7}$)], where t is the year at which the individual is fourteen years old.

[b]Compulsory school years$_t$ = *min* [(education for exemption$_t$), (maximum age of compulsory schooling$_t$ − entry age$_{t-7}$)], where t is the year at which the individual is fourteen years old.

column (1). The introduction of a continuation school law is associated with a 0.15-year increase in schooling for the affected cohorts. Similar to our findings for contemporaneous high school enrollment rates, we estimate larger effects for child labor school years than for compulsory schooling law years, but the impacts of both variables are small and statistically insignificant. State manufacturing employment tends to have a depressing effect on educational attainment, possibly reflecting higher opportunity costs of schooling due to youth employment in certain industries.[34]

Our qualitative findings with respect to the effects of state laws on educational attainment are similar to Lleras-Muney (2002). But we estimate somewhat larger effects of continuation school laws and modestly smaller effects of child labor school years.[35] The estimates in column (2) restrict the sample to the same birth cohorts in Lleras-Muney's sample (born from 1910 to 1925) but use our more accurate measure of child labor laws. The estimates on the restricted sample without the oldest cohorts in column (2) imply that a one-year increase in "child labor school years" increases completed schooling by 0.04 years, similar to Lleras-Muney's baseline estimate of 0.05 years of completed schooling for each additional year required from child labor laws.

The estimates in columns (3) to (6) of table 9.2 show statistically significant, substantial, and rather similar effects of continuation school laws on educational attainment of whites and blacks and males and females. The other aspects of child labor and compulsory schooling laws do not have individually significant effects on any of the groups. The negative effect of manufacturing employment on educational attainment is more substantial for blacks than whites and larger for males than females.

The central message from the estimates in table 9.3 is that state compulsory schooling and child labor laws, despite their expansion, appear to have played only minor roles in the growth of educational attainment for youths from 1910 to 1939 (the birth cohorts of 1896 to 1925). For youths born in 1896, 9 percent lived in states with continuation school laws at age fourteen, 33 percent faced no compulsory schooling law at age seven, 14 percent faced no child labor law at age fourteen, and mean years of schooling required by child labor laws and compulsory schooling laws were 4.6 and 4.9 years,

34. Also, the "automobiles per capita" variable that has large effects on contemporaneous high school enrollment rates has small and statistically insignificant effects on overall years of schooling. But we do find (in unreported regressions) that the automobiles per capita variable has large and statistically significant positive effects on years of high school and the probability of completing nine or more years of education using the same sample. In contrast to the findings in table 9.3 and to our cross-section findings using the high school graduation rate (Goldin and Katz 2009), the manufacturing variable in table 9.2 is not consistently negative.

35. The differences in the estimates from Lleras-Muney (2002) arise from our expansion of the sample to cover earlier cohorts (those born from 1896 to 1900), our improvements in the coding of and specification of the effects of state laws, slight differences in treatment of regional trends, and some small data entry errors affecting the control variables for several observations in Lleras-Muney's published regressions.

respectively. In contrast, for youths born in 1925, 69 percent lived in states with continuation school laws, all states had child labor and compulsory schooling laws, and the mean years of binding schooling requirements from child labor and compulsory schooling laws had both risen to eight years.

Our core estimates in table 9.3, column (1) imply that changes in state laws can explain an increase in educational attainment of 0.145 years with 0.088 years coming from the adoption of continuation laws and 0.057 years coming from the strengthening of other child labor and compulsory schooling law requirements. Thus, about 6 percent of the 2.45-year increase in schooling from the 1896 to 1925 birth cohorts can be attributed to changes in child labor and compulsory schooling laws. The estimated proportional contribution of these laws to the growth of overall educational attainment is almost identical to our estimate of their contemporaneous effects on the high school enrollments for these same cohorts.

9.3   Enforcement of Compulsory Schooling Laws

We have, thus far, used the details of compulsory schooling and child labor laws but not information on their enforcement. The extent of law enforcement, as we previously noted, is difficult to measure and scant information on enforcement procedures is available in the many volumes and documents we have used to compile the laws. One reason is that enforcement often resided in municipalities, whereas the laws were passed at the state level. Expenditures on enforcement, moreover, were not always part of one agency or governmental unit. Rather, the expenditures on enforcing compulsory schooling laws were occasionally at the school district level or in other entities such as the courts. The same was true of child labor laws.

Deffenbaugh and Keesecker, two noted contemporaries of the period who together and separately produced many government documents about compulsory schooling from 1914 to the mid-1930s, noted that school censuses are found in places where compulsory education laws are enforced (1935, 23–24). Thus, to get a sense of the change in enforcement over the high school movement era we have gathered information on which states had laws requiring a school census be taken and with what frequency. The "school census" was a survey, generally taken by the attendance officer (also known as the "truant" officer) of the school district (or in small districts by the teachers themselves), which was intended to include all children within the ages of compulsory education and often those younger and those older up to the age of majority.[36] By knowing which children should be in school within the district, the enforcement of compulsory education laws was made more likely.

---

36. School censuses were also used by various states, both before and after the passage of compulsory schooling laws, to apportion state school funds.

We have found four fairly comprehensive lists of school censuses covering much of the period we explore: 1913, 1928, 1935, and 1945 (listed by the approximate last year of the laws reported). Because every state had a school census by 1928, we compare 1914 and 1928.[37] These years are interesting for our purposes because they cover much of the period of the high school movement prior to the Great Depression and they also cover the years of the greatest expansion of compulsory education laws (see the various parts of figure 9.3).

The 1913 compilation (U.S. Office [Bureau] of Education 1914, table II, 39) of compulsory school laws reported that, among states with a compulsory education law, all but four required a school census. Some required the census only of the larger cities and some may have not required an annual census.[38] The four states that did not have a census (California, Illinois, Louisiana, and Michigan) are a mixed group and contain several that were leaders in education. Michigan may actually have required a census since the Office of Education report (1914) noted that teachers' reports of absence in Michigan required that "the last school census shall be compared with the enrollment."

The 1928 compilation (Keesecker 1929, part I, 20) reported that thirty-nine states required an annual school census, five states required one biennially, one state required one every four years, three states required a census quinquennially, and one (Nevada) required a school census at the judgment of the state board.[39] By 1928 the vast majority of states had an annual school census and all had some type of census.

From 1913 to 1928 the largest change in states having a school census was for those that did not previously have a compulsory education law. Among the states with a law predating 1913, enforcement was potentially enhanced by having a statewide mandate rather than one covering only the larger cities and a requirement to have an annual census. Increased enforcement through the provision of a school census does not appear to have been as great as some have presumed. To the extent that the experts, Deffenbaugh and Keesecker, are correct, there was enforcement of compulsory education laws.

37. The lists that we have not used here are Deffenbaugh and Keesecker (1935, 25) and Proffitt and Segel (1945, table 1). Between these two dates the following states curtailed their state school censuses: Arizona (annually), California (every third year), Delaware (biennially), Indiana (annually), Nevada (annually or as deemed necessary by the superintendent), and New Jersey (quinquennially), where the mandate as of 1935 is in parentheses. Most other states kept the requirement the same as in 1935.

38. The 1913 compilation does not list whether the census had to be annual, biennial, or on another timetable.

39. The states include the District of Columbia. California, included by Keesecker in the "annual" group, did not require a census but rather that parents register children of school age with the authorities. The tabular material appears to contain an error: DC and Florida should be "annual," not "biennial."

9.4   Conclusion

The secondary school enrollment rate of U.S. youth expanded enormously (by over 50 percentage points) during the period of the high school movement, from 1910 to 1940. Changes in child labor laws and compulsory schooling laws motivated by Progressive Era campaigns to reduce child labor, eliminate youth idleness and delinquency, and expand schooling have been credited by many as playing a major role in the rapid rise of U.S. secondary schooling during the first half of the twentieth century. This chapter finds that changes in child labor and compulsory schooling laws had statistically detectable but relatively modest effects on U.S. secondary schooling rates. Continuation school requirements, which were intended to increase the costs to employers of teen labor, had somewhat larger effects on schooling than did other components of child labor and compulsory schooling laws. Our estimates imply that increases in the restrictiveness of state continuation school, child labor, and compulsory schooling laws can account for only about 6 to 7 percent of the increase in secondary school enrollments and ultimate educational attainment of U.S. youth from 1910 to 1939.

If compulsory schooling and child labor legislation had small effects in the United States, why were they passed? The laws had some positive effect on schooling and may have been more effective for certain targeted groups, such as the children of the foreign born in large cities. But as we have noted, many of the laws were not pro-education. They were, instead, antitruancy, antivagrancy laws designed to make certain that teens were either employed or at school and not loitering.

Why does the evidence for the United States differ from that of some other nations? Compulsory schooling laws were expanded and increasingly enforced in many countries in the mid-twentieth century and were apparently effective in increasing enrollment rates. Their effectiveness was greatest when they were accompanied by large increases in educational access and spending, often when the laws bound the state to provide more educational resources. One of the most studied cases is that of Great Britain.

The historic 1944 Education Act increased the age of compulsory education (the school leaving age) in England, Scotland, and Wales from fourteen to fifteen in 1947 and appears to have been rigorously enforced (Ringer 1979). The fraction of those leaving school at age fourteen declined from 57 percent in 1945 to less than 10 percent in 1948 and then to about 5 percent by 1950 (Oreopoulos 2006). The act also included a guarantee that secondary schooling would be free of charge.[40] The compulsory schooling

40. Oreopoulos (2006) discounts the role of guarantees in the Education Act 1944 for free secondary schools because there was little change in the schooling of fifteen-year-olds around 1947 and for many years after. But the lag in the enrollment of fifteen-year-olds probably had more to do with the paucity of educational resources than the lack of initiative on the part of British teens. The state had been forced to provide places for fourteen-year-olds by the act, but

age in Britain was extended only when the educational system had recovered from the war and teachers and schools were available for the increased number of fourteen-year-olds, accounting for the delay to 1947. Large numbers of British school children could not have gone to school past age fourteen in the absence of the act because the resources were not in place before the state was committed to providing them.

In the United States, on the other hand, schools (even secondary schools) were already largely available and free for most students who could have been affected by compulsory schooling laws. The impact of the constraints imposed on youths, employers, and local governments by child labor and compulsory schooling laws were far less important in the rise of the U.S. secondary school. The enormous expansion of U.S. secondary school enrollment was largely due to factors such as the substantial pecuniary returns to a year of school, increased family wealth, and greater school access.

Data Appendix

Construction of State-Level Compulsory Education and Child Labor Laws, 1910 to 1939. (Data are posted at: http://www.economics.harvard.edu/faculty/goldin/data.)

The compilation of state-level compulsory education and child labor laws, from 1910 to 1939, contains the following seven variables:

1. Minimum age of compulsory schooling, known as the school entrance age (also compiled for 1900 to 1909).
2. Maximum age of compulsory schooling, known as the school leaving age (also compiled for 1900 to 1909).
3. Education for exemption from maximum age rule.
4. Age at which youth can obtain a work permit (for work during normal school hours).
5. Education required to receive a work permit (for work during normal school hours).
6. Whether state has mandatory continuation schools.
7. Maximum age of continuation school attendance (and whether the state permitted municipalities to mandate continuation schools).

---

it was not bound to make school accessible to older youths even though the act made secondary school free. Descriptions of the schools and curriculum for the fourteen-year-olds from *The Times Educational Supplement* in 1947 (generously provided by Damon Clark) reveal that classes, particularly in rural areas, were held in temporary structures and were intended for only one additional year of schooling—the year the youths were fourteen years old.

These variables summarize complex laws. The first three variables concern compulsory education laws and the last four are child labor laws. Compulsory education and child labor laws were often two sides of the same coin. They have appeared to latter-day observers to have been inconsistent because the maximum age of compulsory education was often higher than the age at which a work permit could be obtained. But the laws were generally part of the same piece of legislation and had a set of similar goals.

The binding constraint for much of the period we consider was the age at which a youth could obtain a work permit or the education required to receive a work permit. Take, for example, a state with a maximum age of compulsory education of sixteen years, but in which a youth of fourteen can receive a work permit for work during normal school hours if the youth had already completed eight years of school. In that case, the binding constraint would be, most likely, the age needed for the work permit. But if the education required were no more than being able to "read and write," the binding constraint would be the education required to get a work permit. Many states also had a minimum education level to excuse a youth from the maximum age of compulsory education. In certain states and times, this would have been the binding constraint.

Finally, many states adopted laws requiring school districts to establish "continuation schools." The continuation school idea caught on after World War I, although it was first adopted in 1911 by Wisconsin. A mandatory state continuation school law (variable 6) meant that school districts, with a large enough number of working youths under some age, had to establish a continuation school. Youths who did not meet a minimum education standard were required to attend the school for some number of hours per week (for example, one afternoon of four hours) and the employers were often responsible to excuse the youths from work during their school time. Many states, however, did not have a mandatory law but rather had a law setting the maximum age for youths to be in such a school if one existed. That is, variable (6) would be 0 but variable (7) would be some age. If a municipality had a continuation school, the maximum age given in the state law would be binding.

The compulsory education and child labor laws contain numerous complexities that make their coding difficult. Most states, for example, had several exemptions for compulsory education and a detailed knowledge of court decisions is required to assess their importance. For example, "mental defectives" were almost always exempt from compulsory education laws. Similarly, children of impoverished families were often exempt from the education requirement for a work permit. The definition of "defective" and "impoverished" was up to the courts. There is also the difficult issue of enforcement.

Another complexity is that state laws occasionally had different ages for cities and towns than for the rest of the state or for the largest city versus all other places. Our coding used that for the majority of the population. In other cases, the state left the details of compulsory education laws to the school districts and municipalities. Finally, these seven variables omit the details concerning child labor laws, such as the number of hours they could labor and the occupations that were banned for youths of various ages and by sex.

The data on these laws are derived primarily from more than a dozen contemporaneous compilations, often commissioned by the U.S. Office of Education or the Children's Bureau of the U.S. Department of Labor. When a law changed between two of the compilations, the state laws were consulted to find the precise date of change or, when available, information on changes to state laws published by the U.S. Office of Education.[41] In some cases we could not locate the precise date of change. In such cases, the law is generally extrapolated back in time (e.g., if a law changed between 1921 and 1924, the 1924 details are assigned to 1922 and 1923). Because we have major compilations for 1910, 1914, 1915, 1917/18, 1921, 1924, 1927, 1928, 1929, 1935, 1939, and 1945, as well as minor compilations for several other dates, the change dates that we have imputed are probably not too different from the actual ones.

The interpretation of the state laws was often difficult and some compilations were wrong in some of the details. In certain cases, the state laws are difficult to code because they did not apply in uniform ways throughout the state. For example, in some cases the law applied to just the largest city (e.g., Wilmington, DE; New Orleans, LA; Baltimore, MD). In these cases, we have coded the state law rather than that of the city because the majority of the state's population did not live in the largest city. But when the law applied to all cities and towns (say above 2,500 people) we have coded the city laws rather than those applying to only rural areas in the state. In some cases, there was no state law and localities were given discretion to write their own law. In these cases, we coded the state as not having a law. In a few instances the law applied differently to boys than to girls and we have used the restrictions that applied to the former.

The data set is the result of many individual labors. It was begun independently by Claudia Goldin (in 1993) and by Adriana Lleras-Muney (in her PhD dissertation). Stefanie Schmidt took Goldin's initial coding and added others. Stefanie Schmidt's work covered almost the same years that Lleras-Muney's did (1915 to 1935 for Schmidt and 1915 to 1939 for Lleras-Muney). Both used similar sources in most years, but there were some differences. Schmidt relied on state legal documents for the years between the compilations to pinpoint state law changes. Lleras-Muney used more published compilations than did Schmidt and thus encountered fewer changes that had uncertain dates.

41. State law documents include titles such as "School Codes of [State]," "Act of [State] Legislature," "[State] Board of Education," and "Biennial Reports of [State]."

We cross-checked these two compilations (and another by Angrist and Acemoglu, which also covers years after 1940 but contains less detail for the 1915 to 1940 period), checked them against the original documents used, and rectified the differences, as best we could. In addition we extended the Lleras-Muney and Schmidt series back to 1910.

References

*Acemoglu, Daron, and Joshua Angrist. 2000. "How Large Are Human Capital Externalities? Evidence from Compulsory Schooling Laws." In *NBER Macroeconomics Annual 2000,* volume 15, edited by Ben S. Bernanke and Kenneth Rogoff, 9–59. Cambridge, MA: MIT Press.

Angrist, Joshua D., and Alan B. Krueger. 1991. "Does Compulsory School Attendance Affect Schooling and Earnings?" *Quarterly Journal of Economics* 106:979–1014.

———. 1992. "The Effect of Age of School Entry on Educational Attainment: An Application of Instrumental Variables with Moments from Two Samples." *Journal of the American Statistical Association* 87:328–36.

*Bender, John F. 1928. "Criticisms of Attendance Laws." *American School Board Journal* 76:43–44.

Bermejo, F. V. 1923. *The School Attendance Service in American Cities.* Menasha, WI: George Banta Publishing Co.

Bertrand, Marianne, Esther Duflo, and Sendhil Mullainathan. 2004. "How Much Should We Trust Differences-In-Differences Estimates?" *Quarterly Journal of Economics* 119:249–75.

*Bonner, H. R. 1923. "The Conviction of Legislators." *American School Board Journal* 66:45–48.

Clapp, Mary A., and Mabel A. Strong. 1928. *The School and the Working Child: A Study of Fifty School Departments of Massachusetts.* Boston: Massachusetts Child Labor Committee.

§Deffenbaugh, Walter S., and Ward W. Keesecker. 1935. *Compulsory School Attendance Laws and their Administration.* U.S. Office of Education Bulletin, 1935, no. 4. Washington, DC: GPO.

Edwards, Linda Nasif. 1978. "An Empirical Analysis of Compulsory Schooling Legislation, 1940–1960." *Journal of Law and Economics* 21:203–22.

Eisenberg, Martin J. 1988. "Compulsory Attendance Legislation in America, 1870 to 1915." PhD diss., Department of Economics, University of Pennsylvania.

Emmons, Frederick Earle. 1926. *City School Attendance Service.* Teachers College, Columbia University Contributions to Education, no. 200. New York: Teachers College, Columbia University.

Engerman, Stanley L., and Kenneth L. Sokoloff. Forthcoming. *Economic Development in the Americas since 1500: Endowments and Institutions.* Cambridge: Cambridge University Press.

*Ensign, Forest Chester. (1921) 1969. *Compulsory Education Laws and Child Labor.* New York: Arno Press.

Gibbons, Charles E. 1927. *School or Work in Indiana?* New York: National Child Labor Committee.

Goldin, Claudia. 1994. "Appendix to: How America Graduated from High School:

An Exploratory Study, 1910 to 1960." NBER Historical Working Paper no. 57. Cambridge, MA: National Bureau of Economic Research, June.

———. 1998. "America's Graduation from High School: The Evolution and Spread of Secondary Schooling in the Twentieth Century." *Journal of Economic History* 58:345–74.

Goldin, Claudia, and Lawrence F. Katz. 1999. "Human Capital and Social Capital: The Rise of Secondary Schooling in America, 1910 to 1940." *Journal of Interdisciplinary History* 29:683–723.

———. 2003. "Mass Secondary Schooling and the State: The Role of State Compulsion in the High School Movement." NBER Working Paper no. 10075. Cambridge, MA: National Bureau of Economic Research, November.

———. 2008. *The Race between Education and Technology.* Cambridge, MA: Belknap Press of Harvard University.

———. 2009. "Why the United States Led in Education: Lessons from Secondary School Expansion, 1910 to 1940." In *Human Capital and Institutions: A Long Run View,* edited by D. Eltis, F. Lewis, and K. Sokoloff, 143–78. New York: Cambridge University Press.

§Keesecker, Ward W. 1929. *Laws Relating to Compulsory Education.* Bureau of Education Bulletin, 1928, no. 20. Washington, DC: GPO.

Kézdi, Gábor. 2001. "Robust Standard Error Estimation in Fixed-Effects Panel Models." Unpublished Manuscript. University of Michigan, July.

Landes, William M., and Lewis C. Solmon. 1972. "Compulsory Schooling Legislation: An Economic Analysis of Law and Social Change in the Nineteenth Century." *Journal of Economic History* 32:54–91.

Lang, Kevin, and David Kropp. 1986. "Human Capital versus Sorting: The Effects of Compulsory Attendance Laws." *Quarterly Journal of Economics* 101:609–24.

*Lleras-Muney, Adriana. 2002. "Were Compulsory Attendance and Child Labor Laws Effective? An Analysis from 1915 to 1939." *Journal of Law and Economics* 45:401–35.

———. 2005. "The Relationship between Education and Adult Mortality in the U.S." *Review of Economic Studies* 72:189–221.

Lochner, Lance, and Enrico Moretti. 2004. "The Effect of Education on Criminal Activity: Evidence from Prison Inmates, Arrests and Self-Reports." *American Economic Review* 94:155–89.

Margo, Robert A., and T. Aldrich Finegan. 1996. "Compulsory Schooling Legislation and School Attendance in Turn-of-the-Century America: A 'Natural Experiment' Approach." *Economics Letters* 53:103–10.

*Merritt, Ella Arvilla. 1940. "Trends of Child Labor, 1937 to 1939." *Monthly Labor Review* 50 (January): 28–52.

Monthly Labor Review. 1937. "Child Labor: Compulsory School-Attendance Provisions Affecting Employment of Minors in the United States, 1936." February.

*———. 1938. "Labor Laws, State Labor Legislation, 1937." January.

Moretti, Enrico, Kevin Milligan, and Philip Oreopoulos. 2004. "Does Education Improve Citizenship? Evidence from the U.S. and the U.K." *Journal of Public Economics* 88:1667–95.

*National Child Labor Committee. 1927. *Twenty-Third Annual Report of the National Child Labor Committee for 1927.* New York: National Child Labor Committee.

§———. 1928. *Child Labor Laws and Child Labor Facts: An Analysis by States* (November 1927). New York: National Child Labor Committee.

Oreopoulos, Philip. 2003. "The Compelling Effects of Compulsory Schooling: Evidence from Canada." Unpublished Manuscript. University of Toronto, March.

———. 2006. "Estimating Average and Local Average Treatment Effects of Education when Compulsory School Laws Really Matter." *American Economic Review* 96:152–75.

———. 2007. "Do Dropouts Drop Out Too Soon? Wealth, Health, and Happiness from Compulsory Schooling." *Journal of Public Economics* 91:2213–29.

———. 2009. "Would More Compulsory Schooling Help Disadvantaged Youth? Evidence from Recent Changes to School-Leaving Laws." In *An Economic Perspective on the Problems of Disadvantaged Youth,* edited by J. Gruber, 85–112. Chicago: University of Chicago Press.

Organization for Economic Cooperation and Development (OECD). 1998. *Education at a Glance: OECD Indicators, 1998.* Paris: OECD Press.

*Proffitt, Maris M. 1933. *Report on 206 Part-Time and Continuation Schools.* Office of Education Pamphlet no. 38. Washington, DC: GPO.

§Proffitt, Maris M., and David Segel. 1945. *School Census, Compulsory Education, Child Labor: State Laws and Regulations.* U.S. Office of Education, Bulletin, 1945, no. 1. Washington, DC: GPO.

Reed, Anna Yeomans. 1927. *Human Waste in Education.* New York: The Century Company.

Ringer, Fritz K. 1979. *Education and Society in Modern Europe.* Bloomington: Indiana University Press.

Ruggles, Steven, Matthew Sobek, Trent Alexander, Catherine A. Fitch, Ronald Goeken, Patricia Kelly Hall, Miriam King, and Chad Ronnander. 2008. *Integrated Public Use Microdata Series: Version 4.0* (Machine-readable database). Minneapolis: Minnesota Population Center (producer and distributor). http://usa.ipums.org/usa/.

*Schmidt, Stefanie. 1996. "School Quality, Compulsory Education Laws, and the Growth of American High School Attendance, 1915–1935." PhD diss., Department of Economics, Massachusetts Institute of Technology.

§Segel, David, and Maris M. Proffitt. 1942. *Pupil Personnel Services as a Function of State Departments of Education.* U.S. Office of Education Bulletin, 1940, no. 6. Washington, DC: GPO.

Stambler, Moses. 1968. "The Effect of Compulsory Education and Child Labor Laws on High School Attendance in New York City, 1898–1917." *History of Education Quarterly* 2:189–214.

Steinhilber, August W., and Carl J. Sokolowsi. 1966. *State Law on Compulsory Attendance.* U.S. Department of Health, Education, and Welfare, Circular no. 793. Washington, DC: GPO.

Stigler, George. 1950. *Employment and Compensation in Education.* Occasional Paper 33. New York: National Bureau of Economic Research.

§Sumner, Helen L., and Ella A. Merritt. 1915. *Child Labor Legislation in the United States.* U.S. Department of Labor, Children's Bureau Publication no. 10. Washington, DC: GPO.

Troen, Selwyn K. 1975. *The Public and the Schools: Shaping the St. Louis System, 1838–1920.* Columbia: University of Missouri Press.

Tyack, David B. 1974. *The One Best System: A History of American Urban Education.* Cambridge, MA: Harvard University Press.

U.S. Department of Education. 1993. *120 Years of American Education: A Statistical Portrait.* National Center for Education Statistics, Washington, DC: GPO.

———. 2008. *Digest of Education Statistics: 2007* (NCES 2008–022). National Center for Education Statistics, Washington, DC: GPO.

§U.S. Department of Labor, Children's Bureau. 1921a. *State Child-Labor Standards, January 1, 1921.* Chart series no. 1. Washington, DC: GPO.

§———. 1921b. *State Compulsory School Attendance Standards Affecting the Employment of Minors, January 1, 1921.* Chart series no. 2. Washington, DC: GPO.

*———. 1923. *Standards and Problems Connected with the Issuance of Employment Certificates.* Bureau Publication no. 116. Washington, DC: GPO.

§———. 1924. *State Compulsory School Attendance Standards Affecting the Employment of Minors, September 15, 1924.* Chart series no. 1. Washington, DC: GPO.

§———. 1930. *Child Labor: Facts and Figures.* U.S. Department of Labor, Children's Bureau Publication no. 197 (October 1929). Washington, DC: GPO.

§———. 1935. *State Compulsory School Attendance Standards Affecting the Employment of Minors: State Child Labor Standards.* Washington, DC: GPO.

*———. 1938. *Child-Welfare Legislation, 1937.* Bureau Publication no. 236. Washington, DC: GPO.

*U.S. Federal Board for Vocational Education. 1920. *Compulsory Part-Time School Attendance Laws.* Bulletin no. 55. Trade and Industrial Series no. 14 (August). Washington, DC: GPO.

§U.S. Office (Bureau) of Education. 1910. *Education Report, 1910* (Annual Report of the Commissioner of Education). "Compulsory Education and Child-Labor Laws." Washington, DC: GPO.

§———. 1914. *Compulsory School Attendance.* Bulletin no. 2. Compiled by Walter S. Deffenbaugh. Washington, DC: GPO.

*———. 1925. *Important State Laws Relating to Education Enacted in 1922 and 1923.* Bulletin, 1925, no. 2. Compiled by William R. Hood. Washington, DC: GPO.

*———. [various years]. *Report of the Commissioner of Education for the Year Ended [year].* [Annual Report]. Washington, D.C.: GPO.

*———. [various years]. *Biennial Survey of Education, [various years].* Washington, D.C.: GPO.

§1916/18 (1917/18 compendium); also 1920/22, 1922/24, 1928/30, 1930/32.

§Major compilation of compulsory education and/or child labor laws.
*Reference used to construct the Appendix materials, in addition to those with §, or mentioned in the Appendix. Some references used in the Appendix are also mentioned in the text.

10

The Impact of the Asian Miracle on the Theory of Economic Growth

Robert W. Fogel

Before considering the impact of the "Asian Miracle" on growth theory, I need to consider when the term *Asian Miracle* became common among economists and what ideas preceded it. I also need to review the concept of growth theory, tracing its origins and its evolution. This is not an easy task because of the complex way that theory, measurement, and the needs of economic policy have interacted in the work of growth economists since World War II.

Nevertheless, I believe there is widespread agreement that two papers by Robert M. Solow, both published in the second half of the 1950s are nodal points in the huge literature on the theory and measurement of long-term economic growth.[1] They became nodal points despite the fact that similar growth models by others had been published about the same time. Solow (2007) has recently singled out a paper by the Australian economist Trevor Swan (1956) that embodied all of the elements of his model, but that had little impact on subsequent research.

10.1 Aggregate Production Functions, Total Factor Productivity, and Exogenous Technological Change

In his 2007 paper, Solow mused on this discrepancy. Why, he asked, did his paper become so influential? The way to do it, he said, was:

Robert W. Fogel is the Charles R. Walgreen Distinguished Service Professor of American Institutions at the Booth School of Business, University of Chicago; Nobel laureate in economics; and a research associate of the National Bureau of Economic Research.

1. See also Solow (1958).

(i) [K]eep it simple; (ii) get it right; and (iii) make it plausible. (By getting it right, I mean finding a clear, intuitive formulation, not merely avoiding algebraic errors.) I suspect that all three of these maxims were working for the 1956 paper. It was certainly simple; it didn't get lost in the complications and blind alleys that beset Trevor Swan's attempt; and it was plausible in the sense that it fitted the stylized facts, offered opportunities to test and calibrate, and didn't require you to believe in something unbelievable. (Solow 2007, 4)

In his 1957 paper, Solow applied a Cobb-Douglas production function to the explanation of the growth of U.S. output, with the astounding result that increases in the inputs of labor and capital explained only about 13 percent of the increase in output between 1909 and 1949. Eighty-seven percent was unexplained. Solow attributed this unexplained portion to improvements in technology, which he treated as being outside of the model; hence the term *exogenous* technological change.

From an empirical standpoint, perhaps the most important consequence of the Solow papers was to shift the attention of economists from labor productivity to total factor productivity as the principal measure of changes in economic efficiency or technological change. However, Solow's analysis did not emerge, like Athena, fully grown from the head of Zeus.

Economists had been struggling with the concept of total factor productivity for several decades. Some such measure was, as pointed out by Griliches in 1996, much discussed in the 1930s, especially in connection with the National Bureau of Economic Research programs on developing time series in national income.[2] This concern led the Bureau to launch projects that produced long-term time series on the measurement of capital formation in various sectors and in the economy as a whole. An interim report on the progress of this work was published by Goldsmith (1952). Bureau economists were constructing indexes of output divided by total input in the late 1930s, the 1940s, and the 1950s, and they identified such indexes as measures of the efficiency of the economy (see, for example, Copeland and Martin 1938, Stigler 1947, Fabricant 1954, Kendrick 1955).

Perhaps the most important Bureau paper on total factor productivity prior to Solow's work was published by Moses Abramovitz in 1956 under the title, "Resource and Output Trends in the United States since 1870." Making use of Simon Kuznets's data on real national income, he estimated that real net product per capita had increased at an annual rate of 1.9 percent, quadrupling over the seventy-five years between 1869 to 1878 and 1944 to 1953. He also computed an index of all resources, labor, and various forms of property, weighted by their shares in national income. To his surprise,

2. In Europe, Jan Tinbergen, in a 1942 paper published in German, used a Cobb-Douglas function with an exponential time trend, which he interpreted as a measure of changes in efficiency for Germany, Great Britain, France, and the United States. But Tinbergen's paper did not become known in the United States until much later.

this index of inputs explained only 14 percent of the increase in output over the seventy-five years. The remaining 86 percent was due to an unexplained increase in productivity.

The results were not only surprising to Abramovitz, but also defied adequate explanation. He called the unexplained rise in total factor productivity "the residual," and also a "measure of our ignorance." He attributed much of the residual to errors in the measurement of the inputs. With respect to labor, he singled out changes in the age structure of the labor force, which concentrated hours of work at the most productive ages. He also noted the neglect of increases in skills and of investments in health and education and in on-the-job training of labor. On the side of capital, he emphasized the failure to measure the increased stock of knowledge, improvements in the organization and technique of production, and greater investments in research and development. He also pointed to, but did not attempt to measure, the contributions of increasing returns to scale, which Edward Denison later put at 10 percent of the increase in total factor productivity (Dension 1962).

10.2   Convergence and Divergence

In 1945, the idea of high-performing Asian economies was not in the mind of American or European economists. In the United States, economists worried about the problems created by the demobilization of over 20 million people (half from military ranks and half from war industries) and their integration into the civilian labor force. There were widespread fears that America might slide into a severe new depression. In Europe, the central issues turned around the Allied occupation of Germany and Italy and the restoration of the war-devastated economies. In Asia, the central issues were the demilitarization of Japan and the restoration of the nations that had been occupied by Japan. On the horizon were problems related to the dismantling of the colonial empires of Britain, France, and other European powers.

Several events between 1945 and 1950 set the stage for the political economy of the remainder of the twentieth century. One was the outbreak of the Cold War and the strategy of containing the expansionist ambitions of the Soviet Union. Another was the rapid recovery of Western Europe and the transformation of West Germany into an ally in the anticommunist coalition. A third was the communist victory in the Chinese civil war that followed the defeat of Japan. Still another important event was the partition of India into independent Hindu and Muslim nations. There was also the emergence of newly independent governments throughout South and Southeast Asia[3] that were each struggling to find its road to rapid economic growth.

---

3. As used in this chapter, the term Southeast Asia applies to the first group of eight nations in table 10.2.

Table 10.1   A comparison of the per capita income of 15 nations in 1950
                    (International Dollars of 1990)

China	439*
Hong Kong	2,218**
Indonesia	840**
Korea (South)	770**
Malaysia	1,559**
Singapore	2,219**
Taiwan	936**
Thailand	817**
India	619*
Japan	1,926**
France	5,270***
Germany	3,881**
Italy	3,502**
United Kingdom	6,907***
United States	9,561***

Source: Maddison (2001).
Note: Rank by World Bank standards of 1990: *low-income; **lower-middle income; ***upper-middle income.

   As table 10.1 shows, the countries of South and Southeast Asia were at different economic levels in 1950, at the beginning of this quest. Japan, an occupied nation, had suffered severe reversals in fortune and had slipped to a level of per capita income characteristic of a low middle-income economy. Even the more prosperous Asian nations shown in table 10.1 had per capita incomes that were less than a quarter of that of the United States. In contrast, the war-ravaged economies of Europe were by 1950 already on their way to a quarter century of unprecedented economic growth that would raise standards of living, health, and life expectancy for ordinary people to levels that few would have predicted (Crafts and Toniolo 1996). Thus the stage was set for intense debates among economists and policymakers about the way to deal with global disparities. Among the points at issue were the virtues of centralized and decentralized planning and whether international trade was a handmaiden of domestic economic growth or an obstacle to it.

   When Western economists began talking and writing about convergence in the 1950s and 1960s, the focus of their conversation was not convergence between the West and the East, but convergence between Western Europe and the United States. Immediately after World War II, the United States was by far the richest country in the world, not only by per capita income but also by total income. With just 7 percent of the world's population, the United States accounted for a quarter of global gross domestic product (GDP) (Nelson 1991).

   This does not mean that Western economists lost sight of the rest of the world. During the 1950s and 1960s, they developed an increasing interest in the progress of the ex-colonies of Asia, particularly India and China. The political leadership of both countries was heavily influenced by the Soviet model of centralized planning. Both countries developed successive five-year plans for the economic growth of their countries. These plans sought rapid economic growth by placing special emphasis on the rapid development of heavy industry. Both taxed rural areas to subsidize cities and urban industries.

However, India sought to achieve its objectives under a political democracy, in which some industries would have government backing but the bulk of economic production and distribution would be left to the private sector. It also embarked on a protectionist policy aimed at promoting infant industries. New financial institutions were set up that placed the supply of capital largely under the control of the government, which directed investment into sectors given prominence by the plan. The first five-year plan, which ran from 1951 to 1956, was successful in meeting its goals, and private enterprise expanded. As indicated by table 10.2, the annual rate of growth in per capita income during the plan was in the neighborhood of 2 percent. However, annual net investment was in the neighborhood of just 6 or 7 percent (Pepelases, Mears, and Adelman 1961; Malenbaum 1959, 1982).

By the early 1960s, the Indian economy began to stumble. Not all of the problems were due to errors by policymakers. Some problems arose from border clashes with Pakistan and China. Some of the food shortages were due to droughts. But the main pressure on the food supply was due to explosive growth of population as mortality rates fell sharply. As a result of the successful public health measures undertaken during the 1950s and 1960s, such killer diseases as cholera, malaria, and smallpox were brought under control, helping life expectancy at birth to rise from thirty-two to fifty-one years between 1950 and 1968 (Chandrasekhar 1968). Moreover, growth of per capita income also raised the demand for food, putting upward pressure on food prices that pinched both the urban and rural poor. Government efforts at land reform may actually have increased rural inequality (Mellor et al. 1968; Blyn 1971). Attempts at government-controlled industrialization thwarted private investment and promoted uncompetitive enterprises (Shenoy 1968; Sklaeiwitz 1966; Healy 1972; Bhagwati and Chakravarty 1969). As a result, Indian growth slipped badly during the first half of the 1960s (see table 10.2).

Although India and China were the cases most frequently discussed by economists, attention was also paid to other nations in Southeast Asia. During the 1960s, there was considerable pessimism about Indonesia's future. Although there was a spurt of economic growth immediately after independence, during which the nation recovered from the setbacks associated with the Japanese occupation, the economy stagnated between 1955 and 1965, a period long enough to make economists wonder if Indonesia could overcome its problems (Mears 1961). Beginning with the mid-1960s, however, the country began vigorous growth that lasted for three decades (see table 10.2). Malaysia and Singapore also stagnated during the decade of the 1950s, contributing to the sense among some Western economists that adverse institutional factors might thwart their development. But in these countries, fortunes changed decisively in the 1960s.

Table 10.2 shows that eight Southeast Asian nations all grew vigorously from 1965 on, and that several of them (Hong Kong, Taiwan, and Thailand) had vigorous economic growth throughout the second half of the twentieth century. Indeed, their growth rates far exceeded the previous growth rates of the industrialized countries. Few American or European economists anticipated growth rates that would double, triple, or quadruple the long-term rates of the industrial leaders between 1820 and 1950.

The most startling change of fortune was in Japan. With the outbreak of the Korean War, United Nations forces placed large orders with Japan, greatly stimulating its industrial growth. Even after the end of fighting, Japan's economy benefited from large orders for the buildup of the U.S. military establishment in the Pacific region. The Japanese export boom powered the dramatic rise in the Japanese economy. In one industry after another, including scientific instruments, cameras, sewing machines, and shipbuilding, Japanese firms displayed their command of the latest technology. During the 1960s, Japan moved from producing under a half million cars to becoming the world's second-largest supplier, displacing Germany and France, among others. The rise of auto production helped promote the expansion of steel and moved the country toward world preeminence in that basic product (Allen 1972). As table 10.2 shows, from 1950 through 1970, the growth of Japanese per capita income exceeded that of all the other high-performing economies. In the space of two decades, Japanese per capita income increased more than fivefold, a feat that had required more than a century for the nations that led the industrial revolution (Kuznets 1971a; Maddison 1995). Although the growth of Japanese per capita income slowed after 1970, it still increased by about 40 percent between 1970 and 1980, making it the second largest economy in the world, bigger than France and the United Kingdom combined (Maddison 1995).

During the late 1960s and early 1970s, many analysts became alarmed at what appeared to be the unchecked growth of population in Asia. It was widely predicted that such growth would not only swamp the capacity of South and Southeast Asia to feed itself, but would also smother the tenuous economic growth of the region. In the 1950s, many demographers had predicted that population growth would moderate because a decline in fertility would soon follow the decline in the death rate, which had caused the Asian population explosion. That view was called the theory of the demographic transition. But fertility rates remained high through the end of the 1960s, causing some demographers to declare that the theory of the demographic transition was dead (Coale 1975). As it turned out, that gloomy forecast was

Table 10.2   Average annual percentage rates of growth in per capita income 10 HPAEs compared with 5 rich nations by quinquenna, 1950–2005

	1950–1955	1955–1960	1960–1965	1965–1970	1970–1975	1975–1980	1980–1985	1985–1990	1990–1995	1995–2000	2000–2005
China	5.5	3.2	1.0	2.1	2.2	5.1	9.1	6.2	11.1	7.6	8.9
Hong Kong	3.5	3.5	9.0	3.4	4.2	8.9	4.0	6.7	3.1	1.0	3.7
Indonesia	3.3	0.7	-0.6	3.8	4.7	5.9	3.9	5.1	5.8	-0.7	3.3
Korea (South)	6.5	1.0	3.2	8.6	10.1	5.4	6.5	7.8	6.4	3.5	4.0
Malaysia	-1.3	0.9	3.4	2.9	5.0	6.2	3.2	3.1	6.9	2.3	2.4
Singapore	1.2	-0.4	2.9	10.7	7.7	8.2	2.2	6.2	5.9	3.5	2.8
Taiwan[a]	6.0	3.7	6.6	7.7	6.0	8.3	6.7	3.9	5.6	6.8	
Thailand	3.0	2.7	3.9	5.3	2.9	5.6	3.7	8.4	7.6	-0.6	4.3
India	1.8	2.2	0.5	2.4	0.7	0.7	3.3	4.2	3.2	4.0	5.4
Japan	7.6	7.5	8.3	10.4	3.2	3.5	2.6	4.3	1.2	0.8	1.2
France	3.7	3.6	4.4	4.5	2.6	2.6	1.4	2.7	0.7	2.4	1.0
Germany	8.3	5.8	3.6	3.4	2.1	3.3	1.3	2.9	1.8	1.9	0.6
Italy	6.0	4.8	5.1	5.0	2.1	5.8	1.8	3.0	1.1	1.9	0.1
United Kingdom	2.5	2.0	2.4	2.0	1.9	2.1	1.8	3.1	1.3	2.9	2.0
United States	2.7	0.8	3.4	2.3	1.6	2.6	2.1	2.3	1.2	2.9	1.4

Sources: 1950–1975: Maddison 2001; 1975–2005: World Bank, World Development Indicators Online. (http://web.worldbank.org/WBSITE/EXTERNAL/DATASTATISTICS/0,,content MDK:21725423~pagePK:64133150~piPK:64133175~theSitePK:239419,00.html).
[a]1950: Maddison (2001). 1995–2002: Asian Development Bank (2003a, 2003b).

Table 10.3   Secular trends in total fertility rates

	1950	1960	1970	1980	1990	2000	2005	2007
China	6.24	5.93	4.76	2.68	2.10	1.89	1.60	1.60
Hong Kong	4.43	4.97[b]	3.49	2.06	1.27	1.04	1.00	1.00
Indonesia	5.49	5.42	5.10	4.10	3.04	2.42	2.60	2.40
Korea (South)	5.18	5.60	5.24	4.02	1.77	1.47	1.20	1.10
Malaysia	6.83	6.72	5.15	3.91	3.77	2.96	3.30	2.90
Singapore	6.41	5.43[c]	3.10	1.74	1.87	1.44	1.30	1.30
Taiwan[d]		5.79	4.00	2.51	2.27	1.76	1.20	1.10
Thailand	6.62	6.42	5.01	3.52	2.10	1.86	1.70	1.70
India	5.97	5.81	5.43	4.75	3.80	3.07	3.00	2.90
Japan	3.30[a]	2.01	2.07	1.74	1.54	1.36	1.30	1.30
France	2.86[a]	2.80[d]	2.48	1.95	1.78	1.88	1.90	2.00
Germany (West)	2.10	2.41	2.01	1.46	1.45	1.38	1.30	1.30
Italy	2.40	2.42[d]	2.38	1.64	1.26	1.24	1.30	1.40
United Kingdom	2.18	2.82	2.45	1.89	1.83	1.64	1.70	1.80
United States	3.08	3.65	2.47	1.84	2.08	2.06	2.00	2.10

Sources: Keyfitz and Flieger (1990); Population Reference Bureau (see http://www.prb.org/datafind/datafinder.htm; World Bank, World Development Indicators Online (see http://www.worldbank.org/data/wdi2004/index.htm); CIA World Factbook (see https://www.cia.gov/library/publications/the-world-factbook/).
[a]1951
[b]1961
[c]1962
[d]1981

incorrect. As table 10.3 shows, between 1970 and 1980, total fertility rates fell sharply in all Southeast Asian nations. Today all of these nations, except for Malaysia and Indonesia, have total fertility rates below replacement. Indeed, fertility rates in most of these nations are below the fertility rates of three of the five rich nations shown in table 10.3.

The forecast that Southeast Asia would be unable to feed itself because of the unbridled growth of population also turned out be erroneous. Table 10.4 shows the food situation throughout South and Southeast Asia in 1961. Per capita consumption of calories in China, even after the famine, was at or below the level of consumption in England and France toward the end of the eighteenth century (Floud et al., forthcoming). The same desperate situation prevailed in India, Thailand, and Korea. By 2000, the food situation had changed dramatically. Despite the erroneous agricultural policies that precipitated the famine of 1960 and 1961, and again slowed agriculture during the "Cultural Revolution" of 1966 to 1967, China's progress in agriculture between 1962 and 2000 has been remarkable (Clark 1976; Lin 1998). China not only found a way to feed itself, but did so well enough to increase its average daily consumption of calories by 73 percent, despite the near doubling of its population. Although not as dramatic, there were also

Table 10.4   **Trends in caloric consumption**

	In calories per capita per day			Percentage increase		Percentage of calories from animals		
	1961	2000	2003	1961–2000	1961–2003	1961	2000	2003
China	1,725[a]	2,979	2,940	72.7	70.4	3.8	19.4	21.9
Hong Kong								
Indonesia	1,727	2,913	2,891	68.7	67.4	2.9	4.1	4.8
Korea (South)	2,147	3,093	3,035	44.1	41.4	2.7	15.0	6.2
Malaysia	2,401	2,917	2,867	21.5	19.4	10.5	17.8	17.9
Singapore								
Taiwan[a]								
Thailand	1,938	2,459	2,424	26.8	25.1	8.8	11.7	12.5
India	2,073	2,489	2,473	20.1	19.3	5.5	7.9	8.2
Japan	2,468	2,753	2,768	11.5	12.2	9.6	20.5	20.6
France	3,194	3,597	3,623	12.6	13.4	31.7	37.7	36.8
Germany (West)	2,889	3,505	3,484	21.3	20.6	32.7	30.0	30.7
Italy	2,914	3,663	3,675	25.7	26.1	15.5	25.5	25.7
United Kingdom	3,240	3,312	3,450	2.2	6.5	38.8	30.1	30.6
United States	2,883	3,814	3,754	32.3	30.2	35.1	27.4	27.8
World	2,255	2,805	2,809	24.4	24.6	15.0	16.5	17.0

Source: Food and Agriculture Organization of the United Nations (FAOSTAT) nutritional data, 2004 (http://apps.fao .org/default.jsp), using the "Food Balance Sheets" data collection.
[a]1962

substantial gains in caloric consumption in the rest of South and Southeast Asia, ranging from 12 to 68 percent. Another point worth noting is the improvement in the quality of the diet, as indicated by the increase in the proportion of nutrients coming from animals. In China, the rise was from under 4 to over 19 percent of total caloric consumption. Only Indonesia and India still have levels of the consumption of animal products that hearken back to eighteenth-century conditions in England and France (Floud et al., forthcoming). Still another problem is the unequal distribution of food in many of the nations of South and Southeast Asia. In these countries, the proportion of low birth weights is still high, which implies the early onset of chronic disabilities at middle and late ages, a problem that will contribute to the high cost of medical care for the elderly in future years (Barker 1998; Doblhammer and Vaupel 2001; Fogel 2003, 2004b).

Let us now consider expectations of economic growth right after World War II, viewing them from the standpoint of the present. At the close of World War II, there were wide-ranging debates about the future of capitalist economies that pivoted on the Keynesian proposition that a macroeconomic equilibrium is possible at less than full employment and, in particular, the interpretation of that proposition by Alvin Hansen in his 1938 presidential address to the American Economic Association (Hansen 1939). Hansen argued that secular stagnation was likely because of: (1) the end of the fron- tier, (2) the end of rapid population increase, and (3) the end of capital-intensive technological change. The key issue, as the stagnationists defined it, was not whether the growth of the GDP would come to an end, but whether a high level of government spending was necessary to prevent a high level of permanent unemployment, even if GDP did grow.

That such a debate would erupt in anticipation of peace is not surprising. The alarm about massive unemployment was widespread in 1943 and 1944 because the country was demobilizing over 11 million soldiers from the armed forces and there were some 9 million or more workers in defense industries that were simultaneously being let go. So there were about 21 million people thrown on a job market of about 60 million, including the armed forces and the defense establishment (U.S. Bureau of the Census 1955, table 220). But as it turned out, the recession of 1945 only lasted eight months and was followed by a robust expansion that lasted thirty-seven months. Moreover, the recession of 1949 and 1950 lasted eleven months and was followed by another robust expansion that lasted forty-five months (U.S. Bureau of the Census 2003, table 771). The peak came in 1953 after the economy had already absorbed 20 million potentially unemployed workers, and unemployment was below 3 percent by 1953. Total civilian employment was up by 15 percent over the wartime peak (Bratt 1953).

Although unemployment remained over 5 percent during some of the years of the long 106-month Kennedy-Johnson expansion, it dropped to 3.5 percent in 1969. So even a quarter of a century after the war, there were still economists who believed that the United States could not have an economy with both growth and low unemployment unless there was a very big government sector. By the late 1950s, the United States and other Organization for Economic Cooperation and Development (OECD) countries were well into the post–World War II expansion, now called "the Golden Age," with growth rates twice the long-term average of the world leaders during 1840 to 1940. Measured by per capita income, the long-term average growth rate of the leaders prior to 1940 was about 1.9 percent per annum and the growth rate during the Golden Age was, for Western Europe, about 3.8 percent (Kuznets 1971a; Maddison 1995; Crafts and Toniolo 1996). Over the whole period from 1950 to 1999, expansion multiples for GDP averaged about fivefold in Western Europe and the United States (see table 10.5). The wide-ranging debates over the causes for the accelerated growth rates of the Golden Age suggested some points of consensus. These included the reduction of barriers to international trade, successful macroeconomic policies, and opportunities for catch-up growth following the end of World War II, especially in France, Germany, and Italy. The destruction of much of the prewar capital stock, the reconstruction aid that rebuilt industry with a more advanced technology, the successes of macroeconomic policy, the elasticity of the labor supply, high levels of education, and the weakness of vested interests have all been advanced as explanatory factors (Abramovitz 1990;

Table 10.5   Expansion multiples of GDP for 15 economies 1950–1999 (ratio of GDP
                    in 1999 to GDP in 1950, international dollars)

United States	5.07
France	5.22
Germany	5.50
Italy	6.20
Spain	8.39
United Kingdom	3.19
5 European Nations	4.98
China	25.59
Hong Kong	28.01
Indonesia	9.48
South Korea	38.93
Malaysia	15.61
Singapore	36.72
Taiwan	46.84
Thailand	23.68
8 Southeast Asian Nations	24.06
India	8.11
Japan	16.09

Sources: Maddison (2001); World Bank, World Development Indicators Online (see http://
www.worldbank.org/data/wdi2004/index.htm).

Mills and Crafts 2000; Crafts and Toniolo 1996; Denison 1967; Maddison 1987, 1991, 1995; Olson 1982).[4]

The eventual fading away of the stagnation thesis, of the notion that there was something in the operation of capitalistic economies that made them inherently unstable, brought to the fore several new concerns. These included the growing gap in income between developed and less developed nations, and a new emphasis on cultural and ideological barriers to economic growth in poor countries. In contrast to some of the early theories associated with the Harrod-Domar model, which suggested that poor countries would grow rapidly if there were large injections of capital from rich countries, by the 1960s the emphasis was that the export of capital would fail to promote growth unless the deep cultural barriers that made these countries unreceptive to the conditions needed for economic growth were somehow overcome. Some commentators, most notably Gunnar Myrdal, in his three-volume work on the Asian economies, said that India would have difficulty in sustaining high growth because it promoted asceticism and thus undermined the acquisitive culture that spurred Western Europe (Myrdal 1968; Lau 1969).

There was also a shift from worries about oversaving, which I must say,

---

4. When the value of increased longevity and improved health are added to GDP, growth rates increase significantly (Fogel 1989b, 2000, 2004a; Murphy and Topel 2005).

never caught on at certain universities. It did not catch on at Chicago or at Columbia. Nor did it catch on at the National Bureau of Economic Research. Analysts such as Simon Kuznets, Arthur Burns, and others thought that savings were not a threat to economic growth, but were a necessary condition for economic growth because you needed the savings to build both infrastructure in developing countries and also to get a thriving public sector growing (Kuznets 1961; Colm 1962; interview with P. A. Samuelson, conducted by Robert W. Fogel and Enid Fogel, taped recording, 1992).

There was, about this time, a new emphasis on export-led growth. The practice of poor countries selling their exports to rich countries got a bad name during the interwar period and was widely viewed as exploitation of these countries by imperial powers. The later view, looking at the Canadian and American experiences, was quite the contrary (North 1966; Kravis 1970). Selling raw materials and other labor-intensive products to the rest of the world is a way to get capital and entrepreneurship from the developed countries to provide those same talents and qualities to the less-developed countries. One of the great discoveries of economic historians during the 1960s and confirmed in the 1980s and 1990s was that the Hobson-Hilferding-Lenin thesis that English coupon-clippers got rich from investments in poor countries such as India, and then withdrew large sums of annual earnings, was wrong. After the computer revolution, it was possible to put the whole late nineteenth-century portfolio of British overseas investments into machine-readable form (Simon 1970; Davis and Huttenback 1986; Stone 1999). Lo and behold, it turned out that there was a strong correlation between a country's per capita income and the share of the British overseas portfolio invested in it. The United States received the largest share, followed by Canada and Argentina (which at the turn of the twentieth century had one of the highest per capita incomes in the world). Of course, that did not stop diehard critics of Western imperialism, who then denounced Britain for *failing* to have invested in underdeveloped nations (Davis and Huttenback 1986).

10.3   The Asian Miracle

As remarkable as what was widely forecast in the post–World War II debates were the things not foreseen in the 1940s, 1950s, or even the early 1960s. One of these was the extraordinary economic growth in Southeast and East Asia, beginning first with Japan, which in four decades went from a poor, defeated country to the second largest economy in the world, increasing per capita income tenfold. This was a feat that took leaders of the industrial revolution about 150 years to accomplish (Kuznets 1971a). The economic miracle of the high-performing Asian economies other than Japan was also unforeseen, and that state of mind persisted into the 1970s. It was not that economists did not know that per capita income was rising, but there was a widespread opinion that it could not last, that somehow it was a fluke. That view was based on the uneven economic performances of several of the Southeast Asian nations. Indonesia, for example, had some catch-up growth during the first half of the 1950s but faltered in the 1960s. Of the "Four Asian Dragons," only Taiwan did better than Italy or Germany between 1950 and 1970 (see table 10.2). The idea that all of the Southeast Asian nations, including China, were in the midst of an unprecedented expansion that might affect the global economic balance did not emerge until the early 1990s.

So, except for Japan, there was little excitement about the growth rates elsewhere in East Asia until the late 1970s and early 1980s, when some analysts began taking note of the Korean economic miracle (gross national product [GNP] per capita tripled in less than two decades) (Krishnan 1982) and comparable accelerations in the growth rates of Hong Kong, Singapore, and Taiwan. These four economies began to be called the "Four Asian Dragons" or the "Four Asian Tigers" (Hicks 1989).

The phrase "Southeast/East Asian Economic Miracle" and the acronym HPAE (for high-performing Asian economies) were added to the economic lexicon by the World Bank when it published a book, *The East Asian Miracle: Economic Growth and Public Policy,* in 1993. The term was almost immediately embraced by economists, some of whom felt it neatly summarized a new phase of global economic development, and by a few, such as Paul Krugman, who wrote a paper titled "The Myth of the Asian Miracle" (1994), arguing that the marginal productivity of capital would soon decline because the miracle depended mainly on investment in capital and not on efficiency growth. In later work, Krugman modified his predictions (1998, Krugman and Wells 2005), allowing for a longer period of growth, but still maintaining his earlier skepticism.

However, Chinese economic growth did not slow down for reasons delineated by Abramovitz in his 1956 paper. The new investments embodied new technologies that greatly improved the efficiency of the productive process. Moreover, China invested heavily in raising the educational level of the population, concentrating first on primary education. As early as 1980, the gross enrollment ratio[5] of primary schools reached 113 (see table 10.6). The extension of secondary school has also been impressive, with the enrollment ratio rising from 46 in 1980 to 76 in 2006. The sharpest rate of increase has been at the tertiary level (colleges and universities), where the enrollment ratio tripled between 1980 and 1997, and tripled again between 1997 and 2004, reaching 19 in the latter year. This rapid increase in educational levels was promoted both by business and political leaders who recognized not only that they had to expand the supply of highly trained technicians, but that the demand for high-tech consumer products required well-educated consumers.

---

5. Persons in school × 100 ÷ persons of school age.

Table 10.6   **Gross enrollment ratios**

	Primary school			Secondary school			Tertiary school[c]			Age for compulsory attendance
	1980	1997	2006	1980	1997	2006	1980	1997	2005	
China	113	123	111	46	70	76	2	6	19[b]	7–15
Hong Kong	107	94	98[a]	64	73	85	10	22	32	
Indonesia	107	113	114	20	56	64	4	11	17	7–15
Korea (South)	110	94	105	78	102	96	15	68	90	6–15
Malaysia	94	101	101[a]	48	64	69[a]	4	12		
Singapore										
Taiwan[a]										
Thailand	99	87	108	35	58	78	5	21	43	6–14
India	83	100	112	30	49	54[a]	5	7	12[b]	6–14
Japan	101	101	100	93	103	101	31	41	54[b]	6–15
France	111	105	110	85	111	114	25	51	56[b]	6–16
Germany (West)		104	103		104	101	27	47		6–18
Italy	103	101	103	72	95	100	27	47	63[b]	6–14
United Kingdom	104	116	105	83	129	98	19	52	60[b]	5–16
United States	99	102	98	91	97	94	56	81	82[b]	6–16

Sources: National Center for Education Statistics 2002 (1980, 1997); World Resources Institute Earth Trend (http://earthtrends.wri.org/searchable_db/index.php?step=countries&cID[]=63&cID[]=91&cID[]=189&cID[]=190&theme =4&variable_ID=423&action=select_years). Unesco.org (http://stats.uis.unesco.org/unesco/ReportFolders/Report Folders.aspx).

[a]2005

[b]2004

[c]It has been argued that the high U.S. figures for tertiary education are misleading because of the wide range of educational content in U.S. institutions at the junior college and four-year undergraduate schools. While it is true that European gymnasiums provide educations equivalent to the first two years of many U.S. colleges, the elite American universities provide educations that surpass those of the gymnasiums. At the doctoral and postdoctoral level, elite American universities are superb—hence, the large number of foreign students who flock to U.S. programs.

Hence, the marginal productivity of physical capital has risen, not only because of the advanced technology embodied in new physical investment, but also because of the greater investment in raising the quality of labor. The quality of labor has risen, not only because of formal education, but also because of on-the-job training, increased experience, improved health, and increased longevity. Rather than declining, the rate of increase in Chinese per capita income rose to 9.2 percent per year between 1990 and 2005, which is more than a third higher than the growth rate during the previous fifteen years. Indeed, there is no convincing evidence that long-term Chinese economic growth is faltering (Fogel 2007).

10.4   Endogenous Economic Growth

To those who know the nonmathematical literature of the pre-1975 growth theorists, the belief that endogenous theories of economic growth are an invention of the late 1980s is surprising. While it is true that Solow and some other modelers treated technological change as exogenous in papers written in the 1950s and 1960s, verbal theorists such as Simon Kuznets, Moses Abramowitz, Theodore W. Schultz, and Douglass C. North paid a great deal of attention to endogenous technological change, emphasizing the synergies between improvements in the quality and quantity of labor and of physical capital.

Kuznets (1966, 1971a, 1971b), for example, stressed that economic growth both required and produced major changes in the structure of the economy (defined as the distribution of inputs or output among the major sectors of the economy). Not only were increases in agricultural productivity a condition for the rapid growth of manufacturing, but new manufacturing technologies, which produced more efficient agricultural equipment or new varieties of seeds and fertilizer, were major factors in the growth of agricultural productivity and stimulated changes in agricultural technology.

According to Kuznets, many current economic opportunities and problems were determined by economic conditions and relationships that evolved slowly, often taking many decades to work out. At a time when Keynes declared that "in the long run we are all dead," an aphorism reiterated by many economists not only during the 1930s but during the 1940s and 1950s, Kuznets continued to call attention to the role of long-term factors that had to be taken into account by policymakers, factors that led him to conclude that the opportunities for returning to high employment levels and rapid economic growth were greater than generally believed in the decades immediately following World War II.

Current social problems in the late 1960s and 1970s, Kuznets emphasized, were often the result of past growth—the consequence of past desirable attainments, which at a later time produce socially undesirable consequences that require remedial policy action. Of his numerous illustrations of this principle, one is particularly cogent: the explosion of population growth in the less developed nations of Asia, Africa, Oceania, and Latin America in the quarter century following World War II. This population explosion threatened to thwart efforts to raise per capita incomes from their dismally low levels because birth rates remained traditionally high, while public health policies and improved nutrition cut death rates in these regions by more than 50 percent in less than a generation. One obvious solution to the problem was to reduce fertility, yet there was a web of traditional patterns of behavior and belief that tended to keep fertility high. Nevertheless, Kuznets believed that properly designed public policies could hasten the social and ideological changes required to reduce fertility and to lead these societies to prefer a greater investment in a fewer number of children (Becker 1960, 1981; Becker and Lewis 1973). Such a program required not only government and private campaigns to disseminate the technology of birth control but a restructuring of social and economic incentives that would provide rewards for families with fewer children.

Yet, as the experience of the United States and other developed nations has shown, the success of the program to curtail fertility is bound, much further down the line, to create a new set of issues, similar to those that have become the center of the modern women's movement: the restructuring of society in such a way as to promote equal opportunity for women in all occupational markets. The rapid economic growth of 1945 to 1970 also produced new concerns about equity issues, particularly between whites, blacks, and Hispanics, and gave momentum to the movement for equal rights for women.[6]

Economic growth creates social problems because it is profoundly disruptive to traditional values and religious beliefs, to long-standing social and family patterns of organization, and to numerous monopolies of privilege. Despite the fact that modern economic growth has brought with it tremendous increases in longevity and good health, has brought to the lower classes standards of living as well as social and economic opportunities previously available only to a tiny minority, and has greatly reduced the inequality in the income distribution of developed nations, the social restructuring of society required by modern economic growth has been fiercely resisted—sometimes because of an unwillingness to give up traditional values and ways of life, sometimes by entrenched classes determined to protect their ancient privileges. Because of the complex responses to change and because the epoch of modern economic growth was still unfolding, many aspects of the social restructuring that were underway were still obscure and difficult to predict (Kuznets 1966, 15). As late as 1972, Kuznets felt compelled to point out that despite the multitude of tentative partial generalizations, cross-sectional studies, and econometric exercises, there was as yet no "tested generalization, significantly specific to permit the quantitative prediction of aggregate growth, or even of changes in the structural parameters in the course of growth" (Kuznets 1972, 58).

Kuznets was particularly concerned with longitudinal issues, such as the length of the period of observation that was needed to identify the underlying process at work in any specific aspect of economic growth. How, he asked, can one determine whether such a process, once identified, is sufficiently stable to provide a reliable basis for prediction? These problems are illustrated by an issue on which Kuznets was the preeminent investigator of his age: the interrelationship between demographic processes and modern economic growth.

A particularly important aspect of the issue was the concentration of the decline of death rates at early ages, which contributed to the reduction in fertility rates. The reduced fertility rate released a large proportion of the female labor force to gainful occupations, accelerated the transition to modern families, mobile and responsive to economic incentives, and promoted new ideologies conducive to economic growth (1966, 56–62). In subsequent

---

6. Further down the line, the drop in fertility rates creates new problems as the population ages. See Fogel (2003, 2004b), Floud et al. (forthcoming).

work, Kuznets noted the increase in the share of women in the U.S. labor force from 17 percent in 1890 to nearly half in the 1980s, which he attributed to the lower fertility rates, the shift in employment opportunities from manual to service sector positions, and urbanization, which made organized labor markets more accessible to women (Kuznets 1989; Fogel 1989a). He also called attention to the fact that the most rapidly growing occupations—those in the professional, technical, clerical, sales, and other services—were the ones in which women had made the greatest inroads. Nevertheless, in the late 1950s and early 1960s, when the new women's movement was still incipient, Kuznets did not anticipate fully the explosive entry of women into the labor force during the next quarter century, nor the new ideology that would facilitate that development (1966, 193–95).

Ideas of endogenous technological change were also deeply embedded in the work of economists who studied the diffusion of new technologies. Among the earliest of these studies was the dissertation of Zvi Griliches (1956) and papers based on it (particularly in 1957 and 1960), which analyzed the factors affecting the rate of diffusion of hybrid corn. Griliches traced that process from the early scientific research of agricultural experimental stations to the sequential adoption of various strains of these seeds by commercial producers. He also analyzed the rate of spread of this type of seed by farmers, looking at the difference in the characteristics of early and late adopters within and across states. Indeed, it took more than half a century for hybrid corn to displace its rivals everywhere.

Consequently, at any point in time, the existing average technology was a weighted average of technologies of different vintages, not merely of the prehybrid seeds per se. Seed manufacturers produced new vintages of hybrid seeds as technology adapted to the climate and soil types of particular regions and subregions. Griliches also related the educational level, institutional connections, and income of individual farmers to the rate at which they changed over to the new strains of corn.

What Griliches did for the diffusion of new technologies in agriculture, Edwin Mansfield did for diffusion of industrial technologies. Mansfield (1971) measured the lag between invention and innovation for forty-six inventions. The lag varied from one year for Freon refrigerants to seventy-nine years for florescent lamps. The lag for some other notable inventions was twenty-four years for the distillation of hydrocarbons with heat and pressure, twenty-two years for television, twenty-seven years for zippers, thirteen years for radar, and fourteen years for jet engines.

He then turned to the factors that influence the decision to innovate. After emphasizing the risks associated with innovation (only two out of ten new products that emerge from research and development become commercial successes), he set forth the costs and benefits of both leading and waiting for others to lead. The investment needed to bring a new innovation to market is usually in the range of ten to twenty times the original research costs.

Mansfield then analyzed the rates of diffusion of twelve innovations in four industries (coal, iron and steel, brewing, and railroads). He found that the diffusion of a new technique was generally a slow process. Among the factors that affected the rate of diffusion were the size of the firm, the expected rate of profit from investing in the innovation, the growth rate of the firm, the overall profit level of the firm, and the liquidity of the firm.[7]

It was not only characteristics of the firms but also characteristics of the managers that influenced rates of diffusion of new technologies. Presidents of early adopters of complex new technologies were younger and better educated than heads of firms that were late adopters.

In subsequent studies, Mansfield (1980) found that both firm and industry expenditures on research and development had a substantial impact on firm and industry rates of growth in productivity. Both basic and applied research, individually and in conjunction, increased productivity growth. With respect to interfirm, interindustry, and international transfers of technology, Mansfield (1975) delineated among material, design, and capacity transfers. Capacity transfers often involved the transfers of people, since there was often "no substitute for person to person training and assistance" (373). That was especially the case when the transferred technology had to be adapted to take account of local conditions, including differences in relative costs, abilities, cultures, and climates (Mansfield 1972).

The notion of endogenous technological change did not begin with the cohort of Griliches and Mansfield. Walt W. Rostow (1990, especially chapters 15 through 17 and 20) has summarized the known theories of technological change, endogenous and exogenous, going back several centuries. More relevant to the issues in this chapter is the work of Joseph Schumpeter, who was the most important growth theorist between the deaths of Smith and Malthus and his own death in 1950. His earlier work focused on long cycles in economic output, which he attributed to fluctuations in the rate of inventions and innovations (Schumpeter 1934). His analysis led him to single out entrepreneurs as the dynamic agents of change, to point to the equity effects of economic growth (embodied in his concept of "creative destruction"), and to make the creative clusters of innovations inherently inflationary. Later in his career, Schumpeter focused on the conflict between economic concentration and competitive markets, and between the capitalist system of economic organization and the political, social, and intellectual movements that were hostile to capitalism for ideological reasons. It was these conflicts, he argued, rather than the secular diminution of investment opportunities, which threatened the continuation of economic growth under a system of political democracy (Rostow 1990, especially 233–42).

Theodore W. Schultz was another major motivator of the theory of endog-

---

7. See Perkins 2006a and Maddison 1998 for discussions of the lag of China and India in adapting modern technology.

enous technological change. He received the most acclaim for his contributions to the theory of human capital (Schultz 1962, 1971). But that was only one aspect of his broader concern with economic growth and the elimination of poverty. These broader concerns led him to examine closely the impact of government fiscal policies and specific interventions into agriculture in both developed and developing countries, policies that distorted agricultural production and had perverse effects on the distribution of income. Like Schumpeter, Schultz was concerned about new sources of future income growth, and this concern led him to recognize that in the twentieth century, human capital had become more important than physical capital in explaining both economic growth and the inequality of the income distribution. His theory of human capital led him to conclude that unregulated high fertility was a major factor in destabilizing an agricultural sector. Such considerations also caused him to emphasize the importance of the investment in improving nutrition and health as a key to economic growth in poor nations and to identify investment in "allocative skills" as a key to dealing with problems of disequilibria (Bowman 1980).

Schultz was influenced in his thinking about human capital by his experiences with postwar reconstruction. Despite the devastation of Europe, all of the war-ravaged countries experienced rapid economic growth in the 1950s, quickly exceeding their prewar levels. This led Schultz to dwell on the central role of human capital in modern economic growth, to consider the possibility that a significant share of the so-called residual factor in economic growth was due to improvements in the quality of the inputs, particularly in the quantity of capital embodied in human labor. Although his empirical work on this question focused on education, Schultz recognized that improvements in health, in the capacity to process information, in the development of allocative skills, and in on-the-job training might be more important than the effects of formal education per se.

Abramovitz was another of the nonmathematical theorists who grappled with issues of endogenous technological change throughout his career. In papers published in 1972 and 1993, he called attention to the shifting bias of technological change, which was intensive in physical capital between 1850 and 1950 (the era of the building of railroads and the electrical grid) but became human capital-intensive thereafter (Abramovitz 1972). Since 1950, "technological change tended to raise the marginal productivity of capital in the form of education and training of the labor force at all levels; in the form of practical knowledge acquired by deliberate investment of resources in research and development; and in other forms of intangible capital, such as the creation and support of corporate structures and cultures and the development of product markets, which are the infrastructure of economies of scale and scope" (Abramovitz 1993, 229).

Abramovitz also stressed the interdependence of technological progress and both tangible and human capital accumulation. He noted both tangible and intangible capital formation influenced the pattern of technological progress. But he cautioned Lucas, Romer, and other contributors to the "new growth theory" from overemphasizing the impact of capital accumulation on the direction of technological change. Although the bias of technological change was influenced by capital accumulation, it was also influenced by the evolution of scientific and technological knowledge that was "quite unrelated to the terms of factor supply," including the influence of relative factor costs, the evolution of science and technology, and the "impact of political and economic institutions and modes of organization on which the discovery and acquisition of new knowledge depend" (Abramovitz 1993, 237).

10.5   Bridges between Two Cohorts of Theorists on Technological Change

This section compares the work of Zvi Griliches, Richard Nelson, and Dale W. Jorgenson, whose research on technological change spanned the period from the mid-1950s to the present. All of these investigators focused on the difficulties of measuring technological change. All three were concerned with endogenous as well as exogenous sources of technological change. All three were deeply involved in problems of the identification and measurement of endogenous technological change. Although they dealt with national patterns of change, much of their research was focused at the level of industries and on the characteristics of the firms that comprised the industries. All three welcomed the new enthusiasm brought to the studies of technological change and economic growth by a younger cohort of investigators led by Romer, Lucas, Helpman, Barro, Acemoglu, Aghion, Howitt, Krugman, and Young, among others.[8]

Griliches's studies were notable for their display of statistical skills. He made important contributions to econometric modeling of specification biases, to models of distributed lags, and to models that dealt with "unobserved" or "omitted" variables, such as ability. He also developed the hedonic technique for separating changes in the prices of complex products into components due to improvement in qualities of such products (such as automobiles and pharmaceuticals) and to inflation. He was also one of the pioneers in the study of the impact of investments in research and development on productivity at the firm, industry, and aggregate levels. He emphasized that much of the unmeasured residual in productivity gains was due to the "spillover" effects in one firm or industry on the inputs and outputs of other firms and industries (Heckman 2006; Trajtenberg and Berndt 2001; David 2003). These are all key points in the explanation of the Asian Miracle (see section 10.7).

Richard Nelson has been a thoughtful analyst of the economics of inven-

---

8. Helpman (2004) provides an insightful tour of the new growth theory, pointing out its major issues and evaluating its foundations (Helpman 2008).

tion and the processes by which inventions become incorporated in the process of production and marketing. In the late 1950s, he critically surveyed the economic literature on these topics and pointed to numerous unresolved issues. Among the points he stressed were the high risks in research and development, and the few initiatives launched by firms that ever got to the point of yielding commercially viable projects (1959). He also delved into the problem of explaining changes in total factor productivity and attributed much of the difference between Solow and Denison to such issues as the rate of improvement in the quality of labor and capital and the average age of the capital stock. But he also emphasized that interactions between these variables had not been sufficiently explored, and he also stressed the need to focus on the processes, which differed among firms, that affected incentives and their feedback (1964). In later papers (1981, 1988; Nelson and Wright 1992), Nelson stressed the need to focus on the processes that generate, screen, and spread new technology at the firm, interfirm, and inter-industry levels. Along with Stanley Fischer (1993) and others, Nelson placed much emphasis on the role of macroeconomic policy in creating favorable contexts for rapid technological progress. Nelson collaborated with Harold Pack (1999) on an insightful discussion of the interrelationship of the Asian Miracle and Modern Growth Theory with a paper of the same title (see section 10.7).

Jorgenson has been at the forefront of the elaboration of the theory of production and in the measurement of the improvements in the quality of inputs, the improvements in the economic and social organization of production, and the identification of spillover effects that account for a significant part of unmeasured inputs. Jorgenson's early work made important contributions to the theory of economic growth in dual economies: two-sector models with an advanced and a backward sector (1961a, 1961b). Indeed, much of his work has focused on the movement from a highly aggregated level of analysis to disaggregated levels.

Thus, he has placed a great deal of emphasis on moving to the industry and firm levels for purposes of both analysis and measurement, demonstrating that in so doing, one could explain much of Solow and Denison's unmeasured residual. In this connection, he pointed to the need to recognize that much of the change in total factor productivity was explained by measuring the substitution of higher qualities of labor for lower ones as well as the substitution of improved vintages of capital for earlier ones. He also sought to measure unmeasured spillover effects from one industry or one firm to another (1967, with Griliches; 1969, with Christenson; 1980 and 1986, with Fraumeni; and 1980, with Gollup). Jorgenson also called attention to the need to take account of changes in the quality of intermediate goods at the sectoral level, estimating that these changes explained more of the change in sectoral output than improvements in the quality of labor and capital (1990, with Kuroda).

Jorgenson has led the way in explaining the sharp increase in U.S. productivity growth that began in the 1990s. In his presidential address to the American Economic Association (2001) and in papers with Stiroh (1999, 2000), he attributed the rapid diffusion of information technology (IT) between 1990 and 2000 to the decline in IT prices, which he said was triggered by an earlier and even sharper decline in the prices of semiconductors. Moreover, all of the increase in U.S. total factor productivity during 1990 and 1995 and two-thirds of the increase during 1995 and 2000 was due to improvements in IT.

In several of his recent papers (e.g., 2001, 2005; Jorgenson and Nomura), he found that in the United States, IT-using industries were leading economic growth, and through wage effects, were promoting improvements in labor quality, and that IT was having a similar effect on other G7 countries (Crafts 2004). Improvements in the quality of inputs, best measured at the industry level, were major factors in output growth (e.g., 1992, with Gollop; 1999 and 2000, with Stiroh; 2005, with Nomura; 2005).

In a paper with Dougherty (1996), Jorgenson characterized the recent work on endogenous economic growth as an effort to account for spillover effects. He linked unexplained productivity to spillover effects that increase output in unrelated firms and industries but were normally unmeasured. Jorgenson provided a direct accounting of the benefits of such spillovers. In his most recent paper with Vu, Jorgenson finds that the accelerated pace of globalization and IT penetration between 1989 and 2006 may be important factors in explaining the jump in output productivity. He estimates that developing Asia accounted for 40 percent of global economic growth during this period (Jorgenson and Vu 2009).

10.6   The Economic Historians

No students of economic growth have been more absorbed in issues of endogenous technological change than economic historians. Their interest in these issues is as old as the concept of the Industrial Revolution of the second half of the eighteenth and the first half of the nineteenth centuries. They traced out the succession of inventions in textiles and iron that transformed these industries, as well as successive improvements in steam engines going back to the early seventeenth century, that made it possible to substitute mechanical power for human power in mining and manufacturing and animal power in transportation.

This progress turned partly on accidents, but mainly on the creation of an economic, social, and political environment that encouraged and supported new technologies, by ethical and religious dictums and by progrowth ideologies. As David Landes put it, Britain's large lead in technology over France (citing Joel Mokyr [1985] and Walt Rostow [1979]), was no accident. With one innovation after another, repeatedly England was the leader, and France and others were followers.

British inventors, Landes said, were responding to the high cost of labor (in the case of textile inventions) and the vicissitudes of deep coal mines (in the case of steam engines). Moreover, the British pool of skills in such areas as millwork and machine building was apparently larger than in Continental countries. It was not that Britain had a large monopoly of skills, but "the size of the pool, its free, noncorporate character, and direction (provenance) of its efforts and experience. These seem to have made a difference" (Landes 1994, 650; Crafts 1997, 1995; see also Harley 1992 and Temin 1997).

Landes (1994) continued:

> The key invention falls within the Smithian paradigm: the adoption of rural putting-out. This goes back to the middle ages and represents a crucial departure from the town-based, corporate (guild) mode of production. The key is the division of labour and the recruitment into the production process of women and children. Say no more: the effect is to reduce costs and prices, increase demand, widen the market, promote further division of labour, lay the basis in specialization for small but cumulative improvements in technique . . . The effect of this fall in prices and increase in markets at home and abroad was to turn Britain into the workshop of the world. (651)

Among economic historians writing about changes in patterns of U.S. economic growth, no one has done more to emphasize the critical role of institutions in affecting economic growth than Douglass C. North. In an article published in 1968, North estimated the substantial increases in the total factor productivity, on the order of 300 percent, in ocean shipping between 1600 and 1850. The principal technological change was the increase in payload capacity brought about by the changes in the design of the ships, which became larger and swifter. The more efficient ships (called flutes) had been in use in the Baltic trade since the early seventeenth century. Why did it take so long for ships of this design to become dominant in the Atlantic trade? The answer, said North, was the threat of piracy located in the Caribbean. As long as the pirate threat existed, freighters had to be armed, and arming required smaller, sturdier ships that could withstand the recoil of the canons. It was not until the elimination of pirates from their shelters in the Caribbean that the faster, longer, lower-cost ships became dominant in the transatlantic trade.

Two years later, together with Robert Paul Thomas, North published an "Economic Theory of the Growth of the Western World" (1970). In that essay, they argued that changes in product and factor prices, promoted by population growth and the increased size of markets, led to a set of institutional changes that channeled incentives toward "productivity-raising types of economic activity. . . . These institutional innovations and accompanying changes in property rights built productivity into the system, enabling Western man to finally escape the Malthusian cycle" (1). North and Thomas collaborated again on articles explaining the rise and fall of the manorial system (1971) and on the substitution of settled agriculture for hunting and gathering (1977).

In a highly influential paper with Barry R. Weingast, a political scientist, North (1989) investigated the impact of the English Glorious Revolution of 1688, which "fundamentally redesigned" fiscal and governmental institutions to limit the confiscatory power of the crown. The elevation of the role of Parliament and introduction of an independent judiciary "produced a marked increase in the security of private rights" (804). As a result, private capital markets flourished and the government was able, within a decade, to increase borrowing by an order of magnitude. The institution also created more favorable conditions for economic growth, including the growth and development of banks, the creation of new instruments of private credit, and the promotion of a wide array of businesses (North 2005).

Several other economic historians have had a substantial influence on the recent wave of growth theory. Papers by Stanley Engerman and Kenneth Sokoloff called attention to the importance of distant history in establishing institutions and pathways that influence patterns of current economic growth (Engerman and Sokoloff 1997; Sokoloff and Engerman 2000). This theme has resonated with growth theorists such as Acemoglu, Johnson, and Robinson (2000, 2001) and Ray (2008). Paul David's emphasis on the impact of path dependency, which links particular inventions and the large investments by their users to explain the difficulty of getting users to switch to more efficient substitutes for the original innovation, has also been influential (David 1985).

In another important paper, David (1990) explained the long lag between the invention of new technologies and their impact on economic growth using the electrical dynamo as a case in point. Even when engineers correctly foresaw the potential usefulness of electricity, a wide range of businesses were still based on mechanical power, and numerous details had to be addressed to make the new type of power advantageous for many different products and in various locales. Moreover, architects, engineers, and managers had to be trained to design, install, and operate the new systems. The risks perceived by capitalists were large enough to cause many to hesitate to invest. These problems were worked on slowly. It took about four decades to go from the construction of the first generating stations to the 50 percent point in the diffusion of electricity to users.

Economic historians have also made major contributions to the study of industrial organization and its synergy with economic growth. Carefully tracing the growth of big business in the United States, Alfred Chandler Jr., the doyen of managerial history, laid out the circumstances that led to the rise of large-scale enterprises led by professional managerial hierarchies. He also compared the U.S. corporate structure with large enterprises in England and Germany (Chandler 1977, 1990). Chandler had a strong influence on the theory of industrial organization as it was developing during the last third of the twentieth century (Teece 1993; Caves 1990). Efforts to reassess Chandler's legacy began to appear in the late 1990s and have continued, aimed at taking account of new industrial structures brought on by changes in technology, markets, business strategy, and communications (Galambos 1997; Ghemawat 2002).

It remained for Lamoreaux, Raff, and Temin (2003) to provide a new synthesis of the evolution of industrial organization as it stood at the beginning of the new millennium. Their aim was not only to take account of the changed circumstances that led the classical Chandlerian firm—vertically integrated and diversified—to be outperformed by more specialized and vertically disintegrated firms, but to also provide a theory of the new tendencies in firms and markets. They developed a dual perspective that brought to the fore the economic logic behind business choices. Changes in industrial structures and markets reflected the vast increases in per capita income, the huge declines in the cost of processing information, and the large decrease in transportation costs that altered spatial maps and permitted products to be designed again for individual needs.

10.7   The Impact of the Asian Miracle on Growth Theory

The Asian Miracle began to have a profound impact on growth theory well before the full scope of that miracle was apparent. The early papers in the new wave of theoretical work, those that appeared between 1986 and 1990, were responding mainly to European and U.S. developments in the period between 1950 and 1980. When theorists shifted some of their focus to Asia during the first half of the 1990s, they concentrated mainly on the Four Little Dragons, sometimes adding such new contenders for the title of "miracle" as Indonesia, Malaysia, and Thailand. China and India did not move to center stage until the second half of the 1990s.

The extraordinarily high growth rates of China since 1980 and of India since the middle of the 1990s have profoundly challenged the discussion of theorists and policymakers. These extraordinary growth rates, if they persist for two or three decades, will radically alter the global economic playing field, transforming China and India from merely "newly industrializing countries" to titans of the global economy.

Tables 10.7 and 10.8 compare the global economy in 2000 with a possible, perhaps probable, restructuring less than a generation from now. In the year 2000, the global economy was dominated by six groupings of countries: the United States; the European Union (which then consisted of fifteen countries [EU15]); India; China; Japan; and a group of six Southeast Asian

Table 10.7   The global distribution of GDP in 2000, by grouping of nations

Grouping	Population (in millions)	Percent of total	GDP in billions of $ (PPP)	Percent of total
United States	282	5	9,601	22
European Union (EU15)	378	6	9,264	21
India	1,003	16	2,375	5
China	1,369	22	4,951	11
Japan	127	2	3,456	8
6 South East Asian Countries (SE6)	381	6	2,552	6
Subtotals	3,540	57	32,199	73
Rest of the world	2,546	42	12,307	28
World	6,086	99	44,506	101

Source: Fogel (2007).

Note: PPP = purchasing power parity.

countries (Singapore, Malaysia, Indonesia, Thailand, South Korea, and Taiwan [SE6]). As measured by GDP, these six groupings accounted for 73 percent of the world's economic output and 57 percent of the global population (see table 10.7). The balance of the world (including Latin America, Africa, and Eastern Europe) accounted for about 28 percent of GDP and 42 percent of the global population.

Table 10.8 presents a not improbable set of forecasts for 2040. The population forecasts are those of the United Nations. The economic forecasts are mine but were influenced by the forecasts of the CIA and *The Economist.* To my mind, the most unsettling of the forecasts in table 10.8 is the relative decline of the European Union implied by its stagnation in population and its modest growth in GDP.

Although the EU population in 2000 exceeded that of the United States by about a third, by 2040 the EU population will be somewhat smaller than that of the United States. The projected stagnation of the EU15 population is based primarily on the persistence of extremely low fertility rates. The *total fertility rate* (roughly the average number of children a woman is expected to have during the course of her childbearing years) has fallen far below the level required for the reproduction of the population (2.1 children) in most EU15 countries, and has been below reproduction for several decades.

One implication of the low fertility rate is that the population of the EU15 is aging rapidly. In the year 2000, the median age in Italy and Germany, for example, was about forty, which is a decade higher than in China and half a decade higher than in the United States. By 2040, the median age in Italy and Germany is predicted to be about fifty. This rapid aging of many EU15 countries means that their *dependency ratios* (the ratio of economically inactive to economically active persons) will soar. These demographic factors will, by themselves, significantly curtail the capacity for economic growth. However,

Table 10.8   The global distribution of GDP in 2040, by grouping of nations

Grouping	Population (in millions)	Percent of total	GDP in billions of $ (PPP)	Percent of total
United States	392	5	41,944	14
European Union (EU15)	376	4	15,040	5
India	1,522	17	36,528	12
China	1,455	17	123,675	40
Japan	108	1	5,292	2
6 South East Asian Countries (SE6)	516	6	35,604	12
Subtotals	4,369	50	258,083	85
Rest of the world	4,332	50	49,774	16
World	8,701	100	307,857	101

Source: Fogel (2007) and United Nations (2009).

political and cultural factors appear to be reinforcing the impediments to economic growth. These include limitations on the length of the work week and increasingly heavy taxes on businesses to support large social welfare programs (that are nevertheless facing bankruptcy) and are threatening to make EU15 firms uncompetitive in the global market.[9]

I do not mean to imply that labor productivity and per capita income in the EU15 will not grow. They will grow at a rate that, by past standards, was not bad (about 1.8 percent per annum), but they will not be able to match the surge in growth that will prevail in South and East Asia. The European market will be about 60 percent larger in 2040 than it was in 2000. But the U.S. market will be over 300 percent larger, India's will be over 1,400 percent larger, and China's will be 2,400 percent larger. Indeed, the Chinese market in 2040 by itself will probably be larger than the combined markets of the United States, the EU15, India, and Japan. It may well be the case that English will survive as the principal commercial language beyond 2040, but I suspect that there will be an explosion of business managers in the West who also speak Mandarin.

The possibility of such a massive restructuring of the global economy has substantially changed the conversation of growth theorists of the late 1980s. The debates of those years were aimed at altering the canon of growth models to allow for slighted variables (such as knowledge and experience), changed parameters (such as large capital shares and different elasticities), to rethink the implications of returns to scale and externalities in different contexts suggested by new analyses of available empirical information, and

9. The expansion of the EU15 to EU27 will help to invigorate the EU15 through increased cross-country migration. However, it is unlikely that the migration rate will be large enough to offset the low fertility rates in Italy, France, and other EU15 countries. Moreover, resistance to immigration is likely to increase in low-fertility countries as fears of loss of national identity increase.

to introduce such new terminology as "absolute" and "conditional" convergences.[10] The old set of issues has not been abandoned, but the locus has shifted, and a number of new issues have emerged.

One of the central issues among growth theorists is whether increases in factor inputs or in total factor productivity has been the main source of economic growth in the surging Asian economies (Perkins and Rawski 2008). A companion issue is the role of governments and of macroeconomic policy in encouraging, permitting, and sustaining economic growth (Young 1995; Krugman 1994; 1998; Stiglitz 1996, 2001; Kim and Lau 1994; Park 2002). Growth theorists are also grappling with the implications of uneven economic growth across the provinces and socioeconomic groupings of both China and India, for the long-run economic and political stability of both countries (Chaudhuri and Ravallion 2006; Zakaria 2005, 2006; Pei 2006; 2007, Lopez 2004).

Jere Berhman, an old hand in the study of economic growth among developing nations, surveyed the literature (2001) on growth in Asia and elsewhere, pointing out changing viewpoints since the end of World War II. In the 1950s, he wrote, the key issues raised by growth economists were (1) the need to raise capital-to-labor ratios; (2) the problem of overcoming the inefficiency of markets; (3) the key role of industrialization in overcoming low growth rates; (4) the belief that international trade was harmful to developing countries because the benefits of trade were siphoned off by monopolistic producers in rich countries; and (5) the belief that governments were unbiased, had good information, and pursued policies appropriate to promoting growth. By the beginning of the twenty-first century, most of these ideas had been jettisoned. Among the ideas that replaced them were the proposition that merely throwing capital at the problems was not enough, that markets are better than bureaucrats (many of whom were rent-seekers) in allotting resources, and that international trade stimulated rather than retarded growth.

Dwight H. Perkins, who has been studying economic, social, and political developments in China and other Southeast Asian nations for more than half a century, recently put the accelerated growth in Chinese per capita income since 1978 in perspective (2006a). The available evidence suggests that China's decline from relative prosperity in the thirteenth century to relative poverty at the end of World War II was due partly to its lag in applying science to the development of modern technology, partly to destructive invasions, and partly to civil wars that prevented the emergence of a strong central government needed to provide the institutional foundation for modern economic growth. While some of these problems were solved after the

10. See Barro and Sala-i-Martin (2004) for an excellent review of growth theory and its empirical findings. For the foundational basis of the new work, see Romer (1986); Lucas (1988); and Barro (1991); Barro and Sali-i-Martin (1997). See also Jones (1997). For a critique of the empirical underpinning of this work, see Srinivasan and Bhagwati (2001).

accession of Mao Zedong, mistakes in economic policy, combined with Mao's desire to launch a cultural revolution that would transform Chinese values, led to nearly two decades of sluggish growth and to various economic and social calamities.

Perkins attributes the high rate of growth in Chinese per capita income during the past three decades to reforms that began in 1978. As a result of these reforms, the government was able to generate a high internal rate of investment, promote foreign trade, open China to foreign investment (with its accompanying advanced technology and know-how), and transform China into a market economy. However, these processes of transformation are not complete, and the future rate of growth will depend on success in completing the necessary reforms. The main future challenge, he argues, will be "to maintain a stable environment" for economic growth while the Chinese "political system evolves to one more suitable for an educated, increasingly high income country" (Perkins 2006b, 263).

Perkins's historical perspective helps to inform recent efforts to resolve the conflicting views of growth theorists (Maddison 1998). In a 1999 paper, Nelson and Pack stressed that it was not merely the introduction of advanced technology into East and South Asia that accounted for their rapid growth. More crucial was the restructuring of the economy to effectively absorb the new technologies. Such absorption required a policy regime that encouraged the development not only of an educational system that helped entrepreneurs and technicians to begin the process of mastering and deploying the new technologies, but also of an industrial structure that permitted this new cadre to gain the experience needed to effectively exploit the new technologies. "To learn to use new technologies," they wrote, "and to function effectively in new sectors required the development of new sets of skills, new ways of organizing activities, and becoming familiar and competent in new markets" (Nelson and Pack, 418). They also stressed that "only a small portion of what one needs to know . . . is codified in machine manuals, textbooks, and blueprints; much of it is tacit and learning is as much by doing and using as by reading and studying" (418; see also Nelson and Winter 1982; Rosenberg 1994). The usual growth accounting procedures, they argued, "would attribute the major share of growth simply to the growth of capital," when assimilation and industrial restructuring were the main forces driving growth (426).

Beyond these technical issues about how to interpret the available information, there is a lively debate about how long China can continue growth at rates greater than ever before achieved for long periods of time. China has emerged as a major global factor in an array of product markets. Now second only to the United States in oil consumption, and accounting for 40 percent of all the growth in global oil consumption in recent years, China has also become the world's largest consumer of steel, cement, and copper (OECD 2005; Kato 2004; Morrison 2006).

Most of China's growth in terms of per capita income (69 percent between 1978 and 2002) is due to increases in labor productivity. Within industry, the increase in labor productivity was 6.2 percent per annum and 5.7 percent per annum in agriculture. About 30 percent of China's growth rate is likely to continue to come from modest increases in the labor force participation rate and interindustry shifts. Much of China's labor force is still in agriculture, so there is substantial potential for growth through a shift to industry and services as it moves toward the current technological frontier.

Investment in capital—especially human capital—is capable of rapid development in the next several decades. The increases in enrollment ratios outlined in table 10.6, combined with the knowledge that a college-educated worker is 3.1 times as productive (and a high-school graduate is 1.8 times as productive), as a worker with less than a ninth-grade education, underlie the potential for growth (Fogel 2006).

As a result of its rapid growth in per capita income, China has also emerged as a major player in the production and sale of manufacturing products. As indicated by table 10.9, Chinese production of autos in 2007 exceeded all of the major national producers except the United States and Japan. Moreover, given the current rates of increase in the auto production of all the nations, it is likely that China will be the global leader in auto production by 2010 or 2011.[11]

Ownership of other major consumer durable products has also been increasing at spectacular rates. Between 1990 and 2007, Chinese households have increased ownership of air conditioners annually by 15 percent, computers by 32 percent, and cell phones by 48 percent (National Bureau of Statistics of China 2008).

The rapidly expanding economies of China and India have led many analysts to speculate on the reemergence of these two economic giants as global political players. The most recent assessment of the U.S. National Intelligence Council (2008) conjectures that, by 2025, U.S. political dominance will be replaced by what it calls "multipolarity." This multipolarity it predicts is "unlikely to produce a single dominant nation-state with the overwhelming power and legitimacy to act as an agent of institutional overhaul" (81).

However, we are already in a multipolar world, which the United States helped to create. Our ability to influence international affairs is already constrained by the desires of Europe, Russia, India, and China. Diplomacy under the Clinton and Bush administrations was shaped by such recognition.[12]

---

11. Despite the slowdown in the production of China's automobile industry in 2008, it has been estimated by the China Association of Automobile Manufacturers (CAAM) that annual production will increase by 5 percent in 2009 (Li 2009). In February 2009, new car sales increased by 25 percent in China, partially due to reduced sales taxes on small passenger cars (Ying 2009).

12. See Zakaria (2006) and Morrison (2006).

Table 10.9 **Automobile production in Southeast and South Asia compared with five Western nations and Japan**

	Production in 2007 (thousands)	Production Increase over 2006 (%)
China	8,883	22
Hong Kong		
Indonesia	412	39
Korea (South)	4,086	6
Malaysia	442	−12
Singapore		
Taiwan	283	−7
Thailand	1,287	8
India	1,708	14
Japan	11,596	1
France	3,016	−5
Germany	6,214	7
Italy	1,284	6
United Kingdom	1,750	6
United States	10,781	−5
World	73,153	5.7

Source: Organisation International des Constructeurs d'Automobiles, survey for 2006–2007 (http://ww.oica.net).

My own view of future U.S. global influence is more conditional. A lot depends on the future rate of growth in U.S. labor productivity. If that continues at the annual rate of 2 to 4 percent, then it is possible that the United States will remain well ahead of its competitors in economic and political influence down to 2025 and beyond. Much will depend on the willingness of the United States to invest heavily in scientific research and development, and to increase the share of the population educated in the sciences. I am optimistic on both of these counts. Unlike China, whose past growth has depended on its ability to adapt to the existing technology of the United States and other OECD nations to its conditions, the United States is at the current production frontier. Hence, its continued growth depends on the rate at which it can develop new technologies, which requires a plentiful supply of engineers to design new systems of production and distribution, and new science on which these new systems will depend. Industry will respond to the new technologies, as they have in the past, because they will increase labor productivity and raise profits.

10.8   Nota Bene

Three key issues have been raised by readers of the original version of this chapter (as previously noted).

1. Why do I predict that the growth rate of GDP for the EU15 will be only 1.2 percent per annum between 2000 and 2040?
2. Why do I believe that U.S. GDP between the same years will grow at 3.7 percent per annum?
3. Why am I so optimistic about China's future growth rate, which I put at 8.0 percent per annum between 2000 and 2040?

Let me deal first with my optimistic estimate for China. How and why China will become an economic colossus has to do not only with the country's economics, but also with its politics. To begin with, it helps to divide China's economy into three major components: agriculture, services, and industry. Over the twenty-five years between 1978 and 2003, the growth of labor productivity has been high in each of these sectors, averaging about 6 percent each year. At the national level, however, output per worker grew by 9 percent annually over the same period. The national growth exceeded the sectoral growth rates because output per worker was much higher in industry and services than it was in agriculture. So as millions shifted from agriculture—where the bulk of China's labor has been concentrated—to industry or services, the country's annual growth rate rose by an additional 3 percentage points. Between 1978 and 2005, about 195 million workers shifted from agriculture to industry and services. In other words, internal migration accounted for about 47 percent of the labor force in industry and services in 2005. I expect such shifts between sectors to continue to be an important element in China's overall economic growth over the next generation (Fogel 2007).

Many observers believe that social unrest, both active and latent, will retard China's rate of economic growth. Potential pitfalls include the shaky state of the banking system. They also include income disparities between the rapidly growing coastal provinces and the more slowly growing interior provinces, between urban and rural labor, and between highly skilled and manual labor. Other potential flashpoints arise from pressures on fuel supplies and electrical power, the growth of environmental pollution, and the adequacy of water supplies. These problems are well understood by China's leaders and solutions are being actively pursued. So far, the government has managed to head off potential crises.

As a consequence, the polls conducted by reliable agencies reveal a widespread belief among the Chinese that their living conditions have improved and will continue to improve in the future. This optimism reflects the rapid increases in income experienced by the great majority of households for more than a quarter of a century.

Still another possibility is that internal growth will be derailed by international conflicts such as the border disputes over Kashmir with India and Pakistan and disputes over the sovereignty of the Spratly Islands with Malaysia, the Philippines, and Vietnam. But these issues are being treated diplomatically rather than militarily. The most tumultuous dispute, over the sovereignty of Taiwan, now appears to be headed toward a resolution, tentatively endorsed by both China and the incoming KMT (Chinese Nationalist Party) government in Taiwan.

An important factor in sustaining China's high growth rate will be its investments in expanding secondary and tertiary education—another key shift likely to boost labor productivity growth. In a 2006 study, I reported that high school graduates in the United States were 1.8 times as productive, and college-educated workers 3.1 times as productive, as their peers with less than a ninth-grade education. Extrapolating these findings to China, and estimating that the enrollment ratio in high school will grow to about 100 percent and in college to about 50 percent over the next generation, would, in and of itself, add over 6 percentage points to the annual growth rate (Fogel 2006).

These targets for higher education are not out of reach. As recently as 1980, Western European nations had tertiary enrollment ratios (the ratio of the number of students in colleges and universities to the total number of persons at college ages, usually eighteen to twenty-two years old) of about 25 percent; only in the United States was that figure above 50. The movement to from 25 to 50 in Western Europe took place over just two decades at the end of the twentieth century. In the case of Britain, two-thirds of the increase from 19 to 52 percent took place between 1990 and 1997.

The significance of investment in human capital as an engine of economic growth has not eluded the State Council in China. In 1998, Jiang Zemin called for a massive increase in enrollments in higher education, and the response was swift. Over the next four years, enrollment in higher education increased by 165 percent (from 3.4 million to 9.0 million), and the number of students studying abroad rose by 152 percent. Given that the tertiary enrollment ratio increased by about 50 percent between 2000 and 2004 (from 12.5 to 19.0 percent), my projection for 2040 is not overly optimistic. China is already on track to reach it (Fogel 2007).

Next, my forecast for the EU15. Here, demography is the key issue. What is worrisome is not just the zero rate of population growth (the demographic forecasts are not mine but those of the United Nations population division) but the changes in the age structure of the population.

The population of OECD nations has been aging rapidly, and that trend is likely to continue over the next several decades. Columns (1) and (2) of table 10.10 present the forecast of the Population Division of the United Nations on the change in the median age of the five largest West European nations. In Germany, Italy, and Spain, the predicted increases range between eleven and fourteen years. In France and the United Kingdom, the median age increases by six and five years, respectively.

Columns (3) and (4) forecast the change in percentage of the population that will be over sixty-five. For Germany and Italy, the elderly will increase

Table 10.10   Median age and percent of population age 65 and over in five European nations in 2000 and 2040

Country	Median age		Percentage age 65 and over	
	2000 (1)	2040 (2)	2000 (3)	2040 (4)
France	37.7	44.2	16.1	26.5
Germany	40.0	51.2	16.4	31.8
Italy	40.3	50.9	18.4	31.8
Spain	37.6	49.1	16.8	28.1
United Kingdom	37.7	42.3	15.9	22.6

Source: http://esa.un.org/unpp.

Table 10.11   Percentage of women aged 15–49 in 2000 and 2040

Country	2000	2040	Percentage decline
France	47.5	38.3	19
Germany	46.8	34.6	26
Italy	47.0	34.4	27
Spain	50.8	35.8	30
United Kingdom	46.8	41.5	11

Source: http://esa.un.org/unpp.

to nearly one-third of the population. Only in the United Kingdom will the elderly be less than one-quarter of the population.

The basic reason for the rapid aging of the population has been the low level of fertility. In all of these countries, the total fertility rate has been below the level needed to replace their populations for several decades. As a result, the percentage of women in the childbearing ages has declined from about 50 percent in 2000 (it was also about 50 percent in 1950) and is projected to be about 35 percent in 2040. So we have a double whammy (to use American slang): not only will women in the reproductive ages have sharply reduced fertility rates, but the proportion of women who are in the childbearing ages will also have declined sharply (see table 10.11).

Attitudes toward sex have evolved sharply. One-hundred and fifty years ago, it was considered a sin to enjoy sex, the only legitimate purpose for which was procreation. But today, even in Rome, young women respond that sex is mainly a recreational activity. Behind the statistics on trends in fertility is a vast change in ethics embodied in a culture that is much different from that embraced by the generation that fought in World War II, which married early and produced the great baby boom between 1945 and 1965.

The widespread embrace of the ethic that celebrates sex as recreation

Table 10.12   **Predicted changes in the natural rate of increase (per thousand)**

Country	2000	2040
France	3.8	−0.3
Germany	−1.5	−6.2
Italy	−0.7	−4.3
Spain	1.4	−0.9
United Kingdom	1.3	0.7

Source: http://esa.un.org/unpp.

Table 10.13   **Predicted changes in the dependency ratio**

Country	2000	2040	Percentage increase
France	.54	.75	39
Germany	.47	.79	68
Italy	.49	.81	65
Spain	.46	.72	57
United Kingdom	.54	.64	19

Source: http://esa.un.org/unpp (2008 revision).

means that the rate of natural increase (births minus deaths) is likely to decline in the principal EU15 nations. Indeed, even in 2000, the natural rate of increase was negative in Germany and Italy. By 2040, it is likely that natural increase will be negative in all of the designated nations except the United Kingdom (see table 10.12).

Although the twentieth century increase in the share of the population that is elderly is a tribute to the great advances in economic performance, biomedical sciences, and environmental improvements, there is no automatic guarantee of equitable balance between the generations in the future. Indeed, there are new problems that will have to be solved if a third of population in 2040 is over age sixty-five.

Moreover, since younger workers are a major source of new ideas, slowing down the ascendency of the next generation may retard the pace of technological change. The solution to such problems will not be easy. The elderly should not be shunted aside as if they were rotten tomatoes. To force their premature retirement will undermine not only their morale, but also the morale of those who expect to replace them.

As a result of the demographic trends, the dependency ratio is expected to rise sharply in four of the five largest EU15 nations between the years 2000 and 2040, as shown by table 10.13.

The inverse of one plus the dependency rates is a reasonable proxy for the labor force participation rate (which I designate by ρ). Hence, table 10.13 suggests an annual rate of decline of 0.4 percent in the labor force participation rate due purely to changes in the age structure of the population. I allow ρ to decline by an additional 0.2 percent per annum because of a reduction in the length of the work year over the period 2000 to 2040. This allowance raises the annual rate of decline in ρ to 0.6 percent per annum. Since I expect the annual rate of growth in labor productivity of the five nations to average about 1.8 percent, it follows that their annual rate of growth in both per capita income and GDP will average 1.2 percent.

Now let me turn to my forecast for the United States. Although the United States and EU15 growth rates were the same during 1975 to 2005, I do not believe that to be an overriding consideration. The key issue is the slowness of the European Union relative to the United States in adopting the new information technology. Other issues are the greater EU preference for leisure than commodities when compared with the United States, and the decline of the EU's annual rate of growth in labor productivity from 2.4 percent during 1980 to 1995 to 1.5 percent during 1995 to 2004. By comparison, U.S. labor productivity growth increased from 1.5 percent per annum during 1980 to 1995 to 3.0 percent during 1995 to 2004 (van Ark, O'Mahony, and Timmer 2008).

During 1995 to 2004, U.S. GDP grew at 3.7 percent per annum. I believe that this high rate will persist down to 2040 because of continuing technological advances in genetic engineering, health care, information technology, transportation, energy production and consumption, and education (van Ark, O'Mahony, and Timmer 2008).

References

Abramovitz, M. 1956. "Resource and Output Trends in the United States since 1870." *American Economic Review* 46:5–23.

———. 1972. "Manpower, Capital, and Technology." In *Human Resources and Economic Welfare: Essays in Honor of Eli Ginzberg,* edited by I. Berg, 50–70. New York: Columbia University Press.

———. 1990. "The Catch-up Factor in Postwar Economic Growth." *Economic Inquiry* 28:1–18.

———. 1993. "The Search for the Sources of Growth: Areas of Ignorance, Old and New." *Journal of Economic History* 53:217–43.

Acemoglu, D., S. Johnson, and J. A. Robinson. 2000. "The Colonial Origins of Comparative Development: An Empirical Investigation." NBER Working Paper no. 7771. Cambridge, MA: National Bureau of Economic Research, June.

———. 2001. "Reversal of Fortune: Geography and Institutions in the Making of the Modern World Income Distribution." NBER Working Paper no. 8460. Cambridge, MA: National Bureau of Economic Research, September.

Allen, G. C. 1972. *A Short Economic History of Modern Japan.* London: Allen and Unwin.

Asian Development Bank. 2003a. *Asian Development 2003 Statistical Appendix.* Oxford: Oxford University Press.

———. 2003b. *Key Indicators 2003,* volume 34. Manila: Asian Development Bank.

Barker, D. J. P. 1998. *Mothers, Babies, and Health in Later Life.* Edinburgh: Churchill Livingstone.

Barro, R. J. 1991. "Economic Growth in a Cross Section of Countries." *Quarterly Journal of Economics* 106:407–43.

Barro, R. J., and X. Sala-i-Martin. 1997. "Technological Diffusion, Convergence, and Growth." *Journal of Economic Growth* 2:1–27.

———. 2004. *Economic Growth.* Cambridge, MA: MIT Press.

Becker, G. 1960. "An Economic Analysis of Fertility." In *Demographic and Economic Change in Developed Countries,* Conference of the Universities-National Bureau Committee for Economic Research: A Report of the National Bureau of Economic Research, 209–40. Princeton, NJ: Princeton University Press.

———. 1981. *A Treatise on the Family.* Cambridge, MA: Harvard University Press.

Becker, G., and H. G. Lewis. 1973. "On the Interaction between Quantity and Quality of Children." *Journal of Political Economy* 81:S279–88.

Berhman, J. 2001. "Development, Economics of." In *International Encyclopedia of the Social and Behavioral Sciences,* edited by N. J. Smelser and P. B. Baltes, 3566–74. Oxford: Elsevier Science.

Bhagwati, J. N., and S. Chakravarty. 1969. "Contributions to Indian Economic Analysis: A Survey." *American Economic Review* 59 (suppl.): 1–73.

Blyn, G. 1971. "Review of Developing Rural India: Plan and Practice." *Economic Development and Cultural Change* 19:334–37.

Bowman, M. J. 1980. "On Theodore W. Schultz's Contributions to Economics." *Scandinavian Journal of Economics* 82:80–107.

Bratt, E. C. 1953. "A Reconsideration of the Postwar Forecasts." *Journal of Business of the University of Chicago* 28:1–18.

Caves, R. E. 1990. "The Transformation of Corporate Control by Neil Fligstein." *Business History Review* 64:352–55.

Chandler, A. D. 1977. *The Visible Hand.* Cambridge, MA: Harvard University Press.

———. 1990. "Response to Contributors to the Review Colloquium on 'Scale and Scope.'" *Business History Review* 64:736–58.

Chandrasekhar, S. 1968. "How India is Tackling Her Population Problem." *Foreign Affairs* 47:138–50.

Chaudhuri, S., and M. Ravallion. 2006. "Partially Awakened Giants: Uneven Growth in China and India." World Bank Policy Research Working Paper no. 4069. Washington, DC: The World Bank.

Clark, C. 1976. "Economic Development in Communist China." *Journal of Political Economy* 84:239–64.

Coale, A. J. 1975. "The Demographic Transition." In *The Population Debate: Dimensions and Perspectives. Papers of the World Population Conference, Bucharest, 1974,* 347–55. New York: United Nations.

Colm, G. 1962. "Capital in the American Economy: Its Formation and Financing." *Journal of the American Statistical Association* 57:693–96.

Copeland, M. A., and E. M. Martin. 1938. "The Correction of Wealth and Income Estimates for Price Changes." In *Studies in Income and Wealth,* volume II, Conference on Research in Income and Wealth, 85–131. New York: National Bureau of Economic Research.

Crafts, N. F. R. 1995. "The Golden Age of Economic Growth in Western Europe, 1950–1973." *Economic History Review* 48:429–47.

———. 1997. "Some Dimensions of the 'Quality of Life' during the British Industrial Revolution." *Economic History Review* 50:690–712.

———. 2004. "Social Savings as a Measure of the Contribution of a New Technology to Economic Growth." Working Paper no. 06/04. Department of Economic History, London School of Economics, July.

Crafts, N. F. R., and G. Toniolo. 1996. *Economic Growth in Europe since 1945.* Cambridge: Cambridge University Press.

David, P. A. 1985. "Clio and the Economics of QWERTY." *American Economic Review* 75:332–37.

———. 1990. "The Dynamo and the Computer: An Historical Perspective on the Modern Productivity Paradox." *American Economic Review* 80:355–61.

———. 2003. "Zvi Griliches on Diffusion, Lags and Productivity Growth: Connecting the Dots." Presented at the Conference on R&D, Education, and Productivity held in memory of Zvi Griliches, Carré des Sciences, Ministere de la Rechèrce. Paris, France, August 25–27.

Davis, L. E., and R. A. Huttenback. 1986. *Mammon and the Pursuit of Empire: The Political Economy of British Imperialism, 1860–1912.* Cambridge: Cambridge University Press.

Denison, E. F. 1962. "The Sources of Economic Growth in the United States and the Alternatives Before Us." *Supplementary Paper no. 13.* New York: Committee for Economic Development.

———. 1967. "Sources of Postwar Growth in Nine Western Countries." *American Economic Review* 57:325–32.

Doblhammer, G., and J. W. Vaupel. 2001. "Life Span Depends on Month of Birth." *Proceedings of the National Academy of Sciences USA* 98:2934–39.

Dougherty, C., and D. W. Jorgenson. 1996. "International Comparisons of the Sources of Economic Growth." *The American Economic Review* 86:25–9.

Engerman, S. L., and K. Sokoloff. 1997. "Factor Endowments, Institutions, and Differential Paths of Growth among New World Economies: A View from Economic Historians of the United States." In *How Latin America Fell Behind,* edited by S. Haber, 260–304. Palo Alto: Stanford University Press.

Fabricant, S. 1954. "Economic Progress and Economic Change." In *34th Annual Report of the National Bureau of Economic Research.* New York: National Bureau of Economic Research.

Fischer, S. 1993. "The Role of Macroeconomic Factors in Growth." *Journal of Monetary Economics* 32:485–512.

Floud, R., R. W. Fogel, B. Harris, and S. C. Hong. Forthcoming, 2011. *The Changing Body: Health, Nutrition, and Human Development in the Western World since 1700.* Cambridge: Cambridge University Press.

Fogel, R. W. 1989a. "Afterword: Some Notes on the Scientific Methods of Simon Kuznets." In *Economic Development, the Family, and Income Distribution: Selected Essays, Simon Kuznets,* edited by Louis Galambos and Robert Gallman, 413–38. Cambridge: Cambridge University Press.

———. 1989b. *Without Consent or Contract: The Rise and Fall of American Slavery.* New York: W. W. Norton.

———. 2000. *The Fourth Great Awakening and the Future of Egalitarianism.* Chicago: University of Chicago Press.

———. 2003. "Forecasting the Demand for Health Care in OECD Nations and China." *Contemporary Economic Policy* 21:1–10.

———. 2004a. "Changes in the Process of Aging during the Twentieth Century:

Findings and Procedures of the *Early Indicators* Project." *Population and Development Review* 30:19–47.

———. 2004b. *The Escape from Hunger and Premature Death, 1700–2100: Europe, America, and the Third World.* New York: Cambridge University Press.

———. 2004c. "High Performing Asian Economies." NBER Working Paper no. 10752. Cambridge, MA: National Bureau of Economic Research, September.

———. 2006. "Why China is Likely to Achieve Its Growth Objectives." NBER Working Paper no. 12122. Cambridge, MA: National Bureau of Economic Research, March.

———. 2007. "Capitalism and Democracy in 2040." *Daedalus* 136:87–95.

Galambos, L. 1997. "Global Perspectives on Modern Business." *Business History Review* 71:287–90.

Ghemawat, P. 2002. "Competition and Business Strategy in Historical Perspective." *Business History Review* 76:37–74.

Goldsmith, R. W. 1952. *Income and Wealth of the United States: Trends and Structure.* Baltimore, MD: Johns Hopkins University Press.

Griliches, Z. 1956. "Hybrid Corn: An Exploration in the Economics of Technological Change." PhD diss., University of Chicago.

———. 1957. "Hybrid Corn: An Exploration in the Economics of Technological Change." *Econometrica* 25:501–22.

———. 1960. "Hybrid Corn and the Economics of Innovation." *Science* 132:275–80.

———. 1996. "The Discovery of the Residual: A Historical Note." *Journal of Economic Literature* 34:1324–30.

Hansen, A. H. 1939. "Economic Progress and Declining Population Growth." *American Economic Review* 29: 1–15.

Harley, C. K. 1992. "International Competitiveness of the Antebellum American Cotton Textile Industry." *Journal of Economic History* 52:559–84.

Healy, D. T. 1972. "Development Policy: New Thinking About an Interpretation." *Journal of Economic Literature* 10:757–97.

Heckman, J. 2006. "Contributions of Zvi Griliches." NBER Working Paper no. 12318. Cambridge, MA: National Bureau of Economic Research, June.

Helpman, E. 2004. *The Mystery of Economic Growth.* Cambridge, MA: Belknap Press.

———. 2008. *Institutions and Economic Performance.* Cambridge, MA: Harvard University Press.

Hicks, G. 1989. "The Four Little Dragons: An Enthusiast's Reading Guide." *Asian-Pacific Economic Literature* 3:35–49.

Jones, C. I. 1997. "On the Evolution of the World Income Distribution." *Journal of Economic Perspectives* 11:19–36.

Jorgenson, D. W. 1961a. "The Development of a Dual Economy." *Economic Journal* 71:309–44.

———. 1961b. "The Structure of Multi-sector Dynamic Models." *International Economic Review* 2:276–91.

———. 2001. "Information Technology and the U.S. Economy." *The American Economic Review* 91:1–32.

———. 2005. "Information Technology and the G7 Economies." Accessed December 12, 2008. http://www.isae.it/Jorgenson_Information.pdf.

Jorgenson, D. W., and L. R. Christensen. 1969. "The Measurement of U.S. Real Capital Input, 1929–1967." *Review of Income and Wealth* 15:293–390.

Jorgenson, D. W., and C. Dougherty. 1996. "International Comparisons of the Sources of Economic Growth." *American Economic Review* 86:25–9.

Jorgenson, D. W., and B. M. Fraumeni. 1980. "Capital Formation and U.S. Productivity Growth, 1948–1976." In *Productivity Analysis,* edited by A. Dogramaci, 49–70. Boston: Martinus Nijhoff.

———. 1986. "The Role of Capital in U.S. Economic Growth." In *Measurement Issues and Behavior of Productivity Variables,* edited by A. Dogramaci, 161–244. Boston: Martinus Nijhoff.

Jorgenson, D. W., and F. M. Gollup. 1980. "U.S. Productivity Growth by Industry, 1947–1973." In *New Developments in Productivity Measurement and Analysis,* Studies in Income and Wealth, volume 44, edited by J. W. Kendrick and B. N. Vaccara, 17–136. Chicago: University of Chicago Press.

———. 1992. "Growth in U.S. Agriculture: A Postwar Perspective." *American Journal of Agricultural Economics* 74:745–50.

Jorgenson, D. W., and Z. Griliches. 1967. "The Explanation of Productivity Change." *Review of Economic Studies* 34:249–80.

Jorgenson, D. W., and M. Kuroda. 1990. "Productivity and International Competitiveness in Japan and the United States, 1960–1985." In *Productivity Growth in Japan and the United States,* Studies in Income and Wealth, volume 53, edited by C. R. Hulten, 29–57. Chicago: University of Chicago Press.

Jorgenson, D. W., and K. Nomura. 2005. "The Industry Origins of Japanese Economic Growth." NBER Working Paper no. 11800. Cambridge, MA: National Bureau of Economic Research, November.

Jorgenson, D. W., and K. J. Stiroh. 1999. "Information Technology and Growth." *American Economic Review* 89:109–15.

———. 2000. "U.S. Economic Growth at the Industry Level." *American Economic Review* 90:161–67.

Jorgenson, D. W., and K. M. Vu. 2009. "Growth Accounting within the International Comparison Program." *ICP Bulletin* 6 (March): 3–19.

Kato, T. 2004. "Can the East Asian Miracle Persist?" Remarks by Takatoshi Kato, Deputy Managing Director, International Monetary Fund. Accessed February 2, 2009. http://www.imf.org/external/np/speeches/2004/120204.htm.

Kendrick, J. W. 1955. "Productivity." In *Government in Economic Life,* 35th Annual Report, edited by S. Fabricant, 44–47. New York: National Bureau of Economic Research.

Keyfitz, N., and W. Flieger. 1990. *World Population Growth and Aging: Demographic Trends in the Twentieth Century.* Chicago: University of Chicago Press.

Kim, J., and L. J. Lau. 1994. "The Sources of Economic Growth of the East Asian Newly Industrialized Countries." *Journal of the Japanese and Industrial Economies* 8:235–71.

Kravis, I. B. 1970. "Trade as a Handmaiden of Growth: Similarities between the Nineteenth and Twentieth Centuries." *Economic Journal* 80:850–72.

Krishnan, R. R. 1982. "The South Korean 'Miracle': Sell-out to Japan, US." *Social Scientist* 10:25–37.

Krugman, P. 1994. "The Myth of Asia's Miracle." *Foreign Affairs* 73. Accessed November 10, 2008. http://fullaccess.foreignaffairs.org/19941101faessay5151/paul-krugman/the-myth-of-asias-miracle.html.

———. 1998. "What Happened to Asia?" Accessed November 17, 2008. http://web.mit.edu/krugman/www/DISINTER.html.

Krugman, P., and R. Wells. 2005. *Macroeconomics.* New York: Worth Publishers.

Kuznets, S. 1961. *Capital in the American Economy: Its Formation and Financing.* Princeton, NJ: Princeton University Press.

———. 1966. *Modern Economic Growth.* New Haven, CT: Yale University Press.

———. 1971a. *Economic Growth of Nations: Total Output and Production Structure.* Chicago: University of Chicago Press.

———. 1971b. "Modern Economic Growth: Findings and Reflections." Lecture to the Memory of Alfred Nobel, December 11. Accessed December 30, 2008. http://nobelprize.org/nobel_prizes/economics/laureates/1971/kuznets-lecture.html.

———. 1972. *Quantitative Economic Research: Trends and Problems.* Fiftieth Anniversary Colloquium. New York: National Bureau of Economic Research.

———. 1989. *Economic Development, the Family, and Income Distribution: Selected Essays.* New York: Cambridge University Press.

Lamoreaux, N. R., D. M. G. Raff, and P. Temin. 2003. "Beyond Markets and Hierarchies: Toward a New Synthesis of American Business History." *American Historical Review* 108:404–33.

Landes, D. S. 1994. "What Room for Accident in History? Explaining Big Changes by Small Events." *Economic History Review* 47:637–56.

Lau, L. J. 1969. "Asian Drama: An Inquiry into *The Poverty of Nations* by Gunnar Myrdal." *Stanford Law Review* 21:967–76.

Li, P. 2009. "China to Outstrip USA in 2009 Auto Sales." *China.org.cn,* February 11. Accessed March 29, 2009. http://www.china.org.cn/business/2009-02/11/content_17260994.htm.

Lin, J. Y. 1998. "How Did China Feed Itself in the Past? How Will China Feed Itself in the Future?" Second Distinguished Economist Lecture presented at Centro Internacional Mejoramiento de Maiz y Trigo. Mexico, D.F., Medico, January 9.

Lopez, J. H. 2004. "Pro-growth, Pro-poor: Is There a Trade-off?" World Bank Policy Research Working Paper no. 3378. Washington, DC: The World Bank.

Lucas, R. E. 1988. "On the Mechanics of Economic Development." *Journal of Monetary Economics* 22:3–42.

Maddison, A. 1987. "Growth and Slowdown in Advanced Capitalist Economies: Techniques of Quantitative Assessment." *Journal of Economic Literature* 25:649–98.

———. 1991. *Dynamic Forces in Capitalist Development: A Long-Run Comparative View.* Oxford: Oxford University Press.

———. 1995. *Monitoring the World Economy.* Paris: Organization for Economic Cooperation and Development (OECD).

———. 1998. *Chinese Economic Performance in the Long Run.* Paris: OECD Development Centre.

———. 2001. *The World Economy: A Millennial Perspective.* Paris and Washington, DC: OECD.

Malenbaum, W. 1959. "India and China: Contrasts in Development Performance." *American Economic Review* 49:284–309.

———. 1982. "Modern Economic Growth in India and China: The Comparison Revisited, 1950–1980." *Economic Development and Cultural Change* 31:45–84.

Mansfield, E. 1971. *Technological Change.* New York: W. W. Norton and Co.

———. 1972. "Contribution of R&D to Economic Growth in the United States." *Science* 175:477–86.

———. 1975. "International Technology Transfer: Forms, Resource Requirements, and Policies." *American Economic Review* 65:372–76.

———. 1980. "Research and Development, Productivity, and Inflation." *Science* 209:1091–93.

Mears, L. A. 1961. "Indonesia." In *Economic Development: Analysis and Case Studies,* edited by A. Pepelases, L. A. Mears, and I. Adelman, 418–67. New York: Harper and Brothers.

Mellor, J. W., T. F. Weaver, U. J. Lele, and S. R. Simon. 1968. *Developing Rural India: Plan and Practice.* Ithaca: Cornell University Press.

Mills, T. C., and N. F. R. Crafts. 2000. "After the Golden Age: A Long-Run Perspective on Growth Rates that Speeded Up, Slowed Down, and Still Differ." *Manchester School* 68:68–91.

Mokyr, J. 1985. *The Economics of the Industrial Revolution.* Totowa, NJ: Rowman and Allanheld.

Morrison, W. M. 2006. "CRS Issue Brief for Congress: China's Economic Conditions." Accessed February 2, 2009. http://www.fas.org/sgp/crs/row/IB98014.pdf.

Murphy, K. M., and R. H. Topel. 2005. "The Value of Health and Longevity." NBER Working Paper no. 11405. Cambridge, MA: National Bureau of Economic Research, June.

Myrdal, G. 1968. *Asian Drama: An Inquiry into the Poverty of Nations.* New York: Pantheon.

National Bureau of Statistics of China. 2008. *China Statistical Yearbook 2008.* Beijing: China Statistics Press.

Nelson, R. R. 1959. "The Economics of Invention: A Survey of the Literature." *Journal of Business* 32:101–27.

———. 1964. "Aggregate Production Functions and Medium-Range Growth Projections." *American Economic Review* 54:575–606.

———. 1981. "Research on Productivity Growth and Productivity Differences: Dead Ends and New Departures." *Journal of Economic Literature* 19:1029–64.

———. 1988. "Modelling the Connections in the Cross Section between Technical Progress and R&D Intensity." *RAND Journal of Economics* 19:478–85.

———. 1991. "Diffusion of Development: Post–World War II Convergence among Advanced Industrial Nations." *American Economic Review* 81:271–75.

Nelson, R. R., and H. Pack. 1999. "The Asian Miracle and Economic Growth Theory." *Economic Journal* 109:416–36.

Nelson, R. R., and S. G. Winter. 1982. "An Evolutionary Theory of Economic Capabilities." *American Economic Review* 68:440–49.

Nelson, R. R., and G. Wright. 1992. "The Rise and Fall of American Technological Leadership: The Postwar Era in Historical Perspective." *Journal of Economic Literature* 30:1931–64.

North, D.C. 1966. *Growth and Welfare in the American Past: A New Economic History.* Englewood Cliffs, NJ: Prentice Hall.

———. 1968. "Sources of Productivity Change in Ocean Shipping 1600–1850." *Journal of Political Economy* 76:953–70.

———. 2005. *Understanding the Process of Economic Change.* Princeton, NJ: Princeton University Press.

North, D.C., and R. P. Thomas. 1970. "An Economic Theory of the Growth of the Western World." *Economic History Review* 23:1–17.

———. 1971. "The Rise and Fall of the Manorial System: A Theoretical Model." *Journal of Economic History* 31:777–803.

———. 1977. "The First Economic Revolution." *Economic History Review* 30: 229–41.

North, D.C., and B. R. Weingast. 1989. "Constitutions and Commitment: The Evolution of Institutions Governing Public Choice in 17th Century England." *Journal of Economic History* 49:803–32.

Olson, M. 1982. *The Rise and Decline of Nations: Economic Growth, Stagflation, and Social Rigidities.* New Haven, CT: Yale University Press.

Organization for Economic Cooperation and Development (OECD). 2005. "Economic Survey of China, 2005." Policy brief. Accessed February 2, 2009. http://www.oecd.org/dataoecd/10/25/35294862.pdf.

Park, J. H. 2002. "The East Asian Model of Economic Development and Developing Countries." *Journal of Developing Societies* 18:330–53.

Pei, M. 2006. "The Dark Side of China's Rise." Accessed February 2, 2009. http://
www.foreignpolicy.com/users/login.php?story_id=3373&URL=http://www.for
eignpolicy. com/story/cms.php?story_id=3373&print=1.

———. 2007. "The High Cost of Prosperity." Accessed February 2, 2009. http://
www.carnegieendowment.org/publications/index.cfm?fa=view&id=19059
&prog=zch.

Pepelases, A., L. A. Mears, and I. Adelman. 1961. *Economic Development: Analysis
and Case Studies*. New York: Harper and Brothers.

Perkins, D. H. 2006a. "China's Recent Economic Performance and Future Prospects." *Asian Economic Policy Review* 1:15–40.

———. 2006b. "Stagnation and Growth in China over the Millennium: A Comment
on Angus Maddison's 'China in the World Economy, 1300–2030.'" *International
Journal of Business* 11:255–64.

Perkins, D., and T. G. Rawski. 2008. "Forecasting China's Economic Growth to
2025." In *China's Great Economic Transformation*, edited by L. Brandt and T. G.
Rawksi, 829–86. Cambridge: Cambridge University Press.

Ray, D. 2008. "Development Economics." In *The New Palgrave Dictionary of Economics*, 2nd edition, edited by S. N. Durlaf and L. Blume, 468–79. New York:
Palgrave Macmillan.

Romer, P. 1986. "Increasing Returns and Long-Run Growth." *Journal of Political
Economy* 94:1002–37.

Rosenberg, N. 1994. "How the Developed Countries Became Rich." *Daedalus*
123:127–40.

Rostow, W. W. 1979. *Getting from Here to There*. New York: McGraw-Hill.

———. 1990. *Theorists of Economic Growth from David Hume to the Present*. New
York: Oxford University Press.

Schultz, T. W. 1962. *Investment in Human Beings*. Chicago: University of Chicago
Press.

———. 1971. *Investment in Human Capital: The Role of Education and Research*.
New York: Free Press.

Schumpter, J. 1934. *The Theory of Economic Development: An Inquiry into Profits,
Capital, Credit, Interest, and the Business Cycle*. Cambridge, MA: Harvard University Press.

Shenoy, B. R. 1968. "India: Planning for Economic Disaster." *Wall Street Journal*,
May 23.

Simon, M. 1970. "New British Investment in Canada, 1865–1914." *Canadian Journal of Economics* 3:238–54.

Sklaeiwitz, N. 1966. "India's Food Plight." *Wall Street Journal*, June 7.

Sokoloff, K., and S. L. Engerman. 2000. "History Lessons: Institutions, Factor
Endowments, and Paths of Development in the New World." *Journal of Economic
Perspectives* 14:217–32.

Solow, R. M. 1957. "Technical Change and the Aggregate Production Function."
Review of Economics and Statistics 39:312–20.

———. 1958. "A Skeptical Note on the Constancy of Relative Shares." *American
Economic Review* 48:618–31.

———. 2007. "The Last 50 Years in Growth Theory and the Next 10." *Oxford Review
of Economic Policy* 23:3–14.

Srinivasan, T. N., and J. Bhagwati. 2001. "Outward Orientation and Development:
Are Revisionists Right?" In *Trade, Development, and Political Economy: Essays in
Honour of Anne Krueger*, edited by D. Lau and R. Snape, 3–26. London: Pal-
grave.

Stigler, G. J. 1947. "The Kinky Demand Curve and Rigid Prices." *Journal of Political
Economy* 55:432.

Stiglitz, J. E. 1996. "Some Lessons from the East Asian Miracle." *World Bank Research Observer* 11:151–77.

———. 2001. "From Miracle to Crisis to Recovery: Lessons from Four Decades of East Asian Experience." In *Rethinking the East Asian Miracle,* edited by J. Stiglitz and S. Yusuf, 509–26. Oxford: Oxford University Press.

Stone, I. 1999. *The Global Export of Capital from Great Britain, 1865–1914: A Statistical Survey.* New York: St. Martin's Press.

Swan, T. W. 1956. "Economic Growth and Capital Accumulation." *Economic Record* 11:334–36.

Teece, D. J. 1993. "The Dynamics of Industrial Capitalism: Perspectives on Alfred Chandler's Scale and Scope." *Journal of Economic Literature* 31:199–255.

Temin, P. 1997. "Two Views of the British Industrial Revolution." *Journal of Economic History* 57:63–82.

Tinbergen, J. 1942. "Zur Theorie der Langfirstigen Wirtschaftsentwicklung." *Welwirts Archive* 1:511–49.

Trajtenberg, M., and E. R. Berndt. 2001. "In Memoriam: Zvi Griliches, 1930–1999." *Journal of Economic and Social Measurement* 27:93–7.

U.S. Bureau of the Census. 1955. *Statistical Abstract of the United States 1955.* Washington, DC: Government Printing Office.

———. 2003. *Statistical Abstract of the United States 2003.* Washington, DC: Government Printing Office.

U.S. Intelligence Council. 2008. *Global Trends 2025: A Transformed World.* Accessed February 3, 2009. http://www.dni.gov/nic/NIC_2025_project.html.

United Nations. 2009. "World Population Prospects: The 2008 Revision Population Database." Accessed December 27, 2009. http://esa/un.org/unpp/p2k0data.asp.

van Ark, B., M. O'Mahony, and M. P. Timmer. 2008. "The Productivity Gap between Europe and the United States: Trends and Causes." *Journal of Economic Perspectives* 22:25–44.

Ying, T. 2009. "China February Auto Sales Rise 25% after Tax Cuts." *Bloomberg. com,* March 10. Accessed March 27, 2009. http://www.bloomberg.com/apps/new s?pid=20601087&sid=aDCOM2mACDYY&refer=home.

Young, A. 1995. "The Tyranny of Numbers: Confronting the Statistical Realities of the East Asian Growth Experience." *Quarterly Journal of Economics* 110:641–80.

Zakaria, F. 2005. "Does the Future Belong to China?" *Newsweek,* May 9. Accessed February 3, 2009. http://www.fareedzakaria.com/articles/newsweek/050905. html.

———. 2006. "How Long Will America Lead the World?" *Newsweek,* June 12. Accessed February 3, 2009. http://www.fareedzakaria.com/articles/newsweek/ 061206.html.

11

Ken Sokoloff and the Economic History of Technology
An Appreciation

Joel Mokyr

The economic history of technology is a subfield of a subfield, and it is a small enough cell in the table of specialized areas of our discipline for all practitioners to know each other and read one another's work, often as journal referees and book reviewers. In such small fields, it appears there are two equilibria: either the field gets cooperative and friendly so that the participants communicate in an amicable and civilized style and do not let their professional disagreements interfere with personal judgment, or bloody internecine warfare breaks out, creating scenes worthy of a David Lodge. The difference between the two outcomes is often a single person or a few key individuals. A single scholar of impeccable stature, respected and liked by others, sets a tone that leads the participants to reconsider their position rather than be dismissive of other views, and may lead the entire field to a cooperative equilibrium. Alternatively, a leader's intolerance or egomania may create long chains of action and retaliation.

In the economic history of technology, for the period that Ken Sokoloff, myself, and a few others worked in, there was and is quite a bit of difference of emphasis and disagreement, but over the years the field remained cozy and friendly at best, respectful and polite at worst. Sokoloff commanded such widespread respect and affection, and his work was so solid and well-documented, that the entire field ended up for decades in the "good" equilibrium. It is also true, one might add, that the other major players in the area, especially Naomi Lamoreaux and Zorina Khan, as well as some of the

Joel Mokyr is the Robert H. Strotz Professor of Arts and Sciences at Northwestern University, holds a joint appointment in economics and history, and is a Sackler Professorial Fellow at the Eitan Berglas School of Economics at the University of Tel Aviv.

best economists working in the area, such as Manuel Trajtenberg and Ariel Pakes, were his friends and collaborators.

Much of the debate, as might be imagined, was about the question of the sources of technological progress. For Ken Sokoloff, working in applied endogenous growth theory *avant la lettre,* incentives mattered above all. Throughout his extensive work in the area of innovation, a few themes emerged that consistently reflected the way he viewed the economics of technological progress. Invention, he believed, is by and large a rational activity, undertaken by individuals who calculate, at least at some level of approximation, their costs and benefits ex-ante before they decide to engage in the work that leads to invention. He full well realized that this activity, when undertaken at all, was highly sensitive to institutions that organized markets and thus set the rewards structure for would-be innovators, but he firmly believed that on the whole the supply of inventions was quite elastic. Provide this pool of would-be inventors with the right opportunities, Sokoloff argued, and the floodgates of invention will open.

In nineteenth-century America, he believed, these opportunities were provided by two main elements: patents and markets. In a duo of pathbreaking papers with Khan published in the early nineties in the *Journal of Economic History* (1990, 1993), Sokoloff and Khan showed that invention at this time was unique in being accessible and democratic and not confined to a narrow elite. Most American inventors were anything but eccentric cranks; they were by and large rational entrepreneurs responding to market opportunities and looking for profits. They had invested in the kind of human capital needed to develop inventions, mostly artisanal and machinist skills necessary to generate the incremental mechanical devices that were at the heart of American inventive activity in this age. They demonstrated that in the first half of the nineteenth century, the road to patent and benefit from invention was accessible to a significant segment of the U.S. population: artisans and machinists accounted for close to half of inventions. His and Khan's view was that American invention was above all open and competitive, driven by markets and incentives. In short, an "economic" activity in most dimensions.

It would be fair to say that in the literature on the economic history of technological progress, Sokoloff found himself to be a consistent demand-sider. For him, the fact that patents seemed to respond to business cycles and concentrate in areas with good access to markets constituted strong evidence that demand was predominant. This responsiveness to demand condition was for him the conclusive demonstration of the fact that invention was not exogenous (Sokoloff 1992, 354). In his view, those who focused on major technological breakthroughs, unduly focused "attention on the idiosyncratic aspects of all singular events" and "diminished the significance of general mechanisms at work" (347). This is not a wholly uncontroversial position, as it abstracted from the scientific origins of technological change—admittedly a difficult and complex matter, but one in which Sokoloff saw of little interest. At this stage of his career his focus was on the technological development of the United States in the nineteenth century, when for most of the period invention consisted of mechanical contraptions and incremental microinventions that required little direct input of science. With some exceptions, the giants of science whose work was foundational to subsequent invention, men like Oersted, Gay-Lussac, Chevreul, Faraday, Ampère, and Liebig, were working in Europe and their additions to knowledge clearly were exogenous to American inventiveness (Sokoloff 1992, 368). In that sense, Sokoloff's vision of the process on this side of the Atlantic in that period was quite complete.

And yet, he carefully distinguished the American experience from that of other nations, where for one reason or another the opportunities to inventors were more limited to a privileged elite, perhaps less sensitive to market incentives and more driven by internal motives and peer pressures. In one of their best and most persuasive papers, published in the Berg and Bruland volume (1998), Khan and Sokoloff carefully compared the impact of different patenting environments on the nature of invention in the United States and Great Britain. Such comparisons, as they were fully aware of, are hazardous for many reasons, but they must be made nonetheless. In a later paper (Khan and Sokoloff 2004) they added, quite correctly, that it was the American system that was exceptional in its openness and in its recognition that "it was in the wide public interest that patent rights, like other property rights, be clearly defined, well enforced, and easy to transact in" (15). One gets the impression that Sokoloff himself clearly felt that such an open and accessible patent system was desirable and virtuous and the key to sustained invention.

These were and are not uncontroversial views. Patents have been denounced, most recently in a provocative book by Boldrin and Levine (2008), as rent-seeking monopolies, and the exact incentive effect they have on the propensity to invent (as opposed to the propensity to patent) is still subject to much debate (Mokyr 2009). Yet these are all, as the cliché has it, hard and complex issues on which reasonable scholars can disagree without being disagreeable. Ken would not have it any other way.

For Sokoloff, measurement and quantitative analysis was nondebatable. For an economic historian of technological progress, this poses, of course, a dilemma. Fundamentally, each invention is a sui generis and is made only once. Two separate inventions are inherently different, and "counting" them is subject to a number of serious objections. He thought long and hard about this matter, and as was appropriate for a Harvard grad student under the influence of the late Zvi Griliches, in the end he still found the use of patent data attractive; indeed, irresistible. He fully understood, better than most, the limitations of the use of patent data in the economic history of technology (Sokoloff 1992, 350). But he made enormous efforts to correct and adjust for whatever biases these data imparted on the elusive measurement of inventive activity. The economics of the modern patent system is complex, and it was no different in eighteenth century Britain and nineteenth century America. Yet it has always attracted able economic historians (for instance, Rick Sullivan, Harry Dutton, Christine Macleod, and Petra Moser), in that it provides us with a measure at how invention really works on an aggregative and regional level. Much like looking at the night sky with a telescope, we understand that we only see a section of what we would like to see, and in many ways the blunt instrument we are using is distorting reality. But Sokoloff's ingenuity, curiosity, and energy overcame these objections as well as was possible.

The picture he painted of nineteenth century innovative activity is one that was comfortable to economists. Innovation was closely associated with markets—indeed, it itself was a market activity, in which technological ideas were sold and bought. As he showed in his first paper in this genre (Sokoloff 1988), inventive activity tended to be concentrated in areas in which markets were accessible and developed. Equally important, inventive activity followed the market for inventions: as his and Lamoreaux's fascinating paper on the glass industry (Lamoreaux and Sokoloff 2000) showed, not all producers were big inventors and not all inventors were big producers.

Clustering and agglomeration effects are all good and well, but in the Sokoloff view of the historical phenomenon of technological progress, the most important market was the market for knowledge, which he regarded as the key to the successful economy. He and Lamoreaux showed how essential the market for patent assignment became, and how its growth facilitated the growing and inevitable specialization between those who developed the new technology and those who were best positioned to use it (Lamoreaux and Sokoloff, 1996, 1999c, 2001). The existence of institutions in certain core regions that supported the marketing and sale of patents, such as patenting agents and lawyers and the availability of financial backing, was key to this interpretation, and lies at the heart of the geographical persistence of the cores of inventive activity (Lamoreaux and Sokoloff 1999b; 2009). These areas formed the "clusters" of inventive activity, with the agglomeration economies supplied by the institutional infrastructure rather than by some kind of knowledge spillover. More patents meant more assignments, and more assignments in turn helped build the "market" for technology. This in turn attracted more and more inventors to migrate to those regions, creating a positive feedback model of the kind that is used in economic geography.

By the late nineteenth century, in this interpretation, a class of ingenious, productive, full-time specialized inventors had emerged that were a "crucial source of new technological knowledge" (Lamoreaux and Sokoloff 2009, 53). These people lived by and for the patent system, and the better the inventor, the higher was his or her propensity to invent, to patent the invention, and to assign the invention to a producer who could make good use of it. Apart from the fact that the product sold had some qualities that made it an unusual commodity, Sokoloff's work was much in the spirit of William Parker's famous characterization of U.S. economic history: "[W]hen all is said and done, the market did it again." It was a viewpoint consonant with a Northian view that saw growth occurring through better institutions that supported markets, with technological progress just a special case of the beneficial effects of good property rights, personal mobility, and well-functioning information-dissemination. It was a unique vision of the emergence of technological activity and its distribution over time, but one fully backed up by the data.

Yet within this general paradigm, Sokoloff was an empiricist who was professionally committed to let the data speak even when it did not always produce the results he expected. His deep knowledge of the development of innovation in the U.S. at both the national and regional levels forced him to revise his thinking about how American technology evolved: he saw that there was no direct transition between the single lone inventor working from his basement (or workshop) to the large corporate inventors that Schumpeter pointed to. In between there was a sophisticated, competitive, decentralized market, in which ingenious and increasingly professional inventors came up with a stream of inventive ideas, which they sold (or assigned) on the market after securing property rights to it through a patent.

Eventually, however, the American system he admired so much came to an end. The clusters of inventive activity in New England that had persisted throughout the nineteenth century started to decline in the twentieth century as manufacturing activity shifted away and the nature of inventions began to change. The growing complexity of technology required more and more fixed capital, and the old institutions that supplied credit to budding inventors were no longer adequate. Moreover, inventors increasingly needed formal scientific education instead of the informal training or even autodidactism that often sufficed before, and the "burden of knowledge" that successful inventors needed (to use a term employed by Jones [2009]), increasingly imposed barriers to what once was an open market. Rather than a self-employed entrepreneur, the typical inventor increasingly became an employee in a firm that in an earlier age would have licensed or bought his invention. At this stage of history, Schumpeter replaced North in his interpretation (Lamoreaux and Sokoloff 2009), although here, too, Sokoloff's vision was nuanced and sophisticated. Inventors in the twentieth century, much like their predecessors in an earlier age, had choices and exercised options, mostly in the rational fashion that an economist would expect.

Sokoloff was never one to shy away from some scholarly risk-taking and making some assumptions needed to validate his findings, as long as those assumptions, in the best traditions of cliometrics, were fully and explicitly spelled out. Those who had doubts, including myself, were engaged in debate, always agreeable and always informed and thoughtful. It was often more pleasant to *dis*agree with Ken Sokoloff than to agree with other lesser scholars and gentlemen. Moreover, he was invariably generous, always giving other scholars credit for insights (even when those differed from his), always polite and respectful toward opponents. As a scholar, a teacher, and a colleague he led by example. The field of economic history has been impoverished by his untimely death, but his published work will continue to be read and studied, and the small but active field of the economic history of technology continues to thrive thanks to his leadership.

References to Papers by Kenneth L. Sokoloff

Sokoloff, Kenneth L. 1988. "Inventive Activity in Early Industrial America: Evidence from Patent Records, 1790–1846." *Journal of Economic History* 48: 813–50.

Sokoloff, Kenneth L., and B. Zorina Khan. 1990. "The Democratization of Invention During Early Industrialization: Evidence from the United States, 1790–1846." *Journal of Economic History* 50:363–78.

Sokoloff, Kenneth L. 1992. "Invention, Innovation, and Manufacturing Productivity Growth During the Antebellum Period." In *The Standard of Living in Early 19th Century America,* edited by R. Gallman and J. Wallis, 345–78. Chicago: University of Chicago Press.

Khan, B. Zorina, and Kenneth L. Sokoloff. 1993a. "Entrepreneurship and Technological Change in Historical Perspective: A Study of Great Inventors During Early American Industrialization." *Advances in the Study of Entrepreneurship, Innovation, and Economic Growth* 6:37–66.

———. 1993b. "Schemes of Practical Utility': Entrepreneurship and Innovation Among 'Great Inventors' During Early American Industrialization, 1790–1865." *Journal of Economic History* 53:289–307.

Pakes, Ariel, and Kenneth L. Sokoloff. 1996. "Science, Technology, and Economic Growth." *Proceedings of the National Academy of Sciences* 93:12655–57.

Lamoreaux, Naomi R., and Kenneth L. Sokoloff. 1996. "Long-Term Change in the Organization of Inventive Activity." *Proceedings of the National Academy of Sciences* 93:12686–92.

Khan, B. Zorina, and Kenneth L. Sokoloff. 1998. "Patent Institutions, Industrial Organization, and Early Technological Change: Britain and the United States, 1790–1852." In *Technological Revolution in Europe,* edited by M. Berg and K. Bruland, 292–313. Cheltenham, UK: Edward Elgar.

Lamoreaux, Naomi R., and Kenneth L. Sokoloff. 1999a. "The Geography of the Market for Technology in the Late-Nineteenth and Early Twentieth Century United States." *Advances in the Study of Entrepreneurship, Innovation, and Growth* 11:67–121.

———. 1999b. "Inventive Activity and the Market for Technology in the United States, 1840–1920." NBER Working Paper no. 7107. Cambridge, MA: National Bureau of Economic Research, May.

———. 1999c. "Inventors, Firms, and the Market for Technology in the Late Nineteenth and Early Twentieth Centuries." In *Learning By Doing in Markets, Firms, and Countries,* edited by Naomi R. Lamoreaux, Daniel M. G. Raff, and Peter Temin, 19–60. Chicago: University of Chicago Press.

———. 2000. "Location and Technological Change in the American Glass Industry

During the Late Nineteenth and Early Twentieth Centuries." *Journal of Economic History* 60:700–29.

Khan, B. Zorina, and Kenneth L. Sokoloff. 2001. "Intellectual Property Institutions in the United States: Early Development." *Journal of Economic Perspectives* 15:233–46.

Lamoreaux, Naomi R., and Kenneth L. Sokoloff. 2001. "Market Trade in Patents and the Rise of a Class of Specialized Inventors in the Nineteenth Century United States." *American Economic Review* 91:39–44.

Khan, B. Zorina, and Kenneth L. Sokoloff. 2004. "Institutions and Democratic Invention in 19th Century America." *American Economic Review* 94:395–401.

———. 2006a. "Institutions and Technological Innovation during Early Economic Growth: Evidence from the Great Inventors of the United States, 1790–1930." In *Institutions and Growth,* edited by Theo Eicher and Cecilia Penalosa Garcia, 123–58. Cambridge, MA: MIT Press.

———. 2006b. "Lives of Invention: Patenting and Productivity among Great Inventors in the United States, 1790–1930." In *Les Archives de l'Invention,* edited by Liliane Perez, et al., 181–99. Paris: CNRS/Université de Toulouse-Le Mirail.

Lamoreaux, Naomi R., and Kenneth L. Sokoloff. 2009. "The Rise and Decline of the Independent Inventor: A Schumpeterian Story?" In *The Challenge of Remaining Innovative: Lessons from Twentieth Century American Business,* edited by Sally H. Clarke, Naomi R. Lamoreaux, and Steven Usselman, 43–78. Stanford: Stanford University Press.

Other References

Boldrin, Michele, and David K. Levine. 2008. *Against Intellectual Monopoly.* Cambridge: Cambridge University Press.

Jones, Benjamin. 2009. "The Burden of Knowledge and the 'Death of the Renaissance Man': Is Innovation Getting Harder?" *Review of Economic Studies* 76: 283–317.

Mokyr, Joel. 2009. "Intellectual Property Rights, the Industrial Revolution, and the Beginnings of Modern Economic Growth." *American Economic Review Papers and Proceedings* 99:349–55.

12

Kenneth Sokoloff on Inequality in the Americas

Peter H. Lindert

His forays into the comparative history of inequality amply demonstrate Ken Sokoloff's versatility. Ken and his collaborators amassed a novel comparative history with a clear pattern: the explanation of both inequality and slow growth in Latin American and the U.S. South before the middle of the twentieth century lies in the sources of institutional differences, sources that were themselves inegalitarian by design. The main culprit was the concentration of political voice, fostered by accidents of history. Its weapons featured policies toward land allocation, mass education, migration, and the tax structure.

The freshness of this departure would have been less obvious if his previous works had been marching in the same direction, offering previews of this later project. Yet only one of his previous projects adumbrated the exploration of inequality in the Americas that Ken undertook with Stan Engerman and others in his last dozen years of research. That one preview of strong interest in inequality took the form of a solid result rather than a theory or expression of personal preference. His work on patent history, both solo and in collaboration with Zorina Khan, supported a clearly egalitarian finding—relative to the patent systems of other countries, the patent system of early America gave much greater encouragement to technological advances by ordinary people, giving an egalitarian twist to American economic growth up to the late nineteenth century.

Revealing the hidden democracy in America's approach to patents may have encouraged Ken to think further about inequality between the regions of the United States, and between this nation and others. Those topical links

Peter H. Lindert is Distinguished Professor of Economics at the University of California, Davis, and a research associate of the National Bureau of Economic Research.

may have been forged as early as his doctoral thesis. By the end of the 1980s, at least, he was quite prepared to venture into the comparative history of inequality, and was discussing these issues with Stanley Engerman. When Steve Haber approached Ken about contributing to a 1992 conference on how Latin America fell behind, there was no need for Ken and Stan to start from square one, and the first in a cycle of widely cited papers was soon being revised and edited.[1]

This essay describes the evolving project that tied inequality to just about every other major force in the economic and political history of the Americas. Thanks to the richness of their reading of history, Engerman, Sokoloff, and coauthors were pioneers in realizing the value of a cross-sectional analysis of all of the Americas for the purpose of explaining differences in growth and inequality. Like the team of Daron Acemoglu, Simon Johnson, and James Robinson,[2] they exploited exogenous international differences from centuries earlier. Yet they made (most of) their strong prima facie case without econometrics. Rather, they mined the vast expanse of the Western Hemisphere's comparative history for its nuggets of valid approximations to natural experiments. Relative to today's state-of-the-art econometric findings from randomized experiments, their technique traded away from statistical reliability of any one test, toward the stronger suggestive power of a broader historical database.[3] While this strategy makes it harder to fashion short articles that satisfy journal editors and referees, it has the offsetting advantage of sparking a further wave of research.

12.1   The Vast Nexus: Daring to Link Inequality and Growth with Nearly Everything

Scholars who care deeply about the sources of economic development are immediately confronted with the daunting fact that there are so many possible causal links that need testing. At a minimum, scholars as a group must test all of the causal arrows pointing from relatively exogenous variables to endogenous variables in figure 12.1. In slightly greater detail, these are

Causal Arrow A: Accidents of political history shape institutions.[4]
Causal Arrow B: Factor endowments shape institutions (e.g., endowments of land, minerals, forests, sweat-crop geography, skilled labor, and unskilled labor all shape land policy, migration policy, ownership of labor, and tax laws).[5]

---

1. Engerman and Sokoloff (1997). I am indebted to Stan Engerman and Steve Haber for their recollections.
2. Acemoglu, Johnson, and Robinson (2001, 2002).
3. Students have reported that Ken often advised them at the onset of their thesis formation, "Just plot the data and see what they seem to show."
4. Engerman and Sokoloff (2005, 2008, chapter 1, this volume).
5. Engerman and Sokoloff (2008, chapter 1, this volume).

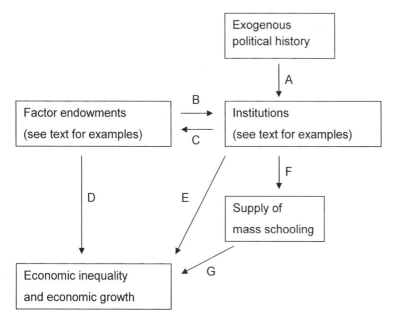

Fig. 12.1   A causal nexus shaping the history of inequality and growth

Causal Arrow C: Institutions shape factor endowments.[6]
Causal Arrow D: Factor endowments directly affect the inequality-growth mix.[7]
Causal Arrow E: Institutions directly affect the inequality-growth mix.[8]
Causal Arrow F: Institutions affect the supply of mass schooling.[9]
Causal Arrow G: The supply of mass schooling affects economic inequality and growth.[10]

6. Engerman and Sokoloff (chapter 1, this volume).
7. Engerman and Sokoloff (1997, 2002).
8. See Engerman and Sokoloff (1997, 2002, 2008) and Sokoloff and Zolt (2006). Their work is used by De Ferranti et al. (2004), Frankema (2009), Nugent and Robinson (forthcoming), and the special issue of *Revista de Historia Económica* (forthcoming), among others. Here I omit any causal arrows running between economic inequality and economic growth. One should avoid trying to draw causal arrows between two endogenous variables that are driven by overlapping sets of exogenous forces. By analogy, one should not strain to decide whether price drives quantity or vice versa, when both are codetermined by exogenous influences on supply and demand. Engerman and Sokoloff and their coauthors also avoid this trap. While certain of their passages might seem to imply that "inequality" retarded economic growth in Latin America, they are careful to link that inequality to its inegalitarian exogenous sources.
9. Engerman, Mariscal, and Sokoloff (2002, 2009); Mariscal and Sokoloff (2000). Their lead has been followed by Latika Chaudhury's (2009) comparative analysis of the institutional determinants of education finance across the regions of India, and also by Go and Lindert (2010), and Lindert (2010).
10. Engerman, Mariscal, and Sokoloff (2002, 2009); Mariscal and Sokoloff (2000); Frankema (2009).

Only the most energetic would succeed in advancing our collective knowledge about all of these. Engerman and Sokoloff have done so in their comparative history of the Americas, exploring all the causal arrows in figure 12.1. These collaborative writings are widely cited, and other authors have followed their lead.

12.2   Which Sources Make the Best Exogenous Instruments?

"Improving our knowledge of whether institutions are exogenous or endogenous, and of how flexible they are in adapting to changes in conditions, is crucial to gaining a good understanding of their role in economic development."
—Engerman and Sokoloff, this volume

It is never easy to sort out such intertwining relationships, and like the human figures in the famous sculpture of Laocoön and his sons, Engerman and Sokoloff had their hands full. Still, it is fair to say that theirs is the best summary of the profession's judgment of the sources of Latin American inequality. Here I offer only some guesses about which of the links they studied are strongest, and where future research efforts are most likely to concentrate.

It seems likely that the arrows on the right-hand side of figure 12.1 will be reaffirmed and reinforced more than those involving factor endowments. Their evidence on the role of political voice continues to stand up under further study, especially in its effects working through the denial of subsidies for mass schooling (arrows A, E, and F, plus the not-so-controversial G). In the next decade, I expect other scholars to reinforce these links with time-series natural experiments to supplement the heavily cross-sectional evidence they produced in such abundance. The enrichment of our knowledge of changes in Latin American inequality over time has already begun, prodded largely by the views of Engerman and Sokoloff.[11] Structural break analysis may soon follow, relating changes in education policies and tax structure to regime changes.

Such an emphasis on the exogenous sources of inegalitarian policies is likely to crowd out the emphasis on the role of factor endowments, featured on the left-hand side. Granted, the Engerman-Sokoloff contribution to this volume plausibly argues that factor endowments help to explain differences in American countries' institutions regarding immigration.

Yet three other sets of comparative studies tend to favor emphasizing the

---

11. For example, Leticia Arroyo Abad (2008) is developing evidence of swings in the relationship of wages to land rents in five Latin American countries across the long nineteenth century. Jeffrey Williamson (2010, forthcoming) uses international regression evidence plus data on some income determinants to argue that Latin American inequalities have had pronounced falls and rises since independence. See also the income gini trends sketched in Baten et al. (forthcoming, figure 3).

role of exogenous institutions in shaping inequality. First, comparing Russia with Western Europe has suggested that political forces were much more important than factor endowments in shaping the institutions that produced inequality and slow growth. If land abundance and labor scarcity led to the attraction of immigrants with better offers to ordinary folk, how are we to explain the fact that the expansion of Russia kept leading to greater oppression and relative stagnation over the centuries up to 1861? As Niebohr, Blum, Domar, and others have emphasized, imperial Russia developed the political strength to fix serfs more tightly to their lords on the new lands. To slide Russian experience onto the same string as the Engerman-Sokoloff contrast among the Americas requires an emphasis on the exogenous-institutions side of their work rather than the factor-endowments side.

A second such comparison is the Central American natural experiment presented by Nugent and Robinson. Factor endowments were very similar in Colombia, Costa Rica, El Salvador, and Guatemala when they achieved independence. All four had land well-suited for coffee, and had broadly similar land areas per capita. Yet Costa Rica and Colombia developed much broader education, stronger urban development, relatively more independent free-holders, less income inequality, and higher gross domestic product (GDP) per capita than did El Salvador or Guatemala. Nugent and Robinson persuasively argue that it was exogenous accidents of political history that sent the two pairs of countries down very different paths, despite the similarities in their initial factor endowments.[12]

A third set of comparisons is emerging from my extending the empirical base for testing the Engerman-Sokoloff hypotheses about the Americas. To test the strength of arrows F and G on the right-hand side of figure 12.1, I have explored differences in public policy toward mass primary education within Latin America and between world regions.[13] This institutional side of the Engerman-Sokoloff is well supported, albeit with a revised geographical emphasis. Throughout the twentieth century, Latin American governments have supplied less financial support for primary education than have governments in other continents. In many cases the Latin American country has had a higher GDP per capita, while spending less of mass education, than a somewhat poorer country on another continent. Figure 12.2 illustrates this point by highlighting the inegalitarian tendency in the region's support for education, starting from the earliest comparative data on primary-school expenditures. Clearly, back around 1900 the same amount of support per pupil was spread over a smaller share of the school-age population in Latin America than in other regions. Argentina, for example, spent relatively heavily per pupil, as one would expect from its prosperity in the belle epoque, yet had low enrollments rela-

---

12. Nugent and Robinson, forthcoming.
13. This paragraph is based on the work summarized in Lindert (2010).

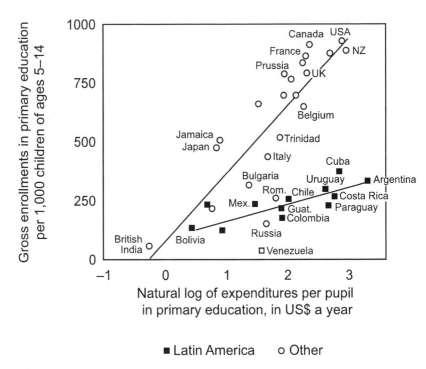

Fig. 12.2   Primary school enrollment outcomes versus expenditures per pupil, c. 1900

tive to many poorer countries, including Cuba, Jamaica, Japan, Trinidad, and much of Europe. The most likely explanation is not that Argentine parents had a peculiarly low demand for enrolling their children in school, but rather that those in control of local state and local governments concentrated the expenditures in Buenos Aires and in the richer neighborhoods, so that fewer children had good local schools. Over the whole twentieth century, Argentina continued to spend less on primary education than its high average income would have predicted. A more serious case is that of Venezuela, especially from the 1930s on, when *caudillismo* produced some of Latin America's lower enrollment levels despite the nation's oil wealth. The source of such low performances seems to have been the source that Engerman and Sokoloff emphasized: a lack of political will to devote tax money to mass education.

A natural experiment of sorts is now in progress for further testing the effects of inegalitarian politics on mass education. Between 1980 and 2000, several Latin American countries shifted toward democracy, with more constraints on executive power and more contestability of elections. Others, like Costa Rica, experienced no such change, since their democracy was already relatively full, while Venezuela retreated from democracy to "Bolivarian democracy."[14] Meanwhile, the region has begun to administer internationally comparable tests of student learning in the middle grades and in secondary school. The test scores correlate with national average incomes, the clearest outliers being high-scoring Costa Rica and low-scoring Venezuela.[15] Will the shift toward democracy deliver improvements in the quality of schooling in those countries where it occurs and is sustained?

12.3 Fiscal Structure

Another promising frontier effort is Ken's unfinished work, with Eric Zolt, on how inequality of power has shaped the institutions of taxation. Here again the evidence is from the Americas. By bringing institutions and inequality to center stage, Sokoloff and Zolt revise the usual thinking about how tax structures are shaped in the long run. The usual thinking links the evolution of tax structures to the development of more progressive and more decentralized government revenue collection.[16] Sokoloff and Holt see greater explanatory power in the concentration of political power. Right from the start, the Latin American countries had tax systems that were more regressive because they had greater concentration of political voice. Given the eternal difficulties of determining the net incidence of taxes (and expenditures) across income classes, Sokoloff and Zolt could only show that, relative to Latin America, the United States and Canada tended to rely more on direct taxes that are at least conventionally thought to be more progressive, such as the property tax.[17]

Sokoloff and Zolt also introduce some clear historical differences in the devolution of fiscal power from the central government to local governments. In the nineteenth century and early twentieth, this decentralization was much greater in Canada and the Northern United States than in the Southern United States, and more in the latter than anywhere in Latin

14. Lindert (2010, figure 8, using Polity data).
15. Hanushek and Woessmann (2009).
16. On the role of revenue-collecting capacities, see Harley Hinrichs (1966) and the many writings of Richard Bird on tax structure and economic development, including his writings specific to Latin America.
17. The Sokoloff-Zolt paper contained an unresolved tension regarding taxes on consumption. These are introduced as prominent distinguishing features of both the "more progressive" tax structures of rich countries and the more regressive systems of developing countries (e.g., on p. 3). Future researchers should be able to ease the tension by noting two basic points about the incidence of consumption taxes. First, a flat and permanent consumption tax is not really regressive in terms of its bite on shares of income tax, as long as the rate of return on savings just matches the rate of discount on future consumption. Second, progressivity and regressivity always need to be defined as effects of both the taxes and the expenditures they pay for. This simple but often-overlooked point allows us to recognize that the consumption taxes of modern welfare states are progressive in that they finance expenditures (e.g., universal public health) that are very progressive, whereas the consumption taxes of Latin American have not been spent in favor of the poor.

America.[18] Similar issues of the evolution of fiscal structure are now being pursued over the breadth of European economic history, partly in response to Ken's work. A leading pioneer exploring this topic is another member of the UCLA family in economic history, Mark Dincecco.[19]

12.4   Conclusion: Political Inequality and the Lack of a Growth-Equality Trade-Off

The pathbreaking work by Engerman and Sokoloff has, in the end, shifted our attention toward political inequality and its institutional manifestations. Granted, some of their writings have invited the interpretation that it is economic inequality, especially inequality in land ownership, that has caused bad growth performance in Latin America. Yet implicit in their emphasis on the role of suffrage institutions is a strong exogenous component of political voice. In terms of figure 12.1, their contrasts within the Americas have effectively spotlighted the causal arrows cascading downward from arrow A, even though they also attempted to find a role for factor endowments. The egalitarian role has been played by the northern U.S. states and the provinces of Upper Canada, where political voice is more local and more equally shared than in the southern U.S. and in Latin America. Their tale of the Americas will probably be read as a story of how unequal political power led to economic inequality and slower growth.[20]

The primacy of political inequality as an influence on both economic inequality and economic growth underlines a commonsense reason for discarding the belief that there is an unavoidable growth-equality trade-off. There could have been an unavoidable trade-off between these two goals only if the political process had already exhausted every opportunity to develop policies that fostered both of them. Yet human history seems devoid of such political perfection. At the egalitarian end of the historical spectrum, even the welfare states of Northern Europe have passed up the opportunity to promote both equity and efficiency by scrapping their agricultural policies that overwhelmingly benefit landowners. At the inegalitarian end, countries that have prioritized the growth goal have nonetheless passed up opportunities to make egalitarian pro-growth investments in the health and education of the masses. This end of the spectrum is well illuminated by the Engerman-Sokoloff tale of political failures in the history of Latin America and the southern United States.

18. Go and Lindert (2010) note a pattern in the locus of government budgetary power that fits well with the hypothesis of Sokoloff and Zolt. They note that power was decentralized more into town and city governments in the northern states than in the South, where state legislatures kept a firm grip on the budgetary and legislative reins.

19. See Dincecco (2009a, 2009b, 2010), and his current book project.

20. This emphasis on the causal role of political, rather than economic, inequality has already been presented in Lindert (2003, especially pages 323–25), and econometrically supported by historical Colombian data in Acemoglu et al. (2007).

References

Acemoglu, Daron, María Angélica Bautista, Pablo Querubín, and James A. Robinson. 2007. "Economic and Political Inequality in Development: The Case of Cundinamarca, Colombia." NBER Working Paper no. 13208. Cambridge, MA: National Bureau of Economic Research, June.

Acemoglu, Daron, Simon Johnson, and James A. Robinson. 2001. "The Colonial Origins of Comparative Development." *American Economic Review* 91:1369–401.

———. 2002. "Reversal of Fortune: Geography and Institutions in the Making of the Modern World Income Distribution." *Quarterly Journal of Economics* 117:231–94.

Arroyo Abad, A. Leticia. 2008. "Inequality in Republican Latin America: Assessing the Effects of Factor Endowments and Trade." Global Prices and Income History Group Working Papers, no. 12.

Baten, Jorg, Peter Foldvari, Bas van Leeuwen, and Jan Luiten van Zanden. Forthcoming. "World Income Inequality 1820–2000." *Revista de Historia Económica.*

Chaudhary, Latika. 2009. "Determinants of Primary Schooling in British India." *Journal of Economic History* 69:269–302.

De Ferranti, David, Guillermo E. Perry, Francisco H. G. Ferreira, and Michael Walton. 2004. *Inequality in Latin America: Breaking with History?* Washington, DC: The World Bank.

Dincecco, Mark. 2009a. "Fiscal Centralization, Limited Government, and Public Revenues in Europe, 1650–1913." *Journal of Economic History* 69:48–103.

———. 2009b. "Political Transformations and Public Finances: Europe, 1650–1913." Paper presented at the International Economic History Congress. Utrecht, The Netherlands, August 3–7.

———. 2010. "The Political Economy of Fiscal Prudence in Historical Perspective." *Economics and Politics* 22:1–36.

Engerman, Stanley L., Elisa Mariscal, and Kenneth L. Sokoloff. 2002. "Schooling, Suffrage, and the Persistence of Inequality in the Americas, 1800–1945." Unpublished Manuscript.

———. 2009. "The Evolution of Schooling Institutions in the Americas, 1800–1925." In *Human Capital and Institutions: A Long Run View,* edited by David Eltis, Frank Lewis, and Kenneth Sokoloff, 93–142. New York: Cambridge University Press.

Engerman, Stanley L., and Kenneth L. Sokoloff. 1997. "Factor Endowments, Institutions, and Differential Paths of Growth Among New World Economies: A View from Economic Historians of the United States." In *How Latin America Fell Behind,* edited by Stephen Haber, 260–304. Stanford: Stanford University Press.

———. 2002. "Factor Endowments, Inequality, and Paths of Development Among New World Economics." *Economía* 3:41–109.

———. 2005. "The Evolution of Suffrage Institutions in the New World." *Journal of Economic History* 65:891–921. Winning article, Arthur H. Cole Prize 2005–2006.

———. 2008. "Debating the Role of Institutions in Political and Economic Development: Theory, History, and Findings." *Annual Review of Political Science* 11: 119–35.

Frankema, Ewout H. P. 2009. *Has Latin America Always Been Unequal? A Comparative Study of Asset and Income Inequality in the Long Twentieth Century.* Global Economic History Series. Leiden and Boston: Brill.

Go, Sun, and Peter H. Lindert. 2010. "The Uneven Rise of American Public Schools to 1850." *Journal of Economic History* 70:1–26.

Hanushek, Eric A., and Ludger Woessmann. 2009. "Schooling, Cognitive Skills, and the Latin American Growth Puzzle." NBER Working Paper no. 15066. Cambridge, MA: National Bureau of Economic Research, June.

Hinrichs, Harley. 1966. *A General Theory of Tax Structure Change during Economic Development.* Cambridge, MA: Law School of Harvard University.

Lindert, Peter H. 2003. "Voice and Growth: Was Churchill Right?" *Journal of Economic History* 63:315–50.

———. 2010. "The Unequal Lag in Latin American Schooling since 1900: Follow the Money." *Revista de Historia Económica* 28:375–405.

Mariscal, Elisa, and Kenneth Sokoloff. 2000. "Schooling, Suffrage, and the Persistence of Inequality in the Americas, 1800–1945." In *Political Institutions and Economic Growth in Latin America,* edited by Stephen Haber, 159–217. Stanford: Hoover Institution Press.

Nugent, Jeffrey B., and James A. Robinson. Forthcoming. "Are Endowments Fate?" *Revista de Historia Económica.*

Sokoloff, Kenneth, and Eric Zolt. 2006. "Inequality and the Evolution of Institutions of Taxation: Evidence from the Economic History of the Americas." Unpublished Manuscript.

Williamson, Jeffrey G. 2010. "Five Centuries of Latin American Inequality." Forthcoming in *Revista de Historia Económica.*

13

Remembering Ken,
Our Beloved Friend

Manuel Trajtenberg

It has been almost three years since Ken succumbed to a long, protracted illness. Three years too many of void and longing for an exceptional human being who shone radiantly in our horizon, only to leave us, his countless friends and disciples and colleagues, far too soon, when he was still in the midst of making economics a better discipline to grasp, and this world a better place to journey.

"*A beautiful mind*" is not just the successful title of an inspiring story, but also a powerful conjunction of words that conjures the image of a great intellect trapped in the grip of mental illness. To paraphrase it, Ken was "*a beautiful soul*" trapped in a treacherous body, which ever since childhood challenged him with pain and ailment, until finally it did him in with precipitous rage. "*A beautiful soul*" made of overflowing kindness, of boundless empathy, of thoughtfulness and softness and loyalty toward his friends—so many of us, so fortunate that fate brought us within the radius of Ken's life.

A beautiful soul **and** a beautiful mind, for Ken brought to bear to our profession as much as to his daily life a powerful intellect, which encompassed far more than that of the run of the mill economist: literature, history, politics, science. There was no subject that was alien to him, no corner of human knowledge or art that escaped his attention and curiosity. As amply demonstrated in this volume, Ken's contributions to economic history left an indelible imprint that will surely reverberate for generations to come. But that is just part of the story: Ken was a great intellectual in the good old sense of the word, far greater than the mere count of published articles or prizes

Manuel Trajtenberg is head of the National Economic Council at the prime minister's office of Israel; professor at the Eitan Berglas School of Economics, Tel Aviv University; and a research associate of the National Bureau of Economic Research.

received or talks rendered—it was through the interaction with students, colleagues, and friends, that the radiance of his beautiful mind showed the most, illuminating our shadows.

I had the tremendous fortune of meeting Ken over thirty years ago, as I arrived for the first time to the United States to study at Harvard. We roomed together for two years: his last two, my first. Our relationship developed into the closest it comes to brotherhood without actual kinship. For virtually all of my adult life Ken was a main pillar of my existence, of my conception of the world, of my notion of what humanity and friendship and affection are.

We had endless hours of discussions about politics, about ideas, about the why and the when and the how, some strident and vociferous, some soft and quiet, always, always inspiring. He was a staunch believer in some basic principles such as democracy, fairness, equal opportunity, liberty, the capacity for progress, the value of knowledge and of the intellect. Even in the darkest days for the polity in America, Ken passionately loved his country and what it stood for, but he could be equally acerbic in criticizing excesses of power at home and abroad, the shortsightedness of government, greed, corruption, unfairness. Having grown up in a less fortunate country, I typically tended to be more skeptical and doubtful than Ken, but he managed to instill in me a set of beliefs that greatly helped me cope over the years with this confounding and cynical world.

Ken followed closely the lives of his friends' families, becoming for our fortunate children the fabled good uncle who arrives every time from distant places, showering them with well thought presents, with tender smiles. As much as each of us would like to think that Ken was uniquely special just for himself or herself, in fact very many of us felt exactly the same. That was one of Ken's greatest gifts: that he managed to be so much for so many, and yet each felt that he was uniquely his . . .

Even as his body shrank to the minimally possible, even as he contemplated the coming end, his worries and thoughts were with us, with the many friends who came to bid him goodbye. As always, Ken wanted to be as fair as possible in allocating his precious last hours, in making sure that each of us got enough attention, even in consoling us. It is impossible to figure out how he managed, in the midst of his tenacious battle with the cruel disease, to display such generosity of spirit, such unselfish love.

Ken was no believer; his was too rational a mind to accommodate religion, and yet there is something almost divine about his life, his qualities, his touch. We all knew he was very special, but it is only when he is no more that we realize how much. *"A beautiful soul, a beautiful mind,"* that is the way we ought to keep his radiant memory in our firmament—perhaps the flame will last for many lifetimes.

With immense sadness but equally boundless love,
Manuel Trajtenberg

Contributors

Dan Bogart
Department of Economics
3151 Social Science Plaza
University of Irvine
Irvine, CA 92697-5100

Dora L. Costa
Department of Economics
University of California, Los Angeles
Box 951477
Los Angeles, CA 90095-1477

Stanley L. Engerman
Department of Economics
University of Rochester
Rochester, NY 14627-0156

Robert W. Fogel
Center for Population Economics
University of Chicago
Booth School of Business
5807 S. Woodlawn Avenue, Suite 367
Chicago, IL 60637

Sebastian Galiani
Department of Economics
Washington University in St. Louis
Campus Box 1208
St. Louis, MO 63130-4899

Camilo García-Jimeno
Department of Economics, E52-380
Massachusetts Institute of Technology
50 Memorial Drive
Cambridge, MA 02142

Claudia Goldin
Department of Economics
Harvard University
Cambridge, MA 02138

Stephen Haber
Department of Political Science
Stanford University
Stanford, CA 94305-6044

Philip T. Hoffman
Division of the Humanities and Social
   Sciences
Mail Code: 228-77
California Institute of Technology
Pasadena, CA 91125

Lawrence F. Katz
Department of Economics
Harvard University
Cambridge, MA 02138

B. Zorina Khan
9700 College Station
Bowdoin College
Brunswick, ME 04011

Sukkoo Kim
Department of Economics
Washington University in St. Louis
One Brookings Drive
St. Louis, MO 63130-4899

Naomi R. Lamoreaux
Department of Economics
Yale University
Box 208269
New Haven, CT 06520-8269

Peter H. Lindert
Department of Economics
University of California, Davis
Davis, CA 95616

John Majewski
Department of History
University of California, Santa
    Barbara
Santa Barbara, CA 93106-9410

Joel Mokyr
Department of Economics
Northwestern University
2003 Sheridan Road
Evanston, IL 60208

Gilles Postel-Vinay
INRA-Lea DELTA
48 BD Jourdan
Ecole Normale Superieure
75014 Paris, France

James A. Robinson
Department of Government, IQSS
Harvard University
1737 Cambridge Street, N309
Cambridge, MA 02138

Jean-Laurent Rosenthal
Division of Humanities and Social
    Sciences
California Institute of Technology
1200 E. California Blvd., MC 228-77
Pasadena, CA 91125

Kenneth L. Sokoloff

Dhanoos Sutthiphisal
Department of Economics
McGill University
855 Sherbrooke Street West
Montreal, Quebec H3A 2T7 Canada

Manuel Trajtenberg
Eitan Berglas School of Economics
Tel Aviv University
Tel Aviv 69978 Israel

Author Index

Note: Page numbers followed by "f" or "t" refer to figures or tables, respectively.

Abad, L. A., 366n11
Abramovitz, M., 9, 320, 323, 329, 330
Acemoglu, D., 14n5, 54, 63n11, 76, 122, 139, 146, 206, 279, 288, 334, 364n2, 370n20
Ackerman, R. K., 26n33
Adams, C. F., Jr., 239
Adams, S. B., 238
Adelman, I., 315
Adelman, J., 33nn50–51, 34n52, 52, 53n6
Ades, A. F., 123, 123n2, 124n3, 125, 128n4, 148
Aguilar, G., 95
Albert, W., 189n19
Allen, G. C., 316
Allen, R. C., 26n33
Allinne, J.-P., 159n3
Alston, L. J., 33n51
Altman, I., 13n2, 17n15, 25n30
Amaral, S., 33n551
Anglade, G., 58
Angrist, J. D., 279, 279n8, 288, 288n17
Appleby, J. C., 17n13
Arora, A., 238
Arrow, K. J., 237n2
Atack, J., 29n43, 30, 33n49
Averitt, R. T., 268n28

Bandeira, M., 55
Bardo, M. D., 115
Barickman, B. J., 33n51

Barker, D. J. P., 319
Barnes, V. F., 26n33
Barro, R. J., 338n10
Barth, J. R., 115
Bartlett, R. P., 13n3
Baseler, M. C., 16n6
Baskin, J., 239
Bateman, F., 29n43, 30, 33n49
Becker, G., 324
Becker, R. A., 146
Belich, J., 51n4
Benmelech, E., 111
Berg, A., 102, 104
Berhman, J., 338
Bermejo, F. V., 282n12
Berndt, E. R., 330
Bernstein, M. A., 268n31
Bernstein, M. D., 57
Berquist, C. W., 37n56
Bertrand, M., 292
Bethell, L., 37n56
Bhagwati, J. N., 315, 338n10
Bidwell, P. W., 26n31
Billington, R. A., 50n2
Bimpikis, K., 206
Bischoff, J., 225n22
Blum, J. M., 269
Blyn, G., 315
Bodenhorn, H., 10, 108, 109, 110, 111
Bogart, D., 184n9, 202n44

Boldrin, M., 206, 357
Bond, B. W., Jr., 26n33
Borgatti, S. P., 166f
Bornstein, M., 105
Boucher, P. P., 16, 17nn13–14, 25n30
Bowling, K. R., 142
Bowman, M. J., 329
Bratt, E. C., 320
Brennan, S., 111, 114
Brenner, R., 54, 76
Brown, R. H., 144n9
Brunt, L., 223
Bulmer-Thomas, V., 37n56
Burroughs, P., 31n46
Burrows, E. G., 143n9
Bushnell, D., 37n56
Butland, G. J., 52n6, 58
Butler, O. R., 238
Butlin, N., 37n58

Cadman, J. W., 198nn41–42
Calomiris, C. W., 113, 114, 241
Campante, F. R., 124n3
Canny, N., 13n2
Caprio, G., Jr., 115
Carey, H. C., 31n46
Carosso, V. P., 240
Carter, S. B., 18n18
Castro, D. S., 33n51
Caves, R. E., 335
Cerutti, M., 95
Chakravarty, S., 315
Chandler, A. D., Jr., 237n1, 259n22, 335
Chandrasekhar, S., 315
Chaudhuri, S., 338
Chaudhury, L., 365n9
Chiver, E. M., 39n64
Christensen, L. R., 331
Christie, K. H., 52n6
Clapp, M. A., 282n13
Clark, C., 318
Clark, G., 15, 189n20, 206
Clifford, F., 191n23
Clodfelter, M., 28n38
Coale, A. J., 316
Coates, T. J., 25n30
Coatsworth, J. H., 37n56, 53n6
Coffman, C., 192n28
Coghlan, T. A., 38n59
Cohen, W. M., 237, 237n1, 242n4
Cole, J. A., 27n36
Colm, G., 322

Condliffe, J. B., 39n63
Copeland, M. A., 312
Cortés Conde, R., 37n56, 126, 140, 144
Costeloe, M., 91
Crafts, N. F. R., 314, 320, 321, 332, 333
Craig, L. A., 192n28
Craven, W. F., 26n33
Crosland, M., 232
Cull, R., 239

David, P. A., 330, 334
Davie, M. R., 19n20, 28n39
Davies, K. A., 37n56
Davis, L. E., 113, 114, 240, 322
Dean, W., 33n51, 52n6
De Ferranti, D., 365n8
Deffenbaugh, W. S., 283, 301, 302n37
Del Ángel-Mobarak, G., 97
De Long, J. B., 239, 240
Denevan, W. N., 16n9, 21
Denison, E. F., 313, 321
De Vries, J., 16n8
Diaz-Cayeros, A., 125
Dietz, H. A., 125
Dincecco, M., 370n19
Do, Q.-A., 124n3
Doblhammer, G., 319
Doghterty, C., 332
Dollar, D., 6, 9
Dorfman, J., 31n46
Duckham, B. F., 189n18
Duflo, E., 292
Duly, L. C., 39n65
Dunn, R. S., 23n27
Dutton, H. I., 208n1

Easterlin, R. A., 5
Economopoulos, A., 111
Edwards, L. N., 288n17
Edwards, R. C., 268n28
Eidt, R. C., 55
Eisenberg, M. J., 288n17
Eisenberg, P. L., 34n53
Ekrich, A. R., 25n29
Elliott, J. H., 16n6, 17n15, 18n16, 22n24,
    23n25
Elphick, R., 39n65
Eltis, D., 20n22, 22
Emmer, P. C., 13n2
Emmons, F. E., 282n11
Engerman, S. L., 1, 3, 4, 8, 13n1, 14nn4–5,
    16n8, 17n12, 23n29, 27n35, 28n40,

34n52, 37n57, 49n1, 50, 76, 91, 105,
109, 139, 146, 177n1, 194n32, 280n9,
334, 364n1, 364nn4–5, 365nn6–10
Ennis, H. M., 148
Everett, M. G., 166f

Fabricant, S., 312
Falconer, J. I., 26n31
Farnam, H. W., 28n40
Federer, J. P., 240
Feinstein, C. H., 39n65, 40nn66–67
Feller, D., 29n44
Findlay, R., 13n1
Fischer, S., 331
Fisk, C. L., 243n6
Fitzgerald, R., 38n61
Floud, R., 318
Fogel, R. W., 321n4, 324, 325n6, 327, 342,
343
Ford, A. C., 26n32, 37n56
Fosfuri, A., 238
Frankema, E., 365n8, 365n10
Fraumeni, B. M., 331
Freeman, L. C., 166f
Freeman, M. J., 178n3
Frencz, I., 19n20, 28n39

Galambos, L., 259n22, 335
Galenson, D. W., 16n6, 25n29
Gallman, R. E., 113, 114
Galloway, J. H., 17n12
Galvez, A., 232
Gambardella, A., 238
Gamboa Ojeda, L., 95
Gans, J., 238
Gatell, F. O., 111
Gates, P. W., 26n32, 28n38, 29n43, 29n45,
33n49
Gerlach, A. C., 56
Ghemawat, P., 335
Gibb, G. S., 258
Gibbons, C. E., 282n13
Gibson, C., 22n24
Giliomee, H., 39n64
Gillespie, C. D., 227
Glade, W. P., 37n56
Glaeser, E. L., 123, 123n2, 124n3, 125,
128n4, 148
Go, S., 365n9, 370n18
Goldin, C., 8, 279n7, 289n20, 292, 292n25,
293n27, 294, 296n30, 300n34, 306
Goldsmith, R. W., 312

Gollup, F. M., 331, 332
Gomberg, A., 93, 94
Goodrich, C., 181n5
Gordon, T. F., 192, 192n26
Graham, D. H., 24
Graves, A., 38n61
Gray, L. C., 26n32, 38n61
Green, C. M., 146
Gregson, M. E., 192
Griliches, Z., 327, 331
Grinath, A., 109
Grubb, F., 17n14
Gudmundson, L., 37n56

Haber, S., 4, 94, 96, 97, 98, 102, 104, 105
Hall, C., 57
Hammond, B., 109
Hanley, A. G., 101, 103
Hannah, L., 240
Hansen, A., 319
Hanushek, E. A., 369n15
Haring, C. H., 17n15
Harley, C. K., 333
Harlow, V., 39n64
Harris, M., 26n31
Hartz, L., 49n1
Hawke, G. R., 39n63
Healy, D. T., 315
Heckman, J., 330
Heckscher, E. F., 16n7
Hellman, E., 39n65
Helpman, E., 330n8
Henderson, J. V., 123, 123n3, 128n5
Hennessy, C. A. M., 51, 51n3, 57
Heywood, C., 26n33
Hibbard, B. H., 29n41
Higman, B., 23n28
Hilt, E., 193n30
Himmerich y Valencia, R., 27n36
Hinrichs, H., 369n15
Hintz, E. S., 236, 239
Hochschild, A., 15
Hoffman, P. T., 5, 92, 158n1, 159, 161, 163,
164, 167n11
Hofstadter, R., 50n2
Holden, R. H., 35n54, 93
Horn, J., 13n2, 17n5, 25n30
Hounshell, D. A., 238
Hughes, T. P., 236, 237nn1–2
Hurst, J. W., 201n43
Hutchinson, E. P., 28n40
Huttenback, R. A., 322

Jacobson, N., 37n56
Jefferson, M., 5, 52, 121
Jewkes, J., 237n1
Johnson, S., 14n5, 54, 63n11, 76, 77, 122,
    139, 146, 334, 364n2
Jones, B., 359
Jones, C. I., 338n10
Jones, R., 18n18
Jorgenson, D. W., 331, 332
Jourdain, W. R., 32n47
Jupp, P., 194nn33–34

Kandell, J., 125
Kato, T., 339
Katz, F., 93, 293n27, 296n30
Katz, L. F., 8, 279n7, 289n20, 292, 294,
    300n34
Katzman, M., 56
Keesecker, W. W., 283, 301, 302, 302n37
Kendrick, J. W., 312
Keyssar, A., 27n35, 50, 109
Kézdi, G., 292
Khan, B. Z., 7, 177n2, 205, 206, 210,
    215n10, 221, 221n15, 356, 357
Kim, J., 338
Kim, S., 122n1
King, A., 39n64
Klein, D. B., 183n7, 187n15, 192n29
Klein, H. S., 28n37, 37n56, 97
Klepper, S., 237n1, 265
Knight, F. W., 23n28
Knowlton, E. H., 258
Kravis, I. B., 322
Kremer, M., 223
Krishnan, R. R., 323
Kropp, D., 288n17
Kroszner, R. S., 107
Krueger, A. B., 279n8, 288n17
Krugman, P., 323, 338
Kuczynski, R. R., 15, 24
Kuroda, M., 331
Kuznets, S., 9, 312, 316, 320, 322, 324, 325,
    327

Lamoreaux, N. R., 7, 110, 113, 206, 215n10,
    236, 238, 239, 240, 243n6, 245n9,
    248n10, 250, 253, 258, 263, 265n25,
    269, 335, 358
Landes, D. S., 332, 333
Landes, W. M., 288n17
Lane, C., 109
Lang, K., 288n17

Lanjouw, J. O., 250, 255
Lau, L. J., 321, 338
Lazonick, W., 237n1
Legler, J. B., 108, 111
LeGrand, C., 52n6
Lerner, J., 223, 242n4, 250, 255
Leslie, S. W., 238
Levenstein, M., 7, 240, 245n9, 253, 263,
    265n25, 269
Levin, R. C., 237
Levine, D. K., 206, 357
Levine, R., 115
Levy, J., 92
Lewis, H. G., 324
Li, P., 340n11
Libecap, G. D., 33n51
Lindert, P. H., 185n12, 194n35, 365n9,
    367n13, 369, 370n18, 370n20
Lindo-Fuentes, H., 37n56
Lipartito, K., 238
Lipset, S. M., 49n1, 50n2
Livi-Bacci, M., 16n9
Lleras-Muney, A., 279, 279n8, 287, 293, 300,
    300n35, 306
Lochner, L., 279n8
Lockhart, J., 24, 37n56
Lopez, J. H., 338
Lora, Q., 58
Lucas, R. E., 338n10
Ludlow, L., 95

MacLeod, R. M., 208n1, 225n21, 232n27
Maddison, A., 16n10, 18n18, 19n21, 124,
    141, 316, 320, 321, 328n7, 339
Mahoney, J. L., 52n6
Maine, H. S., 210nn6–7
Majewski, J., 108, 183nn7–8, 187n15,
    192nn28–29, 193n30, 195n38
Malenbaum, W., 315
Mamalakis, M. J., 24
Mann, C. C., 49
Mansfield, E., 327, 328
Marichal, C., 93, 95
Mariscal, E. V., 3, 8, 365nn9–10
Markiewicz, D., 93
Martin, C., 33n50
Martin, E. M., 312
Martin, J. G., 239
Martin, R. M., 15, 40n66
Martin du Nord, N. M. F. L. J., 159n3
Maurer, N., 93, 94, 95, 96, 97, 98, 223
McBride, G. M., 35n54

McCreery, D., 37n56, 52n6
McDonald, J. D. N., 32n47
McEvedy, C., 18n18
McGreevey, W. P., 37n56, 122n1
McLauchlan, G., 38n62
McNeil, I., 216n12
Mears, L. A., 315
Mehlum, H., 54n8
Mellor, J. W., 315
Merrick, T. W., 24
Middlebrook, K., 97
Miller, D. H., 51n4
Milligan, K., 279n8
Mills, T. C., 321
Miranti, P. J., Jr., 239
Mitchell, B. R., 184n11, 190n22
Moch, L. P., 13n2
Moehling, C. M., 195n36
Moene, K. O., 54n8
Mokyr, J., 206, 332, 357
Moretti, E., 279n8
Mörner, M., 13n2
Morrison, W. M., 339, 340n12
Morse, R. M., 122n1
Moser, P., 223
Moses, B., 18n17, 23n25
Moskowitz, T. J., 111
Moss, D., 111, 114
Mowery, D. C., 237, 237n2, 239, 258, 269
Moya Pons, F., 37n56
Mueller, B., 33n51
Mullainathan, S., 292
Murphy, K. M., 225, 321n4
Musacchio, A., 105
Myers, D. J., 125
Myrdal, G., 321

Navin, T. R., 239
Neal, L., 240
Nelson, R. R., 237n2, 242n4, 314, 331, 339
Nettels, C. P., 26n33
Ng, K., 111
Nicholas, T., 223, 236, 239, 241, 250, 257, 257n20
Nickson, R. A., 125, 146
Normura, K., 332
North, D. C., 140, 141, 146, 206, 322, 333, 334
Nugent, J. B., 14n5, 365n8, 367n12

Ochieng', W. R., 39n64
O'Mahony, M., 346

O'Neill, H., 111
Oreopoulos, P., 279n8, 288n18, 290n24, 303, 303n40
O'Rourke, K. H., 13n1
O'Sullivan, M. A., 236, 240, 241
Oveda, J., 95
Ozdaglar, A., 206

Pack, H., 331, 339
Pakes, A., 356
Palacios, M., 37n56
Palmquist, R. B., 192
Park, J. H., 338
Parker, W. N., 29n43, 30, 33n49
Parry, J. H., 18n17, 23n25
Parsons, J. J., 52n6
Pei, M., 338
Peláez, C. M., 99, 101
Pepelases, A., 315
Pérez-Brignoli, H., 37n56, 57
Perkins, D. H., 10, 328n7, 338, 339
Perry, J. R., 25n29
Petersen, M. A., 112
Piketty, T., 160
Pineo, R. F., 37n56
Pinto, S. M., 148
Pomfret, R., 33n50
Portes, A., 122n1, 126, 145, 146
Porto, A., 148
Postel-Vinay, G., 5, 92, 158n1, 159, 160, 161, 163, 164, 167n11
Potash, R., 92
Powell, J. M., 32n47, 38nn59–60, 51n4
Prichard, J., 16n6
Priestley, J., 186n13, 192n26
Proffitt, M. M., 302n37

Quintyn, M., 116

Raff, D. M. G., 335
Rajan, R. G., 112
Ratcliff, R. E., 128n6, 145
Rausch, J. N., 51, 51n3
Ravallion, M., 338
Rawski, T. G., 338
Ray, D., 334
Razo, A., 93, 94, 97, 98
Reed, A. Y., 283
Reich, L. S., 237, 250
Resnick, M., 124n3
Reynolds, R. L., 25n30
Richards, J. F., 51n4

Richardson, G., 184n9
Rife, C. W., 26n31
Ringer, F. K., 287n16
Ripley, W. Z., 261
Risch, E., 28n40
Robb, J. F., 258n21
Robbins, R. M., 29n41
Roberts, S. H., 32n47
Robinson, J. A., 14n5, 54, 63n11, 76, 77,
    122, 139, 146, 334, 364n2, 365n8,
    367n12
Robinson, W. G., 258n21
Rocki, D., 143
Rockoff, H., 109, 111
Rodríguez López, M. G., 95
Romer, P., 338n10
Romero Ibarra, M. E., 95
Roseberry, W., 37n56
Rosen, K. T., 124n3
Rosenberg, N., 269, 339
Rosenbloom, R. S., 238–39
Rosenthal, A., 24, 164, 167n11
Rosenthal, J.-L., 5, 92, 158n1, 159, 160, 161,
    163
Ross, R., 39n65
Rostow, W. W., 328, 332
Rousseau, P. L., 110, 115
Rout, L. B., 18n19, 28n37
Ruggles, S., 299
Rusk, J. G., 27n35

Sala-i-Martin, X., 338n10
Samper Kutschbach, M., 37n56
Sánchez-Albornoz, N., 16n10, 18n17
Sawers, D., 237n1
Schankerman, M., 250, 255
Scherer, F. M., 237
Schmidt, S., 279, 287, 288n19, 289n21, 306
Schmooker, J., 5
Schultz, T. W., 329
Schumpeter, J. A., 236, 237, 328
Schwartz, S. B., 23n27, 24, 33n51, 37n56
Scobie, J. R., 143, 144
Scotchmer, S., 223
Sears, M. V., 239
Segel, D., 302n37
Sewell, J. E., 259n22
Shavell, S., 223
Shaw, A. G. L., 38n59
Shead, J., 186n13
Shenoy, B. R., 315
Shishido, H., 124n3

Shleifer, A., 225
Shlomowitz, R., 38n61
Sidney, S., 225n20
Simon, M. C., 240, 322
Simpson, L. B., 27n36
Sinclair, K., 39n63
Sinclair, W. A., 38n59
Sitterson, J. C., 38n61
Sklaeiwitz, N., 315
Skowronek, S., 125
Smith, A., 39n64
Smith, A. E., 16n6, 17n14
Smith, J. K., 238
Snowden, K. A., 156
Sobel, D., 223n16
Sokoloff, K. L., 1, 3, 4, 5, 6, 7, 9, 13n1,
    14nn4–5, 27n35, 34n52, 37n57, 49n1,
    50, 76, 91, 105, 109, 125, 139, 146,
    155, 177, 177nn1–2, 194n32, 205,
    206, 212, 215n10, 236, 238, 239, 240,
    243n6, 245n9, 248n10, 250, 253, 258,
    263, 280n9, 334, 356, 357, 358, 364n1,
    364nn4–5, 365nn6–10, 369
Sokolowsi, C. J., 278n4
Solberg, C. E., 33nn50–51, 53n6
Solomon, L. C., 288n17
Solow, R. M., 9, 311, 311n1
Southworth, C., 15
Spencer, W. J., 238–39
Srinivasan, T. N., 338n10
Stambler, M., 282n13
Steckel, R. H., 195n36
Steinhilber, A. W., 278n4
Stephenson, G. M., 29n41
Stern, S., 238
Stigler, G., 288n17, 312
Stiglitz, J. E., 338
Stillerman, R., 237n1
Stiroh, K. J., 332
Stone, I., 322
Strahan, P. E., 107
Strong, M. A., 282n13
Summerhill, W. R., 33n51, 101, 140, 141
Suzigan, W., 101
Swan, T. W., 311
Sylla, R., 108, 109, 110, 111, 112, 114

Tannenbaum, F., 35n54
Taylor, G. R., 50n2
Taylor, P. E., 188n16
Teece, D. J., 237nn1–2, 335
Temin, P., 109, 333, 335

Tenenbaum, B., 92
Thomas, R. P., 206, 333
Thompson, L., 39n65
Thorne, R. G., 196n39
Timmer, M. P., 346
Tinbergen, J., 312n2
Toniolo, G., 314, 320, 321
Topel, R. H., 321n4
Topik, S., 104
Torvik, R., 54n8
Townsend, M. E., 15
Trajtenberg, M., 330, 356
Triner, G. D., 104
Troen, S. K., 279n6
Trudel, M., 27n34
Turner, F. J., 50, 52, 55
Tyack, D. B., 279

Usselman, S. W., 238, 242n4

Vamplew, W., 37n58
Van Ark, B., 346
Van Zwanenberg, R. M. A., 39n64
Vatter, H. G., 269
Vaupel, J. W., 319
Verdier, G., 116
Viotti da Costa, E., 32n48, 33n51
Vishny, R. W., 225
Vu, K. M., 332

Wa-Githumo, M., 39n64
Walker, D. W., 92
Wallace, Mike, 143n9
Wallis, J. J., 108, 109, 111, 125, 181n4,
    192n28, 195n37, 197n40
Walsh, J. P., 242n4
Walsh, M., 50, 50n2
Walter, R. J., 128n6, 145
Wang, T.-C., 110

Ward, J. R., 189n18
Washburn, W. E., 28n38
Wasserman, M., 93
Watts, D., 24
Weber, D. J., 51, 51n3
Weingast, B. R., 140, 141, 334
Weiss, T., 192n28
Wellington, R. G., 29n44
Wells, R., 323
Wettereau, J., 109
Wheaton, W., 124n3
White, E. N., 113, 114, 240, 259, 261, 269
White, R., 239
Willcox, W., 19n20, 28n39
Williams, M., 32n47
Williams, R. G., 52n6
Williamson, J. G., 185n12, 366n11
Wilson, M., 39n65
Winks, R. W., 51n4
Winter, S. G., 339
Wise, G., 238
Woessmann, L., 369n15
Womack, J., 93
Wood, G., 195n38
Wright, B. D., 223
Wright, G., 331
Wright, R. E., 187n14

Yared, P., 63n11
Yarrington, D., 37n56
Ying, T., 340n11
Young, A., 338
Ypersele, T. v., 223

Zagarri, R., 144n10
Zakaria, F., 338, 340n12
Zeckhauser, R., 237n2
Zeitlin, M., 128n6, 145
Zolt, E. M., 125, 146, 365n8, 369

Subject Index

Note: Page numbers followed by "f" or "t" refer to figures or tables, respectively.

Aboriginal populations: in Australia, 37–38; estimated distribution of, in New World, 21t; in New Zealand, 38
Abramovitz, Moses, 329–30
Africa, European movements into, 14
Aggregate production functions, 311–13
Albany Regency, 111
Americas, European movements into, 14. *See also* Central America, frontier in; North America; South America, frontier in; Spanish America
Argentina: case study of urban primacy in, 142–45; cities in, 145; frontier land in, 52; landholding in rural regions of, 36t; land laws in, 33–34
Asia, European movements into, 14
Asian Miracle, 9, 311, 322–24; economic growth theory and, 9–10; impact of, on economic growth theory, 335–41. *See also* South and Southeast Asia
Asian Tigers, 9
Australia: aboriginal population in, 37–38; British movements into, 14; land policies of, 38; Wakefield's policies and, 38
Autocracy index, 63–64

Bank charters, 107–8
Banking systems: in Brazil, 98–105, 100f, 102t; in Mexico, 92–97, 95t, 98t; in United States, 105–15

Bank of North America (BNA), 106–7
Bank of the United States (BUS), 107, 108–9
Berhman, Jere, 338
Bessemer, Henry, 216
Black Death, 54
Brazil, 27–28; banking system in, 98–105, 100f, 102t; financial incumbents in, 98; influence of Wakefield's ideas in, 32; political elites in, 98
Britain. *See* United Kingdom

Canada, 27; landholding in rural regions of, 36t; land policies of, 33; measuring frontier in, 56–57. *See also* New World; North America
Capital cities, 121, 122; data for estimating impact of, on urban primacy, 123–24; identifying impact of political factors on population concentration, 128–39; patterns of political centralization and development of, 122; urban primacy and, 128–39
Carey, Henry Charles, 31
Central America, frontier in, 57, 62f. *See also* Latin America; New World
Centralization. *See* Political centralization
Chandler, Alfred, Jr., 334–35
Charter bonuses, 109
Charters: bank, 107–8; U.S. vs. British corporation, 6. *See also* Transport charters

Child labor laws, 278; aspects of, 1910–1939, 284–85f, 286–87; compliances and constraints of, 290, 291t; effects of, on contemporaneous high school enrollment, 292–97, 294t; effects of, on eventual educational attainment, 297–301, 299t; federal government and, 278; impact of, on schooling and educational attainment, 287–301; types of, 281–83. *See also* Compulsory education laws; High school movement in U.S.; Secondary schooling

Child Labor Tax Law (1918), 278

China, economic growth and, 10, 315–16, 338–40. *See also* South and Southeast Asia

Cities, authority of, in U.S. vs. Argentina, 144–45

Colombia, frontier land in, 52

Compulsory education laws, 278; aspects of, 1910–1939, 283–87, 284–85f; compliances and constraints of, 289–90, 291t; effects of, on contemporaneous high school enrollment, 292–97, 294t; effects of, on eventual educational attainment, 297–301, 299t; enforcement of, 301–2; impact of, on schooling and educational attainment, 287–301; previous findings and empirical strategies for, 287–89; types of, 281–83. *See also* Child labor laws; High school movement in U.S.; Secondary schooling

Conditional frontier thesis, 4, 53–54. *See also* Frontier thesis

Constraints on the executive variable, for political institutions, 62–63, 63f

Costa Rica, frontier land in, 52

Cowper-Coles, Sherard, 216

Credit, notarial, 159, 161. *See also* France

Credit markets, French, 155; externalities in, 162–74. *See also* France; Notaries

Credit transactions, French, 5

David, Paul, 334

Decentralization of political authority, transportation revolution and, 198–201

Democracy, transportation revolution and, 180, 194–98

Democracy index, 63–64

Development, 5–6; institutions and, 6–7; patent systems and, 7

Díaz, Porfirio, 92–93

Dominican Republic, frontier in, 58

Dominion Lands Act of 1872 (Canada), 33

East Africa, land distribution in, 39–40

Economic growth, 280; impact of inequality on, 89; in Mexico, 91–97; role of institutions in, 37; total factor productivity and, 338; transportation revolution and, 178

Economic growth theory: Asian Miracle and, 9–10; economic historians and, 332–35; impact of Asian Miracle on, 335–41

Economic historians, 332–35

Economic history of technology, Sokoloff and, 355–60

Edison, Thomas, 216

Educational attainment, impact of child labor laws and compulsory schooling laws on, 287–301

Education laws. *See* Compulsory education laws

Elites, 4. *See also* Political elites

Ellis, Carleton, 216

Encomienda system, 16, 27

Endogenous economic growth, 324–30

Entrepreneurial firms. *See* Small and medium enterprises (SMEs)

Equity markets: companies' access to, in 1929, 262t; and inventive activity, 259–65. *See also* Credit markets, French; Securities markets

European colonial domains, population composition in, 15t

European Union (EU), economic forecast for, 336–37

Exogenous technological change, 311–13

Factor endowments, 3, 6–7; transportation revolution and, 178

Fair Labor Standards Act (1938), 278

Financial incumbents, 90; in Brazil, 98; in Mexico, 92–93

Four Asian Dragons, 323

Four Asian Tigers, 323

France: cantons in, 158–59, 160f; mortgage lending estimates in, 1840–1865, 161t; mortgage loans in, 5, 163–72; mortgage markets in, 157–61; notarial credit in, 159–61; population composition of colonial domains, 15t. *See also* Credit markets, French; Notaries

Free banking, 111–12
Frontier, 3–4; alternative data for measuring, 62–68; in Americas, 59t; classification by subnational administrative units, 78–85t; descriptive statistics, 65t; empirical results for, 68–74; introduction to, 49–55; land allocation and understanding, 51–52; in Latin America, 52; measuring, 55–56; measuring, in Canada, 56–57; measuring, in Caribbean republics, 58; measuring, in Central America, 57; measuring, in South America, 58–62, 61f; measuring, in U.S., 56–57; in North America, 60f; sources for, 77t
Frontier thesis, 49–51; applicability of, to Latin America, 51; land allocation and, 51–52. *See also* Conditional frontier thesis

Geography: importance of, for inventions, 236; institutions and, 177; and U.S. vs. British transportation systems, 6
Germany, population composition of colonial domains of, 15t
Graduation Act of 1854, 30t, 31
Great Britain. *See* United Kingdom
Great Depression: distribution of patents by type of company before, 243–45, 244t; effects of, by type of firm and region, 265–69, 266–67t; organization of inventive activity before, 243–48
Griliches, Zvi, 327, 330
Growth. *See* Economic growth
Growth theory. *See* Economic growth theory

Haiti, frontier in, 58
Hamilton, Alexander, 142–43
Headright system, 26
Hidalgo Rebellion, 91
High school movement in U.S., 275–76; graduation rates by region and, 275, 277f; role of federal government and, 276–77; state governments and, 277–79. *See also* Secondary schooling
Homestead Act of 1862, 30t, 31, 33, 51–52
Homestead Act of 1884 (Argentina), 33

Immigration, 3. *See also* Migration
Immigration policies: continuity of U.S., 28–29; industrialization and, 28; single European women and, 23n28; Spanish, 21–23, 23n26

Indentured servitude, institution of, 17; Spanish colonies and, 18; in Virginia, 26
India, economic growth and, 10, 315. *See also* South and Southeast Asia
Industrialization, as factor of immigration and land policy, 28
Industrial research labs. *See* In-house research laboratories, large firms'
Inequality: effect of, of power on institutions, 369–70; impact of, on economic development, 89; in Mexico, 91–97; political, and lack of growth equality, 370; Sokoloff on, in Americas, 363–71
In-house research laboratories, large firms', 7–8, 235–36; literature on, 237–39; securities markets and, 239–42; significance of inventions of, vs. small firms, 248–59. *See also* Inventions; Inventive activity
Institutions, 280; development and, 6–7; geography and, 177; inequality of power and, 369–70; measuring political, 62–64; in Mexico, 91–97; role of, in economic growth, 37
Inventions: importance of geography and, 236; introduction to, 205–6; prizes and, 207; protection of property rights and, 206; U.S. education system and, 8. *See also* Patents; Prizes
Inventive activity: data sources for, 242–43; organization of, before Great Depression, 243–48; reorganization of, 265–69; role of equity markets and, 259–65. *See also* In-house research laboratories, large firms'; Patents; Patent systems
Inventors: college attendance and occupations of fathers of British and U.S., 220–21, 221f; determinants of prizes of U.S., 229–31, 230t; great British, 215–16; great U.S., 214–15; prizes and, 222–31; social backgrounds of British and American, 216–21, 217t; types of returns for, and distribution of British, by education, 218–20, 220f; types of returns for, and distribution of U.S., by education, 218–20, 219t
Italy, population composition of colonial domains of, 15t

Japan, economic growth and, 316. *See also* South and Southeast Asia
Joint Companies, 198
Jorgensen, Dale W., 330, 331–32

Keating-Owen Child Labor Bill (1916), 278, 278n5
Kenya, land distribution in, 39–40
Kuznets, Simon, 325–27

Labor supply, American colonies and, 20–27
Land allocation, frontier thesis and, 51–52
Land disposal policy: industrialization and, 28; migration and, 14–15
Land distribution, 3; in Australia, 38; in East Africa, 39–40; in New Zealand, 38–39
Landes, David, 332–33
Land laws: in Argentina, 33–34; in Latin America, 34; U.S., 1785–1916, 30t
Land Ordinance of 1785, 52
Land ownership, North American vs. European, 26–27
Land policies: in Mexico, 34–37; as policy instrument for size of labor force, 33; regional development and, 15; in U.S., 35–36
Land values, U.S., transportation improvements and, 192–93
Large firms: 2, 266–67; effect of Great Depression on, by region, 265–69; role of equity markets and, 259–65. *See also* In-house research laboratories, large firms'
Latin America: applicability of frontier thesis to, 51; capital cities and urban primacy in, 128–39; continuity in, 19; frontier land in, 52; immigration and, 19; importance of national and provincial capital status on population concentration in, 124; land laws in, 34; Sokoloff on inequality in, 363–64. *See also* New World; South America, frontier in; Spanish America; *and specific countries*
Lister, Samuel, 216
Loans. *See* Mortgage loans, French

Madison, James, 142–43
Maine, Henry Sumner, 210
Mansfield, Edwin, 327–28
Maoris, 38
Mexico: banking system in, 92–97, 95t, 98t; financial incumbents in, 92–93; financial markets in, 96–97; inequality, institutions, and economic growth in, 91–97; landholding in rural regions of,

35, 36t; land policies in, 34–37; political elites in, 93
Migration: centralization of political authority and, 18; within Europe, 13–14; European, into Africa and Asia, 14; land disposal policy and, 14–15; U.S. and Canadian policies of, 18–19
Morgan, J. P., 240
Mortgage loans, French, 5, 163–72. *See also* Credit markets, French; France
Mortgages, as component of European financial system, 157
Multipolarity, 340
Mushet, Robert, 216

National Industrial Recovery Act (1933), 278
Nelson, Richard, 330–31
Netherlands, the, population composition of colonial domains of, 15t
New World: British migration policies for, 17; distribution and composition of populations in, 24t; estimated distribution of aboriginal population in, 21t; European directed migration to, by nation and continent of origin, 22t; labor supply in, 16–17, 20–21; population concerns in, 15–16; role of industrialization and migration to, 28; slave labor in, 20–21; Spanish migration policies for, 17–18; Spanish migration polices to, 21–23. *See also* Central America, frontier in; Latin America; North America; South America, frontier in; Spanish America
New York Stock Exchange (NYSE), 239–40
New Zealand: aboriginal population of, 38; British movements into, 14; land distribution in, 38–39
North, Douglass C., 333–34
North America: accessibility of land and immigration to, 25–26; composition of population of European descent, 24–25, 24t; frontier in, 60f; immigration to northern part of, 23–27; land ownership in northern part of, vs. Europe, 26–27. *See also* Canada; New World; United States
Notarial credit, 159, 161. *See also* France
Notaries, 172; data collected for, 158–61; in France, 157–58; as intermediaries, 156; role of, 5. *See also* Credit markets, French; France

Open-source movement, 206

Patent data, 242–43
Patenting: in Britain, 210, 211f; in U.S., 210–14, 214f
Patents: characteristics of, by assignee, 245–48, 246t, 247t; distribution of, by type of company before Great Depression, 243–45, 244t; increase in inventions and, 206; rates of, by region, 248, 250f; regional distribution of assignee companies by type, 252t; significance of, and technological sector, 248–59; by U.S. regions, 248, 249t, 251t. *See also* Inventions; Inventive activity; Prizes; Property rights
Patent systems: development and U.S. vs. British, 7; in early industrializers, 208–14. *See also* Inventive activity; Property rights
Perkins, Dwight H., 338–41
Political centralization, 18; analytical framework for, 126–28; capital city development and patterns of, 122; regional development and, 15; transportation revolution and role of, 198–201; urban primacy and, 124–25, 126–28
Political decentralization, 125, 144
Political elites, 90; in Brazil, 98; in Mexico, 93; in U.S., 106
Political inequality, lack of growth equality and, 370
Population concentration, urban primacy and, 124
Portugal, population composition of colonial domains of, 15t
Preemption Act of 1841, 29, 30t
Prizes: determinants of, for U.S. inventors, 229–31, 230t; inventions and, 207; in U.K. and U.S., 222–31. *See also* Inventions; Patents
Property rights, 7; inventions and protection of, 206. *See also* Patents; Patent systems
Public land laws, U.S., 30t
Public lands, supply of, 32–33

R&D facilities. *See* In-house research laboratories, large firms'
Regional exchanges, role of, and inventive activity, 261–65
Research laboratories. *See* In-house research laboratories, large firms'

Rostow, Walt W., 328
Royal Society, 225–27

School districts, in U.S., 276–77
Schooling laws. *See* Compulsory education laws
Schultz, Theodore W., 328–29
Secondary schooling, 8–9; state governments in, 278; U.S. enrollment and graduation rates, 275, 276f. *See also* Child labor laws; Compulsory education laws; High school movement in U.S.
Second Bank of the United States, 109
Securities markets, 239–42; large firms with in-house research laboratories and, 239–42
Slavery, in New World, 16–17, 20–21
Small and medium enterprises (SMEs): effect of Great Depression on, by region, 265–69, 266–67t; inventions and, 241–42; inventive activity and, 259–65; role of equity markets and, 259–65; significance of inventions of, vs. large firms, 248–59
Sokoloff, Kenneth L., 1–3; economic history of technology and, 355–60; on inequality in Americas, 363–71; personal remembrance of, 373–74
South Africa, land distribution in, 39–40
South America, frontier in, 58–62, 61f. *See also* Latin America; Spanish America; *and specific countries*
South and Southeast Asia: annual percentage rates of growth in per capita incomes in, 316, 317t; growth in education levels in, 323–24, 324t; per capita incomes of, in 1950, 314, 314t; population growth of, 316–18; post–World War II economic growth in, 319–22; secular trends in total fertility rates, 318t; trends in caloric consumption in, 318–20, 319t. *See also* Asian Miracle
South Korea, secondary schooling in, 275. *See also* South and Southeast Asia
Spain, New World migration policies of, 21–23, 23n26
Spanish America: composition of population of European descent, 23, 24t; historical roots of urban primacy in, 140–41; land policy in, 27; pursuit of European migrants in, 17–18. *See also*

Spanish America (*continued*)
    Latin America; New World; South
    America, frontier in
State-chartered banks, U.S., 107–10, 108f,
    112–14, 113f
State governments, secondary schooling
    and, 277–79

Technological advances. *See* Inventions
Technological change, bridges between two
    cohorts of theorists on, 330–32
Technology, economic history of, 355–60
Thomson, Elihu, 216
Total factor productivity, 9, 311–13; eco-
    nomic growth and, 338
Transportation corporations, 6
Transportation improvements, U.S. land
    values and, 192–93
Transportation investments, urbanization
    and, 179–80
Transportation organizations: background
    history of, 181–82; in U.K. vs. U.S.,
    178–80
Transportation revolution, 178; creating
    organizations for, 181–82; economic
    growth and, 178; inter-city competition
    and, 192–94; role of democracy in,
    194–98; role of political decentraliza-
    tion and centralization and, 198–201
Transport charters: costs of, in U.K., 184–
    86; and degree of democracy and eco-
    nomic equality in U.S. and U.K., 195–
    98; differences in democratic political
    systems and, 180; low price of, in U.S.,
    182–84; urbanization and, 186–92; in
    U.S. vs. U.K., 179–80. *See also* Charters
Turner, Frederick Jackson, 4, 49–50, 52, 53
Turner, Walter, 216

Uganda, land distribution in, 39–40
United Kingdom: costs of transport char-
    ters in, 184–86; democratic political
    systems and transport charters in, 180;
    great inventors of, 215–16; patenting
    in, 210, 211f; population composition
    of colonial domains of, 15t; role of
    democracy and transportation revo-
    lution in, 194–98; transportation char-
    ters in, 179–80; transportation corpora-

tions in, 6; transportation organizations
    in, 178–80
United States: banking in early republican,
    108, 108t; banking system in, 105–15;
    capital cities and urban primacy in,
    128–39; case study of urban primacy
    in, 142–45; centralization of political
    power in, 125; cities in, 144–45; com-
    mercial banks in, 113t; continuity of
    immigration policies of, 28–29; demo-
    cratic political systems and transport
    charters in, 180; great inventors of,
    214–15; historical roots of urban
    primacy in, 139–40; importance of na-
    tional and state capital status on popu-
    lation concentration in, 124; invention
    and education system of, 8; future of
    global influence of, 341; landholding in
    rural regions of, 35–37, 36t; land laws
    of, 1785–1916, 30t; land policies in,
    35–36; low price of transport charters
    in, 182–84; measuring frontier in, 56–
    57; patenting in, 210–14, 214f; political
    decentralization in, 144; political
    elites in, 106; role of democracy and
    transportation revolution in, 194–98;
    state-chartered banks in, 107–10, 108f,
    112–14, 113f; transportation charters
    in, 179–80; transportation corporations
    in, 6; transportation organizations in,
    178–80. *See also* North America
Urbanization: transportation investments
    and, 179–80; transport charters and
    role of, 186–92
Urban primacy, 4–5; analytical framework
    for, 126–28; capital cities and, 128–39;
    case study of, in Argentina, 142–45; case
    study of, in U.S., 142–45; data for esti-
    mating impact of capital cities on, 123–
    24; historical roots of, in Americas, 139–
    41; introduction to, 121–26; per capita
    income and differences in, between U.S.
    and Latin America, 124; political cen-
    tralization and, 124–25, 126–28
Urban structures, 5

Wakefield, Edward Gibbons, 31–32, 38
Westinghouse, George, 216
Wood, Henry A., 216